Subjects of Terror

SUBJECTS OF TERROR

Nerval, Hegel, and the Modern Self

Jonathan Strauss

Stanford University Press
Stanford, California

Stanford University Press
Stanford, California

© 1998 by the Board of Trustees of the
Leland Stanford Junior University

Printed in the United States of America

CIP data appear at the end of the book

To My Father
To My Mother

Acknowledgments

Countless remarkable people have made this book possible, and it is bound to them through ties of admiration, friendship, and gratitude. Mitchell Greenberg has watched over its slow transformation from early sketches to a finished manuscript with a deep and unwavering personal concern. His intellectual contributions, the inspiration of his own work, and his persistent support have made him an embodiment of humane scholarship and a wonderful friend. He has taken on himself the often thankless task of sternness when it was necessary, and for this perhaps most difficult and tangible sign of his constancy I wish to express my special gratitude. James Creech has repeatedly lent his brilliant skills as a reader to early drafts of the book, but perhaps more important, his own recent work has served as an essential reference point for the most fundamental questions of ethics and identity that the current study addresses. Without Denis Hollier, who guided the initial and most inchoate stages of this project, it would never have come to fruition, and I want to thank him for his help not only in shaping its most basic ideas but also for his patient, decisive instruction in the art of scholarly writing. Other invaluable aid in this respect came from Peter Brooks, Kevin Newmark, and Karsten Harries. Thomas Trezise has repeatedly intervened at crucial stages in the manuscript's development, each time providing insight, criticism, and the renewed conviction that the project was in fact valuable and worth pursuing. Ross Chambers has generously taken the time to read an earlier version and has given both encouragement and stringent criticism, without which the book would have been at once much narrower in scope and more diffuse in argument.

André Green, Scott Durham, Peter Rose, Steve Nimis, Bruno Bosteels, Eric de Chassey, Joshua Landy, and Yve-Alain Bois have all given significant help on particular points of the manuscript. In a more general but just as real sense, my colleagues in the Department of French and Italian at Miami University have provided encouragement, support, and intellectual breadth during the writing. Marie-Claire Valois in particular has been a rich source of information, and has frequently opened my eyes in more subtle ways to different approaches to conceiving of problems. Her intelligence and ethical engagement have in themselves been an inspiration. Among the many students who have provided perspective and insight into ideas that were often first worked out in seminar, Laura St. Pierre has played an especially important role. Miami University has given very significant assistance to the completion of this project, most materially in a CFR grant, which allowed for manuscript research at the Spoelberch de Lovenjoul collection of the Bibliothèque de l'Institut in Paris, and through a leave of absence. Early work was made possible through the generous support of the Mrs. Giles Whiting Foundation.

Claire de Chassey has aided me both materially and immaterially by providing a place to stay and write in peace during the most decisive moments of authorship. She lent me her house in Paris, where the chapter on *Aurélia* was written, and I hold that inimitably humane and generous environment largely responsible for the shift in tone which that chapter marks, for it was the study of Nerval's last work that held the keys to a passage out of death-based theorizations of subjectivity. Bruno Bosteels, at another crucial point in the manuscript's completion, very generously offered me the undisturbed use of his office in Cambridge, with its summery view over one of the oldest cemeteries in the United States. Johanna Damgaard Liander gave me invaluable help with the collections at Harvard's Widener Library.

Helen Tartar of Stanford University Press has shared her breadth of knowledge and subtlety of insight; I have also learned to admire her tact and determination. Readers would join me in thanking Nathan MacBrien and Ann Klefstad at the Press if they knew the clarity those two have brought to moments of opaque and charmless prose. They have been gracious, firm, and excellent company. Diane Brown meticulously and single-handedly prepared the index.

More than anyone else, though, it is Gabriela Basterra who is responsible for what seem to me to be the work's real merits, perhaps invisible to others. As an interlocutor, especially on Kant, Levinas, and tragedy, she has brought a depth and significance to the book which it otherwise would have lacked. Most important, however, it has been my hope to write something that might at least bear in mind the generosity, intelligence, and deep human goodness she personifies.

These names speak for themselves: the final shortcomings are only my own.

J.S.

Contents

	Preface	*xi*
1.	History and Romantic Self-Identity	*1*
2.	Death-Based Subjectivity	*23*
3.	Nerval in Context: The Authority of Madness	*74*
4.	Playing with Death: *Les Faux Saulniers*	*98*
5.	The Subject Writes After Its Own Death: "Le Christ aux Oliviers"	*134*
6.	The Lyric First Person: "El Desdichado"	*155*
7.	*Aurélia*: The Signs of Others	*206*
8.	Death and Its Alternatives	*269*
	Notes	*291*
	Works Cited	*361*
	Index	*371*

Preface

"Know thyself," read the inscription over the entrance to the Oracle of Delphi, the ancient navel of the world and the temple whose voice would send Socrates forth to lay the foundations of Western philosophy. Probably the god had meant that we should be aware of our indignity as mere mortals, but Socrates' was only the first in more than two thousand years of misreadings, two millennia of misinterpretations that slowly invented and disposed of the self. Know thyself—as if one did not already, and as if the self was something to know, rather than to experience. The oracle pronounced the self to exist on the level of everything else as an object of investigation, submitted to the rules of knowledge that brought the world into order. A self, then, that had to be brought into order for itself, a self that had to be subject to the order of knowledge. The inscription comes not as a call but as an imperative: know thyself. And yet, reading in a particular way, one might detect a certain generosity. More important than anything, it could seem to say, is the knowledge that comes from the self. The oracle asserts the validity of the self as an origin for knowledge, as though knowledge came from the intimacy within, the touchless contact inside that could bring about a world. Perhaps it is not an imperative after all but a calling and an offer of the world: know thyself. Written over the spreading door from which a voice issues, a mute inscription calls out to the self the secret of the self: that through it the world is springing up, that life and its plenitude are not elsewhere but already within, emanating out, overflowing. The inscription calls the self to the self, as its own origin, welling up too, like the world, within. Take pleasure, it says, not later, not elsewhere, but here, and now. And the self, ever since, has hesitated between these two interpretations, between a call and an imperative, between the imposition of an ideology and the overflowing of joy, long suspecting that although profoundly contradictory, they were both right.[1]

More recent than this uncertainty is the conviction that one simply is one's self and that one should expect from others a recognition that is somehow inherently owed that self. We are growing more accustomed to the idea that one's identity is something to be expressed not merely by ourselves but also, derivatively from that, by others. How does one know, however, when that self has been recognized? Does this not imply some innate sense of it, a primordial knowledge? Or perhaps one is driven to know *more* about one's self by investigating the forces that have somehow determined it as it is: cultural, economic, racial, sexual, and so on. But does this not presuppose that one is determinate, a precise and available being, already somehow known to oneself, if only vaguely? A product?[2] What is sought in this book is not the genealogy of any particular subjectivity, or a history of how it came to be, but a certain history of how people *go about* thinking of themselves. It is a limited investigation of what have been dictated or presupposed as the very conditions of being a subject, of having an identity. One forgets that these conditions are open to discussion. Even the oracle itself, while treating the self as something that remains to be known, gave not the slightest hint at how one might go about fulfilling its injunction, as if the self remained to be known but the deeper questions of *how* and by *what means* to know it went without saying.

Such is the basic issue of this book: *how* does one have an identity? There is no single answer, but the sheer plurality of the responses is of interest, for they reveal the way in which the most fundamental structures of individuality are open to change, suasion, violence, and human intervention in general. The specific forms of those plural answers indicate, as well, the sheer range of pain and hope that this freedom of the self entails. The book concentrates on certain figures as representative of a larger recent history of subjectivity, and argues that the writings of the romantic poet Gérard de Nerval can be read as a significant and specifically literary resistance to what could be called an ideology of self-experience. The particular ideology in question is a radically negative model of self-understanding and self-awareness that gained cultural dominance during the period from the French Revolution to the mid-twentieth century, and it remains key to contemporary theories of subjectivity. This model was most thoroughly articulated in Kant and Hegel and, later, by Heidegger and Lacan. Nerval's writings, often at the brink of madness, show that this negative self-construction, which so often passes itself off to be as inevitable as death, not only determines self-*understanding* but that it also determines self-*experience* or, in other words, how it *feels* to be a subject in this cultural and historical context. That feeling is, fundamentally, terror, and the context is still in many ways our own.

Concentrating on one writer as representative of a generalized problem allows one to address the issue of subjectivity at the point of its practical enactment: that convergence of theory and experience that is an individual. Some readers will not be so interested in the work of a French poet and will want to bypass the more literary parts of this book, which concentrate on his writings. Others will be concerned with Nerval and will look for those passages that might offer insights into his aesthetics or life. Although this study is meant to bridge the gap between those two sorts of readers and to show the importance of the most poetic aspects of literary writing for a basic philosophical issue, an outline of the overall text will allow those picking it up for the first time to map their own itinerary through it, one that will lead eventually across it all.

The first chapter contextualizes the overall question of subjectivity by looking at early theorizations of the French Revolution that viewed it as the beginning of history. For the nineteenth-century historian Jules Michelet, it was an event that left in its wake an empty sense of self that something must fill—the feeling of the loss of feeling, of the loss of self. For Kant, history was dependent on a subject, but who that subject might be and how it related to the individual remained to be seen. The self-conscious or apperceptive subject that he set forth as the guarantor of experiential coherence evaporates, under scrutiny, into an empty proposition, while the aesthetic subject, the self of sensation and individuality, finds its true being in the experience of the sublime, which, through an identification with the impersonal abstraction of freedom, constitutes the individual's annihilation *as* individual. Hegel saw this confrontation, this sublimation, as instantiated both in the Terror of the French Revolution and in the relation between sensuous experience and language.

The second chapter describes "death-based subjectivity" as a historically specific model of self-identity that understands the persistence of the self, its identity over time, as absolutely other than momentary and sensuous experiences, of which it is the negation. It is the constant living of the sublime moment in all its terror. The example of the guillotine shows how this could be worked out in social practice and argues that public execution was a mechanism for spectacular subjectification. The examples of Hugo, Zola, Théophile Dondey, and Mallarmé show a more intimate instantiation of this coercive and terrifying model of self-experience. Readings of Kant, Hegel, Nietzsche, Kojève, and Heidegger allow a theorization of this experience and demonstrate the apparent inevitability of understanding one's self as a source of annihilating terror.

Chapter 3 begins to consider the significance of Nerval's writings within this context by addressing the question of his insanity, which by his own accounts seemed indissociable from the question of writing and his sense of identity. His madness was literary, his writing mad, and his subjectivity somehow inseparable from his delirious poetic production. This insanity can be understood, however, in a larger sense as the resistance to death-based subjectivity. Nerval speaks of literature as a game space in which the self is created and where its relation to the world and to others is put into play.

The fourth chapter examines the "eccentric" feuilleton *Les Faux Saulniers* to show how it toys with the possibilities of death and madness that literature had come to represent for Nerval. In this tour de force of ludic digression and rhetorical indeterminability, Nerval attempted to construct an identity as an evasion of the legal, historical, and other institutional discourses that would be ready to determine and dominate it. The self that emerges here is a labile series of metamorphoses that play on the undecidability of stylistic tricks and whose permanence is similar to Lacan's idea of the subject as a pun.

In the fifth chapter, a reading of the sonnet series "Le Christ aux Oliviers" shows the relation between Nerval's aesthetics and Hegel's pronouncement that art was, as of his writing, no more than the empty tomb of dead human historical Spirit. In these poems Nerval does not resist such an approach but in fact embraces it, turning to literature in search of an afterlife, or a life in death. In a fantasy of God's demise, he imagines a material, self-disappropriated subject existing as incoherent objects and a fragmentary poetics that would instantiate an incomprehensible self.

Chapter 6 construes the sonnet "El Desdichado" as an enactment of the aesthetics and world vision sketched out in "Le Christ aux Oliviers." Approached through its very incoherence and poetic meaninglessness, the poem reveals itself not as a self-representation but a self-*creation* in which the poem is itself the subjective model articulating experience in an open-ended and nontotalizing way. The self functions here as an alienated and impossible rhetorical figure that begins to break with Hegel and death-based subjectivity in general.

Chapter 7, a study of Nerval's last work, *Aurélia*, shows how this description of his periods of madness, hallucination, and confinement in asylums argues for the significance of a subjectivity understood not only as linguistic and open-ended but also as a communality called into being by others. This self differs importantly from the Lacanian idea that subjectivity is based on castration and fear.

The final chapter looks at the implications of this open, poetic self that is called upon by others and that slips out from the seemingly inevitable grasp of death-based subjectivity. Something similar has been theorized by Kristeva, Althusser, the psychoanalyst Piera Aulagnier, and by Emmanuel Levinas, but Nerval's painfully defiant self differs from that of these thinkers, too, and in its sybilline utterances it still remains new and unread.

A brief note on conventions used in the text: in quotations, spaced ellipsis points (. . .) indicate omissions of portions of original text; closed suspension points (...) replicate ellipses in the original.

Subjects of Terror

1. History and Romantic Self-Identity

> Hegel, whom we must always cite when it is a question of aesthetics . . .
> —*Gérard de Nerval*

> . . . a universe of death . . .
> —*Edmund Burke (quoting Milton)*

In 1831 the historian Jules Michelet caught a personal and introspective moment in his journals:

> I am deeply affected by having seen my little child standing rapt in front of the ocean. . . .
>
> Seeing on the one hand that terrible image of the infinite and on the other my daughter, and that force that calls us back into the depths of nature, I felt the fiber of my individuality tear apart. The general, the universal, the eternal, these are man's homeland.
>
> It is from you that I shall seek comfort, my noble country; you must take the place of the God who has fled, must fill the incommensurable void that Christianity's passing has left in us. You owe us the equivalent of the infinite. We all feel individuality perishing in us. May there begin in us again the feeling of social generality, of human universality, of the world! Then perhaps will we rise again toward God.[1]

Perhaps more than anyone else, Michelet attempted to create that "noble homeland," with a lifetime of tireless labor, endless years in archives, and the staggering, single-handed and unprecedented production of a twenty-seven-volume history of France. Though he had not created an image of eternity in his work, he had nonetheless depicted a social collectivity with a coherent past and a bearing on the future. Under his pen France emerged as a document and a labor, a construct that took up the life of its author; but if Michelet sacrificed himself to the Herculean task of writing France into being, of creating a coherent documentary homeland that was still lacking, he did not view his undertaking as a personal loss. On the contrary, it represented a protection of his person, a shield against the vanishing of an individuality that, curiously—what was, in fact, the sensation?—he felt shredding away inside himself. It is in this intimate entry from his journals that one can see an explanation for the drive that led him to spend his life in archives and writing, in carefully constructing a single long narrative of one character, one country. That drive, it would appear from this passage, came from a feeling, the sensation of his selfhood disappearing, an experience he can barely mention without calling out, as if apotropaically, the succoring names of the general, the universal, the eternal, of *la patrie*. These are the appellations invoked to turn away a danger that has its own name: facing the individual, like the ocean before a child, is the terrible infinite, a void left by the Revolution's abolition of Christian faith, a void that abolishes, in its turn, the individuality of the one who gazes on it. The corrosive image of this void enters the eye and dissolves the fibers of personhood, the very stem of the self. Against this Moloch-like emptiness stands a single child, and as the ocean is the dreadful image of the void, so is she the image of the author and of us all as solitary figures before the world. There is the need for something, as vast as the ravaging infinite, which would protect us from its pointless and endless negativity, and it is this protective structure of general intelligibility, in which the individual can be mapped and preserved as individual, that Michelet calls homeland, social generality, human universality. There must be something under these names, he asserts, that is as meaningful and positive as the rational aftermath of the Revolution is meaningless and negative. That something, one could say, is what he wrote in the volumes of the *History of France*.[2] It is history that protects the individual from the infinite, and one writes history to take a place and fill an annihilating void, a void one can feel within oneself, already beginning to take one's self away. That feeling, more than the narratives it generated, would be the place to look for the character of Michelet's historical period, for it was just such an experience of fear, of the terrible, that marked his contemporaries' theorizations of the relation between individual and collective time.

It was the Revolution which, in instituting the cult of Reason or the vacuous Supreme Being, brought an end to the relation between God and humanity and as such was the very period that laid waste Christian hope and opened humanity's eyes to the abyssal infinitive that would consume it individual by individual.[3] Michelet will begin writing his *Histoire de la France* for personal reasons, from an inner sense of loss and fear stemming from the events surrounding 1789. Kant, in the *Conflict of the Faculties*, will for theoretical ones situate the inauguration of historical consciousness in a feeling or *Affekt* (of disinterested empathy) provoked by an event such as (and he uses this single example) the Revolution.[4] Though they operate from the two opposing poles of the argument—Michelet, driven by the sensation of his own perishing selfhood, representing individual motivation, and Kant pushed by the impersonal dictates of Reason—both thinkers locate the origin of the historical articulation between human particular and totality in the French Revolution.

Kant's project in philosophy, not unlike Michelet's in history, was to demonstrate the existence of a coherent totality, a project that, in the 1781 *Critique of Pure Reason*, took the form of an argument for the existence of a priori synthetic judgements, that is, of determinations which, without being based on empirical evidence, could offer more information about concepts than could be provided analytically, through their separation into constituent parts. The impossibility of such judgements would leave human beings confronted by the world—or nonworld—of isolated sense data imagined by the British Empiricists, a congeries of information in which one could not legitimately identify any necessary objective laws of connection, such as causality. Kant's counter-argument, in the "Transcendental Aesthetic" section of the first *Critique*, was that space and time were both a priori and synthetic. They were not derived from empirical experience because all empirical experience presupposed them, and they were synthetic because they did not derive from the dissection of another, compound concept. One could say that they were synthetic in another sense, however. By demonstrating the necessity of time and space for all subjective empirical experience, even while bracketing their objective existence as unknowable, Kant seemed to show that the unknowable objective world was bound together in being perceived by certain necessary laws of thought. Thus intelligences, to the extent that they were intelligences, existed within a coherent, ordered totality of intelligible and sensual experiences; in short, they lived within a synthetic world.[5] Underlying the unifying structures of time and space, however, there was for the author of the first *Critique* another, fundamental figure of synthesis: if, for Michelet, it was the historical collective that held the individual together, for Kant it was the Subject that brought the world, and even its time, into a unified manifold.[6] One might be an individual only insofar as one is a historical individual, but, according to the German, there is no history without a subject of history.[7]

Despite the apparent symmetry between Kant's and Michelet's attitudes toward the relation between human part and whole, one should not confuse the former's notion of Subject with the latter's idea of individuality. Kant, in fact, recognized the relation between subject and individual as one of the most vexing of his time, and his discussions of it, for all their negativity and rigorous skepticism, are some of the rare passages in the first *Critique* in which the author demonstrates any affect toward his topic, speaking of "the highest interests of humanity" and of an argument not merely incontrovertible but also "powerful" for the immortality of the soul.[8] Why, one might ask, should the relation between subject and individual be so highly interesting to humanity? Why should it call for arguments not merely incontrovertible but also powerful, why should it call for a reasoning not merely true but also forceful in its expression? Why should it bring to bear on the philosophical text both emotion and rhetoric? One can provisionally respond that this problematic moment of articulating between individual and Subject is analogous to the aporetic attempt to articulate between intuitable experience and conceptual subjectivity, an attempt we shall refer to below as the sublime and which is always marked by affect, even if it is the terrible feeling of the end of feeling. For the moment, however, this sudden expression of Kant's concern for his material need only serve as an index of the importance of this question and an indicator that, through the very modality of its expression, it is tied to other moments in his aesthetic writings where feeling plays a significant and intelligible role.

At the crux of the difference between the Kantian idea of a Subject and what someone like Michelet may have meant by an individual is the impossibility, for Kant, of knowing the subject in itself. The Subject is, first of all, a self-knowing, and Kant refers to it as apperceptive; it holds together thought as the constant operator "I think" which can always be appended to any of its propositions, thereby grounding them in the unity of a thinking first-person agency.[9] Like the objective *noumena*, or things-in-themselves, of the external world which we encounter only as perceptions and transfigured by the laws of perception, but never as they are in themselves, the Subject, although it is structured as self-consciousness and though it is the single basis of experience or intuition, can never in and as itself be intuited but can only be known, even by itself, as a representation. This is not as paradoxical as it seems.

> It is evident that rational psychology owes its origin simply to misunderstanding. The unity of consciousness, which underlies the categories, is here mistaken for an intuition of the subject as object, and the category of substance is then applied to it. But this unity is only unity in *thought*, by which alone no object is given, and to which, therefore, the category of substance, which always presupposes a given *intuition*, cannot be applied. Consequently, this subject cannot be known. The subject of the categories cannot by thinking the

categories acquire a concept of itself as an object of the categories. For in order to think them, its pure self-consciousness, which is what was to be explained, must be pre-supposed.[10]

As the eye can see only the visual effects or images of its activity but can never see the act of seeing in itself, since to see that act, if it were physiologically possible, would presuppose it and would render it, insofar as it was observed, as a *seen* seeing, that is to say, not in itself but as altered according to the laws of visual perception, and therefore as the object rather than the activity of seeing, so the subject, as that which underlies the forms of all possible thought and perception, can never be thought in itself, but only as thought transformed by the laws of thinking, which Kant calls categories. Unlike the objects of sense perception or of thought, however, there is no intuition that underlies our knowledge of the subject; rather, it is discernable only as the intuitionless structure of thinking. Whereas there might be certain physiological processes in seeing that would be the basis of intuitions transformed by perception, in the subject there is no intuition, only form. The form that the unknowable subject gives in the very act of thinking is unity itself.[11] The subject that establishes the coherence of all thought is, as Kant puts it, self-consciousness, but a self-consciousness that does not know itself, which is conscious of itself only as a representation, of a representation not of any*thing* but rather of the formal unity of thought. The Subject is self-knowledge, but only as the representation of the principle of coherence itself, expressible as "I think."

One is inclined to think of the unified and unifying "I" of apperception as an individual, that is, as something like a Cartesian *res cogitans* or that which Michelet felt vanishing in himself, but this cannot be, since the Kantian subject is explicitly described as neither thing (*res*) nor object of possible intuition (or feeling). The pure subjectivity of the subject has certain significant consequences. Because it can never be given as an object of knowing, one can make no objective judgements about the subject. One cannot, for example, say that objectively it would be permanent, substantial, or simple, or even that as representation it figures something with those qualities.

> It has . . . been proved that the concept of a thing which can exist by itself as a subject and never as mere predicate, carries with it no objective reality; in other words, that we cannot know whether there is any object to which the concept is applicable—as to the possibility of such a mode of existence we have no means of deciding—and that the concept therefore yields no knowledge whatsoever. If by the term 'substance' be meant an object which can be given, and if it is to yield knowledge, it must be made to rest on a permanent intuition, as being that through which alone the object of our concept can be given, and as

being, therefore the indispensable condition of the objective reality of the concept. Now in inner intuition there is nothing permanent, for the "I" is merely the consciousness of my thought. So long, therefore, as we do not go beyond mere thinking, we are without the necessary condition for applying the concept of substance, that is, of a self-subsistent subject, to the self as a thinking being. And with the objective reality of the concept of substance, the allied concept of simplicity likewise vanishes; it is transformed into a merely logical qualitative unity of self-consciousness in thought in general, which has to be present whether the subject be composite or not.[12]

In making this argument for the unknowability of the apperceptive agency, Kant moves from speaking of the subject as consciousness of my thought to referring to it as the unity of thought in general. If the subject is to be considered the consciousness of my thought, the latter can only be deemed to be *my* thought because *I*, as subject, am conscious of it, but since the nature of the "I" is what is to be explained in such a determination, the fact that it must be presupposed (in the concept of the *mineness* of my thought) makes it impossible, without falling into a *petitio principii*, to adduce the apparent objective unity of those thoughts, derived from their being mine, as evidence for the simplicity or the substantiality of the subject. The significance of this begins to become apparent if one recalls that the "I" unifies all propositions and possible conscious events insofar as they can all be predicated of the statement: "I think (or am conscious) that… "[13] The problem that Kant addresses in the above paragraph is the tendency to take this apperceptive formula as a synthetic rather than an analytic judgement; to understand it as the former is to suppose that some further knowledge can be derived from the formula than is available from the mere identification of its necessary constituent elements, but Kant here states explicitly that the concept of the pure subject "yields no knowledge whatsoever." If the "I think" is to be considered as analytic, however, it can be reformulated, more exactly, as "It is (here, in this stating) stated that… " where "it," "here," and "this" only indicate what is already analytically implicit in the act or fact of the statement itself. The problem of presupposing the "I" in the statement of its nature is avoided, but the subject is reduced to something like the proposition: "this is a proposition." This purely analytic subject, strange as it might appear, would conform to what Kant seems to mean by the expression "purely logical." What the subject, were it knowable, would designate cannot be said, and therefore one cannot know whether the subject, as anything other than pure propositional positioning and self-indexing, is in itself composite or simple. Since the idea of individuality supposes that simplicity, one cannot say that Kant's subject is an individual. According to his reasoning, the subject of experience is purely propositional, logical, almost grammatical.

Insofar, then, as there is a world in which the individual can exist, that world is held together by the subject, but that subject is, as far as it can be known, purely propositional, the mere self-deixis of expression that creates an abstract here and now of its own auto-referentiality. The knowable subject of experience, insofar as that experience is coherent, is thus impersonal and representational (but of no*thing*, of nothing knowable except as that representation), something like the sheer words themselves of the formula "I think." Who then feels, one might legitimately ask? A stranger, an alien? And how does one make sense of Michelet's feeling that he was losing himself? One could say that Michelet's consciousness of his own annihilation before the terrible image of the infinite was his feeling the subject—that which gives coherence and representability to the whole world at the sacrifice of everything in it, including himself—as knowable object of experience. This idea of feeling the subject is not so absurd or paradoxical as it may at first sound. In fact, it was theorized by Kant—and many of his contemporaries—under the name of "the sublime," and as such it became a conceptual cornerstone for romantic aesthetics and ideology. It is something like the affectively marked passage from a sentient agent of experience to an intelligible and coherent subject, and one could say that even now it continues to underwrite some of the most significant and influential, if also perhaps the most barren, theories of subjectivity and selfhood.[14]

The Sublime Subject and the Terror: Kant and Hegel

By defining the human, in "On the Sublime," as that which wills to do rather than that which must do, Friedrich Schiller found in the imperious necessity of death, which he called that "single terror, *which he [i.e. the human individual] simply must do and does not will*," an apparent dehumanization of the human.[15] Because he must die, no individual can be considered human. In willing to die, however, that same individual regains his humanity, asserting his superiority over the natural and material through a sacrifice of self-interest. There will thus be instances—indeed one can say that it is the human condition, the condition of humanity before death—in which one will in fact have to kill oneself:

> Cases occur in which fate surmounts all the ramparts upon which man founds his security and nothing else remains but for him to flee into the sacred freedom of the spirit… and no other means of withstanding this power of nature than to anticipate her, and by a free renunciation of all sensuous interest to kill himself morally before some physical force does it.[16]

The individual's humanity resides here in his ability to assert his freedom over physical constraints through an act of moral suicide. This makes of freedom the moral negation of material self-interest, a pitting of the spirit against the concrete and material. It also ensues from this that if freedom and the human can be bought at the price of individual death, they must exceed the concrete particular existence of the individual: in the willed, human death, one therefore dies not for one's own freedom or the freedom of another, but for freedom itself, for humanity itself. One annihilates one's living self for an idea, becoming a negative sign of that which cannot be figured. One becomes, in Kant's terms, sublime, and the human itself is thus the sublime.

It is precisely in terms of the sublime that Schiller himself understands this freedom. For him, the sublime is to "stand face to face with the evil fatality. Not in ignorance of the dangers which lurk about us—for finally there must be an end to ignorance—only in *acquaintance* with them lies our salvation. We are aided in this acquaintance by the magnificent spectacle of change which destroys everything and creates it anew, and destroys it again . . . "[17] This confrontation is, however, salvation only on the level of another faculty—that of Reason—for if the individual encountering such a spectacle of the terrifying destructiveness of nature

> willingly abandons the attempt to assimilate this lawless chaos of appearances to a cognitive unity, he will abundantly regain in another direction what he has lost in this. It is precisely the entire absence of a purposive bond among this press of appearances by which they are rendered unencompassable and useless for the understanding (which is obliged to adhere to this kind of bond) that makes them an all the more striking image for pure reason, which finds in just this wild incoherence [*wilde Ungebundenheit*] of nature the depiction of her own independence of natural conditions. . . . Thus reason combines in a single unity of thought within this idea of freedom, which she supplies from her own resources, what understanding can never combine in a unity of experience; by this idea she subordinates the infinite play of appearances to herself, and simultaneously asserts her power over the understanding as a sensuously limited faculty.[18]

This unity of thought, this idea that brings together in a unified and coherent whole the lawless destructiveness which we confront in the sublime, is freedom, which ultimately instantiates itself as a radical refusal of self-interest expressed as suicide. What is gained in the intellectual unity of the idea of reason, in the transformation of nature into a unified concept of lawlessness, is not gained on the level of the material individual, but rather on the level of the impersonal moral law itself. The sublime is freedom, which in turn is the will to die, instantiated ultimately, in certain cases, by self-destruction in the name of a coherent idea.

The full negative force of sublime freedom is less immediately apparent in Kant's *Critique of Judgement* than in Schiller, partly because the overall argument in the "The Analytic of the Sublime" is more highly elaborated than Schiller's. First, for Kant, the experience of the sublime, or at least of the dynamic sublime, involves the question of freedom, although the relation between the two seems of secondary importance when first mentioned. According to Kant, in an experience of the dynamic sublime, the mind is capable of appreciating the overwhelmingly destructive forces of nature or the divine without fear of their potential damage to its personal, material interests. This distinction between appreciation and fear of overwhelming force is referred to as a state of freedom. As Kant writes: "The man that is actually in a state of fear, finding in himself good reason to be so, because he is conscious of offending with his evil disposition against a might directed by a will at once irresistible and just, is far from being in a frame of mind for admiring divine greatness, for which a temper of calm reflection and a quite free judgement [*ganz freies Urtheil*] are required."[19] This freedom of judgement would seem at first to be of a very different nature than Schiller's human freedom of the will, insofar as it is not initially cast as a sacrifice of self-interest through a voluntary embracing of what is most negative to self-interest (a willing what one fears), but rather as a securing of self-interest through moral behavior. Kant's appreciator of divine sublimity is free from fear not because he wills the terrible to himself, but because he knows that his acceptability to God will turn away from him the divine wrath visited upon other, less pious souls. Kant continues the above passage by explaining that "only when he [the man who is in a state of fear] becomes conscious of having a disposition that is upright and acceptable to God, do those operations of might serve to stir within him the idea of the sublimity of this Being... "[20] Whereas freedom in Schiller would be a heroic assertion of the will, in Kant it seems to be a form of humility. In the former freedom is freedom from self-interest ultimately instantiated in moral suicide, in the latter it seems to be the securing of self-interest from fear through servile uprightness. And yet it should serve as a clue to the profound identity of the two approaches that one can imagine a humility which would amount to a willing of what one must anyway undergo, a free subservience. And ultimately this is what Kant's sublime moral freedom amounts to.

The true and profoundly negative nature of Kant's concept of freedom can begin to be seen at the end of the section of "The Analytic of the Sublime" that speaks of the difference between fear and admiration. He writes:

> Everything that provokes this feeling [of our superiority over nature] in us, including the *might* of nature which challenges our strength, is then, though improperly [since the sublime is subjective, and only apparently objective], called sublime, and it is only under presupposition of this idea within us, and in relation to it, that we are capable of attaining to the idea of the sublimity of that Being which inspires deep respect in us, not by the mere display of its might in nature, but more by the faculty which is planted in us of estimating that might without fear, and of regarding our estate as exalted above it.[21]

Two things are to be remarked here. First, that the human ability to appreciate the power of nature places the human in a position of superiority in regard to nature. Second, this appreciative superiority is an *idea*, and it is only under the presupposition of this idea that we can attain such superiority. Thus, human freedom derives from the opposition of idea to nature and is in fact itself the idea that is opposed to nature.

This opposition between the idea of freedom and nature takes the more precise and radical form of a negation of the material or sensible, as Kant makes clear in the pages following the above paragraph. "The beautiful," he writes, "prepares us to love something, even nature, apart from any interest: the sublime to esteem something highly even in opposition to our (sensible) interest."[22] In fact, this opposition to material interest is the essence of the sublime: "The *sublime* is what pleases immediately by reason of its opposition to the interest of sense."[23] Now, this very negation of sensible interest, which constitutes the sublime, is explicitly characterized by Kant as a moral law which in turn constitutes a form of freedom:

> The object of a pure and unconditioned intellectual delight is the moral law in the might which it exerts in us over all *antecedent* motives of the mind. Now, since it is only through sacrifices that this might makes itself known to us aesthetically, (and this involves a deprivation of something—though in the interests of inner freedom [zum Behuf der innern Freiheit]—whilst in turn it reveals in us an unfathomable depth of this supersensible faculty, the consequences of which extend beyond reach of the eye of sense), it follows that the delight, looked at from the aesthetic side (in reference to sensibility) is negative, i.e., opposed to this interest, but from the intellectual side, positive and bound up with an interest.[24]

Thus, the might that makes the human transcendent over natural necessity (Nature's destructive forces) is a moral law which makes itself known aesthetically (materially, or figurably) only through negation or sacrifice of sensible interest. The positive side of this sacrifice, its interest, is purely intellectual and is specifically freedom itself. The uprightness of the individual acceptable to God, that which makes the human capable of recognizing the sublime, is not the securing of personal (sensible) interest but the sacrificing of it in the name (literally) of the purely intellectual idea of uprightness itself, that is, the moral law.

It is with this understanding of freedom and the moral law that one can now make sense of a dense passage that links the sublime to terror and subjectivity, thereby opening the way to an appreciation of Hegel's reading of the Terror of the French Revolution as a sublime and annihilating mediation between absolute freedom (freedom as absolute) and the concrete particular individual. The paragraph in question begins: "Thus, too, delight in the sublime in nature is only *negative* (whereas that in the beautiful is *positive*): that is to say, it is a feeling of imagination by its own act depriving itself of its freedom by receiving a final determination in accordance with a law other than that of its empirical employment."[25] One cannot, in view of other sections of the same text previously quoted and discussed, understand this loss of freedom in the sublime as an absolute loss; rather, the negativity of the sublime is a loss of freedom on the empirical level, a loss recompensed by a final determination on a higher level—that of law, of the moral. But this higher level, this determination in accordance with the moral, is itself a higher level of freedom, since, as has been previously discussed, the morality of the sublime is precisely an intellectual and pure freedom. Or, as Kant will put it a few pages later, "aesthetic finality is the conformity to law of judgement in its *freedom*."[26] The passage continues:

> In this way it [imagination] gains an extension and a might greater than that which it sacrifices. But the ground of this is concealed from it, and in its place it *feels* the sacrifice or deprivation, as well as its cause, to which it is subjected. The *astonishment* amounting almost to terror [die an Schreck gränzt], the awe and thrill of devout feeling, that takes hold of the viewer [der Zuschauer] when gazing upon the prospect of mountains ascending to heaven, deep ravines and torrents raging there, deep-shadowed solitudes that invite to brooding melancholy, and the like—all this, when he knows himself to be in safety [bei der Sicherheit, worin er sich weiß], is not actual fear.[27]

Either a hesitation or an apparent contradiction troubles Kant's text: here he states that the terror of the sublime is aesthetically appreciable at its true value only insofar as one is assured of one's own safety, which is to say one's interest, and yet elsewhere he contends that the sublime is precisely the negation of at least sensible interest. The apparent paradox can be resolved by considering the safety said to be assured here not as *sensible* interest but as *intellectual* interest, since, as we have seen, the former is held to be sacrificed to the latter in the experience of the sublime.[28] There is no reason to believe that Kant *wants* to say this, that there is not a genuine hesitation in his text, but it is the only way to resolve the apparent antinomy of freedom here, and it is how Hegel will resolve the problem of freedom, to say that in this passage the "he" who is assured of safety, or the preservation of interest, can only be a "he" who has identified with the abstract, negative principle of moral law: freedom itself.[29] It should also be noted that Kant describes the feeling of the sublime conversion of the "he" from material to idea as precisely not fear but as something bordering on *terror*.[30]

This feeling of astonishment close to terror, which would be felt as terror were the observer not socialized through a submission to moral ideas, did the observer not in fact identify himself with the moral as idea, which is to sacrifice material interest in favor of an abstract and idealized interest— this near-terror marks the submission of the individual to the principle of freedom.

> But acting in accordance with principles of the schematism of judgement, (consequently so far as it is subordinated to freedom,) it [imagination] is at the same time an instrument of reason and its ideas. But in this capacity it is a might enabling us to assert our independence as against the influences of nature, to degrade what is great in respect of the latter to the level of what is little, and thus to locate the absolutely great only in the proper estate of the Subject.[31]

Thus, the sacrifice of material self-interest in favor of intellectual and idealized and universal interest (the moral law) is a sacrifice in favor of freedom, but since this sacrifice is, as has been said, an identification (the "he" who identifies with the moral law), one can say that the one who triumphs over nature's forces is only the one who has sacrificed himself as particular individual and has identified himself as freedom itself. This is what Kant here denominates as "Subject." The sublime subject is thus impersonal and abstract, the negation of concrete materiality. It is literally no one.

In the *Phenomenology of Spirit*, Hegel too will link the absolute, freedom, and terror in a moment that annihilates the concrete individual. The discussion here, although it does not make explicit reference to the sublime as such, functions according to its terms and structures as determined by Kant in his aesthetic writings. Hegel entitles the section of his work devoted to the French Revolution "Absolute Freedom and Terror" (Die absolute Freiheit und der Schrecken) and he characterizes the period of Jacobin ascendancy as the sacrifice of individual consciousness to an abstract and absolute notion of freedom. During this period the "Notion"

> comes into existence in such a way that each individual consciousness raises itself [sich erhebt] out of its allotted sphere, no longer finds its essence and its

work in this particular sphere, but grasps [erfaßt] itself as the *Notion* [*Begriff*] of will, grasps all spheres as the essence of this will, and therefore can only realize itself in a work which is a work of the whole. In this absolute freedom, therefore, all social groups or classes which are the spiritual spheres into which the whole is articulated are abolished; the individual consciousness that belonged to any such sphere, and willed and fulfilled itself in it, has put aside its limitation; its purpose is the general purpose, its language universal law, its work the universal work.[32]

The freedom of the Terror thus pits the absolute against individual consciousness. It is the infinite expansion, or de-limitation, of specific articulations into a universal notion, the elevation of the particular into the undifferentiated and purely ideal. In the Terror, therefore, the individual consciousness grasps, or *comprehends* (*erfaßt*) itself as a universal Notion, and its language becomes universal law.[33] Since it is from the archaic form of the past participle of the verb Hegel uses for this elevation (*erheben*) that the German word for the sublime (*Erhabene*) comes, it would be no undue violence to the language to translate as a "sublimation" this raising up of the individual consciousness into a purely absolute and notional essence.

Although the term "individual consciousness" is here taken in the sense not of any particular individual but of distinct social spheres or classes, in other passages from this same section it becomes clear that such a particular individual is in fact the true object of negation, the one who pays the ultimate price of sacrifice to the absolute. The leveling of class difference, which in Hegel's terms is the "destruction of the actual organization of the world," would be only a preparatory step to the real and final act of negation, that of the atomic self-consciousness: put concretely, it is always some *one's* head that must fall beneath the blade of the guillotine. Hegel describes the historical moment of this apogee of universal freedom as follows:

> And, moreover, by virtue of its own abstraction [um ihrer eigenen Abstraktion], it [the universality of universal freedom] divides itself into extremes equally abstract [in ebenso abstrakte Extreme], into a simple, inflexible cold universality [Allgemeinheit], and into the discrete, absolute hard rigidity and self-willed atomism [Punktualität] of actual self-consciousness. Now that it has completed the destruction of the actual organization of the world, and exists now just for itself, this is its sole object, an object that no longer has any content, possession, existence, or outer extension, but is merely this knowledge of itself as an absolutely pure and free individual self. All that remains of the object by which it can be laid hold of [an was er erfaßt werden kann] is solely its *abstract* existence as such. The relation, then, of these two, since each exists

indivisibly and absolutely for itself, and thus cannot dispose of a middle term which would link them together, is one of wholly *unmediated* pure negation, a negation, moreover, of the individual as a being *existing* in the universal. The sole work and deed of universal freedom is therefore *death*, a death too which has no inner significance or filling, for what is negated is the empty point of the absolutely free self [der unerfüllte Punkt des absolut freien Selbsts]. It is thus the coldest and meanest of all deaths, with no more significance than cutting off a head of cabbage or swallowing a mouthful of water [also das Durchbauen eines Kohlhaupts oder ein Schluck Wassers].[34]

The use of a metaphorics of eating and drinking, of cabbages and mouthfuls of water, to describe the death of the self, introduces the question of materiality into the opposition between atomic individual consciousness and abstract Notion.[35] This atomic, individual self-consciousness is, by now, actual only in an immaterial sense. The world has divided itself into the abstract concept of absolute freedom, on the one hand, and the absolutely pure and free individual on the other. The latter is, in other words, the individual consciousness, the person, who has identified with the principle of freedom, who has submitted to what Hegel had earlier called "the universal law."[36] And for these very reasons, because of this identification of himself as abstract principle of freedom, because of his identification with a universal moral law, this individual that is no longer an individual but rather a universal is the same as Kant's sublime Subject.[37] And like Kant's sublime subject, Hegel's absolutely pure and free individual self has arisen through a sacrifice of sensible interest, through a sacrifice of its own materiality. Having identified with the abstract principle of absolute freedom, it has reduced itself to "an object that no longer has any content, possession, existence, or outer extension." The use of the term "no longer" is worth noting, because it indicates that the absolutely free and abstract individual arises out of one which, like Kant's interested and terrified presublime self, has extension, possession, content and existence, which is to say, material actuality.

The atomic absolutely free self, which would correspond to Kant's sublime subject, differs from the notion of freedom itself not materially, but pseudo-materially, so to speak, through the pure punctuality of its atomism. It is the "empty point of the absolutely free self," what Hegel will soon after call the "insubstantial point [substanzlose Punkt],"[38] and like the geometrical point, the free self immaterially indicates material position, designates in its punctuality only its merely theoretical objectivity from absolute freedom itself. As individual self-consciousness raises itself up to a mouthpiece of the language of the universal law of freedom, it has sacrificed an actual, concrete, material particularity to become a "point," which is to say an abstract concept of the specific.

Having identified with freedom itself, it is *only* as such a punctuality that the individual can now be "laid hold of."[39]

Hegel insists heavily on the meaninglessness of the death of the atomic individual, describing it in the above passage as having no more significance than the cutting off of a head of cabbage. Later, in speaking of the sacrifice of all marks of concrete particularity which self-consciousness must undergo to become atomistic, he again returns to this theme of absolute negativity: "All these determinations have vanished in the loss suffered by the self in absolute freedom; its negation is the death that is without meaning, the sheer terror of the negative [der bedeutungslose Tod, der reine Schrecken des Negativen] that contains nothing positive, nothing that fills it with a content."[40] Now, this death of the atomic individual is meaningless for two important reasons. First, because it is already dead: it has already sacrificed its actuality to abstraction, its specificity to universality, its finitude to the infinite, so that it is merely that which speaks the language of universal law. Second, it is meaningless because this death is not a sublation or *Aufhebung*. There is, as Hegel puts it, no mediation between the two absolutes (abstract freedom, and the abstract individual): "The relation, then, of these two, since each exists indivisibly and absolutely for itself, and thus cannot dispose of a middle term which would link them together, is one of wholly *unmediated* pure negation, a negation, moreover, of the individual as a being *existing* in the universal."[41] Where there is no mediation, there is no determination of the negation, no dialectic, no progress. In the name (literally) of absolute freedom, the concrete, material determinacy of the individual is abolished and his head guillotined as indifferently as a head of cabbage, because that materiality and determinacy have already been abstracted in the individual's identification with absolute freedom. And because there is no mediation, there is no sublation, no *Aufhebung*, and consequently the negation of the execution leads to a dead end, dialectically. The feeling evoked by this faceless confrontation with the sheer, meaningless negativity of a death that has already happened is designated by Hegel as pure terror, "der reine Schrecken."[42]

In Kant, terror is the uncultured feeling that precedes one's individual identification with the moral law, the law that offers intellectual positivity in exchange for a sacrifice of sensible interest. In Hegel, however, the sacrifice offers precisely nothing in return because submission to "universal law," to absolute freedom, has nothing positive about it. It is simply death, meaningless death. Therefore, for Hegel, terror is not the feeling that is sublated in an identification with the notional and abstract positivity of freedom as moral law, for absolute freedom and the law which is its language are purely negative. Rather, terror for Hegel is the feeling of recognition that the sublimation of the concrete individual in an identification with absolute freedom is entirely negative, is simply meaningless death. Hegel's reading of the Jacobin reign during the French Revolution is thus a rereading of Kant's aesthetics of the sublime which resolves what we have described as a hesitation in the earlier text. The lability of Kant's ideas of positivity and safety, his apparent indecision whether what turns away the terror of the sublime is safety from individual immolation in the absolute or safety in the ability to consider that self-immolation as positive on a higher, impersonal level—that lability is resolved by Hegel as pure negativity. Utter disinterest cannot be considered positive, in Hegel's terms, and the ambiguity that cordoned the sublime off from the terror of absolute death is removed. The difference between Kant's sublime and Hegel's Terror is that Hegel's individual is aware that his personal, material sacrifice of himself as finite, atomic consciousness on behalf of a sublimation into absolute freedom is not a sublation, has nothing positive about it, but is a pure dead end in which he will, as finite individual consciousness, simply and sheerly die. The sublime Subject, the utterly free I, is simply a grammatical construct which can be grasped only in moments and places like the cold embrace of the guillotine, while its approach can be felt in the feeling of terror, the feeling of the end of feeling. This seems to have been the sensation that Michelet knew when, standing by the edge of the sea, he faced that image of the end of images, of the end of imagination and the imaginable world, "cette terrible image de l'infini."

The Linguistic Sublime: Hegel and Sense Certainty

To ward off that terror Michelet turned to writing, but writing contains its own inherent dangers for the individual subject of experience. Hegel, in fact, advanced a theory of language which could be called the linguistic sublime—although he himself never used the expression.[43] In a passage from the *Phenomenology of Spirit*, published one year before Nerval's birth and seventeen years after Kant's *Critique of Judgement*, Hegel pitted the sensuous against abstraction, as Kant did in the third *Critique*'s discussion of the sublime. What is of particular interest here is the role of writing in the convergence of several different issues: the relation between permanence and the here and now, the annihilating character of this relationship, and its connection to the "I." Taking truth to mean essence, or that which, unlike the accidental or contingent, remains unvaryingly predicable of something, Hegel uses the example of a scrap of paper to demonstrate that the truth of the here and now is the abstract and universal. At midnight, the observation "Now is the night" had been jotted down, and it is read later, at noon:

> The Now that is Night is *preserved*, i.e. it is treated as what it professes to be, as something that *is*; but it proves itself to be, on the contrary, something that is *not*. The Now does indeed preserve itself, but as something that is *not* Night; equally, it preserves itself in face of the Day that it now is, as something that also is not Day, in other words, as a *negative* in general. This self-preserving Now is, therefore, not immmediate but mediated; for it is determined as a permanent and self-preserving Now *through* the fact that something else, viz. Day and Night, is *not*. As so determined, it is still just as simply Now as before, and in this simplicity is indifferent to what happens in it; just as little as Night and Day are its being, just as much also is it Day and Night; it is not in the least affected by this its other-being. A simple thing of this kind which *is* through negation, which is neither This nor That, a *not-This*, and is with equal indifference This as well as That—such a thing we call a *universal*. So it is in fact the universal that is the true [content] of sense-certainty.[44]

One can say of the now that it is Night and that it is Day and both will be, at the appropriate time, true. But the now, in its truth, that is to say in its persistent or self-preserving sameness to itself, is neither Night nor Day. One cannot simply say that it is both Night *and* Day, since these are mutually exclusive predications: the now is, rather, *either* Night or Day. The persistent self-sameness, the essential or true identity of the now cannot be found in any of its infinite possible predications because each one is contradicted by all of the others. The truth of the now is thus the negation of all particular predications that can be applied to it insofar as they are particular, and it is in this sense that the now is something negative in general, or, as Hegel also puts it, a universal. The universal, through its persistent self-identity, is thus the negation of the particular. Similarly, Hegel argues, the "I" of sense certainty is, in its truth, impersonal, for when I attempt to give utterance to myself as "I," "I say in general all 'Is'; everyone is what I say, everyone is 'I,' this singular 'I.' Consequently, the 'I' is merely universal like 'Now.'"[45]

Now, the place in which this self-sameness is revealed, the medium of its appearance, is language. The self-sameness of the observation "Now is the night" is maintained and made manifest by being written down. It is important to understand that Hegel does not mean that it is the materiality of the paper on which the observation is noted which guarantees its durability, since it is precisely the material, the sensuous, which is being volatilized in this demonstration. Rather, it is language itself, since language, by its very nature, substitutes a generic sign for the specific object intended by sense-certainty.[46] It is through language, and writing, that we make manifest to ourselves the annihilating force of our own abstract faculties in relation to our sensuous ones. Hegel asserted that language, by its very nature, could express nothing but the annihilation of the particular, because linguistic expression invariably universalizes the object it is intended to designate by forever abstracting away its concrete specificity. In attempting to speak of the finite, individual particulars of sensual existence, he wrote, "we do not *envisage* the universal This or Being in general, but we *utter* the universal; in other words, we do not strictly say what in this sense-certainty we *mean* to say. But language, as we see, is the more truthful; in it, we ourselves directly refute what we *mean* to say."[47] In other words, although we intend to express the finite particular we instead give utterance to its nullity in respect to the universal truth which it instantiates and which negates it.

In the "I," in the name, or in the entire creation of a written self, the particularity of the self is lost, becoming a locus of substitution that can designate each and every individual, but in a sort of pseudo-individuality, a generalized and categorical individuality; language is the death of the particular, and the written subject remains eternally preserved only as an abstract universal.[48] Consequently, according to Hegel, by the very nature of language, in saying "I" one is always inevitably saying "I am nothing," for the truth of the individual—instantiated *as* truth in language—is precisely *not* the individual. To the extent that the faculty of reason, as described in Kant's theory of the sublime, can be understood as a sublation (a death and preservation) of sensual, imaginative individuality and as the abstraction of the sensual world into the conceptual infinite, it is structurally equivalent to language as described by Hegel. In both cases the individual particular of sensual experience is preserved *only in its infinite or universal* annihilation—that is, not as an individual at all. One must therefore wonder in what sense this can be considered "preservation" and, therefore, determinate negation and *Aufhebung*, for the negation exercised here is precisely the negation *of determination itself*. The Kantian triumph of the individual in the sublime and his Hegelian truth in language are therefore anything but individual. They are merely abstract negation, what Hegel, in his discussions of the guillotine and the Master/Slave dialectic, describes as death: the simple, unrecuperable end of consciousness.[49] The *Phenomenology* has, in short, extended from the sublime moment to *all* moments the annihilating confrontation between particular and abstract universal. This moment involves the "I," is indeed the truth of the "I," of the "I" as self-identity. Because the self, insofar as it is constant, is the annihilating other of its own sensuous experiences, sublime reason and language cannot be said to save the individual but to end him or her.

The absolutely negative relation between the sensuous and its abstraction set out by this chapter of the *Phenomenology* is not resolved through later dialectical mediations. It is an indication of the troubling effects of sublimation in the

Phenomenology that both the role of language in "Sense Certainty" and the chapter on the Terror in general are described by Jean Hyppolite as particularly problematic aspects of the system.[50] Furthermore, Hegel's analysis of the Terror, as we understand it, is an application to the relation between state and individual of the relation between sensuous particular and abstract language—it is in this sense that the citizen becomes a mere expression of the language of the law, as Hegel puts it. It will become apparent, from our discussion of Alexandre Kojève in the next chapter, that the role of abstraction and sublimation has troubling implications for Hegel's system as a whole. In other words, the difference between a terrible sublimation of the sensuous and its recuperative dialectical sublation is not necessarily as secure as Hegel would have us believe, and the death that he proposes as the basis of the human may not, in fact, be as hospitable to the individual it inhabits as he wants to argue.

Literature in the Episteme of Written Subjectivity

Michel Foucault described the scission between expression and thing, between *les mots et les choses*, as the defining characteristic of an essential shift in the eighteenth-century paradigms of the relation between individual and world. It is precisely the newly determined incongruity between representations and the objects of those representations that constituted, for him, the change of episteme between classicism and the modern period. Although he tracks the signs of this rupture in three different intellectual domains—economics, natural history, and linguistics—it seems to bear most significantly, and most fundamentally, on the relation between the individual and the subject. First of all, this advent of a new episteme is not merely a historical event. It is meta-historical, for it was in allowing a difference between the structures of representation and those of the represented (for instance, between the structures of grammar and those of thought, which the earlier *Logique* of Port Royal had taken to be homologous) that the expression of human time came to be understood as history rather than sheer order.[51] History, as an expression of human time with its own material density and opacity—a density and opacity that have nothing to do with the nature of what is represented but which originate in the exigencies of representation itself—is thus premised on a structure, or rather *is* a structure, that will prove to be similar to the relation between individual and language. This fact puts one in the curious position of being able to determine a writer's historical *con*text primarily by reading his or her *texts* themselves.

The relation between individual and language in what Foucault calls the new episteme becomes most apparent in juxtaposing his analyses of economics and linguistics. In the former domain, with the theories of Adam Smith, a model based on barter in which goods represent each other, is replaced by one in which goods get their value from an irreducible constant: labor, which is not itself a representation of something else, but whose finality is based on the finality of human existence, the fact that it can be used up (as death) and that it *is* used up in labor, which Foucault calls "toil and time, the working-day that at once segments and uses up a man's life."[52] As a result, the study of wealth and exchange tends toward a study of the human itself: "it is already pointing in the direction of an anthropology that will call into question man's very essence (his finitude, his relation with time, the imminence of death)."[53] What that anthropology of labor reveals about the human—but reveals only in its premises—is that the latter's foundational element is "*a* man," the individual, that this individual is established through his relation to death, and that the determining, defining irreducible of the anthropological individual is death. The finitude by which the latter can be defined—the terminus, or term, by which he is determinable—is death, and what labor thus reveals, without ever *meaning* anything, is that one is by essence always the one who is dying.

In linguistics, on the other hand, and especially in the writings of Bopp, language passes from being itself an instantiation of the basic organization or *form* of thought, varied into different languages only by the force of events over time, to being one *object* of thought among others. But in a sort of aesthetic compensation, as language loses its unique and privileged status as a universally determining formality in scientific discourse, or the "discours d'idées," according to Foucault it gains in autonomous finality as literature, which supposes and embodies, rather than demonstrates, the primacy of language. That presupposed primacy of language is precisely its subjectivity, and so, as language becomes object of knowledge in the work of philologists, it becomes subject of knowing in literature. What that subject knows, however, is only itself, as literature, and with the change in the episteme, with the reduction of language to object of scientific interest, literature

> breaks with the whole definition of *genres* as forms adapted to an order of representations, and becomes merely a manifestation of a language which has no other law than that of affirming—in opposition to all other forms of discourse—its own precipitous existence; and so there is nothing for it to do but to curve back in a perpetual return upon itself [retour sur soi], as if its discourse could have no other content than the expression of its own form; it addresses itself to itself as a writing subjectivity, or seeks to re-apprehend the essence of all literature in the movement that brought it into being; and thus all its threads converge upon the finest points—singular, instantaneous, and yet

absolutely universal—upon the simple act of writing. At the moment when language, as spoken and scattered words, becomes an object of knowledge, we see it reappearing in a strictly opposite modality: a silent, cautious deposition of the word upon the whiteness of a piece of paper, where it can possess neither sound nor interlocutor, where it has nothing to say but itself, nothing to do but shine in the brightness of its being [scintiller dans l'éclat de son être].[54]

What Foucault describes is not merely the dead end of peevish literary effeteness expressed—as, say, the doctrine of "l'art pour l'art"—by authors narcissistically wounded to find their medium reduced, among certain of their more influential contemporaries, from the form of truth to its object. What he is arguing, one could say, is that there was one discipline at this moment that took as its object that which can never be an object; that literature is the field in which the strictly propositional subject of Kant's first *Critique* unfolds itself in the appearance of its being, of its being as appearance, or *Schein*, or *éclat*. Despite what Foucault says, literature, viewed in this way, is not therefore a retreat from science or the "discours d'idées," but is the engagement of its most troubling issue, that of the subject; and one cannot say that Kant's work does not fall under the heading of science, or that one is using the expression "discours d'idées" promiscuously to include him, since it is precisely his critical philosophy that inaugurates, for Foucault, the intellectual paradigm shift that is the new episteme.[55] In its subjective "return upon itself" literary discourse—or literary *writing*—is not a shrinking away from science, rather it is a reflection on its very possibility, in the form of the subject. Thus it is that Hegel, in his lectures on aesthetics, will refer to poetry as not only the highest of the arts, but also as subjectivity expressing itself not merely through, but always already as language.[56]

What is most significant in this is the idea that the nature of the subject, which for Kant had exhausted its philosophical interest in the sheer propositionality of "I think," will now be revealed in literature. Not merely in literature, but in literature as a mode of writing that here comes to instantiate the impersonal detachment that, for Saussure, distinguishes *langue* from *parole* or, in Kant, subject from individual.[57] In the first *Critique* the subject has become the unknowable essence of all possible coherence, world, and form. It is the simple, empty, almost grammatical starting point of world-historical Spirit's self-development in Hegel's *Phenomenology*. Here this subject has fallen to literature, and there it has been taken up as the fundamental issue.[58] The subject that writing has inherited in this philosophical age is none other than its own being, and the issue that emerges to confront authors is the self-annihilating force of their own words, dissolving them as individuals. The writer is one who dies before the labor is done, who dies, even before laboring, in the simple immediacy of the self-reflexive text. Two deaths stake out the field of authorial existence: the death that is the labor of writing, and the death, sooner, more abrupt, that is the recognition of that labor's negative mode of existence. On the one hand the experiential individual, the one who can feel, feels always through death, through his or her own finitude; on the other hand the subject has no place for the individual, since it is the sheer reflection of language on itself—a language that excludes the individual through annihilating him or her. It is this aporia of a scriptural subjectivity that finds no space for life, that premises all in death, and ends it in death, it is this subject that can make no sense of life without killing it off that will trace itself across Europe in the two centuries following the French Revolution.

2. Death-Based Subjectivity

> Clearly my ability to speak is connected to my lack of being. I name myself and it is as if I were speaking my death-song: I separate myself from myself, I am no longer my presence or my reality but an objective, impersonal presence, the presence of my name, which surpasses me and whose petrified immobility fulfills for me exactly the function of a tombstone weighing down against the void. When I speak, I deny the existence of what I say, but I deny also the existence of the one who speaks: my words, while revealing being in its nonexistence, affirm that this revelation depends on the nonexistence of the one who reveals, on his power to distance himself from himself, to be other than his being.
>
> —*Maurice Blanchot*

When Emile Zola lay awake long into the hours of the night, gripped with the fear of death, he was not alone in his presentiments of the void. Once more, he was expressing, if only to himself, the feelings of an age, feelings that Michelet too had tried to put into words in his own intimate journals, but that now returned less as an inner sense of pain and loss than as pure, wracking fear. Something had taken shape at about the time of the French Revolution, something involving death, writing, and the sense of self. Were we not still part of the same period in too many ways, we might look back and wonder why the era that began at the end of the eighteenth century was so profoundly negative and why it offered up such a bleak image of self-identity. Among all the artistic currents and conflicting ideologies of the last two hundred years, one concept of individuality seems to have dominated, casting a pall over these centuries with its particular bleakness and pervasiveness. And although, certainly, the nineteenth century did not invent the fear of death, it made it its own in a way that had not been seen before, placing death in its utter emptiness at the heart of subjectivity, institutionalizing the identification between individual and nothingness in art, theory, and social practice. The dreadful separation Zola was feeling in the dark, a loneliness so profound and terrible it often led to bouts of weeping, was an intimation of that death that is the subject. It was, I think, himself he sensed.

Part of the period's negativity expresses itself in pronouncements of the death of God, or in reaction to them. The cry of the German poet, Jean Paul, that God is dead sounded throughout the nineteenth century, echoing in Nerval and Nietzsche but also in the very structures of life, and the violent secularization of the state during the Revolution institutionalized a loss that was repeated more privately in endless inner colloquies, in verses, and in philosophical tracts. The poems of Théophile Dondey, hidden throughout his life, reveal a long and ultimately vain personal struggle against atheism which stretched across the middle of the nineteenth century and left him facing death as a bitter nihilist at about the same time that a mortal insomnia was awakening Zola in the night. Later, in the 1930's, Alexandre Kojève will look back at the revolution that was Hegelianism and find in its theorization of subjectivity a death sentence for both God and humanity. According to Kojève, to be human, for Hegel, was to recognize one's death and to identify with it, not as a dying into God, but as simply dying. In the personal poems of a Jeune-France turned bureaucrat, in the sleeplessness of a novelist, in the vast edifice of Hegelianism, in lectures at the Ecole des Hautes Etudes, in a historian's walk on the beach with his young wife and daughter, the death of God returns in its terrible emptiness time and again as the human condition.

By speaking of the negativity of these two centuries, I am less concerned with their mourning for a dead God than with the idea of subjectivity associated with it, the product of a change in self-perception that acquired its own significance and history. In casting about for a way to stage this change concretely to ourselves, to draw up a series of images that would condense for us the institution of this new subjectivity and its effects on the individual, we can turn to one of the great rituals of state power, an event that, before vanishing from the city centers and then from sight altogether, underwent a massive conversion in its procedure and meaning. This change in individual identity is exemplified in the movement from torture-execution to the guillotine, in the passage from a theatrical, state-imposed individuation based on pain to subjectification based on the weight of abstract and absolute death. But this is only a symptom of something larger, for beyond the Place de Grève there is an overwhelming pressure in the form of social, philosophical, aesthetic, and cultural forces and discourses to understand oneself in this way, to conceive of one's sameness to oneself as overwhelmingly, absolutely negative. By this I mean that in thinking of ourselves as individuals, we have, since the Revolution and in ways shaped during and around it, a tendency to think of our identity, the who we really are, as absolutely different from any of our experiences. There is an "I" who remains permanent throughout all my experiences, and for this reason I can think of them as mine. But this "I," by its very permanence, is irreconcilably different from any of those experiences, which are passing or momentary. This subject, this self-identity that is always in me, that is me and which frames my experiences as mine, is also absolutely other than them because, while they are specific, it is absolute. The subject is that aspect of me that is no one event but is also everywhere else—it is the me that is absent from the event and in this sense, in making the event its own, my own, the subject makes the event abstract, absent, theoretical. Any experience is, as subjective experience, subsumed into the timeless other that is "I" and that makes of it my experience. In this way, I am constantly accompanied by another who takes up the events of my life, as they happen, and abstracts them away from me. Few, too, are the experiences in which this "I" is not stronger than the event, or in which I forget that the experience is happening to me, and it strikes me as coming to no one in particular. Perhaps orgasm, perhaps certain dream or psychotic states might free us from the apparently primordial grip of our self-identity, but it is the very inconstancy, the very vagary of such moments that allows them to go unnoticed for so long as forms of resistance to the subject, or as glimpses of its possible facticity. Instead it is the subject that prevails across these long years as the negation of its own experiences, of its own living.[1]

As an identification with this abstraction, I am, moreover, an identification with that last of abstractions, my own death, the death of my living. Kojève, paraphrasing the preface to Hegel's *Phenomenology of Spirit*, will declare, in his last lecture for the academic year of 1933–34, "Thought and discourse, which reveals the Real, spring from the negating Action which realizes Nothingness by annihilating *Being*: Man's given-being. . . . This amounts, therefore, to saying that human beings themselves are nothing more than this Action; Man is death which lives a human life."[2] This, Kojève argued, before what were (or were to become) some of the most significant intellectuals of his time, was the Hegelian Subject, the "abstract-I." His influence on the postwar period in France was enormous, but he was not, I want to argue, expressing in this anything that had not already in a certain way been sensed and publicly articulated during the nineteenth century. Long before those meetings at the Ecole des Hautes Etudes, something similar had been argued in different terms. In 1831, the year of Hegel's death, a journalist at the Parisian newspaper *Le Figaro* had, for instance, drawn this sarcastic portrait of a Jeune-France, one of the band of obstreperous second-generation romantics that included Nerval, Gautier, and Théophile Dondey: "The *Jeune-France* is gay, but his is a putrid gaiety. During the day he has visited the Catacombs, Père-Lachaise cemetery, the House of Lords; he holds forth on the gibbet at Montfaucon and the anatomy clinic; to the young ladies he shows a bone and tells them: 'You have as much beneath your gauzes and muslins. So you are always walking in the company of a skeleton, you have death beneath your skirts: let's have a look at death.'"[3] For all its facetiousness, this sketch gives expression to a significant reappropriation of the medieval *memento mori*: one's death is, like one's skeleton, something at the core of one's person, a permanence that holds one together, but at the same time it is something other, in whose company one always walks. Unlike a medieval dance of death, this is not a fantasy of flesh awaiting resurrection, or a minatory lesson in morality, but rather the identification with an unredemptive and alien ending of oneself. It is, in part, the voice of Hegel one detects in the young aesthete's lascivious jeering, but under the lifted skirts one gets, too, a brief glimpse of another future of the deadly subject of self-permanence: its return as castration anxiety in the Lacanian symbolic system.

With the loss of God, Michelet called for something to take His place in the very fiber of individuality. Among the responses to that call the most persuasive and the most terrible was nothingness itself. This theorization of self-identity that sees it as the abstraction of all particular lived experiences, as an identification not only with an abstraction but with an absolute abstraction—death—was, and still is, a pervasively adopted idea of subjectivity.[4] By "adopted" I mean that this theorization represents, for all its abstractness, an ideology that has altered the way we view ourselves and thus has altered the self. It has consequently had material and experiential effects on those who have subscribed to it—a significant number, if not the majority. The modern self traced out here is a death machine whose distribution can be attested, as we shall see, in philosophical and aesthetic discourses.[5] This assimilation of a new and radically negative self-identity on the part of the individual, however, was not painless. On the one hand, there is a broad network of coercive social, aesthetic, and theoretic powers enforcing such a subjectification. But against these pressures one discovers also forms of resistance, a resistance that expresses itself in terror toward that identification with death or, in more positive terms, as attempts to construct selfhood in other ways. Writers such as Piera Aulagnier, Julia Kristeva, Emmanuel Levinas, and Gérard de Nerval will offer glimpses of other approaches to thinking of self-identity and will help to contextualize the negativity of the modern self as one possibility among others, as a historical event rather than an ontological necessity.

The Guillotine and Its Theorists

Hegel, apparently referring to the French Revolution, spoke of his own period as a "birth-time" in which long years of presentiment and decay had been "cut short by a sunburst which, in one flash, illuminate[d] the features of the new world."⁶ This brilliant beginning also had its darker side, however, for at about the same moment as Hegel's historical epiphany the theorization of self-identity and individuality took an extremely negative turn, which expressed itself throughout social behavior. According to Foucault's analysis, Adam Smith's economic theory represented, for example, a fundamental change in occidental thought—what he termed the advent of a new episteme at the end of the eighteenth century. By basing his economics on the principle of labor rather than exchange, Smith, according to Foucault, "formulates a principle of order that is irreducible to the analysis of representation," which analytical order had characterized the classical period previous to it.⁷ The fixed grounding point of Smith's system, that which would put an end to the potentially limitless play of classical representational exchange and ground it in an irreducible other, is the finitude of the human being who must work, and as a result his economics "is already pointing in the direction of an anthropology that will call into question man's very essence (his finitude, his relation with time, the imminence of death)."⁸ As an attempt to limit an entirely discursive epistemological order through a referential grounding, the modern notion of labor produces a single referent: death. It is death alone that puts an end to the metaphoric conversions of exchange, death alone that cannot be ascribed a value and that therefore determines the value of everything else. To labor within a capitalist, bourgeois economics is thus not to understand one's activity in terms of pleasure, satisfaction or need, but to inscribe it within the abstract notion of one's own mortal finitude, and thereby to understand one's agency as grounded in one's death. We can get a further idea of the historical specificity of this new understanding of self-identity, although not of the wide range of its implications, by considering a material change in civic behavior whose significance was well attested by its contemporaries and which still seems to be a defining point in our own social identity. This event is the passage from torture-execution to the guillotine. It is a shift that allows us to see an originary moment in the practice of state-imposed death, but it is only one of the most spectacular manifestations of that imposition, while the concept of the abstract subject is, I think, among the most subtle of those manifestations. This precise event marked succeeding generations theoretically and imaginatively to such an extent that one can say, in regard to the sense of self, we have never really gotten over the invention and institution of the guillotine.

In the pre-Revolutionary torture-execution, the identity of the individual was expressed, and enforced, through physical agony. The victim, alone in the crowd, felt a pain that was the object of the entire spectacle and which differentiated him or her from everyone else. While separating the sufferer as *different* from others, however, the pain conversely designated his body as the *same* as that of the criminal and enforced the continuity of individual identity between perpetrator and victim, for the torture comprised an important symbolic element that sought to reproduce the crime on the body of the punished. This symbolic component included such simple cruelties as tearing out the tongues of blasphemers or severing the murderous hands of parricides, but it often took the form of complicated reenactments. The most famous single example is probably the regicidal dagger that was affixed to Damiens's hand while executioners burnt his skin and tore at it with pincers prior to his being drawn and quartered.[9] The description of Damiens's 1757 punishment became a reference point for following generations, and has undoubtedly marked the imaginations of all those who have come across it in the opening pages of Michel Foucault's *Discipline and Punish*. Less familiar, but just as significant for our present concerns, are other more elaborately staged executions which were perhaps less cruel but which went further in explicitly revisiting the particulars of the crime on the victim of its punishment. In this regard, Foucault cites the practice of exposing the body of the punished at the place of the crime, or of holding the execution itself there.[10] Still more spectacular in its encryption of a crime on the person of the criminal is the sentence handed down, fifteen years after Damiens's death, to a servant found guilty of murdering her mistress. It decreed that

> a gibbet was to be set up "at the foot of which will be placed the same chair in which the said Laleu, her mistress, was sitting at the time of the murder; and having seated the criminal there, the executioner of the High Court of Justice will cut off her right hand, throw it in her presence into the fire, and, immediately afterwards, will strike her four blows with the cleaver with which she murdered the said Laleu, the first and the second being on the head, the third on the left forearm and the fourth on the chest; this done, she will be hung and strangled on the said gibbet until she be dead."[11]

Three things are to be remarked here. First, the punished is different from other people. These are not mass executions. Each victim is alone in the crowd by virtue of the fact that he or she, and no one else, is punished. The punishment separates the punished from everyone else, and in this sense it individuates its victim, who becomes a spectacle of isolation. Second, there is, especially in the more symbolically charged executions, an emphasis on continuity: the victim of the punishment is the same person as the criminal. This may seem obvious, but if it is so obvious, why is there such need to represent that identity through the careful repetition of the crime in its atonement? This element of continuity can be summed up in the concept of responsibility: the victim and the criminal are one and the same person, and the victim is responsible for the actions of the criminal. Identity is staged here as self-sameness over time and this identity is the access point, the handle which the social collective, or the state, has on the one who must respond for the actions of the criminal. The execution is, in this respect, a theatrical representation of the response-able one, of the one who bears an obligation to the state to respond. The symbolic ordeal pronounces the individual to be the same person over time and it asserts that the individual, as continuous over time, owes the state an answer. Particularly striking to us now, who are accustomed to the idea of a punishment calibrated to the character of the criminal and the nature of the crime (with heavier sentences, for example, assigned to a depraved disregard for human life than for violent bursts of jealous fury), is the role of materiality in establishing that individuality. Between crime and punishment it is the same place, the same chair, the same weapon, the same gestures and wounds. Above all, the body of the criminal is the same as the body of the punished. As such, it is the support of individuation in two senses. Materially it is constant over time: the gestures and wounds of the execution may be representations of elements of the crime, but the body of the punished is the very body of the criminal, and it is thus that justice has its claim to it. Furthermore, in its sentience, the body establishes a difference from other people, for no matter how far one might go in redistributing the borders of individuality—conceiving of single persons as converging processes within desiring machines that exceed them, or as the self-experiencing of an impersonal ideology—pain effects a separation, for while one person suffers another simply does not.[12] It is thus through the body that the torture execution grasps the individual, drawing from him or her the response that is owed. Third, while in these symbolically charged punishments the same crime is more or less meticulously repeated, in the second instance it is not a crime, for the executioner is, in the methodical application of the punishment, held innocent of it. What this indicates is that while the material is a support for individuality and an access to the response which the individual owes the state, it is not in itself sufficient to establish that individuality. As if to mock the first two points observed above, in what is represented as symbolically and materially the same crime, the executioner is not held responsible, though he labors physically at it. In its vigor or debility, his body may play a role in the execution, and an observer of Damiens's torture could remark, "though *a strong, sturdy fellow*, this executioner found it so difficult to tear away the pieces of flesh that he set about the same spot two or three times," nonetheless the executioner does not labor, somehow, for himself.[13] He acts impersonally, as a non-agent, or as the agent of another will. He is not assigned to take any pleasure in the act or to have any direct interest or investment or anger beyond the scrupulous application of the sentence. Even in cases of personal cruelty or spitefulness on the part of the *bour-*

reau, his actions, whether or not they are punished as lapses in his official obligations, were not enough to make him guilty of the same crime as the criminal he inflicted them on.[14] The willing agent of the punishment is not the person incarnate in the body of the executioner, but is the sovereign. The public torture scene thus comprises two symmetrically opposed sets of activities: a physical individuation of the victim and an ideological depersonalization of the *bourreau*, an imposition of responsibility on the punished and an effacement or withholding of responsibility on the part of the executioner in a scene that is typically intended to represent or reenact the original crime. The crime, as act, is reread, and what is changed, above all, in its repetition is that agency for it is assigned in an ostentatious contrast: the state decides, through exercise upon the body, that one is responsible and an agent while the other is not responsible—a non-agent *for the same act*. The scene is, therefore, about individuation and responsibility, about the state's control of individuation as responsibility. It is about the creation of an individual.

With the Revolution, this all came to a rapid end. On December 1, 1789, Joseph Ignace Guillotin proposed six articles concerning legal punishment to the Constituent Assembly, the last of which stated that the "method of punishment shall be the same for all persons on whom the law shall pronounce a sentence of death, whatever the crime of which they are guilty. The criminal shall be decapitated. Decapitation is to be effected by a simple mechanism."[15] The first five articles of his proposal, concerning the rights of the punished and their families, were rapidly adopted, but the sixth was not even brought to debate until March 1792. This delay, as Daniel Arasse observes, can be understood as an indication of the profound break with the past that Guillotin's proposal for capital punishment represented.[16] One can easily imagine why there might be hesitation: the sheer act of debate would necessarily bring forth a public reconsideration of the nature and ends of state-imposed death, for the adoption or rejection of the machine would have to be argued on the basis of its relation to the goals and nature of the republic, which were still being formed. The state, consequently, would not merely be a criterion to determine the fate of the machine; the machine, for its part, would also become a criterion by which to shape the nature of the state. Nor, in this, were the representatives of the people considering the expulsion of death from the mechanics of the new republic, for the issue here was not capital punishment itself, although that had been and would continue to be a subject of public debate; Guillotin's proposal concerned instead the means for including death within that mechanism. Rather than a banishing of death from the city, a turning away from it, he proposed an ideological confrontation with death as a defining element in the identity of the state. How immediate that confrontation would be and how defining it would become were probably beyond the wildest dreams of the hesitant legislators and even of Guillotin himself. For all that the Revolution brought with it, for all it renewed or originated, the single image most indelibly associated with it in most people's minds is probably that of a machine it did not even invent, but which it debated, adopted, and set before itself as an icon of the body politic.

The guillotine was envisioned as a humanitarian reform. Guillotin's proposal called for a death that was simple, uniform, and mechanical, which would do away with the class distinctions and symbolic individuations associated with existing torture-executions. As a machine, it would deliver the same death to all, and would do so instantaneously and painlessly. In an unfortunate burst of rhetorical enthusiasm that would make him the butt of endless public mockery, Guillotin described the action of his "simple mechanism" in the following terms to the Assembly: "The mechanism falls like a thunderbolt, the head flies off, the blood spurts forth, the victim is no more."[17] Although probably exaggerated to play up the grotesque effect of Guillotin's oratory, another published account, from the *Moniteur* of December 18, 1789, indicates his insistence on the painlessness as much as the rapidity of the device: "Gentlemen, with my machine, I can have your heads off in the twinkling of an eye and you will feel not the slightest pain" and "The form of death I have invented is so gentle that, were one not expecting to die, one would scarcely know what to say of it, for one feels no more than a slight sensation of coolness at the back of the neck."[18] Still, more than the purported painlessness of the guillotine, it is its rapidity that seems to have caught the imagination of its contemporaries. This is what Arasse calls the "terrible instant" and "the blind spot" of the operation, the fact that "the blade fell so swiftly as to be *invisible*."[19] He quotes Cabanis's *Note sur le supplice de la guillotine*, in which the doctor, who had been present at initial testings of the mechanism, asserted that it "strikes heads off faster than the eye can see" and that the "spectators see nothing. For them there is no tragedy; they have no time to be shocked."[20]

At least in theory, with the adoption of the guillotine, capital punishment entirely lost its component of physical pain, that access that the *ancien régime* had maintained to the individuality of the condemned and, potentially, to everyone. Death itself had become the punishment. It fell in all its absoluteness and impersonality, with a mechanical indifference to the particularities of the condemned it clutched. The victims were now ushered quickly to the *bascule*, the executioners were strictly forbidden to prolong or otherwise theatricalize the event. Death's visitation was no longer a labor, but the matter of an instant, there was no work to be done with it, no struggle with its personification in the executioner, no scenes of physical agony or listening for its rattle, since it came now immediately, with nothing intervening, from one moment to the next.

Death had drawn absolutely near. No longer a mediated process, execution by the guillotine, coming in an instant, physically changed the relation to the absolute: it was made present as a particular now in a particular place. The spectators literally, as Cabanis put it, saw nothing. The absolute intervened in the physical world, taking it away in a vacuous, invisible present. The public watched the end of the visible world, the end of watching. Despite the blood and brief, closely policed final gestures of its victims, this is what the spectacle at its heart had become: a manifestation of the end of seeing. Nothing happened: the guillotine was the happening of nothing, nothing as an event.

This simplification of capital punishment was contemporaneous with an abrupt change in the attitude toward death itself. One of the entries on the subject from the *Encyclopédie* of 1765, for instance, had argued that death should not be considered an absolute and that it was instead only a single element within a long and graduated series that included other aspects of life such as youth and senescence.[21] Extinction was not, in this sense, the intervention of a perfectly alien other, but rather the final gesture in a familiar process, an event that had been preparing itself, indeed occurring, since birth and which had insinuated itself into the very fabric of life. Viewed from an anthropological point of view rather than a medical one, the end of life comes slowly and tranquilly: "*Death* is not armed with a cutting instrument [un instrument tranchant], nothing violent accompanies it, for one ends life by imperceptible degrees."[22] Far from the romantic marker of the sublime that it would become in Schiller or the dreadful human essence that Hegel would make of it, death was presented by the encyclopedist as an integral part of life which seemed terrible only through one's misunderstanding of it. "Men fear *death*," he wrote, "as children fear the dark and only because their imaginations have been frightened with phantoms as empty as they are terrible [des fantômes aussi vains que terribles]. The process of leave-taking, the tears of our friends, mourning and the funeral ceremony, the convulsions of the failing machine, these are what tend to frighten us."[23] It is not, in fact, death itself that frightens, but the events associated with it: the strange, autonomous activity of the body and the alienation of an otherwise long-intimate and organic process through the ritualized *adieux* imposed on the dying through the force of social custom. Once these ritualized estrangements have been recognized for what they are, the author contended, death loses its terror. That sanguine attitude does not, however, seem to have survived the invention of a mechanism for delivering a physically painless death, free from physical convulsions and the body's consciousness of its own disintegration, an end that struck its victims with an inconceivable, apparently transcendental instantaneity. Armed clearly and publicly with a blade that separated the living from the dead in an imperceptible moment, the sheer abstract imminence of death was now viewed as itself the source of terror and pain. This can be seen in a letter to Roederer, the *procureur général syndic*, concerning a condemned man who, as the result of an emergency decree mandating the development and construction of a humane means of capital punishment, had been awaiting his execution for two months while such a machine was sought. Justice Moreau wrote of the prisoner that "every moment by which his wretched existence is prolonged must be another death to him" and pointed to the need, "in the name of justice and of the law, in the name of humanity to put an end to the effects caused by this delay, which are detrimental to the law, to the safety of the public, to the judges and indeed to those under sentence."[24] Another contemporary asserted that "the worst of the ordeal for the condemned man will be his own fear of death, a fear more painful to him than the stroke that deprives him of life."[25] This all was put much more vividly in a report by the executioner himself, Charles Henri Sanson. The Assembly had solicited his opinion about the practicality of decapitation as a universal means of punishment in the case of death sentences. He argued against the proposal, asserting that the signs of death's imminence would be too clear, too spectacular, and incontrovertible even if the method itself was physically the quickest and caused the least suffering; it would consequently be almost impossible to manage the condemned, since they would be in the grip of their natural fear of death and would not be in control even of themselves. "A further consideration," he wrote, "is that, when there are several condemned men to execute at once, the terror of the execution, caused by the vast quantities of blood, will bring terror and faintness to the hearts of even the most intrepid of those to be executed."[26] Charles Henri, who had assisted his father in the drawing and quartering of Damiens, was convinced that even a humane and reformed capital punishment that confronted its victims only with their own extinction would elicit a response of overwhelming terror in them. In placing the mechanics of death outside of the body, in making its intervention painless and instantaneous, the guillotine had laid death bare, and it was seen to be terrifying in itself. This is the new death that had come into the heart of the city, where the guillotine, its blade alone removed, remained permanently at the ready in the Place du Carrousel.

The guillotine differed from similar machines in other countries, many of which preceded it, in that it was integrally connected to a self-conscious shift in the global ideology of the state and the relation of the individual to it. This change is particularly clear from the arguments that were advanced for the initiation and continuance of the Terror. At the outset, the stewardship of death did not seem to be more than a peripheral element in the renovation of society. Robespierre was, in fact, originally against capital punishment and argued for its suppression before the Convention. Even later, with the killing well under way, the death penalty was justified on brutally pragmatic grounds, with Marat, for instance, calling for tens of thousands of executions which, he argued, would not have been necessary had a handful been done in time.[27] But with the arguments for the judgement and execution of the king, and even more, with the Terror, the administration of death began to take on an almost spiritual necessity within the state. It was no longer merely a practical solution to very real threats to the nascent republic, it was also the mechanism for an inward, moral shift in the citizenry. In a speech to the Convention on April 15, 1794, for instance, Saint-Just argued that "a revolutionary man is a hero of good sense and probity," and spoke of the "vehemence of a pure government" to justify his call for a rigorously punitive application of the law, which in practice meant tumbrils and decapitation.[28] The sword of justice was both the instrument by which the new social order had been brought into being and the guarantee of its preservation, for through surveillance and sharp reprisals men would be enthralled "to the duties and reasonable obligations with which liberty cannot dispense."[29] By treating it as a privileged instrument of universal liberty, Saint-Just's enthusiastic conception of the guillotine is not far from Hegel's grim theorization of it in the *Phenomenology of Spirit*. In both cases, the device represents the equality of all citizens in the pure or absolute exercise of their freedom. The philosopher had contended that the identification between the individual and absolute freedom entailed the meaningless abstraction or sublimation of the individual. The statesman had assumed that impersonal, ideological identification as his own, giving voice to his own abstraction by declaring: "You will never see me oppose my particular will against the will of all [opposer ma volonté particulière à la volonté de tous]. I shall want what the French people, or the majority of its representatives, wants."[30] This, for Hegel, is what is terrible about the guillotine: it is the instantiation of a social structure that generally, everywhere and for everyone, annihilates individual particularity and experience in the identification with the absolute. It is internalized, in other words, as the principle of liberty itself.

It is in this sense that the guillotine is sublime: it makes manifest the incompatibility between the abstract absolute and the material particular, subtracting away the presence of the present into the invisibility of the instant in which nothing comes, with annihilating immediacy, to a single person. While both Camille Desmoulins and Robespierre referred generally to the sublimity of their undertaking and the sacrifices that it entailed,[31] Arasse connects the execution itself to Kant's reference to terror in the third *Critique*, asserting that, "like the Kantian spectator of a violent storm, the spectator of the Terror shuddered at the *terribilitas* of what he saw, yet enjoyed the knowledge that it could do him no harm."³² Arasse's masterful work on the material and imaginary functioning of the guillotine and the extraordinary insight he brings to bear on his readings of it do not, however, prevent him from misconstruing both Kant and the sublimity of the Terror's executions. It is a significant, almost unavoidable misconstruction because it is based on precisely that passage in the third *Critique* where Kant himself is ambivalent about the nature of self-interest in the sublime. To be consistent with the rest of Kant's argument, one must understand this safety from harm, this securing of self-interest, to function not on the level of the individual but on the level of the impersonal. This is how Hegel appears to have read this situation, and the result is his depiction of the Terror of the French Revolution as the universal exercise of an absolute and meaningless death, visited on individual citizens, whether or not they were guillotined, through their identification with the abstract principle of the state. But it is difficult to read the passage that way because it is both rebarbative and paradoxical to speak of securing personal interest only on the level of the impersonal. The text is, at that particular point, ambiguous, and Kant is apparently ambivalent. Arasse has followed one of two possible readings of the meaning of self-interest there and Hegel the other, but within the larger argument of the *Critique* Hegel's is the only one that makes sense. The sublimity of the guillotine is not that it strikes another, as Arasse contends, but rather that it reveals, in the theatricalization of an ideological structure, that one has oneself already been struck. The moment of the guillotine is every moment. It bares the individual first before death in general, but also, more specifically and pervasively, before death as an ideological abstraction.

The internalization of this sublimation as the basis of individuality produces a highly theorized and frequently attested sense of self-identity which we have termed death-based subjectivity. By this is meant the generalization throughout the moments of a life of an isolating and self-constituting face-to-face with impersonal abstraction. It is the identification of oneself, as a self, with the endless repetition of that moment of sublimation that abstracts lived experiences into a higher order coherence grounded in persistence. This abstraction entails negating the concrete specificity of those experiences, and in this it voids them of precisely those characteristics that make of them experiences and life. It is in this sense that subjectivity grounded in abstraction is grounded in death. And, as will be seen, this identification with one's own death, or with death in general, this disappropriation of all of one's momentary experiences, pleasures or pains, the voluptuousness of existence, is associated, both theoretically and aesthetically, with terror.

As we have seen in the preceding chapter, the sublime moment of Kant's writings expresses the incompatibility between aesthesis and abstraction, and represents the triumph of abstract reason over sensuous imagination. Moreover, it is a moment in which the "I" identifies with an abstraction and in so doing negates the individual that it had previously been. The sublime moment is thus a self-identification in which an abstract and impersonal self rejects a sensuously identified and personally interested self.[33] This triumph is felt as terror, which in itself indicates a profound aversion or resistance to this sublimation on the part of the individual. There are, as we have seen, two passages from Hegel's *Phenomenology of Spirit* that are of particular interest in this respect, in that they seem to develop this aesthetic insight on the levels of the State and of general sensuous experience. In the "Absolute Freedom and Terror" section, Hegel describes the French Revolution as the historical moment in which the depersonalization of the sublime is instituted as state policy, in which the state becomes the abstract principle of generalized freedom or *volonté générale*. Here the individual is sacrificed to the abstract universal both in ideology and in concrete terms, which take the form of the guillotine. Hegel is very clear about the absolute meaninglessness of this loss, its undialectical pointlessness, and where Kant, in the *Conflict of the Faculties*, sees the origin of history, Hegel sees its abeyance. The sublimated or *erhabene* subject is, in Hegel's terms, not merely a subject born in terror or who inspires terror, but also a subject of *the* Terror. Although he viewed the French Revolution as a dialectical dead end, Hegel did in fact argue elsewhere, and very problematically, that *every* subject is already, by its very nature, a sublimation, since "the self only knows itself as transcended self."[34] The reason for this is set out in the section on "Sense Certainty" from the *Phenomenology*, which describes the relation between language and sensuous experience as an annihilation of the particular in the universality of its abstract representation. By identifying itself through language as its persistent self-sameness, the "I" constructs itself as the negation of its own inviduality, very much as Kant's sublime individual understood itself as an abstract principle inimical to its own personal interests. The theoretical groundwork was by this point in place for conceiving of subjectivity and writing as terrifying and voracious sublimations of living experience.

The philosophical writings of Kant and Hegel discussed so far represent the explicit, if problematic, theorization of a new approach to subjectivity which made itself felt materially and socially. Certainly, no single document formulates what we have termed "death-based subjectivity," but by drawing connections among these various texts it is possible to imagine a background conception, a synthetic construct of self-identity that finds expression in these various sorts of discourse, whether theoretical, literary, or social. The most spectacular instance of this expression was probably the guillotine, but it also manifested itself in writing. Writing was, I would argue, that other Place de Grève where the sublime took hold, a place that immediately involved everyone literate and in which the dead could speak, a place where, indeed, they could do nothing but speak and where only the dead could speak.

The Literary Void

Victor Hugo's second novel, originally published in 1829, took as its subject the thoughts and experiences of a prisoner in the days before his execution at the guillotine. Written in the first person and inspired by the sight of the Place de Grève thronged with crowds awaiting a beheading, the book was intended as an argument against capital punishment, an attempt to lay bare the cruelties inherent in a supposedly painless procedure. This cruelty occurs not as a physical suffering, Hugo contended, but in the constant rebelling of the mind against the idea of its own end.[35] As the fictional prisoner himself puts it: "my spirit is imprisoned by an idea. . . . I have but one thought, one conviction, one certitude: condemned to die! Do what I might, there it is . . . like a leaden specter at my side, jealous and solitary, chasing away all distractions, face to face with wretched me."[36] Like the skeleton of the caricatural Jeune-France, the thought of death permanently accompanies the prisoner, and in its certitude, this single idea subsumes all other thoughts or feelings, excluding the prisoner from them. His condition is an extremely explicit example of death-based subjectivity, in that the isolation of the subject, its independence from the surrounding world, is established through a continuous consciousness of its experiences as being, first and foremost, its own, and to this extent, disappropriated and negated. The idea *of* death here becomes the idea *as* death, for it separates the prisoner from his life insofar as life is anything but the immediate and abstract identification with one's own inscrutable nonexistence as *néant*, or void.[37]

The idea of such an overwhelming of life by an abstraction comes to strike the prisoner as hideous, even if the abstraction in question is a putatively positive one. Somewhat like Hegel in his reading of the Terror, the prisoner is brought, by his unusual awareness of his own relation to death, to see in the concept of liberty a lifeless universal capable of devouring particular human existences. Running his eyes over the walls of his cell, he tries to decipher the graffiti left by its previous occupants, all of whom have, by now, met the end awaiting him. A particular inscription incites his indignation and pity: "A Phrygian cap engraved quite deeply in the stone, and underneath: *Bories. The Republic*. He was one of the four sergeants of La Rochelle. Poor young man! How appalling their supposed political imperatives are! for an idea, a dream, an abstraction that horrible reality called the guillotine!"[38] There is a revealing dialogue between these two sections from the novel. It seems to be the prisoner's own experience of the disappropriating force of the idea of death which incites his indignation at the thought of perishing for an idea, and the power that an abstraction could wield over life consequently becomes grotesque for him. What the prisoner considers horrible in both these passages is the confusion of the abstract and the "real," the overwhelming of the concrete, particular experiences of a sentient individual by an impersonal generality. The character's indignation and horror at the guillotine are also, in this sense, a horror and indignation at the conclusions that Hegel drew in the "Sense Certainty" chapter of the *Phenomenology*, for he revolts, here, against the sacrifice of lived experience to an abstract universal.

In *Le Dernier Jour* as in the *Phenomenology*, language plays a privileged role in this confusion of concrete and universal, for it is the site of a confrontation between the material particulars of life and their own abstraction, a confrontation in which the individual is annihilated. In the preface to the second edition of *Le Dernier Jour*, Hugo described his novel as an attempt to lay death bare, to strip it of the rhetoric with which prosecutors disguised it when seeking the guillotine. While Maurice Blanchot, in a close reading of Hegel's "Sense Certainty" chapter, would later declare that "of course my language does not kill anyone," Hugo here contends just the opposite: language, through its figurativeness, literally produces death.[39] He describes the activity of the prosecution in a style that, through a grotesque mixture of the literal and the metaphoric, imitates the very intervention of death in the living which the prosecutor seeks to conceal:

> In debate he pulls for the guillotine, for that is his role, his purpose. The closing statement is his work of art and he decks it out in flowery metaphors, perfuming it with quotations. . . . He abhors the literal almost as much as the disciples of Delille. Fear not that he should call things by their name. For shame! For each idea whose nudity might revolt you he has a full costume made of epithets and adjectives. He can make Mr. Sanson presentable. He has gauzes to hide the blade. He can soften the swinging-plank's hard lines. He can wrap the red basket in a periphrase [Il entortille le panier rouge dans une périphrase]. You won't know what it is. . . . Look at him sawing at some wretch's neck with an ill-made law [Le voyez-vous scier avec une loi mal faite le cou d'un misérable]. Have you noticed how he soaks a couple or three venomous texts in a muddle of tropes and synecdoches so that laboriously he can extract from them a man's death?[40]

Hugo's style relies on the grotesque confusion of abstraction and concrete particular that the prisoner had described as hideous and terrible. The (obscured) difference between the linguistic and the nonlinguistic, between the abstract and the "real" which the prisoner observes in the markings on his wall, is here captured in the violent juxtaposition of signifiers that designate other signifiers ("périphrase") and those that designate signifieds (the "panier rouge"). This technique of fatal confusion comes to a climax in the impossible image of a prosecutor sawing off a prisoner's head with a law. The prosecutor's argument relies on a certain gauzy opacity of language to obscure his true intentions, and it is this opacity that leads the tribunal and the public to forget the referential significance of his speech. State-sponsored death is, in this respect, a product of the independence of language, of its abstraction from what it represents, and this independence, considered in itself, is described by Hugo as literature. Literature is, it would then seem, the place in which one forgets the specifics of life and death and in this way produces death.[41]

Hugo's prisoner spoke of his death sentence as a prison that separated him from his own life, and this idea of death as a severing is an extremely important aspect of the novel. It takes, of course, the concrete form of the guillotine's blade itself, which by cutting into the flesh severs it from life, but it also has a less material sense: it is the isolation of the prisoner from others. By virtue of his relation to death he is unlike the rest of the world: "Until the death sentence I had felt myself breathe, pulse, live in the same environment as other men; now I could make out something like a barrier between the world and me."[42] This isolation becomes evident throughout the novel in the various appearances of crowds of spectators who have been brought together out of an interest in the protagonist's death. In no case is this interest seen as compassion, but rather as pleasure. He is severed from the world of the living in that he, alone among them, does not want his death and in that they, in looking at him, see him characterized only by his death. The surrounding world of others has, in this way, objectified the prisoner's own identification with the void through a hostile turning away from him.[43] Death, as identification with abstraction, thus involved a separation from others, and it is precisely this aspect of mortality that will, as we shall see, allow Emmanuel Levinas to speak of all death as being felt as murder, as a hostility from others.[44]

Zola, like Hugo, depicted the immanence of death as the terrifying proximity of the void, and, like Hugo, he conceived of it as particularly frightening because of the isolation it entailed. And also like Hugo, who had been driven to write *Le Dernier Jour d'un condamné* by his own fear of death, his inability to keep himself from identifying, throughout the day of a public execution, with what he imagined to be the thoughts and emotions of the condemned, Zola had attributed to his character Lazare, from *La Joie de vivre*, a terror before death that was born of the author's own experiences, from his own fear-ridden insomnia and panicked bouts of weeping.[45] Zola takes as his starting point a scene that might have been a page out of Kant's third *Critique*, but unlike Kant or Hugo, he makes of this confrontation with a transcendent, terrible, and annihilating alterity an event at once profoundly intimate and perfectly common, moving the staging of the encounter from turbulent scenes of nature's wildness and Alpine fastnesses, or the extraordinary and spectacular circumstances of a public execution, to the banal setting of a bourgeois interior in the calm of night. Certainly, the first indications of Lazare's troubled mind appear as a reaction to what is a perfectly Kantian example of the mathematical sublime:

> One evening as they lay side by side, [Lazare] looked up at the stars that were emerging like pearls of fire against the dimming sky. . . . He let silence fall again. His merriment no longer rang so sure, an uneasiness within him clouded his eyes opened wide. Above, in the sky, the stars swarmed thicker with every passing moment, like glowing embers shovelled across the infinite.
>
> "No one's ever taught you about it, you don't know," he murmured at length, "Each star is a sun with machines like the earth rolling around it. There are billions of them, and behind them, still more, and behind those… "
>
> He fell silent, then spoke again in a shuddering, constricted voice: "I don't like to look at them… It frightens me."[46]

The scene ends with Lazare bursting into tears and crying out: "Oh! death, death!" As presented by Zola, it is the sheer weight of infinity intimated to Lazare by the expanse of the night sky that evokes in him the idea of his own mortality, as if there was something inherently unbearable in its mere idea, as if a pure concept could damage the one who conceives of it. Picking up on the ontological proof of the existence of God in Descartes's *Meditations*, Levinas will similarly single out the infinite as a concept that exceeds its thinker and thus constitutes an alien presence within the subject, but he will conceive of that inherence of the other with the subject as grounding the self in an ethical relation to others. Zola, on the other hand, here depicts that alien conceptual presence as an inherence not of living others with their primordial claims on one's goodness, but rather of an inhuman no one with claims on one's very existence.

This hostile other that is the thought of death will stay with Lazare throughout his life, growing more persistent as he ages, so that the momentary pleasures of life, the voluptuousness of existence, eventually evaporate before this abiding "nightmare of the void."[47] In the face of this simple abstraction, the present moment seems to fail, as if he were, in his obsessive morbidity, consciously enacting on the sensible world the abstracting negation which Hegel had determined to be the essence of sensuous experience and had discerned in the functioning of language. Lazare's fear of death "threw him into dark brooding, a seething hatred towards existence. He looked on life as a sham if it were not to last forever."⁴⁸ In its evanescence, the moment becomes odious and alien to Lazare, who values only that which is eternal, and, like Hegel, who speaks of the truth of things as their unvarying essence, Zola's character treats the passing instant as a deception. Like his biblical namesake, he passes through his own existence like the living dead. He sublimates his own experiences into the thought of death, holding the varying concrete particulars of his own life as void and the void of death as real. What had been dispassionately theorized in Hegel's "Sense Certainty" chapter as a dialectical necessity on the part of human Spirit working its way toward self-knowledge is here described in terms of an emotionally charged first-person experience of self-destruction: Zola represents the negation of experience in favor of abstraction as a painful and terrifying pathological condition. Nor is this simply a fictional representation. According to Edmond de Goncourt's journal, Lazare acts as a mouthpiece for Zola's own fears, which he summed up in a note to himself during the planning of the novel: "The particular family destroyed so that it might be taken back up into the great family of beings. The disappearance of the 'I,' that is what is terrible."⁴⁹

Unlike the Hegel of the opening chapter of the *Phenomenology*, Zola extended this negation from the relation to inanimate objects of experience to the relation with other people, seeing this rejection of moment-to-moment existence in favor of abstract permanence as entailing a terrible isolation of the individual from others. The disappearance of the "I" into the impersonal generality of being is conceived as an element, albeit the most terrible, of the sublimation of the particular family, as if the relation to one's immediate others was somehow primordial to one's relation to oneself, and as if self-identity and its destruction were contingent on another, more fundamental relation. It is in this other, more basic relation that Levinas will see the play of the infinite as ethics and goodness, whereas for Zola the infinite—the "great family of beings"—threatens one's connection to others as much as it does one's connection to oneself, bringing an end to the experience of genuine human alterity rather than grounding it. This fear of separation plays a predominant role in Lazare's crises, and is summarized in Zola's terse remark about the character: " …brutal, eternal separation. It was against this that all his being rose up in outrage."⁵⁰ In willingly identifying with a permanence that will always escape him, in considering the truth of himself to consist in an unvarying essence that will always lie elsewhere, Zola's character morbidly and pathologically alienates himself from his own passing experiences, treating the sensible voluptuousness of his own existence as a void and his relations to others as falsified by an absolute and insuperable distance. The fact that Zola represented Lazare's condition as pathological is in itself highly interesting, in light of the fact that it was a pathology he apparently shared: he must have viewed the condition as at once unavoidable—the human condition, what he must fear—and at the same time abnormal.[51] While identifying, in nightly terror, with his own death and the isolation it entailed, Zola still confusedly sensed that this identification was unnecessary. This, one could say, is the act of resistance that Lazare is incapable of—the pathologizing of his own subjectivity.

Hugo and Zola represent extreme cases of a certain relation between the individual and the absolute. In one novel the individual in question is a man condemned to die, in the other he is, though bourgeois, homebound, and a spokesman for the author's own experiences, clearly depicted as grotesquely sick. And yet, in both cases the writers seemed to be making a more generalizable point about self-identity. For Zola, it was the terrifying disappearance of the "I" into the abstract generality of beings, while for Hugo it was the hideous sacrifice of life to abstraction. A similar approach to the question of subjectivity can be seen in the poetics of this period, displaced onto the relation between a poet and his or her poetry. To illustrate this, we can take two examples, one well-known, the other almost entirely forgotten.

Théophile Dondey, known also under his anagrammatical pseudonym of Philothée O'Neddy, published only one thin collection of poems during his lifetime. Entitled *Feu et flamme*, it appeared in 1833, three years after the tumultuous premiere of Hugo's *Hernani*, which had cemented the friendship of a small circle of aspiring poets and artists revolving around the haughty and imposing figure of Petrus Borel.[52] Among their number figured Théophile Gautier, Gérard de Nerval, and the painter Célestin Nanteuil. According to Gautier, no one in the group seemed so fully to embody their aesthetic ideals as Dondey, but after publishing *Feu et flamme* at age 22, he quickly disappeared into a life of what even he himself seems to have considered bourgeois mediocrity. His father having died in the cholera epidemic of 1832 one year before qualifying for a pension and survivor's benefits, the young poet found himself obliged to support his mother and sister. He consequently spent the rest of his life working in the Ministry of Finance, publishing a handful of stories and theatrical criticism in newspapers, and privately producing a small body of poetry that was only published two years after his death in 1875. His writing momentarily excited the attention of Valéry Larbaud, who in 1935 published a short essay on Dondey, largely concerned with establishing the name he should be known under. Otherwise he received virtually no attention.[53] But in his poetry, Dondey explicitly made out the confrontation with death to be the fundamental characteristic of the human condition. The role of negation as a universal principle of self-identity is worked out much more clearly than in his contemporaries such as Hugo,

Zola, or Mallarmé, and for this reason his writing serves as a sort of catalyst, helping to crystallize the significance of the other authors' relation to death and personhood. The connection between this construction of subjectivity and the act of writing is much less developed than in, say, Mallarmé, but it can be glimpsed indirectly and constitutes one of the most striking and original elements of his poetry.

For most of his life Dondey believed in God in a devout if unorthodox way, but this yielded, in his last years, to an utter, even cynical skepticism, and one can trace in his poetic practice an ongoing but ultimately unsuccessful struggle against an atheistic construction of subjectivity in which the infinite *moi* of God was replaced by the Absolute of death.[54] Early in his life, Dondey defined his poetic project, and that of his entire generation, as being the transcription and laying bare of his *moi*.[55] This process of poetic introspection revealed that self-identity demands an absolute—indeed, *is* an absolute—but this left open the further questions of what absolute it is that constitutes subjectivity and what it implies to be an absolute. At first, the jubilant response came in the form of a Cartesian assertion of the certitude of thought:

> *Je doute, donc je pense*. Entre nous, j'ai grand'peine
> A croire qu'une chose *absolument* certaine,
> Dont l'évidence éclate en *absolus* rayons
> Ne soit pas *absolue* elle-même. —Voyons:
> La négative ici peut-elle être sensée?...
> Nous tenons l'absolu, frères! c'est la pensée!
>
> *I doubt, therefore I think*. Between us I've a hard time
> Believing that something that is *absolutely* sure,
> And whose necessity streams out in *absolute* rays
> Is not to be thought *absolute* in itself —Consider:
> Can the negative make any sense here?...
> We've grasped the absolute, brothers, and it is our thought![56]

What is to be proven in this passage is the existence of the self, and it is demonstrated through the indubitability of doubt itself, which in turn proves that the "I" thinks. The key element here is that this evidence of the self's existence to itself should be certain. As much an image of the unhappy Lazare from Zola's *Joie de vivre* as he is of the Descartes of the *Meditations*, coming to grips with the possible intervention of a *malin génie* or evil spirit, the poet requires that his self-immanence be absolute. Given his emphasis on the word and the enthusiasm with which he greets its apparent discovery, Dondey seems unwilling to be satisfied with anything less than an apodictic justification of his own existence to himself. Once established, this certitude of the self to the self is taken as a guarantee of the permanence of the "I":

Je pense, donc je suis. —Verbe de l'évidence!
Fiat lux de la raison prouvant sa transcendance!
Si je suis, quelque chose a donc toujours été.
Ex nihilo nihil. C'est vieille vérité.
De l'être la pensée étant preuve absolue,
Une autre certitude en demeure conclue:
C'est que, si quelque chose a toujours existé,
Quelque chose a pensé en toute éternité.

I think, therefore I am. —The truth made word!
Fiat lux of reason as it proves its transcendence!
If I am, then something has always been.
Ex nihilo nihil. This truth is age-old.
Since thought is of being an absolute proof,
Another certitude can be held without doubt:
That if something has always existed,
Something has thought for all eternity.[57]

Through the *cogito*, the self proves its existence to itself, and its existence is demonstrated, through the absolute, to be persistent, that is to say, self-identical over time. In this sense, as subject, the self is held to be transcendent and Descartes, as the discoverer of subjectivity, is said to be sublime.[58] Self-permanence, or subjectivity, is thus construed as a transcendence or sublimation, an absolving, or absolution of the relation between the subject so constituted and all that is not certain. The self now stands as utterly different from what is not it, and it is only through this utter difference that the *ex nihilo nihil* argument for its permanence can work: the distinction between the self and what is not it must be understood to be no mere transformation; it is as perfect as the difference between being and not being. But the subject as absolute self is also entirely different from its self as the contingent experience of accidents befalling it, and in this sense, as transcendent, the self is absolved even from itself.[59] Grounding self-identity in a transcendental absolute carries with it certain dangerous potential consequences, however. Although, in this passage from *Véilléités philosophiques*, Dondey triumphantly demands, "Can the negative make any sense here?", with the passage of time he came to lose his confidence concerning the response to that question. In the years subsequent to these optimistic affirmations of the eternity of thought, Dondey resisted, with diminishing success, the apparently necessary conclusion that the absolute is absolute negativity, and his understanding of the indubitable moved from doubt and suffering to eternal night and, finally, to the "néant" of death. The idea that thought is absolute had, by this point, become far from appealing, and its reassurance had turned to something more terrible. A passage added years later to the fragments of the *Véilléités philosophiques* attests to this shift:

> L'absolu! l'absolu!... n'ai-je pas souvenir
> D'un vers déterminé qui prétend le tenir?
> Je ne sais; mais ce soir, ma muse est peu pressée
> De crier: l'absolu, frères, c'est la pensée!
> Les deux *critériums* grâce auxquels nous restons
> Certains que nous pensons, certains que nous sentons,
> Comment s'appellent-ils? *Le doute et la souffrance.*
> *Je souffre, donc je suis. Je doute, donc je pense.*
>   ...Alors—oui, c'est fatal, de toute éternité,
> Quelque chose a souffert, quelque chose a douté.
> Logique, allons, tais-toi. Ta fièvre me déroute.
> Non, l'Absolu n'est pas la souffrance et le doute.
>
> The absolute! The absolute!... Don't I recall
> A resolute verse that believed it within grasp?
> I don't know; but this evening my muse is little rushed
> To cry out: the absolute, brothers, it is our thought!
> The two *criteria* by which we can be sure
> That we think, sure that we feel,
> What are they called? *Suffering and doubt.*
> *I suffer so I am, I doubt therefore I think.*
>   ...So—yes, it is fate, for all eternity
> Something has suffered, something has doubted.
> So logic, be quiet. Your fever drives me astray.
> No, the Absolute is not doubting and pain.[60]

The *cogito* has turned into the triumph of immortal doubt, a conclusion that can only be avoided by a rejection of absolute certitude itself, but once established in the poet's mind this now unwelcome guest is not easily chased away, and it remains, like Lazare's idea of the infinite, turning existence into doubt and suffering. By the end of Dondey's life, this identification of the "I" with absolute conviction had slipped even from pain and dubiousness, which still preserve some connection with the voluptuousness of sensuous existence, to pure and absolute negation, with the poet finally exclaiming: "O terreur! l'Absolu, c'est peut-être la nuit ! [Oh terror! perhaps the Absolute is night!]"[61] One can only wonder whether Dondey's funeral, in 1875 at Saint-Etienne-du-Mont, and his burial in the Montparnasse cemetery, represent a death-bed conversion to hope or merely the wishes of his sister, but one can trace, in the poetry he composed for himself alone over the course of his adult life, an identification with a subjectivity that, in its permanence, constituted a transcendental absolute absolutely other than the variorum of its own experiences.[62] By the end of his life the poet would view with alarm and then terror this abstraction that was himself.

There is a scene in one of Dondey's poems which suggests that for him, as for Hegel, language was the privileged medium of abstraction. The poem is the 1859 "Post-Scriptum" added to his *Rhapsodies du Vidame*, which were composed from 1838 to 1846. The lyrical addendum that closes them shows the older poet looking back over the work of his more youthful self and finding it haunted by his own enduring but alienated consciousness:

> L'autre nuit, sous ma lampe, énervé de tristesse,
> Je tenais dans mes mains ces pages de jeunesse...
> 			. . .
> J'écoutais ce penser, qui m'habite et me mord:
> —Etre mort dans la vie et vivre dans la mort!—
> 			. . .
> Pourtant, à l'épilogue, un ris silencieux
> Au lecteur—de la part d'un rimeur philosophe
> Me gagna: je trouvais bizarre une apostrophe
> Qui, dès ce temps lointain, savait très-bien déjà
> Que l'ombre réclamait ses vers—surtout ceux-là;
> Et qu'il n'était pour eux d'autres lecteurs possibles
> Que les dieux, les esprits, les morts,—les invisibles.
> A peine avais-je ainsi pensé—qu'il me sembla...
> Ah! personne pourtant, personne n'était là!
> Il me sembla—charmé de deuil—navré de joie—
> Entendre le frisson d'un vêtement de soie—
> Et le soupir d'un sein gonflé d'émotion.
> Ces plis frôlés, ce bruit de respiration,
> C'était tout contre moi... Je tremblais comme un saule...
> Je sentais regarder par-dessus mon épaule.
> Une haleine offensa ma joue—et je surpris
> Comme un toucher vivant parmi les cheveux gris.
>
> The other night, by my lamp, worn down by sadness,
> I held in my hands these pages from my youth
> 			. . .

> I listened to a gnawing thought, which dwells within me:
> To be dead in life and to live inside death!
>
> . . .
>
> And yet, at the epilogue, a silent laugh
> To the reader—on the part of a philosopher poet—
> Brought me round: an apostrophe struck me as bizarre
> Which, since that distant time, was quite fully aware
> That its words fell by rights to the dark—above all the ones that I read—
> And that for them no other readers could there be
> But the gods, the spirits, the dead—all those we can't see.
> Scarcely had it occurred to me—or at least so it seems—
> Ah! But no one was there!
> It seemed to me—in raptures of mourning—wounded by joy—
> I heard the rustling of silken clothes
> And the sigh of a breast that heaved with emotion.
> The folds that brushed by, the sound of a breath
> It was all right against me... Like a willow I shook...
> I sensed a gazing over my shoulder,
> A breath trespassing on my cheek—and I caught
> Something like a living touch among the grey hair.[63]

The act of rereading his own verses evokes in the poet the thought of a living death, although it is not clear at the beginning why this should be so. As the poem progresses it becomes increasingly evident that it is not the themes of his early writing that elicit this response in him, but rather their form—there is something in writing itself, rather than in what it refers to, which makes the poet think of a living death. This becomes most acute in an apostrophe by the young poet to his reader, which causes his older self to reflect on the relation between reader and writer, between himself in his maturity and himself in his youth, in what amounts to a delayed inner colloquy. The poet who wrote the lines is gone, replaced by them and his reader, and in this sense the verses represent a living death, the speaking out of the dead to those who come after. More striking, however, is the fact that the reader is himself also addressed as the dead, for the young author is said to know full well that they are his only possible audience. One is accustomed to thinking of dead authors, but the idea of a dead reader seems much more disturbing—yet it is only the converse of the former. As the public thinks of an author whose works it reads as dead, so does the author think of his public: he is speaking to them through death, and for that reason they are the invisible, the unknown, the abstract. In lending an ear to the written call of his younger self, the older poet places himself in the position of the dead, for he is the one who occupies the abstract space of reader, who identifies with the invisible and indeterminable other to whom the call addresses itself. This identification evokes the allegorical figure for the apostrophe itself, which takes the form of a ghostly presence who, invisible but manifest, watches the reader reading. The apostrophe from the dead always comes as a *quod sum eris*, always identifies the one interpellated with the dead, making one, in one's listening, more dead than they. It is the moment that reveals, to the poet who observes his own listening, that writing intervenes as death in life, as the impersonal persistence of thought beyond the accidents of its momentary thinker. The poetic self is an absolute, fleetingly occupied by the predications that are reader and writer, but only insofar as they assume their own death, only insofar as they conceive of themselves as dead. The written self is, in this sense, the paradigm for Dondey's understanding of all subjectivity.

The absolute negativity that Théophile Dondey struggled against almost his entire life seems to have formed the ground of Mallarmé's poetics. In an 1867 letter to Eugène Lefébure he wrote: "I have created my works entirely by *elimination*, and every truth I have gained was born from the loss of an impression which, having flashed a moment, consumed itself and allowed me, thanks to the shadows which it released, to proceed deeply into the feeling of absolute Darkness. Destruction was my Beatrice."[64] As he conceived of it, his work was, then, an ongoing, absolute negation of evanescent impressions undertaken in order to reach, like Dante, ever deeper into death. Probably the most extreme and pure expression of this descent was achieved in the posthumously published fragments for *Igitur ou La folie d'Elbehnon*, which depict, in a puzzling allegory, the descent of Igitur, a personification of the absolute, down the stairway of the human spirit to what Mallarmé, in a note to himself, describes as "the bottom of things."[65] The narrative begins at the stroke of midnight, but it is a midnight that strangely persists, trapped in a closed room where time seems to have become absolute: "Et du Minuit demeure la présence en la vision d'une chambre du temps où le mystérieux ameublement arrête un vague frémissement de pensée . . . cependant que s'immobilise (dans une mouvante limite), la place antérieure de la chute de l'heure en un calme narcotique de *moi* pur longtemps rêvé."[66] The visionary room is itself a metaphor for the pure "I" in which the moment fixes itself, where the movement of thought is halted, brought into the mobile limit of an absolute subject persisting across the passage of time through which it moves. The evanescent moment, whether the chiming of the hour or the flickering of thought, is always anterior, because it is the moment that, in its evanescence, has not yet been sublimated, that has not yet been subsumed into the pure "I." Another object in the room also condenses the immobilizing temporality of absolute subjectivity: "C'est le rêve pur d'un Minuit, en soi disparu, et dont la Clarté reconnue, qui seule demeure au sein de son accomplissement plongé dans l'ombre, résume sa stérilité sur la pâleur d'un livre ouvert que présente la table."⁶⁷ The absolute subject is figured as a book on which the sterility of the sublimated moment is preserved.

Igitur ou La folie d'Elbehnon can be read as a sort of preface to Mallarmé's most famous poem, for Igitur's purpose in descending the stair of the human spirit to "the bottom of things" is to accomplish the preordained task of casting dice on the tombs of his ancestors. It is, in the lingering midnight of the allegorical room, an event that takes place in absolute, eternal circumstances, but it is also, as the poet puts it, a useless act: "Le personnage qui, croyant à l'existence du seul Absolu, s'imagine être partout dans un rêve (il agit au point de vue Absolu) trouve l'acte inutile, car il a y a et n'y a pas de hasard—il réduit le hasard à l'*Infini*."⁶⁸ By identifying with the absolute, Igitur treats the events of his own life as a sort of pointless dream, something like Lazare of Zola's *Joie de vivre*, and this negative understanding of his own actions is justified through Mallarmé's idiosyncratic conception of chance. A comparison with his outline for *Igitur* clarifies some of the reasoning behind this cryptic passage, for in his notes to himself the poet had written: "L'infini enfin échappe à la famille, qui en a souffert,—vieil espace—pas de hasard. Elle a eu raison de le nier, sa vie—pour qu'il ait été l'absolu. Ceci devait avoir lieu dans les combinaisons de l'Infini vis-à-vis de l'Absolu."⁶⁹ Here, chance is connected to the infinite and opposed to the absolute. The family, which has preordained that Igitur should cast dice on the tombs of his ancestors and thereby identify with the absolute, has, in this, denied *hasard*; this negated chance which thus stands opposed to the absolute is, as an apposition reveals, the protagonist's life itself, and for this reason Mallarmé will speak of Igitur's breath as "son souffle qui contenait le hasard [his breath, which had chance in it]."⁷⁰ This absolution of his own life comes in Igitur's reduction of the potentially limitless accidental particularity of his own existence to the abstract concept of infinity.

The absolute and useless act of human introspection theorized and staged in *Igitur* became the subject of Mallarmé's most controversial poem, which took the form of a calligrammatic glossing of the proposition: "Un coup de dés jamais n'abolira le hasard [a throw of the dice will never abolish chance]."⁷¹ This act, as we know from *Igitur*, is the self-interrogation at the base of the human spirit, and the poem, like *Igitur*, is concerned with a casting of lots which occurs "dans des circonstances éternelles [in eternal circumstances]." These conditions are no longer the funereal silence of a nocturnal room and a subterranean tomb, but a shipwreck, a *topos* of the sublime, in which the infinite fury of natural forces devours a solitary ship that, subsequently, reveals itself to be an isolated person: "naufrage cela direct de l'homme sans nef [a direct shipwreck that of man without a ship]." Here, the number thrown by the dice is described as "un roc faux manoir tout de suite évaporé en brumes qui imposa une borne à l'infini [a rock false manor immediately turned to vapors when it set a boundary-stone against the infinite]." The casting of the dice is intended to place a limit on the infinite, to interrupt it with the particularity of its sentence, which comes not from immutable laws but through the sheer unpredictability of material existence, the accidental as opposed to the essential. But this limit to the infinite is vaporized, incapable of withstanding the forces of the sublime moment, and shifts, through a further metaphoric substitution, into a mere feather "flétrie par la neutralité identique du gouffre [wilted by the identical neutrality of the abyss]." A cast of the dice cannot abolish chance, though the player seeks to impose a term on the limitless happenstance of life, because chance is and is not, as Mallarmé puts it in Igitur: it *is* in the sense that there exists the variorum of accidents that make up existence, while it is *not* in the sense that these can, in their variety, be reduced to the idea of the Infinite, much as Schiller had reduced the wild chaos of nature to the concept of freedom.[72] And while all that takes place, as Mallarmé concludes in "Un coup de dés," is the place itself, or the "circonstances éternelles," he reserves the possibility—"peut-être"—of a single exception. This potential remnant is at such an altitude that it fuses with the beyond, and it is this very liminality that prevents one from determining whether there really does remain some residue of the particular in this sublime encounter. It is a something that, like Kant's post-terrified subject of the sublime, lies beyond interest: "hors l'intérêt," and thus partakes in the vaporization of the personal. It is a "constellation froide d'oubli et de désuétude pas tant qu'elle n'énumère sur quelque surface vacante et supérieure le heurt successif sidéralement d'un compte total en formation [cold constellation of forgetting and disuse not to the point but that it numbers on some vacant and superior surface the starry successive jostle of a total reckoning under way]." It is writing that remains in its ambiguous materiality; this is the site of forgetting the particular, the blank space of the open book in Igitur, the jostling or *heurt* of words in which Mallarmé had, elsewhere, seen the "disparition élocutoire du poète [the elocutory disappearance of the poet]."[73] But most significantly, this empty and forgotten residue of sublimation is not merely the poetic condition, although writing in its cold permanence makes especially manifest to us the sublime shipwreck of the particular in the purity of the lingering "I"; rather, this empty, residual lingering is the human condition, since, as Mallarmé concludes the poem, every thought is a throw of the dice.[74]

Like Zola, Hugo, and Dondey, Mallarmé saw a certain horror in this *face à face* with the immanence of abstract subjectivity, and he evoked it in a scene of Igitur observing his own face in a mirror jusqu'à ce qu'enfin, mes mains ôtées un moment de mes yeux où je les avais mises pour ne pas la [i.e., ma figure] voir disparaître, dans une épouvantable sensation d'éternité, en laquelle semblait expirer la chambre, elle m'apparût comme l'horreur de cette éternité. Et quand je rouvrais les yeux au fond du miroir, je voyais le personnage d'horreur, le fantôme de l'horreur absorber peu à peu ce qui restait de sentiment et de douleur dans la glace, nourrir son horreur des suprêmes frissons des chimères et de l'instabilité des tentures, et se former en raréfiant la glace jusqu'à une pureté inouïe.[75]

This is self-identity, the terrifying specular moment in which the abstract devours sensation, the lingering death of the self-consuming subject. It is hard to imagine a grimmer depiction of self-experience than this, and yet, generally, for one who made this negativity into the basis of his poetic practice and understanding of self-identity, Mallarmé does not come across as particularly horrified. The tone of his poetry seems, on the contrary, perfectly disengaged, characterized by a sort of glacial urbanity that appears far closer to the attitude of the mirror than of the frightened Igitur. This impassivity before what he acknowledges to be the horror of subjectivity could be what the poet had intended by "un calme narcotique de moi pur"—a stupifying of the senses, even of horror, a subsequent dullness, an indeterminate state bordering, perhaps, on spleen. However this condition might be characterized, in Mallarmé one sees a certain dampening of the sublime terror of the subject, its sublimation into something else, something like a narcotic indifference to the world—or something like writing.[76]

The primary point in reading Mallarmé here has not been, however, to demonstrate his negativity, since his poetry has already given rise to one of the richest and most intelligent bodies of literary criticism in existence, a body bearing predominantly on the idea of Mallarmé as poet of the absolute.[77] The concern here is, instead, first to demonstrate that Mallarmé did not see this absolute negativity as the effect of some particular poetic practice, but rather that poetic practice revealed for him the essentializing nature of subjectivity itself, that every thought emits "un coup de dés."[78] The second, more consequential issue is to situate that negativity within a larger intellectual context. This context has gone largely unnoticed, leading to the impression that Mallarmé had somehow mysteriouly reinvented Hegel in his poetic practice. One sees this in Paul de Man's unpublished doctoral dissertation, for example, which devoted an entire chapter to the attempt to establish Mallarmé's exposure to Hegel on the basis of his readings and conversations, an attempt which concludes that Mallarmé must have come to his apparent Hegelianism through some idiosyncratic journey of his own.[79] That Mallarmé made negativity his own, that he appropriated it as the basis of an original poetics, is not in question here. I am merely contesting the supposition that it was not part of a more pervasive understanding of the relation between self and experience. Mallarmé, as much as Zola, was giving voice to a period; but, more than Zola, he seems to have been shaping also the future of affective reactions to subjectivity. In following years it is less the weeping and terror and obsessive-compulsive behavior of the novelist that seem to mark intimations of the subject, and more an icy, dulling fear, somewhere between narcosis and a primary, inexpressible anxiety over expression itself.

If the face in Igitur's mirror represents a vanishing resistance to the horror of persistent self-identity, a philosophical voice was raising itself in protest and scorn against this absolution of the self from its own experience. It did not prevail, and, like Nerval's, eventually disappeared into incomprehensible madness, but not without first giving utterance to a remarkable insight into the potentially arbitrary nature of subjectivity and into the possibility of understanding human experience in its concrete plenitude without abstracting it into the appropriated and sublimated content of a persistent self, judicially answerable, theoretically void, experientially terrified or narcotic. In his first published work, *The Birth of Tragedy*, Nietzsche had asserted: "It is only as an *aesthetic phenomenon* that existence and the world may be eternally *justified*."[80] Something of an inversion has occurred, for instead of looking for the truth and meaning of sensuous existence and later conceiving of moral behavior on that basis, as Hegel did, Nietszche construed the question of existence in terms of justification; as if the rightness of the world were more basic than its meaning or truth, and as if ontology and epistemology were not the most primordial aspects of our being but were themselves grounded in ethics.[81] The discourse of this primordial aspect of existence is not metaphysics, but a phenomenal aesthetics, the discourse of the artistic manipulation of the sensuous world. Certainly, Nietzsche's conceptualization of that primordial phenomenology was not unambiguous or unproblematic. In the *Birth of Tragedy* itself he described concrete individuality as antagonistic to art and the aesthetic.[82] Later in his life, he would refer to an inherent scriptural quality in even prelinguistic experience, contending that "all our so-called consciousness is a more or less fantastic commentary on an unknown, perhaps unknowable, but felt text."[83] And Paul de Man's reading of *On Truth and Lie in an Extra-Moral Sense* has shown the tropological structures that underlie the essay's understanding of the most basic human experience.[84] Still, there is an ongoing attempt in Nietzsche's work to formulate the necessity and importance of nonlinguistic experience, and the genealogy of the subject went hand in hand, for him, with what he described as a vulgar need for language. Mallarmé's horrible mirror of self-identity reappears in Nietszche, but now only to have its inevitability derided. In 1882, thirteen years after Mallarmé sketched out *Igitur* and sixteen years before "Un coup de dés" appeared in print, Nietzsche published the following lines in *The Gay Science*:

> The problem of consciousness (more precisely, of becoming conscious of something) confronts us only when we begin to comprehend how we could dispense with it. . . . The whole of life would be possible without, as it were, seeing itself in a mirror. Even now, for that matter, by far the greatest portion of our life actually takes place without this mirror effect; and this is true even of our thinking, feeling, and willing life, however offensive this may sound to older philosophers. *For what purpose*, then, any consciousness at all when it is in the main *superfluous*?[85]

Since, Nietzsche observes, consciousness is thought that has taken the form of words, he concludes that it is the product of a need for communication, which would, by allowing human beings to supplement each other's weaknesses, have compensated for the physical shortcomings of the species and secured its survival.[86] Consciousness is thus language and therefore constitutes a communality within the individual. It is that within a person that comes from elsewhere as an alienation of the self into the general; unlike Lazare in Zola's *Joie de vivre*, or Mallarmé's Igitur, however, this alienation of the self, this presence of a generalized other at the heart of self-consciousness, is only an element within human experience even though, as an evolutionary imperative, it has "lorded it over" individuals since time immemorial, dominating the other aspects of their existence. This imperative character of consciousness as linguistic self-identity recalls the coercive aspect of subjectivity that is revealed in state-imposed punishment and in the conception of the individual as a responsible entity; it also foreshadows, if indistinctly, both the Freudian paternal interdiction, insofar as it is an injunction to the individual to enter the social and symbolic, and Althusser's conception of subjectivity as the interpellation, from an internalized agency of state ideology, that calls on the individual to be self-same.[87] Unlike the other writers considered so far, Nietzsche does not see this identification with the universal as a relation to the sheer absolute entailing an utter separation from others, since it is for him, on the contrary, a connection to others, a communality. Although one can discern in this the outlines of a possible ethical relationship, an inherence of the interests of the other within the individual, Nietzsche views linguistic communalization as something of a degeneration from a more direct relation to individual experience, and holds it, consequently, in some contempt, as the following passage from *The Gay Science* indicates:

> My idea is, as you see, that consciousness does not really belong to man's individual existence but rather to his social or herd nature; that, as follows from

> this, it has developed subtlety only insofar as this is required by social or herd utility. Consequently, given the best will in the world to understand ourselves as individually as possible, "to know ourselves," each of us will always succeed in becoming conscious only of what is not individual but "average." Our thoughts themselves are continually governed by the character of consciousness—by the "genius of the species" that commands it—and translated back into the perspective of the herd. Fundamentally, all our actions are altogether incomparably personal, unique, and infinitely individual; there is no doubt of that. But as soon as we translate them into consciousness *they no longer seem to be*.[88]

Language is a dissolution of experience into the vulgarity of the universal. The individual is, therefore, individual only through the momentary particulars of his or her experience and actions. In opposition to this generalizing vulgarity, and to the abstraction of Mallarmé's midnight, Nietzsche offers high noon, the moment that seems to linger eternally not by its abstraction but through the very plenitude of its voluptuousness. This is the now that leads Zarathustra to cry out: "Leave me alone! Still! Did not the world become perfect just now? Oh, the golden round ball!"[89] And this pleasure in the moment, this identifying with its depth, becomes a willing that it be so and not otherwise, that it linger in its plenitude and evanescence, and this is the Eternal return, the willing that the moment be just so. "Against the paralyzing feeling of general dissolution and incompletion," Nietzsche wrote, "I uphold the *Eternal Return*!"[90]

Between Hegel and Mallarmé, on the one hand, and Nietzsche on the other, it seems, however, to have been the former who most clearly articulated the future of self-identity.

The Theorization of Subjectivity and Death

From 1933 to 1939 Alexandre Kojève gave a series of lectures on the *Phenomenology of Spirit* at the Ecole des Hautes Etudes in Paris. It would be difficult to exaggerate their influence on postwar French thought. True, it was not really Kojève himself who first salvaged Hegel from the neglect into which his reputation as a bourgeois philosopher had sunk him, since that honor, in this century at least, probably falls to Jean Wahl's *Le Malheur de la conscience* or the special 1931 issue of *Revue de métaphysique*; but more than anybody else it was Kojève who made Hegel's work the seemingly necessary reference point for several generations of intellectuals. The list of those who attended his courses is especially revealing, for among them figured an astonishing concentration of the most influential thinkers of the years to come, such as Jacques Lacan, Pierre Klossowski, Alexandre Koyré, Eric Weil, Maurice Merleau-Ponty, Raymond

Aron, André Breton, and, intermittently, Emmanuel Levinas.[91] What is most striking in these seminars, aside from the sheer fact of reading Hegel's work as an end in itself rather than as a powerful precursor of other thinkers such as Marx, is the emphasis Kojève placed on the role of mortality in his understanding of Hegel. With Kojève, Hegel would become again a dominant, if not domineering, intellectual figure, but the idiosyncratic nature of Kojève's interpretation was often obscured by his sheer mastery of the materials, and this appears nowhere more clearly or significantly than in the importance he placed on death and in his troubling reading of the *Phenomenology*'s analysis of the Terror. Whatever the causes that might have led to them, the biases of Kojève's reading represent an explicit centralization of death and terror within the theorization of subjectivity, and what had been oblique or confused in writers like Mallarmé or Zola here becomes brutally systematic.

One can get a sense of Kojève's general take on Hegel by looking at the two epigraphs for his *Introduction à la lecture de Hegel*, the assemblage of both his own and students' notes of the courses he taught at the Ecole des Hautes Etudes. The first epigraph, taken from the 1806 Jena lectures, shows Hegel self-consciously situating himself at the beginning of a new historical period, the advent of a new appearance of Spirit. The passage, as Kojève quotes it, begins:

> Gentlemen! We find ourselves in an important period, a fermentation in which Spirit has made a leap forward, casting off its previous concrete form and taking on another. All the mass of ideas and concepts which held currency up until now, the very bonds of the world, have dissolved and fall away of themselves like visions in a dream. Spirit is preparing to appear anew.

For Kojève, the historical originality of which Hegel speaks here consists largely in the advent of Hegel himself—his having been the first philosopher to recognize the defining importance of death in the essence of the human, the first, that is, to recognize the human as a specific relation to death.[92] It was Hegel, according to Kojève, who finally bestowed on human beings their mortality, freeing them, in this way, for a consciousness of their nature and initiating them, consequently, as historical beings, since history, for Kojève's Hegel, is only possible in an atheistic world where people recognize their finitude.[93] The German philosopher would thus mark not merely a significant moment *within* history, but the beginning of history itself in the appearance of Man as a consciously historical being, as a being who identifies with history and becomes its subject. As Kant saw in the disinterested interest of observers toward events like the French Revolution a sublimation of personal interest into a concern for the good of humanity in general, and, from there, the origin of History, Hegel, conversely, would have seen that origin in the determination of the particular person, in an individuation effected through a conscious relation to death.[94] As will be seen, however, these two positions amount to more or less the same thing, since the essential piece that Kojève brings to an understanding of the role of negation in subjectivity is the explicit characterization of abstraction as both a uniquely human faculty and a form of death. The historical individual is thus, in both cases, one who has identified with its own vanishing into abstraction.[95]

In Kojève's reading the human is also placed under the sign of the sublime, for the second of his epigraphs quotes a statement made by Hegel in 1816. "Man," the passage reads, "since he is Spirit, can and should consider himself worthy of all that is most sublime. He can never overestimate the grandeur and the power of his spirit." Although Kojève does not explicitly develop the significance or implications of this assertion, it is not merely a bit of rhetorical flair, for the sublime, as a relation to concrete experience, plays an integral if unspoken role in the very structure of Hegel's formulation of subjectivity.

To understand why death and the structures of the sublime play such an important part in Kojève's conception of Hegel—indeed, *how* they play such a role—one must retrace the steps in his reasoning, starting with his formulation of the difference between essence and existence. Kojève defines the essence of a thing as its persistence over time and opposes it to the thing's actual existence. The result of this is that one can say that a thing, in its essence, does not exist, and that the persistence of something over time is the persistence of a void or a pure abstraction.[96] Now, it is the very essence of the human to see things in this way, as abstract essences, since Hegel, according to Kojève, defines Man by his understanding, the faculty that separates him from his existence in the *hic et nunc*—which separates him, in other words, from existence as such. This abstract human essence manifests itself, Kojève asserts, as discourse:

> Hegel tells us that the Understanding (= Man) is an "*absolute* power," which manifests itself in and by "the activity of *separation*," or better yet, as the "act-of-separation" (Scheiden). But why does he say this?
>
> He says it because the activity of the Understanding, that is to say human thought, is essentially *discursive*. . . . The absolute force or power of the Understanding which Hegel has in mind are, in the final analysis, none other than the power or the force of *abstraction* which is found in Man.[97]

Even actions, according to Kojève, are subject to this principle of abstraction since they are executed in time and in view of a persistence over time: an action acts towards the future, as an intention, and thus refigures the present in terms of the not-yet, the merely potential, the abstract. Although the act might be understood as a realization, or making real of the "void of being" that is, in Kojève's terms, the future, the future is instead conceived here as the abstract sense of the act and as such only really present in discourse.[98] Instead of realizing the future, the act abstracts the present into intention and sense. As Kojève succinctly puts it: "Discourse (= Subject) . . . Discourse (= Man)."[99] To be human is, in short, to transform oneself into concept and abstraction, and things persist in the understanding, acts are possible as human acts, only because the understanding, the faculty of abstraction, is other than the evanescent *hic et nunc*.

This discursive persistence or essence cannot be thought of as substance, according to Kojève, but must be understood as negativity, since the latter, he writes, "is 'the energy of thought' which releases the sense of Being [qui dégage le sens de l'Etre] by separating essence from existence. It is this negativity that is 'the energy of the pure abstract-I' which engenders 'thought,' which is to say, the 'Understanding' and its discourse."[100] Persistence, the abstraction of existence into its discursive essence in a pure "I," is thus derivative of negativity, the uniquely human faculty to see what is not, to live in a world that is not. We might imagine the opposition between natural substance and the human through the difference between a painter and a poet both attempting to express the specific concept of a not-a-tree. The poet can simply state: "It is not a tree," while the painter will be confronted with a perplexing challenge. Man, in his essential and definitive discursivity, lives, as it were, insofar as he is human, in a not-a-world since he is in the paradoxical position of being dependent on the world, of being pure nothingness away from the sensuous and substantial, and yet, precisely, separating himself from that world. Man, according to Kojève, "is pure nothingness outside the natural World. And yet he *separates* himself from this World and sets himself in *opposition* to it."[101] Man is, as Man, the pure nothingness that is his discursive persistence. The linguistic "acte de séparer" or "Scheiden" from the sensuous world constitutes the human as a void. In this respect, the separation of Kojève's human being can be compared to the *Spaltung* of Lacan's split subject insofar as the latter originates the individual within the symbolic through the loss of everything that it represents.[102]

This insubstantial negativity that is the essence of the human might be impossible to isolate and discern did it not reveal itself as a phenomenon within the sensuous materiality of the real world. This is the moment when what we have described, loosely, as the painterly world is interrupted by the intervention in it of the abstract not-world. This is the moment of death. As Kojève writes: "'The true being of man is his *action*,' says Hegel. Now, Action is the realization of Negativity, which manifests itself on the 'phenomenal' level as death."[103] Or, as he puts it elsewhere: "the real penetration of the Universal into the Particular is the finishing-off of the latter's finitude, or in other words its effective death."[104] The finitude of the human, that which makes the human human, is thus the intervention of the absolute in the real, that is, in the variorum of existence. The historical character of Man is based on this intervention which is death. Moreover, the essence or sense of action, insofar as it is human action and thus a work of negativity (which is to say an unmaking and a submitting of the present to the void of being that is the future) also manifests itself phenomenally as death. As readers of Kojève, we might recall that the guillotine had made this intervention spectacularly real to its contemporary commentators by instituting, in the public square at the heart of the city, a machine that revealed the abstractness of the present moment in an invisible *hic et nunc* that brought the absolute to bear on visible, sensuous, and ethical existence. The human is thus identified with that which is known in the world as death; and we are, as subjects, as persistent, human actors, death to ourselves. For this reason, Kojève will speak of us, to the extent that we are historical agents and human beings, as a sort of living death:

> This amounts, then, to saying that the human being itself is none other than that action; it is death which lives a human life.
>
> The human being, since it is thus, if you will, a differed death, or an affirmation of the Void by the negation of what is given, or once again: *creation*, is not therefore a *given-being*.[105]

Certainly, what Kojève is attempting to do, like Hegel and Heidegger before him, is to restore to the moment its lived evanescence by preserving a constant awareness of its transience, and in this sense his analysis of Hegel could be considered a true phenomenology and not a metaphysics, were it not that this very attempt entailed also an identification of the self, as that which persists among vanishing experience, as itself death. Death is human transcendence of the living animal connection to the world; it is the sublimity of the human.[106] This is why Kojève will characterize Hegel's dialectical philosophy as a "philosophy of death" and why he will see human consciousness, in its humanity, as a consideration and discussion of death: "since Man is born from finitude, it is only by thinking of death and by speaking of it that he is truly what he is: discourse conscious of itself and of its origin."[107]

The effect of action as a recasting of the present through the potentiality of the future is not far from Heidegger's concept of "thrownness," much as the refusal to confront death, which is represented by Beauty for Hegel and Kojève, will recall his analysis of *Gerede*, or "idle talk." But before turning to a consideration of *Being and Time*, we should not forget the significance of Kojève's reading of Hegel. Death, which here becomes the defining characteristic of human subjectivity, is not merely a metaphor. Rather, in its material brutality, it is the manifestation of the essence of human action and history, indeed, of human consciousness in general. It is for this reason that Kojève speaks of war as the most human of activities. And insofar as the individual is a synthesis of universal and particular, he or she maintains them only in their opposition, which is to say that this "synthesis" implies the persistence of a negative relation between the individual as discourse and subject on the one hand, and as lived experience on the other. We might, in this context, recall the very beginning of Kojève's lectures, where he had heralded the end of history as the appearance of absolute philosophy; this was to be the synthesis of essence and existence, in which Spirit would be perfected through the integration of natural, sensuous, aesthetic content into the human.[108] Kojève returned to this question in his lectures from the end of the same year, where he clarified the meaning of that synthesis. Hegel, Kojève writes,

> says that "Spirit" *is* "Science," that it is "Science" which is the only "objective reality" of Spirit. Now, that "Science" is none other than Hegelian philosophy itself, which appears at the heart of the natural World when Man's historical becoming comes to an end. Spirit is, consequently, none other than the spatiotemporal totality of the natural World, to the extent that this totality is entirely revealed by the discourse of the perfect (= satisfied) man, or of the Sage, while this discourse is itself a simple integration of the true sense of all discourses pronounced by men over the course of History.[109]

The spatiotemporal entirety of the world is revealed and reintegrated into absolute philosophy, which summarizes history, bringing back the whole of the aesthetic in the sense of the sensuous: this is the end of history, the goal of the *Phenomenology*, the final synthesis in which human Spirit perfects and fulfills itself. But absolute philosophy brings history back only discursively, as sense rather than sensation. If we recall that for Kojève, sense is the abstraction of essence from the here and now, it becomes evident that absolute philosophy restores the sensuous only as an abstract and universal category, like Kant's transcendental aesthetic or Mallarmé's infinite *hasard*. So, while it is true that Kojève speaks of Nature as the abstract negation of essence and asserts, at the opening of his analysis, that absolute philosophy only concerns itself with the concrete totality formed by the synthesis of essence and existence, it is also true that by the end of the same year, in the discussion of death that closes the published version of his courses, Kojève identifies absolute philosophy with the abstraction of existence, with the discursive negation of the here and now in its "sense." He identifies absolute philosophy, in short, with death. To this extent, Kojève appears to have deviated, over the course of his lectures, from the original promises of his interpretation.

To put this into practical and concrete terms, we can say that the guillotine, for example, as *the* machine for the intervention of the absolute within the real and therefore the machine of the subject and of history, brings the absolute to bear immediately and irreparably (as Hegel himself argues in the Terror section of the *Phenomenology*) on the living and cannot, for that reason, be synthetically reintegrated into life. As absolute difference, this intervention cannot lead to progress, it can only be repeated. This is the Terror, the endless compulsion to repeat the meaningless moment of the absolute in a perpetually frustrated attempted to integrate it into life. This too is Zola's obsessive-compulsive "arithmomania," which constantly repeats the moment of leavetaking from life throughout the actions of the day.[110] It is, not least of all, the fulfillment of philosophy at the end of history in Kojève, which takes the form of the endless repetition, as discourse rather than action, of all of human history, reduced to the ceaseless rereading of the *Phenomenology*.[111] Levinas, speaking of the transcendental relation to the Absolute, will attempt to draw a way out of its stuttering impasse by understanding it as an ethical relation in which alterity comes not as death but as a living other in the expressiveness of a human face. Kojève's subject of history, whose sense is fulfilled in absolute philosophy, constitutes rather a theorization of the persistent subject that had appeared in Zola, Dondey, and Mallarmé—it is an abstraction opposed to existence insofar as existence is experience of the momentary both in its evanescence and in the plenitude of its senselessness. The identification with the subject, in Kojève, is what is most terrible in life, for the human condition, when considered in itself, is lived, experienced, and known as terror by the existent, nonessential part of the human, that part which feels. The subjectivity that Kojève draws from Hegel here is a self that feels itself as terror, and its history, the only history, is the history of terror. This terror, as Kojève explained at the Ecole des Hautes Etudes in the years before the Second World War, is what it feels like to be human.

It is hard to imagine a more brilliant reader of Hegel than Kojève, but this should not blind us to certain idiosyncrasies of his approach, and one of the key problems of the Kojévian interpretation, pregnant with consequences for an entire period, is its curious deformation of the value that the Terror held for Hegel. One can wonder how he could remain so blind to the letter of Hegel's text, entirely ignoring those statements in it which seem directly to contradict his own conclusions. Other readers have had difficulties with the Terror analysis in the *Phenomenology*. Hippolyte, for instance, was confused by this section of the book, but he, at least, recognized that confusion.[112] Blanchot seemed to comes closer to Hegel's actual text, but even he ignored the full scope of the conclusions Hegel drew from his readings. Perhaps this resistance to the absolute and meaningless negativity of the Terror for Hegel is the necessary result of the way that this generation made sense of Hegel in rediscovering and reappropriating him. With the centralization of death in the conceptualization of human identity, the Terror, and its Hegelian theorization, took on a particular and ambiguous importance as the enactment of death-based subjectivity in state policy. It was perhaps the case, too, that for this generation of French readers the Terror was a moment which, as French, made a particular and not entirely negative sense.

Kojève understood Hegel's analysis of the Terror to be the realization, on the social level, of absolute liberty as death. In the unmediated opposition between individual and universal that constituted, for Hegel, the heart of the Terror, Kojève saw the resistance of "the isolated particulars towards the universal which is incarnated in the State. They set themselves against it in absolute opposition, wanting to negate the given State in an absolute manner by completely annihilating it."[113] In our own interpretation of the same immediate opposition, we had seen a somewhat more complicated scenario than this personal resistance to the State, and had argued that the conflict is between the evacuated remains of the individual, described by Hegel as an "insubstantial point," and his or her own self as identified with the state, that is to say, as a conflict between two modes of self-representation within the individual, rather than between the individual and something external. Our reading was much closer to that of Maurice Blanchot, who, ten years after the end of Kojève's lectures and three after Hyppolite's publication of the *Genèse et structure de la phénoménologie*, would gloss this same passage as meaning that in identifying themselves with the abstract universal of absolute liberty, individuals identify with the universal incarnate in the State. It is for this reason, according to our own reading and to Blanchot, that their deaths are without significance: the individuals have no content (which is that which makes individuals of them in the first place); they are no longer separate from the State, which now incarnates absolute negativity in its ideology. According to Blanchot's "Literature and the Right to Death," perishing by the guillotine is insignificant because it is nothing more than the "manifestation of the fact that such a freedom is still abstract, ideal (literary), that it is only poverty and platitude. Each person dies, but everyone is alive, and that really also means everyone is dead."[114] Kojève, on the other hand, conceived of the Terror as a moment that gives sense to human life, in that it takes the individual seriously, recognizing, so to speak, his or her humanity. This, for Kojève, is the positivity of the Terror, and the individual's "political right to death" amounts to the State's fatal respect for the humanity of that individual through his or her execution.[115] And yet Hegel himself had already utterly and explicitly rejected Kojève's positivist interpretation of this passage. How, one wonders, can Kojève, given his reading, pass over in silence Hegel's remark that the guillotine is "the coldest and meanest of all deaths, with no more significance than cutting off a head of cabbage or swallowing a mouthful of water."[116] Even Hyppolite, despite his avowed perplexity before this section of the *Phenomenology*, understands it as an interpretation of "the failure of that revolution."[117] Death in the Terror, contrary of Kojève's position, is precisely a death that does *not* take the humanity of the individual seriously, to the extent that his or her death is utterly void and empty of sense. It seems, however, that Kojève *must* misinterpret this passage, because to understand it otherwise, to understand it as the text itself seems to read and as Blanchot understands it, would mean that his death-based interpretation of the Hegelian system would be an espousal of the meaningless Terror as the human condition, as the work of history, and that this senseless, void Terror would itself be "death that lives a human life." It would mean that absolute philosophy was the absolutely empty action of the guillotine in the Terror.

This misreading of the Terror as a positivity works its way into Kojève's analysis of the role of war in understanding history and the human, and there one gets a clearer idea of the importance of this bias to his global approach. As a passage Kojève quotes from Hegel's lectures of 1805–6 indicates, war is structured like our understanding of the Terror in the *Phenomenology*, since the death its spreads is coldly impersonal and represents an identification of the individual with the absolute liberty of the state.[118] As in his reading of the Terror, Kojève understands this impersonal death of an abstracted individual as dialectically positive, and indeed, identifies it as the essence of history and the human:

> It is thus deadly war which assures the historical freedom and the free historicity of Man. Man is only historical insofar as he actively participates in the life of the State, and that participation finds its culmination in the voluntary risk of life in a purely political war. So it is that man is only truly historical or human insofar as he is at war, at least in potential.[119]

No matter how convincing Kojève's arguments might be that Hegel did understand war this way, he gives no mention of Hegel's own rejection of the historical positivity of cold, impersonal death when it had appeared in his analysis of the functioning of the Terror, a fact that would, at the very least, indicate an extreme ambivalence on Hegel's part toward the value of state-imposed death. And yet Hegel had been explicit and repetitive: death under the Terror "is the death that is without meaning, the sheer terror of the negative that contains nothing positive, nothing that fills it with a content."[120] These are scarcely the terms in which he might be expected to describe the recognition of a putative right to death or the State's celebration of individuality, let alone the essence of the human and the historical. The stubbornness with which Kojève ignored Hegel's own conclusions about the meaninglessness of impersonal death and the vacancy of the individual that identified with it as an abstract universal indicates the curious bias of his readings of the *Phenomenology*. Kojève's espousal of death as the essence of the human is, in this sense, an exaggeration of elements within the original system, elements toward which Hegel himself expressed a genuine resistance, or which he condemned as insignificant and undialectical. Kojève's reading of Hegel is an astonishingly grim and negative one, which confronts and appropriates, in its understanding of subjectivity, a Terror and a death from which Hegel himself had shrunk. And yet it is not, for this, necessarily a *wrong* interpretation. One can argue, instead, that his reading is in fact more resolute than Hegel's own, that it was Kojève who, more than Hegel, was capable of tarrying with the negative in its dreadful reality. It was this resolute tarrying that allowed Kojève to conceive of the abstract impersonality of the State and the vacant death it imposed as legitimate manifestations of subjectivity. In a way that Hegel himself had not, Kojève demonstrated that by accepting the subject as the basis of individuality, one accepted also the guillotine as a recognition of that individuality.

At the heart of history according to Kojève lies war, and at the heart of the human subject is the terrible confrontation with death. To be human is, in his analysis of Hegel, to feel the immanence of oneself as terror. This fear that seems, since the time of the Revolution, inalienable from the concept of subjectivity is never really taken as an object of philosophical inquiry in its own right. Or, at least, it is not so treated until Heidegger turns to the question of anxiety in *Being and Time*. Concerned to analyze human self-identity in its lived plenitude rather than as a metaphysical abstraction, Heidegger's phenomenological approach seems in many respects very similar to Hegel's intentions in *The Phenomenology of Spirit*, at least when considered in a pre-Kojévian way. Both seek to describe the human significance of concrete experience and view it as indissociable from the true essence of humanity. Absolute philosophy, for Hegel, concerns itself only with the synthetic union of intellectual abstraction and concrete or natural existence, while for Heidegger, the authentic human self cannot be understood as a universal alienated from the worldly engagements that constitute its activities and life. For Hegel, however, that experiential component manifested itself, above all, in the history of humanity or *Geist*, whereas for Heidegger its most significant expression was in the small events of daily life that are most intimate to people. For Heidegger, the human individual has no sense, indeed no existence, outside of the world in which it exists. He therefore designates human beings with the term "Dasein," which means "being-there" or "presence": the human is one who is "there" in the world of events and beings in relation to which it exists and outside of which it has no existence. On this basis, it would seem that Heidegger offers a genuine alternative to the profoundly negative conception of self-identity that had troubled European thought since the time of the French Revolution, given that instead of viewing the persistent individual as the negation of its own experiences, he was proposing that it be viewed as intelligible, real, and self-same only *in* those experiences. Among the intimate events that befall all Dasein and that constitute its specific way of being, Heidegger pays particular attention to moods, an element that goes largely unexamined in previous analyses of the most fundamental structures of self-identity, since those previous approaches treated them as accidental rather than essential. Among these moods, which reveal the most basic functioning of the self by revealing the particular ways in which Dasein exists in the world, Heidegger devotes special attention to anxiety, which emerges as fear before the most primordial type of being that characterizes Dasein.

The significance of Heidegger's attempted break with abstract or transcendental subjectivity should not be dismissed. His approach not only marks a recognition of the problems inherent in the sublimation of the self, it also offers, despite its problems, a highly elaborated analysis of those shortcomings. The originality of his method stems from Dasein's being "there" in the world, from its primordial involvement in other beings and other Dasein, an involvement conceived by Heidegger in terms of care. Care is consequently the mode of being peculiar to Dasein, and only on its basis can one understand Dasein's self. The failure to recognize this constitutes, therefore, the principal shortcoming of those models of selfhood that conceive of its persistence only in terms of an abstracted subjectivity. As Heidegger himself frames the issue:

> Ontologically, Dasein is in principle different from everything that is present-at-hand or Real. Its "subsistence" is not based on the substantiality of a substance but on the "*Self-subsistence*" of the existing Self, whose Being has been conceived as care. The phenomenon of the *Self*—a phenomenon which is included in care—needs to be defined existentially in a way which is primordial and authentic, in contrast to our preparatory exhibition of the inauthentic they-self. Along with this, we must establish what possible ontological questions are to be directed towards the "Self," if indeed it is neither substance nor subject.[121]

By approaching the question of selfhood "ontologically," Heidegger means understanding Dasein not as simply one more being or entity in the world, but as one with a distinctive relation to Being itself. The "there" of Dasein is not merely a relation to other entities within the world, but constitutes Dasein as fundamentally different from them, a difference that cannot derive from its relation to those other entities (since it would therefore be only a more elaborated relation to them) but in reference to something else. That something else than beings is Being itself, and Dasein, though it may, for moments or centuries, forget the fact, is unique in the world in that for it Being as such is an issue. While

Dasein, as "essentially" existing, cannot be thought of as an abstract essence in negation of the world, neither can it be conceived of like other entities, such as rocks or hammers, within the world. By the term "present-at-hand," Heidegger means that particular mode of being through which philosophers have traditionally understood the existence of entities and Dasein itself.[122] It is an understanding of beings that "thematizes" them, or, in other words, seeks to grasp their reality by isolating them as specific objects distinct from the world in which they are involved through such connections as function, use, suitability, intention, and so on. Dasein, in its peculiar and authentic way of being, does not exist as present-at-hand but as a concernful connection with the world, and it is "there" in the world as care. In this authentic, concernful way, it does not relate to entities in the world as objects of scrutiny, but circumspectly encounters them as "ready-to-hand."[123] Now, while the persistence of Dasein is not to be understood in terms of a sublimated abstraction, neither is it to be conceived of as the subsistence of a substance, for it is not related to itself like other entities in the world; rather, its identity over time is grounded in its unique relation to Being as such, a relation that plays on Dasein's potential for Being and for not-Being. It is this distinctive relation to the world as potential for Being or not-Being that is, as we shall see, the source of anxiety in Dasein, and it is to forget this anxiety that the individual turns from confronting its authentic mode of Being and loses itself in inauthentic modes of self-understanding. In thus fleeing from itself, Dasein falls into the anonymity of the "they-self," which is its alienation from itself in a community of unappropriated activities and beliefs which come from nowhere in particular but which seem valid by the sheer fact of their pervasiveness. Dasein runs from itself toward the "they" because it is, in short, aversive to itself. This aversion of the self to itself should strike us as remarkable despite its recurrence in all of the authors studied so far, indeed *because* of its recurrence, for it serves as an initial indication of the persistence of terror and sublimation even within those models of self-identity that seek to break with subjectivity and to ground the human individual in existence rather than essence. In Heidegger, Dasein's anxious aversion to itself stems from this: despite the facts that its peculiar way of being is care and that care entails an involvement in the world, authentic Dasein is primordially alone. And Dasein is alone, as we shall see, because care is Being-toward-death.[124]

By briefly examining the steps in Heidegger's discussion of selfhood, we can get a sense not merely of the powerful centripetal pull of death-based subjectivity, but also a preliminary notion of alternative approaches, which will find a fuller development later, in our readings of Nerval, Kristeva, and Levinas. Heidegger himself brought attention to the fundamental originality of his approach, as in his assertion that "defining the structure of care has given us a basis on which to distinguish ontologically between existence and Reality for the first time. This has led us to the thesis that the substance of man is existence."[125] Dasein, in other words, is neither abstract nor substantial, it is existential, and that which is persistent and fundamental in it is the sheer fact of existence itself. One must be careful, however, not to understand this existence in the way of metaphysical philosophers or the "they," since Heidegger distinguishes Dasein's characteristic type of existence from Reality, which is the traditional way of construing existence as presence-at-hand. Dasein exists in relation to its possibilities, which can either be or not be, and in this way, in its relating to the world, it relates to it primordially and authentically in terms of its Being or not-Being, that is to say, in the way of existing that is peculiar to it. In other words, Dasein's distinctive way of being is to live as the existing of a potential. This can be seen in the following passage from *Being and Time*:

> In being its *Self*, Dasein is, *as* a Self, the entity that has been thrown. It has been *released* from its basis, *not through* itself but *to* itself, so as to be *as this basis*. Dasein is not itself the basis of its Being, inasmuch as this basis first arises from its own projection [*Entwurf*]; rather, as Being-its-Self, it is the *Being* of its basis. This basis is never anything but the basis for an entity whose Being has to take over Being-a-basis.[126]

In authentically being itself, Dasein does not "fall" but projects, or throws, itself onto its possibilities for being, and this projection is its actually being them. We do not say that it is their "realization," since that would imply an understanding of Dasein's existence based on traditional concepts of Reality as presence-at-hand. Instead, authentically, Dasein *is* its possibilities in the way that is peculiar to it: it lives them as possibilities, that is, as things which are but which could or could not have been. They are lived authentically, in other words, as putting Dasein's relation to Being itself into play. In this sense, Dasein, by living, brings its "basic" or original self into being: it is the *Being* of its basis, or potentialities-for-Being. While Heidegger maintains that Dasein is its basis, he also contends, somewhat confusingly, that Dasein is *not* its basis, insofar as the latter arises from Dasein's *Entwurf*, or projection. Dasein is *not* its own basis in the sense that, as thrown, Dasein lives as the *Being* of possibilities, and that in this condition of possibility, even as "realized" possibility, the possibility of *not* having been realized or not having existed is fundamental. This is clarified somewhat by the fact that *Entwurf* has the further sense of "project" or "outline" for something to be completed later: as an ongoing and underlying—or basic—project, Dasein is constantly in the state of potentiality, although in living it brings that potentiality into *Being*. This basis of Dasein must not, in Heidegger's terms, be thought of as the persistence of an essence that is realized in existence or as the subsistence of substance, for insofar as it is *not* in Dasein's *Being* it simply is not. There is no "someplace else" for it to be, and so this basis, understood as "ground" of Dasein's specific kind of being *is null and empty*. For this reason Heidegger states that "in itself, being a basis *is* a nullity of itself. 'Nullity' does not signify anything like not-Being-present-at-hand or not-subsisting; what one has in view here is rather a 'not' which is constitutive for this *Being* or Dasein—its thrownness."[127] The "substance" of Dasein is its existence, and in existing Dasein makes itself not as the realization of a pre-existent "basis" or plan but as the choosing or acting of itself, and it is for this reason that Heidegger can speak of Dasein as grounded in a void.

Dasein's authentic way of Being, its thrownness onto its potentialities, can be understood most fundamentally as a relation to time, and for this reason, Heidegger asserts that "*Temporality reveals itself as the meaning of authentic care.*"[128] In conceiving of Dasein's authentic way of being as temporality, however, we must be careful not to understand it in terms of the notion of time as it is generally understood by the "they." In living as the Being of its potentialities, in projecting itself or making a project of itself, Dasein constantly and most primordially lives toward a future. The future is somehow implicit in Dasein's actions, because they are part of the project that is its existence. Furthermore, the future is primordial because it grounds Dasein's actions to the extent that they are potentialities: insofar as actions are futural their being or not-being remains open. As Heidegger puts it:

> By the term "futural," we do not here have in view a now which has *not yet* become "actual" and which sometime *will be* for the first time. We have in view the coming [*Kunft*] in which Dasein, in its ownmost potentiality-for-Being, comes towards itself. Anticipation makes Dasein *authentically* futural, and in such a way that the anticipation itself is possible only in so far as Dasein, *as being*, is always coming towards itself—that is to say, in so far as it is futural in its Being in general.[129]

In its authentic temporality as the basis for care, the future is not an empty theoretical moment that will eventually arrive, like a deferred Hegelian "now," for that moment, as authentically lived by Dasein, will be lived in its own potentiality as a convergence of engagements in the world projected toward its own futural possibilities. Dasein's authentic temporality is thus conceivable only if we understand *all* of its moments as futural, and if, as thrownness, the present moment can be thought of as the anticipation of further anticipation. But in thus being futural, Dasein is not moving away from itself, it is rather coming toward itself as the *Being* of its potentialities: when the moment comes Dasein will be its potentiality. This futurity, thus, also involves a relation to the past, for in coming to itself, Dasein is, in a certain sense, coming *back*, but it is a return that, in conformity with Dasein's authentic temporality as thrownness onto potentialities, is itself fundamentally futural. In Heidegger's words:

> Only in so far as Dasein *is* as an "I-*am*-as-having-been," can Dasein come towards itself futurally in such a way that it comes *back*. As authentically futural, Dasein *is* authentically as "*having been*." Anticipation of one's uttermost and ownmost possibility is coming back understandingly to one's ownmost "been." Only so far as it is futural can Dasein *be* authentically as having been. The character of "having been" arises, in a certain way, from the future.[130]

In being itself, in existing as the being of its basis, Dasein returns, in some sense, to what it has already been. We have already seen that for Heidegger, that basis is in itself a nullity. The authentic past cannot, therefore, be thought of as a present that has slipped away, and Dasein as a continuity, part of which is no longer so accessible to it, like a rod partially dipped in water; the "having been" must instead be understood in terms of potentiality.[131] The present, as projected, is an anticipated anticipation, it is the once-futural possibility that might or might not have been, and in this way the relation to the past is grounded in the future or arises from it. Dasein returns to itself as that which was anticipated but might or might not have been and which continues to project itself, as anticipation, on other possibilities. In seeing time in these terms, Dasein recognizes in its own temporality its specific relation to Being as a concern for the possibility of Being or not-Being.

Initially, this approach to existence seems significantly different from Kojève's understanding of action. Kojève's reading of Hegel sees the present as abstracted into its "sense" by its projection, through intentional action, onto a future, and he asserts that "Negativity is thus nothing but the *finitude* of Being (or the presence in it of a genuine future, which will never be its present)."[132] Heidegger seems, on the other hand, to conceive of action as the *being* of potentialities: in this sense the future seems *to be* in the act. The implications of this understanding of human existence need to be drawn out, however, for there is a natural tendency to think of possibility inappropriately in terms of a simple presence-at-hand that has not yet come about, and this is far from Heidegger's intention. And these implications tend toward an ever-increasing insistence on the role of nothingness and negativity in Dasein's mode of being. We have already gotten a sense of this from Heidegger's discussion of the "nullity" of Dasein's basis, but he pursues this question much farther. By authentically Being, that is, in its thrownness or projection as the *Being* of its potentialities, Dasein is fundamentally free, but it is free, in its authenticity, actually to be only *one* of those possibilities, and consequently it is *not* as all of its other potentialities. As Heidegger puts this: "Dasein is its basis existently—that is, in such a manner that it understands itself in terms of possibilities, and, as so understanding itself, is that entity which has been thrown. But this implies that in having a potentiality-for-Being it always stands in one possibility or another: it constantly is *not* other possibilities, and it has waived these in its existentiell projection."[133] This is what it means to live as projected, to *be* authentically: to understand that in being grounded as potentiality in the issue of Being or not-Being, one understands oneself not only as *Being* but also as *not-Being* all those other possibilities that might have been. To live authentically is to be concerned by this not-having-been, to view it as somehow primordial to one's *Being*, for in the complex temporality of care, it is always the persistent nullity of what is not that prevents the potential from slipping into a modality of presence-at-hand. To live authentically is to be profoundly concerned, then, with the *not* or the negative. It is for this reason that Dasein feels a fundamental sense of guilt, which is the feeling toward that which one might have been but is not and that which one could be but will not be.[134] For this reason, in authentically *Being*, Dasein confronts what is not and wants to have a conscience.[135] Conscience is the awareness of one's guilt in being projected.

It is not yet clear why these projects and actions should be determinative of a *particular* Dasein or why they could not be thought of as general needs or urgings that come from elsewhere. Hegel cast this same situation in terms of recognition in his analysis of the master/slave dialectic, where the slave exists at all only insofar as it does the will of the master, but even there it is still a question of some*one*'s will, even if that someone is someone else. Heidegger, on the other hand, understands the situation in more mundane but more impersonal terms. Dasein is, by its very nature, open to the possibility of thinking the thoughts and enacting the projects of the anonymous "they" whose constant, uninvestigated opinions and idle chatter make up the everyday world. In Heidegger's approach, this thinking and doing what "they" think and do is an inauthentic way of being for Dasein insofar as it is a turning away or fleeing from Dasein's most primordial structures.[136] The "they" does not own up to its fundamental guilt, since it never acknowledges the finite limitations of *Being* one's potentialities. By virtue of its indistinctness and anonymity, the "they," unlike the individual, always has time to do whatever it is that might be done or knows that there is always someone left to do it. As a result, the way of being that characterizes the "they" never forces the issue of not-being. In confronting its authentic way of being, Dasein consequently turns away from the "they" and toward its limited self, in which potentiality takes on its full ontological significance through *Being* or *not-Being*. For Dasein, therefore, being authentically means being "resolutely."

What Heidegger understands by this is that in its commitment to itself, and its recognition of its consequent guilt, Dasein attains that persistence that makes of it a finite individual self. "Existentially," Heidegger writes, "'*Self-constancy*' signifies nothing other than anticipatory resoluteness. The ontological structure of such resoluteness reveals the existentiality of the Self's Selfhood."[137] In this assertion, it seems that we have finally drawn close to a conception of persistent individual identity that would construe it in terms of existence rather than essence; in short, as something other than death-based subjectivity or the negation of lived experiences. But we must look more closely at what resoluteness means in terms of Dasein's specific sort of existence in order to determine the genuine originality of this approach and its value as an alternative to the models we have examined so far. First of all, we must recognize that for Heidegger, the self and self-constancy are grounded in care, not vice versa.[138] The mode of care in which the self exists is resoluteness, which is to say one is oneself and one has an identity not simply as a pregiven something which one manifests through being, but only insofar as one exists resolutely. Resoluteness, as a mode of care, therefore grounds the self as a way of being in the world, rather than as an abstraction inimical to it. In Heidegger's words: "In resoluteness the issue for Dasein is its ownmost potentiality-for-Being, which, as something thrown, can project itself only upon definite factical possibilities. Resolution does not withdraw itself from 'actuality,' but discovers first what is factically possible."[139] What we need to remember in this is that even if the self is a "product" of care's projection (and this is not to be understood in terms of a finished product that is present-at-hand), it is only as an individualized self that Dasein authentically exists as care. Now, at bottom, resoluteness is the commitment to one's own, finite, untransferable and inalienable potentialities. It is, as Heidegger puts it, a being-towards that which is one's ownmost. While one could perhaps imagine other untransferable moments such as pain or pleasure, Heidegger is interested in something that places the whole of one's being in question and which, consequently, constitutes one as a finite totality. It is not entirely clear *why* Heidegger rejects such experiences as pain and pleasure, but one can imagine that while they might put the whole of one's being, or indeed the world, into question, they do so in a way that dissolves the "I" rather than confirming it in its isolation. In pleasure, I disappear into the world; in pain, it is the world that is annihilated.[140] According to Heidegger, that which puts the Being of the whole of the world at issue while isolating the "I" as an individual is death. For this reason, he states: "Care is Being-towards-death. We have defined 'anticipatory resoluteness' as authentic Being towards the possibility which we have characterized as Dasein's utter impossibility."[141] Resoluteness is resoluteness toward the future as a possibility, and in its most authentic sense it is resoluteness toward a definite possibility, that is to say, one that defines or delimits Dasein while never losing its fundamental potentiality and thereby simply appearing as present-at-hand. Death is that one possibility that, while certain, still remains a possibility, for while death itself is inexorable, the moment of its coming always remains unknown. It is this constant certainty of a possible death, the knowledge that it could come from one moment to the next, unannounced and total, that gives to the self its persistence. Resoluteness is merely the confronting of this constancy of death:

> The holding-for-true which belongs to resoluteness, tends, in accordance with its meaning, to hold itself free *constantly*—that is, to hold itself free for Dasein's *whole* potentiality-for-being. This constant certainty is guaranteed to resoluteness only so that it will relate itself to that possibility of which it can *be* utterly certain. In its death, Dasein must simply "take back" everything. Since resoluteness is constantly certain of death—in other words, since it *anticipates* it—resoluteness thus attains a certainty which is authentic and whole.[142]

The self is self insofar as it is always at risk of not being, and it is only in this way that Dasein can have a permanence that is specific to its peculiar way of being. This is not a subject or a substance, because this death is the constantly impending possibility of what simply is not, which is neither existence nor essence. One's authentic anticipatory being is thus, most fundamentally, an anticipation of one's not being at all, and it is through this "at all," or the utter end of all possibilities, that death gives to Dasein not only its constancy and end, but its totality. In death, it is not just this or that possibility that is at stake, but all possibilities—it is the constant possibility of impossibility. This individual wholeness which resoluteness reveals in and to Dasein is, however, wholly empty, since it is grounded in the absolute nothingness of death. The pure nonbeing of its basis is made manifest to Dasein, which thereby appropriates and identifies itself. Insofar as it is authentic and resolute, Dasein, consequently, *is* the nullity of death. As Heidegger states:

> When Dasein is resolute, it takes over authentically in its existence the fact that it *is* the null basis of its own nullity. We have conceived death existentially as what we have characterized as the possibility of the *im*-possibility of existence—that is to say, as the utter nullity of Dasein. Death is not "added on" to Dasein as its "end"; but Dasein, as care, is the thrown (that is, null) basis for its death. The nullity by which Dasein's Being is dominated primordially through and through, is revealed to Dasein itself in authentic Being-towards-death.[143]

Death is grounded in care, but death reveals the depth and immanence of Dasein's not-Being, so we must not think of care as some more fundamental positivity of which death is merely an epiphenomenon. Rather, as Heidegger contends, in death one is one's ownmost, meaning that in facing it one returns from one's lostness in the "they" toward that possibility which is not only definite and determining, but is also *only* one's own. No one else can die in one's place, and it is in this sense that death is nonrelational. Being toward death is, in this way, what constitutes one *as* an individual.[144] Now, it is only as an individual that Dasein authentically *is* in the manner that is specific to it. Consequently, as Kojève asserted that the essence of the human is death and that Man is the death that lives a human life, for Heidegger, Dasein's peculiar way of being—what makes human beings human—is the individual's awareness of its own impending death and its identification with the nullity that constitutes that death. Humanity, for Heidegger, is grounded in the finite individual and the finite individual is, in turn, grounded in death. It is this that anxiety reveals:

> Thrownness into death reveals itself to Dasein in a more primordial and impressive manner in that state-of-mind which we have called "anxiety." Anxiety in the face of death is anxiety "in the face of" that potentiality-for-Being which is one's ownmost, nonrelational, and not to be outstripped. That in the face of which one has anxiety is Being-in-the-world itself. That about which one has this anxiety is simply Dasein's potentiality-for-Being. Anxiety in the face of death must not be confused with fear in face of one's demise. This anxiety is not an accident or random mood of "weakness" in some individual; but, as a basic state-of-mind of Dasein, it amounts to the disclosedness of the fact that Dasein exists as thrown Being *towards* its end. Thus the existential conception of "dying" is made clear as thrown Being towards its ownmost potentiality-for-Being, which is non-relational and not to be outstripped.[145]

One is anxious about Being-in-the-world itself, for that is what is at stake in death, in its utter impossibility of being. But in anxiety one is also troubled by the very nature of potentiality itself, the nullity at the basis of and throughout Dasein's existence as care. One is anxious too about the individual isolation that dying reveals to be the condition of human existence. And because that isolating persistence of death in the individual *is* the human condition, anxiety is not a passing or occasional mood. By its very nature Dasein is always anxious. It is always anxious about the nothing that is itself and which hangs over every moment, bordering Dasein down into an absolutely nonrelational existence. Terror, one could say, has retreated from the world of beings into the issue of Being itself, where it has taken on a more primordial, more basic role as the constant revelation of humanness to the human. The absolutely alone individual is the one who feels this humanity that is nothing other than itself. Like Hegel's historical *Geist*, Dasein as individual receives its identity not from a faceless crowd but in a face to face with death.[146] I, one could say, receive my face by confronting that which has no face. Or I am given a face only to look at that which has none. I am I through a faceless other. So say all the authors we have read, except perhaps Nietzsche.

On the basis of Heidegger's analysis, we might still wonder how it is that we are so certain about death that it should be the very basis of our being. Far from the most certain aspect of our existence, might we not instead say that it is the most mysterious? And what is to make us believe that because others die, so must we? To answer this, we must understand that for Heidegger, death is the name that we give to the awareness that we are not the overwhelming majority of the possibilities that we might be, the awareness of our finitude. It is, more specifically, the conviction that from one moment to another we will not be. We do not discover death by living. Because it is untransferable and nonrelational, we cannot gather its certainty from another. Rather, death is the primordial certainty of our finitude, our knowledge that we are *as* potential. The conviction that we are certainly going to lose all potential from one moment to the next, that we are absolutely potential, is, according to Heidegger's reasoning, that which allows human life, because human life is human only as this potentiality, only as this placing Being and not-Being at issue. Human beings do not, according to Heidegger, discover death through life, but rather life through death.

In Heidegger's understanding of human existence, one is caught, therefore, between two deaths: between one's volatilization in the "they"—as no one in particular, as not really being anyone—and the isolated confrontation of one's own nonexistence. *Being and Time* represents an attempt to understand human identity in terms that would break with the model of death-based subjectivity which has returned incessantly in countless forms since the end of the eighteenth century, leaving its trace in social institutions, constitutional reform, poetics, history, pathology and philosophy. And yet this attempt fails. Fear returns as the human condition and the self reveals itself once more as death. It is because of this persistence that one must look elsewhere, to another sort of authority, if one is to discern a significant resistance to this model of human existence and the seeds of an alternative way of understanding the self. One such elsewhere is in the long process of an aesthetic self-understanding shot through with the incomprehensible language of a poetic madness. It is in the works of Gérard de Nerval, born one year after the publication of *The Phenomenology of Spirit*, that we will try to find the traces of another self.

3. Nerval in Context: The Authority of Madness

> If ever a writer . . . sought to define himself painstakingly to himself, to grasp and bring to light the murky shadings, the deepest laws and most elusive impressions of the human soul, it was Gérard de Nerval.
>
> —*Marcel Proust*

> Yes, there is in my head a storm of thoughts that ceaselessly dazzle and exhaust me; there are years of dreams, of projects, of torments that jostle for expression in a single line, a single word.
>
> —*Nerval*

"In those days of literary eccentricity, among the fads, the freaks and the outrages both voluntary and involuntary, it was quite difficult to appear extravagant, for every madness seemed plausible," Théophile Gautier wrote of Paris in the early 1830's, when a small band of young artists, known variously to themselves as the Petit Cénacle, the Jeunes-France, or the Bousingos, and to later critics as the Petits Romantiques, were drawn together by a common lionization of the slightly older generation of romantic writers such as Hugo and Lamartine, as well as by a general desire to shock their complacent bourgeois contemporaries through transgressive behavior.[1] Their socially confrontational activities seemed for a long time to predominate over serious aesthetic contributions to any established genres, with almost all the members of the group, though determined to be artists of one sort or another, hesitating among different callings, with Petrus Borel, for instance, undecided between architecture and poetry, Gautier between painting and literature.[2] Yet, as Gautier later wrote, from the beginning Gérard de Nerval stood out among these rebellious aesthetes by having dedicated himself to a specific vocation. Not only was he devoted to literature, but even as a student at the Lycée Charlemagne he had already established a reputation for himself as a writer, with published poems and a translation of *Faust* that would later earn him praise from Goethe himself.

Further distancing himself from his publicity-hungry peers and friends, Nerval displayed an almost pathological discretion. According to Gautier, "if he heard his name spoken, he disappeared at once,"[3] and "in those eccentric days . . . Gérard dressed in the simplest, least noticeable manner, like a man who desires to mingle with the crowd without attracting attention."[4] A third distinguishing trait would occur to Gautier in retrospect, several years later. Unlike his fellow members of the Jeunes-France or the other voluntary eccentrics of the period, who devoted much of their energies to acts of apparent lunacy, Nerval did not merely feign madness. It was difficult to notice at first, given the tenor of the period, but he was really going mad.[5]

The Silence of Insanity

The importance and complexity of Nerval's role as a mad writer have evolved over the years since the evening of late February 1841 when, following the appeals and declination of a certain star hanging over the horizon, he wandered naked through the streets of Paris, into the arms of the night patrol, and into what was to be the first of a long series of voluntary and involuntary confinements. When Jules Janin described the incident with a lengthy feuilleton installment in the March 1 issue of the *Journal des débats*, an article to which Nerval would later refer as a "premature biography" and which Janin himself called a "posthumous elegy," he presented his friend's mental crisis as the tragic end of a literary career: Nerval's death, if not in body, at least to literature.[6] Yet, ironically, the works for which Nerval is now best known, those which have won him a prominent and enduring position in the French literary canon, are precisely those that follow that initial attack and which seem to bring his madness to expression. It is in light of just such works that Michel Foucault, for example, has situated Nerval at a turning point in the history of madness's ability to speak in a voice that is authentically and essentially its own.

Nerval himself was not the first to speak in public about his illness—that role probably went to Janin—but he was undoubtedly the first to argue that its expressions had a legitimate authority all their own, and he contended toward the end of his life that the story of his mental crises "has not entirely lacked reasoning even if it has always been free of reason [n'a pas été entièrement dépourvue de raisonnement si elle a toujours manqué de raison]."[7] Starting during the writer's own lifetime and continuing through the years beyond Foucault, other critics have attempted variously to understand or to discredit this idea of a "raisonnement" entirely free of reason, and it is consequently possible to trace the development of an increasingly complex understanding of Nerval's madness and its peculiar alternate discourse or "reasoning." Among these other readers there runs a tradition that observes a fundamental split in Nerval, a split articulating a critical distance of self-observation following along the lines of madman *and* writer, experience *and* testimony to that experience; accordingly, Théophile Gautier, one of the earliest and most consistent writers to credit Nerval's claim to voice the experience of madness, imagined that voice to emerge out of a communication between two opposite aspects of his friend's psyche, represented in an unbalanced, half-blind and half-mute dialogue between a pair of allegorical figures. He wrote the following assessment of what he described as Nerval's lucid madness:

> It has been said that *Aurélia* is the poem of Madness [Folie] telling its own story. It would have been more accurate to call it Reason [Raison] writing the memoirs of Madness at the latter's dictation. In it, the cool-headed philosopher beholds the visions and hallucinations of his counterpart. He does not contradict them, he does not battle them; he explains them, showing their point of departure and tracing their line of thought [il les explique, il en montre le point de départ, il en suit la filiation], determining their relation to the situations, circumstances, accidents, existing conditions, and memories of his dreams and waking life.[8]

In its respect for the voice of madness, in its attempt to reintegrate the irrational utterances of that sybilline voice into a rational and comprehensible etiology, in its use of a network of pyschic interconnections moving in multiple directions through dream and waking life, and in its attempt ultimately to cure Nerval's madness by rationalizing it in these ways, Gautier's portrayal of his friend's literary technique comes across as an anticipation—in some ways an eerily accurate anticipation—of the psychoanalytic session, with Folie in the place of the analysand and Raison in that of the analyst. For Gautier construes the relation between these two aspects of his friend's personality as neither antagonistic nor symmetrical. Here, Raison neither combats nor belies the reminiscences of Folie, it does not function to contradict madness but instead adopts the somewhat subservient role of its audience, scribe, and exegete. The difference between reason and unreason is not seen as a state of absolute mutual alterity, and although they are perhaps fragmentary, the hallucinatory visions of Nerval the mad poet are not disrupted by voids or silences that would subtract them forever from rational discourse but constitute, at least implicitly, a linear narrative that reason can retrace. For Gautier, connectedness and a continuous line of reasoning are not absent from the memoirs of madness but are simply left as yet unstated, and the remarkably passive role of reason in rendering the reminiscences of madness intelligible consists principally in following and unfolding them (*suivre* and *expliquer*), exposing their continuity (*filiation*), and in identifying the causal structures underlying them (as in his reference to a *point de départ*). Discourse and coherence are not things that Nerval's philosophical acumen lends to his madness; they already lie before it objectively, albeit dimly. In fact, Gautier often remarked on his friend's surprising clearness of style, its *clarté* even during bouts of insanity,[9] and the metaphorical implications of this conception of Nerval's literary technique as a sort of lucidity reappear in this passage and underlie the depiction of Raison's transcriptions. The latter are a sort of luminous transparency that reveals its object without distorting it, for aside from following and exposing, they show (*montre*) the origins and determine the connectedness of what lies before them. Reason throws light on the parts of discourse that invisibly exist before its intervention, and Nerval's madness appears in this context as a sort of excessive discretion, a discourse that leaves too much implicit, which reveals too little of the line that connects its parts.

If Folie is thus an excess of discretion in recounting itself, in narrating its memoirs, its cure will lie in exposition, in Nerval's patient, written self-analysis. Ultimately, however, for all the amicable consideration he grants to Nerval's record of his experiences in insane asylums, Gautier minimizes the authority of his mad "raisonnement" as an original expressive force in his writing, reducing the divergence between the discourses of Folie and Raison to something like a stylistic flaw, a confusing ellipsis on the part of the former. In Gautier's lopsided allegory of Nerval's language, reason withholds its version of madness's dictations from Folie's view and review, offering them to the public without first submitting its altered version to the approval of the one whose words it supposedly represents; the text is copiously altered in its supposed transcription and the final judge of its meaning, even of its wording, is Raison. For Gautier, Nerval's writing is something like an attempt to expose lucidly his own implicit coherence to himself, but it does so in a scene of dictation in which the scribe (re)establishes its own language, the language of reason, in the language of madness, finding in it what it is accustomed to finding.

To use a metaphor from textual criticism, Gautier's is a conscious application of *lectio facilior*, a principle used since the Middle Ages to guide the philological reconstruction of documents. When there are divergent versions of the same text in different manuscripts, the editor assumes a bias toward the more unusual reading, the *lectio difficilior*, working on the assumption that it is the natural tendency of a scribe to miscorrect to a less unusual or complex grammatical or semantic structure, that he instinctively reads into a text what he already assumes it to contain and thereby levels its originality. This idea of a coherence and a continuity underlying Nerval's *œuvre*, both in its madness and its lucidity, this reading of its discontinuities as ellipses to be exegetically smoothed out and its obscurities as flaws to be corrected, continues even now, as we shall see, to guide key readings of Nerval, but it has not gone uncontested. Although Proust repeated many of Gautier's points in his own commentary, and his writing on Nerval is considerably shorter and sketchier than Gautier's, he offered a much richer and more troubling image of the relation between Nerval's madness and his art, while attributing to the poet and his work a far broader importance in the history of literary self-awareness. "If ever a writer . . . sought to define himself painstakingly to himself," Proust wrote in *Contre Sainte-Beuve*, "to grasp and bring to light the murky shadings, the deepest laws and most elusive impressions of the human soul, it was Gérard de Nerval."[10] Like Gautier, Proust saw Nerval the writer as often the witness and recorder of his own madness, but these critics differ in two significant ways when addressing this subject. First, for Gautier, Nerval's Folie, though capable of discoursing, cannot be said to have a discourse that is genuinely its own, while for Proust, Nerval's madness was the elaboration of something essential to his literary originality and in turn gave rise to more writing, to a simultaneous recording of his experiences of that madness. "This madness," he wrote, "is so utterly the offshoot of what is most essential to his literary originality, that he describes his madness even as he experiences it."[11] In short, while Gautier sees in Nerval's madness an expository deficiency that is to be cured by an unusual literary lucidity, Proust sees that madness as an organic development of Nerval's literary originality. He does not record it, according to Proust, because it is a flaw in his literary abilities, but because it is an expression of them; he is a great writer not in spite of but through his madness. Second, Proust sees Nerval's development of his madness less as an exercise in pathology and cure than as an integral and key part of a personal introspection. As Nerval's madness was, in Proust's eyes, an elaboration of his literary originality, so was it an elaboration of his subjectivity in general, and he spoke of Nerval's attacks as "a sort of excessive subjectivism." In recounting his insanity, Nerval was thus not simply abolishing it, he was also recounting himself, bringing himself into view. For Nerval, to know himself was in part to know his madness, its laws, its nuances, its impressions, and to fix them in writing. Without demonstrating precisely how it was to be done, Proust asserted that despite all that is jarring and incomprehensible in them, Nerval's texts should be read rather than corrected, thus introducing, probably for the first time, the need for a *lectio difficilior* into the critical legacy of his literary madness.

The three terms that will broadly define the field occupied by the present study of Nerval—insanity, self-knowledge, and writing—are thus already set out in *Contre Sainte-Beuve* as integrally related to one another. A consideration of self-knowledge and writing in the context of Nerval's works compels one to examine the concept of autobiography and to determine the sorts of relations that can obtain between an individual's life and his writing of it. In Nerval, this difference between life and literature is attenuated, for the author had a tendency, as he himself asserted, to live his life literarily and to attempt to experience, understand, and organize it in terms of written models. Because here both the writer's life and his work are artistic constructs, and because the relation between *l'homme* and *l'œuvre* is therefore already a literary one, in this particular case one can analyze that relation without recourse to non-Nervalian or nonliterary texts. Consequently, one can be interested not so much in the difference between an actual, historical Nerval and the works he produced, as in the difference between life and work that he elaborated *in his writings*. And if Nerval is of interest in relation to questions of literary coherence and fragmentation, if he can throw an important light on them and become in some way exemplary, it is because in his feverishly active literary self-reflections he introduced a concept of the autobiographical self that is thoroughly fissured by a highly elaborated and vertiginously distributed series of self-distancings, introspections, and ironic self-criticisms originally intended to preserve the very coherence of his authorial self. Another reason is that there is undoubtedly at play a complex relationship between literary self-dispersion and literary self-containment in an author who seemed, in the eyes of one of his closest friends, to "find pleasure in taking leave of himself [à s'absenter de lui-même], in disappearing from his work, in leading the reader astray,"[12] and yet who, to the continued mystification of his colleagues, was prey to an active and lifelong anxiety over the need to find legal methods to control the proliferation of unauthorized versions of his own works, thereby manifesting a belief (for which he was roundly criticized by other authors, who felt creations of the spirit to be the property of all) that an author, as a person, is sufficiently invested in his works that he can in some way lay claim to their exclusive possession.[13]

Among those writers who have taken Proust's proposed approach to heart, Michel Foucault stands out in his *Histoire de la folie à l'âge classique* as the most richly suggestive, though he was far from the most intimate or comprehensive reader of Nerval. His interpretations demonstrate the influence of Martin Heidegger's readings of certain poems by Hölderlin, a German romantic and quasi-contemporary of Nerval who, much like the younger French writer, also went insane. Certain key structures, such as an anxiety over the relation between the subjective particularity of a poet and the abstract universality of the work he created, which Foucault identified in Nerval's writing and which are discussed at greater length below, were already articulated by Hölderlin in reference to his own poetry and analyzed in that context by Heidegger;[14] other insights in Foucault's work recall the propositions set forth in Heidegger's more strictly philosophical texts, as in the way that Foucault's formulation of the relation between

Nerval's immediate subjective experience and its mediate, universal expression draws on the bifold, or *zwiefältig*, structure of the ontico-ontological difference.[15] Foucault's principal failing in his handling of Nerval, however, lies precisely in the alien origins of his approach, which stems more from Hölderlin, Heidegger, and his own history of madness than from Nerval's writings themselves. Yet even though he treats the poet and his texts as more exemplary than original, Foucault offers certain invaluable insights into how that originality might be discerned.

To understand the importance as well as the idiosyncratic singularity of Nerval's expressions, to hear that authentic voice of madness which speaks in his works, *Histoire de la folie* contends, it is necessary to situate him in a precise historical context. Accordingly, Foucault offers a two-point positioning of Nerval within a double chronology of madness. On the one hand, he locates Nerval as significantly apart from and disruptive of a positive, historically specific and externally imposed conception of madness that emerged at the end of the eighteenth century and developed during the course of the nineteenth. On the other hand, he integrates Nerval into a silent and continuously sustained experience of unreason that reached from Diderot's *Neveu de Rameau* to Antonin Artaud.[16] It is this dual chronology, split between scientific positivism and an "experience of unreason," to which Foucault is referring when he writes:

> The return to the immediate in Hölderlin's last poems, Nerval's sacralization of the sensible, these can only yield an altered and superficial meaning to those attempting to understand them through a positivist conception of madness: their true sense must be gathered from that moment of unreason in which they are set. For it is from the very center of that experience of unreason, which is their concrete condition of possibility, that one can understand the two movements of poetic conversion and psychological evolution.[17]

It is the positivist, pathological conception of madness, embodied in such men of science as the Dr. Esprit Blanche who treated Nerval for mental illness, that covers over (or "recouvre," as Foucault puts it) the hidden, shadowy, and silent history of *déraison*. In his chapters on the nineteenth century, he attempts to demonstrate how scientific approaches to madness led their proponents to view the latter as a positive entity with an ontogenesis and logic comparable to those of physical ailments and how those approaches reduced or ignored the radical negativity of what madness said by considering those utterances as *positive* signs, or symptoms, developing organically and causally in the course of an identifiable illness rather than as a *negative*, hidden, shadowy, and silent—"sourd"—alternative to rational discourse. Consequently it is to this latter "expérience de la déraison," and not to a pathology of madness that we must turn if we are to approach the possibility of an alternate and silent history of madness in its own right. But, if Foucault's concern is to explore the way in which, by insisting on a positive semantics grounded in causal and organic coherence, medical discourse of the nineteenth and twentieth centuries covered over a radically negative and paradoxically silent discourse that threatened to undermine and fragment that semantics, our interest is not to reconstruct that argument, but to examine the ways in which Nerval treated his own, and critics', predispositions to understanding literature in terms of coherence and how he placed those predispositions into conflict with a growing suspicion that writing offers only a semblance of unified meaning to an essentially meaningless and fragmentary subjective existence. The modality of that relation between language and the individual experience it is meant to represent, and in representing organize, is at the core both of Nerval's personal literary drama and of the significance of his work as a specifically poetic response to the philosophical context of subjectivity in which he was working, and in which we still live.

Foucault conceives of the turning point, or conversion, represented by Nerval's and Hölderlin's poetry as a double movement whose original binary unity breaks apart in madness. On the one hand, Nerval's radical newness is based on an experience of unreason that is an immediate encounter with the fulguration of sensuous existence, described by Foucault as "the intoxication of the sensible, the fascination of the immediate . . . , the dizzying force of the sensuous . . . , the delirium of the real, of glittering appearance [l'ivresse du sensible, la fascination dans l'immédiat, . . . le vertige du sensible . . . , le délire du réel, de l'apparence scintillante]," but which on the other hand, precisely as an experience of the immediate, that is, of that which *as* immediate is non-exchangeable and non-iterable, excludes the poet from language and community, thrusting him into the isolation of madness. The experience of unreason underlying the poetic conversion is thus structured as a reciprocal movement—working like the opposite sides of a folded page and similar to the Heideggerian *Zwiefalt*—of opening to the immediate and of closing off mediations, such as language, that would draw the poet out of his reclusion, out of "the solitude of delirium." Consequently, "the moment of *Ja-sagen* to the sensuous burst of light [l'éclat du sensible], is in itself also a withdrawal into the shadow of madness."[18]

The oneness of this moment, its ironic and "fearful unity," is too difficult for us, for the pathologists of the nineteenth century, even ultimately for the poet who risks himself in apprehending it, and it falls ineluctably apart into its constituent movements, expressible only through a metaphorics of exclusion. "But for us," Foucault writes, "these two moments are distinct and distant, like poetry and silence, day and night, the fulfillment of language in its manifestation and its loss in the limitlessness of delirium." But it is precisely in the experience of that unity that the poets Hölderlin and Nerval, like a series of other artists and thinkers who followed them, have risked themselves and then, because the double moment was too difficult to be maintained in its unity, lost themselves as it broke off and veered toward isolating madness. In a move that is rich in significance for readings of Nerval's descriptions of his own madness, Foucault describes the existences of these poets, who wagered and lost their entire beings in the experience of unreason, as reduced to a word or idiolect. "And each of these existences," he writes, "each of the utterances that these existences are [ces paroles que sont ces existences], repeats, in the insistence of time, this same question." The question that they repeat, the question incessantly offered up by the idiolect to which their existences have been reduced, is the question of their own muteness, their inability to speak. It is the question: "Why is it not possible to remain within the difference of unreason? Why must it always break off from itself . . . ? How could it be that this experience is so robbed of language [privée de langage]?"[19] For Foucault, Nerval's existence thus foundered in the endless return of the question of why he could not speak, of why he could not bring into words a unitary experience of unreason whose fulguration he had glimpsed, the untiring and interrogative enunciation of a single, specific absence—that of language. For Foucault, he had become a witness, a word, bearing testimony to his own experience of a silence beyond reason, a silence capable of penetrating and perforating aesthetic and rational discourse.[20]

Foucault's study insists on nothing so much as the difficulty of hearing the voice of madness, whose paradoxical silence withdraws it from notice; and, consequently, if one is to appreciate what is original in Nerval, not merely in his uncanny ability to speak from beyond the tomb of his own reason or in the strange beauty of some of his later works, but also in his insights into selfhood and subjectivity and how they might be integrally related to writing, then it will be necessary to perceive the new in his writings without assimilating it too readily into traditions that are already known and familiar. One will need constantly and vigilantly to remain open to that *lectio difficilior* through which the expression of Nerval's originality emerges from his texts, for that originality and that subjectivity develop out of a dialogue with madness in which the poet comes face to face with the possibility of an incoherent and meaningless self. But *Histoire de la folie* goes further. The originality and historical importance of Nerval's writing are grounded for Foucault in a silent and unbearable unity, and any reading fully sensitive to that ground would be a *lectio difficilior* in the sense of one that was too difficult, even for the poet himself.

Nerval's psychotic episodes came at a particularly interesting moment in the history of insanity, one that had witnessed a sea-change in the role of madness within society. Much has been written about Pinel's liberation of the inmates of the Salpêtrière in Paris and his institution of humane, medical approaches to their treatment. And if, as Hegel contended, the Revolution drove many mad by laying waste the foundations of civil society, it also laid the groundwork for a more enlightened handling of their needs. On March 27, 1790, the Revolutionary Constituent Assembly announced a law mandating that individuals "detained because of a state of insanity . . . will be examined by doctors who . . . will enquire into the true situation of those sick so that, in accordance with the decision taken about their condition, they are either freed or cared for in hospitals that will be designated for this purpose."[21] Although, in certain circles, madness continued to be theorized as a metaphysical problem, under the Revolution it had come to be *treated* as a problem of public health, and the discourse that could best make sense of the mad was now considered to be a medical one.[22] This discursive and practical shift in the social role of insanity was, like the guillotine, instituted by legislators of the Revolution as a move toward a more humane state, but like the guillotine it also represented the displacement and sublimation of a form of violence. Surprisingly, Althusser does not number medicine in his (admittedly partial) list of state ideological apparatuses, and this fact perhaps indicates the impression of transparency that medical and scientific discourses have long enjoyed in European society, even if they are inextricably linked with juridical practice and theory (as Althusser himself would come to learn first hand).[23] This apparent ideological transparency has made resistance especially difficult, since there does not seem to be anything to resist: a discourse *against* pathologization may not appear as language at all, since it seems to be refusing not *medical* language, but language itself.

If the utterances of madness do indeed constitute a language staked out against coercive ideological structures, we must still wonder: in the name of what and against precisely what was it speaking? The relation of insanity to the issues of subjectivity we have been discussing is not most clearly theorized in works by doctors, for the emphasis there tends to be on procedure and practice rather than on primordial issues of self-identity. Although Pinel's *Traité médico-philosophique sur l'aliénation* is, for instance, rich in historical significance concerning the treatment of patients in asylums, anyone seeking philosophical insight from it will be sadly disappointed. And while we might find Zola's doctor treating his *arithmomanie* as a medical concern, he entirely ignores its subjective implications and their relation to death, although these were the most significant aspects of the condition for Zola himself.[24] It is consequently better for us now to turn to the metaphysical tradition examined in the preceding chapter, if we are to get an idea of how mental illness fit into issues of self-identity during Nerval's life.

The remarkable similarity between Gautier's description of Nerval and Hegel's discussion of madness from the *Philosophy of Mind* suggests that certain basic characteristics of a "rational" understanding of insanity were broadly diffused throughout Europe. Hegel argued, for instance, that because "insanity is not an abstract *loss* of reason . . . but only derangement" it has "the healthy, intellectual consciousness . . . for its presupposition."[25] As a mere disruption of another, meaningful discourse, madness has, in other words, no language or significance of its own. Nor can it exist independently, according to Hegel's formulation, for it never entirely loses contact with reason; instead, it is inscribed within rational communication as a lack of meaning, or, to be more exact, as a lack of discourse itself. Consequently, madness is only knowable, for Hegel, by relation to reason, a condition that he represents in terms strikingly similar to Gautier's scene of Nerval's *Folie* dictating to his *Raison*:

> The insane subject is . . . in communion with himself in the negative of himself. . . . Consequently, though the insane person is *in himself* or *implicitly* one and the same subject, yet he does not know himself objectively as a self-accordant, inwardly undivided subject, but as a subject disrupted into two different personalities.

> [The insane "I"] is driven out of its [rational] mind, shifted out from the centre of its actual world and, since it also still retains a consciousness of this world, has two centres, one in the remainder of its *rational* consciousness and the other in its *deranged* idea.[26]

The mad person is, quite literally, of two minds, like Gautier's Nerval and like Foucault's *zwiefältig* impasse of mediated immediacy. But if madness itself has no language, it nonetheless has a "center" of its own, its own personality, its own "idea," even if they are conceived of as negative and deranged. The mad self, unlike mad discourse, is not the lack of a self, it is rather a self that lacks language. It is unspeakable and unspeaking, existing elsewhere than in its expression. It expresses itself only as a gap or an interruption, as those places where expression leaves off under the pressure of what is but does not communicate. The mad self is, in short, a refusal of sublimation. It is for this reason that Hegel speaks of it as an obstruction to totalization, since the mad, nondiscursive self is a self that cannot come together into a coherent and finite whole, it is a self that cannot be brought into a synthetic meaning, but which merely exists in the abrupt insignificance of the material.[27] When discourse is understood and enforced as the sublimation of existence into terror and death, the resistance to it will sometimes operate as silence, the mute interruption of insanity.

Mad Writing: The Preface to 'Les Filles du feu'

Although he avoided referring publicly to his mental disturbances as illness, preferring to describe them allegorically as a "descent into Hell," Nerval did in fact speak about his madness and its relation to his writing. Events and word in the press forced his hand somewhat. For some time before the publication of *Les Filles du feu* (The daughters of fire) he had begun to lose control of his reputation and image in the public eye. On December 10, 1853, for example, in the midst of Nerval's second major mental breakdown and during his institutionalization in the clinic of Dr. Blanche, his longtime friend Alexandre Dumas had published an article in *Le Mousquetaire* both lauding Nerval's literary achievements and describing the degeneration of his mental condition. Nerval, who later called this piece the "epitaph of my mind"[28] much as he had referred to Jules Janin's account of his first crisis as a "necrological entry,"[29] published an extensive quotation from Dumas's article in the preface to *Les Filles du feu*, following it with an attempt to explain in his own terms the onset of his illness. The document that ensued constitutes perhaps the single most important reflection by Nerval on the relations linking his self-consciousness, his madness, and his literary vocation, and as such provides, as will be seen, an invaluable access to reading both the late, visionary *Aurélia* and an earlier and extremely complex work, *Les Faux Saulniers* (The salt smugglers). The former attempts an explanation of the relation between the first person and the experience it represents, while the latter represents a working out, rather than a detached self-analysis, of Nerval's literary subjectivity in its relation to coherence and fragmentation.

It is revealing of Nerval's own concerns that the only section of Dumas's article quoted in the preface to the *Filles du feu* focuses on the relation between madness and writing, which Dumas, like Proust, saw as indissociable in Nerval. The real issue for the latter, if one is to judge from the preface as a whole, is not so much to demonstrate whether he was insane or not as to discuss the relation or relations between unreason and literature, for although Nerval steadfastly refused to dismiss his own behavior as merely mad and meaningless, his response to Dumas justifies this position only by first addressing the apparently more immediate question of how an author, especially an irrational author, writes. For Dumas, Nerval's condition stems from and expresses itself as literary production, but as a sort of pointless, if pleasurable, creation. As he explains his friend's condition, Nerval's crises are provoked by an excessive involvement in his writing: "from time to time," Dumas writes, "when some bit of work has especially preoccupied him, his imagination, that resident lunatic, takes over and for a moment succeeds in driving out reason, who is mistress of the house; then the first remains alone and all-powerful in that mind fed on dreams and hallucinations."³⁰ And if these crises originate in literary production, that is also where they tend, for they lead the author they have mastered into an extraordinary and brilliant if useless creativity, in which mad imagination, "vagabond that she is, casts him into impossible theories and books that cannot be done [livres infaisables]." If these books are unworkable, if his mad theories are impossible, they are nonetheless described by Dumas as both strangely seductive to others and as essentially and superlatively poetic:

> On another day he believes himself mad and recounts how it happened, and he does it with such a hearty joy, by way of such amusing adventures, that each listener wants to fall mad too that he might follow this guide leading them into the land of illusions and hallucinations full of oases fresher and shadier than those that rise along the burning route from Alexandria to Ammon; or then again, melancholy is his muse, and hold back your tears if you can, for never Werther, never René nor Antony had more poignant plaints, sadder weeping, more tender words, more poetic cries!³¹

Writing or speaking under the sway of madness, Nerval produces a discourse that, although impossible, proves extraordinary for its affective power, its allure, and its pure poetry, a discourse surpassing its literary models and antecedents to become more literary than any literature known, than any book actually written. The pure discourse of madness is, in Nerval's case, the quintessence of the poetic, but in expressing itself finally in its essence this poetry must, seemingly paradoxically, express itself as unrealizable projects, scraps of conversation, that is, as fragments and aporias. According to Dumas, literature, as revealed by Nerval, makes no sense, has no coherence, is structured as a paradox, and can only move and seduce.

If Dumas seems to credit the authentic voice of madness in Nervalian discourse as the essence of the literary, he sees it as totally disconnected from reason, for it is only when madness has chased the latter from the poet's mind that these episodes can occur. In Dumas's understanding of his friend's work, there is no need for a *lectio difficilior*, because there is no opposition between forces, between Reason and Madness, between mediation and immediacy; there is only *Folie*, and her discourse is not merely easy, it is almost irresistible. Although he described his episodes as a "descent into Hell," Nerval did not dispute, in his response to Dumas's assessment, that there was pleasure in his imaginative experiences, or that the process of writing exercised a kind of seduction even over him; nor does he contradict his friend's contention that his writing was intimately connected, even identified with unreason. Where he does take issue with Dumas is in the latter's contention that the discourses of unreason and reason have nothing in common, that the *ja-sagen* to the sensible should, as Foucault put it, always be the refusal of the intelligible. Nerval, in answering his colleague with a rhetorically subtle and self-ironic argument, promotes his unreasonable poetic experiences as a form of thought with its own legitimacy, which he calls "raisonnement." Although entirely without reason, his quintessentially poetic discourse is a sort of reasoning. As such it exists in some form of connection to other, more accredited discourses, to which it stands not in a relation of pure mutual exclusion but of critical distance. This, then, would be the significance of Nerval's poetry: not so much its seductive pleasurableness as its inherent but alternate legitimacy as a form of thought and knowledge, especially self-knowledge. It is a discourse that derives its authority from its own sources but which can nonetheless enter into critical dialogue with other, rational modes of expression which it thereby limits and contextualizes. It is this rationally accessible explanation of his *raisonnement* which Nerval undertakes in his response to Dumas, where he plots the relation between reason and unreason through a discussion of his experiences of writing, and, in particular, through the story, as Dumas puts it, of how he became mad, of how he himself passed subjectively from reason to unreason. The unstated but clear argument that comes out of an examination of his response to Dumas holds that his literary experience is, *in itself*, the proof of the connectedness between reason and unreason, even if that connectedness is, in rational terms, impossible, unmappable and unthinkable.

Nerval begins the story of his slide from sanity to madness with this injunction: "Now . . . that I have recovered what is vulgarly called reason, let us reason," and he finishes it by promising that someday, when he has written the full history of his descent into the netherworld of unreason, "you will see that it [his account] has not entirely lacked reasoning though it has always been free of reason [n'a pas été entièrement dépourvu de raisonnement si elle a toujours manqué de raison]."[32] The mere fact that he speaks in his own name is significant, for in retelling the story of his crisis, in moving from his status as the material of another writer's description to the position of subject of his own recounting of the same incidents, he takes a first step toward appropriating the authority to speak of his own madness, at least in retrospect. He *can* speak of his madness because he *does* speak of it, even if, unlike his contemporaries, he does not refer to it in public as madness or illness, preferring to write in the preface of the *Filles du feu* of a "descent into Hell" from which he had in time emerged.[33] After beginning obliquely, speaking in the third person of "certain storytellers," Nerval will soon number himself among them and assume the narrative "I" of his experiences while institutionalized. This very appropriation of the first person, while establishing an identity, or at least a direct filiation between the subject of previous mad experiences and a present narrator, nonetheless masks an enterprise of subjective distancing which Nerval, by his own account, was undertaking in writing of his "descent." As is clear from certain of his letters, he felt that by writing, by proving his ability still to write, he would also establish his sanity and his remove from madness.[34] Through the labile "I" to which he will turn in the following passages, Nerval thus sought to establish both a split and an identification between the past self of his experiences in insane asylums and the presently writing self: the first person establishes a continuity between the two moments while its function as evidence of the ability to write it distinguishes them. The fact of the written first person thus posits the authority of the Nervalian subject by allowing him to articulate, and in articulating recognize, the paradoxical connection and disconnection of reason and unreason.

This use of the first person both to differentiate and to identify went beyond the reappropriation of his past alienated self to become, as he will assert, the key first to his ability to write and later—as its tenuous binary status began to fold in favor of identification rather than distinction—to the outpouring of madness. Paul de Man has drawn attention to a particular mode of the literary sublimation of the self, "that of the author as he is changed and interpreted by his work."[35] Few authors have been as instinctively and intellectually aware of such a transformation of themselves through their writing as Nerval, who intentionally used literary structures to shape his inner life even as he remained conscious of the possibility that such an undertaking could lead to a *Walpurgisnacht* of fantasmatic self-representation. Both Proust and Gautier saw in Nerval a certain division, a self-critical distance that allowed him to be at once hallucinatory and reasonable, both madman and writer. For Gautier, and in a more complex manner for Proust, Nerval the writer was somehow detached from Nerval the madman whose behavior that writer observed and recorded. By his own account, however, Nerval was troubled by the difficulty of maintaining a distinction between himself and the object of his writing, with the result that even when discussing other people, or the fictional creations of his imagination, his natural tendency should be to identify with them and to believe that in expressing the various elements and characteristics of their being he was expressing those of his own. It was, he contended, the very lability of his use of the first person and his adoption of literary personae that led to his first attack of madness, and in the preface to the *Filles du feu*, he accordingly began his explanation of that madness by asserting: "There are, as you know, certain storytellers who cannot invent unless they identify with the characters of their imagination."[36]

Nerval thus construed his recent "descent into Hell" as precisely a problem of selfhood, asserting that his mental crisis originated in an identification, the collapse of a certain critical distance, a loss of distinction between writer and written; it began with what might be described, in Proust's terms, as an excess of subjectivity, for he found himself rapidly and uncontrollably assimilating another person into himself and thereby negating that other person's alterity. The source of his literary originality—that without which he said he was incapable of invention—is therefore also represented as the source of his madness, for both invention and the loss of reason stem from the same process of identifying with his character. In the continuation of the passage cited above, Nerval addresses the question of how to control the movement between these two results, between madness and originality, and after an anecdote depicting Charles Nodier as an author losing his own identity in that of his characters, Nerval's response to Dumas continues:

> Well, you should understand that the momentum of a narrative [l'entraînement d'un récit] can produce a similar effect, and that one ends up, as it were, embodying the hero of one's imagination, so that his life becomes yours and you burn with the artificial flames of his ambitions and loves. And yet this is what happened to me when I undertook the story of a character who, I am quite sure, figured in the time of Louis XV under the name of Brisacier. Where did I read that adventurer's fateful biography? I tracked down the abbé de Bucquoy's, but I seem to be quite incapable of fixing the slightest historical proof to the existence of that other, illustrious mystery [renouer la moindre preuve historique à l'existence de cet illustre inconnu]! What would have been no more than a game for a master like you—who play upon our chronicles and memories with such skill that posterity will no longer know how to untangle the true from the false and will burden with your inventions all the historical characters you have called on to figure in your novels—had become for me an obsession, a fever [un vertige].[37]

He is referring here principally to two of his own texts, one concerning the Abbé de Bucquoy, which he had completed and published three and a half years earlier, in 1850, under the title of *Les Faux Saulniers*, and another concerning a certain Brisacier, which for reasons given in the passage itself—such as his inability to find historical documents and, more seriously, the mental crisis provoked by writing the story—he was forced to leave unfinished. He describes how, in the case of Brisacier, and through an implicit parallelism in the case of the Abbé de Bucquoy as well, he had identified with a character whose story he had undertaken to write. Brisacier was not, however, purely Nerval's creation, and his historical existence independent of Nerval seemed to irritate the author as he repeatedly failed to establish any objective proof of his hero's autonomy from his own invention. The identification at some unspecified point apparently took a turn for the worse, since at the end of the passage Nerval describes the degeneration of his control over his own creative processes, an obsessional vertigo that he will, later in the same preface, describe as his "descent into Hell." Whereas in the later passage he will describe the experiences of his crisis in some detail, here its nature is almost entirely left to surmise. Besides presenting the conditions of its onset in the process of writerly identification, Nerval here gives an initial intimation of some of the characteristics of his "vertige" by contrasting it with Dumas's writing technique, and he thereby offers a negative and elusive glimpse of his madness. Dumas is master of a distinction between subjective authorial invention and objective historical record, between truth and falsehood, between novel and history. So clearly is he said to control these differences that confusing them in the eyes of others like Nerval, touching even their memories themselves, has become a game for him. In contrasting his own "vertige" with Dumas's control, Nerval portrays his obsessional self as an author who has lost the ability to distinguish between novel and history, between objective fact and subjective invention, and who by venturing too far into a game whose rule lies in the fluidity of such distinctions, whose goal is to redefine them masterfully, has lost the ability to untangle (*démêler*) truth and falsehood.

The term "historical" here is placed in opposition to authorial invention and thus, in reference to Nerval, has the sense of that which is not part of his own hypertrophied, imaginative self but which lies outside or anterior to him. As literary creation is for him a pseudo-autobiographical account of a person he believes himself to be, and therefore a subjective writing, historical existence is conversely objective to him. Gautier was consistent with Nerval's own views in saying "he was more subjective than objective," but this should not be taken to mean that Nerval was unaware of a distinction between subject and object, since this page demonstrates that it is his very need for this distinction, combined with his inability to draw it, which he considered to be the essence of his vertiginous decline.

The point at which play turned into vertigo is spelled out in the continuation of the passage above. Already the structure of the section cited, where a sentence about his inability to find objective proof of Brisacier's existence is followed by another describing his slipping into obsession, strongly suggests a causal link between the two, and this would in turn explain why Nerval was able to finish his biography of the Abbé de Bucquoy—he found historical evidence of his existence in the form of an earlier biography—whereas he left that of Brisacier, for whom he found no biography or any historical proof of any kind, unfinished. Developing this implied causality in the lines that follow his reference to the onset of an obsessional delirium, Nerval depicts the moment when his frustrated attempts to prove Brisacier's historical existence suddenly engendered a sort of epiphany. "Inventing, a moralist has said, is basically remembering, and unable to find proof of my hero's material existence," he writes, "I came to believe, on the spot, in the transmigration of souls." This original extension of his own existence to include past lives sets in motion an expansion of his subjectivity which reaches its all-pervasive and all-consuming apogee in an identification with God himself. "From the moment that I thought I could grasp the series of all my previous experiences," he asserts, "it cost me as little to have been prince, king, magus, genius, and even God, for the chain was broken and marked the hours as minutes."[38] The appropriation of a single object in Nerval's identification with Brisacier has given way to a megalomaniacal identification with all of creation, leaving Nerval as comprehensive, and as solitary, as God.

Nerval's "descent into Hell" thus begins as a state of indeterminacy between himself and another, a state that develops as he undertakes to write, a state that is presupposed by all acts of literary creation but which here exceeds Nerval's mastery when he is unable to tie (*renouer*) his subject matter to an objective existence. In this case, the absence of a thread, or the disruption of a nonsubjective continuity that he cannot re-establish, is the catalyst for his degeneration from invention to obsession. This lack of filiation is as central to his depiction of the onset of his madness as its restoration will be to his cure and to the eventual recovery of a critical, reflective distance in regard to himself. Much as the key to the beginning of his crisis lay in an inability to connect and tie together, in a failure to link the character of Brisacier to historical evidence, the decisive moment in his return to lucidity is represented as the recovery of a thread. After describing the beginning of his attack in the passage examined above, Nerval offers a fragment from the text on Brisacier he was writing when the attack occurred and then comments on it with the following remarks, which recount, in highly symbolic form, the events of his return to reason:

> Once convinced that I was writing my own story, I set about translating all my dreams, all my emotions and, yielding to that tender love for a fugitive *star* [*étoile*] which abandoned me in the night of my solitary destiny, I wept and I shuddered at the vain apparitions of my sleep. Then a ray of divine light shone into my Hell; surrounded by monsters against which I dimly struggled, I seized Ariadne's thread and since that moment all my visions have become heavenly. Some day I shall write the story of that "descent into Hell [descente aux enfers]," and you will see that it has not entirely lacked reasoning though it has always been free of reason.[39]

What had begun as the loss of a single object—proof of Brisacier's historically independent existence—and had then expanded into the Godlike pervasiveness of Nerval's subjectivity, is shown here generalized into the reduction of all objectivity to the vague but painful awareness of its loss. In the depths of his crisis he thus finds himself overwhelmed by a solitude in which the absolute absence of alterity is particularized in the image of a fugitive *étoile* which has abandoned Nerval to himself. The experience of divine plenitude has turned into an *enfer* of isolation in which every trace of an objective world has dwindled to the point where Nerval finds himself alone among the empty creatures of his imagination, and his writing becomes the translation of a solipsism troubled by a lack, by the memory of a vanished star. What Foucault has referred to as a vertigo of the immediate, Nerval portrays as a vertigo of limitless self-representation.

The elements that had precipitated his decline are still present in somewhat different form at its nadir: an overwhelming subjectivity and the absence of an object (Brisacier and the *étoile*). The reference to Ariadne's thread reveals a further elaboration of the metaphoric structure underlying Nerval's public understanding of his "descent." He had originally referred to the relation between subjective invention and historical objectivity as a literary game he had failed to master, which he had been unable to "tie up" (*renouer*), whereas here, some pages later, he conceives of it as a maze whose thread he has lost. Underlying the shift from game to labyrinth is the idea that neither, regardless of its complexity, is in itself an image of madness, for the game can be mastered (by someone like Dumas), and the maze can be traced (by someone like Theseus). The labyrinthine game turns to madness at the point where Nerval loses control over it, when a thread—the thread that attaches Brisacier to a historical existence, the thread that communicates between the inside and the outside of a maze—is broken and a linear continuity is severed.

The terrain itself, the game or labyrinth where madness takes place, is essentially literary, for the identification that hangs by a thread between madness and lucidity, that identification whose nuanced mastery sets the possibilities of originality and insanity both into play, is what Nerval described earlier, in the passage where he spoke of "certain storytellers who cannot invent unless they identify with the characters of their imagination," as both the source of his literary invention and a condition that develops out of the "momentum of a narrative," in short, as *a written movement toward further writing*. To the extent that they function as metaphors for his process of inventive identification, the maze and the game constitute images of literary creation, ways of imagining a writer's relations both to his text and, through that text, to historical characters. They also constitute, in a broader sense, an image for the textual relation between self and other, because the split between original invention and historical record elaborates a more fundamental distinction between subjectivity and objectivity, a distinction that breaks down in a "descent into Hell" at precisely that moment when mastery over the separation between history and invention falters.

Although Nerval never finished the text on Brisacier, he did complete a part of it, a letter from prison written in Brisacier's name but drawing on the events, the characters, and the tone of Scarron's unfinished *Roman comique* in such a way as to suggest a continuation of the earlier novel. Nerval included the fragment in the preface to the *Filles du feu* as part of his response to Dumas, and two points should be made concerning this insertion. First, incomplete as the extant portion of the Brisacier text may have been, Nerval made other attempts to incorporate it in openly fragmentary form within a larger work, and among the manuscripts in the Spoelberch de Lovenjoul collection at the Bibliothèque de l'Institut there exists under the title *Aurélie* an introduction to a story of Brisacier which is followed by the words "la lettre." Presumably the letter which was to follow was that which Nerval published in the *Filles du feu*, accompanied by the long analysis of its relation to his madness. At the end of the unused introduction to the Brisacier text, Nerval offered the following justification for its publication: "To my mind, certain passages retraced the ideal portrait of Aurélie, the actress, sketched out in *Sylvie*. That connection can alone lend some worth to such an incomplete fragment."[40] The reference to *Sylvie* indicates that the introduction was originally intended as a means to incorporate the Brisacier passage into the *Filles du feu*, a role ultimately played by the analysis of the "descent into Hell" in the preface; however, the unused text, unlike the published version, offers an important glimpse into Nerval's understanding of the coherence of his writing, demonstrating that he sought at least once to incorporate a fragment *as such* into one of his works, although what Nerval might have meant by the terms "fragment" and "incomplete" remains to be seen. What is more, the different *justifications* for the inclusion of the Brisacier text in a larger work are not merely plural, they are also presented in such as way as to make them incompatible, for in the unused version Nerval notes that a resemblance to *Sylvie* "can alone [peut seul]" justify the publication of the Brisacier text, whereas in the final version he does in fact find another justification—its value as part of a self-analysis—and entirely omits any reference to a resemblance between *Sylvie* and the Brisacier fragment. Even without reading the "peut seul" in an overly rigorous sense, the discrepancy between the two arguments speaks of a desire on Nerval's part to publish the incomplete segment before having found any publicly acceptable reason to do so. It further indicates that although Nerval was ready to use a fragment as such, he was also at some pains to disguise that fact, attempting in one way or another to minimize its apparent heterogeneity. An illusion of continuity could thus disguise a more fundamental discontinuity in a text, a discontinuity perhaps perceptible as such to its author alone.

The second point about the fragmentary letter is that it reveals Nerval's awareness that an apparent aesthetic coherence—here, of the character Brisacier and the continuity of his story—could link, ground, or mediate a split between authorial subjects. For, even after publishing what he had written of the Brisacier story, Nerval maintained the hope of one day extending it to the point where his friend Dumas could complete it. In a letter written June 1, 1854, to Georges Bell, Nerval asked his correspondent to tell Dumas "that I think from time to time of continuing the adventures of Brisacier, especially since he promised to finish them."[41] Despite his identification with his hero, Nerval did not view himself as indispensable to the invention of his story, thus demonstrating, after having recovered from his mental crisis, that in his own eyes Brisacier was objective in at least the minimal sense of being a possible, coherent creation with an inherent, autonomous structure sufficient that it could be further elaborated by another writer. His hero's unity of character, even if it originated in Nerval, did not depend continuously on Nerval's own subjective unity, but—even if only in a potential sense—lay outside of him, apprehensible by a third party. The continuation of the Brisacier story, its continuity, could mask a discontinuity between its authors. The "I" of its first-person narration could be adopted by both Dumas and Nerval, and Nerval thus acknowledged the existence in writing of a coherent objective subject, a subject in which he could participate but which would exceed him, and which he could not exhaust, an agency that in its scriptural impersonality could be said to resemble the pure propositionality of the Kantian apperceptive subject.

Further in this line, but more radical in its implications for the relation between subjective and literary coherence, is Nerval's suggestion in another work (ironically, a much more fragmentary one), that a literary text, drawing as it does on a tradition of aesthetic coherence, offers the possibility of papering over inconsistencies, discontinuities, and lacunae within the subjectivity of a single author. In one of the so-called *Lettres d'amour* (Love letters), he had written, "My ideas are singular; my passion surrounded by much poetry and originality; and I intentionally arrange my life like a novel, for the slightest discordance shocks me."[42] Few authors have referred as explicitly as Nerval to writing's effect on the self-apparent coherence of their own individual existences; even fewer have also embraced the possibilities of literary incoherence, openly allowing fragments, discontinuities, and lacunae into their work. When Nerval poses questions—theoretically or in practice—about literary coherence, he is also questioning the coherence of a life, and of the subject that perceives it as its own.

In looking back with a little detachment over the prefatory letter to the *Filles du feu*, one can easily detect something cautiously playful in its tone, a certain apparent lack of earnestness that could lead one to dismiss its significance the way its author refuses, at the end, any value to his *Chimères* (Chimeras) other than the inexplicable beauty of their expression. There is a rhetorical appeal, an attempt at conciliation and agreement in the letter, not merely in Nerval's willingness to couch his response to Dumas in terms of a continuation or amplification of his friend's assessment of him, but also in the very levity ("I, for my part, was embroidered on all my seams," for example) with which he describes what he will, after all, at the end of the preface call a descent into hell. There is in his response, in his explanatory description of an experience that will, by the end of the preface and certainly in *Aurélia*, bear more resemblance to a harrowing than to a shady oasis, something of the incongruously "hearty joy" which Dumas had remarked in Nerval's accounts of his madness, and something even, in the enthusiasm with which he recounts his "descent into Hell," of their seductive attraction. In this tone it is hard not to hear also a falsifying attempt to please his audience by rendering more palatable and commercial, more light and popularly entertaining, what in other texts he will reveal to have been a traumatically nightmarish encounter with the troubled mysteries of his own subjective nature and origins. To a less blithe, more informed reader, who is looking for more than entertainment in these pages, there is also a disorienting irony in the tone of this piece, which might lead one to wonder to what extent, or on what level, Nerval's assertions are to be credited. The first, dedicatory lines are, for example, particularly densely perverse. Nerval dedicates the present volume to Dumas as he had dedicated another to Jules Janin, whom he says he had to thank "for the same service as you [au même titre que vous]." The connection is that after his mental breakdowns both had written biographies of their friend, in which, for all their flattery, they took manifest pleasure in exercising their literary skills on a depiction of Nerval's charmingly poetic madness. Nerval, in the beginning of the preface, points to the similarity between the two articles and thanks Dumas for having "devoted a few of your most charming lines to the epitaph of my mind," much as he had, a year and a half earlier, in the preface to *Lorely*, thanked Janin for "honors which I can recall only in blushing."[43] The hypocrisy of the gratitude Nerval heaped on his overly hasty biographers only barely matches the hypocrisy of the flattery it recognizes. In a letter, Nerval bitterly reproached Janin for his article and demanded a retraction, asserting that as a consequence of its showily poetic description of his institutionalization, "I shall never be able to present myself anywhere, never marry, never make people listen to me seriously."[44] One consequently approaches the Nervalian text with a justifiable caution, never entirely certain of how seriously to take any assertion or proposition. As much as any text by any eighteenth-century skeptic, Nerval's apparent earnestness can reveal itself to be as duplicitous as it is alluring, and that is, undoubtedly, part of the famous charm of his writing, its ability to deceive, to mislead, to confuse, and to seduce, with a mastery that undoubtedly surpasses Dumas's on another level.[45]

And yet, despite all that is troubling or potentially disorienting in the tone of the preface to *Les Filles du feu*, a certain basic train of thought is discernible there. Behind the irony and behind the alluring stylistic dissimulation, which argues against the importance of his madness by saying that it meant nothing, and which dismisses it as a nonevent with no bearing on his rational character, there is another, incompatible argument contending that his madness was a crucially revealing event bearing on the very essence not merely of his subjectivity but potentially of all subjectivity. Yes, Nerval agrees, writing for him is intimately associated, even in some way identified, with an experience of unreason; and yes, this unreason is fundamentally alien to a rational discourse—it is different, it is other. Where Nerval's response to Dumas differs from his friend's account of his madness, and from the lightly self-dismissive tone of his own prose, is in the contention that this experience of unreason, for all its alterity, for all its refusal to submit to rationalization, is something more than an enticingly pleasurable diversion or a series of insignificant digressions. There is, he insists, something legitimate and important in his unreason, for it is an authentic form of subjective knowledge that asserts itself in his inexplicable writings, a knowledge he describes not as reason but as *raisonnement*. What this later might be is hinted at in his descriptions of his unreasonable texts and of his process of composing them. Writing appears not merely as a *description* of subjective states but as a *self-creation* in language; as Nerval describes the ludic or labyrinthine field of literature, the subject does not precede its writing. Rather, it is negotiated, gambled with, contested, and mapped in writing, and it is in literary production that the mobile relations between subjectivity and objectivity, between subject and world, subject and history, subject and other, are played out, won or lost, mastered or submitted to, linked or broken, tied and dissolved. The connections elaborated in this game-space seem to give coherence and intelligibility to the world by, for example, leading the a-mazed author from a labyrinthine hell. They also seem to exceed the *individual* subject, as in the case of Brisacier, and are capable of coming undone and losing the writing "I" in the field of literature, sweeping him into something like a psychotic episode in which everything appears to be an extension of the subject. The living specificity of others is then reduced to the mere and utterly abstract awareness of alterity's lack.[46]

If one is even provisionally to take Nerval seriously—and why should one not? by what authority does one refuse his claim to *raisonnement*?—then the act and matter of writing pose certain fundamental questions for subjectivity and self-knowledge. One will want to know how the field of literature is inherently prearticulated, how subjective experience is related to it, and how it involves others. In the next chapter, Nerval will be seen to engage these questions by approaching narrative as a means to generate experiential coherence. He will attempt to use literary structure as subjective structure. This attempt will fail under the force of his own style, which, in becoming more self-conscious and more propositionally apperceptive, becomes also more incoherent, driving the autobiographer into a more disturbingly aporetic but also more dynamic conception of writing and, from there, subjectivity.

4.   Playing with Death: *Les Faux Saulniers*

> I have become the living tomb of the Gérard de Nerval you loved.
>
> —*Nerval*

In discussing the sublimation of the self in writing, Paul de Man conceived of modern literary theory as caught between two opposing tendencies, one an effort to read in works the plenitude of a lived personal experience, the other deciphering in them the barrenness and asceticism of a transcendental, impersonally exemplary self that would lead to insights about the nature of being itself. As he put it:

> Some of the difficulties of contemporary criticism can be traced back to a tendency to forsake the barren world of ontological reduction for the wealth of lived experience. Because it implies a forgetting of the personal self for a transcendental type of self that speaks in the work, the act of criticism can acquire exemplary value. Although it is an asceticism of the mind rather than a plenitude or a harmony, it is an asceticism that can lead to ontological insight.[1]

Michel Foucault, as we have seen, described Nerval's madness in somewhat similar terms as the untenable attempt to express the immediacy of sensuous experience through the mediation of discourse. De Man was writing of the difference between two ways of reading a text, while Foucault was concerned with the opposition between discourse and something irreducibly alien to it, but both authors nonetheless offered models of a subjectivity caught between the fullness of its own experiences and the loss of that fullness in language. In setting up this opposition between experience and its communication, between lived plenitude and an empty language of the self, Foucault and de Man both inscribe the relation between self-identity and its linguistic expression within the larger structures of what we have called death-based subjectivity. By emphasizing the impersonality a subject can acquire in writing, de Man proposed a kind of literary interpretation that would recognize the inevitable self-transcendence of the author in his or her own writing, and his exemplary critical approach consequently construes literary self-representation as a sublimation of the self into an abstract revelation of impersonal being. This idea of a self-disappropriation inherent in writing was echoed by Lacan when he spoke of verbalization as an alienation of the self. In discussing the frustration often experienced by an analysand during a psychoanalytic session he wrote:

> Is it not rather a matter of a frustration inherent in the very discourse of the subject? Does the subject not become engaged in an ever-growing dispossession of that being of his, concerning which—by dint of sincere portraits which leave its idea no less incoherent, or rectifications that do not succeed in freeing its essence, of stays and defences that do not prevent his statue from tottering, of narcissistic embraces that become like a puff of air in animating it—he ends up by recognizing that this being has never been anything more than his construct [œuvre] in the imaginary and that this construct disappoints all his certainties? For in this labour which he undertakes to reconstruct it *for another*, he rediscovers the fundamental alienation that made him construct it *like another*, and which has always destined it to be taken from him *by another*.[2]

This *œuvre* of the self is, as Lacan will write in the next line, the *moi* or ego, a provisional identification of the subject with a unified image of itself. This image, for all its coherence, will frustrate the subject in its alienation as image and will therefore only satisfy *an other* than the subject, an other constructed in and as discourse. The talking cure is, in this sense, an interminable failure, since its goal, that which the subject seeks to fix in words, always escapes in them toward a purely verbal other. For the subject, language thus constitutes the field of an endless desire and an interminable loss of itself. De Man's understanding of literary subjectivity, Foucault's unbearable division between mediation and immediacy, and Lacan's description of language as an inevitable but necessary self-alienation, all closely parallel Nerval's own fears concerning self-representation and his conception of the effect that authorship had on his perception of himself and his world. The poet was aware of writing's inherent potential to reduce the immediacy of lived experience to the lifelessness of abstract individuality; he was conscious, too, that the price of lending literary coherence to his own life, of understanding his self-identity in terms of aesthetic structures, was the possible revelation that his life was nothing more than a textual impersonation of particularity. What makes Nerval especially interesting in this respect is that despite this awareness he persisted in attempts to evoke the fullness and specificity of himself in certain of his works, to entrust himself living to the anonymity and death that writing came to signify for him. It is this conscious striving to evoke the living individual and the plenitude of his particularity within the abstract coherence of a text that became the subject, in a variety of senses, of the feuilleton *Les Faux Saulniers*. It situates Nerval at the center of what Foucault described as an epochal shift in the literary experience of madness and what de Man identified as the crucial difficulty of interpreting subjectivity in twentieth-century literary theory. Most significantly, this "mad" longing also reveals Nerval to have been concerned with the basic issues of death-based subjectivity and textual sublimation.

As we have seen, the relation between concrete individual and abstract absolute lay at the heart of German romanticism. It appeared with its annihilating horror in theories of the sublime. It is figured in the recurrent scenario of Isis's unveiling and the subsequent destruction of the worshiper who had dared to view face to face the principle of universality itself.[3] It was the irritating seed from which the *Phenomenology of Spirit* was born. The various conceptual premises, tendencies, and anxieties that govern Nerval's construction of a literary subjectivity derive largely from the theoretical parameters of romantic individuality as it was determined by thinkers such as Kant, Schiller, and Novalis. In fact, the central issues of his elaboration of such a written subjectivity constitute a relocation of the sublime relation between individual and absolute from the realms of nature, spirituality, and death—where it had presided for the Germans—into a purely linguistic realm. He was, in other words, somehow conscious of and troubled by what we have called the linguistic sublime. The absolute no longer appears primarily in the form of a deity, a force of nature, or the great movements of history, but rather in the intimate relation between a person and the language he uses to express even his own particularity. The speaking individual, and especially the writing individual in Nerval's works, has no need to lift his eyes to the stars to fear himself in the presence of his own mortality, his own insignificant absence; he is already inhabited by it, he endlessly utters it, and the more he constructs himself as a linguistic property, the more he attempts to know himself in his own writing, the more too death comes to be the stem of his selfhood. And although they tapped anxieties which were shared by his age, Nerval's attempts to remain personally in the generality of language, to bend the laws of linguistic death against themselves so that in their field of impersonal permutations an individual self could be maintained and remembered, nonetheless distinguished Nerval from his contemporaries, making of him an object of wonder and ridicule.

Fleeing Sublimation: The Debate over Literary Piracy

This association of language with the death of the individual manifested itself throughout Nerval's writings and life. It seems to have found one of its most dramatic expressions in his theories about intellectual property. Ora Avni has discussed these issues in reference to Nerval, viewing the conception of language underlying his persistent promotion of antipiracy laws as a form of madness in itself, and her remarks offer a useful context for approaching the question. In *The Resistance of Reference* she contends:

> Writing poetry becomes madness only when one believes that it can be owned; when one believes that there is a proper way to own discourse (original authorship) and an improper way (plagiarism); when one believes in an original—and therefore true—instance, whose claim to regulate linguistic exchanges extends beyond the temporal constraints of enunciation (*énonciation*) and remains intact throughout subsequent transactions or readings; in short, when one believes that the centrality of the subject is crucial to the legitimacy of his discourse and that any offense against this centrality is or should be punishable by law.[4]

Although the antinovelistic stance of the *Faux Saulniers* ostensibly defies any need for a central subject, and although the key to its continuity is, as will be seen, presented within the text not as Nerval himself but as a role that the author among others can fill, Avni's analysis of literary ownership and exchange nonetheless offers a useful model for the interrelationship of the authorial self and the impersonality of writing. The possibility that literary proprietorship could extend beyond the temporal constraints of enunciation, or that an abiding connection between an own(ing) self and its discourse could perdure in the communality of subsequent communications exercised a control over almost all of Nerval's literary œuvre as well as his mystical and religious investigations. It also played a significant and legible role in the *Faux Saulniers*. This longing for a literary continuance of ownership, for an unbroken link to an original self, can be understood as a reformulation of the *zwiefältig* structure of Nerval's madness as it was conceived by Foucault: as a longing to resolve the unbearable irreconciliation between the immediacy of individual, *personal* experience and the communal mediacy of language.[5]

While it is not entirely clear what his feelings about plagiarism were, numerous documents attest to the continuing importance of the subject for Nerval and they reveal, as Avni states, his belief in a continuing subjective presence in writing, in a persistent attachment of discourse to an original enunciator, as well as his unflagging concern over the question "of a property which, as Alphonse Karr put it, people have always neglected to declare *property*."[6] Furthermore, Avni's association of antipiracy law and madness is given empirical support by one of the more curious moments in Nerval's public life, an event described at length in Jules Janin's feuilleton from the March 1, 1841, issue of the *Journal des débats*. The article, which Nerval later viewed with horror as something close to a necrology and which he privately denounced to Janin as an unconscionable public condemnation of his suitability for the society of anyone but poets and lunatics, gives something of a biography of Nerval from after the death of his faculties of reason and includes a detailed description of events leading up to his first episode of madness. According to the paper, Nerval had spent the afternoon before his attack engaged in a heated debate with friends about plagiarism and piracy. "What interested him above all during the nearly three months since he had returned from Belgium," wrote Janin, "was the great question of literary property." The views of Nerval, who alone held that foreign *contrefaçon*, or piracy, should be legally abolished, are not well represented in the article, apparently because Janin had been on the other side of the argument, but the terms of the discussion and the general positions of the speakers are visible enough to throw light on Nerval's opinions. For his interlocutors, the power, even the paradoxical legitimacy of *contrefaçon*, derived from its universalizing nature ("it is to piracy, above all, that the French language will one day owe its universality"), from its ineluctable tendency to popularize and distribute and thereby to recognize in great works of the human mind their transcendence of the immediate concerns of the individual who created them. Such creations are, Janin's friends contended, by their very nature impersonal, and any attempt to stem the material realization of this fact by controlling their distribution would be sheer pusillanimity, a misunderstanding of genius. Masterpieces cannot be owned because, virtually by definition, they surpass the scope of any individual: "No, no," reasons one unnamed popular author, "you will never reduce a man of genius's work to a thing like *property*, which is to say a thing subject to the whims, the egotism, the ignorance of a single man, subject to his personal use, subject to his abuse." Evidently a "man of genius" is both "man" and "genius"; squalid, ignorant, capricious, and insignificant insofar as he is the former, transcendental and universal insofar as he is the latter. His works do not belong to him or his descendants, "but to all of humanity, that haughty and imposing sole legatee [*légataire universelle*] of all great ideas, of all masterpieces." The argument extends from masterpieces to any creation of the mind, for "one cannot make a trade and an eternal merchandise of thought."

Taking at the same time a second approach which seems profoundly incompatible with the first, Nerval's friends argue for the benefits of piracy to the original author, and generally agree that although a writer may lose some income to unauthorized editions of his work, this deficit is more than compensated by an increase in popularity. His name is disseminated throughout the world of letters. "For the little bit of money he loses to it," they contend, "he gains from it an immense popularity; his name and glory . . . go out hither and yon into the most inaccessible corners of literate Europe." Later, this question of the name returns, and here piracy is seen to allow it to triumph over time, with one of Nerval's friends pointing to an apparently fundamental difference between owning a building and possessing a great name:

> Though the property does not change, the proprietors change without cease or respite by death, by marriage, by the survival of children and who knows what. It seems to me, on the contrary, that once your name has been placed at the head of a good book, you stay master of it right to the end of time. You grasp its glory, if not its profits [vous en toucher la gloire, sinon l'argent].

But it is precisely this question of touching the name, maintaining contact with it and continuing to master it, which remains unanswered in such a response, for as Nerval will be seen to demonstrate in the *Faux Saulniers*, the name *is* like a building—or a set of clothes—in that it can be inhabited by various people. Nerval's madness will lie in his insistence on keeping in touch with his own name, even as it increases in geographical distribution and threatens more and more seriously to exceed him temporally. Or rather, his madness will lie in this insistence on maintaining such mastery in the face of a growing awareness of its impossibility. As he pursues his point, Nerval's colleague adjusts the tack of his argument slightly but significantly: "You grasp its glory, if not its profits, *and not only you*, but your offspring, and each child has a fair share, the same share, in the spoils of paternal glory [cette curée de la gloire paternelle]" (emphasis added). All that had gone before is undermined by this continuation, since as the train of thought progresses, it becomes apparent that rather than retaining mastery over his name an author loses it to his children, who descend on it like a pack of hounds at a kill, all feeding on it equally. For the "curée," which derives from the word "cuir" (the skin of a deer), is that part of the beast thrown to the dogs. It is a sloughed-off hide whose owner has lost touch with it, belonging to no one in particular because it belongs equally to all: since thought and language are universal, an author has no particular right even to his own name.

Nerval's own objections to these positions were brief, according to Janin, and they concentrated mostly on the possibility of assuring some sort of immortality by combating piracy. He asserted that his interlocutors had "their own reasons for not wanting to be immortal" and concluded with a justification for extending property rights to an author's estate: "Fifty years, that sounds good in a law; and, all things considered, when you die you won't be displeased to have fifty years ahead of you." Taken altogether, the opposing positions seem clear enough: for Janin and his friends, *contrefaçon* is acceptable because it simply replicates the disappropriation, even the self-disappropriation, that is the essence of thought and writing, whereas for Nerval the struggle against piracy is a struggle against death, against the loss of self implicit in authorship.

That night Nerval lost his mind, and, according to the article, in the ensuing madness "no longer [knew] his name, nor the name of his friends, nor the beloved name that every man keeps hidden there deep in his soul—his smile alone remained."[7] Even if Janin's record is accurate only in its rudiments, it still offers the following suggestive scenario: Nerval is profoundly exercised by the possible permanence of the relation between his present creating self and the enduring communally exchanged product of that creation, between himself and language. He defends such a possibility alone against a group of friends (a scene already structurally like the scene of writing in its confrontation between the individual and his plural audience of other literati, other writers; structurally, it is as if writing itself is speaking to him) who contend that such creations are the property of all, and thus, that in the intimacy of invention—even in the invention of himself—Nerval is instantly losing his language to the universality of his possible readership, that the link between individual author and language is no sooner made than it is broken. That night, Nerval, mad, can no longer attach names to friends or self. His colleagues have, by force of numbers—in instantiating a plurality representative of writing's impersonality—won an argument whose profundity they could not grasp. His entry into language, they have said, is his death, and Nerval has withdrawn himself from language. That Nerval should later have referred to Janin's article as "necrological" and a "premature biography" takes on a particular significance when compared to the feuilleton itself, for Janin and his friends had been arguing all along that *all* writing was precisely that.[8]

In madness and in lucidity, in silence and, as we shall see, in writing, Nerval persistently rebelled against the idea that an author must necessarily lose his works, and an autobiographer his carefully constructed self, to the abstract universality of language. And he was in fact predominantly an autobiographer, constantly reshaping and recasting himself, incapable of inventing or recounting the existence of another—such as Brisacier, or the Abbé de Bucquoy—

without personally appropriating that other person's experience. His mute madness, in which, as Janin puts it, even the name engraved most deeply in the heart of his being is forgotten, constitutes one act of refusal, one withdrawal from the death of onomastic impersonality. His writings, especially those from the important period of self-examination which Jacques Bony has described as "the conquest of his 'I'" and whose first major work is *Les Faux Saulniers*, attempt, conversely, to embed the author more firmly in his works and to renegotiate the links between language and subjectivity in favor of a concrete specificity of the latter. The apparently aimless wanderings, the seemingly pointless musings and conjectures that fill the pages of the feuilleton represent in fact a supple but continuous examination of different literary and rhetorical models for constructing a self that could permanently uphold the contact between the particularity of the author and the universality of his writing, between the mute Nerval of his mad experiences and the lucid Nerval of his later accounts of them, between the plenitude of his unspoken life and the communication of that plenitude.

Structure and Genesis of the Text

Unlike the story of Brisacier mentioned in the preface to the *Filles du feu*, Nerval finished that of the Abbé de Bucquoy, but the events of its composition and publication are nonetheless complicated. On September 29, 1850, the *National*, a Parisian paper, published the following notice: "Aussitôt après les Souvenirs dans l'Exil [de Mme. de Belgiojoso], le National publiera: Études Historiques: Les Faux Saulniers (Extrait de la *Vie et des Aventures de l'abbé Bucquoi* [sic]), par Gérard de Nerval." The said feuilleton began on October 24 with an account of the origins of Nerval's interest in the abbot: while visiting in Frankfurt he had found a biography that seemed a promising basis for a historical study, but the exaggerated price of the volume had persuaded him not to buy it on the spot and instead to borrow a copy at one of the Paris libraries on his return from Germany. The library system was more idiosyncratic, the book more elusive than he had expected, and with the first installment of the feuilleton due he had still not found the biography on which it was to be based. As things turned out, it was not until November 30 that he was able to lay his hands on the document he would describe as "the work which was supposed . . . to be the basis [of his feuilleton], that is to say, the *official* history of the Abbé de Bucquoy,"[9] and to begin his reworked version of the Abbé's life. In the intervening month he was thus obliged to find other material to fill his pages, and his options were limited by the constraints imposed on periodicals by the recent passage of the Riancey amendment, which placed a prohibitive surtax on papers publishing novels in feuilleton form.[10] Nerval, finding himself short of copy and legally limited in his literary invention, turned to the events of his search for the "official" biography of the Abbé, to the question of where the border between (legal) history and (forbidden) novelistic invention lay and who was to adjudicate it, as well as to diverse other stories read or overheard from various sources.

The obviously heteroclite nature of the materials, the reflections on the distinction between novel and history, the ludic role-playing and irony of the narrator in the *Faux Saulniers* all conform to the labyrinthine image of literature that Nerval would later sketch out in the description of his "descent into Hell." Accordingly it is here if anywhere among Nerval's works that one can expect to find him elaborating and controlling the game of subject and object as well as the play of fragment and coherence. Yet the work in which Nerval might be expected to have elaborated a powerful mastery of literary unity began to fall apart soon after its publication and by its author's own hand, for the very diversity of its elements allowed him to break off sections of the *Faux Saulniers* and publish them separately in other volumes; in this way most of the story of his search for the elusive biography of the Abbé was reworked to become *Angélique* in the *Filles du feu*, while certain of its sections were incorporated into *La Bohême galante*, and the biography of the Abbé itself was reprinted in *Les Illuminés*. It was these apparently definitive versions that prevailed in the public eye, and for over a hundred years, from the original *tiré à part* following its publication in the *National* to its inclusion by Jacques Bony in the 1984 Pléiade edition of Nerval's *Œuvres complètes*, there was only one edition of the *Faux Saulniers* (Michel Lévy in 1867–68), the text lying otherwise untouched and essentially forgotten.[11]

Before embarking on Nerval's treatment of subjectivity and objectivity and of literary coherence and incoherence in this complex text, it will be useful to give some idea of its overall shape and to summarize the narratives that weave through it. The feuilleton falls easily into two major sections of unequal length: the historical account of a certain Abbé de Bucquoy and his escapes from prisons during the waning years of Louis XIV's reign is preceded by a section roughly twice as long which describes Nerval's day-to-day attempts to find a copy of the abbot's biography. This earlier section is by far the more eccentric and incorporates a heteroclite assortment of stories of varying length that draw on a wealth of sources. These stories are all more or less associated with the principal themes of the fugitive abbot and his elusive history, but insofar as the work and its various parts are held together thematically, it is only loosely, through the character of the abbot and the motif of a search for something evasive. The first installment describes Nerval's discovery of the biography, his decisions to use it as the basis of his feuilleton but not to buy it on the spot, and the first indications, once he has returned from Frankfurt to Paris, that the book will be very difficult to find. "Excuse these digressions," he concludes, setting the tone and program for the pages to follow, "—and I will keep you abreast of the voyage I am undertaking in pursuit of the Abbé de Bucquoy.—This eccentric and eternally fugitive character cannot forever escape a rigorous investigation."[12] Visits to the Bibliothèque Nationale, the Mazarine, Arsenal, and Versailles libraries as well as to various antiquarian book dealers fail to produce the book, raising instead a host of questions about the abbot, including the spelling of his name, whether someone impersonated him, the nature and breadth of his travels, and so on. The events of the search give rise to numerous anecdotes, reflections, and reminiscences, including a purportedly true ghost story, a visit to the Palais de Justice, various stories about amorous seals ("Histoire d'un phoque"), and accounts of Nerval's life in theater, while the archives themselves produce two documents whose contents the author finds sufficiently interesting to recount in detail. The first of these, found among the police dossiers in the Bibliothèque Nationale, is the "Affaire Le Pileur," a brutal struggle over an inheritance. The second, much longer, are the memoirs of Angélique de Longueval, great-aunt of the abbot; this account of her elopement, her wanderings across Europe in the train of her feckless husband, and her sad end exercised such a fascination over Nerval that, "pursuing *the Bucquoys* in all their forms," he abruptly left Paris for the Valois region, scene of Angélique's youth and elopement. The reworking of the memoirs is interwoven with descriptions of Nerval's own travels through the countryside in which they took place. The inscribed rocks and landscapes of this countryside suggested models of scriptural permanence to the aimless writer; incorporated too are remembrances of his own youth there, a visit to Rousseau's tomb, the outline of a drama based on the last days of the philosopher's life, and countless lesser anecdotes, reflections, responses to readers' letters, and observations on narrative techniques. The story of Angélique draws to a close, Nerval returns to Paris, purchases the abbot's biography at an auction, and reflects that as "Ulysse a fini par trouver Ithaque" he has recovered the Abbé de Bucquoy. The second section of the *Faux Saulniers*, interrupted by occasional considerations on the nature of historiography, then follows, telling the story of the abbot's numerous escapes from various prisons, notably the Bastille.

The Invention of a Coherent Subject

While critics generally agree that the texts that originally constituted the first part of the *Faux Saulniers* put Nerval's identity somehow on stage, into question, and ultimately at stake, the conclusions drawn from these observations are widely divergent. Insisting heavily on what he refers to as the "coherence" of the narrative, Raymond Jean, for instance, asserts that "it seems that in composing *Angélique*, Gérard never ceased to be aware of the unity of the pages he was writing in a *humorous* and *ironic* vein,"[13] and ultimately concludes that the playful complexities of the text eventually restore Nerval to himself. "Let us add that in this *game*," he writes in reference to the ironic and critical tone of *Angélique*, "Nerval seeks and finds himself."[14] He understands the author's search for the abbot's biography as a "movement towards himself" passing along "the path of memory"[15] and views the critical distance in Nerval's ironic posture as a Hegelian movement of the self into objectivity so that it can return to itself. "Humor, as he practices it," Jean writes, "rests on a 'duplicity' of spirit. . . . This mechanism of the spirit is described by Hegel during the same period as a capacity for installing the subject inside the object."[16] Nerval's "installation" in his text is, he contends, manifested in those moments when the latter reveals its contingency in relation to his authority: the more aesthetically discontinuous the text, the more fragmentary or polysemous it is, the more it reveals itself as the creation of an author's mastery. In every interruption, digression, and irony of the text, Nerval "shows clearly that he has chosen to place himself *inside* his narrative and that he is at every moment master of destroying it just as much as of producing it."[17] Without referring directly to him, Sarah Kofman takes issue with Jean's proposition that in writing this text Nerval recovered a self that was never really lost or at risk, and while agreeing that *Angélique* is essentially about Nerval himself, that "the Abbé de Bucquoy is the paradigm of the author, of Nerval," she nonetheless draws from this premise conclusions diametrically opposed to his. Explicitly rejecting any reading of *Angélique* which would view it as the story of a subject strengthening its identity with itself, she maintains that Nerval, "by identifying with his characters, by the imitation of multiple literary models, loses all identity of his own."[18]

The diversity of its materials, its wandering, skipping style (if it may be called a style), and the plurality of its different versions under different titles, all make it difficult to speak of the *Faux Saulniers* as a single text, especially since, as Kofman contends, even the project of self-identification, which might draw the work together into a subjectively unified whole, is potentially undercut in the very process of writing. Whether or not, however, the feuilleton is ultimately unified, it periodically raises the question of its own unity, thereby introducing the category of coherence at least thematically among its literary and subjective concerns. One particularly salient example of this theme occurs in a parabasis entitled "Observations," from the second half of the feuilleton. Here Nerval describes, at some length, the novelistic version of the abbot's life he would have liked to have written but could not, because of the Riancey amendment. The fictional additions he proposes to the documents handed down by history are almost entirely concerned with lending continuity to their narrative and establishing motivation for characters and events. Still, for all the causal connectedness of "the lovely novel that could have been made from these materials," which Nerval sketches out in these pages, the author asserts that this continuity will be insufficient, and that "it will be said, 'But this love, this despair, these assorted changes of state, all of it is too vague to become the subject of a novel; there passion must dominate.'"[19] The force that furnishes structure to the novel—allowing one to begin to speak meaningfully of narrative coherence rather than simply wholeness, unity, or connectedness—is described by Nerval as a "subject [*sujet*]," and is contrasted with two specific emotions ("love" and "despair"), and "changes of state," all of which are generally treated as "vague." A subject, it appears from this passage, unifies and subordinates individual elements of a whole under its single principle. It is not merely continuous, it is also not vague. It dominates, lending the text a central authority. The word itself condenses much of the discreet but abiding imagery through which Nerval, in the preface to *Les Filles du feu*, elaborated his conceptions of genre and the relation of writing to nonliterary events, for *sujet* comes etymologically from the Latin *sub-jectum*, meaning that which lies under or is thrust upwards. It is a substrate, a playing field whose territory must be cast up and seized by the players. The choice of the word also sheds light on Nerval's proclaimed need to identify personally with the heroes of his works, since novelistic coherence depends on the idea of a human subject, a personal identity: by treating passion as necessary to the structure of the novel, Nerval presents narrative coherence and narrative subject as indissociable from the idea of human affect.

What "passion" and "a subject" are remain to be clarified, but from the present material one can distinguish certain characteristics that situate them within larger, ongoing problematics in Nerval's work. First, they are somehow related to the novel. Second, they give a unified wholeness to a text. This relation between the novel and coherence, alluded to in the "Observations" section of the *Faux Saulniers*, is representative of an underlying theoretical construction that remained fairly stable throughout Nerval's writings; in the so-called *Lettres d'amour*, for example, the author exclaims: "People accept confusion and incoherence in conversation, but written lines become eternal witnesses. . . . The lovely novel that I would write for you, if my thoughts were calmer."[20] The missing term from the compound chiasmatic structure subtending these lines would be the novel's coherence: as conversation is incoherent and its speaker troubled, so is the author calm and his novel coherent. The third characteristic of the subject that comes out in the "Observations" is that it is *in* the text, not somewhere outside of it. This again is consistent with other passages from Nerval's writings, such as this one from the end of the *Voyage en Orient* (Voyage to the Orient) in which he cited the lack of linearity in his narrative, the fact that it could not be tied and untied like a thread, to distinguish its form from the novelistic and to attest to its "reality": "The letters and recollections from my travels brought together in these two volumes," he wrote, "since they are the simple accounts of real adventures, cannot offer that regularity of action nor those knotty twists and turns [ce nœud et dénouement] that belong to novelistic form."[21] Earlier in the same work, he had given a clearer idea of the stylistic effect that the nonnovelistic real would have on a text, contending that the force of events themselves revealed itself in the writing through its very inconsistencies—which guaranteed their origination in the experiences of an "I." The latter are diffuse, much as the nonnovelistic structures of a narrative are said in the "Observations" to be vague without the intervention of a subject: "What interest could you find in these jumbled, diffuse letters, mixed with fragments from travel diaries and legends picked up by chance? This disorder is itself the guarantee of my sincerity, for what I have written I have seen, I have felt."[22] According to these lines, the experiencing subject can no more ground the coherence of a narrative than can events themselves, for the subject and his experiences mark themselves in the text as precisely the opposite of such coherence: they are legible in its disorder and fragmentation. The subject, or passion, as something that gives unity to a written work cannot therefore be drawn from outside of it; passion cannot be thought of as a nonliterary affect, but rather as a literary invention. As that which masters the text—dominates it, as Nerval states in the "Observations"—it is entirely text-immanent. While Jean's image of a masterful, coherent, but nontextual author who marks the imposition of his will on a text through its disorder is nowhere attested in Nerval's theorizations of writing, the contrast between an incoherent nontextual experience and a text-generated, novelistically coherent subject pervades them.

The passages quoted above from the *Voyage en Orient* offer another, complex—even in an etymological sense (as multifold)—image of coherence. Nerval's oft-repeated fantasy, quoted by Gautier—that he would like to travel freely over the face of the earth, noting his impressions on a ribbon that continuously folded itself to produce, at his journey's end, a volume of a single line[23]— would, it seems, have found its realization in the two volumes that bound together the various letters and memories of his travels in the Middle East, but the author apologizes for them on the ground that they lack precisely that simple, threadlike linearity that the fantasy book was supposed to provide. The cohesion of the text, the passage from the *Voyage en Orient* indicates, would come not from the volumes, but from a novelistic strategy, and this, it seems, is because the simple is not so simple as it seems. Somewhat paradoxically, both the thread that holds the story together, its *nœud* and *dénouement*, and the rulelike linearity of the narrative derive from twists and folds. Yet another model of novelistic coherence is sketched out in these brief remarks, one that seems to play on the etymological roots of the word, the Latin *co-haerere*, which means to cling to one another, for the text is said here to find its unity in hanging together like a knot. Unlike a stable ground, or *terrain*, the knot does not exist before what comes together in it, it is no-place in itself. It is rather the cohesion generated through the crossings of heterogeneous lines, through their exchanges and substitutions, the no-place where issues join without blending, touch without fusing. The linearity of the novel would come from their tying and untying, their *nœud* and *dénouement*, from their very instability, from the process itself of drawing together and then separating what has been drawn together, like the loom of Penelope. These slipping knots would here be a formulation of literary coherence, of passion, of the subject.[24]

Naming Death

To appreciate the complexity and specificity of Nerval's idea of literary subjectivity in *Les Faux Saulniers* it is first necessary to consider certain earlier texts in which he thematized the relation between writing and death, for they make apparent how, even early in Nerval's career, language came to represent for him a loss of the individual. This is the darker, more austere face of his writing, the side of despair and endless, irreparable loss. Although it can be obscured in later works by their ironic tone or apparent levity, it nonetheless continued to guide his thinking about his personal relation to his texts. A theatrical review for the July 19, 1839, issue of *La Presse* is particularly revealing in this regard; in it Nerval analyzed a play, entitled "Le Mort-Vivant" (The living corpse), which was as remarkable for the nature of its material existence as for its unusual subject matter. "The feuilleton which we are beginning," he wrote, "and the analysis which we are undertaking do not refer to any performance that has been given or, indeed, to any performance that is possible." The available evidence strongly indicates that "Le Mort-Vivant," from which Nerval cites long passages in verse, is, like the story of Brisacier from the preface to the *Filles du feu* and the impossible historical novel which he described in the "Observations" section of the *Faux Saulniers*, another in his line of *livres infaisables*, or "books that cannot be done"—a work of his own invention which he describes and critiques, from which he quotes, but which otherwise does not exist. Although here he does not attribute the work to anyone in particular, its manner of impossible presentation, the concerns evoked even in the title, the novelty of the idea, remarked on by Victor Hugo, all point to Nerval's authorship.[25] It depicts the story of a desperate young poet who believes himself witness to a series of events after his death which, at the play's conclusion, turn out to be no more than the opium-induced illusions provoked by his attempted suicide. Before poisoning himself in the third scene, the protagonist utters the following lines: "Qu'est-ce donc que la mort? / La mort, nom sans objet, qu'on la craigne, ou l'envie / C'est pure abstraction. . . . "[26] Death is conceived of here as a linguistic operation, a pure sign without a referent and, moreover, as an act of abstraction. Conversely, it can be inferred from these lines that linguistic abstraction, if taken to the point that a word (or name) loses its object, if it becomes pure abstraction, constitutes a kind of death, and the intelligibility of the monologue thus turns on a conception of language which views its inherent generalization of particularity as an annihilating process.

Nerval again took up and further elaborated the relation between death and language in a story entitled "Isis," first published in 1845 and later reedited for *Les Filles du feu*. In a particularly significant passage, adapted from a section toward the end of Apuleius's *Golden Ass*, the goddess Isis addresses the story's metamorphosed hero with a long self-identification that Nerval rendered with these words:

> I, the mother of nature, mistress of the elements, the first source of the centuries, the greatest of the divinities, the queen of the manes; I who mingle in myself both gods and goddesses; I whose unique and all-powerful divinity the universe has adored under a thousand forms. Therefore am I called in Phrygia Cybele; in Athens Minerva;[27]

followed by a long list of divine appellations attributed to the goddess in the idiolects of different peoples, authors, and places. Motivating the passage from which the above quotation is drawn is a consideration of the distinction between the uniqueness of a referent—the goddess—and the seemingly inexhaustible plurality of names that can designate it, and the narrator traces two different attempts to narrow that dichotomy between sign and referent, to impose on language the singularity of that which it represents. Thus it is that "Apuleius, in giving her [the goddess] all these names, most readily calls her Isis; this is the name which for him sums up all the others; it is the primitive identity of that celestial queen, with her diverse attributes and her changing mask!"[28] It was not, however, Apuleius who, according to the narrator, took this process of linguistic stabilization furthest, but rather Christ, whom Nerval referred to as the most intrepid of the deity's initiates. "So, beneath the efforts of modern reason perished Christ himself," he wrote, "this last of the enlighteners, who in the name of a higher reason had earlier depopulated the heavens [qui, au nom d'une raison plus haute, avait dépeuplé les cieux]. . . . In raising your sacred veil, goddess of Sais! did the most daring of your followers find himself face to face with the image of Death?"[29] Like Apuleius, Nerval's Christ was engaged in a process of summarization which would reduce all divine names to one; but with Christ, the movement from a plurality to a single name entails a correlative movement from people to reason: the skies are *dépeuplés* in favor of single name and a "raison plus haute." As language is stabilized in relation to its referent, as the changing mask of Isis takes on the features of an original and unaltering face and a multiplicity of names is reduced to a primitive, nominal "identity," the various gods of antiquity are simultaneously abstracted from their roles as individual "people" into the impersonal force of modern reason. The movement from idiolects to a universal language is thus accompanied by both an increased understanding and a dehumanizing intellectualization of the object of those idiolects, culminating in a final, immediate encounter with the original face of reason: the name that condenses all names, language in its abstract universality, names only death.

In "Isis," the progress toward a single, stable name for a unique referent reveals or renders that referent as death itself. This offers some clue to the significance of the fact that in 1850, five years after writing the first version of "Isis," Nerval was forced by circumstances to overcome his mania for pseudonyms and choose a single, unvarying byline for himself.[30] This was the year in which he wrote and published *Les Faux Saulniers* and it proved to be decisive in the development of his literary subjectivity, a fact that he himself addressed and which he attributed to certain convergent legal developments. Bound by the recently passed Riancey amendment, which placed a prohibitive surtax on novels published in feuilleton form, and by the Tingy amendment, which, as part of the "law of July 16, 1850," forced individual writers to sign their articles in their own names, Nerval found himself obliged to reconsider the line between his literary and nonliterary personae.[31] Although the events of 1850 made it necessary for him to assess and take conscious action on the way he presented himself in writing, it was a question he had already been reflecting on, and the year before, in a letter to the editor of an arts review, he had commented on the distinction between his public and private selves:

> Every man of literature, like every artist and every politician, belongs to the public sphere [appartient à la publicité]; it is actually difficult to trace clearly, in the case of the latter, the line which separates public life from private life; and yet such a line exists, a bit vague, somewhat unstable, it is true, but it is barely permitted [il n'est guère permis] for any but friends to cross it at several points.[32]

Writing, according to Nerval, had always threatened to transform the writer into a creature purely for others, into a being who belonged more to "publicité" than to himself, but the movement between his outward and inward existences was controlled, even if only in an unstable way, by the convention and decorum embodied in the impersonal statute: "il n'est guère permis." Now, however, with passage of the Riancey amendment, which restricted writers' ability to attribute their own opinions and musings to fictional characters, and the Tingy amendment, which forced them to sign their writings in their own names, the law threatened to efface entirely the "line," which had already been disquietingly vague and mobile, between private and public life, between one's existence for oneself and one's existence for others. Nerval reacted publicly to the legal changes in a drama review written for *La Presse* on September 30, 1850, the day before *Les Faux Saulniers* was announced in *Le National*. "Now that the law obliges all journalists to sign their articles," he wrote, "the personality of each writer risks growing out of all proportion. Without being forced, perhaps, to tell the story of his life, one finds oneself drawn to *pose* more before the reader."[33] Compelled to reveal his name, Nerval responds by asserting that the *moi* of the writer will become a role, a pose that one can adopt ("Let us put on then, to try it out for a moment, that terrible 'I' [ce terrible *moi*] of Montaigne and Pascal," he writes in the following paragraph), that the writer himself will still escape into the impersonality of a stance which has outgrown him individually. Between May 1849 and November of the following year, Nerval thus changes his opinion about the relation between an author and his works: no longer does he see the author as disguised by withholding himself from his texts and his public; he now considers the very act of writing, of going public, to be itself a disguise. Moreover, it is a disguise of excess, of surpassing the limits of the self, of a *moi* that becomes anonymous as it develops "outre mesure," or "out of all proportion"; by its very nature, Nerval here contends, writing threatens to say too much and to abstract the individual out of existence, to depersonalize him.

In the section entitled "Observations," from the second half of the *Faux Saulniers*, Nerval acknowledges that the Riancey amendment prevents him from using the sole model of literary coherence he has identified—the novelistic subject—to structure his feuilleton; but earlier, in the first part of the text, when he had not yet found the abbot's biography and was under pressure to develop material to fulfill his obligations to the *National* and his readership, Nerval did in fact assert that something held the text of the *Faux Saulniers* together, something subjective and peculiar to him, whose irrationality, obstinacy, and force over his will make it resemble a passion. At the beginning of a passage entitled "Réflexions," from the November 15 installment of the feuilleton, he writes: "Despite the digressions which are natural to my way of writing I never abandon an idea; and whatever one might say, the Abbé de Bucquoy will turn up in the end."[34] What counteracts the self-consciously disruptive style of the *Faux Saulniers* is not merely a singular idea but also the narrator's personal attachment to that idea. The writing is digressive but the author is consistent, and Nerval points up the opposition at work between the two forces by his use of a concessive syntax structured around the words "despite" and "whatever." Moreover, whereas in the "Observations" section Nerval will refer to himself with the detached ambiguity of "we" or "the author," here, in its first part, to identify the unifying force of the *Faux Saulniers* he speaks as "I"; that force of coherence is presented as an element or aspect of the "I," and the "Réflexions" thus convey that the *Faux Saulniers* arise from the conflict between a first person and the digressive, fragmentary discursive style which is natural to it. Installed within the text itself and guiding its elaboration is then the difference between the writing itself—as "way of writing"—and its author, who is accordingly legible in the text both through its continuity and as one of its characters. While with his failed novel on Brisacier Nerval had been unable by his own account to preserve a distance between himself and his text, coming to believe that he was what he wrote, with the *Faux Saulniers* he depicts himself as aware of the difference between himself and his writing, a subtlety that is thrown into relief by its contrast with his reference to the "abbé de Bucquoy," which identifies the abbot with his biography.[35] The continuity of the impassioned author is itself, however, a literary construct.

The complexity of the first person and its relation to the continuity of the text are thematized by Nerval in a passage entitled "Autre digression forcée" (Another forced digression) from the October 31 installment of the *Faux Saulniers*, and it is accordingly here if anywhere in the text that one can expect to find an opening toward his understanding of how subjectivity and coherence functioned in the feuilleton. He writes:

> I am once again obliged to speak of myself and not of the Abbé de Bucquoy. It is scant compensation. The public must admit, however, that the impossibility in which we find ourselves of writing *novel* forces us to become the heroes of the adventures that daily befall us, as they do every man—and whose interest is undoubtedly highly contestable the most part of the time.
>
> In short, we are testing ourselves on mobile and slippery ground [nous nous essayons sur un terrain mobile et glissant]—we must be guided or warned.[36]

There is, it appears, a position in the text which can be filled by either the authorial "I" or the Abbé de Bucquoy. While, by the narrator's own assessment of the situation, the abbot fills the role better and Nerval is a somewhat unsatisfactory substitute, the latter is nonetheless a passable understudy and can function in the role—or perhaps more accurately, the narrative can function with him standing in. The character itself is modeled on the hero of a novel, and there is thus in the *Faux Saulniers* a principal narrative position which can be distributed among various persons, which is indissociably attached to none of them, and which would lend to the writing a certain novelistic structure, if not interest.[37] Unlike the Brisacier story, Nerval maintains his awareness (and his reader's) of the distinction between his hero and himself, identifying not with the abbot but with the function he serves in the text. Or, rather, it is not so much an identification as a subordination, an intentional structuring of his relation to the events of his daily life on a literary paradigm. This transformation of the first person from the subject of daily experiences to the equivalent of a novelistic hero, this process of imagining one's own life as a novel, is figured in the metaphor of a terrain that allows circulation between different roles and functions, which permits a certain convertibility between the abbot and the "I," between hero and Everyman, between the first persons singular and plural. There is, so to speak, a more fundamental connectedness among the various roles and persons of the author in relation to his text, a more profound and substantial coherence underlying the various manifestations of subject in the feuilleton; but this terrain is unstable. Not only is it described as "mobile et glissant," it is also represented as being beyond the control of the author himself, who appeals to his readership to aid him in his efforts to master written subjectivity. The literary subject as a site of coherence is thus depicted here as mobile, slippery, and dialogic; that is, dominated only by means of an interaction with readers, who are called on to warn and advise.[38]

Though it is not immediately apparent, Nerval continues to probe these questions of subjectivity, convertibility among individuals, and textual role-playing in the digression that follows his assertion "I am once again obliged to speak of myself and not of the Abbé de Bucquoy," for the incident he then relates concerns precisely the possibility of two separate individuals being considered identical simply because they share the same textual function. Here, however, the function he focuses on is not that of a role—like the protagonist of a novel—but that of a name. "A newspaper for which I worked in the past . . . — *Le Corsaire*," he writes, "reproaches me today with having changed color," by which was meant political allegiance.[39] In responding to the accusation, he first points out the seriousness of the charge, remarking that while the "apparent variations" in the political tone of a periodical result normally from a shift in owners or directors, "for a writer, the reproach is more serious." To exculpate himself of this seeming "change of convictions" he provides the following information:

> There has been, in the information which the editor of the *Corsaire* has been able to gather, confusion between two names. I am not the same as the Mr. Gérard who was part of the staff of *Public Spirit* and who, undoubtedly, wrote according to his personal opinions. A stranger to all party struggles, I must even say that I have met that homonym, whom my name may have damaged in his own party, as his could risk doing to me today—if I belonged to a party.[40]

Nerval is attempting on the one hand to establish his independence both from any political party and from his own name, and on the other to prove the invariability of his convictions. In thus arguing for his detachment and consistency he contrasts his personal stance with that of names and newspapers, both of which only apparently change opinion because, in their impersonality, they can be inhabited by different individuals. By establishing his own independence, Nerval also establishes that of his name: the two, he contends, are not necessarily linked. This arbitrariness of names, which is manifested in their ability to be general signs of the particular (with a single name designating a plurality of individuals as individuals) and to be chosen freely and interchangeably to designate an individual, made them the object of Nerval's lifelong fascination.[41] In the "Autre digression forcée," he again demonstrates an ability, reminiscent of the elusive abbot's numerous prison escapes, to evade the law and to reassert his independence in the arbitariness of names. He may be Gérard, but then, he contends, so are others. His name, like the *moi*, is an artifice of individuality, or personal subjectivity.[42] It is like a role, like the hero or the subject of a novel, like the continuity of the *Faux Saulniers* itself, to which personal subjectivity can subject itself.

The choice of this particular anecdote is not as arbitrary or circumstantial as the author pretends in describing it as one of those "adventures that daily befall us, as they do every man," for the awareness of the detachment between an individual and his name which Nerval displays in the above passage, as well as his facility with pseudonyms, constitute a common point between the author and the elusive hero whose role he must play. The abbot's name has been fluid at best throughout the search for his biography, leading Nerval to remark at one point: "I arrived yesterday at Compiègne, pursuing *the Bucquoys* in all their forms," and later, "the old names have no spelling."[43] During his examination of the police documents in the Bibliothèque Nationale, Nerval had discovered a reference to a "*self-styled* [*prétendu*] Count de Bucquoy," which led him to speculate:

> Could it be a fake Bucquoy—who would have been passing himself off as the other... for some purpose it would be hard today to appreciate? Could it be the real one, who might have hidden his name beneath a pseudonym? Reduced to

this single piece of evidence the truth escapes me—and there is not a jurist who would not be within his rights to contest even an individual's material existence!⁴⁴

It is not merely the actual use of pseudonyms that can throw the material existence of an individual irretrievably into doubt, but also their potential use; names, in their promiscuity, cannot preserve a material individual from the imposed forgetfulness that is legal skepticism, and they function as a site of substitution, a place where one individual can take the place of another and a false Bucquoy can pass "for the other." The name is a dramatic function in the text, a mask behind which various individuals can hide, an impersonal image of an individual, and Nerval speaks of it with such language, announcing at one point: "I've received a letter today from a Paris library to the effect that there existed two Abbés de Bucquoy—a true one and a fake. . . . We shall attempt later to unmask [*démasquer*] the intriguer who seems to have substituted himself for the descendant of his Lord, Count de Bucquoy."⁴⁵ A false Bucquoy passes for the real one, as one Gérard hides another. Nerval has shown a consistent fascination with the abbot's elusiveness, with the fact that he is "eccentric and eternally fugitive,"⁴⁶ with the endless deceptiveness of his very name, and when he identifies himself as posing in the role of the abbot, he does so precisely as one whose textual identity is also unstable, is similarly detached from "an individual's material existence." Their relations to their names thus function as a legible model for their relation to the text itself, to the role that they play in it, to the function of continuity that they lend to it as its "main motive."⁴⁷

The name, like the role, is an abstract figuring of particularity, a locus of substitution and passage, which by identifying individuals one with another asserts their communality, their sameness, and constitutes of them a group, a totality, a unity. The "main motive" of the *Faux Saulniers* is a personification of precisely this lability, for the distinguishing characteristic of the abbot, that behavior which, when adopted by Nerval, allows him to impersonate the abbot and to adopt the leading role of his own feuilleton, is precisely his ability to pass for another, to impersonate. The central character of *Les Faux Saulniers* is thus a figure for substitution among individuals, a figure for the characters' relations to their own names and thereby to their integration into language. For that reason, the onomastic musings that appear as one more form of digression in the text are in fact central paradigms of its unity. And among these seeming digressions, among the various pseudonyms and divergent spellings that serve to identify his hero, one in particular appears to have caught the author's attention, for twice Nerval mentions in the *Faux Saulniers* a piece of information given only once in the original version of the biography: the abbot at one point chose to call himself "le Mort," or "the Dead Man." The earlier account, from the first half of the feuilleton, describes the circumstances under which the abbot adopted this name:

> Having escaped as if by miracle from a great danger, he took a vow to leave the world and to retire to a Trappist monastery. The Abbé de Rancé—about whom Chateaubriand wrote his last book—sent him away, on the grounds that his faith was not strong enough. He put back on his decorated outfit, which he soon traded for a beggar's rags.
>
> Following the example of fakirs and dervishes, he travelled through the world, thinking to give examples of humility and austerity. He took as his name *the Dead Man* [*le Mort*], and even led a free school in Rouen under this name.
>
> I shall stop here, for fear of deflowering the subject [de peur de déflorer le sujet].[48]

The abbot at first withdraws to a place of reclusion where already another abbot is "making a name for himself"—the Abbé de Rancé, who will become the subject of an entire book by Chateaubriand. He is soon expelled back into the world, however, and here, following other examples ("of fakirs and dervishes") he himself becomes an example; he becomes, in other words, a particular which stands not for itself, but for the abstract principle that identifies it with other individuals, or in this case with other examples—a paradigm. At the same time, finding himself obliged to change guises, he trades one set of clothes and one appearance for another and in so doing he adopts another name. The name functions here in parallel to a costume that can be put on and removed or worn by various individuals, and the name he does choose at this moment of self-imposed exemplarity and abstraction is precisely one which will at some point designate every man ("le mort"). Moreover, this name, which refers to one who is eternally absent or "eternally fugitive," allows him both to absent himself—to disappear as the criminal Abbé de Bucquoy—and to identify himself precisely as an absence. *Le Mort* designates an absolute abstraction of the individual into perfect generality and the consequent impossibility of distinguishing him;[49] it indicates his loss as an individual, his utter anonymity, and in this way the abbot's newly adopted name both hides him and reveals him as the hidden one. This is more apparent in the later version of the same incident, which, while substantially identical to the above, also explains the signification of the appellation "le Mort": "This name symbolized for him the forgetting of life's sorrows and the desire for eternal rest." The name is not merely the trace of forgetting—"the forgetting of life's sorrows"—it is also the symbol of the desire for what is missing, "the desire for eternal rest." The abbot, in playing with names, thus identifies himself as an eternally lost object of desire, and it is at this point that something new has become legible in Nerval's reasoning on names and language, for the commentary on why the abbot chose such a name and what it signified were Nerval's personal additions to this episode as it is described in the original (1719) version of the abbot's biography: the name does reveal, if not what has been lost, at least that it is lost.[50] The abbot, Nerval shows, has found a name that in the abstracting death that is language both reveals the nature of language and marks the absence of an individual. In le Mort, death names itself and in naming itself comes as close as it can to designating something beyond its own generality: an absent abbot, "eternally fugitive" like the "fugitive *star*" of Nerval's descent into Hell, "which abandoned me in the night of my solitary destiny";[51] and Nerval himself, who must structure himself according to the role left by the absent abbot, and who immediately "fills" it by demonstrating his own ineluctable elusiveness in relation to his own name, his own absence from a text which would seem to designate him in his individuality. "Le Mort" offers the possibility of maintaining, if only negatively, if only through the designation of his loss, an attachment between language and a specific individual. Such a negative construction was not, however, a satisfactory solution to the problem of literary subjectivity. It was only a designation of despair, a recognition of the inability of language to preserve anything but the trace that marks the loss of the plenitude of immediate subjective experience.

Nerval's references to a unifying force in his heteroclite feuilleton and his uses of pseudonymy represent only the first stages in an increasingly elaborate and disjunctive practice of self-representation and self-construction through literature, but their significance should not be slighted. He identifies as a force of coherence in writing and in daily life (in "the adventures that daily befall us, as they do every man") a certain kind of subjectivity, which functions as a mobile locus of substitution, an eternally absent object of desire that continuously marks itself as withheld from discourse, a loss that is subject to a potentially limitless series of metamorphoses, whose most precise name, le Mort, is also exactly the most general and forever expresses the annihilating truth of language. One can say that at this stage in his exploration of literary selfhood, Nerval isolated that ascetic quality of language that de Man asserted was one of the two poles of literary subjectivity as it has come to be known to modern literary criticism: the self stripped of the plenitude of its immediate experience and reduced to an exemplary reflection on primary ontological questions, a sort of Heideggerian rebus; at this stage, where he identifies himself in writing as the death that is writing, Nerval's voice rises to the pitch of that single question which Foucault heard echoing solitary through his later madness: how can it be that the attempt to maintain oneself in the divergence between immediate experience and its loss in the abstraction of language could itself be so deprived of expression that all one can do is let death call out its own name?

Writing Beyond Return: Memory as Palimpsest

If writing is the loss of oneself into the anonymity of death, then self-preservation would seem to lie in muteness, in the retreat from words that had characterized Nerval's first psychotic episode. It is not clear, however, that there is anywhere to return to, for, as appears from the feuilleton, the self, in its self-identity as a continuity over time, is already textual, and as such, it merely perpetuates that hazardous objectification that places sanity and death at stake. In a counter-intuitive mimesis, Nerval offers a concept of memory that is grounded not in the individual's immediate experience of himself as a temporally extensive consciousness (if such an immediate knowledge could be possible), but in his enduring objectification.[52] The individual, as he is known to himself in memory, is structured like a document.

The scene takes place during Nerval's wandering in the Valois region, where he is pursuing traces of his own and the Abbé de Bucquoy's histories. It is All Hallows, the day of the dead, and the author is listening to an ancient air sung by a group of local girls. He remarks: "Yet another song from my cradle. Childhood memories come back to life [se ravivent] when one has reached the midpoint of one's existence. They are like a palimpsest [un manuscrit palympseste] whose lines are made to reappear through chemical procedures."[53] What of the self has been lost to the self comes back to life (*se ravivre*) because it has been preserved in a book, but this is not the volume of a single continuous line which Nerval had contemplated openly before Gautier and his other friends; here it is a document that is troubled by erasures, loss, overwritings, a book to which the self has been consigned also *in its absence* as a notation that has provisionally disappeared. It is a book to which the author is entrusted and yet from which he has, as Gautier put it, withdrawn himself, where the author can temporarily undergo death and forgetting and be written over and nonetheless still be recalled to life. Nerval's memory of himself is fragmentary and allusive, its various elements open to reanimation through the intervention of another hand or voice, through the metaphorical application of chemical agents that reveal what has been lost or covered over, by the voices of singing girls which draw up a recollection from the past. The self revives because it listens and responds to events in the present, and it can do so because it is structured like a fragmentary, open-ended text precisely *without* a linear narrative; because it is constructed as a compilation that can be entered at any point and followed through by any number of different itineraries. In this particular model of subjectivity, the self, insofar as it is structured and apprehensible, is always already a wandering, is always partial, incoherent, digressive, awaiting reformulation, and, above all, written.[54]

Writing appears here as the metaphor for a medium in which the self can be preserved, but, according to this model, in order for the particularity of the individual to persist for itself, there must be textual forgetting as well as textual remembering, there must be the inscription of a loss or annulation, of a forgotten moment or aspect, and this trace must be subject to recall; moreover, this is not merely the sign of loss, but also a loss of the sign, since the trace of the past, its memory, vanishes also and can only be rediscovered through a chemical intervention. By its very nature the writing is riddled with functional blanks, loss, and erasure. The image of self-consciousness that figures here in the metaphor of the overwritten book comes out also in Nerval's description of his madness, when his theories of authorship slip vertiginously into the experience of a solipsistic identification with all of human history and the ecstatic culmination of his idiosyncratically syncretic spiritualism. There, he speaks literally of reincarnation, of reawakening the entire chain of his various individual existences, and he does so in terms that are structurally almost identical to the image of the palimpsest which he uses to describe the processes of memory in the *Faux Saulniers*. It is in the preface to the *Filles du feu* that Nerval recounts this manic experience of himself in both his plenitude and his fragmentation. There, he describes how, in writing the story of Brisacier, which was published as a fragment in collection with the letters entitled *Un Roman à faire*, he suffered a trauma that indicated to him the possibility of an articulation between the individual and the general:

> Inventing, a moralist has said, is basically remembering, and unable to find proof of my hero's [Brisacier's] material existence, I came to believe, on the spot, in the transmigration of souls no less firmly than Pythagoras or Pierre Leroux. . . . From the moment that I thought I could grasp the series of all my previous experiences, it cost me as little to have been prince, king, magus, genius, and even God, for the chain was broken and marked the hours as minutes.[55]

Here, it is not language that constitutes the terrain on which the sublime and annihilating confrontation of the individual with the universal is played out; rather, it is in the realm of history. Still, the underlying structures of memory are virtually identical in both cases. In his madness, Nerval himself is each particularly and also every one generally, as a potentially limitless series of individuals in which it costs nothing to be one more, and as God himself. The articulation between individual and universal is constructed around a process of forgetting and remembering, a passage through death and then a restoration to life in which one mortal is replaced by another and which can be recalled in its entirety and *its diversity* by the "inventing" author. It is a continuous series that is also discontinuous, punctuated by death. To exist as finite particulars, the various historical identities must undergo erasure, death, forgetting, and replacement; but it is only a provisional annihilation, and in his mania, Nerval can recall the divergent, overlaid lives. By being a palimpsest, by erasing and preserving the erased, he can be both mortal and immortal, finite and infinite.

This articulation between individual and universal that is represented both in the image of the palimpsest and in Nerval's visionary experience of his plural individualities was to become a global discursive model for the elaboration of the authorial subject throughout the *Faux Saulniers*. For the feuilleton itself constitutes a sort of palimpsest. It draws on a profusion of distinct narratives culled from different sources and written by various authors which often bear virtually no relation to one another; it is a text punctuated by stops, inconsistencies, and rebirths; its digressions, shifts of focus, and substitution of characters one for another are so many rupturing passages through a nothingness of forgetfulness in which the self is constantly dying and being reborn in a text that figures itself as only part of a continuum starting with an endless tale woven by Penelope and tending forever forward. In the fragmentation of the text, the novelistic subject of coherence returns constantly to life, passes in protean fashion through a multiplicity of individual identities. But the fragmentation of the text, in introducing the finitude of the individual into it, also rejects finitude, inscribing the *Faux Saulniers* into an ongoing writing, as part of an endlessly digressive story begun by Penelope and continued on through countless other writers. In its fragmentariness, the *Faux Saulniers* already inscribes into itself its potential for reappropriation, a potential that Nerval himself, paradigmatically, put to service when he divided them up and reused them in other texts. The text is discontinuous, even though Raymond Jean argues for the paradoxical continuity of its antinovelistic form, and Jacques Bony sees this discontinuity as narratively and stylistically belied by the near-perfect dominance of a single narrative voice.[56] The text's discontinuities are positioned by the writing itself, when read in conjunction with other of Nerval's works, as points of genuine and radical stoppage, moments of death and forgetting that incorporate the need for constant reappropriation, reorganization, and reconsideration into the dismembered body of the feuilleton. Or rather, it is not a text which is dismembered, since it never constituted an integral whole, but is instead one that is always in the process of being (re-)membered. The *Faux Saulniers* is marked by a discursivity that constantly and firmly rejects any final mastery, which remains always to be narratively recast, reworked, recontextualized, and recommenced.

Consequently, the image of the subject that emerges in these pages is that of an endlessly incomplete narrative project.

A passage entitled "Réflexions" from the end of the first section of the *Faux Saulniers* thematizes the text's status as part of a longer, ongoing process of writing. It mediates between the preceding installments, which had been given over to an abundance of divergent narrative elements intended to fill copy until the elusive biography could be found, and a recounting of the contents of the biography itself. The passage also serves to assess the text in its entirety, to conclude and summarize it. This last liminal installment is written in part as a conversation between two unidentified persons, letting the narrative thread fray into a final admission of its persistent polyvocality; the text is summarized, identified in its wholeness, not as a single line of thought enunciated from a single voice, but in a dialogue between voices which situates that textual whole in an antiphonal literary tradition whose continuity lies in a pattern of assertion and response, imitation and renewal. Nerval's *Faux Saulniers* bears the impress of a literary history that it preserves by renewing and reanimating, which survives in its transmission through different voices and spontaneities; and this voice speaking in other voices is inscribed discursively into the text itself through its summary dialogic structure, much as the death of the author is inserted into it through its ruptures, discontinuities and digressions. In these two respects, polyvocality and rebirth, the *Faux Saulniers* becomes a microcosm of the tradition into which it insinuates itself. The passage in question, which thematizes the relation between feuilleton and literary history, reads:

> "And then… " (That's how Diderot would begin a story, you'll say.)
> "Go on!"
> "You have imitated Diderot himself."
> "Who had imitated Sterne… "
> "And he had imitated Rabelais… "
> "Who had imitated Merlin Coccaïe… "
> "And he had imitated Petronius… "
> "Who had imitated Lucian. And Lucian had imitated a lot of others… If only the author of the *Odyssey*, who sent his hero wandering for ten years about the Mediterranean, only to lead him finally to that fabled Ithaca, whose queen, surrounded by dozens of pretenders, undid each night what she had woven during the day."
> "But in the end Ulysses found Ithaca again."
> "And I have refound the Abbé de Bucquoy."
> "Tell us about him."
> "I have been doing nothing else for the last month."[57]

The comparison with Ulysses is disingenuous, for Nerval, who has forced himself to wander as the "hero" of his own life, returns to his Ithaca to reveal not himself among a group of pretenders, but the Abbé de Bucquoy, who had himself, as is pointed out in the following paragraph, been deemed by the police to be a pretender: the self-styled or "*prétendu* abbé de Bucquoy." He has not brought an end to the plurality of those who would assume the role of the wanderer, but even here, at the end, has riven it in two, distributing it between the voices of a dialogue; furthermore, he has identified the *promeneur*-narrator as himself a pretender, for his wanderings have been, he asserts, part of the story of the abbot, of whom, he contends, he has spoken exclusively since the beginning of the feuilleton. This final disclosure of the entirety of the text is, in short, a false identification and a false conclusion to the narrative it summarizes, and in its falsity it leaves the *Faux Saulniers* open-ended, an incomplete part of a literary tradition and a subjective identity which remain continually "à faire" and "à parfaire," still to be done and finished; and in this respect the ending recalls Nerval's idiosyncratic tendency to publish unfinished works, like his numerous projects for novels.[58] This is the terrain on which Nerval inscribes himself, a terrain constructed in the past and future transactions of language, and in which the memory of an individual identity is eternalized by imprinting itself, as surreptitiously as one of Dumas's creative additions to historical record, into the very process of literature's renewal and reinvention. It is the elaboration of an individuality that constantly defers its death by incorporating it through fragmentation, by remaining irreparably incomplete.

As Jacques Bony has shown in *Le Récit nervalien*, 1850—the year in which Nerval wrote *Les Faux Saulniers*—constituted a turning point in the author's literary life, when he consciously attempted to master the first person and to work out the relation between writer and text, between his creative individual identity and its written representation. The feuilleton, like other texts from the same period, stages both the relation and the difference between author and writing. With Nerval, and perhaps with any writer, that relation is not merely one of representation, of sign and referent, because the representation is conceived as changing what it represents, as altering the author's self; but this is not the change that de Man and Binswanger, or in a more consciously Hegelian way, Raymond Jean, had spoken of, for the altered self of Nerval is not intended to return *from* the text as if the latter were an excursion through an alterity that could be entered and left.[59] Rather, in writing, Nerval consciously recognizes his own inherent textuality, at first staging a nontextual existence in order to submit it to the regularity, the coherence, the continuity of a literary work and to the permanence of writing, but ultimately concluding that the most valid model for articulating self-knowledge over time is primordially textual: a discontinuous, palimpsest-like document that, forever incomplete, insinuates itself into a dialogic or polyvocal tradition that will continually renew it. While it is true that a palimpsest implies a single piece of paper on which it is written, and its complexities would seem to be supported by an unvarying substance, the feuilleton consistently undermines any such notion of an underlying substantiality in sign systems, and the text instead promotes a model of permanence based on a mobile locus of substitutions, the endlessly vagrant crossing of its various narratives, styles, voices, and identifications.

The question, raised in discussion with Jules Janin and described as madness by Ora Avni, of permanently attaching a specific individual to a name or an utterance has shifted its focus between the crisis of 1841 and the writing of the *Faux Saulniers*. In the latter it is no longer a question of maintaining a permanent attachment between the individual and something outside of himself—such as a (literary) property, a possession—but rather of maintaining such an attachment inside the individual, that is to say, to himself. Memory, the permanence of the individual, its persistence over time, Kantian inner sense, is identified here as necessarily a form of writing, a palimpsest. There is therefore a paradox at the heart of the concept of individual identity, for insofar as one is a self-same individual one must be so over time, but to endure is to be written, and to be written is to be annihilated in one's individual specificity. As that which remains of the individual, as that which persists over time, every subject, therefore, is sublime, a textually sublime subject. There is no other possible model. The problem of madness, between immediacy of experience and the mediation of language, is not merely about expressing something—one thing—to others; it is also cast here as the problem of the self, any self.

Hegel's 'Aesthetics'

Similar questions of subjective text-immanence come out in Hegel's lectures on aesthetics, where they play a curiously disruptive role in the overall argument of the work and exemplify the troubling volatility of literary subjectivity within epistemological systems supposed to be stable. These formulations of what Hegel calls "poetizing subjectivity" arise from a discussion of the lyric, but they are sufficiently close to Nerval's model of written self-identity in the *Faux Saulniers* to demonstrate the extent to which the *feuilletoniste* was engaged in the most troubling theoretical issues of aesthetics and subjectivity of his period. The similarity between their separate understandings also indicates Nerval's potential for elaborating a significant alternative to what became the dogma of subjectivity in the romantic and post-romantic periods. Rather than being simply different from Hegel's approach, Nerval's diverges from it, and as such attains a critical rather than merely alternative value.

Much like Nerval, Hegel saw in the subject a force of cohesion in works of art; unlike the author of the *Faux Saulniers*, however, he understood the paradigm of that work of art to be lyric poetry and the subject the concrete individuality of the creating poet. Although the concreteness and individuality of the author will become increasing problematic as the argument proceeds, one can appreciate the degree to which Hegel's "poetizing subjectivity" resembles Nerval's *sujet de roman* as a formally unifying force:

> But the proper *unity* of the lyric is not provided by the occasion and its objective reality but by the poet's inner movement of soul and his way of treating his subject. For the single mood or general reflection aroused poetically by the external stimulus forms the centre determining not only the colour of the whole but also the whole range of particular aspects which may be developed, the manner of the exposition and linkage, and therefore the plan and connection of the poem as a work of art.[60]

Or, as Hegel will put it a few pages later: "as the center and proper content of lyric poetry there must be placed the poetic concrete person, the poet."[61] In both Nerval and Hegel the subject is that which unifies and centers, from which everything else depends as an elaboration, but in the latter's formulation the subject appears not merely as formal principle, but as concrete content. The coherence of the lyric artwork is thus, for Hegel, grounded in the experience of the specific individual author, for content and the concrete signify, in the Hegelian system, precisely such particularized experience.[62] Much like Nerval's novelistic *sujet*, which is held synonymous with passion in the "Observations," the Hegelian lyric subject is largely identified with affect; the poet's soul, Hegel contends, "must so expand as to absorb a rich world of ideas, passions, situations, and conflicts."[63] Or, as he puts it in another, earlier passage, lyric poetry gains its content, that is to say its individual specificity, from the soul of the poet, and this finds, in turn, its own content predominantly in feelings, although these latter are not necessarily limited to passions:

> The genuine lyric, like all true poetry, has to express the true contents of the human heart. Yet, as contained in lyric, the most factual and fundamental matter must appear as subjectively felt, contemplated, portrayed or thought.
>
> Further, here it is not a matter of the bare expression of an individual's inner life, of the first word that comes directly to mind as an epic statement of what the thing is, but of a *poetic* mind's *artistic* expression, an expression different from an ordinary or casual one.[64]

The task of poetry is the expression of human spiritual content, but no matter how positive and concrete the latter may appear to be, it only becomes *true* content, only *truly* becomes positive and concrete, when it is shaped or "imprinted" by subjective affect, impression, imagination, or reflection. In short, content—the ground of lyric unity—becomes content in being experienced as such by a subject. It is at this point that the problem arises, for elsewhere Hegel, completely consistently with this passage, has described experiential content as the product of the finite individual.[65] He does not abandon this position, but he modifies it disastrously: the content of lyric poetry, its coherence, is the exteriorization of individual (or finite) interiority, but, he qualifies, it is not a *simple* exteriorization. The exteriorization is an *artistic* one, rather than an ordinary or accidental one, not because it deforms its content but because its content, the soul of the poet, is itself *already* poetic. The coherence of lyric poetry thus lies in the true content of the individual human soul, but the truth of the human soul, its individual coherence, is already poetic, and what the lyric exteriorizes is therefore not the human soul in its individual specificity but in its truth, which is lyricism itself.

Hegel probably added this caveat about the poetic soul to avoid the trap of madness that Foucault identified in the work of Hölderlin and Nerval, for if the poet simply, that is *immediately*, expresses his interiority, in what sense can his expression be said to be language, which is by its nature mediate?[66] He skirts this problem by describing the poet's soul as already mediated by poetry, but this leads to a construction of the lyric as the expression not of content but of mediation itself. What is glimpsed but repressed in this passage is an image of exteriorization which does not work according to a positivist construction of representation in which entities are figured more or less adequately, which is to say, according to an idea of truth as *adequatio intellectus ad rem*.[67] Rather, when human content is *truly* represented here, all that is represented is representation itself. Now, this would not be a serious problem for the Hegelian system, if this particular moment were not integrated into a larger dialectical progression passing through art and other disciplines such as history, philosophy, and theology; since the lyric is so integrated into this system, and since the progress that incorporates it is structured as the increasing adequation of representation to represented, any moment in that structure which functioned according to a fundamentally different representational plan, such as the representation not of a positive entity but of representation itself, would fall outside of the logic of the dialectic, would leave a gap in its progress. Because that gap would come from a certain moment's nonintegration into the premises of the system as a whole, the universality of those premises would be disproved, and, in the present case, the Hegelian dialectic would be shown structurally incapable of accounting for constructions whose legitimacy it recognized—such as poetic subjectivity. But it is just such a construction, a text-immanent coherent subject, that Nerval proposes in the *Faux Saulniers*, and it is in this passage from the *Aesthetics* that it can be said to gain the recognition of its philosophical legitimacy as well as its critical value as an alternate formulation of the subject. The circularity of such a text-immanent subject mines the ground of the Hegelian system, but it is precisely such a subject that Nerval elaborates in his own writings.

The Subject as a Lacanian Pun

If it is possible to determine some of the implications of such a text-immanent subject for a system which, like Hegel's, would attempt to integrate phenomenal content into its model of subjectivity, we might still remain less confident about *how* such an utterly insubstantial and interminable subject would establish its continuity and self-identity. The conclusion that for Nerval the subject is inherently textual and as such gains persistence through its role as a mobile locus of substitution does not amount to a theorization of that subjectivity, and there is as yet no compelling reason to think that such a model can in fact be expounded. Although innumerable readers have attempted to make sense of Nerval's literary self-constructions, it will not be until nearly a century after his death that a theory is elaborated which can systematically articulate a construct of identity that understands it as linguistic, vagrant, and traversible—which can account, in short, for the self that Nerval asserts is at stake in *Les Faux Saulniers*. In Book II of his *Seminar* Lacan described the subject as a locus generated through substitutions. It is, he contends, an identity whose coherence or "mastery" lies, precisely, in its ability to undermine models of meaning (*sens*) founded on the existence of a stable signified underlying the signifier. The subject accordingly appears as a process (of substitution) rather than a position (masterfully underlying discourse or underwriting a text):

> Can an interrogation even be sustained concerning this ultimate *quod*, which is the experience of the unconscious subject as such [l'expérience du sujet inconscient en tant que tel], concerning which we no longer know who or what it is? In this respect the evolution of analysis itself places us in an especially tricky situation [embarras], inasmuch as it takes as an irreducible given those tendencies of the subject which on the other hand it shows to be permeable, crossed and structured like signifiers [perméables, traversées et structurées comme des signifiants], operating, beyond the real, in the register of meaning, on the equivalence of signifier and signified in its most material aspect as wordplay,

puns, witticisms [dans son aspect le plus matériel, jeux de mots, calembours, mots d'esprit]—which ultimately leads to the abolition of the human sciences, insofar as the last word of the witticism [le dernier mot du mot d'esprit] demonstrates the supreme mastery of the subject [la suprême maîtrise du sujet] in relation to the signified itself, since it puts it to all kinds of use, since it plays with it essentially in order to annihilate it.[68]

Lacan, like Nerval, sees an annihilating power in language, in the word itself, which, he contends, operates against the signified—the meaning or *sens*—of language and problematizes the model of subjective experience as a unified, irreducible ground underlying discourse (that Lacan speaks of an unconscious subject does not much matter here, since he nowhere places it into opposition with a conscious one—the Unconscious for him simply is the place of the subject). The clinical experience of psychoanalysis shows that such a coherent, prediscursive subject is itself a permeable structure of crossings that is always already organized like a signifier. This linguistic force annihilates meaning by undermining the distinction between the signifier and its sense: by showing, as Lacan says elsewhere, that there is no other word than the word, that before language as communication of information there was already language as the structure of the subject supposed to underlie communication. And the utterance that reveals this most clearly is the *mot d'esprit*—which itself puns here by bringing together the ideas of *Witz* and *Geist*, both translated into French by a single term said by Lacan to be the word both of humor and of the subject: *esprit*—for the joke, in its absurdity, reveals a different way of making sense, another need or use in language. This other discourse is that of the Unconscious, which speaks its desire in the *calembour*, in the point of crossing, where one word gets taken for another because materially they sound the same. The subject, when it draws attention to itself in the absurd materiality of language, reveals what Lacan calls its symbolic structure, which he describes as the "symbolic knot of resemblance, of identity and of difference."[69]

The *embarras* or paradox of the Lacanian subject described above is that while it must be considered the irreducible ground of identity, it also reveals itself to be permeable and crossed, which is to say derivative or reducible. The coherence of this paradox—in other words, how its two elements or sides necessarily go together—is suggested obliquely in other paragraphs from the same seminar, and it is to them that one must look for a further elaboration of the coherence of this ludic subject. Later on, for example, Lacan identifies language as a sort of ground for objects, which gives them their independent permanence over time, and it would thus be the word that is the self-identity of the object in distinction or isolation from the subject.

> It is through nomination that man makes objects subsist with a certain consistency. If objects had only a narcissistic relationship with the subject, they would only ever be perceived in a momentary fashion. The word, the word which names, is the identical. The word doesn't answer to the spatial distinctiveness of the object, which is always ready to be dissolved in an identification with the subject, but to its temporal dimension. The object, at one instant constituted as a semblance of the human subject, a double of himself, nonetheless has a certain permanence of appearance over time, which however does not endure indefinitely, since all objects are perishable. This appearance which lasts a certain length of time is strictly only recognisable through the intermediary of the name. The name is the time of the object. Naming constitutes a pact, by which two subjects simultaneously come to an agreement to recognise the same object. . . . That is the joint, the emergence of the dimension of the symbolic in relation to the imaginary.[70]

It is in the self-identity of the word that the object finds its own self-identity. That this self-identity should be contractual and not materially inherent is in itself significant, since it indicates that the ground of objective permanence is *established*, that it is so established on the symbolic level, and that consequently it is so dialogically through a process of interconnection, difference, and mediation. The permanence of the object may well be generated onomastically in distinction to the subject but it is nonetheless dependent on the latter and is, consequently, dialogically mediated rather than materially positive. On the other hand, and more significantly here, if the object derives its permanence from the word, which is established intersubjectively, the subject, which is structured linguistically, would also seem to derive its own permanence from a similar nominative procedure, since it too, as has already been argued, is a word: the *mot d'esprit*. The subject is a word that, like the object-guaranteeing nomination, does not derive its identity from a stable notion of materiality, but instead constantly and ludically undermines such notions by pointing up its own permeability.[71] As the traversability of the objective word is constituted by the intersubjective pact that grounds it as ground, so is the paradoxical irreducibility of the subjective *mot d'esprit* grounded in the intrasubjective differentiality of the signifier.[72]

In the following paragraph of the seminar, Lacan illustrates the relation between the imaginary and the symbolic orders described above by referring to his own meta-analysis of Freud's self-interpretation of the dream of Irma's injection, the "dream of dreams," as Lacan puts it—the initial or initiating dream of psychoanalysis in that it revealed to Freud the key to dream interpretation. Here again, the subject appears in a word, in a *mot d'esprit*, which now takes the form of the curious, impersonal appearance of a written chemical formula:

> This point is designated by the AZ of the trimethylamine formula. That's where the *I* of the subject is at that moment. And my suggestion to you is that you see in that that the dream's last word wasn't said without humour, nor without hesitation, since that is almost a *Witz*. Just when the hydra has lost its heads, a voice which is no longer anything more than the *voice of no one* [*voix de personne*] causes the trimethylamine formula to emerge, as the last word on the matter, the word for everything. And this word means nothing except that it is a word.[73]

The word that is the word of the *I*, that *is* the *I*, means only that it is a word: the meaning of the *je* is only its self-indexed materiality *as* word. This is the permanence of the subject, behind the hydra-headed multiplicity of ego identifications, beyond its identifications as coherent images of a self.[74] And that word is like a *Witz* or a *mot d'esprit*, which reveals the materiality of sense, the identity of signifier and signified, and which by its nature asserts that there is no other word than the word, that the meaning of the word is only the word itself. It is in this self-referentiality of language to its materiality, then, that would lie the permanence of the subject: in the impersonal *voice of no one* that is only language referring to itself. The self-identity of the word itself—the material self-sameness of the pun—is, however, problematic and mediated, according to Lacan, for, as he had asserted earlier in the same seminar, the signifier is itself permeable and crossed. The permanence of the subject lies, then, in a word, in a *je*, whose own permanence is grounded in the possibility of punlike equivalences; it is a permanence made of nothing but crossings, interpenetrations, and substitutions, something like a *calembour* and a knot. Or to put it differently, the subject is like a pun, grounded in the materiality of a pun, which is itself only grounded in another pun, and so on indefinitely.

It is as if Lacan had taken Kant at his word, literally, when the latter had identified the apperceptive subject as the possibility of appending the formula "I think" to every cognition. Here the subject's propositionality can only derive its own self-identity, from one predication to the next, out of the permanence of the "I," which corresponds to what Lacan would call the apparently necessary irreducibility of the subject. What Lacan does that is different from Kant at this juncture is to conceive *explicitly* of the "I" and its permanence as entirely discursive rather than referential, as that which, in fact, abolishes referentiality in discourse: it is through the punlike materiality of the propositional "I" that the subject finds its self-sameness, its subjectivity, for Lacan. And if the Lacanian subject inscribes itself extravagantly but coherently within a half-occulted philosophical tradition of propositional subjectivity, the power of the "I" to abolish referentiality resembles, furthermore, the annihilating force of language that one finds in Hegel's chapter on sense-certainty in the *Phenomenology of Spirit*, in Nerval's review of "Le Mort-Vivant," and in the arguments of Janin and friends; the knotlike structure of the "I" is, on the other hand, similar to the subject of the novel used by Nerval as a paradigm for the role of authorial subjectivity in *Les Faux Saulniers*, a subjectivity whose name, like the Lacanian name, functions as a *Witz* or pun where one Gérard can be confused with another, a false Abbé de Bucquoy can pass "for the other," and "le Mort" can trade the living for the dead. And yet, for all the suggestive richness and impenetrable coherence of this ludic construction of discursive subjectivity, it is essentially lacking, for it is permanently alienated and evasive, an annihilating *nein-sagen* to the plenitude of immediate experience which refuses the immediacy of self-identity even in the situational self-sameness of its mobile knots. Lacan himself was still working on them at the end of his life in models growing ever more complex and opaque, still attempting to track their fugitive traces.[75] Nerval, too, was unsatisfied with his own desiring narrative subject as a construct of self-identity. The following chapters will consequently trace Nerval's relinquishment of the attempt to master the subject's irreducible reducibility, its endless evasiveness as mobile locus of substitutions in wordplay, pun, and the inextricable tangle of differences and identifications that create narrative and subjective coherence. It was this difficult renunciation, this passing through death, that would allow him to conceive of self-identity as meaningfully open-ended, but it was only by first understanding himself as dead and by poetically elaborating that self-experience that he was finally able, in *Aurélia*, to espouse, almost literally, the fragmentary materiality of the signifier as the model of the self. And yet, if at the end he will return to an ostensibly Lacanian construction of subjectivity, it will only be to refuse and displace both it and its Kantian and Hegelian predecessors.

5. The Subject Writes After Its Own Death: "Le Christ aux Oliviers"

> On the one hand, saying "I die" is the condition of possibility of any "I" whatsoever; on the other hand, "I die" is not anything that can be said *by* an "I" since death can have no, *is* no, subject.
> —*Andrzej Warminski*

> God is dead!
> —*Jean Paul*

> It seems to me that I am dead and that I am fulfilling this second life of God.
> —*Nerval*

Art as an Empty Grave in Hegel's 'Aesthetics'

The relation between subjectivity and narrative structure, which dominated the pages of *Les Faux Saulniers*, was contextualized by Hegel within a historically specific, aesthetic expression of human self-consciousness. Overall, in his lengthy series of lectures on the history of art, Hegel had been concerned to show the possibilities and limits inherent in various art forms for the objectification of an increasingly complex human consciousness, and he divided these forms into three major categories or historical periods, designated as symbolic, classical, and romantic. While his analyses of the first two epochs concentrated on sculpture, the third is characterized instead by its narrative forms, which are consequently examined in great detail.[1] Both the terms "romantic" and "narrative" are used in an unusually broad sense: for Hegel, the former begins with and is epitomized by the romances of the Middle Ages, while the latter is taken to include not merely written accounts of adventures but also pre-textualized undertakings, such as the Crusades. Although he situated it chronologically well ahead of his own time, the romantic period represented for Hegel the historical end of the aesthetic as a valid expression of human spirit or *Geist*, since he viewed it as characterized by a dismembering force that led to "the decay and dissolution of art itself [die Zerfallenheit und Auflösung der Kunst selbst]."[2] This fragmentation that brought down art itself, that had, in fact, already brought an end to the epoch of the aesthetic, was itself the result of an irreconcilable split between art, especially literature, and the subjective content it sought to represent, and it is this loss of meaning that is signified to the philosopher in the fragmentary structures and incoherences of romantic narratives. If Hegel's reaction to the increasingly manifest discrepancy between material aesthetic form and spiritual content was to denounce art as a valid expression of the latter, Nerval instead chose to pursue the subjective and experiential possibilities of a non-representational language, a language that had outlived the deaths both of the individual it was supposed to mean and of art itself as a representation of living spirit. In this posthumous poetics, he began to adumbrate the possibility of another construct of the subject, one that parts with the Hegelian tradition, not by looking death in the face, as Hegel had described the dialectical principle of world-history in the preface to the *Phenomenology of Spirit*, but by looking out through the face of death, by being death, by writing as the dead.[3] It is not surprising that the point at which their ways part should be a tomb—that of spirit itself.

While treating the Crusades as the fullest realization of romantic narrative structures, the *Aesthetics* also finds in their problematic apogee a revelation not of the limits of *Geist* itself but of the capacity of art to express it as coherent historical human subjectivity, and Hegel consequently describes them as the "collective adventure of the Christian Middle Ages; an adventure, inherently fragmentary [gebrochen], and fantastic."[4] Construed in this way by Hegel as a lived narrative, as a historical event cast as literary construct, the Crusades could be understood to offer a model for reconciling writing and experience, literature and life, abstract absolute and concrete individual, a reconciliation that would give a central phenomenological importance both to Nerval's assertions that he consciously organized his life as a novel and to the whole project of the *Faux Saulniers*.[5] Instead they are taken as a paradigm for precisely the opposite: the disclosed inadequation between the aesthetic and the spiritual, between literature as formal expression and spiritual content to be expressed. Their fragmentation is the symptom of a deeper failing: their inability to integrate life and its manifestation. Their *Gebrochenheit* is thus again the Foucaultian moment of madness in Nerval and Hölderlin, the impossibility of mediating immediately between the immediacy of experience, of the individual in the plenitude of life, and the abstract mediation of language. Under this pressure they fall to pieces, for there is nothing left to hold them together, no living individual, no stable and authentic underlying meaning. They have become an empty tomb, an epitaph for no one, a memory without a remembered. Consequently, for Hegel the Crusades are "of a spiritual tendency, and yet devoid of a truly spiritual aim," because

> Christendom is supposed to have its salvation in the spirit alone, in Christ who, risen, has ascended to the right hand of God and has his living actuality, his abode, in the Spirit, not in his grave [the Holy Sepulchre] and in the visible immediately present places where once he had his temporal abode.[6]

The Crusaders' mistake was to seek redemption—the reconciliation between their individual existences and the divine absolute—through immediate physical contact with the material remains of Spirit, that is, by attempting to recapture Jerusalem, instead of somehow through Spirit itself. It is precisely this substitution of outside for inside, of tomb for spirit, of material trace for spiritual meaning, that makes, according to Hegel, for the "fragmentary and fantastic" tone of the Crusades. From this it follows:

> In these opposed elements [the accidents of individual behavior not unified by a true spiritual goal], deeds and events with one and the same end turn out after all to lack all unity and consistency of leadership: the whole collection of Crusaders was scattered, split away into adventures, victories, defeats, and various accidents, and the outcome does not correspond to the means used and the great preparations made. Indeed the aim itself is cancelled by its achievement.[7]

As a paradigm for romantic art in general, and for romantic narrative in particular, the Crusades represent a destructive concentration on the particularity and substantiality of signs, a moribund and deadly literalism that annihilates what it would represent. For the absence of the living Christ from the Holy Sepulchre is itself only an emblem for another, more fundamental absence that, according to Hegel, ails romantic art in general, and leads ineluctably to its fragmentary incoherence: the absence of the living Spirit from its work.

> As we have seen several times already, a fundamental characteristic of romantic art is that spirituality, the mind as reflected into itself, constitutes a whole and therefore it is related to the external not as to its own reality permeated by itself, but as to something purely external separated from it, a place where everything goes on released from spirit into independence, and which is a scene of complications and the rough and tumble of an endlessly flowing, mutable, and confusing contingency.[8]

Romantic art thus reveals a split inherent in the aesthetic, a split between living spirit, or self-knowing soul, and its expression; this mutual externality, this separation leads to a fragmentation of art into an incoherent materiality, which, in turn, not merely fails to express spiritual content adequately, but somehow actually annihilates it. And at the same time, very curiously, as spirit is killed by the letter, the latter, material representation, takes on a life (or afterlife) of its own. It goes its own way as a fluid, complicated, and contingent objectivity. The art object, as object, lives on after the death of spirit, after the death of the subject, as something fragmentary, fluid, and mobile. Where these two paths separate is also where Nerval and Hegel part company. The latter will try to find other models of adequate spiritual self-expression, while Nerval will turn to examine in his poetry the afterlife of the object, the restless, mobile ways of the signifier. The subject, accepted now in its pure propositionality as a radicalization or literalization of the Kantian apperceptive subject, will be construed, quite rigorously, as an art object, and dead literature will be shown to lead an afterlife as the self-sameness of the self, as individual identity.

The Abstract World of Nerval's Early Poems

If Hegel was concerned with universal Spirit, the totality of human experience in its overarching coherence, while Nerval concentrated on the experiences of a single individual—himself—the latter's tendencies toward megalomania, combined with his questioning of the relation between himself and an objective world, tended to narrow and periodically abolish that difference of scope between the two writers. This is particularly evident in works such as the poem "Le Christ aux Oliviers" (Christ on the Mount of Olives), where Nerval speaks in the voice of Christ to declare the immanence of his own death and the consequent annihilation of all creation. The vacant first person of this poem, originally published in 1844 (some seven years before *Les Faux Saulniers*) represents a particularly significant moment in Nerval's exploration of written subjectivity, not merely because of his grandiose pretensions and their Hegelian scale, but also because it represents an evacuation of the speaking subject accompanied by a movement toward a poetics that describes itself as the impersonal and incoherent verbal remains of an abolished subject, the beginning of attempts by Nerval not to avoid his own death in writing, but somehow to write *after* it, in the vacuum of a lost subjectivity and coherence. Thematically the poem represents a development of images that had, since Nerval's earliest verse works, been used to represent his subjective relation to an objective world, but it also opens the way to the impersonal, disjunctive poetic description of the subject which forms the material of his last sonnets. As, over the course of his life, Nerval's poetry grew to embrace death and to recognize an isolation of the lyric "I" from any nonlinguistic referent, the triumph of death over life accompanied by a willingness to continue writing after that death, he was also moving toward a high point in the self-disclosure of written subjectivity. In this sense, the late sonnet "El Desdichado" constitutes a culmination of the self-representation undertaken in prose works like *Les Faux Saulniers*. In order, however, to appreciate the sonnet's relation to such nonlyrical works, one must be able to read its imagery and allusions, and this can be done only by situating it in the context of Nerval's earlier poetry.

The only instance of poetic juvenilia that Nerval published again later, the poem "Pensée de Byron" (Thinking of Byron) first appeared in print in the *Élégies nationales* of 1827, when Nerval was nineteen years old, and was incorporated some twenty-five years later into the feuilleton *Petits Châteaux (Bohême galante)* of 1852, and again, the following year, into the book *Petits Châteaux de Bohême*. The poem introduces the germ of a theme which would remain with Nerval throughout his life, a fact that may account for the unique significance he attached to it, for it sketches out the idea of a void standing between the author and something else. Reflecting on his unrequited love for an unnamed woman, he writes: "L'espérance a fui comme un songe… / Et mon amour seul m'est resté! / Il est resté comme un abîme / Entre ma vie et le bonheur."[9] This image of an absence (*abîme*) interfering with the author's appreciation of something else underwent a significant elaboration when in 1831, at the age of 23, Nerval published a poem entitled "Le Soleil et la gloire" (The sun and glory), also later republished in the *Petits Châteaux (Bohême galante)*, and *Petits Châteaux de Bohême*, under the title "Le Point noir" (The black dot). An adaptation of a sonnet by the German poet Bürger which Nerval had translated in his *Poésies allemandes* of 1830, the poem evidently maintained some validity or force over the course of his life, causing him to translate and then adapt it at the beginning of his literary career, then, two decades later, at the end of his life, to republish it, then republish it again. While the poem remained substantially the same over the years, its significance changed and developed in respect to the shifting context of its author's further literary production, and certain of his later poems, including his most famous, "El Desdichado," by readopting and reworking its themes and imagery can be seen to represent various exegeses of its fundamental poetic and subjective insights. The poem clarifies the nature of the disruption between the *I* and his "happiness," which had been touched on in "Pensée de Byron," by working it into a figure for the difference between subjective and objective worlds:

> Quiconque a regardé le soleil fixement
> Croit voir devant ses yeux voler obstinément
> Autour de lui, dans l'air, une tache livide.
>
> Ainsi, tout jeune encore et plus audacieux,
> Sur la gloire un instant j'osai fixer les yeux:
> Un point noir est resté dans mon regard avide.

Depuis, mêlée à tout comme un signe de deuil,
Partout, sur quelque endroit que s'arrête mon œil,
Je la vois se poser aussi, la tache noire!

Quoi, toujours? Entre moi sans cesse et le bonheur!
Oh! c'est que l'aigle seul—malheur à nous, malheur!—
Contemple impunément le Soleil et la Gloire.

Whoever has stared fixedly at the sun
Seems to see around him, before his eyes, in the air,
A livid stain that obstinately flies.

And so, still young, I too audaciously
Dared for a moment to fix my gaze on glory:
In my avid sight a blackened spot still remains.

Since then, always included like a sign of mourning
Everywhere, on whatever place my eye should stop,
I see it also rest, the blackened spot!

What, forever? Between me always and happiness!
Oh! It's that the eagle alone—alas for us, alas!—
Can contemplate the Sun and Glory without harm.[10]

Over everything the poet considers another image superposes itself, distorting his perception of the world and his basic subject-object relationships. This blinding image is the mark left by an earlier experience, that of contemplating another object, glory, which in its effect on the intelligence is compared to the sun in its effect on the eye. What thus interposes itself everywhere, forever coming between the "me" and everything else (*tout*, *partout*) is not a thing itself, not the sun or glory, but the sign (*signe*) of a thing, and specifically, the sign of its absence, a "sign of mourning" which not only signifies a signified (glory or the sun), but also signifies it *as a thing that is absent*, as a dead thing, something that must be mourned. To pursue the solar metaphor, what is represented by the dark spot is the sun, an experiencing of the sun, and the absence of those two things; and the sun, as that which permits all visibility, is the possibility of perceiving other things, the punctual, concentrated potential for seeing at all, visibility *in abstractu*, and the act of looking at the sun is the act of looking at vision itself. As the sun is to the world of visible objects, so is glory to the world of what one might call "good" or "happy" objects, for it obstructs the perception of all items on which the poet rests his attention, coming between his "me" and "happiness." What is universally perceived is not objects, but the impossibility of happiness, the absence (or afterimage) of the possibility of happiness, and the poet, consequently, can perceive no object in its objectivity but sees only the sign he bears subjectively in his cognition itself. Furthermore, he can see no object in its particularity, since the "point" superposes itself over all that is detached from the generality of the objective world, over everything that would otherwise be grasped punctually in its isolation from the continuity of its spatial surroundings or the flow of time. The loss of vision derives from fixing the sun for an instant (*un instant*) and reappears whenever the eye stops (*s'arrête*); the poet can only register the objective world as constantly in motion, without isolated objects or individual points, which is to say as a cognizable whole without cognizable parts, or, in other words, abstractly. He perceives the world only as a generality punctuated at a center that corresponds objectively to the poet's subjectively central position, always following his gaze and inscribing it into his surroundings as the sign of the loss of the particular. The mark of loss is the mark of the poet in the objective world, for the black "point" corresponds to his punctual subjectivity, his particularity: it memorializes a moment of his life; it mixes (*mêler*) his subjective perceptual defect into the objective world; it traces his viewpoint across that world, ceaselessly following his gaze; and it forms the only articulation in that abstracted objective world, offering a center point that corresponds to the subject's position in the world he perceives. The eye, or the inner eye, in thus continuously marking the subject onto an abstracted objectivity, marks him only as a sign of something that is gone. The "point noir" thus constitutes an inscription of the subject onto an apparently objective surface, an autobiography in its simplest, brute state, but an autobiography that can only be read by its author, since the surface on which the inscription is made lies in the perception of objectivity, not in the objective realm itself.

Poetry of an Incoherent World

Nerval returns to the metaphors and themes of these early poems in "Le Christ aux Oliviers," a series of five interconnected sonnets first published in 1844 and later included among the *Chimères* of the 1854 *Filles du feu*. Here, he develops the idea in its epigraph "God is dead! the heavens are empty" (quoted from the German poet Jean Paul) into an inward, psychological drama of cosmic significance. The poem depicts Christ in the garden of Gethsemane at the moment when, certain of his impending material death, he casts into doubt the existence of a spiritual life or of a higher significance to the world than is already immanent in it. Nerval insists on Christ's dual identity as God and representative of God, describing him in the poem's opening line as "the Lord" but then emphasizing his materiality with a reference to "his thin arms" and his individuation from the godhead with a reference to his supplicant position before the divine ("raising his thin arms to the sky"). This paradoxical duality of an incarnate god, both lord and supplicant, who addresses himself as another in prayer and can throw that other, divine, truer existence into doubt, forms what one might call the epistemological spine of the poem, for it allows Nerval to articulate the relation between subjective and objective worlds, which he had already begun to examine in previous works, from the position of the one historical individual for whom those two realms were at once separate and legitimately identical, in respect to whom all objectivity—even in the eyes of others—is a modality of subjectivity. The "I" of the poem no longer expresses the first person of a particular individual in face of the universal and the objective; instead, it now expresses an absolute subjectivity, something like the absolute Spirit that passes through progressive stages of objective self-knowledge in Hegel's *Phenomenology*. This subject not *in* but *of* history is compared to a poet:

> Quand le Seigneur, levant au ciel ses maigres bras,
> Sous les arbres sacrés, comme font les poètes,
> Se fut longtemps perdu dans ses douleurs muettes,
> Et se jugea trahi par des amis ingrats;
>
> Il se tourna vers ceux qui l'attendaient en bas
> Rêvant d'être des rois, des sages, des prophètes…
> Mais engourdis, perdus dans le sommeil des bêtes,
> Et se prit à crier: "Non, Dieu n'existe pas!"
>
> Ils dormaient . . .
>
> When the Lord, raising his thin arms to the sky
> Beneath the sacred trees, had lost himself,
> As poets do, in voiceless pains
> And judged himself betrayed by thankless friends,
>
> He turned towards those who awaited him below
> Dreaming of a future as kings, sages, prophets…
> But numbly, lost in a bestial sleep,
> And he set to crying, "No, God does not exist!"
>
> They slept on . . . [11]

The act of supplication to a higher sense than can be found in the world is somehow poetic, for the gesture is made "as poets do," and the series of sonnets thus not only examines the relation of absolute subjectivity to itself, but also takes as its starting point a poetic stance. Absolute self-knowledge, however terrible its consequences may prove to be in these sonnets, begins poetically in a gesture toward a higher meaning. But Christ, in this posture, does not address the divine in words, and if he poetizes, it is silently, for he is "lost in voiceless pains." He finds words only when he turns from God, when he abandons the poetic stance and faces his followers, but in turning from one void he encounters another, for his followers have fallen into a bestial sleep, and the expression of his insight, his discovery of the meaninglessness of the world-historical poetic stance, falls only on his own ears. The painful silence of the poet before the loss of an absolute meaning is put into words, but they communicate nothing, because there is no one to receive them, neither god nor human being. Addressing his sleeping disciples in the last tercet of the first sonnet, Christ proceeds to describe his experience of God's nonexistence, using three times—almost talismanically, as if there were no other possible expression for it, as if language had come to a stuttering halt—the word that Nerval had employed in "Pensée de Byron" to describe his relation to the world:

> Ils dormaient. "Mes amis, savez-vous *la nouvelle*?
> J'ai touché de mon front à la voûte éternelle;
> Je suis sanglant, brisé, souffrant pour bien des jours!
>
> Frères, je vous trompais: Abîme! abîme! abîme!
> Le dieu manque à l'autel, où je suis la victime...
> Dieu n'est pas! Dieu n'est plus!" Mais ils dormaient toujours!

> They slept on. "My friends, have you heard *the news*?
> With my brow I've touched the eternal vault;
> I am bleeding, broken, and sick for days on end!
>
> Brothers, I deceived you: Abyss! abyss! abyss!
> I am victim at an altar that has no god...
> God is not! God is no more!" But still they slept!

The expression "God is dead" indicates that the god who has died never existed, for it effaces the distinction between the human and the divine; as Kojève writes, "there are no *mortal* gods."[12] But to say that God is dead or no more, rather than simply "God does not exist," indicates that even if God never existed, he has somehow been withdrawn, that his nonbeing is perceived as a loss. While the earlier poems represented a relative absence, something (love and glory) which was missing in respect to the poet but could be found elsewhere by others, Nerval here confronts an absolute absence, the disappearance of something that is nowhere and never was. Like the afterimage of the sun in "Point noir" this absolute absence is perceived as a mark left on the eye, and the description of this ultimate "sign of mourning" constitutes one of the most powerful and—ironically—visionary moments in Nerval's writings. The second sonnet of the poem is a reprise of the insight offered in the opening one and consists of Christ's expression to his sleeping disciples of his experiences while in the "mute agonies" of the poetic stance:

> Il reprit: "Tout est mort! J'ai parcouru les mondes;
> Et j'ai perdu mon vol dans leurs chemins lactés,
> Aussi loin que la vie, en ses veines fécondes,
> Répand des sables d'or et des flots argentés:
>
> Partout le sol désert côtoyé par des ondes,
> Des tourbillons confus d'océans agités...
> Un souffle vague émeut les sphères vagabondes,
> Mais nul esprit n'existe en ces immensités.
>
> En cherchant l'œil de Dieu, je n'ai vu qu'un orbite
> Vaste, noir et sans fond; d'où la nuit qui l'habite
> Rayonne sur le monde et s'épaissit toujours;
>
> Un arc-en-ciel étrange entoure ce puits sombre,
> Seuil de l'ancien chaos dont le néant est l'ombre,
> Spirale, engloutissant les Mondes et les Jours!"

> He began again: "All is dead! I've travelled across worlds;
> And I've lost my flight in their milky ways,
> As far as life, in its quickening veins,
> Spreads golden sands and silver tides:
>
> Everywhere the desert strand fringed in waves,
> And the confused swirlings of troubled seas...
> A vague breath moves the vagabond spheres,
> But no spirit exists in these immensities.
>
> In seeking God's eye, I found only a socket,
> Vast, black, and bottomless, from which an inhabitant night
> Spreads over the world ever-thickening beams;
>
> A weird rainbow circles round this dismal well,
> The threshold once of chaos, whose shadow is the void,
> A spiral swallowing Worlds and Days!"

What seemed to be signs of life, the products, like oceans and golden sands, of its fecund veins, has been revealed to be dead, empty (*désert*) and in a state of agitated confusion. The wind that blows over the face of the world and moves its spheres, bearing momentarily a promise of life, is itself empty (*vague*), and the *spiritus* (*esprit*), or animated breath, which it suggests does not exist. Breath itself is vacant and dead, and the poet's words too, therefore, are borne like planets in a vacuous confusion that only seems alive, that is hollow at its center. These empty words turn, in the tercets, to describe that empty center, and the imagery shifts from the pneumatic to the visual. What Christ was looking for is made explicit: in the poetic stance he had been seeking God's eye, the divine viewpoint, the perspective around which the absolute subject organizes his perception and cognition of the world. By making his God cyclopean, in giving him but one eye (reduced later to one empty socket), Nerval offers an image of the divine view-point as a unique center for the universe, a solitary and unified position for thinking it in its entirety. This absolute subject, this cognitive unity of the world, like the errant wind and the poet's voice, is lifeless; but although it is in a certain fundamental sense hollow, it is not precisely empty, and the poet-savior describes what he has found looking into the empty eye of God. The eyeless socket is described as a dark well inhabited by night, but this nocturnal darkness, this nothingness is itself not the farthest reach in his exploration of God's death, for the void is only a dark image, a shadow cast by something else which Nerval calls "l'ancien chaos." As far as can be seen, literally, the unified intelligibility of the world, the absolute subject, has been lost to a fundamental disorder, and the poet has discovered that the world and his words are at bottom incoherent.

The image of a hollow eye socket radiating darkness over the world recalls and recasts the "point noir" of Nerval's earlier poem, but in "Le Christ aux Oliviers," the poet considers the blinding mark of absence not from a subjective viewpoint, as he did before, but from an objective one. The poem's epistemological spine, as has been remarked, is the dual status of Christ as subject of the world and as objective event in that world, as Lord and supplicant. Like the "livid stain" that floats as a sign of the subject in the objective world of "le point noir," inscribing that subject and his viewpoint into his surroundings, Christ incarnate is a projection into the objective world of the divine, absolute subject; he is himself the "stain" on God's eye. It is the floating spot of the earlier poem that now speaks in the first person; it is the subject objectified into the world that expresses itself in this sonnet, and what it expresses is the death of its own central, coherent subjectivity. All that remains, all that speaks and poetizes here *is* objectivity, and all it expresses is the loss of the coherent subject, its replacement by the contingent, the chaotic, the incoherent. All that remains of the subject is its expression, its objectification, the fragmentary "news" of its nonexistence. What is new here is not an atheism. This is not merely an atheistic poem, for there can be other, nondivine orders to the universe; the poem is more troubling, for it does not replace God with another structure, such as dialectically progressive *Geist*. What is new is the idea of a subject that would always have been speaking after its own death and that could lucidly express its own fundamental incoherence, a subject whose incoherence would not be violated by its poetic textualization but would instead be preserved by it. It is the position of one who recognizes that self-verbalization is death but continues to speak of himself, and in speaking elaborate himself.

The scene in the garden of Gethsemane is only a *moment* of doubt, but Nerval has his Christ, as he emerges from it, wonder whether it is a moment that can ever be reconnected with time; whether, in some sense, it has not brought time to a standstill, making any further events illusory. At the beginning of the third sonnet, the poet apostrophizes what remains after the death of God with a triple appellation: *Destin*, *Nécessité*, *Hasard*. When the first two can also go under the name of the third, it means that the direction and force of events in time have been given over to chance, with one moment aleatorically succeeding another, and the first-person Christ raises the question of whether order can be reborn out of this aimless succession, whether the chaotic subject can transmit an immortal breath from the old, dead order to a new one. Christ's words continue:

Immobile Destin, muette sentinelle,
Froide Nécessité!... Hasard qui, t'avançant,
Parmi les mondes morts sous la neige éternelle,
Refroidis, par degrés l'univers pâlissant,

Sais-tu ce que tu fais, puissance originelle,
De tes soleils éteints, l'un l'autre se froissant...
Es-tu sûr de transmettre une haleine immortelle,
Entre un monde qui meurt et l'autre renaissant?...

O mon père! est-ce toi que je sens en moi-même?

Unmoving Fate, mute sentinel,
Cold Necessity!... Chance who, advancing
Among worlds that lie dead beneath eternal snows,
Chills, by degrees, the paling universe,

Do you know what you are doing, primal force,
With your burnt-out suns jostling one another...
Are you sure to transmit an immortal breath,
From a dying world to another being born again?...

Father! is it you whom I feel in myself?

These quatrains offer a glimmer of hope, but express it only in a question. The possibility is raised that the breath of life, the center and guarantor of coherence, can be passed from the deceased divine order to a new one; that a living, organized world can be born from another; and that from the death of a first universal subject a second one will arise. Were this the case, death, rather than immortality, would be proven illusory, would appear as a moment in life, a stage of dialectical negativity in the forward progression of living self-knowledge and time. This possibility, however, arises only out of the question of whether life can be *transmitted*, that is to say, sent over or communicated, across an abyss of death; whether the forward, linear, coherent progression of time can connect two instants across a moment that has been withdrawn from time; whether life can send itself out into death and timelessness and later reestablish itself.

The concerns motivating these questions and the understanding of life, temporality, and transmission which they reveal bear a precise resemblance to the concerns about writing, subjectivity, and death which arose in certain of Nerval's prose works such as *Un Roman à faire*, published in 1842, two years before "Le Christ aux Oliviers."[13] There, Nerval had spoken of a waylaid letter and a lock of hair sent from one person now dead to another, a letter that had been written by one in life to another in life but that got caught in its transmission, that never reached its intended audience, that continued, as if subtracted from time, to repeat the same words across the passing moments, and that survived after both its addressor and addressee had disappeared into the anonymity of death. There, Nerval had wondered how much life remained in the letter, how that life could best be preserved and nurtured, how best it could be brought to reveal and express itself, and ultimately he had argued for preserving the document as a suggestive fragment. Here, in "Le Christ aux Oliviers," he confronts a message from a similar moment, a voice of a vanished living world lost in transmission among the timeless dead, offered to another living world that may never exist. Unlike the letter in *Un Roman à faire*, however, the voice of the poem actually addresses the status of the misplaced moment by openly articulating the disjunctive temporality of its present, by thematizing its own waylaid condition, and by speaking in the awareness that it expresses a dead subjectivity. It identifies itself, in short, as a post-subjective self-consciousness.

After the third sonnet's octave questions whether order can be (re)established among the random juxtapositions of aimless, vagabond spheres in an atomistic world, the sestet has the poet-savior identify the vessel to which divinity, the "immortal breath," has been entrusted: he himself is its bearer.

> O mon père! est-ce toi que je sens en moi-même?
> As-tu pouvoir de vivre et de vaincre la mort?
> Aurais-tu succombé sous un dernier effort
>
> De cet ange des nuits que frappa l'anathème...
> Car je me sens tout seul à pleurer et souffrir,
> Hélas! et si je meurs, c'est que tout va mourir!

> Father! is it you whom I feel in myself?
> Have you the power to live and to conquer death?
> Or have you succumbed beneath a final attempt
>
> Of that angel of night whom anathema smote?...
> For I feel alone in my pain and my tears,
> Alas! and if I die, so will all else die too!

In so identifying himself, Christ also reestablishes himself as an object among others, as the site of the objectification of the divine after the death of the divine, coherent subject. Without being able to resolve the question of whether the transmission has been successful, whether God the Father has been consigned, living, to an object in the world, the son is able to establish the significance of His having been *un*successful. The moment of doubt has questioned whether death underlies life, or whether life underlies death—which, in an etymological sense, is the subject of the world. More radically, it has raised the possibility that no such subject exists, that the world is bottomless and without center, for it has also asked whether a fundamental coherence underlies apparent disorder, or whether coherence is only a contingent illusion; it has entertained the doubt that there exist connections among the atomistic particulars of the objective world, and proposed, conversely, that they may be so many independent fragments among which no coherent transmission can be made. If Christ does not bear the "immortal breath," then the moment of doubt, of subjectlessness and death, will be eternalized, time will be proven a fiction, it will be established that there is not, and consequently never was, immortality. It is in this sense that the sonnet's final line is to be construed: if the vessel is empty, if life cannot be transmitted in death, then everything, sooner or later, will die. The words "if I die, so will all else die too" do not represent an apocalyptic vision of the abrupt end of the world, rather they recognize that nothing will be immune to reverting to the incoherent fundamental state underlying being itself and that there is no subject or history to the world. Among these objective fragments of an incoherent world one distinguishes itself as the self-conscious voice of the poem; but what makes the poet-savior distinct, what characterizes him, is his status as what could be called, oxymoronically, an absolute fragment, because he is here something whose self-identity expresses itself as an awareness of its own incompleteness and incoherence, as something that cannot be thought in its specificity and unique difference except as incomplete, and yet for which there exists no whole into which to be integrated. To poetize oneself this way is to situate nonidentity—lack, loss, difference—at the core and ground of self-identity, and to dissolve the self-sameness of both subject and individual. Not only are the latter different from each other, they are different from themselves, and at the heart of the same—of the *moi-même*—there is no heart, no *même*.

In the poem's last two sonnets the position of the first person shifts, and, except for a quatrain in which he calls for Judas to betray him, the voice of Christ falls silent as the poem continues in a third-person narrative interrupted twice by the brief, first-person exclamations of Pontius Pilate and Caesar. Furthermore, the poet gradually retreats from the moment of hyberbolic doubt that was described in the first three sonnets, although, because of the complexities in Nerval's use of mythological reference, the final status of Christ after his immolation remains ambiguous at the poem's end. Thus, while the meaning of the reference to "l'éternelle victime" in the first line of the fourth sonnet, coming as it does immediately after the climax of doubt, remains for the moment undecided—is he eternal because caught in the supratemporality of the Godhead, or because, in the moment of doubt, time has lapsed and events no longer lead from one another but stand unconnected and as if arrayed in space like planets?—the opening quatrain of the fifth and final sonnet identifies the sacrificed poet-savior with Greek mythological characters to whom Nerval seems to attribute a triumph over death. After a fourth sonnet that depicts Christ's appeal to Judas to betray him, Judas's refusal, and Pilate's command: "Allez cherchez ce fou [Go fetch me this madman]," the octave of the final sonnet depicts the efforts of others—Pilate and Caesar—to make Christ speak, treating him and his death as a sort of oracle; but the poet-savior has returned to the muteness that marked the beginning of the poem.

C'était bien lui, ce fou, cet insensé sublime…
Cet Icare oublié qui remontait les cieux,
Ce Phaéton perdu sous la foudre des dieux,
Ce bel Atys meurtri que Cybèle ranime!

It is indeed he, this madman, this sublime lunatic…
This forgotten Icarus who climbed the skies,
This Phaëton lost beneath bolts of heavenly fire
This beautiful, broken Attis whom Cybele revives!

It is difficult to determine what degree of ambiguity should be read in Nerval's use of the references to Icarus, Phaëton, and Attis. On a mythological level they offer at best a very troubling idea of rebirth. The Icarus myth, as recounted by Isidore of Seville, Hyginus, and Ovid, makes no mention of a resurrection or a second journey to the skies;[14] and it seems as if Nerval sought, after the original publication, to minimize the possibility of interpreting the line as a reference to such a second ascension, changing the original wording "qui remontait *aux* cieux" of the first edition to "qui remontait *les* cieux" in subsequent ones. "Remonter aux" implies "to climb again to" whereas "remonter les cieux," with the verb used transitively, has the sense of traveling not *again* but *against* the normal flow of something, as in a movement toward a source; thus the later version could be a reference to Icarus's one known flight, described as the fatal attempt to scale the heavens to the source of life. Similarly, the character of Phaëton, who was entrusted by his father Helius one day with the chariot of the sun and who was subsequently destroyed by one of Zeus's thunderbolts when his inability to govern his horses threatened to set the earth on fire, does not represent in the myths a figure of rebirth, and Nerval gives little indication in the poem, except by the context, that he should be understood in such terms here.[15] The case of Attis is more complex. In what is referred to as the "Phrygian" version of the myth, Attis does attain, in a certain sense, to immortality, but even there it is of a very limited and questionable sort. Giulia Gasparro has described the aspect of renewal in this myth with the following words:

> Unlike the Lydian version, however, the accounts of Pausanias and Arnobius contain an attempt to modify this doleful conclusion [the death of Attis] by reviving Attis. Although this does not actually take place, a form of survival after death is indeed accorded to him: his body does not decay and his hair continues to grow while a finger remains in motion, a sign that Attis is not completely dead.
>
> So if we cannot talk of the youth's return to life or "resurrection," the mythical tradition attested by the two authors has an outcome which, even if it is characterized by *pathos* and by mourning, guarantees a positive prospect for Attis, since he is saved from complete annihilation. In this manner the youth obtains a subsistence beyond death, or rather what we would be entitled to call a subsistence "in death."[16]

If, in literature, these three myths offer nothing by the slimmest, most macabre suggestion of rebirth or immortality, they are nonetheless very closely associated with those ideas in mystic and ritual traditions. All three have been identified with the figure of the *interrex*, the youth chosen annually as a surrogate king to be sacrificed at the close of a one-day reign after which the true king would return from hiding in a simulated resurrection.[17] The myth of Attis gave rise, in fact, to the Roman festival of the Hilaria, a week-long celebration of death, renewal, and rebirth which took place in March and probably constituted a model for the Christian rites of Easter.[18] Perhaps the most striking aspect of the Hilaria was, however, the violent ritual self-castration of the Corybants, or followers of Cybele, figures who will reappear in the last fragmentary pages of *Aurélia*, and here again, the idea of rebirth, even at its most celebratory, is associated with that of damage and centralized loss and with the impossibility of transmitting life from generation to generation.[19] As a whole, although the use of the word *ranime* or "revives" in the last line of the first quatrain suggests that the figure of Attis is to be taken in its positive ritualistic sense, rather than in its negative literary one, and the entire passage seems intended to bring closure to the hyperbolic doubt of the preceding sonnets through an affirmation of life over death, the choice of mythological characters remains a curious and ambiguous one; they seem closely associated with ideas of resurrection, but offer only the hope of a grim, mutilated afterlife.

The poem ends with a mutism similar to that which began it. Again the savior-poet has fallen silent in an experience of death, and the first person of the poem is passed on to his successors, but now, at the poem's close, he no longer attempts or is able to bring utterance to that experience. Unlike the scene in the first sonnet, it is the audience, not Christ, who attempt to establish some communication; far from falling asleep, they try to question the divine, to read it:

> L'augure interrogeait le flanc de la victime,
> La terre s'enivrait de ce sang précieux…
> L'univers étourdi penchait sur ses essieux,
> Et l'Olympe un instant chancela vers l'abîme.
>
> Réponds! criait César à Jupiter Ammon,
> Quel est ce nouveau dieu qu'on impose à la terre?
> Et si ce n'est un dieu, c'est au moins un démon…
>
> Mais l'oracle invoqué pour jamais dut se taire;
> Un seul pouvait au monde expliquer ce mystère:
> —Celui qui donna l'âme aux enfants du limon.

> The augur questioned the victim's flank,
> The earth was drunk with his precious blood…
> The stunned universe tilted on its axis
> And Olympus for a moment teetered over the abyss.

> "Answer!" cried Caesar to Jupiter Ammon,
> "What is this new god imposed on the earth?
> And if not divine, then at least it's a demon..."
>
> But the oracle invoked had forever been silenced;
> One alone could explain to the world this mystery:
> —He who gave a soul to the creatures of dust.

The victim represented here is not necessarily Christ himself, although that is possible on a metaphorical level—and is in fact somewhat predetermined by earlier references to him as "the victim" (sonnet 1) and "the eternal victim" (sonnet 4). What is significant here is the silence that has overtaken the earth. The voice of the poet-savior has fallen mute, and the oracles will never speak again, while the moment of hyperbolic doubt is recalled in the "instant" during which Olympus wobbles eccentrically on its axis. But the poetic stance that questions the coherence of the world is taken up by another, by one whose being, unlike Christ's, does not articulate between the objective and subjective worlds, and who can never, consequently, affirm to himself a universal coherence through his own existence. Caesar, like anyone who is not Christ but nonetheless inquires as a poet into the identity of the world subject, must await a sign from the only one who can say whether there is immortality and central coherence—an eye and an axis—to the world. The poem identifies who that individual is: Christ, the doubter. But the poem does not give an answer, withholding at the end his voice and even the sign of his survival. All that remains is a lifeless object, a body with a mute flank. And in this respect, by explicitly refusing to answer the question that it explicitly poses, the poem never really emerges from the moment of hyperbolic doubt. The subject that it presents remains unresolved: absolutely fragmentary and different from itself. Like the answer to the question of coherence, like atomic particles in a liquid, the self of this poem remains in suspension, ungrounded. In a world from which the *souffle*, or breath, of Spirit has passed, the "I" has found its identity in its own inadequacy to itself, and in so doing it has taken leave of those mimetic models of subjectivity that underlie Hegel's concept of *Geist*'s self-manifestation. It has turned to the afterlife of empty words, empty eye sockets, empty flanks: pillaged tombs, in short.

The poet-savior is characterized as mad. He is referred to twice in rapid succession as "fou" (in the last line of the fourth sonnet and the first line of the fifth) and then as "cet insensé sublime." These epithets suggest a discreet autobiographical turn to the poem, an identification between the author and the figure of Christ that extends beyond the savior's poetlike posture in the first line, for they repeat a vocabulary that had come to be associated with Nerval himself and with his particular variety of eccentricity. In a letter to Jules Janin of August 24, 1841, three years before he published "Le Christ aux Oliviers," Nerval had responded with some bitterness to the account of his mental breakdown published in the *Journal des Débats*.

> for seven months I have passed for *a madman* [*pour fou*] thanks to your March 1 necrological entry.... I am, as always, no less grateful than touched to pass for a *sublime madman* [*fou sublime*], thanks to you, Théophile, Thierry, Lucas, etc., I shall never be able to present myself anywhere, never marry, never make people listen to me seriously [me faire écouter sérieusement].[20]

The identification between the poet-savior and Nerval is reinforced by the latter's perceived inability to make himself heard ("me faire écouter sérieusement") and its resemblance to his insistence, in the poem, on the bestial sleep that prevents Christ's disciples from hearing him, Judas's indifference to his plea to be betrayed, and the victim's final muteness. Moreover, the same themes that appear in the sonnet sequence figure prominently in a collection of Nerval's notes to himself published four months after his death under the title "a notepad found on G. de N. the day of his death."[21] One fragment, which recalls the moment of hyperbolic doubt, reads: "The reign of God is over, it shall be born again.—Christ is the second love." Another fragment, the first in the published collection, shows Nerval situating himself in the specular relation which in "Le Christ aux Oliviers" allows an objectified self to observe his own death, although here the author sees himself objectified as God: "It seems to me that I am dead and that I am fulfilling this second life of God." The similarity among the Christ figure of the poem, the "fou sublime" from which Nerval wished to distance himself publicly, and the Nerval of the final carnet suggests that the poet-savior of "Le Christ aux Oliviers" represents a mode of alienated subjectivity which Nerval identified at least occasionally as his own, that the sonnet cycle is in part autobiographical, and that the poem's moment of hyperbolic doubt could be read as a dissimulated analysis of Nerval's 1841 bout of madness, an incident he would be able to recount openly only in 1854, when in the preface to the *Filles du feu* he described what he then referred to as his "descent into Hell" and in *Aurélia* he recounted the events of his passage through institutions for the insane.[22]

In "Le Christ aux Oliviers," madness appears as the visionary condition of the poet-savior, a moment of radical doubt, and the opening to a possible rebirth through the annihilation of subject, time, and coherence. It is a movement of primary self-investigation by which the subject, in a poetic stance, consigns himself to a lifeless objectivity where words are borne on an inanimate breath and the very principles governing the structure and intelligibility of the world are fragmented. When Nerval describes Christ as a "sublime" madman, the adjective should be taken in a strong and historical sense, for it is the romantic sublime that is making itself felt in these sonnets, the sublime that Kant describes as jeopardizing the particular individual by confronting it with the absolute, and which he sees best exemplified in the veiled image of Isis. The sublime madman is the individual who lifts the veil of Isis and views absolute death eye to eye—the death of the absolute and death as the only absolute in this world (that which underlies being itself, that which will consume all, when, as the poet-savior asserts, "tout va mourir"). According to Arsène Houssaye, Dr. Esprit Blanche, who treated Nerval in his sanitorium, would write later to the archbishop of Paris: "Your Grace, Gérard de Nerval hanged himself because he saw his madness face to face";[23] but the poem indicates, conversely, that Nerval went mad because he saw death face to face, that madness is precisely such a face-to-face encounter with the loss of coherence. It is a more radical sublime than Kant speaks of, for "Le Christ aux Oliviers" represents a confrontation not with the absolute, but with the loss of the absolute and its replacement by chaotic, atemporal fragmentation.

In reconsidering the specular structure of the subject and its objectification in "Le Christ aux Oliviers," it is apparent that the possibility that the divine subject *as divine subject* could die necessarily implies that the divine subject never existed (since immortality is inalienable from the deity), and that a God speaking after his own death is the speaking of a subject that could only ever have existed posthumously *in that very speaking*. In identifying, personally, with such a divine subject (as he seems to have done in the letter to Jules Janin and in the fragments from his notebook discussed above), Nerval identifies with a written subject that has no unwritten original. Moreover, the writing that figures here represents a radical loss of coherence, an afterlife in a subjectless, unintelligible, and chaotic world. The Nerval that is suggested in the notebook supposedly found on his body the day of his death and in "Le Christ aux Oliviers" is thus a fragmentary, written simulation of an unwritten original that never otherwise existed. By indicating that seemingly rational, coherent discourse is premised not on order but on chaos, the poem identifies an onto-epistemological status in which atomistic words are borne on a fundamentally lifeless breath and suggests the subsequent necessity of characterizing the poem itself by such a status. This inverts the romantic sublime by reasserting the dominance of the concrete individual over his linguistic annihilation insofar as the sensuous immediate cannot be reduced to abstraction within the conceptually universalizing mediation of writing. In asserting the fragmentation of the world and history and consequently of his poem, Nerval identifies language and reason not as an organizing mastery of the sensible world, but rather as subject to the "lawless chaos" and "wild incoherence" which for Schiller were the essential characteristics of nature and the material.[24] The writing subject has, in this poem, reasserted the immediacy of the sensuous within language, but at the cost of abandoning its claims to coherence and intelligibility. Rather than existing as the cognizable truth of an abolished individual, the poem offers itself as the material instantiation of an individual who, in order to live, has disappropriated himself as subject. This material instantiation was already signaled in the second sonnet by the talismanic use of the word "abyss," which only signifies the loss of intelligibility, the loss of the semantic itself. This self-disappropriating subject uses grammatical constructions of subjectivity, such as the first person pronoun, only to undermine their intelligibility and to lead the semantic level of the poem always back to the specificity of its material existence as linguistic artifact: this is a senseless, sensible subject that lives in linguistic death through an insistent incoherence. This is the reason too why Nerval's most famous, late sonnets remain firmly ensconced within the French literary tradition but at the same time frustrate, as we shall see, all attempts at their intelligibility: they lead back untiringly to their specific meaninglessness.

6. The Lyric First Person: "El Desdichado"

> Your Grace, Gérard de Nerval hanged himself because he saw his madness face to face.
>
> —*Arsène Houssaye*

> Le monde est plein de fous... et qui n'en veut pas voir
> Doit rester dans sa chambre et casser son miroir.
>
> —*Nerval*

The sonnet "El Desdichado," beginning with the first person pronoun, presents itself as a lyric self-identification and a sort of testament of its author. Nowhere else in the history of French literature have the words "I am... " been more puzzling than here. Nowhere else have these words so thrown self-identity and poetry into question. Although it opens with what seems to be a classic lyric statement of a speaking self unified under a single title and in respect to a unique object of desire, the poem soon shifts to modes of self-representation that proceed by detached details, allusions, and images, lent an almost Symbolist quality by their seeming independence and density of significance.[1] The mood moves from statement to imperative to question and back to statement while the punctuation, rhythm, and metrical caesurae of the sonnet take on a primary, quasi-semantic significance. It is a poem difficult to read in any detail, because it is arcane and allusive; and because of the terse way in which it draws on a personal symbolic language, elaborated from a complex network of various mythological and oneiric sources, which Nerval began to use more and more publicly in his last years. This hermetic aspect of the poem has undoubtedly contributed to its enduring relevance, as successive generations of critics have read it as an allegory of various subtexts—autobiographical events, esoteric knowledge, or the process of poetic inspiration—and have attempted to recover the key that would unlock its enigmas. What is most troubling about the sonnet, however, is the absence of such a key, for the poem, in a very meaningful way, does not make sense.

The Critical History: Imposing Unity

The body of work on this sonnet is vast. Some is excellent, and over the last sixty years or so, very considerable progress has been made in meticulously establishing the intertextual resonances, if not the meanings, that the poem's various epithets and symbols would have held for Nerval. Such readings have gone far in certifying the allusive richness of the poem and its lapidary density, but with few exceptions such interpretations have tended to slight the allegorical images in favor of what they represent, to read not the sonnet but through it; they have tended, in other words, to concentrate on the information imparted by the poem rather than on the process by which it is imparted, neglecting the way in which that information is poetically transformed. If Georges Le Breton's limited but influential reading of "El Desdichado" sees it as the encoded description of an alchemical process which "describes in allegorical form the different phases in the transmutation of base metals into gold,"[2] if Jean Richer conceives of it as a meditation on its author's natal horoscope, or Jacques Dhaenens takes it to be Nerval's account of an intuitively Hegelian passage through death to an enriched reunion with his muse, none of them satisfactorily explains the relation between the poetry and its encrypted narrative content, or whether that transformation could have an effect on its content; all seem to agree that the same meaning could be expressed in another form with no significant loss, that the message and its expression are separable. For such critics, and they are by far the majority, the subjective persona advanced in this poem is not essentially literary; it is only expressed literarily.

Le Breton, who speaks of the poem as an "enigma in the precise sense given the term by alchemical authors," does in fact make an attempt to account for the allegorization of its message, by contending at the end of his interpretation that "it was a matter of creating a hermetic poetry which would be taken for pure poetry and a literature which, once the key had been hidden, would be taken for dream literature."[3] It would be difficult, however, to agree with such a reading, which views the poetic interest of the sonnet, and the enduring fascination it has exercised over nonalchemists, as accidental. Moreover, by contending that the poem in its superficial unintelligibility gives the appearance of a "dream literature," Le Breton's analysis inadvertently signals how misleading such a neglect of the unallegorized (but allegorizing) and "purely poetic" aspects of the sonnet can be, for Nerval clearly and repeatedly articulated his interest in the language of dreams, in their effects on his writing and life, and in what he described as the "overflowing of dreams into real life."[4] The interpenetration of sense and nonsense, reason and unreason, madness and lucidity, dream and reality, which Le Breton identifies with the distinction between literary form and its content, was precisely that discursive region that most fascinated Nerval, especially at the late point in his life when "El Desdichado" was written. To speak of the dreamlike elements of the sonnet as an unanalyzable mask hiding a core narrative at once draws attention (by at least identifying them as such) to the importance of nonsense and the nonsemantic in this poem, and at the same time dismisses it. This process of encoding, allegorizing, and inscribing is itself, however, of primary significance in "El Desdichado," and the sonnet ultimately reveals itself to be a meditation on and an enactment of a purely written subjectivity.

This neglect of the most immediate face that the poem presents, the attempt to pass through it to the meaning it conceals, almost invariably entails for critics an impatient hermeneutic passage from an apparent, surface incoherence to a supposedly more profound and more legitimate unity. Rare is the critic who devotes more than a sentence or two to the significance of that most striking aspect of this poem, its uneasy fragmentariness; and yet almost all make some note of it.[5] Concerned, above all, with determining the semantic level of the poem, readers tend to dismiss its incoherence out of hand; one is left with the impression that literary criticism is fundamentally and endemically a process of synthesis rather than analysis. This apparent predisposition is raised to the status of postulate by Jacques Dhaenens when he argues, in his book-length study of "El Desdichado," for the a priori integrity of any significant work of art:

> We are, on the other hand, convinced that every great work presents its internal coherence, that it is only great to the extent that it conceals [recèle] a coherence. . . .
>
> This coherence exists in art, it exists in society insofar as it is a collectivity, it does not exist in the life of individual men. The artist subsequently feels the absence of coherence as the void to be filled by a work and his finished project thereupon becomes the work of a collectivity (coherent even if not always clearly drawn [bien dessinée]).[6]

If the sonnet, or any great work of art, hides its coherence, as Dhaenens contends, and if that coherence can be described as "internal," the only explanation can be that such works are not manifestly coherent and that they are in fact superficially incoherent. The critic accounts for this divergence between apparent and underlying form by establishing a difference between coherence and its literary expression: the fundamental unity of a work may not be immediately visible because the text that embodies it is not "bien dessiné." It is worth noting how little critical thinking on literary incoherence has changed in the century between Théophile Gautier and Jacques Dhaenens, for much as the romantic poet had seen the difference between Nerval's lucid writing and his madness as the stylistic variance between an unflawed and an overly elliptical account of the same essentially consequent narrative, Dhaenens describes the distinction between fragmentary form and coherent message as a defect of execution, an inadequation between expression and what is to be expressed.

Dhaenens expands on the relation between the subject and coherent totality, and his argument for synthetic criticism turns on his contention that subjectivity structures history and literature:

> Rejecting the need for a structural and explicative elucidation of a literary work amounts to denying that the world is a totality and that it is a totality structured by men, subjects of history [sujets de l'histoire]. To reject it is to limit oneself to describing reality (sometimes with brio) and is, moreover, to deny the role of men and history. We know that this negation of the subject is in fashion.[7]

Even disregarding the circularity of the argument (the work of art lends unity to fragmentary individual existence; "men," as subjects of history, lend unity to the literary work), Dhaenens's reading demonstrates just how inaccessible Nerval's insights into writing and selfhood remained, even one hundred and twenty years after his death, for it was precisely this "subject of history" which the poet placed in doubt with the poet-savior figure of "Le Christ aux Oliviers." By meditating on the implications of the death of God, Nerval had already thrown into question that very subjectivity which Dhaenens uses as the foundation and guarantor of intrinsic, hidden literary unity. This questioning is not, as the critic asserts, a simple negation of subjectivity, for Nerval continues, perhaps more so here at the end of his life than ever before, to explore the limits of autobiographical discourse and the lyric first person (in *Aurélia* and "El Desdichado" for example); rather it is part of a reevaluation and restructuring of the category of selfhood, a process that in "El Desdichado" focuses more on the literary than the divine attributes of the poet-savior figure and attempts to elaborate a truly written self.

More recent critics have begun to address this question of the scriptural quality of the subject which appears in Nerval's late writings, to consider it less as a poetic description than as a literary construct. Taking as a starting point Nerval's complaint that in writing *Aurélia* he found himself turning in a "tight circle," Jean-Pierre Richard describes the Nervalian text's "disseminated unity" and its author's search for a written identity as a vertiginous circulation, a process of constant displacement and exchange:

> But he turns in it [in the "tight circle"], and it is the volubility, the verbal diversity and rapidity of this "turn"—Nerval would also say, perhaps, of this "round"—which constitute the life, the vertiginous life of what one can, through the cybernetic game of writing and in the deployment of its infinite capacity for *exchange*, continue to name his identity.[8]

The very movement of displacement that, for critics like Dhaenens, disrupts the text is seen here to identify it with, or rather *as*, a certain individual and to animate it, imparting to the writing something like a life. This unending process is structured, according to Richard, not only by the various means of displacement and linkage that are available through tropes (and here he closely follows the rhetorical displacements that Freud identifies in the dream-work: metonymy, metaphor, analogy, synecdoche, paronomasia, etc.) but also by literary forms, especially the sonnets that Nerval wrote at the end of his life:

> This vertigo of the I, of the I of writing [du moi de l'écriture], knows yet another element of regulation, that of the *form* or of the genre in which it is written.... In a sonnet from the *Chimères*, for example, the temptations of parallelism, the force of couplings, the internal order of the line or the stanza—in short all the regulated or instinctive legality of the poem—set against its inherently literal lability an ensemble of constraints in which that lability is compelled to organize and estheticize itself.[9]

Richard has parted ways with more traditional critics like Dhaenens by viewing the subject of literature not as something held and imparted in writing, but as the very organization and activity of a text, its constant, lifelike movement of displacement and deferral, an Abbé de Bucquoy who escapes always across the level of the signifier, through its permutations and suggestiveness. One never gets through a text, either to its end or to what it hides, since its subject is, for Richard, the very process of hiding and disclosure, repeated endlessly according to the laws of prosody and figurative speech. This recognition of an animate movement to Nerval's text, of the importance of its unstable allusiveness and fragmentation, and of the possibility of an exclusively written subjectivity, represent a major breakthrough in Nerval studies. At the very least, Richard's essay has insisted on looking at the disjunctive surface of the poem as not merely an envelope but as significant in its own right. He has opened the way to an appreciation of how the sonnet elaborates what he describes as the "I of writing."

Following this approach, Julia Kristeva has also addressed the importance of the nonsemantic aspects of the poem in relation to self-identity. She sees the sonnet as the mourning of a lost prelinguistic relationship to objects ("To speak, to place oneself, to establish oneself within the legal fiction known as symbolic activity, that is indeed to lose the Thing").[10] Like Richard, she considers the fragmentary and diffuse nature of the first-person self-identification to be structured and contained by the formalism of poetry, the "phonic and rhythmic coherence, which at the same time limits and permits the free associations inspired by each word or name."[11] The relative abundance of names, as well as epithets, used to identify the first person of the sonnet renders them, in Kristeva's eyes, too polysemous to represent anything but a repetitive series of empty deictic gestures toward a prelinguistic state that is eventually incorporated into the language of the poem itself. This incorporation takes place on the nonsemantic level of the sign:

> "El Desdichado," however, like all Nerval's poetry and poetic prose, attempted a tremendous *incarnation* of the unbridled significance that leaps and totters within the polyvalence of esoterisms. By accepting the dispersal of meaning—the text's replica [réplique] of a fragmented identity—the themes of the sonnet relate a true archeology of affective mourning and erotic ordeal, overcome by assimilating the archaic state into the language of poetry. At the same time, the assimilation is also accomplished through oralization and musicalization of the signs themselves, thus bringing meaning closer to the lost body. At the very heart of the value crisis, poetic writing mimics a resurrection.[12]

The only significant problems with Kristeva's extremely forceful reading of this poem—and they will be discussed later—are her insistence on its oral qualities and her idea that the subjectivity constructed in it imitates (is a replica of) a primary, nonscriptural identity.

Traces of an Abolished Subject

The sonnet "El Desdichado" was first published in the *Mousquetaire* of December 10, 1853, and reappeared in 1854 at the head of the collection of poems entitled *Chimères*, which was included at the end of the *Filles du feu*; there exist, in addition, two manuscript versions of the poem, one of which was once in the possession of Alfred Lombard, the other in that of the poet Paul Eluard. The four versions differ, sometimes significantly, especially in punctuation and the use of capitalization, dashes, and italics. The one presented below is that of *Les Chimères*. Jean Guillaume argues persuasively in his authoritative edition of these poems that the *Mousquetaire* version represents the most primitive known state of the sonnet, followed in chronological succession by the Lombard draft, the Eluard draft, and the version published in the *Filles du feu*.[13] The Lombard manuscript is in red ink with several corrections and additions in black, while the Eluard manuscript, which includes several marginal annotations in the hand of the poet himself, is entirely written in red. In relation to the vast body of criticism that has been accorded it, the text itself always surprises by its brevity:

El Desdichado

Je suis le ténébreux,—le veuf,—l'inconsolé,
Le prince d'Aquitaine à la tour abolie:
Ma seule *étoile* est morte,—et mon luth constellé
Porte le *Soleil noir* de la *Mélancolie*.

Dans la nuit du tombeau, toi qui m'as consolé,
Rends-moi le Pausilippe et la mer d'Italie,
La *fleur* qui plaisait tant à mon cœur désolé,
Et la treille où le pampre à la rose s'allie.

Suis-je Amour ou Phébus?... Lusignan ou Biron?
Mon front est rouge encor du baiser de la reine;
J'ai rêvé dans la grotte où nage la syrène…

Et j'ai deux fois vainqueur traversé l'Achéron:
Modulant tour à tour sur la lyre d'Orphée
Les soupirs de la sainte et les cris de la fée.

I am the dark one,—the widowed—, the disconsolate,
The prince of Aquitaine of the abolished tower:
My only *star* is dead,—and my constellated lute
Bears the *black Sun* of *Melancholy*.

In the night of the tomb, thou who hast consoled me,
Give me back the Posilipo and the Italian sea,
The *flower* which so pleased my desolate heart,
And the trellis where the vine and the rose unite.

Am I Love or Phœbus?... Lusignan or Biron?
My forehead is still red from the queen's kiss;
I have dreamt in the grotto where the siren swims…

And I have twice in victory crossed the Acheron:
Tuning in turn on the Orphic lyre
The sighs of the saint and the fairy's cries.[14]

Three of the four original versions of the poem bear the above title, which is Spanish for "the disinherited"; the word most likely came to Nerval's attention through a character in Walter Scott's *Ivanhoe* who, stripped of his ancestral lands by his father, adopts a coat of arms bearing an uprooted oak tree and the device "El Desdichado."[15] The Eluard draft alone bears the variant title "Le Destin" (Destiny). The latter choice suggests the culminating and guiding moment of a personal narrative, the point toward which an individual life tends and in which it finds fulfillment; but *as* a culminating point, it also suggests the end of that personal temporality, the term of an organized individual narrative, and consequently a moment at, or after, the end of personal time (which recalls the atemporal moment of hyperbolic doubt in the "Christ aux Oliviers").[16] If "Le Destin" suggests a moment from which there is no future, the title "El Desdichado" evokes, conversely, a loss of the past, the disruption of a lineage, or linearity, that binds an individual to what has preceded him.[17] In either case, the individual's relation to time's continuity has been compromised, and the title indicates a subjective moment somehow cut adrift. Unlike "Le Destin," however, the title Nerval ultimately chose is strongly negative in tenor and consequently accords more faithfully with the overwhelmingly dark tone of the first stanza.

The first two words of the poem situate it within a lyric tradition of self-identification, an affiliation that the subsequent lines serve only to strengthen, but it is a shadowy identity, marked by loss, negation, and sorrow that is presented here. The "ténèbres" which first qualify the "je" set the general tone of what is to follow while suggesting, more specifically, the shadows of death and the underworld which will return in the "nuit du tombeau" of the fifth line and in the descent into Hades evoked in the last tercet. The epithet "veuf" reintroduces the theme of a loss of family that first appears in the title and strengthens the image of the lyric subject as one who is essentially dispossessed. "Inconsolé," the most forceful of the attributions given the first person, is generally neglected in analyses of the poem, largely because it tends to undermine readings that argue for an ultimately redemptive thrust to the poem. The argument that the poet has passed through the night of negativity into a higher-order, aesthetic self-affirmation (as Dhaenens, for example, does with his Hegelian reading of the sonnet, or Kristeva with her view of its musicality as an incorporation of the lost prelinguistic object into the very materiality of poetry) becomes extremely problematic in the face of this adjective, which depicts the lyric subject as still unreconciled to his loss. Moreover, while the expression "inconsolable" would have indicated a static point, in which the poet had become sufficiently reconciled to his disconsolate condition to adopt it as his future, "inconsolé" indicates that the poet has not gained this stability, but leaves open the possibility that he will change, that he will eventually be consoled. The poetic "now" of the opening self-declaration, indicated in the present tense of the verb, is thus lent a certain uneasy, provisional quality, and has injected into it a notion of deferral, an impression that the subject of the poem has perhaps not yet found his final form. This incompleteness of the first person's self-identification and the uncertain temporality that the title suggests are underscored by the hesitant, stuttering movement of the first line, for, as Emilie Noulet points out, "the long pause after *veuf* throws off the meter in the second hemistich";[18] the progressive quality of the alexandrine rhythm, which tends to incorporate the pauses in speech into a forward, metrical, and linear movement, is troubled, and instead the interruptions themselves are given preeminence: the meter puts into question the easy flow of time from one syllable (or from one instant) to another while introducing palpable disjunctions into the presentation of the lyric subject. The dash after "veuf," adopted in the second version of the poem and then consistently retained, draws attention to the articulating spaces of the poem and points up their tendency to disarticulation.

The second line can be decomposed into its constituent hemistichs. The "prince d'Aquitaine" suggests, at first sight, that Nerval has simply adopted a poetic stance, a role that he fills with his ventriloquism, but it is a role, or identity, which he adopted on at least one other occasion as well. A letter of November 22, 1853 (eighteen days before the poem's publication in the *Mousquetaire*), from Nerval to George Sand is riddled with indications of madness and signed "Gaston Phœbus d'Aquitaine."[19] The choice of Aquitaine seems to stem from the fact that Nerval, according to the idiosyncratic, personal "genealogy" which he drew up at some unknown point in his life, believed his paternal family to originate in Périgord.[20] The first hemistich would thus reintegrate the poet into that lineage and restore to him that nobility of which the title seems to dispossess him.

The second hemistich, which serves as an attribute to the first, at once strengthens this identification and places it under the sign of negation. The same "fantastic genealogy" which traces Nerval's ancestors back to Périgord also associates them, both geographically and etymologically, with towers. Close to the beginning of the document Nerval notes: "In Périgord, little distance apart and on both banks of the Dordogne [drawing] are the three former towers of Labrunie (so spelled)." A few lines later, while discussing the etymology of Labrunie (his father's family name), he adds, "*Brown* or *Brunn* signifies tower and barley-kiln [*tour et touraille*]"; a few lines later still one finds, "Browning or Brownie in Ireland. The Brownie, spirit of towers and bridges." A place near the center, or starting point, of the genealogical tree itself bears the notation "Tower and bridge" accompanied by a drawing of them.[21] The "tower" of the second hemistich thus appears to recall those towers situated on the banks of the Dordogne which geographically located Nerval's ancestral origins and shaped his name. The significance of towers in Nerval's writings seems also to have had more general resonances, and in his analysis of the genealogy Jean-Pierre Richard notes the "power of affirmation, for Nerval, of towers and all upright objects (columns, triumphal arches, pyramids, mountains), their positive quality of identification."[22] In keeping with this positive, identificatory aspect of vertical figures, the image of the tower often also serves in Nerval's writings to symbolize a commanding point which is the culmination of a confusing journey and which provides a clear, synthetic, and synoptic view of the paths that have led to it. In *Lorely*, for example, Nerval writes of the "steeple at Strasbourg," identifies its summit as the terminal point of a long and arduous journey ("the traveler's legs shudder when he considers that he has easily a league to go in a horizontal line, but that from the foot of the church he will have nearly another league in a perpendicular line"), and describes the view it offers of the surrounding countryside;[23] more telling is the description of the same tower in an article for *Le Messager*, where he writes, in an extended metaphor about human life, of

> the man who knows how to escape sometimes from the soft constraints of habit and who, after a harsh climb, turns around and succeeds in looking at his life from a single and sublime point, as one follows with one's eyes, from the summit of the steeple at Strasbourg, the road just laboriously traveled during a long day.[24]

The image of the tower thus suggests at once origin and end: on the one hand the point from which a family stems and on the other the terminus toward which an individual life tends and from which it can be seen in its linear entirety. The tower is a link that connects a person with the past and the future along an unbroken chain. It is a figure for the connectedness and directedness of his life and an image for his place within a longer lineage. In using the term "tour abolie," Nerval lays waste this symbol of time's linearity and of the continuity of an individual life. The "prince d'Aquitaine *à la tour abolie*" is thus one cut off from past and future, from both family and destiny. The attribute given in this hemistich also helps clarify the choice of title, for while "destin" evokes a moment at the end of time or out of time, it also implies an end that lends structure and direction to the existence that preceded it, and Nerval here dispossesses himself of such a *telos*. Furthermore, much as "El Desdichado" of Scott's *Ivanhoe* identifies himself as the one who has lost his ancestral identity, the poet here adopts the stance of a Prince d'Aquitaine who identifies himself as one who has lost all title to being Prince d'Aquitaine. Whatever particular individual Nerval might have had in mind when writing this line, whether it is "Waifer (or Guaifer) of Aquitaine who, pursued by Pepin III, the short, hid in the forests of Périgord," as Kristeva asserts, or one of the other historical personages whom critics have proposed on the basis of extremely slender evidence, he is an "abolished" Prince d'Aquitaine, one who can identify himself only negatively as what he is not and through what he no longer has.[25]

This curious ontological status of the Prince is remarked by Emilie Noulet in reference to the tower that is attributed to him: "*abolie*, this word rarely found at the rhyme, this passive sense which implies at once the presence and the absence of the tower."[26] The tower is preserved in its negation. It is only insofar as it "is" not. The difference between "tour" and "tour abolie" is thus the difference between a real, physical tower which can be located geographically (like the three Nerval situates on the banks of the Dordogne in the "fantastic genealogy") and a tower that, since negated, "exists" only in language. Consequently the modifier *abolie* displaces the discursive modality of the word *tour* from the descriptive to the emblematic, and the poem shifts from a primarily referential to a primarily symbolic language; the *abolie* thus marks (although it does not initiate) the introduction of the elaboration of subjectivity into a language whose referential function is exclusively negative and which cancels the existence of anything beyond the symbolic order; in other words, it draws attention to a series of gestures that serve to deny the first person's nonlinguistic existence, which tend to elaborate the speaking subject as an *exclusively* linguistic construct, but which have been viewed uniformly by critics as signs and epithets with a biographical, referential import.

It is not the "tour abolie" alone that functions in such a way, for this promotion of the symbolic aspect of language continues in the last two lines of the first quatrain. The "étoile" of the third line has been identified by biographically inclined readers, often in arguments of great ingenuity, with different women whom Nerval loved at one point or another during his life.[27] Dhaenens, on the other hand, sees it as a figure for the poet's muse, who has withdrawn her inspiration.[28] For Kristeva, it is a proto-linguistic object of infantile desire, a Kleinian maternal body which is lost with the child's entry into language and the symbolic.[29] In all cases, the star is taken to be the focus of the poet's longing, an object that gives direction to his will and desire, and it is in this most abstract sense, in its effect on the poet's sense of directedness, that the "étoile" is best understood here. Such an interpretation is corroborated by a passage from the preface to the *Filles du feu*. In it Nerval responds to the commentary by Alexandre Dumas which accompanied the sonnet's publication in the *Mousquetaire*. Describing his descent into and eventual recovery from a period of madness, the author of "El Desdichado" wrote:

> Yielding to that tender love for a fugitive *star* [*étoile*] which abandoned me in the night of my solitary destiny, I wept and I shuddered at the vain apparitions of my sleep. Then a ray of divine light shone into my Hell; surrounded by monsters against which I dimly struggled, I seized Ariadne's thread [le fil d'Ariane] and since that moment all my visions have become heavenly. Some day I shall write the story of that "descent into Hell."[30]

The loss of one light (the "étoile") plunges the author into a hell of his own subjectivity, while another one (the "ray of divine light") rescues him from it. The symmetry between these two heavenly bodies and their effects on the poet indicates that the loss of the "étoile" described here also entailed a loss of something comparable to the "fil d'Ariane" which the "rayon" restitutes, and with it the loss also of the linear order and direction, the minimal but essential structure which that "thread" seems, in this passage, to have lent to his inner world. To be dispossessed of his "étoile" means forfeiting a (perhaps only rudimentarily) organized subjectivity which moves forward toward an ascertainable end; this loss is the night, or negation of destiny, the loss of an object toward which one advances and which when attained will, like the steeple of Strasbourg, retrospectively reveal the coherent sense of the progression toward it. The loss of the *étoile* is the night of destiny, because both *étoile* and destiny represent the same thing: an object of desire and volition that, simply because it *is* an object of desire and volition, confers reason, coherence, and direction on the one who longs for it.[31] Almost by definition, an object of desire is an absent object, but here, it has been lost altogether. Thus the death of his "étoile" has another, related effect on the author's self-knowledge: it consigns him to an entirely subjective realm which confronts him with inchoate and fragmentary self-representations ("vain apparitions," "monsters," and "visions") that, in offering themselves apparently spontaneously, exceed his attempts to master them. The restitution of a light, on the other hand, allows Nerval eventually to integrate those representations into a narrative ("Some day I shall write the story of that 'descent into Hell'"). The death of the star thus thrusts the poet into a nonnarrative discursivity of spontaneous, unmastered, and fragmentary subjectivity; this is the "now" that he adopts in the first stanza of "El Desdichado." There, the ambiguous tense of the verb ("est morte"), which unlike the simple past (*mourut*) can be understood either as a present description or a past event but in either case grammatically implies a continuance into the present, serves also to undermine any possible narrative thrust to the stanza.[32]

The "luth constellé" of the same line prefigures the "lyre d'Orphée" in the last stanza, since after his death Orpheus's lyre was placed in the heavens as a constellation.[33] While the Orphic aspects of the sonnet will be discussed below, some of the signification of his lyre is indissociable from the first stanza's reference to the "luth constellé." In the esoteric texts with which Nerval seems to have been well acquainted, the lyre of Orpheus is generally taken as a symbol of universal or human harmony;[34] by extension the lute, in many of these works, acquired a similar significance. Guy Le Fèvre de La Boderie's introduction to his 1581 French translation of the *Trois livres de la vie* by the Florentine neo-Platonic philosopher Marsilio Ficino (to whom the lyre of Orpheus was often emblematically attributed and to whom Nerval himself refers in the *Illuminés*) uses it as an analogue to the properly functioning human body, or "Instrument humain":

> in your *lute and Pandora*, if the strings and cords are not duly tuned as a group, so that the E-strings answer appropriately to the lower ones, the seconds to the fourths, and all of them one to the other, there results a dissonance to offend delicate ears.[35]

It is on the basis of such evidence as this that the prominent Nerval critic Jean Richer is led to assert that the lute of "El Desdichado" has the sense of a "human microcosm."[36] More significant than La Boderie's parallel between the human body and the musical instrument, however, is the way in which he describes the lute's harmonic functioning: when correctly tuned, the strings and pitches respond to one another, setting off sympathetic vibrations according to the harmonic series. It is thus a locus of *many* threads (or strings), of a complex and multiple linearity that is brought into a shifting unity through the way in which the vibrations affect each other and the strings mutually respond. The "soleil noir" of the stanza's last line can be assimilated with the dead star of the third line, which cannot be located in the simple linearity of a narrative and which in fact disrupts such narrative, since it is carried by the lute, symbol of the harmony among different and discrete lines. What Karlheinz Stierle calls the poem's *mosaikhaft* structure—the ability of its various literary allusions and Nervalian echoes to interact with one another to create other, larger, and unexpected images in the same way that individual tesserae combine to form figures—largely conforms to La Boderie's description but represents the poem as static and stonelike. Nerval's own image of a stringed instrument, while not necessarily allegorical of the poem itself, suggests a more dynamic model of nonnarrative unity and of the controlled interplay among individual elements.[37]

The "soleil noir" of the fourth line recasts the "étoile morte," which it associates lexically and symbolically with another context, that of the moment of doubt represented in "Le Christ aux Oliviers." There it is the "orbite noire" and the "soleils éteints" which come to represent the disruption of linear temporality and the loss of a coherent (world-historical) subjectivity. The juxtaposition of "étoile morte" and "soleil noir" thus sets into motion what one might, in keeping with the lute image of the third line, describe as a harmonic series linking Nerval's meditation on the death of God to the disjunctive sense of self he experienced in his "descent into Hell." The lute which "porte le soleil noir" is thus surrounded and constellated by annulled stars; it does not shine with heavenly bodies but bears them black and dead in their negation; it is an instrument that supports them, holds them in their nonexistence, their extinction. It is a "surface" capable of preserving what is not.

From the first stanza there remains only the word *Mélancolie*, the most telling of the poem for Kristeva, who views the sonnet as both an expression of the melancholia ensuing from the loss of the prelinguistic object and as an attempt to incorporate that infantile object into the phonetic and symbolic levels of poetic language.[38] Given the overwhelmingly negative, even annihilating tenor of the referential aspect of the first stanza, its refusal of the real in favor of the symbolic through the expressions "tour abolie," "étoile morte," and "soleil noir," which refer to things that exist only on the symbolic level, any attempt to read these lines as part of a reintegration and preservation of the real in the symbolic seems highly problematic. A more promising approach can be found in a text by Marsilio Ficino, with whose works Nerval professed to be acquainted.[39] The historian André Chastel describes it in the following words:

> Book 13 of his *Theologia platonica* is a repertory of the powers of the imagination, of visions, premonitory dreams, all the psychic prodigies which ultimately are, for Ficino, the normal exercise of consciousness purified by asceticism and meditation, or duly exercised in its hidden powers. One of the phenomena which occupy him at length is the *vacatio mentis*, in which the soul frees itself of its corporeal attachments; there exist seven types of it: "by sleep, by syncope, by melancholic humor, by even temperament, by solitude, by astonishment, by chastity."[40]

The idea of melancholy as a *vacatio mentis*, or an abandonment of the corporeal, is in almost direct contradiction to Kristeva's understanding of the term, since she views melancholy as a recuperation of the real in the linguistic order, but it seems consonant with the refusal of the physically present or presentable in favor of the purely intelligible which marks the various negated elements of the stanza. Furthermore, the context in which the idea is proposed by Ficino—the relation between vision, imagination, and dreams on the one hand, the normal functioning of consciousness on the other—seems especially Nervalian, an echo of the "the overflowing of dreams into real life" from *Aurélia*.

The first stanza as a whole, then, rapidly exposes certain essential elements of a poetic self-representation. First, it is a subject that is elaborated negatively, through death, dispossession, and annihilation, a subject known through nonexistence and loss. Second, this negativity engenders a subject knowable only on the symbolic level, a purely poetic or written subject. It is in this sense that the present reading comes close to agreeing with Jean Richer's assessment that "*El Desdichado*, Plutonian sonnet, is like *Artémise* a stele for the poet, or more exactly, an alchemical Tomb."[41] Without being an alchemical tomb, the poem nonetheless does function as a "tombeau," preserving the subject, like the "tour abolie," in a purely linguistic negativity, memorializing it in its death. It is not an alchemical but a literary tomb. Third, it is an unfinished, fragmentary, and nonnarrative subjectivity that the poet ascribes to himself here, a subjectivity that evokes the unmastered and disjunctive self-representations of his "descent into Hell," produced in a poetic "now" cut free from its ties to the past and future, yet still incomplete, open to alteration and consolation.[42] This subjective disorder is reinforced through the paratactic syntax of the stanza, which simply places the various self-attributions together without expressing the relations that bind them one to another.

The second stanza introduces an entirely new set of references and a more optimistic tone. Speaking in flowers, the poet evokes an idyllic setting whose very name—Pausilippe (in Italian "Pozzuoli")—derives from a Greek word meaning "the cessation of sadness." The solipsistic tenor of the first four lines seems broken by the introduction of a second figure, the "toi," and the imagery is at once more specific and less emblematic. The possibility of a restitution of a lost past is evoked. With the mention of precise locations, the language appears to tend back toward the referential, and in some way to restore (or "rendre") what had been lost in the abolitions of the first stanza. In fact, these lines do seem to refer to events in Nerval's life, to the extent that all the elements of the last three lines can be read as a condensation of an incident that the author relates in the purportedly autobiographical pages of *Octavie*, also from *Les Filles du feu*. The similarity between the two works is so pronounced that it is worth recalling the prose version. There the poet, traveling in order to find solace for his unhappy love for "the only woman who existed for me, and who was not aware that I so much as existed," wanders through the streets of Naples, where he meets a woman whose language he does not understand. She leads him back to her home, where they sleep together beneath a figurine of Saint Rosalie. Awakening before dawn, the poet leaves his "easy conquest," crosses the sleeping city, climbs the "Posilipo above the grotto," where, on reaching the summit, he reclines "deliciously beneath the trellises of the villas." He is soon overcome, however, by feelings of despair that lead him twice to attempt suicide by throwing himself from the edge of the promontory. "Twice I hurled myself down," he writes, "and some unknown force cast me back alive onto the ground, which I kissed."[43] Naples and the surrounding regions seem, like the Valois, to have been an area of deep personal and mythic significance to Nerval, for he returns to them repeatedly in his writings, but, because of the number of lexical identities between the two texts, it is the version of his experiences which appears in *Octavie* that bears the closest ties to "El Desdichado." The words "Pausilippe" and "treille" appear in both, the "grotte" that he mentions in the prose work appears in the eleventh line of the sonnet, the name of the saint whose statuette kept watch over him during the night is hidden in the last words of the stanza ("rose s'allie"), and the "pampre [vine]" appears in the form of "one of those enormous clusters of grapes," with which the poet refreshes himself after abandoning the idea of suicide.

More important than the events that Nerval recounts in *Octavie* is the significance that he attributes to them, for despite their idyllic appearance he sees them as the theater in which a personal confrontation with death takes place. The two attempts at suicide form, for the author, the core of his Neapolitan experiences, whose narrative he prefaces with the following words, addressed to the woman because of whom he had nearly thrown himself from the cliffs of the Posilipo:

> Death, great God! why does that idea come back at every turn, as if only my death could equal the happiness you promised? Death! and yet the word casts no darkness among my thoughts. She appears to me crowned with pale roses, as if at the end of a feast; I've sometimes dreamed that she was waiting for me, smiling at the bedside of a beloved woman, after the happiness, after the ecstasy, and that she said to me: "Let's go young man! you've had your full share of joy in this world. Now, come sleep, come rest yourself in my arms. I am not beautiful—not I—but I am good and succoring, and I give not pleasure but eternal calm."
>
> But where then had that image already come to me? Ah! as I told you, it was in Naples, three years ago.[44]

Despite what the last two sentences would lead one to expect, the image of death described in such detail in the above paragraph does not reappear in the narrative that follows it, but is only hinted at in the strange appearance of the unknown woman with whom he sleeps and in the two suicide attempts themselves. Still, Nerval is explicit: the passage concerns a face-to-face encounter with the image of death; it is apparently this confrontation, transpiring in the author's momentary resolve to kill himself, which lends its deep, personally mythic importance to this landscape. The promontory is the site of an abandonment of life and an embracing of death, for it is only through the power of a mysterious agency, by "some unknown force," that the author does not actually succumb. Whether or not Nerval did in fact try to take his own life in the circumstances he describes is of no interest here. What does matter is the significance that he attached to these surroundings as the place where he consigned himself, if only for a moment, to the arms of death. In a scene that seems to prefigure the twelfth line of the sonnet ("J'ai deux fois vainqueur traversé l'Achéron"), the Posilipo thus represents a double acceptance of death, from which, for unknown reasons, the poet emerged unscathed, alive, triumphant.[45] The stanza, then, constitutes an appeal for the restitution of this triumph over death and all its trappings. But as the conquest of death only comes in resolving to die, so does the hoped-for restitution come only "dans la nuit du tombeau."

Although with its use of the word "Pausilippe" and its references to flowers, consolation, and the landscape of southern Italy, the tonality of the poem shifts dramatically between the first and the second stanzas, the opening words of the fifth line nonetheless serve to link the two quatrains and, by belying the radicality of the tonal shift, cast a pall over the luminous imagery. Even if one ignores the parallels with the text of *Octavie*, the idea of a preservation in death or of a poetic tomb which is suggested in the first quatrain finds explicit expression here, for while it is unclear whether it is the "je" or the "toi" that inhabits the "nuit du tombeau"—and critical opinions have been inconclusive and varied on the question[46]—and unclear whether the poet's consolation took place in life or death, the second stanza nonetheless clearly represents the possibility of a restitution after death (the poet's or that of the "toi"). Furthermore, and more significantly, all that the poet asks be restored—the Posilipo, the Italian sea, the flower, and the vine—must be restored "dans la nuit du tombeau": as in the first quatrain, all that is presented here is presented under the sign of the negative, is memorialized in the realm of the dead. This parallel between the two quatrains suggests a second one: if the negativity of the first stanza entails a refusal of the nonlinguistic, an abolition of the referential in favor of the symbolic, is a similar sublimation suggested in the second stanza? It is not merely suggested, but even thematized in the ambiguity of the word *rendre*, which can mean "return" or "restore," but also "translate," or "express in language."[47] The "tombeau" would thus also signify a place in which the images of the second stanza are "translated" into linguistic expression, in which they are rendered into poetry. Moreover, the tomb of the second stanza—the place in which life is preserved in death, just as on the Posilipo life had prevailed by embracing nonexistence—would then also indicate the poem itself, the site of a lyric translation of subjectivity into language, the elaboration of a purely symbolic self. The second stanza is thus an appeal to repeat the events of the Posilipo on the level of poetry, that they be rendered into verse.[48]

The individual elements of the last two lines of the stanza are suggestive and seem to acquire an independent significance that could not be limited to their possible relation to an incident in Naples, but it is difficult to determine precisely what it is that they suggest. The imperfect of the third line evokes an entire period during which the poet's heart was at once pleased and devastated, for, as Dhanaens points out, grammatical consistency requires that the past participle "désolé" be read as simultaneous with the main verb "plaisait."[49] "Désolé" means "ravaged" and "empty" but etymologically also signifies "left by oneself" or "isolated." All these meanings seem to be in play here, making the moment in question one remarkable for a sense of isolation, despair, and emptiness at the center or "heart" of the poet's being (for he refers to his "*cœur* désolé"). Thus read, the epithet evokes again the scene of doubt from "Le Christ aux Oliviers" insofar as both poems represent a moment of solitude in which the subjective centerpoint and the core of one's being (respectively the poet's "cœur" and the "œil de Dieu") are found to be empty. This uncentered self, or this self whose center has been evacuated, who exists only eccentrically and dispersed, further recalls the first person of the first stanza, who is portrayed in a state of extreme, solipsistic isolation no longer unified by any single principle (such as the "étoile"). There, as in "Le Christ aux Oliviers," the principle of internal coherence was located not in the subject, who found himself mired in the nightmarish landscape of his own disjunctive self-representations, but in an external object: the guiding star of the "descent into Hell" which resurfaces negatively in the first stanza, and the eye of God in "Le Christ aux Oliviers." In those two passages, Nerval displays a sense of self that does not hope to find its core of coherence and unity within itself but in an *object* toward which it tends, whether that be through desire (as in the star) or through the force of events (as in "l'œil de Dieu"; and to this one can also add the suppressed title "Le Destin" and, metaphorically, the "steeple at Strasbourg"). In the seventh line of the sonnet, this heartless solitude is similarly tempered, if not broken, by an object of pleasure or fascination, the "fleur qui plaisait." Once again, in the seventh line, the poet seems to imagine an object external to himself that holds the key of his inner being, an object that, since it is external, can be irretrievably lost: Nerval does not, in these passages, view his essence as inalienable from himself. The plea for the restoration of the flower would thus be a plea for the reestablishment of an essence to his being—and this in the negativity of the "nuit du tombeau."[50]

For structural or intertextual reasons, virtually all other critics of the poem have also viewed the "étoile" of the first stanza and the "fleur" of the second as parallel designations of the same referent;[51] most have also given close attention to the notation "ancolie" which accompanies the word "fleur" in the Eluard manuscript. The critic Rousseaux has found the species designated as a "symbol of sadness" and an "emblem of madness" in texts available to Nerval.[52] While such resonances are not inconsistent with the reference to the "cœur désolé" of this line, they offer little clarity or focus. The name seems just as strongly motivated by the rhyme with "mélancolie," a fact that, along with the emblematic quality of the word, would indicate that the choice of vocabulary here was being determined not by reference as much as by the interplay of the words themselves on the level of the signifier (the nonsensical or "masking" level of the poem, which critics have almost uniformly slighted).

The reference to "ancolie" would seem, further, to exclude identifying the "fleur" of the seventh line with the "rose" of the eighth. The significance of this latter element is especially vague, and references to other texts serve only to heighten the uncertainty. For instance, in the sonnet "Artémis," also from the *Chimères*, the word "rose" appears four times in a context referring explicitly to Naples. This would seem to clarify the meaning of the term in "El Desdichado." But in "Artémis," it is not the flower itself that signifies so much as the differences among its various possible colors and varieties. The rose held in the hands of "la mort—ou la morte [death—or the dead woman]" is the "Rose trémière" or hollyhock, while the "Rose au cœur violet [purple-hearted rose]" is attributed to Saint Gudule, and the "roses blanches [white roses]," apparently intended to signify Christian saints, are said to insult the gods.[53] This catalogue of roses indicates that they were emblematically significant for Nerval, but in such a context, the semantic field defined by the word "rose" becomes too broad and contradictory to offer a single stable meaning. In its generic form, undifferentiated by color, the word comes across as a potent but empty emblem, an important sign of something unclear, unstable, and indeterminate. The significant attribute of the flower in "El Desdichado," the element that inflects it and lends it meaning, would be its union with another element, the "pampre [vine]." A similar juxtaposition involving an otherwise uninflected "rose" comes at the end of *Sylvie*, where the narrator speaks of a window "framed in grapevines and rose" as part of a setting in which his earlier emotional conflicts had finally found resolution. But the window is, specifically, part of a room described as "one last return to the bric-a-brac which I long ago abandoned."[54] If the rose and the vine represent union, in this case, it is as part of a setting remarkable for its confused juxtapositions and its connection with an abandoned past: they are not so much the signs of stable union as of a once-acceptable disorder. In both *Sylvie* and "El Desdichado" the rose and the vine represent a return of the past; in the former case it is a disorderly past of haphazard couplings while in the latter it is a past incorporating elements of unstable, contradictory, and indeterminate significance. In neither case is the period evoked stable, orderly, definite, or fully determinable.

Altogether, the second stanza not only evokes a place where life can be preserved, it also offers an image for a surface that can unify such disparate elements, and maintain the disjunctions that intertextual allusions such as "rose" and "pampre" introduce into the sonnet. The events of the last three lines of the stanza are localizable within a specific and nonfigural terrain, while their elements (the trellises, the Italian sea, the Posilipo) can be imagined to be deployed as parts of a landscape, held together, imagistically, on a geographical surface.[55] This is in striking contrast to the abyssal confusion of the first stanza, where the closest the poet comes to offering an image of underlying substance is the lute bearing the black sun of melancholy. Here, on the contrary, Nerval grounds his objects in an identifiable region. The stability of such a localization is undercut, however, by a disorienting notation at the end of the stanza in the Eluard manuscript: "Jardins du Vatican." The connection between the events of the Posilipo described in *Octavie* and the second stanza of the sonnet may be highly determined in respect to lexical choice and underlying concerns, but in the eyes of its author the significance of the passage is also strongly associated with the gardens of the Vatican (although there is little intertextual evidence to explain why this would be the case). The marginal note thus dislocates the principle of an underlying unity, such as would support the various elements of these lines in their diversity, from the topographical to another level. What that other level might be is suggested in the culmination of these descriptive lines, where a second image of a unifying surface is offered: the trelliswork arbor itself, which binds and unifies what grows on it. Like the lute, it is a multilinear surface, but unlike the musical instrument of the first stanza, the "treille" is a network that supports and links a diversity of organic life rather than simply producing vibrations or, in its constellated form, shimmerings. The second quatrain thus appeals for a poetic surface—a surface "dans la nuit du tombeau"—which would be analogous to the trellis, a multilinear (and therefore nonnarrative) system that could maintain *in their disjunction* an indefinite and indeterminate confusion of symbolic elements: the Posilipo, the Italian sea, the flower, the arbor, the vine, the rose, and all that they allusively insinuate into this stanza.[56]

The second quatrain thus constitutes a plea for a conquest of death in death, for a restitution of life in the tomb, which recalls a victorious embracing of nonexistence that came to be symbolized for Nerval by the Neapolitan landscape. It is also a plea for the restoration of an objectified sense of inner unity, "la fleur," which pleases even, or only, when the poet is in a state of uncentered dispersion (his "cœur désolé"), and which can maintain him in this unpleasant condition. It is a plea for an insubstantial, nonnarrative network that would support the various aspects of the poet's past and present life in their haphazard disjunctiveness. It is a plea to poetize the events and places of subjective experience, and an attempt to incorporate them into a more symbolic, less referential discursivity, where the past is preserved in the negativity of death, and a landscape becomes delocalized and emblematic. Here the imperative "rends-moi" is particularly rich in sense. It is a call for restoration. It is also a call for translation, the appeal that the world of the poet's experience be "rendered" into linguistic expression, into verse. And in this light, the imperative "rends-moi" has the sense not only of "give back *to* me" but also "render me" all these things, translate me too into verse, into the timeless disorder of a lyric conquest of death in the negativity of a tomblike language.

As important as any of these aspects of the stanza is the fact that it *is* framed in the form of a plea *to* another, and this gesture toward an interlocutor seems an integral aspect of the events of the Posilipo, for each of the three known versions of the incident are given in epistolary form and as an appeal to a "vous."[57] Here, the poem has shifted from a constative to an imperative register and addresses itself to an unnamed "toi," whose introduction in the fifth line breaks the sonnet out of the solipsistic isolation of the first quatrain. The principal interest this line has held for critics has lain not so much in the reference to the "tombeau," which has generally received rather scant attention, as in the difficulty of identifying the "toi." Attributions to various women in Nerval's life or to mythical figures and deities have been advanced by almost all of the earlier specialists. For Geninasca, it is the beloved "morte" represented by the "étoile" of the first stanza and the "fleur" of the second, while for Dhanaens, it is the double of the poet.[58] Kristeva alters the terms of the discussion by viewing the "toi" as representative of what is precisely indeterminable and unidentifiable:

> Who is this "thou"? scholars have wondered, and the answers flow in—it is Aurélia, the saint, Artemisia/Artémise, Jenny Colon, the dead mother... The undecidable concatenation of these real and imaginary figures flees once more toward the position of the archaic "Thing"—the elusive pre-object of a mourning endemic to all speaking beings and a suicidal attraction for the depressive person.[59]

While substantiating Kristeva's remarks about the undecidability of the "toi," the context of the poem, as examined so far, undermines her interpretation of that undecidability as a movement toward a prelinguistic object. The first two stanzas have been overwhelmingly concerned with a sublimation of the prelinguistic, the referential, and the "real," and there is no evidence to suggest that the fifth line marks a sudden and radical departure from this program of negativity, emblematized in the reference to the "tour abolie." In attempting to find a non- or prelinguistic meaning for this pronoun, Kristeva remains firmly aligned with the long tradition of scholarship on "El Desdichado." The word, however, does not only refer, it also enacts. It does not merely designate another, it also creates that other. Certainly, the "toi" indicates someone or something that comforted the poet in the past, something or someone held to preexist the poem. But it also constitutes a poetic re-creation of that object. In simply writing "toi" the poet addresses himself to another, situates himself and his discourse in relation to an interlocutor who becomes the destination, the *telos*, of that discourse. As virtually everybody reading it has remarked, the poem chronicles the isolation of the poet and his loss of an object; no one, however, makes any note of the fact that in using the second person the second stanza functions *as if* that object had been restored. The "toi," whether living or dead, whether in the Vatican gardens, Paris, or the tomb, can still perform the role of the object of the poet's self-defining lyric address. By employing the "toi," the "je" creates the effect of another through language and gives his language the simulacrum of an object.[60] By this simple vocative, the sonnet creates an empty, negative "translation" of the "fleur," a goal toward which it can orient itself and order its discourse. Although the "toi" is an imitation—of the flower and the star, for instance—it is no longer an imitation of anything specific, it no longer has an original. As a vocative, and part of an appeal, it does not *recall* the past but *calls* to the future, positing through its own verbal force a recipient, a destination, and a destiny for itself. This performative use of the "toi" to restitute the desired "fleur" is signaled and substantiated by its role in a passage notable for its effective use of language, a passage framed in the imperative as if to effect, or provoke, a restitution through its very discursivity.

Expression and Silence

The grammatical mood of the poem, declarative in the first stanza, imperative in the second, shifts briefly to the interrogative at the beginning of the tercets, then the sonnet's last five lines return to the declarative, recalling three different scenes from the poet's past life, the last of these, given a fuller expression than the first two, taking up the whole of the final stanza. The relation of the interrogative ninth line—"Suis-je Amour ou Phébus?... Lusignan ou Biron?"—to those that follow is syntactically and semantically unclear. Some critics have attempted to view the three scenes as answers to the questions framed in the ninth line; others see them as a move to narrative discourse that salvages the poet from the feelings of doubt and aimlessness that had characterized the poem up to the tenth line.

No other line of the poem seems more to define the field of possibility for identifying and stabilizing the lyric "je" than the questions that Nerval poses at the heart of his poem—the site, between quatrains and tercet, of the *volte* in the traditional sonnet. Yet, for all its apparent specificity, no other line has raised more inconclusive speculation than this. Research by earlier commentators has produced a list of possible references for each of the four personages mentioned. *Amour* would appear to refer to the figure of Eros in Apuleius's tale of Eros and Psyche in *The Golden Ass* (a work frequently cited by Nerval), although André Lebois has also suggested the allegorical figure from the *Roman de la rose* on the basis of the supposedly medieval tone of the verse.[61] *Phébus*, spelled *Phœbus* in the first three versions of the poem, has been identified with the Greek god of the sun, as well as with the fourteenth-century Gaston Phœbus, comte de Foix, whom Nerval seems to have numbered among his Aquitanian ancestors and with whose name he signed a letter to George Sand dating from the same period as the sonnet.[62] *Lusignan* would designate an Angevin family which Nerval believed related to his own and whose founder is perhaps best known for his legendary wife, the fairy Mélusine, half woman, half snake or siren. The latter, in an attempt to hide her dual identity, forbade her husband to view her on Saturdays, when her monstrous form manifested itself, but he, breaking his vow, surprised her while bathing, discovered the truth, and lost her forever, although she long returned to announce calamities to the house of Lusignan by filling their castle with "cris de Mélusine [cries of Mélusine]."[63] The last name, *Biron*, has also been the richest in possible references, but the most significant is the English romantic poet Lord Byron, an attribution facilitated by the facts that the *Mousquetaire* version of the sonnet gives the name as *Byron* and that in a youthful poem (*A Napoléon. Traduit de Lord Biron*.) Nerval similarly misspelled the name.[64] Almost as important as the four characters themselves are the female figures associated with them. *Amour* is coupled with Pysche, Phœbus with Daphne, and Lusignan with Mélusine. "Biron" has proved less amenable to such an association but has, almost by default, been paired with a "reine" believed to reappear in the following line.[65]

The problem of choosing among the various possibilities for these names would be less intractable if it were possible to establish the syntactic and logical relations among them, but here again, further ambiguities arise. First, is there equivalence or disjunction between the terms in each pair, and between the two pairs themselves: in short, does each "ou" have the same meaning, and is that meaning simply "or" or is it sometimes "in other words"? Second, if there is a correspondence between the elements of the two pairs and not a mere enumeration of possibilities—if the second pair paraphrases the first—is that correspondence based on chiasmus or not?: are those relations A (Amour) : C (Lusignan) :: B (Phœbus) : D (Biron) or rather (with chiasmus) A : D :: B : C ? No line of the poem is richer in meanings than this one, no line draws on a wider network of Nervalian significations, none alludes to more historical and literary precedents or beckons more to exegetical madness. Nonetheless, it is possible to unravel the principal threads that connect it to the last lines of the sonnet and to articulate certain oppositions and identities at work among the various personages, thereby mastering, to a limited but necessary degree, the ambiguities and polyvalences of this line.

First, it is clear that the choice of characters in these lines is partially motivated by purely onomastic links with individuals representative of either a personal or a national past. The name as a name establishes a convertibility, if not an identity, among widely disparate cultural and historical entities. *Phébus* is at once Apollo, but also the medieval comte de Foix, and thence an ancestor of Nerval and the poet himself, who signs a letter with the name. Biron is a series of noble descendants closely associated with Chantilly and the Valois (the heart of France, in *Sylvie*, and the site of Nerval's own past), but also the English poet, and, perhaps, thence Nerval himself, who furthermore numbers among his ancestors the house of Lusignan. In this play of interconnecting names that resonate with one another through the associations and sounds they evoke, the ninth line resembles a miniature and lapidary version of the "fantastic genealogy" which the poet drew up for himself and where, Jean-Pierre Richard contends, "in that space of seemingly lost wandering, a writing, in search of an identity, forms, perhaps, a knot, attaching itself ever more firmly, more necessarily, weaving itself. Textile-tree. Leaf-family."[66] The paranomastic play of the signifier thus sets up a network that functions as a "disseminated unity" (in Richard's words), a mythic family that is not so much elaborated in a linear descent across time but generated ahistorically through names and geography.

Second, with the exception of Biron, these four names are all connected with stories of transformations, the passage of an individual from one state to another seemingly irreducibly alien one. They are stories of becoming *other*. In Ovid's *Metamorphoses*, Daphne, to escape the love-stricken Apollo, is changed into a laurel tree. The story of Eros and Psyche comes from the *Metamorphoses* of Apuleius, also known as *The Golden Ass*, which Nerval knew intimately and which concerned the transformation of a blasphemer into a donkey, his experiences in that state, and his rehabilitation by the goddess Isis. Lusignan is married to a *fée*, or fairy, who reverts to a half-woman, half-snake state once a week. Biron is not associated with any particular fable of metamorphosis, and yet he is perhaps the most significant in this respect, given the context of the second stanza's "rends-moi," for as a poet, he is one who is both the hero and the scribe of his own transformation: he has rendered himself into poetry. As the legendary Biron of folk songs, he exists only as a poetic character. The line is thus heavy with concerns about self-objectification, a passage into the state of being alien to oneself; in the reference to Biron, it also suggests that lyric poetry is such a self-alienation.

Third, this question of a poetic self-objectification, raised in the name of Biron, opens onto another set of interconnections among these names. The stories that they evoke all concern ways of knowing another or the forbidding of knowledge of another, and certain oppositions between cognitive modes start to assert themselves: vision versus blindness, verbal versus nonverbal. With Amour and Lusignan, it is a question of the gaze and visibility. Pysche loses Eros because she sees him. Lusignan loses his wife Mélusine because he breaks his word and looks at her on a Saturday. The stage is thus set for the appearance of Orpheus in the last tercet, since he too was under an interdiction: he was forbidden to look at his wife, Eurydice.[67] Amour, the lover that must be known only in darkness, who can never be seen, contrasts with Phœbus Apollo, who, as sun god, is the very principle of light and visibility. The correspondence between Phébus and Biron is revealed in a passage from Nerval's study on his friend Heinrich Heine, the German poet. There he establishes a near-familial link between the two figures, referring to "Lord Byron, who, born in foggy England, is still no less a child of the sun."[68] The connection Phébus-Biron is further determined by the fact that Apollo is also the god of music and poetry, thus corresponding to the English poet as well as to Orpheus of the last tercet, who, like the sun god, bears a lyre as symbol of his lyrical prowess. Both pairs (Amour-Phébus / Lusignan-Biron) thus emblematize a distinction between not-seeing and seeing, with the latter further associated with poetry itself.

If Amour and Phébus represent invisibility versus visibility, or darkness versus light, Lusignan and Biron also represent nonverbal versus verbalized knowledge. In the original fourteenth-century fable *Mélusine* by Jehan d'Arras, it is not at the moment Lusignan sees his wife bathing that he loses her, even though she is aware that he has broken his vow. They never mention the incident, maintaining a tacit but mutual vow of silence on the subject, until in a fit of rage the husband blurts out the truth. It is at this point, on the point of a passage from preverbal to verbalized knowledge, that the crime is committed, and the fairy, heaving unearthly and inarticulate cries of misery, is forced to vanish. The two pairs of oppositions in this line thus both set up a contrast between, on the one hand, a transgressive passage from one form of knowledge to another, a passage entailing an abolition of the object of knowledge, and, on the other hand, the glorification of that transgressive mode of knowledge in a figure associated with poetry. Psyche loses Eros by looking at him, but Phœbus represents the apotheosis of sight. Lusignan loses his wife by uttering their common knowledge of a crime, but Biron represents the word "laureate," the public acceptance and consecration of speech in poetry. These losses have a particular significance in the context of the poem, since in the cases of both Lusignan and Amour, the object of knowledge is specifically a love-object, which has already come, in the first two stanzas, to represent the alienated or objectified subjectivity of the poet. Thus focused, the question posed by the line becomes, "in confronting myself face to face in verbalized form, have I simply abolished myself, or have I glorified myself?" Or, in other words, the poet asks, "to be I, must I poetize or remain silent?" The rest of the poem offers illustrations of these two options and a final vision of a surface on which they can be, if not synthesized, at least preserved in this disjunction, a surface that is capable of maintaining the word "or" as well as the emphasized caesura of the ninth line.

The second line of the first tercet—"Mon front est rouge encore du baiser de la reine"—introduces another character, whom Nerval annotates in the Eluard manuscript with the words "Reine Candace?" Candace was the generic name of the queens of Ethiopia, who appear, in the form of the queen of Sheba, throughout Nerval's works, notably in the tale of her meeting with King Solomon in the *Voyage en Orient* and in an abortive and financially ruinous play whose title role had been intended as a vehicle for Jenny Colon (with whom Nerval was in love and ostensibly the woman for whom he had attempted suicide on the Posilipo). The "reine" in this light would thus represent a mythic form of the poet's idealized love-object. More significant, however, is the manner in which she appears in the poem itself. Nerval may identify the personage in notes to himself, but in the poem this figure is determined only as one who has left a mark on the poet's forehead. The line does not memorialize the act of kissing, the moment of a union, but the trace of that union, the remembrance of that act. The queen herself may be alive or dead; all that is known of her, here, is the record she has left of a single gesture. She is present in the poem only through this memento, which thus becomes the sign of the queen as well as of her absence. This sign, more than the kiss itself, which draws together two people present to one another, creates a bond, for it joins the present with the absent, that which is and that which is not, and links the past with the present, that which is with that which is no more. The "je," like the lute of the first stanza, is symbolically emblazoned with the sign of loss, has become a symbolical repository. Like the wife of Mausolus, who mixed the ashes of her husband's corpse with wine and drank them, Nerval here makes of his body a tomb, the site where a loved one is preserved in her absence, but unlike Artemis, Nerval preserves not through incorporation but through inscription—a red inscription, like the sonnet itself, whose manuscript is penned in red ink.[69]

The line also finds an echo in the second line of "Antéros," another sonnet from the *Chimères*, but there the reddening of the forehead by the impress of lips more explicitly represents the sign of abolition and absence, for it is identified as the mark of Cain, the mark of death that indelibly stains the face of the first human being, according to the Bible, to confront death, the first to incorporate into himself its memory:

> Oui, je suis de ceux-là qu'inspire le Vengeur,
> Il m'a marqué le front de sa lèvre irritée,
> Sous la pâleur d'Abel, hélas! ensanglantée,
> J'ai parfois de Caïn l'implacable rougeur!
>
> Yes, I am one of those whom the Avenger inspires,
> He has marked my brow with his angry lips,
> Beneath Abel's—alas! bloodied—pallor,
> I sometimes have Cain's implacable red.[70]

The importance the figure of Cain bore for Nerval, and the heroic stature the poet attributed to him as a forceful, inventive, and ultimately redemptive rebel, is amply illustrated in other works—*Aurélia*, and the "Story of Solomon and the queen of the morning" from the *Voyage en Orient*, for example. Cain is not merely the first to bear the sign of the dead, to memorialize the original abolition of another; he also figures in Nerval's works as the archetype of the artist, both as solitary creative genius and as the socially recognized master of the mechanical skills requisite for material expression, and while this binary role tends to displace individual artistic genius toward impersonal *techné*, it is a displacement that will return in the last tercet with the figure of the lyre of Orpheus.[71] Cain comes in this way to represent the marked artist, whose very body has become a repository for signs. In the sonnet, the image of the poet as the bearer of the memorializing inscription of a loss, the absence of a queen, refers back, however, to the preceding line, and serves as an illustration of one of the choices that "je" hesitates between: here is the poet as inscription, the poetized poet, the Biron who bears the sign of the absent on himself and thus symbolically incorporates his abolished alienated essence onto his own person. This is poet as apotheosis of the word, the poet as sonnet.

If the tenth line represents an illustration of the poetic, Apollonian/Byronesque option of self-identification, the next line—"J'ai rêvé dans la grotte où nage la syrène… "—offers an image of the nonverbal option that Nerval had associated with the name of Lusignan. There are two salient features of this line: the revery of the poet and the silence of the siren. Mythically, the siren is associated with song and death, for she lures the navigator to his doom, giving direction not only to the ship on the sea, but also to all of life as a movement toward a specific demise. Instead of turning to celestial aids, instead of following stars, the sailor turns to a voice in song to guide him across the unarticulated, unintelligible, unmapped surface of the ocean. Overwhelming, replacing the shipmen's willpower, the song acts like a star, drawing them on toward a silence that will prove to be their annihilation and destiny, returning them to the depths of the mute, the unspoken, the unfathomed, the inarticulate. The sirens bury sailors in the final anonymity of the sea, like the Dubourjet whose posthumous letters became the substance of Nerval's *Un Roman à faire*.[72] The song of the sirens is a surrogate star that lends a destiny to an ocean-going life; the destiny that it promises, however, is the silence of a nameless tomb, an abolition *without a trace*. The song of the sirens, like the *étoile* of the first stanza, articulates a life and lends it linearity, but the culmination it offers abolishes everything that went before, drowns the trip with the sailors, for nothing is memorialized, and there is no moment when the traveler can turn back to review, in its articulated, intelligible directedness, the whole of his life as he is able to do from the summit of the steeple at Strasbourg.

Here, however, the siren does not sing but swims, or as the Eluard version has it, *verdit*, "turns green." She is shown as integrated into her element, whether that integration be effected, as in the published version, through her immersion and interaction with it or, as in the Eluard version, through the way in which it alters her physical appearance with marine colors. The *grotte* thus represents a place where the siren has fallen silent, where she is reincorporated into the anonymous unintelligibility of the ocean, into the place of nameless death, the tomb that does not preserve but simply abolishes. Like the "grotte, fatale aux hôtes imprudents [grotto, fatal to imprudent guests]" of "Delfica," the fifth sonnet of the *Chimères*, this is a fatal place, in the sense that it is a place of destiny and a place of death. It recalls the events alluded to in the second stanza, which in *Octavie* took place on "the Posilipo, above the grotto," and foreshadows the descent into the underworld of the last stanza. But the scene also echoes a passage from Jehan d'Arras's *Mélusine*: the transgressive moment of illicit viewing that ushers in the unspoken rule of silence between the ill-fated couple. The passage recounts how Raimondin de Lusignan pierced a hole in the door to an enclosure his wife had built around the spring next to which they had first met:

> In this part the story tells us that Raimondin so paced and turned back and forth that he ended up making a groove in the door with the point of his sword, through which he could view everything that was in the room, and he saw Melusine, who was in the vat up to her navel in the form of a woman [jusques au nombril en signe de femme], and she was combing her hair; and below the navel she was in the form of a snake as thick as a herring-barrel, and her long tail did writhe greatly in the water, so that it splashed up even to the vaulting of the room.[73]

Both the text by Jehan d'Arras and the line from the sonnet depict an enclosed space in which a man observes a siren-figure in the water, and in both a necessary, fatal silence reigns. It is a silence that extends to the poet himself, for he is not represented speaking or poetizing, but rather lost in revery, a word that seems to have had a special significance for Nerval: it symbolizes on the one hand the nonlinear, atemporal landscape that Rousseau generated in his *Rêveries d'un promeneur solitaire*, which describe walks in the Valois region, and, on the other, a general refusal of literature.[74] At the end of the *Roman à faire*, Nerval contrasted musing and writing, justifying his fragmentary presentation of Dubourjet's letters with the remark: "And besides, does the world not have enough novels already? Here is one less to read and one more to dream of [un de plus à rêver]."[75] This opposition between writing and revery seems operative here too, making of the *grotte* a place of muteness, a locus of the unwritten which contrasts with the inscription evoked in the preceding line. While the tenth line represents the poet-as-poetry, the eleventh line, drawing on associations with classical myth, the medieval tale of Mélusine, and the underworld, depicts a wordless place where poetry and song fall silent and the individual draws close to anonymous death—the death of being utterly unarticulated, unconstructed, and uncommunicated. A double bind is thus established: the first two stanzas represent language and poetization of the subject as an annihilating tomb, while the final line of the first tercet represents silence as a dissolution of the individual in the infinite aimlessness of the ocean. Whether in language or in avoiding it, the individual faces only its abolition.

Figure of the Nonsynthetic Self

If the tenth line elaborates on the significance of the names Phébus and Biron, while the eleventh line elaborates on that of Lusignan, the last tercet of the poem offers a resolution of the contrasting self-identifications—one verbal, the other mute—which the poet has hesitated between at the beginning of the third stanza. The twelfth line—"Et j'ai deux fois vainqueur traversé l'Achéron"—clearly represents a journey into the underworld, for according to classical mythology Achéron was the turbulent river across which Charon ferried the souls of the dead into Hades; the crossing of its waters in the poem would thus represent a literal or metaphorical death. It is not immediately apparent, however, in what way the reference to "deux fois" is to be understood, whether it indicates a single round trip or two distinct descents. The use of the words "Achéron" and, in the next line, "Orphée," suggests that it is among the myths of antiquity that the key to the line's meaning will be found. The list is not long of those mortals who in one way or another cheated or despoiled death, who passed from the underworld back into the realm of the living: Orpheus, Aeneas, Theseus, Hercules, Adonis, and the Dioscuri: Castor and Pollux. Because he is mentioned in the following line, Orpheus seems to be the most probable choice, but since his two journeys into Hades would have been his failed attempt to retrieve his wife and his actual death, the epithet "vainqueur" seems inappropriate. The choice of Aeneas as an antecedent is supported by lines 133–36 of Book 6 of the *Aeneid*, where the expression "deux fois" becomes the word *bis* (twice); there the sybil instructs Aeneas:

> quod si tantus amor menti, si tanta cupido est
> *bis* Stygios innare lacus, *bis* nigra uidere
> Tartara, et insano iuuat indulgere labori,
> accipe quae peragenda prius . . .

> But if in your spirit the love be so great, the desire so great, *twice* to navigate the Stygian mere, *twice* to see gloomy Tartarus, and if it please you to indulge in a mad labor, learn what must be done first . . . [76]

On the basis of such a subtext, the line from the sonnet might be understood to refer to two separate victories over death, such as the two unsuccessful suicide attempts on the Posilipo, or, taken metaphorically, Nerval's two bouts of madness, which were later described by the poet himself as a "descent into Hell." Again, however, it would be difficult to reconcile such a reading with Nerval's use of the expression "vainqueur," since the latter implies a contest and a violence against death which are absent from Virgil's account; furthermore, as with Orpheus, the sybil's reference to a second trip clearly signifies not a conquest of but a final submission to death.

In a letter to Georges Bell, from June 1, 1854, Nerval will speak of his own descent into Hell, drawing on allusions to the *Aeneid* and making an explicit comparison between himself and Theseus:

> Did I let this *sacred fire* die out altogether?... It's fine for the vestal of the *boulevard de l'Hôpital*! I am not waiting for the goddess's belated aid, I'm making my way upstream by oar. I have sung too often in the gloom:
> *Let my tears move you,*
> *Shades, larvae, terrible specters*!
> Clearly I am not a hero with the strength of Theseus or Peirithous,—nor of Paganini, but I aspire to become strong like a Turk. With a little help, I shall succeed.[77]

In placing Paganini on a continuum with Theseus and Peirithous, Nerval seems to reveal a belief that the artist, like the Greek heroes, confronts death and journeys to the underworld, and art, in this regard, is thus depicted as a grappling with one's own annihilation. Theseus's somewhat humiliating adventures in the underworld are inextricably intertwined with those of Hercules, to whom the epithet "vainqueur" could easily apply: Hercules did in fact do violence—physical or metaphorical, depending on the version of the myth—to death, engaging in a struggle, according to some, with Pluto himself; he also dragged Cerberus into the upper regions as a trophy. A version of the myth in Dom Pernety's *Les Fables égyptiennes et grecques*, a book with which Nerval was well acquainted and to which he made reference at several points in his works, gives a special emphasis to this triumphant aspect of Hercules' undertaking, for it represents the hero stopping on his return to the world of the living to make a crown for himself.[78] This account of the myth is especially interesting in the present context, since seemingly alone among those descriptions of descents into the underworld which would have been available to Nerval, it specifically mentions two crossings of the river Acheron. On his way down, Hercules, according to Pernety, "passed the Acheron and the other rivers of Hell," while on his return journey, upwards, "he brought Theseus away with him and at the same time led Cerberus to Eurystheus. While crossing the Acheron he found there a white poplar and cut from it a branch to make himself a crown."[79]

With the exception of Adonis and the Dioscuri, who will be discussed in relation to the next line, the accounts of these heroes had already been drawn on and, to a certain extent, synthesized by a post-classical precursor of Nerval. Dante's extensive borrowings from Book 6 of the *Aeneid* for his description of Acheron in Canto 3 of the *Inferno* are well known; significantly, Dante places limbo on the far side of Acheron, which thus would have been the only infernal river that Christ crossed in the harrowing of hell, an incident which is alluded to in the next canto (4) by the following exchange between Dante and Virgil:

"Dimmi, maestro mio, dimmi, segnore,"
comincia' io per volere esser certo
di quella fede che vince ogni errore:

"uscicci mai alcuno, o per suo merto
o per altrui, che poi fosse beato?"
E quei, che'ntese il mio parlar coperto,

rispuose: "Io era nuovo in questo stato,
quando ci vidi venire un possente,
con segno di vittoria coronato . . ."

(ll. 46–54)

> "Tell me, my Master, tell me, sir," I began, seeking to be assured of that faith which overcomes every doubt, "did ever anyone, either by his own merit or another's, go out hence and come afterwards to bliss?"
>
> And he, who understood my veiled speech, replied: "I was new in this condition when I saw a mighty one come here crowned with a sign of victory . . ."[80]

Like Hercules, Dante's Christ is shown crowned with victory. Like the poet of the tenth line, too, he bears a sign (*segno*) on his forehead. With this passage from the *Divine Comedy*, much of the syncretic Christian appropriation of the classical *topos* of the journey into the underworld had already been done, centuries before Nerval drew on it in his sonnet; it would be virtually impossible, afterwards, not to see these myths through the filter of Dante. Nor would it have been foreign to Nerval to adopt the role of Christ for himself, since already in "Le Christ aux Oliviers" he had assumed the voice of the savior-poet in the garden of Gethsemane, two days before his descent among the dead. And in speaking of his "descent into Hell" in the preface to the *Filles du feu*, he had written:

> From the moment that I thought I could grasp the series of all my previous experiences, it cost me as little to have been prince, king, magus, genius, and even God. . . . It would be Scipio's Dream, Tasso's vision, or Dante's *Divine Comedy*, had I succeeded in concentrating all my memories into a masterpiece.[81]

Taken in this light, the reference to a double crossing of Acheron would refer not to *a* conquest of death but to *the* conquest of death, the definitive and exemplary triumph of life in the pre-apocalyptic world; it would symbolize both the passage to the lowest point of God's descent into the realm of nonbeing and his resurrection. It is the death of God, followed by his restoration and the resolution of the moment of hyperbolic doubt Christ had passed through during the night before Golgotha.

To say that such an interpretation takes this line out of the realm of personal history into that of world history understates the case. In appropriating the role of Christ as conqueror of death, Nerval depicts himself as the one who through his acts has restored the historical order after it fell into doubt with the death of God. He reaffirms himself here not as a subject *in* history but as the subject *of* history, the one that guarantees its coherence and continuity. All that was lost in Gethsemane is restored in this line. But it is restored altered, otherwise, displaced, impersonal, as the final lines will show.

The colon at the end of the twelfth line indicates that what follows is an explanation, a paraphrase of the line; it is a sign of equivalence between what comes before and after it. The double journey into the underworld and back thus *is* the act of modulating voices on the lyre of Orpheus. Setting aside for a moment the question of the identity of the two female figures of the last line and the opposition between them, what is modulated on the lyre are two voices, or, more specifically, the nonverbal, unarticulated sounds that are produced by two breaths: a *soupir* and a *cri*. The choice of the word *moduler* seems determined at least in part by an intentional archaism, for the Latin verb at its root, *modulari*, was used in classical texts to describe the playing of the lyre.[82] It also signified, however, the putting of words into meter, or versifying, and thus drew together the image of the lyre with the idea of ordered expression, a particular convergence of image and concept that was widespread in texts that Nerval consulted. Dom Pernety, for example, unites them under a common origin when he speaks of the god Hermes, who

> was the first to show men the way of setting their thoughts in writing and of placing their expressions in order, so that a coherent discourse should come of them.... He gave appropriate names to many things . . . , invented music . . . , the three-stringed lyre.[83]

The French word lost any association with a particular musical instrument but maintained the sense of regulating, inflecting, or, in other words, articulating and submitting to formal expression. To modulate shrieks and sighs is thus to give aesthetic form to the preverbal, to articulate the inarticulate, to make an utterance of an unreflected, unthought, and wordless breath. In fact, the Eluard manuscript shows the word "Fée" annotated with the remark, "Mélusine ou Manto." The cries of the fairy, which have entered into the French language as the "cris de Mélusine," were those she let out after her husband had denounced her in public; they were the brute, unconsidered expression of a grief so overwhelming that it reduced the sufferer to a virtually inhuman state. At this point in the text by Jehan d'Arras, Mélusine is seen reverted to an animalistic form, and the howls she lets out, though in a woman's voice, seem to have the force of a natural cataclysm rather than that of human expression:

> Then the lady, so transmuted in the shape of a snake, as it is said, turned thrice about the fortress, and with each time she passed before the window she heaved a cry so wondrous that each one wept for pity of it, and they perceived she was greatly troubled to leave the place and that it was by constraint. And then she made her way towards Lusignan, bearing through the air such great fright in her furiousness that it seemed to all on earth that lightning and tempest must fall from the sky.[84]

Like the siren of the eleventh line of the sonnet, Mélusine is shown in this passage reintegrated into the natural realm, and she moves over the earth in the form of a snake and with a voice that seems to articulate less a human affect than an inhuman disaster. The lyre of Orpheus, that could charm the animals, here seems to give them, if not expression, at least shape, articulating the brute cries of something without language. Manto, on the other hand, was the name of two sybils in antiquity, and evokes in this passage what Dhanaens refers to as "the cries of inspiration (incoherent utterances) pronounced by the Python above a crevasse from which cold mists emerged."[85] Here, they are not so much cries as a stream of words that have no meaning because they are unshapen as discourse, because, though words, they are among themselves unarticulated, unmodulated, cast in an unfathomable disorder like the leaves that the Cumaean sybil threw to the winds. In giving form to these cries, this unintelligible verbal stream, the lyre of Orpheus referred to in the penultimate line maintains the two subjective options set forth in the ninth line, for it is the instrument on which poetic articulation—the Apollonian and Byronic—is given to the nonverbal cries associated with Lusignan's wife. The lyre gives order to disorder by modulating that which has no words: meaningless animal cries, the sigh and the wail. It cadences a language that, when understood in terms of Manto and Mélusine, has failed either under the sybilline pressure of a divine message and a meaning that is more than human or under an unbearable grief that seems beastly and less than human. When language fails before something the lyre takes up the remains and modulates them. At the end of meaning, after meaning, it takes the breath that is left—the *cri* and the *soupir*, the *souffle* absent from "Le Christ aux Oliviers"—and lyricizes it. It is a postverbal poetry, made after a meaning that cannot be borne by language, a sense too high or too low, too bestial or too divine, and it is from the poetry of this damaged language that the subject is made.

While the identity of the *fée* of the last line is suggested in Nerval's annotation to the Eluard manuscript, that very identification indicates that she represents something more abstract and general than a specific mythological, biographical, or folkloric character, for even Nerval hesitates in his attribution, unable to choose between Manto and Mélusine. Similarly, while numerous *saintes* appear in the *Chimères* (and elsewhere throughout Nerval's works), there is no reason to believe that any one of them is the saint of this last line. Like the *roses* discussed earlier, the *saintes*, neither positive nor negative in themselves, seem to have taken on their value and significance through their context or through the epithets attributed to them. In the sonnet entitled "Artémis" alone the word appears four times, with very different connotations. Again, like the *rose* and the *pampre* whose conjunction closes the first half of the poem, these two female figures from the last line of the second half seem to signify more by their opposition to each other than in their own right. They are the masks of a single feminine principle, which Nerval sometimes names Isis and who is the personification of fate, destiny, and death, the ultimate abstraction, the final object of desire, but also the first, since she is the mother of all beings, their origin and original. Too abstract in themselves and differentiated only in their juxtaposition, they can be construed with certainty only as two aspects of the feminine object of desire that haunted Nerval and which has already appeared in the sonnet under the guise of the *étoile*, the *fleur*, the *reine*, the *sirène*, and *toi*. Like the *stella maris* and the siren song that lead the seafarer across uncharted waters, like the *étoile* that leads the poet from the chaotic "enfer," or "Hell," of his unstructured self-representations to their eventual narrative expression, the *sainte* and the *fée* in their femininity represent a principle of directedness and will towards something, linearity and subjective organization, the objectified essence of the inward unity and structure of the self. The attempt, that reappears throughout Nerval's works, to synthesize the various women he loves into simulacra of each other is always an attempt to unify his own subjectivity by identifying with one another these disparate feminine representations of his own internal coherence.[86] For there is a paradox at work here: although they each represent subjective unity—the underlying selfhood of the self, its structure, its self-sameness—these feminine figures are also plural and different, which suggests that the poet's principle of subjective coherence is itself multiple and potentially incoherent. What is problematic, then, in this line is above all the difference between the *sainte* and the *fée*, the fact that as disparate embodiments of Nerval's identity they represent a potentially plural subjective unity.

This disjunction would appear, however, to be resolved in the last tercet through the reference to poetic harmonization: since they are personifications of Nerval's objectified subjective unity, the modulation of the two feminine voices would seem to represent the articulation of the poet's different possible self-constructs into a higher level of subjective coherence. Such a resolution would, however, merely give expression to the fundamental unity that already underlay the multiple feminine masks and identified them as variations of the same: the objectified essence of subjectivity, whose loss is mourned and whose restitution desired throughout the sonnet. The lost subject would thus be returned as the poem itself, figured in the lyre. The two divergent representations of inward coherence, the *sainte* and the *fée*, are, in this reading, brought together on an instrument that modulates them, as two voices, "tour à tour." Originally the line had read, "Modulant et chantant sur la lyre d'Orphée [Tuning and singing on the Orphic lyre]," but in the Eluard manuscript and the *Filles du feu* edition it became "Modulant tour à tour sur la lyre d'Orphée [Tuning in turn on the Orphic lyre]." The original use of the verb *chanter* strengthens, of course, the idea of a verbal, poetic articulation of the preverbal. It was rejected, however, for a more impersonal construction that placed the articulation, the locus of conjunction between poetic and preverbal subjectivities, not in a human voice but in an impersonal and inhuman *instrument*.[87] With the verb *chanter* elided from the line, and the singing voice thus removed from the text, the site where the disparate halves of a fissured subjectivity converge is no longer located in the person of the poet himself, but in a mechanical device; although it represents the human articulation of the inhuman or proto-human elements of subjectivity through the verbalization of the nonverbal, the lyre is not itself a living human being but rather an artifact and a machine. The "place" that underlies the two halves of the self, the substance and subject of the self in their most profound form as that which grounds and unifies the different aspects and self-representations of the self, would thus be objectified out of the poet himself into a machine linking the nonverbal to the verbal. This, to borrow de Man's vocabulary, joins the "barren world of ontological reduction" with "the wealth of lived experience," and expresses the immediacy of sensuous experience in the mediation of discourse. Here, on this instrument, the sensuous muteness of the siren is brought together with the written impress of its absence, or the "baiser de la reine." It is a lyre that outlives Orpheus to fall into the hands of the poet-*je* of the sonnet, a lyre eternalized in constellated form while the body of its original player, torn into fragments by the Maenads, is cast into the anonymous sea.[88] As such, it would seem to be a slight displacement, to the poem itself as field or surface on which ("*sur* la lyre") diversity is maintained, of the substantial subject that links madness to its lucid expression and the multiple expressions of the self into an individual: it would be the lyre-ic *je* that supports the various, divergent principles of selfhood that the poet has elaborated in the rest of the poem.

In the lyre one would seem to be confronted, at last, with an allegorization of the purely propositional subject, an underlying coherence of subjective experience which would function solely on the level of language—indeed, one would finally have to admit, on the level of a meaningless language. For death and the negative are not used in this poem in any sort of progressive sense; they are not the dark articulations of a dialectical self-understanding; rather, they lead to a loss of sense, and a reversion of subjectivity toward a meaningless sound, what Hegel had called a *sinnloser Laut*. As has been remarked, the use of a colon to end the first line of the last tercet indicates that the modulation of the "soupirs de la sainte et les cris de la fée" represents the double journey into the underworld and back. This triumph over death occurs in the alternation of two voices, for the *soupirs* and the *cris* are modulated "tour à tour." The use of the latter expression indicates two things. First, that the voices are not integrated into one another, that they are not synthesized but are rather placed in circulation on a lyre-ic field that can support them both in their mutual exclusion. One voice is expressed while the other is held in reserve, and the lyre must be capable of performing both these functions: it must be both the fatal *grotte* where the song is withheld and the reddened impress that poetically bespeaks. Both voices must pass through death and silence to reemerge in articulate utterance, or to rephrase this in the vocabulary suggested by the stanza itself, one voice must "die" while the other is being modulated and then be "resurrected" when, its own turn for expression come, it is recalled. Consequently the lyre represents a place of linguistic reticence and expression that is metaphorized in a cycle of death and rebirth. Second, the words "tour à tour" indicate an indefinite repetition of this alternation. The two distinct voices of the *sainte* and the *fée* continuously circulate on the journey through death, disappearing and reappearing, one after the other. The triumph over death is not, therefore, a dialectical progression of subjectivity through negativity to a fuller, positive self-identification, as a Hegelian reading like Dhanaens's argues, but rather the mutually exclusive deployment of life and death on an impersonal instrument such that the various aspects of the self—here represented by the *sainte* and the *fée*—can circulate between them without prejudice or advantage to either. There is no sense of progress here, but rather a figure of the endless circular displacement of mutually exclusive elements (the shrieks and the sighs) through mutually exclusive states (death and life).

If such an interpretation of the last stanza should seem improbably abstract, an overly ontological reading of a poet who, after all, speaks of Hegelian philosophy only as an illustration of mystification (his *Chimères*, he says, "are hardly more obscure than Hegel's metaphysics or Swedenborg's *Memorabilia*"),[89] one can nonetheless point specifically to a precise and concrete literary image, an antecedent from classical mythology which leads one to the same conclusions about the model of poetic subjectivity set forth by Nerval in this stanza. A similar image of a divided, doubled self caught in endless circulation through life and death appears in certain of the texts that manifestly influenced the present passage. When, in a conversation with the Cumaean sybil from Book 6 (ll. 119–22) of the *Aeneid*, Aeneas depicts the lyre of Orpheus as the very force that allowed the Thracian hero to triumph over the underworld, he also mentions Pollux, who had achieved a more ambiguous but more sustained victory over death. Aeneas asks why he cannot enter the underworld

> si potuit manis accersere coniugis Orpheus
> Threicia fretus cithera fidebusque canoris,
> si fratrem Pollux *alterna morte* redemit
> *itque reditque uiam totiens* . . .

> if Orpheus, placing his faith in a Thracian lyre and its singing chords, was able to summon the shade of his wife, if Pollux, *travelling again and again so many times the way* [to Hades] redeems his brother with *an alternating death*.[90]

The Dioscurus Pollux is able to redeem his twin brother Castor's life through a pact with the god of the underworld: he shall descend on a regular basis into Hades so that his brother may, during those periods, rejoin the living. This is the alternating death or *alterna mors* that leads Pollux to travel ceaselessly back and forth along the paths between the upper and lower worlds.[91] The Virgilian text obviously resonates throughout the stanza, even in the key points of its vocabulary (*bis*, *Acheron*, *Orpheus*, *cithera/lyre*, *alterna*), and the image of such a doubled self was a constant of Nerval's writings.[92] Moreover, during the same period in which the sonnet was written, Nerval signed his delirious letter to George Sand with the words: "Gaston Phœbus d'Aquitaine / pour copie: / Gérard de Nerval / Dioscures."[93] The last stanza represents, in short, a self-construction as an impersonal binary movement through life and death, devised on the model of Castor and Pollux but construed as an endless, mechanically repeated displacement of mutually exclusive articulations of desire figured as two female personae, the *sainte* and the *fée*.

The Sonnet as a Hegelian Misstep

Nerval then, at the end of the sonnet, proposes a subjectivity that contains its own death within it, that incorporates into itself a place in which the unexpressed and inarticulate is held in forgotten-ness but can be recalled. It is a self that bears in itself another, a place of silence, forgetting, and annihilation, a hidden, timeless place that prefigures the Freudian unconscious. Here, death loses its finality, for instead of moving toward an ultimate and fatal destiny (instead of drowning in the siren-sea), the disinherited subject lives alongside it, as in the *grotte* of the siren. The lyre-ic subject bears its own abolition, it lives with it, incorporates it. In its use of negativity, this seems to be a resurfacing of the fundamental structures of German romantic philosophy and, specifically, an eminently Hegelian image of the self, for it is indisputable that the model of a lyric subjectivity articulated around an *alterna mors* which appears in the final stanza of the sonnet seems close to the Subject described in the following passage from the Preface to the *Phenomenology of Spirit*:

> That an accident as such, detached from what circumscribes it, what is bound and is actual only in its context with others, should attain an existence of its own and a separate freedom—this is the tremendous power of the negative; it

> is the energy of thought, of the pure "I." Death, if that is what we want to call this non-actuality, is of all things the most dreadful, and to hold fast what is dead requires the greatest strength. Lacking strength, Beauty hates the Understanding for asking of her what it cannot do. But the life of Spirit is not the life that shrinks from death and keeps itself untouched by devastation, but rather the life that endures it and maintains itself in it. It wins its truth only when, in utter dismemberment, it finds itself. It is this power, not as something positive, which closes its eyes to the negative, as when we say of something that it is nothing or is false, and then, having done with it, turn away and pass on to something else; on the contrary, Spirit is this power only by looking the negative in the face, and tarrying with it. This tarrying with the negative is the magical power that converts it into being. This power is identical with what we earlier called the Subject, which by giving determinateness an existence in its own element supersedes abstract immediacy, i.e. the immediacy which barely is, and thus is authentic substance: that being or immediacy whose mediacy is not outside of it but which is this mediation itself.[94]

Hegel here describes the "pure 'I'" and the "Subject" as the power to tarry with death, to abide with the negative, to face it. But this negative Subject, this pure "I" that lives in death, is, according to Hegel, the principle of mediation itself. The self that thus maintains itself in death, that passes into death, is the self that mediates itself, for it is no longer simply immediately itself, but itself *through* another, that is, mediately. Through its own death, through its own abolition, through its negation, it relates itself to itself, comes to know itself not abstractly but as an authentic substance. Originally the Subject is simply posited, and as such, is unmediated (something like a sound without referential content); but here, in facing its death, in becoming that death and maintaining itself in it, the Subject objectifies itself, takes on content, and consequently substantiates itself. By thus contextualizing itself with itself, by seeing itself in relation to itself through the mediation of its own negation, the self passes into an entity not merely posited but situated (in respect to the context of itself) and thus passes also from the entirely abstract to the at least minimally specific (contextualized), from the entirely empty to a Subject that knows itself as its own content. The entire movement of the *Phenomenology* functions through the mechanism of "determinate negation" described in this passage, and presents itself, on this basis, as a process of self-knowledge capable of incorporating its own death into itself and of passing from the abstract universal to the specificity of a substantial subjectivity.[95] These are, of course, Nerval's concerns too, as these chapters have tried to demonstrate: the attempt to specify and substantiate the abstract emptiness of a merely posited name (whether that be "je" or the "abbé de Bucquoy" or "Gérard"), the attempt to triumph over death by incorporating it, and the desire to elaborate a self through its objectification.

Though there is a striking communality between the Subject of this passage from the Preface of the *Phenomenology* and the Nervalian subject of "El Desdichado," the two constructs remain fundamentally different. Most significantly, Hegel offers the image of a subject that gains in self-knowledge, specificity, and content by passing repeatedly through its own negation: by rethinking itself, by objectifying itself, Hegelian Spirit moves forward. The Nervalian subject, however, does not move forward, but rather circulates as a series of objectified self-representations supported by an impersonal artifact. These self-representations do not increase in specificity or content, they merely displace themselves, moving on a circular track between life and death. With Hegel, the subject becomes its own death by being negated, moving through its negation, and therefore elaborating itself in a progressive series of alternating steps that pass through a negativity that is generated by and determinate to each position that self-defining subjectivity reaches. Nerval's lyre-ic subject, however, does not elaborate itself through death, but holds death within itself, not as a dynamic force but as an unresolvable, immediate other. The Nervalian self does not elaborate its death, nor, consequently, itself; it remains as a place that holds both death and life, but as nonintegrated, and undetermined by each other. In a word, for Hegel there is progress, for Nerval alternation. Life and death, positive and negative, the sensuous and the articulated, are not mutually determined in the lyre-ic *je*, and they can never, therefore, be synthesized according to any Hegelian model; rather they are juxtaposed, held in their mutual exclusivity as the circuitous structure of a subject that, as supported on the lyre-poem, remains irreducibly plural, that always involves indeterminate fragmentation and a pointless displacement, a twin- or Dioscuri-structure. In its disarticulation, in its maintenance of mutually exclusive predications such *sainte* and *fée*, dead and alive, speaking and silent, tower and its abolition, the lyre-ic subject breaks down its own meaning, situating its coherence elsewhere than in the self-conformity of its sense.

This purely propositional elsewhere is itself, like the referentially substantial subject-as-meaning it displaces, highly problematic. It persistently undermines a tradition of death-based subjectivity, reaching from Hegel to Heidegger, that would seek precisely to control it, and it eludes even the labile consistency that Julia Kristeva, one of the most intellectually supple readers of poetic discourse, would attempt to find in construing "El Desdichado" as the aesthetically material—and thereby essentially non-sensical—recompense for a lost nonverbal meaning. For what, in all this, is particularly troubling about Nerval's poetic structure of subjectivity is that one of the terms that circulate on the lyre—expression or modulation—is the lyre, or the poem itself: although the sonnet may be neatly allegorized in the final image of an instrument that gives measured linguistic shape to the inchoate preverbal, that shaping is nonetheless only one of the modalities of the lyre; its other is silence, retention, the swimming of the siren in the meaningless, voiceless sea, the end, in short, of language. With this recognition, the aesthetic ground gives way beneath the self-identified *je* of "El Desdichado," for it is undermined by the *grotte* that reaches down endlessly into the sea. But really, no image or visual figure of the subject works any longer, now that even the substantiality of the poem itself as aesthetic object is rejected as a basis of self-sameness: the subject's structure, that of the poem, is monstrous, caught between the imaginable and the unimaginable, between a picture of the lyre as substantial object underlying the circulation of diverse subject identifications, and the unpicturable discursive construct of a lyre that circulates on itself. It is shaped—if one uses that word both literally and figuratively, in other words, monstrously—as creature both of the imagination and of its sublime unimaginable end, cast in a language that both makes a sense that refutes the senses and sensuously refuses to make sense.

In the lyre-ic subject of "El Desdichado," Nerval did not, however, merely devise a particularly artful rhetorical conceit; by elaborating and allegorizing a purely discursive selfhood incapable of unified self-determination, he produced a model of subjectivity that, while remaining propositional, cannot be exhaustively interpreted as sublime or utterly abstracted. This construct, futile as it may seem, has very serious implications for the Hegelian tradition.

Before proceeding further with the contextual importance of this poem, it is probably useful to recall the broad outlines of the present reading. The first quatrain determines that the sonnet will be an introspection, and its principal objective is to establish a subjective identity. The self that is depicted here, however, is one surrounded and defined by abolished objects, objects that exist only in a symbolic register. Moreover, since one of these negated, symbolic elements, the *étoile*, represents the objectified principle of the poet's subjective coherence, the lyric self that emerges in these lines is itself abolished, negative, and symbolic. In the following stanza the imagery lightens, and the hope is expressed that life can be restored beyond the tomb, that in a dramatic triumph over death the plenitude of sensuous existence can be restored within the barren negativity of language. In the second half of the poem the relation between death and writing shifts; whereas the written and the symbolic had been associated with death and negativity in the quatrains, in the tercets death—denoted by the *grotte* and the underworld—comes to represent the pre- or nonverbal, the non-symbolic. In the first tercet, the poet explicitly places his identity at issue, asking, among other questions, whether his is a sensuous, preverbal existence, or a poetic representation of something absent and unrestorable. The question itself is grammatically articulated by two disjunctive iterations of "ou?" which are never resolved. Rather, they are maintained as mutually exclusive in the alternating structure of the poetic subjectivity proposed in the last stanza. Metrically the question is arranged around a caesura reinforced by the punctuation (" ... "). This, coming at the very center of the poem, serves to emblematize the fundamentally fissured nature of the lyric self constructed in the sonnet. With the lyre of Orpheus, the final stanza allegorizes the lyric subject of the poem as the poem itself, construed as the breaking down of the unity of its meaning through the maintenance of a dense convergence of noncompossible predications functioning on a variety of levels. First, the coherent essence of the subject is expressed not as a unity but as a plurality, diversely objectified as *sainte* and *fée*. Second, the subject that so variously identifies itself *in absentia* as a lost object of desire is further categorized as paradoxically both alive and dead, caught in a cyclical *alterna mors*. By modulating wordless sounds, the shrieks and sighs of two female personifications, the lyre also figuratively supports a third opposition between the nonverbal and the poetic, which is hyperbolized into the polarity between speech and silence in the "tour à tour" cyclical structure of the lyre, which alternately expresses and silences each of the two inarticulate female voicings. This latter opposition between language and nonlanguage can be mapped, retrospectively, onto the opposition between the impress of a kiss and the mute siren, which in turn develops the difference between Lusignan, representative of the unspoken, and Byron, a metonymy of the poetic. These incompossible predications of the subject are themselves grounded, or supported, in a figure of the aesthetic materiality of the poetic which is itself rhetorically monstrous, since it is neither entirely imaginable nor entirely abstractly intelligible: the image of a lyre circulating, dying and resurrecting, being and not being, on itself. The instrument of Orpheus is an image of the impossibility of the image, but also of the impossibility of discarding utterly—sublimating—the image. It is the image, on the one hand, of a sustained if inconstant reincorporation of the sublime into that which the sublime annihilates: the imaginary. On the other, it evokes the necessary resurgence of the imaginary within the intelligibility of the abstract. Most important, it is, as allegory of the subject, not merely allegory, for it is the self-identification of the poem, which is in turn the self-identification of the lyric self; the impossible figure *is*, in short, the subject as well as its representation. Nerval's literary introspections led to the conclusion that insofar as I am self-same, I am written; the last tercet of "El Desdichado" gives the figure of that writing and is that writing.

One can agree with Kristeva that the loss mourned in the first half of the poem would be that of the nonverbal or preverbal, something like the endlessly fugitive Lacanian "real," or the elusive object of insatiable desire figured by the *object little a*.[96] Speaking of the unmasterable allusiveness of the various figures in the poem, she writes: "The undecidable concatenation of these real and imaginary figures flees once more toward the position of the archaic 'Thing'—the elusive pre-object of a mourning endemic to all speaking beings."[97] The sheer, immense volume of literature devoted to this one sonnet attests in part to this undecidability, whose structural poetic necessity has been the object of the present reading. Over the long decades that this sonnet has been able to maintain its allusive impenetrability, it has become apparent that in general the most fruitful readings of Nerval's most hermetic works, such as Kristeva's, are those that have not attempted to repair this indecision or to reduce it to a single, stable, and hidden meaning behind the words; instead they have sought to describe the functioning and limits of this undecidability as a dynamic process that generates rather than stops effects of meaning or subjectivity. But the demands of such a continued polysemy have been enormous, and even Kristeva's reading, as remarkable as it is, has not been able to sustain the madness that deforms, rather than sublimates or disembodies, this poem's figures. What she does not consider, but what the sonnet and the rest of Nerval's literary work make clear, is that the lost object of which she writes, the "archaic 'Thing,'" is not merely what is represented by the *object little a*, it is not really an object at all, but rather the subject in its self-sameness, the longing of the self for its impossible self, there conceived, as she otherwise accurately determines, as the preverbal, that which is sublimated in language and abolished. Kristeva understands the poem's undecidable polysemy, and the indeterminability of the lyric first-person position, to be structured as mourning around, or toward, a singularized but absent objectivity, a *Chose* or Thing that flees forever like the elusive Abbé de Bucquoy. For all the unmasterable semantic plurality of the sonnet, it does not, in Kristeva's reading, break with a tradition of subjectivity reaching back to the more naïve and original understandings of the Kantian apperceptive subject, for she still sees self-identity (and self-identification) as the organization of predications around the ipseity of a mysterious, apparently noumenal subject-as-referent. Such an interpretation of the poem can only be sustained by ignoring the shift that takes place in the final stanzas from *je* as inconsolable mourning for itself, to *je* as victor of death; here the sonnet identifies the subject as immanent to the poem itself, allegorized in the figure of the lyre, and the pretense of a referential substantiality is abandoned in favor of a purely linguistic afterlife, a sheerly propositional subject. When Kristeva reads the sonority of the sonnet itself as a substitute for the missing *Chose*, she grounds the subject in the materiality of its own language, the meaningless, sensuous concreteness of its prosody and music; but as an impossible figure, caught monstrously between the figurable and the unfigurably semantic, the lyre that circulates on itself belies such a substantialization of the integrity of the poem and the subject it instantiates. What holds the poem together, what holds the subject together, is not the materiality of its acoustic qualities, but the self-identifying figure of the lyre. This is what the poem identifies as its first person, as the *je* gathering its incompossible, proliferating attributions. To this *je*, this impossible figure, are given meanings, but according to what law, in the name of what or whom, and by what rights? The poem answers: not by any law of identity, but by word play, by allusion and paranomasia, by sound determining meaning and meaning determining sound, as in *rose s'allient* = *Rosalie*, in the permutations of the name, like Phébus or Biron/Byron, in the discordant field of incompatible meanings which a single word can cover, like *rose* or *sainte*, or *fée*, and by rhetorical figure, like the lyre. The poem answers: I, but really I and not the mere image of an I, am structured and self-similar in these jokes and monsters that are only words.

There was always, however, a counter-voice to tell Nerval otherwise, starting with his father and Dr. Blanche—he speaks openly of this in *Aurélia*, as will be seen in the next chapter. This voice continues in literary critics who have not been able to bear reading the surface of the poems themselves, who have continued to rush past them looking for a fugitive Nerval, an "archaic 'Thing,'" whom they determine to be the masterful author of these words. But that is not where the author has escaped—like the purloined letter of Poe's story, he has been too visible, too much in evidence; unlike the Poe story, however, the idea of presence, of material surface, is itself put into question and escapes, for the lyre too disappears. The idea of a subject that exists only in language, as an ungrounded proposition, has always troubled even the very philosophical tradition that comes closest to recognizing its necessity as construct. Kant does not accept it, nor in the end does Kristeva seem to. One can say that there is a place for the Nervalian subject in this history, for there has been an attempt to control it, but it has not been an altogether successful attempt, and this failure has had serious implications for the general systems that it marks. In the Preface to the *Phenomenology of Spirit*, to take only the handiest example, Hegel had himself already sketched out a description of the subject, a subject that, for all its apparent coherence and centrality to the larger project of his dialectical system as a whole, will be curiously unsettled by the lyric "I" of Nerval's sonnet:

> The need to represent the Absolute as *Subject* [als *Subjekt*] has found expression in the propositions: *God* is the eternal, the moral world-order, love, and so on. In such propositions the True is only posited *immediately* as Subject, but is not

presented as the movement of reflecting itself into itself. In a proposition [Satze] of this kind one begins with the word "God." This by itself is a meaningless sound, a mere name [ein sinnloser Laut, ein bloßer Name]; it is only the predicate that says what God is, gives Him content and meaning [erst das Prädikat sagt, was er ist, ist seine Erfüllung und Bedeutung]. Only in the end of the proposition does the empty beginning become actual knowledge [ein wirkliches Wissen]. This being so, it is not clear why one does not speak merely of the eternal, of the moral world-order, and so on, or, as the ancients did, of pure notions like "being," "the One," and so on, in short, of that which gives the meaning without adding the *meaningless* sound as well. But it is just this word that indicates that what is posited is not a being, or essence, or a universal in general [oder Allgemeines überhaupt], but rather something that is reflected into itself, a Subject. But at the same time this is only anticipated. The Subject is assumed as a fixed point [als fester Punkt] to which, as their support [als ihren Halt], the predicates are affixed by a movement belonging to the knower of this subject, and which is not regarded as belonging to the fixed point itself; yet it is only through this movement that the content could be represented as Subject.[98]

The Subject of the *Phenomenology* thus begins as a meaningless sound, the simple positing of a name that is determined through predications belonging not to the meaningless sound itself, but to the knower of the Subject. Another example one might adduce would be the clustering of attributions around the "I" of "El Desdichado," which could be understood to begin as pure contentless sound that subsequently takes on sense through predication. However, something significantly skewed is happening in the sonnet's determination of its original subject, since the predications simply articulate—or modulate—rather than end the indeterminacy of their subject, which is itself precisely that which should be at the very root of determinacy according to the *Phenomenology*.

One must understand why this is so, why it is that the Subject should have this crucial, determining role in the Hegelian dialectic, to appreciate why Nerval's elaboration of the first person of his sonnet serves as such a radical critique of the very ground of Hegel's system. The "Subject" or *Subjek* referred to in the above passage is not merely the logical or grammatical partner of a predicate, since it refers at the same time to "something reflected into itself," and Hegel's preceding paragraph has defined it as both the beginning and the goal or purpose of the dialectical process described in the *Phenomenology*. The Subject is "what is immediate and *at rest*, the unmoved which is also *self-moving*" and the term is treated as synonymous with "self (*das Selbst*)."[99] The dialectic of the self, the dialectic of the Subject, is thus homologous in its general outlines with the linguistic process of predication that might be instantiated in a poem such as "El Desdichado."

According to the Preface to the *Phenomenology*, the *Subjek* as individual self-consciousness has the function of lending through its experience concrete specificity or content to the abstractions of the Absolute (*Geist* or Spirit), and in this way plays a role in relation to the Absolute that is broadly analogous to that which exists between subject and predicate as described above. In other words, much as a predicate gives "content and meaning" (readable as "content *as* meaning") to the meaningless sound that is its subject, so the individual gives content, in the sense of concrete actuality, to the abstract absolute (making "Spirit" out of "spiritual Substance").[100] Without the experience of the individual self-consciousness, in short, the Absolute that is the goal of the world-historical dialectical process described in the *Phenomenology* would remain abstract, a "meaningless sound [ein sinnloser Laut]." In the youthful but already Hegelian words from Nerval's review of "Le Mort-Vivant," without individual self-experience, the goal of the *Phenomenology* would remain death: "nom sans objet" and "pure abstraction."[101]

This characterization is reinforced by the fact that Hegel describes the Subject as "Substance";[102] and insofar as it is "*Pure* self-recognition in absolute otherness,"[103] it is "the ground and soil of Science or *knowledge in general*."[104] A few lines later, speaking of the individual, Hegel asserts that

> because this self-consciousness [the "*Individuum*"] has the principle of its actual existence in the certainty of itself, Science appears to it not to be actual [trägt sie... die Form der Unwirklichkeit] since self-consciousness exists on its own account outside of Science. Science must therefore unite this element of self-certainty with itself, or rather show *that* and *how* this element belongs to it. So long as Science lacks this *actual* dimension [Wirklichkeit], it is only the content as the *in-itself*, the *purpose* that is as yet still something *inward*, not yet Spirit, but only spiritual Substance. This *in-itself* has to express itself outwardly and become *for-itself*, and this means simply that it has to posit self-consciousness as one with itself.[105]

In the self-determination of Spirit, one can then say, it is the individual alone who actualizes the abstraction which is the Absolute in its initial, purely posited state, and the individual does this through its finite determination of the experience of itself. In other words, the individual's self-experience gives content and concrete determination to the abstract absolute, and it is therefore the individual self-consciousness whose experience of itself must determine the predication of the meaningless name with which the universal absolute begins.

In the following paragraphs of the Preface, however, Hegel asserts that the individual's experience of itself is not always purely immediate, and that in some instances it is already the product of history or culture. Whereas World-Spirit itself has the patience to pass through and linger on each individual shape of its increasingly rich self-determination, and, as Hegel puts it "to take upon itself the enormous labor of world-history,"[106] the individual self-consciousness does not have such time, and yet it remains untroubled by such constraints because much of this determination has already been "*implicitly* accomplished; the content is already the actuality reduced to a possibility, its immediacy overcome, and the embodied shape reduced to abbreviated, simple determinations of thought."[107] These "simple determinations of thought" are the as-it-were predigested stages of self-experience that the universal individual, or world-historical Spirit, has already passed through and whose content the finite individual receives as the artifacts of a cultural tradition in games, through education, or in general interaction with others.[108] These previously experienced shapes of universal self-consciousness constitute what Hegel describes as the "inorganic nature" of the individual, which he must take possession of or "devour [zehren]."[109] The single individual, which itself is described by Hegel as "incomplete Spirit,"[110] is partially in ignorance of itself, and partly constituted by elements unexperienced by it that, although "natural" to it, are also "inorganic" and therefore alien to it. These elements are the received tradition of a culture that has been reduced to inactual potentialities and "abbreviated, simple determinations of thought." Which is to say, they are simple denominations, empty words.

The individual, or that which gives concrete content to Spirit through experience, finds the origin and possibility of its separate and finite existence in death; as pure immediacy to itself, Spiritual substance remains motionless and therefore unremarkable in the pure constancy of its essential being, but what is astonishing, for Hegel, is that a nonessential element of this universal immediacy should gain independance as a separate, autonomous, individual being. This freedom of an accidental aspect of abstract Spirit is its isolated self-identity, but it is possible only through mediation—the relation of the accident to itself *as* self-identical, or as both self and that which is the same as it. Whereas Spirit as mere abstract spiritual substance is immediately one and therefore unmoving or in rest, the individual accident of Spirit finds its ipseity through its consciousness of itself, that is, as subject and object of its knowing, or Understanding. This difference from itself in its self-sameness is nothing positive or real, but is rather the formal, quasi-logical condition of its identity; more than that, it is in fact the negative as such, the very possibility of difference, the condition of finitude, and Hegel calls it death:

> The circle that rests [ruht] self-enclosed and, as substance, holds its moments together, is an immediate relationship, one therefore which has nothing astonishing about it. But that an accident as such [Akzidentelle als solches], detached from what circumscribes it, what is bound and is actual only in its context with others, should attain an existence of its own and a separate freedom—this is the tremendous power of the negative; it is the energy of thought, of the pure "I." Death, if that is what we want to call this non-actuality [Unwirklichkeit], is of all things the most dreadful, and to hold fast what is dead requires the greatest strength. Lacking strength, Beauty hates the Understanding for asking of her what she cannot do. But the life of Spirit is not the life that shrinks from death and keeps itself untouched by devastation, but rather the life that endures it and maintains itself in it.[111]

This aporia of individual consciousness—that to be identical is for it to be different from itself—is what gives motion to Spirit and motivates history as the subject attempts to reconcile itself with itself, attempting to reduce object to subject across the progress of its self-desire. This individual that gives motion and content to Spirit is grounded in its own death, which constitutes its freedom or *Freiheit*, and consequently this latter concept is again, as in the Kantian sublime, contingent on the annihilation of the finite particular consciousness of sensuous experience. The somewhat mysterious reference to Beauty in the midst of this seems best explained by its unmentioned partner, the sublime, for while Beauty, in Kant's third *Critique*, is a harmonization between the faculties of understanding and imagination, in the sublime judgement the faculty of imagination figures the annihilation of the finite, sensuous figurability of apprehension or, in other words, the imaginable itself. Beauty, in Hegel's terms, hates the Understanding because in constituting the individual through the awareness of its abstract negation or death, the Understanding premises the aesthetic in its conceptual negation. Beauty would be the attempt to reconcile the abstract negativity of difference with the positivity of the aesthesis it makes possible, while the sublime would be Understanding's recognition that the sensous, figurable, concrete world of finite apprehensible accidents is possible only through its continuous negation in the abstractions, or *Unwirklichkeiten*, that are difference, freedom, limitation and death. The individual, and the apprehensible world of the senses, is possible only through a constant, vigilant holding fast of their negation in death, and this power of death is precisely what Hegel calls the Subject.[112] The latter is thus the abiding negation of the individual that makes it possible, its permanent sublimation.

This construct of individuality has had, as we have seen earlier in this book, a long and tenacious life. As merely one of the more striking examples of its persistence, one need only observe how it resurfaces, one would think quite anomalously, in the twentieth century as an integral part of a philosophical project that attempts to break with the abstract nature of the metaphysical tradition and to determine in so-called Dasein an alternate to subjectivity and the paradigmatic limitations and aporias it entailed. Hegel's inorganic elements function in relation to the actualization of the individual much as the idle talk of "the They" (*das Gerede* of *das man*) functions in relation to Dasein in Heidegger's *Being and Time*. For Heidegger, *das Gerede* is precisely those opinions received from the anonymous crowd of humanity and accepted without full consideration by the individual, which distract him from his fundamental isolation in face of his own death. Because it is unappropriated by the finite individual Dasein, idle talk leaves the latter ungrounded, and in such discoursing, "things are so because one says so. Idle talk is constituted by just such gossiping and passing the word along—a process by which its initial lack of grounds to stand on [Bodenständigkeit] becomes aggravated to complete groundlessness [Bodenlosigkeit]."[113] This received information that has not been made one's own distracts Dasein from its inherent isolation as one who must die and in whose place ultimately no other can die, an isolation that is, on the other hand, revealed by a mode of being Heidegger describes as anticipation. The latter, in disclosing Dasein's true grounding or supportedness in its own isolation, also discloses both the basis for Dasein's ability to appropriate (which is to ground in itself) and Dasein's inherent and legitimate freedom from the idle talk of the "they":

> We may now summarize our characterization of authentic Being-towards-death as we have projected it existentially: *anticipation reveals to Dasein its lostness in the they-self, and brings it face to face with the possibility of being itself, primarily unsupported by concernful solicitude, but of being itself, rather, in an impassioned* freedom towards death—*a freedom which has been released from the Illusions of the "they", and which is factical, certain of itself, and anxious.*[114]

For both Heidegger and Hegel, unappropriated cultural material disrupts the actuality of the individual, robbing him of his specificity and finitude, which must be restored through his acceptance of death. For Heidegger the legitimacy of Dasein, for Hegel the ground of the world-historical process that shapes Spirit, lie in the individual's appropriation of its own experience through a self-identification as one who must die. Like the sublime subject of terror in Kant and Hegel, Dasein determines its individual specificity through an appropriation of its death. This appropriation, termed freedom by all three philosophers, is, however, precisely the self-disappropriation of the individual into utter abstraction, and the aporia of the individual subject remains for Dasein, as it had for the earlier constructions it was meant to supplant.

In the sonnet "El Desdichado," however, the subject is not predicated in the sense that Hegel uses, but is instead named and renamed as a series of empty sounds. The vacant nomination that was death in Nerval's early review of the nonexistent "Le Mort-Vivant" has not merely been confronted, it has been identified as the lyric subject, the "I" that maintains itself in death through the circulation of incompossible attributions on the impersonal, polysemous and rhetorically undecidable figure of language, on the poetic place of pure position or pure positing that is allegorized by the lyre of the last stanza. The allusions in the poem to literary and historical *topoi* and figures can be seen as the maintenance of inorganic elements within the poetic construction of the subject. They are maintained, and not incorporated, into that individual subjectivity, because the referent of the allusions remains indeterminable (which Love, which Phébus, which star, being or not-being, life or death, voice or silence, etc.?). The inorganic material is therefore pseudo-determined as subjective content: determined because it does refer to specific traditions, *pseudo*-determined because they, in an undecidability maintained as the alternation of incompossible attributions in the rhetorical material of the lyric surface, do not determine an individual subject as the immediate experience of itself. The individual subject, in other words, identifies itself in this poem as constituted by a language it does not understand, and which experientially exceeds it.

The sonnet "El Desdichado" is an artifact of self-alienation insofar as it instantiates the inscrutability of the self in its own legitimate representation, and it becomes, in its turn, an element of the progress of Spirit. Its status in this context is problematic, for although it is an element of culture and a form of knowledge, it is one that can never be known, for although it is an artifact of individual subjective experience, it is an artifact of the individual subjective experience of non-self-experience, the experience of the non-experiencing of the self, the knowledge of self-ignorance. As such it becomes a constitutive misstep in the progress of Spirit, a stumble that cannot be reincorporated into the experience of the world-historical self-determination of the absolute individual, since this misstep is an essential de-concretization, or a giving away of content, of precisely that element of Absolute subject which is considered to determine—to concretize—the Absolute. Experience, in this late sonnet of Nerval, is experienced as less constitutive of the individual than is poetic discourse, and the particular subject thus knows itself as alien, meaningless, open to—indeed, made up of—an infinite series of potential substitutions and as essentially fissured by aporia. In poetizing experience and accepting its consequent alienation from a finite individual self-consciousness, "El Desdichado" opens up the concept of subjectivity to the otherness of a discursive community that the philosophical tradition of death-based individuation had aggressively excluded as inorganic or inauthentic, and it is this opening to a primordial linguistic communalism that is set forward as the ground of the *moi* in *Aurélia*. In Nerval's last work the subject will not merely accept itself as structurally and materially language, it will understand itself as the discourse of others.

7. *Aurélia*: The Signs of Others

> What I like most of all in traveling . . . is to blend, unrecognized, into that mottled crowd that murmurs with a foreign language, to take part, for a day, in its eternal life.
> —*Nerval*
>
> I had wanted a material sign.
> —*Nerval, 'Aurélia'*

In the sonnet "El Desdichado," Nerval instantiated a lyric subjectivity fragmented by the incorporation of organically unassimilable, alienated cultural artifacts. This poetic subject stood as a critique of the metaphysical tradition of death-based subjectivity that found its roots in Hegelian dialectics and that extended past Nerval's suicide at least as far as Heidegger. The self of "El Desdichado" accepted and incorporated its status as an individual that is not one, that is not an individual to the extent that the word has come to be identified with a specific metaphysical and critical tradition, since the lyric self-identification set forward in the sonnet was held together not by the self-sameness or even compossibility of its predications or the coherence of the experience it represented, but only through the rhetorical figure of an unreconcilable ambiguity. The poem thus constituted a self-identification not as an individual person but as the impersonal subject of linguistic processes; the "I" is a self-construction not through or in face of death, for it is, instead, irremediably alienated as death itself, as the subtle, destroying angel that is language. As if unsatisfied with such open-ended negativity, however, Nerval returned in *Aurélia* to the question of the individual and took up thematically the issue of the first-person singular in an attempt to work out its relation to the discursive community at large and to account for the accession of experience to language or how the "I" in its originality and specificity came into speech. This was not a turning away from the revelations of the sonnet nor a return to a naïve self-construction that might have preceded it, but a displacement and refashioning of individuality after the apocalypse of "El Desdichado." *Aurélia* also represents, then, a return to some of the fundamental questions of the present study—namely, the possibility of mediating between the immediacy of experience and the mediation of language without losing the immediacy of the lived world; how to insert oneself into discourse—or accept oneself as discourse—and account satisfactorily there for one's experience, one's particularity and originality; how to do this in a medium which by its nature abolishes immediacy, originality, and specificity. The question returns under a different guise, and Nerval can again take up this primordial concern because, by the time of his writing "El Desdichado" and *Aurélia*, he had changed his understanding of the connection between language and subjectivity. The relation between the two is no longer construed in the simple polarity of self and other, of particular and absolute, life and death. Instead, the subject is now seen as infinite and mobile, constituted primordially in relation not to *an* other but to others, instantiated always already within the subject as a linguistic field that supports its experience and sense of self. Subjective experience, including therefore the subject's experience of itself, is always already linguistic, always mediated through language and the community of others—one is, at every moment, structured in relation to a living world, and not in respect to death. One is built as nonintegral, and the perceived need to turn away from language and toward a *ja-sagen* of life is therefore premised on a false dichotomy: there is not a split between common language and individual experience, because one is structured discursively as among, through, and toward others. One is ethically engaged, therefore, to others, not to the isolation of death, as Hegel and Heidegger and Sartre would have it. This engagement, this responsibility, this living of the self in the field of language, this introspection into this field and its consequences for the self, are the matter of *Aurélia*, which examines this condition in terms of the question, never stated as such but always subtending the text: "How did I come to language?"

Madness and the Discourses That Would Master It

The first paragraph of *Aurélia* sets out several of the key guiding terms of the work:

> Dreaming is a second life. I have never been able to crack, without a shudder, those gates of ivory or horn that separate us from the invisible world. The first

instants of sleep are the image of death; a cloudy numbness takes hold of our thought and we cannot determine the precise instant when the *I* [*moi*], in another form, continues the work of existence [l'œuvre de l'existence]. It is a dim underworld that lightens little by little and where the shadows and the night release the pale, grimly motionless figures who inhabit this space of limbo. Then the picture takes shape, a new light illuminates these bizarre apparitions and sets them into play—the Spirit world opens up for us [pour nous].[1]

From the outset, the text promises what would appear to be a vast development of the last stanza of the sonnet "El Desdichado": the exploration of a second life that returns recurrently, nightly—another life that is as much ours as our waking existence but that is lived out among the dead and as the dead. What might, in the sonnet, have passed for the metaphorical appropriation of a simple mythological *topos*, is here identified as an integral if alienating part of the most common daily existence. It is not just mad poets that must live the self-alienated, recurrent dissolution of the lyre-ic *je*, this paragraph suggests; rather, it is the common lot that the world of spirits should open "pour *nous*" and that at a certain, unsituable, unmappable moment, the *moi* should take on another form and become other in order to continue, in death, the work of existence. Nor is this the *travail* or *besogne* of existence, but its *œuvre*—not so much the labor, the pure brute expenditure of force against the wasting resistance of death, but the production and creation of existence, its fashioning into artifact or *œuvre*, its poetry, in the etymological sense of *poeisis* as that which produces the work as well as the work that is produced.[2] Life is at work, *à l'œuvre*, here. Life is that which, in its self-alienation, its incessant, cyclical passage between dream and waking, death and life, produces, sets forth the work, poetizes. And it is through the *moi*, the only italicized word of the paragraph, that life circulates, creates, produces *l'œuvre*. The first-person singular holds together the work of existence by its unmappably labile capacity to change form through the passage between incompossible predications, between the living and the dead. Nerval does not appropriate the first person, does not speak immediately through it, as if it represented him in his singularity. Rather he sets it off diacritically, not as *je*, the first-person subject pronoun, but as *le moi*. This word is mentioned, not used in the text, emptied of specific attribution, so that it is not *je*—easily misconstrued not as the signifier but the referent—who allows the passage of existence through life and death, but rather *le moi*, the linguistic subject, the first-person singular, considered as a relational verbal position.[3]

Such are the life and subject of which the text promises to speak, and such are the caveats one should first read before venturing further, at the risk of forgetting the long and difficult lessons of "El Desdichado." The risk is high. The tendency is to read *Aurélia* first, and to explain the sonnet through it, to find in the shorter, more hermetic work the condensed indexing of anecdotes and experiences largely revealed in the longer prose version. The advantage of reading "El Desdichado" first is, however, the possibility of establishing a specifically poetic *je* as the model for subjectivity in *Aurélia*, the possibility of thereby reading the latter text for its specifically poetic logic, its different logic, a logic its author argues to be legitimate even if apparently mad. To read the other way around—to read "El Desdichado" in terms of *Aurélia*—is to risk missing the importance and originality of both and to give too free rein to a predisposition to understand the visions of the later and the hermeticism of the former as symptoms of a medical condition whose only positivity lies in its own organic etiology and progression, whose symptoms have no referential value except in terms of the course of illness, as medical artifacts rather than as introspections into the nature of selfhood.

The opening paragraph is the first of several calls by the author to pay attention to how one reads, and not to accept the easy and familiar limitations of medical, scientific, and metaphysical discourses when trying to come to terms with his text. Already, by arguing that dreaming and the alienation involved in it are paradoxically integral to self-knowledge, Nerval separates himself decisively from the modern history of subjectivity that has preceded him. In Descartes's *Méditations*, to cite only the originary moment of the tradition, it is precisely the possibility that one is dreaming (or that one is mad—the two states, madness and dreaming, function homologously in respect to the argument as a whole) which constitutes the constant threat to the legitimacy of self-knowledge and, a fortiori, objective science. It is only through the exclusion of such a possibility that subjectivity, as the certitude of self-presence, can be established.[4] This attitude persisted up through the romantic period, with both Kant and Hegel referring to madmen as waking dreamers.[5] In the simple act of asserting the legitimacy of dream experience as self-experience, Nerval posits the legitimacy of a fundamentally other and historically excluded model of subjectivity. As a positioning of the terms of introspection in the text that follows it, the opening paragraph also bears polemical weight by situating *Aurélia* differentially and critically in respect both to other paradigms of self-knowledge and to the kinds of discourse that would help determine their structure.

Again, more explicitly, at the end of the fifth chapter of the first section of *Aurélia*, Nerval argues for another kind of logic, and he asserts that the real intelligibility of his text depends on the eschewing of scientific or medical models of expression. Speaking of the series of visionary experiences which led to his first institutionalization, he writes:

> Such was that vision or such, at least, were the principal details which I have been able to remember. The cataleptic state in which I had found myself for several days was explained scientifically to me, and the stories [récits] of those who had seen me thus caused me a kind of irritation when I saw that they attributed to the aberration of my mind the movements or words which coincided with the diverse phases of what constituted for me a series of logical events.[6]

Two narratives or *récits* of the same occurrences are set in opposition: on the one hand there appears to the *moi* a series of logical events with its attendant movements and words, while on the other hand there appear to scientific interlocutors the hallucinations of an aberrant mind, held together not by a legitimate inner order but only as the traces left by successive phases through which an organic *dis*order progresses. Nerval does not deny having been sick, or that his sickness should be medically comprehensible; rather, he argues for an independent legitimacy of the intellectual experiences associated with his cataleptic state, a legitimacy and logic whose intelligibility have no necessary causal relation to the medical condition that accompanied them.[7] The relation between the illness and the visions is rather one of coincidence: they occur at the same time and to the same individual, but one cannot be explained through the other in any significant way. Yet this is precisely what his doctors wish to do. The irritation Nerval feels in the face of this would seem to be a frustration at being told that the *récit* of his subjective experiences was neither subjective nor original, that it was already known and written in medical texts, and that insofar as there was a subject to his experience, that subject was only the illness itself. In this context, Nerval's opening paragraph takes on the critical value of the argument: "If that is the case, then you cannot consider your dreams as part of your subjectivity, and nightly you die and are not yourself."

Nerval's experiences, he argues, cannot be understood through medical discourse as the progression of an organic disorder, nor, he later contends, can they be comprehended in philosophical terms.[8] The following exhange takes place between Nerval and a character in one of his early visions:

> "We are seven," I told my uncle.
>
> "That is indeed," he said, "the typical number of each human family, and, by extension, seven times seven, and so on."
>
> I cannot hope to make that answer understood, and even for me it remained very obscure. Metaphysics offers me no terms for the perception which then came to me of the relation between that number of persons and the general harmony.[9]

In contradistinction to medical discourse, metaphysics does not seem to bear a merely coincidental relation to the significant content of the author's visions, nor does it seem to irritate him by the blind facility with which it would appropriate the logic of his own experiences. If medical discourse goes *too far* in explaining Nerval to himself, metaphysics is incapable of going far enough. It has not the vocabulary, or terms, to express a relation he has perceived, and to the very extent of this deficiency Nerval acknowledges that his experience remains obscure to him, and that he remains alien to himself. It seems at first too tempting to see in this passage the indication of a conscious attempt on Nerval's part to situate his textualized experience outside of the modern tradition of death-based subjectivity and to read his use of the word "metaphysics" here as a reference to Hegel. With Nerval, it would seem more cautious to construe the term as bearing on esoteric knowledge or illuminism, and yet such cautiousness would probably be misdirected, for at the end of the preface-letter to *Les Filles du feu*, written during the same period as *Aurélia*, Nerval uses this very word to describe the Hegelian system, even if he gives no indication that he grasps its content. And in that same reference it is precisely the *obscurity* of Hegel's metaphysics that is of interest to the poet and which constitutes for him the quality that allows a comparison between his poems and the philosopher's works: they are both "obscurs."[10] Metaphysics, and especially Hegelian metaphysics, would then be that which textualizes the obscure, which finds terms that can bring into words what remains shadowy and which can respect the alienation of experiences even in their expression. And yet the present passage from *Aurélia* is too "obscure" for even metaphysics to be of help; rather, it situates a precise moment when Nerval distinguishes his project in relation to a metaphysical and probably Hegelian model of self-knowledge. The critical value of that distinction can only be determined through the reading of Nerval's texts themselves. What is of interest here is that he should come so close to openly naming this critical distance, to identifying his relation to the tradition of metaphysical subjectivity and to construing it in terms of linguistic expression. The problem of this alternate model of self-knowledge is a discursive one. Moreover, that discursivity understands itself as intentionally, and therefore significantly, different from other institutionally certified languages of subjectivity. If that difference is legitimate, it will mean that Nerval's work critiques other subjective models.

Some other language is called for, then, a language that is neither scientific nor metaphysical, and which can express both the logical rigors and the obscurity of his subjectivity. Or rather, the choice of language has already been made; what was lacking was its defense in the face of a medical discursive mode that would not have recognized its legitimacy and its distinction from an insufficient philosophical discursive mode with which it might have been confused. As one might expect on the basis of "El Desdichado," the language in which the author's subjectivity will be expressed is literary, and more specifically, poetic. This is made explicit in the second paragraph of *Aurélia*, where Nerval addresses the question of style and genre:

> Swedenborg called these visions [of the Spirit world] *Memorabilia* and he owed them to revery more often than to sleep; Apuleius's *The Golden Ass* and Dante's *Divine Comedy* are the poetic models for these studies of the human soul. I am going to try, following their example, to transcribe [transcrire] the impressions of a long illness which took place entirely within the mysteries of my spirit—and I don't know why I use this term "illness," for never, in respect to myself [quant à ce qui est de moi-même], have I ever felt better.[11]

Nerval's models for the transcription of the human soul will be poetic. And this term "transcription" is significant, since it suggests not a putting into words for the first time of something that was originally nonverbal, but a putting into other words or even a copying of words, a passage or transference from text to text, as if the impressions he had were already structured according to their own discursivity, their own textuality even, as if they had an original scriptural quality. The problem then, for the author, would be to find in what language, according to what model, they were already written. Not so that he could write them, but so that he could read them most comprehensibly. Just as Nerval's *récit* of his visions is already verbal, but unintelligible if read in terms of the language of medical science, so, this passage suggests, are his impressions themselves already textual; the problem is one of finding the genre, the discursive mode of their intelligibility. They are most rigorously significant, most logical, he asserts, if understood in terms of poetry, a genre that has its own validity in critically differential relation to philosophy and science, whose equal or superior it is in possibilities of self-knowledge.

This idea of an initial poetic quality to subjective experience, of which actual poetry would be a transcription, might come across as merely the product of an excessive emphasis on one word—*transcrire*—did it not seem peculiar to theorizations of the relation between poetry and subjectivity. Hegel himself, in a somewhat tortured passage from the *Aesthetics*, seems to be drawn almost despite himself into such a conception of a primordial scriptural quality to the subject, a quality simply made manifest in poetry. For Hegel, in the section of the *Aesthetics* entitled "Poetizing Subjectivity," poetry differs from the other arts in its material aspect, in its unique immateriality, which is language. Consequently, "poetry, by being expressed in words, should not try to reach that complete perceptibility which the visual artist has to give to his subject-matter as its external form, nor can it remain satisfied with the wordless depth of feeling, the expression of which in soul-laden notes is the sphere of music."[12] While the other arts must concern themselves with finding an adequation between inner spiritual content and its plastic exteriorization, poetry is somehow already spiritual and interior. And this inherent absence of a concrete, sensuous exteriority (even the musical aspect of poetry is of an accidental importance) is what confers on poetry its preeminence among the arts, since the immateriality of language allows interiority to appear most clearly. For this reason the shape and matter of poetry are determined only by the subjectivity of the poet, his or her interiority, rather than by the objective constraints of form and material. This difference between poetry and the other arts is further developed in the following passage, where Hegel asserts that thanks to the immateriality of language,

> the poet is able to penetrate all the depths of the contents of the spirit and can bring out into the daylight of consciousness whatever lies concealed there. For however far in other arts the inner life must, and does actually, shine through its corporeal form, still the word is the most intelligible means of communication, the most adequate to the spirit, the one able to grasp and declare whatever lies within consciousness or pervades its heights and depths.[13]

Of all the means of communication it is language that most adequately makes subjective experience intelligible, and it is in fact capable of *completely* expressing human interiority, for it can grasp *everything* that occurs in consciousness.[14] Because of this perfect adequation between poetic language and inner experience, the latter must already be structured poetically. Subjectivity would thus be primordially linguistic, and poetry would therefore be the expression of expression, the making apparent of making-apparent, the appearance of appearing. What subjectivity would be in itself, beyond its appearance, becomes extremely difficult to say: something hidden, and therefore hidden from expression, but, curiously, what must be brought forth into appearance or into the light of consciousness is said to be already perfectly adequately poetic; since it is thus already appearance itself and necessarily no different than its appearance to consciousness it must consequently be, as it were, hidden *in the light of consciousness* itself. Like Eluard's paradoxical "light in relief," the depths of Hegel's poetic consciousness would seem to be functions of its heights, created as shadows of light cast on light by light; for if consciousness is to be understood as visibility, its hidden recesses must not be consciousness and therefore cannot exist as *its* depths except insofar as they are mere appearances.[15] All that is hidden in the depths of consciousness, then, is that hiding itself is simply an appearance and that nothing is hidden. The secret of the soul that poetry discloses would thus be that there is no secret, that the supposed secret has already been disclosed, and that despite all appearances there is nothing more to say and nothing left unsaid. The secret of the soul is nothing other than this: that poetry is the manifestation that subjectivity is poetic manifestation.

Perhaps as interesting as this formulation of the "poetizing subjectivity" is the resistance it seems to elicit in Hegel himself. Later, in the section on "Lyric Poetry" from the *Aesthetics*, he will back off from this radical construction, and construe the content of poetry as subjective affect, sentiment or passion.[16] What *Aurélia* represents, as these initial, metapoetical anabases indicate, is an attempt to follow the path that Hegel identified but from which he retreated: the proposition that subjectivity most adequately reveals itself not only through but *as* poetry. Such a construction would offer the solution to the impasse of madness as formulated by Foucault—that it is the impossible attempt to present the immediate in its immediacy through language, an impasse that collapsed always into the wordless isolation of the question "How can this madness be so deprived of speech?" If, on the other hand, the immediate is already language, the only mediacy would be the illusion that one is anything else, that subjective experience is anything but poetry, that one could ever possibly have been isolated from the communality that is language. Such is the promise of *Aurélia*, but it is not arrived at easily.

Genesis and Structure of the Text

Aurélia is as disjunctive, narratively, as *Les Faux Saulniers*, but this is hidden by a more restrained repertoire of literary sources and materials, and by a more refined, more supple style of exposition, which is closer to the almost oneiric technique of *récit* which marks *Sylvie*. As Proust observed of the latter text, it is virtually impossible not to lose track of chronology in the apparent vagaries of this style, which reveal, under examination, an extraordinary literary mastery, a complex and original way of thinking of narrative, time, and order.[17] To avoid coming to grief in attempting a close reading of this text, it is worthwhile to recall the broad outlines of the work, which has always been divided—whether in accordance with its author's intentions or not remains unknown—into two different sections.

The first of these two parts begins by identifying the work as an investigation into the nature of the *moi*, based on the impressions left on the author by a long sickness, the story of which begins with his loss of a beloved woman, whom he chooses to call Aurélia. To cheat his grief at her rejection of him, he throws himself into a life of travel and shallow pleasures, and even begins a brief affair with another woman in an attempt to convince himself that he never really was seriously in love. Having disabused himself of these self-deceptions, and while in the first stages of an amicable reconciliation with his lost love, he notices the street number of a house and takes it as an omen of either his death or hers. That night he has a dream that he is in an enormous and complex edifice, where he sees an angel struggle in the air and fall to the ground. The next day, in a scene that is perhaps his account of the gathering described by Jules Janin in his report of Nerval's madness for the *Journal des débats*, the author, knowing now that he is destined to die, visits his friends to take secret leave of them. That evening he begins to walk toward the Orient, fixing his direction on a star that, he felt, "had some influence on my destiny." "Here," he writes, "begins the overflowing of dreams into real life [l'épanchement du songe dans la vie réelle]," and all of life takes on a double appearance. Having stripped off his clothes, he is stopped by the night watch and taken into custody, where he begins to have visions, first of a divinity letting drop a succession of masks, and then of his own double. His friends come to collect him, he is transported to a clinic, and he falls into a crepuscular state of consciousness in which, he says, "everything was transfigured to my eyes." At this point begins a series of loosely interconnected visions, the first of which starts on the banks of the Rhine, in the house of a maternal uncle. From there, he falls into an abyss filled with streams of souls in fusion like molten metal, from which he emerges in a countryside that reminds him of the part of Flanders where certain of his relatives are buried. He then enters a room filled with a tremendous gathering of people resembling the members of his family, and among them he finds his dead uncle. When the author takes this assembly as proof of the immortality of the soul, his uncle explains to him that the world of the living is a theater that affects the destinies of the dead, and that matter is a composite of souls. He also reveals to the author the relation between race and individual, which provokes, within the dream, a vision of the infinite expansion of his own family, through a process of multiplication and repetition. There then follow two other dreams, the first of a visit to a city, inhabited by people dressed in white and who live a life of "simple mores." In the second he encounters three women whose features shift like the contours of a flame, one of whom leads him into a garden, where she grows into a personification of nature itself. The author, pausing to reflect on the significance of his experiences and dreams, then reveals that he later learned that Aurélia had died at about the time of his visions. He describes the gardens of the clinic, and his decision to write down the history of the world, as it is revealed to him in cabala and visions. He then recounts his version of the origin and earliest epochs of the earth. Released from the clinic, the author has the misfortune to fall into a feverish delirium, provoked by an accident. In a vision he sees his double, and is led to wonder if he is the good or the bad half of himself. In another dream he then comes across the preparations for the marriage of his double with Aurélia, which he attempts to interrupt by displaying a mystical sign that he discovers himself unable to utter.

 The second division of the work begins with a reflection on the nature of his relation to the Christian God, in which he questions the connection between human knowledge and sin and undertakes to rediscover the sign whose absence has thrown the world into disharmony. Again he offers an account of the origins of the world, this time much shorter and somewhat different from the original version in the first part of the work. His very sadness fills him with compassion, and he visits a sick friend, but in feeling his friend close to God, the author becomes only the more conscious of his own distance from the divine, which drives him further and further into dejection. It is during this period, while wandering through the streets, that he encounters a funeral procession, which he follows to the cemetery where Aurélia is buried. He returns then to the Valois region outside of Paris and has a dream, which introduces into the narrative the important question of whether the author can be pardoned for a fault which is never clearly articulated. In an attempt at expiation he burns the letters and talismans that remain from his love for the dead Aurélia. In this state of sadness and anxiety, he considers his lack of religious training, and his thoughts return to memories of his earliest childhood—the mother he never knew, the uncle that raised him, his first readings. To draw himself out of this melancholy, the author travels with a friend through the Valois, but he speaks in incomprehensible fragments and is unable, himself, to understand his companion. On returning to Paris he attempts to visit his father, then, wandering through the deserted night streets of the city, has a hallucinatory vision of the end of the world, viewed from the Place de la Concorde. He is again sent to a clinic. After his release he takes lengthy walks in and around Paris, and begins again to write, but another delirious episode sends him to the Hospice de la Charité, and from there, to the clinic of Dr. Blanche, in Passy, where he covers the garden walls with drawings representing characters from his dreams. During this period he has a vision in which the interconnective structure of the universe is revealed to him as a magical web. He installs the material remains of his peripatetic life in his room at the asylum. There is a gap here in the text that was filled in the original, posthumous publication by certain of the *Lettres d'amour*, a practice modern editors have not followed. After this break, the narrative resumes with the description of two more visions. The first takes place one night when, having begun to speak and sing in a sort of ecstasy, the author is taken from his room and locked in a summer house in the gardens of the asylum, whereupon he sees the history of the world written in "strokes of blood" and the dismembered bodies of women. The second vision, much more optimistic, seems to be provoked by the growing sympathy and compassion Nerval feels toward another inmate, named Saturnin. It begins with the author climbing and descending the endless stairs of a tower reaching between heaven and earth. A brother, in the guise of Saturnin, appears and releases him through a lateral door, upon which the two wander through a starlit field and are greeted by a female deity who tells the author that his trials have come to an end. The text then promises to recount the impressions left by several dreams, which it groups under the general title of "Mémorables," but at this point another manuscript section ends, leaving a new gap in the text, and the original editors, on the advice of Théophile Gautier, here appended, in a practice that has become standard for this work, a section of very dense and lyrical visionary experiences that break more or less into two parts. The first and more poetic of the two seems to be an extension of the dream involving the endless tower and is structured as a series of repetitions and echoes, involving the creation of the world, the triumph of immortality, the arrival of the Messiah, and a generalized forgiveness that extends even to the Norse gods. The second part evokes images of Central and Eastern Europe, a return in spirit to Zaandam and Vienna, a cataclysm in the Baltic, and a vision of the female members of the Russian royal family, which offers the promise of peace. The author then turns, briefly, to reflect on the sense of his dreams, and decides to write them down, as a testament to the workings of another world, a real one, and the record of his "descent into Hell."

Aurélia was the last of Nerval's works to be published during his lifetime. It was, in fact, during the period between the publication of the text's first section, in the January 1 issue of *La Revue de Paris*, and the appearance of its second section in the February 15 issue of the same magazine, that the author hanged himself, on the night of January 25, 1855. While the first part can consequently be considered to have reached a definitive state, the same cannot be said of the second division, which the author left in some disarray at his death, and which went to press accompanied by a proviso from the editor Ulbach reading: "We are publishing the work of Mr. Gérard de Nerval as he left it and are respecting, as is our duty, the lacunae which it was his custom to remove from the proofs."[18] While some question remains as to the author's intentions in respect to certain passages of the second section, and whether he would have remained faithful to them up to the moment of publication, the general trajectory of the work seems to have been more or less fixed by the time of his death.[19] Even concerning the insertion and location of the particularly disjointed fragments published at the end under the heading "Mémorables" there seems legitimate cause for confidence as to their conformity to Nerval's intentions, in view of the editorial arguments of Gautier, who was involved in the preparation of the text for press.[20]

Evidence for the chronology of the conception and composition of *Aurélia* comes mostly from letters indicating that Nerval was at work either writing or correcting the text during a period at the end of his life marked by two lengthy episodes of institutionalization at the clinic of Dr. Blanche in Passy and interrupted by two relatively brief periods of release, during the first of which the author made his final journey to Germany. Work would have taken place, then, during the same period as the probable composition of the sonnet "El Desdichado" and the letter-preface to *Les Filles du feu*, as well as the publication of the latter collection. The events themselves are as follows. From August 27, 1853, to May 27, 1854, Nerval was hospitalized in Passy. On the second of December, 1853, he wrote a letter to Blanche that refers to a project seeming to correspond to what will eventually become *Aurélia*. Seven days later, in the December 10 issue of Dumas's literary review *Le Mousquetaire*, the sonnet "El Desdichado" makes its first appearance. Some time between the December 10 printing of *Le Mousquetaire* and January 28, 1854, date on which *Les Filles du feu* was registered in the Bibliothèque de France, Nerval had to have written the preface, since it is constructed as a response to the article with which Dumas accompanied the poem's publication. Some time shortly after his release from Passy in late May, 1854, Nerval left for Germany, and it must have been during the period of confinement preceding his departure for the East that Nerval composed most of *Aurélia*. In letters written to Blanche and to his father and dating from early December, 1853, the author speaks of having undertaken to put into writing the "dreams," "impressions," and "visions" provoked by his illness.[21] Much later, in a letter of June 25 to his doctor, Nerval will refer to "what had been written in Passy." Starting as early as the end of May, only days after his release, letters from various points in Germany will make reference to the progress not of writing but of revising and reworking what the author will now describe to his father as "a remarkable . . . work," to Blanche as "a book," and to Franz Liszt as an "I know not what novel-vision in the style of Jean-Paul."[22] According to Jean Guillaume, who established the text of *Aurélia* for the most recent edition of the Pléiade, by the time Nerval returned to Paris some time around July 20, the text of his manuscript already corresponded closely to the proofs that would later be sent him by the *Revue de Paris*. In late July Nerval would write to Louis Ulbach, the director of the review, "I have done the editing of my work, I am mentally finished. There only remains to tidy up the pieces."[23] On the eighth of August, however, Nerval was taken back into confinement in Passy, which lasted until the fifteenth of October. By the end of this period he had begun to express doubts about the form of the work, writing, on October 13, to Maxime Du Camp that he was still copying and correcting and to Ulbach that he had reservations about dividing the final version into two different sections. Sometime during the autumn of 1854 *Pandora* was written, but aside from a letter to Ulbach requesting seven sets of proofs and probably dating from early November, there is little more information about *Aurélia* until the publication of its first part on January 1, 1855.

Thus, when Nerval wrote at the end of the preface to *Les Filles du feu*, "some day I shall write the story of that 'descent into Hell'" whose onset he had used in attempting to plot the continuity between madness, literature, and subjectivity, he had already recently begun work on keeping his promise, composing the first rough sketches of the work that, little more than a year later, would end with the line "I compare this series of trials which I have passed through to what was represented, for the ancients, by the idea of a descent into Hell." Despite the wide divergence of length and format, the texts of the letter-preface and *Aurélia*, as well as that of the sonnet "El Desdichado," demonstrate a clear thematic unity on several points. First, and most strikingly, in all three works there is the use of death and the underworld as metaphors for alienated subjectivity, and there is the reference to the loss of a star as the precipitating cause of the author's descent into a realm of negativity and despair. All three works draw on a rich matrix of mythological allusion and reference to express this realm of self-knowledge and self-alienation—the labyrinth it is compared to in the preface to the *Filles du feu* evokes the figure of Theseus, who mastered it, and who also descended to and returned from Hades, where he left his unfortunate companion Peirithous. The "ancients" are invoked in the last line and throughout *Aurélia*, whose second sentence mentions the gates of horn and ivory that lead to the underworld in the *Aeneid*. The second section begins with the epigraph "Eurydice! Eurydice!" followed by the line: "Lost a second time!" as if, in describing his otherworldly experiences, Nerval wished to identify himself with Orpheus, as he had done in "El Desdichado." In both the preface and *Aurélia* Nerval cites, among other poetic models, the *Divine Comedy* as a paradigm for the expression and comprehensibility of his self-revelations while ill, and it is Dante's syncretic model of Christ's harrowing of Hell that seems to have informed the image of the Orpheus-figure in the sonnet. Finally, in all three works the project of identifying and controlling a literary subjectivity that can pass between the living and the dead is plotted on a dynamic understructure or field. In "El Desdichado" it is the harmonic, multilinear trelliswork of the lyre itself which figures the poem as subjective instantiation. In the preface, the relation between writing and self-knowledge is construed as both a game-space, such as Dumas himself had been able to master, and as a labyrinth, which Nerval, like Theseus, was eventually able to conquer. All three of these models of written subjectivity will find a dense reformulation in the pages of *Aurélia* and will lead eventually to a radically new conceptualization of self-knowledge.

Structures of Intelligibility

The first-person voice of *Aurélia* repeatedly attempts to identify the underlying structure of the universe, moving through various but not necessarily mutually exclusive models to formulate eventually a dynamic but defective system that would draw all existence and experience together into an intelligible and unified whole and that would determine the relations of the world's various atomic parts—including the *je*—among themselves and to that unified whole. The manifest homologies between this text, the sonnet, and the preface suggest that the attempt to find such a universal understructure can also be understood as the search to determine and master a substantial field that would somehow articulate between writing and experience, between the work and the individual; in this way, the desire to master the intelligibility of the universe that shapes *Aurélia* would not only situate the work within the same subjective problematic that underlies "El Desdichado" and the preface to *Les Filles du feu*, it would also offer an access to the legibility of that *other*, poetic reading of legitimate if alienated subjective experience in which, according to the text itself, the work's true originality and legibility lie.

Nerval uses a semiotic or alphabetical model to represent the ordered intelligibility of the world, as is seen in a passage near the beginning of the second part of *Aurélia* which projects a terrain—a city—that will result from the self-determination of a cycle of unity and disunity, springing from and in a certain sense resuming them both: "perhaps we are touching on the prophesied age when science, having completed its entire circle of synthesis and analysis, of belief and negation, will be able to purify itself and bring the marvelous city of the future up out of the disorder and ruins."[24] After hesitating for a moment, shocked by his own hubris in believing that humankind by itself could, through science, achieve such a self-transcendence, Nerval returns to the idea, framing it now in terms not of a city, but of a kind of writing in which human knowledge would draw together its disparate elements and regain its spiritual force:

> Still, I told myself, it is certain that these sciences are mixed with human errors. The alphabet, the mysterious hieroglyph come down to us only incomplete and falsified, either by time or by those who themselves have some stake in our ignorance; let us rediscover the lost letter or the effaced sign [la lettre perdue ou le signe effacé], let us recompose the dissonant scale and we shall draw force from the spirit world.
>
> So it was that I believed myself able to perceive the relations between the real world and spirit world. The earth, its inhabitants and their history were the

theatre in which physical actions came and played themselves out, thereby preparing the existence and situation of the immortal beings attached to its destiny.[25]

The city is also a hieroglyph, or an alphabet that articulates between the intelligent and the physical worlds, between spirits and matter, and the science of the world, which would reveal the intelligibility of its material structure, is thus a kind of writing comprising in part the dramatic, gestural language by which human beings, whether consciously or not, control the destiny of immortal beings. But if the world and human behavior are a kind of language or text constantly being composed and through which each individual has the care of immortal destinies, this language is, in its available form, defective—for what seems to be a single letter or sign is missing. This remains a mystery, and throws off the harmony and intelligibility of the entire universe, robbing individuals of power and blinding their relations to the immortal fates in their care. The question is what sign is missing, and where, that the world which so manifestly has meaning to others—perhaps hostile others, who would attempt to preserve our ignorance—should be without meaning to us. The loss of a single sign from the system, its obvious existence somehow dissimulated from us, prevents us from understanding our primordial relations to others and from mediating between material experience—our physical actions—and their significance as intelligible gestures in an interconnected, linguistically structured universe.

The intelligibility of the material world is formulated in much more complex and dynamic terms toward the end of the text. Again Nerval is writing of his experiences in the asylum, where he suddenly finds himself capable of grasping a sort of universal language in which "secret voices sprang from the plant, the tree, the animals, the humblest insects." Infiltrated by an invincible force, he is able to perceive the harmonious relations among all the various objects of sensory existence, from the arrangement of stones to smells and the shapes of leaves, and the language of his companions reveals to him its secrets, the "mysterious turns [des tours mystérieux], whose meaning I understood." In this condition, when the world takes on voices and language itself reveals its mysteries, the author begins to marvel that he ever considered himself anything other than nature, that he ever viewed himself as separate from it.

> How, I said to myself, have I been able to exist for so long outside of nature and without identifying with her. Everything is alive, everything acts, everything corresponds; magnetic rays emanating from myself [de moi-même] or others cross unhindered through the infinite chain of created things; it is a transparent web [un réseau transparent] that covers the world and whose loosened threads communicate from one to the next, reaching to the planets and

the stars. Captive for the moment on earth, I speak with the chorus of the stars, and it takes part in my joys and my sorrows![26]

Once revealed, the intelligibility of the world proves to be structured as a dynamic living chain or network held together by a sort of harmonic intercommunication that allows the universal transmission of affect. But what is revealed is not only the intelligible structure of the world, significant as that insight may be, it is also the fact that the *je* is identifiable with this structure, that the identity of the first-person voice lies neither in a resistance to the universal nor in the death-mediated dialectic between particular and absolute, but already as the living of the world itself. There is still a *moi-même*, but it is an infinitely open, infinitely traversed *moi-même*, whose own intelligibility is inalienable from that of the universe at large, who is already infinitely penetrated by and infinitely projected among others. And this disclosure of the mutuality between the secrets of the universe and the secrets of the self only occurs when the world begins to speak, or rather when its secret voices finally become audible to the *je*. The communicative structure of the universe and the projective status of the *je* become apparent when the world comes into language, that is, when the language of all the objects of experience as well as the secret twists or *tours* of speech itself manifest themselves. The passage is thus constructed as a process of progressive manifestation in which the disclosure of voices leads to the disclosure of the secrets of language, which leads to the disclosure of the structure of the universe, which reveals itself as integral to the self-appearance of the first person. It is only through the unfolding of the principles of communication, through the self-presentation of language, that the underlying form of the world and the subject can be expressed. The *réseau* shapes appearance but is itself invisible and manifests itself only through and in appearance, only in and through the self-disclosure of linguistic expression. And what it finally reveals is that the *je* and the universe are constructed as forms of expression, as systems of communication. Language reveals not an annihilating antagonism to the material world, but its own original and universal presence in it.

It is this model of universal intelligibility as apparent in and immanent to language, and this particular articulation of that model, that represents the fullest and densest development of Nerval's conceptualization of the comprehensibility of the world. This concept consequently forms the magnetic pole that will guide any reading of subjectivity in *Aurélia*. This paradigm also brings with it certain implications that Nerval felt himself compelled to address immediately. Through its interconnectivity, through its very universality, for example, the expressive system that structures the *je* and the material world and which articulates between them, revealing their profound identity, bears also the seeds of its own destructive subversion, and the immediate reaction of the poet to this epiphany is one of despair bordering on terror: "Immediately I shuddered [j'ai frémi], imagining that this mystery could be discovered. If electricity, which is the magnetism of physical bodies, I told myself, can be subject to a directionality which imposes laws upon it, all the more so must hostile and tyrannical spirits be able to subjugate intelligences and make use of their divided forces in the interest of domination."[27] What horrifies the visionary is the realization that the structure and intelligibility of the universe could also imply the existence of certain *laws*, understood perhaps at first in the sense of laws of nature, such as the directionality of the flow of electrical current. This primary, neutral sense of law as necessary condition then apparently suggests another meaning, however: the law as imposition of an alien will and as a forced submission. The necessary material conditions of intelligent existence might not be equally and uniformly distributed, there might be certain peculiarities or inequivalencies in the structure of the universe, like the unidirectional flow of electricity or the secret *tours* of language, peculiarities that could allow certain individual elements, or *esprits*, to convert law as natural condition into law as domination of one will over another. What, in the preface to *Les Filles du feu*, had been an innocent game of history and invention that Dumas, "the master," could dominate, has here taken on the proportions of the fate of the universe, played out against unidentified "hostile and tyrannical spirits."[28]

If this domination by an alien will seems at first merely potential and vaguely formulated, and if these hostile spirits remain at first completely unidentified, the danger quickly takes on a certain specificity and historicity. In an almost humorous turn possible only in such a visionary state, Nerval consults what seem to be his personal recollections of the ancient world, which recall to him previous instances of such tyranny, and the nature of the Nervalian visionary universe begins to take on a particular form. Of special interest here is the way in which the author now recasts this question of universal domination in terms of a subjugation of the individual, and his localization of a specific point, both spatial and temporal, as the site of subjective vulnerability to such a subjugation. It becomes apparent that much as the *réseau* of the universe is characterized by certain identifiable irregularities so are the *je* and its relation to the dynamic system of intercommunication. The passage continues:

> That is how the old gods were conquered and subjugated by the new gods; that is how, I went on to myself, consulting my memories of the ancient world, the necromancers dominated entire peoples, whose generations followed one another in captivity beneath their eternal scepter. O misery! Death itself could not free them! for we live again in our sons as we have lived in our fathers—and

the pitiless science of our enemies can recognize us everywhere. The hour of our birth, the point on earth where we appear, the gesture, the name, the room [le point de la terre où nous paraissons, le premier geste, le nom, la chambre]— and all those consecrations and all those rituals imposed on us, all this sets up a fortunate or a fatal series on which the whole future depends.[29]

The capacity to dominate is a form of intelligence or *science*, while the tendency to *be dominated* links, or rather identifies, fathers and sons with each other. It is curious that there should be no reference to mothers in this passage—since, after all, there is no a priori reason to suppose one could not already have lived in one's mother as well as in one's father—that this submission to the law of another should pass entirely patrilineally, should, insofar as it is transmitted, be imposed exclusively through the individual's relation to his father. The law of subjective submission is in this sense a paternal law, a law of the father, and it takes hold of the individual at and through the moment of his birth, his entry into the intercommunicative world. How and when one enters the discursive game-space that structures the world determines one's degree of empowerment in relation to it, one's degree of autonomy or subjugation, and therefore, if somewhat paradoxically, one's potential for uniqueness and originality. The moment in question, on which the originality of the subject hangs, is the moment of his appearance, "où nous paraissons," a gestural moment, a name: it is the moment when he appears and in appearing signifies. This curiously paternal birth, when law gains access to the individual, is the birth of the subject into the linguistic or proto-linguistic expression which is the structure and secret of the universe, it is his birth into language's preexistent hold on him. The individual's birth as *je* and his relation to his father determine in some way, then, whether the discursive intelligibility that structures the material world relates to him as natural law or as law of subjugation.

In the continuation of the same paragraph this relation is further specified in terms of guilt and responsibility:

But if that is terrible enough by human reckoning alone, imagine what it must mean when reconnected to the mysterious formulas that set up the order of the worlds. It has been rightly said that nothing is indifferent, that nothing is powerless in the universe; an atom can dissolve everything, an atom can save everything.

O terror! here is the eternal distinction between good and bad. Is my soul the indestructible molecule, the globule swelled by a bit of air but which refinds its place in nature, or is it that void itself, that image of nothingness which disappears into immensity? Or again could it be the fatal particle destined to suffer, through all its transformations, the vengence of powerful beings? I came to the point of asking myself for an account of my life [me demander compte de ma vie], and even of my previous existences. In proving to myself that I was good, I proved also, as a consequence, that I had always been so. And if I had been bad, I told myself, was not my present life sufficient expiation?[30]

Nerval is first concerned with the possibility of subjective sublimation into the void of limitless immensity. Like Zola's Lazare, this prospect fills him with terror, but Nerval quickly passes to a more significant way of formulating the relation between individual and world, between existence and essence.[31] The distinction between absolute dissolution and absolute salvation could depend, theoretically, on any element in the system, no matter how apparently insignificant; since all is interconnected and since, consequently, even the least atomic particle could ruin the universal harmony, the threat to the whole could stem from the *je* as well as from certain "hostile spirits," and the former could, in short, play an active rather than a passive role in the possibility of tyranny or cataclysm. One is neither impotent nor indifferent in relation to the system, and Nerval is led by these reflections to consider himself ethically in order to determine whether or not he has committed an act, a wrong, which might require expiation. The fate of the world may, then, hang on the *je*, on his rectitude, or on the pardoning of an act. He might be, in other words, at fault in relation to a world dependent on his expiation. If he is at fault, that indicates a precedent responsibility, an ethical obligation to the world. And if it is a fault he cannot find, if he is unable to conclude either in favor of or against his own innocence, it is certainly because, according to the logic of the passage as a whole, he could not have committed the fault himself: if the fault entails that the *je* must "subir les vengeances des être puissants" as expiation, and if that subjugation is itself determined at the moment of birth, at the moment of origin, the fault itself must be original, must stem both from the moment and circumstances of the subject's entry into discourse and from an ethical responsibility to that discourse, a responsibility from before the origin of subject.

One can scarcely exaggerate the dominant role within *Aurélia* of this idea of a primordial fault, or how ubiquitously it structures the text as a problematic of guilt and pardon; as early as the third paragraph Nerval evokes his own mysterious, unspecified culpability, describing himself as "condemned by the woman I loved, guilty of a fault for which I no longer hoped to be pardoned [coupable d'une faute dont je n'espérais plus le pardon]."[32] But the issue of guilt is too exaggerated, too pervasive in the text—the word "pardon" alone appears in at least ten different passages—it is too deeply imbedded in the author's relation to the world, since it is, in fact, virtually the modality of his relation to the world, for it to be explained through any action or misdeed within that world, as he affirms at the outset. In this respect the passage on expiation cited above is particularly significant because it reveals not only that the absence of a sign missing from the mysterious hieroglyphics is itself the fault ("it is certain that these sciences are mixed with human errors [erreurs]. The alphabet, the mysterious hieroglyph come down to us only incomplete and falsified [faussés] . . . ; let us rediscover the lost letter or the effaced sign"), but also that the sign that is in default, the sign whose loss renders the world dissonant, would be that of the subject. It is the *je* which cannot be accounted for, and whose loss has troubled the universal harmony, blocking the articulation between matter and meaning, between experience and its communication. "I came to the point of asking myself for an account of my life [me demander compte de ma vie]," Nerval writes, but a possible wrong stands in the way, an original guilt that would require expiation prevents him from making sense of his existence. The "account" that must be given in this passage is obviously a tallying of good and evil, a summary, but it is also an accounting-for, an explanation of how such a thing could exist. The *faute*, or fault, what excludes the *je*, what subtracts it from the universal language that in some ways so obviously includes it (Nerval does, after all, write in the first person), is the original and originary impossibility of explaining—or accounting for—*how the* je *could exist and how it came into existence*. Whatever its wanderings and eccentricities, this is the central issue of the text as a whole: the need to find the necessary but missing sign on which its intelligibility hinges, the point that would articulate between subject and discourse, between experience and mediation. This is the *faute* which must be repaired, the missing sign of the subject's birth.

Such a reading seems confirmed when compared to the two other passages in which Nerval speaks of his relation to universal harmony, and where he casts himself as somehow responsible for its dissonant, defective state. In the last chapter of the second section, a few paragraphs before describing his vision of the *réseau* structuring the world, he writes of discovering, among the inmates at Passy, that "an error had slipped into the general combination of numbers, and from there stemmed all the evils of humanity. . . . It seemed to me that my role was to re-establish universal harmony through cabalistic art and to find a solution by evoking the occult forces of the various religions."[33] If he is responsible for reestablishing the harmony of the world, it seems to be because it is through his fault that it has been lost; at the end of the first section he had written, concerning his actions in a visionary dream: "What had I done? I had troubled the harmony of the magic universe from which my soul drew its certitude of an immortal existence. I was perhaps damned for having offended divine law in my desire to pierce a fearful mystery. Henceforth I could expect only anger and scorn!"[34] What he had in fact done in the latter passage was give a *sign*. Attempting to interrupt the marriage between Aurélia and his own double, the dreaming Nerval had cried out, "I know full well that he has already struck me with his weapons, but I await him without fear and I know the sign that must conquer him." Pressed by a crowd that seemed to mock his *impuissance*, or impotence, Nerval performed the symbolic gesture that would reestablish his power: "I raised my arm to make a sign which seemed to me possessed of a magic power [une puissance magique]. The cry of a woman, distinct and thrilling, imprinted with a rending sadness, awoke me with a start! The syllables of an unknown word I was on the point of uttering died on my lips."[35] If it was by recovering the lost letter or the erased sign that, as Nerval had said, "we shall draw force from the spirit world," here it is by the revelation of a magical sign, an "unknown word," that he will convert *impuissance* into *puissance*. But if in the passage that spoke of the hieroglyphs the power conferred by the lost sign would restore universal harmony, here that sign and that power serve only to disrupt it, and they are seen as an offense against the divine law. The fault here, that for which expiation must be made, is not the loss of the sign, but its attempted recovery and expression by the *je*. The first person finds himself damned, literally, if he does and damned if he doesn't recover the lost sign. The key to salvation and escape from the tyrannical law is the recovery of a word somehow associated with the raising of his arm and the conversion from impotence to potency. It is the word whose attempted recovery offends divine law and brings upon the author damnation, anger, and contempt.

The law of the father forbids that one learn how one entered into the law. It threatens impotence for those who would learn the phallic origins of legislation, and it exacts expiation for the expiation of another, more original lack—the incapacity to explain how one entered into the law of nature, into the primordial language that holds the world together in sympathy and mutual understanding.[36]

And in this economy of men, of fathers and sons, what was the woman's cry that stopped the word in the dreamer's mouth, that woke him from his vision, that seemed to him to have echoed even in the world of the living? It is the sound of a woman being torn to pieces by pain. And what was the unspoken word it stopped, the sign that would have articulated between matter and intelligibility, between the *je* and the world? A clue is offered at the end of the passage about the *réseau magique*. After having described the potential for a universal tyranny passed on from fathers to sons, and of the possibility that one atomic particle, the *je*, might bear responsibility for the dissonance of the world, a moment of hope comes to the author, condensed into the form of a single name:

> In proving to myself that I was good, I proved also, as a consequence, that I had always been so. And if I had been bad, I told myself, was not my present life sufficient expiation? That thought reassured me but did not free me from the fear that I had been forever classed among the unfortunate. I felt myself plunged into cold water and a water colder still streamed over my forehead. My thoughts turned to the eternal Isis, the mother and the sacred spouse, and all my aspirations, all my prayers joined in that magical name; I felt myself come back to life in her [je me sentais revivre en elle]. Sometimes she appeared to me in the guise of ancient Venus, sometimes with the characteristics of the Christian Virgin. The night brought that beloved apparition back to me more distinctly, and still I said to myself: What can she do, overcome and perhaps oppressed, for her poor children? Pale and rent [pâle et déchiré], the moon's crescent was growing smaller every night and soon would disappear.[37]

Through the name of Isis life returns to the visionary, he feels himself *revivre en elle*. Before, when he had spoken of the transmission of subjugation from generation to generation, it had been because "we live again in our sons as we have lived in our fathers."[38] Here, on the contrary, the rebirth in Isis draws together his aspirations and prayers, combining them into a single, magically powerful name that syncretically figures a series of female deities including the Virgin Mary and Venus. This name that brings together rebirth, longing, hope, and diverse goddesses stands in apposition to another epithet: it also means the mother and sacred spouse. The name that would situate the advent of the *je* in a rebirth integrating him into the law of nature rather than the tyrannical law of the father also serves to identify a female principle as at once maternal and the object of sanctioned libidinal desire, as both mother and wife. In respect to whom she plays these roles is not specified; she does so absolutely, as *the* mother and *the* sacred spouse. To say that the name, the sacred sign, is incest is perhaps to sensationalize the situation, but it does capture some of the anxiety, the terror and ambivalence, that the sign provokes in the visionary.

There is another force, a negative one, that makes itself felt here, that is conquering and oppressing the maternal figure, shrinking her and withdrawing her from her children; her emblem is pale, ragged, dwindling. And the word *déchiré*, describing the moon, recalls the "douleur déchirante" that wracked the shrieking woman of the earlier passage and the cry of womanly pain that stopped the missing sign on the dreamer's lips, the cry that brought him once more under the law of the father when he had been on the point of conquering it, of reestablishing and entering into the law of nature. Both here and there someone shreds a woman. Both here and there that violence brings an abrupt halt to the visionary's attempt to integrate himself into the language of the world by making his origin intelligible within the law of nature. The question remains of who would want to harm the mother. And there remains also the unexplained significance of the cold water that precedes her appearance. Perhaps it is only the cold shower periodically imposed by Blanche to restore reason to the visionary at the heights of his paroxysms, to force him to submit to the vocabulary and intelligibility of science.[39] But perhaps too it is the icy waters of the Bérésina, in which all the relics of his mother were lost after her death— "in a cold German land," "in cold Silesia"—of a fever caught while crossing another river.[40] "My father," Nerval wrote in *Promenades et souvenirs*, "forced to rejoin the army in Moscow, later lost her letters and jewelry in the waves of the Berezina." A few paragraphs later he refers to the "waves of the icy Berezina."[41] Are these the cold waters through which she must pass to return to him, or that he must cross to relive in her, to rejoin a maternal presence he says he never knew, the frigid waters in which his father had lost her even to her memories after taking her from her son and to her death? What, in other words, is the relation in this text between "*la* mère," who appears almost everywhere throughout Nerval's writings, and "*ma* mère," whose story is only hinted at in a handful of scraps like these?[42] And if Nerval speaks of "*mon* père" in the text, does he also, in some way, speak of "*le* père"? The clues to the origin of the *je* seem to lie somewhere in the history or prehistory of this strange family made up partially of relatives, partially of absolutes, a family troubled by secrets, violence, death, humiliation, and longing, but certainly still a family, after all.

The question of subjectivity here is first and foremost a question of reading, a question of finding the style and vocabulary for making a subject apparent and intelligible to itself. This idea of reading certainly includes the limited sense of an encounter with a text like *Aurélia* drafted in a language like French by an author like Nerval and published by editors like those of *La Revue de Paris* or the Pléiade, but it also has a much larger meaning, which would be something like the hidden but apprehensible structure of the universe. In this latter sense, the possible self-legibility and self-appearance of a subject cannot be dissociated from its relation to the communicative system of the universe at large, a relation that hinges above all on the point of entry, both spatial and temporal, into discourse. That point is the moment when movement becomes gesture, cry becomes name, and in explaining how it came to be, how such an event could be possible, how I could be original and unique in a discourse that prefigures me, that shapes my existence even before that existence is mine or there is an I to exist, I answer the question of what language has to do with me by an affirmation of the possibility of my living *in* language. The problem of self-knowledge, of self-existence even, is, however, that others hold the keys to the intelligibility of the subject's entrance into alterity, into his existence as matter structured by language. Those others seem, above all, to be a mother and a father.

Families

The nuclear family, or any kind of family at all, does not fare well in Nerval's writings. Nor is it frequently represented. As Jacques Bony has remarked, the only couple with a child depicted in his works consists of a drunken soldier, a greedy seamstress, and, literally, a little green monster.[43] *Aurélia* is unique in the extent to which it discusses families and family relations, bringing them more or less to the center of the text's global intelligibility by identifying them, in their expanded, mystical forms, as variations of the universal structure of significance and legibility that have already been discussed. The theme, if it can be so called, takes various more or less dissimulated forms that, through the very divergence of their registers, offer an idea of the multilinear links that establish the field on which Nerval attempts to plot the advent of the *je* in a discursive universe. The metamorphoses of the family pass from direct mention of his own immediate relatives and distant ancestors, to religious or esoteric formulations (such as the "mother and sacred spouse" represented by Isis, or the figuration of the paternal order as the sun), to the extreme abstraction of mother and father into interdependent principles of generation in a series of creation myths that are acted out in the author's visions. And through these metamorphoses, the family and its members trace out a semiology to account for or efface the birth of the *je*, or, in other words, the articulation between individual material existence and its intelligible significance.

Because the very structures of universal intelligibility of which Nerval speaks are often represented as material and, as such, gendered, they already contain, implicit in even their most abstracted formulations, notions of sexual desire and anxiety that are then elaborated into theorizations of the family and its internal affective dynamics. In the visions of *Aurélia*, one recurrently encounters, for example, descriptions of masses of souls in fusion, masses that seem, through the very density of their living community, to form material substance, something like aggregates of Leibnizian monads.[44] One of the most striking of these passages, from the fourth chapter of the first section, appears in the *mise en abîme* of a dream within a dream:

> I imagined that I had fallen into an abyss that crossed through the globe. I felt myself carried painlessly by a current of molten metal, and a thousand similar rivers, whose colors indicated their chemical differences, furrowed the bosom of the earth like the vessels and veins that snake among the lobes of the brain.

They all flowed, circulated and vibrated in this way, and I had the impression that these currents were composed of living souls in a molecular state, which only the rapidity of my travel prevented me from distinguishing. A whitish light filtered little by little into these conduits, and I saw at last, opening before me like a vast cupola, a new horizon dotted with islands surrounded by luminous waves. I found myself on a hillside lit by this sunless daylight.[45]

The rivers of souls that interconnect like an arterial web are themselves supported by another kind of substance and incorporated into a higher order of organization. They trace over the earth, which is here represented as something like a human body. It is a grotesque human body, certainly, made up of veins, a breast, and a brain, but these various attributes are significant, for the breast, even if used in a cliché, nonetheless genders the body as feminine, and draws it into the maternal metaphorics that structure Rousseau's image of the providing earth in *Les Rêveries d'un promeneur solitaire* [Reveries of the solitary walker]. This is a metaphorics that is all the more pertinent for coming in a text that manifestly influenced Nerval at other moments.[46] As important as this gendering of the earth, however, is the indirect attribution to it of an intelligence through the metaphor of a brain. This is an extraordinarily unspiritualized image of human intelligence, especially in Nerval's works, marked by a pathologist's attention to the materiality of the organ of thought, but it is precisely this materiality that is important here, since the whole passage concerns the relation between the spiritual and the physical. By comparing the organic substantiality of the brain to the organization of the earth, Nerval suggests an argument not only for the intelligibility but also the *intelligence* of the material world: if sentient beings can agglomerate to form masses in the same way that points with no inherent extension can agglomerate to form lines, and if the organic mass that is the brain can be sentient, why should all of matter not be sentient? In this way, the physical universe, or at least the earth, would not merely be gendered as feminine, it would also be inherently intelligent, which is to say, it would not need to seek elsewhere a spark of life to become animate. Also remarkable in this description, and related to the inherent sentience of the material world, is the manner of the latter's visibility. There is no sun, and instead light originates from the animate, molecular streams themselves, which, by the end of the passage, have flowed together into "luminous waves." Visibility comes from the body itself; it is not localized into a single abstracted and alien point, as in the poem "Le Point noir," but is instead inherent to and diffused throughout the earth, illuminating through emanation rather than propagation.

In this light but sunless world, hidden in a dream within a dream, the visionary is led by a male ancestor into a room filled with people who resemble both him and each other. They are the dead members of his family, and after a "paternal greeting," he meets his departed uncle, with whom he is able to converse wordlessly. When the *je* expresses his delight at the proof of immortality which the assembly of his ancestors seems to represent, his interlocutor cautions him that the situation is more complex than it appears, and to explain this he describes the organization of the world. The earth, he says, "is itself a material body whose soul is the sum total of spirits. Matter can no more perish than can spirit, but it can be modified for good or for evil. Our past and our future are one. We live in our race, and our race lives in us." There is nothing particularly new here, except the explicit fusion of the animate corporeality of the earth with the idea of a universal material substrate contested by forces of good and evil; in the struggle between the *je* and the forces of tyranny, it is the gendered body of the sentient earth that forms both the place of encounter and the stakes between the two contenders.

The relation among the spirits who make up the animating force of the world is sketched out in this passage. They are held together by race and ancestry, through principles of resemblance and repetition: the family members gathered in the room share traits and characteristics that regroup them, while race and individual are said to live reciprocally in each other. This latter idea is not merely communicated to the visionary, it is also illustrated:

> That idea turned immediately into sensation for me, and, as if the walls of the room had opened out onto infinite perspectives, I seemed to see an uninterrupted chain of men and women in whom I was and who were myself; the costumes of every people, the images of every country appeared distinctly all at once. . . . My astonishment grew when I saw that this immense enumeration was composed only of the persons who found themselves in the room and whose images I had seen divide and combine into a thousand fugitive appearances.[47]

The sentient materiality of the world derives from the consolidation of masses of souls, which consolidation is, in turn, effected through the action of resemblance, repetition, and replication theorized in the principle of race. The relation of the *je* to universal discursive structures is thus mediated through his relation to an extremely extended notion of family. Curiously missing from this family, as it is theorized here, are the figures of the mother and the father. One can explain the absence of Nerval's father from the assembly gathered in the room—he was, after all, not dead at the time of the dream—but the absence of his mother is more remarkable. The only trace that seems to remain of her existence in this section is an oblique reference to a painting. Before he falls asleep and enters into the dream within a dream, the visionary converses with an ancestor concerning the members of his family and he is told: "'You see that your uncle took care to do *her* portrait ahead of time . . . now *she* is with us.'" He raises his eyes to view the portrait in question, "which represented a woman in old German costume bent over the river's bank, her eyes caught by a tuft of forget-me-nots. Meanwhile, the night was darkening little by little, and appearances, sounds and the impressions of places grew confused in my somnolent spirit; I imagined that I had fallen into an abyss. . . . "[48] Dressed in the costume of the country where his mother died, the woman in the portrait bends over *the* river, a river that seems to need no name, whose identity goes without saying, as if there was only one river that a *she* could be looking at. The only member of the family not present, she exists now only in a likeness, like one of the portraits Nerval's father lost in the icy waters of the Berezina. Whereas the other lost relatives return in the flesh, *she* returns only as a lost painting.

The vision within a vision begins with the liminal representation within a representation of his mother. The vision, as well as the chapter, ends with an evocation of the mother and father. They appear, finally, but more transfigured than any of the other members of the family.

> One can easily imagine the father and mother as analogous to the electrical forces of nature; but how is one to conceive the individual centers that emanate from them—from which they emanate, like a collective *figure* of souls, whose combination would be at once multiple and limited? One might as well ask the flowers to account for the number of their petals or the divisions of their corolla . . . the ground for the figures that it traces, the sun for the colors that it produces.[49]

The mother and father are also principles of nature, like the currents of electricity used to figure the benevolent law of nature in the "magic web" passage, and there exists a reciprocal process of emanation between them and the various individuals that compose the world. Individuals emanate from the father and mother, but, curiously, in return the father and mother emanate from their own offspring as the principle or figure of their collectivity. In this sense, parents live in their children as children live in their parents. The difficulty in all of this is the problem of establishing how the individual derives from these principles, since, as Nerval writes, the relation between the originary electrical forces and what emanates from them is impenetrable. This is, of course, the primordial *faute*, the missing sign. If the analogy at the base of this passage holds, this is the same as saying that the relation between parents and children is impenetrable and that the question "Where do children come from?" is an insoluble mystery, and the *faute* would be its very insolubility. But Nerval's own question—"How is one to conceive the individual centers?"—should, perhaps, not be taken figuratively to mean: "It is impossible." Perhaps it should be taken literally, for at the end of *Aurélia*, the numbers of the petals of the flower, the figures of the ground and the colors of the sun are all explained by the vision of the "magic web" in the garden of the asylum at Passy. How that vision might have explained his own birth to him, his entry into a preexistant familial discursive world, can be traced out by following the metamorphoses of the mother and father and, later, of the parental couple in its analogous form as abstract principle of cosmic origination.

Fathers

Nerval does refer to his own father on a few occasions in the text, and these are undoubtedly significant, especially to a historical or psychoanalytic understanding of the author or his work.[50] Such readings have, however, a tendency to revert to the positivist, scientific approach that Nerval repeatedly attempted to refuse, if not refute, in the very act of writing, since they look through the text to the psyche that it would represent. Such attempts, though often of clinical value and frequently of tremendous finesse, are nonetheless premised on what can only be called a certain naïveté, if one takes seriously Nerval's polemical proposition: that he knows what he is talking about.[51] The author does not exclude the possibility of reading or even interpreting or analyzing his work; in fact he invites such attention, but he insists that such analysis cannot pass directly from the text to the psyche that created it; that it must, first of all, pass through the meta-text, which is the argument that the author laboriously constructs for his own relation to his representation, and that the reader must in some way account for Nerval's story of his own relation to discourse before being able to read him. To do otherwise is naïve because, premised on an unexamined model of the relation between subject and language, it would presuppose a knowledge of precisely that which it is attempting to discover: the subject of this language. That subject, Nerval contends, is not knowable outside its own work with language, its own construction of its own intelligibility, its own poetics or self-*poiesis*. Because the subject is not discernible through but in the poetry and the meta-poetry it generates in attempting to identify itself for itself, to read through the poetry is precisely to miss the originality and uniqueness of the *je* that emerges in it. It is to reduce it to a preexistent paradigm, to explain the nonexistent. The poetry and the meta-poetry are the subject, as Hegel discovered and forgot, and to read otherwise is, for reasons that will be explained later, to read psychotically, or at least psychotogenically. The goal here will be, accordingly, to read poetically, in the belief that such a reading has its own value as an epistemological model, and that bypassing this model would falsify the objectivity of any psychological or philosophical inquiry not only into Nerval's subjectivity but also, to the extent that Nerval is, as he contends, exemplary, possibly into any subjectivity whatsoever. For this reason, this reading concentrates not on Nerval's real father, but on the ways in which the *je* elaborates a poetic paternity.

As one might expect after reading "Le Christ aux Oliviers," the figure of the father in *Aurélia* tends to be identified with punctually synthetic images or personages, and the most obvious of these is his apotheosis. In the first chapter of the second section, Nerval speaks of the possibility that God might appreciate and encourage the potential of human reason and *science* to regain a lost paradise by bringing an end to the vicissitudes of history, and in so doing he casts the relation between the human and the divine in terms of a benevolent familiarity between fathers and sons. "We must not discount human reason so far," he writes, "as to believe that it gains something from entirely humiliating itself, for that would amount to accusing its celestial origin. . . . God will undoubtedly appreciate the purity of the intentions, and what father would be content to see his son abdicate before him all reasoning and all pride [tout raisonnement et toute fierté]!"[52] God is represented as a father who would delight in his son's rise from humiliation to pride through independent exercise of his inherited faculties. Here, in this optimistic scenario, *fierté* seems to signify less violent self-conceit than a sense of the value of the individual in his originality. This sanguine view of the paternal relationship does not last long, however, for in the following lines the author realizes with horror that even supposing such an attitude on the part of God is criminal: "What have I written here? These are blasphemies. Christian humility cannot speak like this." Apparently God, the father of fathers, is the sort of father who *would* in fact be pleased to see his son renounce his own reason and sense of self-worth in favor of humiliation. The order of the passage dissimulates a reproach, formulated as the question to God of what father would act like him and delight in the subjugation of his offspring, or more specifically, his son. And yet the recognition that a restitution of paradise through human knowledge is a criminal desire does not stop Nerval from attempting it. After the—apparently hypocritical—cry "o science! o vanity!" the author turns immediately to a description of his attempts, through reading cabalistic volumes, to gain a complete understanding of the esoteric history of the world, and how this study led him to the realization that a crucial sign or letter was missing from the universal language. The attempt to determine the origins of the *je* in discourse is thus undertaken in seemingly conscious defiance of a divinely paternal will to subjugate the son. Not only does the law of submission pass through fathers, it also originates in *the* Father, whose interest appears to lie in preventing his son from acceding, through an explanation of the advent of his *je*, to science and the pleasurable estimation of his own originality.

The hostility of God to his son, for which there is no a priori motivation, as Nerval suggests in his open-ended question "what father… ?" is to some extent explained by the rivalry between the two for a female love-object, namely, *Aurélia* herself. In a paroxysm of helpless, unexpiable guilt, the author becomes aware that his moment of possible redemption has passed, and that the attempts by the love-object to rectify his relations to God have, because of him, come to a necessary end. "From the heights of heaven," he writes of the dead Aurélia in the description of his crisis, "she could pray to the divine Spouse for me. . . . And what did my salvation matter anyway? The abyss has received its prey! She is lost for me and for everyone!"[53] His sense of guilt is directed toward the divine husband who has taken Aurélia away from him into death; the adversarial God who punishes his son's independence is also the spouse who kills the son's beloved. This is not the first "spouse" in the text, nor is it even the first to take Aurélia from the author. The note of despair on which the first section had ended was provoked by the vision of Aurélia's immanent marriage to another, who is only later revealed to be God himself.[54] "They were speaking of a marriage and a spouse who, it was said, was supposed to arrive and announce the start of the celebration," Nerval writes. "Immediately a mindless rage seized hold of me. I imagined that the one they were waiting for was my *double*, who was supposed to marry Aurélia, and I created a scandal that seemed to perturb the guests."[55] It is the groom who will take Aurélia away from the author, but he is also another self, an externalization of the *je* who, in the still-unexplained world of object relations, will take possession of the beloved's body. The scandal that the *je* will provoke to halt the wedding is the already analyzed attempt to manifest the sign of his own origination; he will regain the power to enter into possession of the love-object by asserting the sign of his own originality and value, the sign that validates the pleasure of subjectivity, or *fierté*, as the mode of relation to others, including the relation to the intelligent, gestural, human body of the beloved. The sign comes in immediate response to an armed threat, an ithyphallic weapon raised above the visionary's head. It is a castrating danger, which leaves the *je* momentarily impotent:

> one of the workmen from the studio I had visited on entering appeared, holding a long bar [barre] whose tip was composed of a ball still red from the fire. I wanted to throw myself on him, but he menaced me with the ball, which he held constantly pointed at my head. Those around me seemed to mock my powerlessness [mon impuissance]. . . . Then I backed up against the throne, my soul filled with an unspeakable pride [d'un indicible orgueil], and I raised my arm to make a sign [un signe].

What will be called *fierté* later in the text is described here as an unspeakable *orgueil*, a pride on the point of finding expression and entering into discourse. The advent of the *je* is the semiotization of the pleasure of the *je*, the empowering satisfaction of being as a mode of linguistic existence. But the hidden sign is not revealed. A woman's cry wakes the sleeper, who must accept his unsuccessful violence as a crime. The violent attempt to regain Aurélia has been an offense against "the divine law." It is the father who wishes to withhold the beloved, as it is, indirectly, the father who raises the castrating phallus that prevents the *je* from establishing his relation to discourse and from legitimating his own pleasure in himself. Like the postlapsarian entrance to Eden, the gateway to the pleasures of both a woman's body and discourse are guarded by a divine weapon.[56]

This hostile ambivalence to the father appears in the material genesis of the text itself. Vacillating between an annihilation of the father and his apotheosis, motivated, perhaps, by the various forces of fear, resentment, and rivalry that will later mark his relations to God in the text, Nerval, toward the beginning of *Aurélia*, rewrote a significant passage concerning the existence of a divine principle to read precisely the opposite of the initial version. It is during the period after his first series of visions, when the author attempted to share them with others only to find himself misunderstood by his doctors, as they reduced his experiences to a study in pathology. The ability of a friend to seize the importance of what his dreams had revealed to the *je* makes the latter weep with joy for the certitudes he has now gained. He is moved to embrace his interlocutor, and they hold each other "like two brothers." The passage, as printed, reads:

> More [than my doctors] I liked those of my friends who, through patient indulgence or as the result of ideas analogous to mine, had me give long accounts of the things that I had seen in spirit. One of them told me in tears: "Isn't it true that there is a God?" "Yes," I told him, with enthusiasm. And we embraced each other like two brothers from that mystical homeland which I had glimpsed. What happiness I found at first in that conviction! And so that eternal doubt about the immortality of the soul, which affects the best minds, found itself resolved for me. No more death, no more sadness, no more worry.[57]

A manuscript version of the same passage, however, reads quite differently after the affirmation of God's existence:

> "Yes," I told him, with enthusiasm. [But that idea provoked in me instead ~~the conviction~~ strange doubts. Supernatural life had been proven to me, but not the existence of a single, all-powerful being. I placed no impiety, no rebellious-

ness, in this grim reasoning. It was a painful fear and not the shadowy hope of an evil-doer who dreads the hand of God. Undoubtedly, I told myself] What happiness . . . [58]

The first word to go, apparently, is *conviction*, but the conviction of precisely what cannot be said. Certainly not the certainty of the existence of God, because of the concessive structure of the sentence. Grammatically, it would have to be the conviction of something contrary to the existence of God. Conviction is replaced by doubt, specifically of God's existence, which is, in turn, replaced with certitude in the published version. These reversals accord with the attempt to disavow a possible interpretation of his motives, an interpretation he contends would be the reverse of his true intentions and feelings. On a question of the utmost importance, Nerval is unable to decide yes or no, for doubt or certainty, and yet, in both of these two diametrically opposed cases, the affective reaction is the same, for in both versions the answer is met with tears of joy and a fraternal embrace. In all three stages of this segment, Nerval affirms the existence of God, he and his friend hug each other tearfully "like two brothers," and at the end he speaks of the happiness he feels to be assured of the immortality of the soul. If, however, one constructs, on the basis of the erasures, the probable development of this passage, one sees it pass from an original version in which Nerval, after affirming God's existence to his friend, expresses to the reader his conviction to the contrary, through an intermediate version in which he expresses only his doubt of what he had affirmed, to a published version in which he lets the affirmation stand as is. In all three variants the convalescent feels brotherly communion and the joyful certitude of immortality, but in the process from the first to the third version, he has effaced his certainty of the death of a father figure. The process of rewriting serves, above all, to efface the absence of the father from an initial, ecstatically happy vision of an immortal world of endless delight. It is as if the anxiety of the original passage, witnessed in the attempts to clarify his motives, had prevailed, an anxiety that this absence or potential absence of the father might be construed as voluntary on the part of the *je* or that it might answer his desires. Here, guilt effaces a sign, a sign whose restitution would free Nerval from the law of the father and initiate him into an eternal Edenic fraternity. The sign that he has effaced, that he has voluntarily forgotten here, is his knowledge that there is no father.

Mothers

The earth is a maternal body, as has been seen, emanating its own light, dependent only on itself to be intelligible, made of souls in fusion. And as the father most often appears in this text under the guise of God, the mother is also present in Isis, the goddess of varying masks and appellations. Unlike the Christian deity, whom Nerval calls "that solitary royalty," the divine mother is, in herself, more like a crowd than an individual.[59] Her very mention almost always provokes a series of names in apposition.[60] More than anything else, before anything else, it is this metamorphic quality that seems to distinguish the mother goddess, this process of repetition, figuring, and endless disclosure, as mask after mask falls. When the final veil of Isis is pulled aside in German pre-romanticism and romanticism, in Kant, Novalis, and Schiller, what is revealed is only nothing, but an annihilating nothing, a sublime nothing, the nothing that is death as an active, captivating, crushing force defining the individual in his individuality only at the moment of his abolition. The German Isis revealed the subject to himself as a metaphysical principle, in a moment of disclosure as brief and decisive as the fall of Hegel's guillotine. But Nerval's Isis never strips off a final mask, and even when, in *Octavie*, a goddess-death appears to him, she is still heavily figural, since the description lingers on the physical details of face and appearance.[61] In Nerval's work Isis is always appearing, always replacing mask by mask, name by name in a process which, while supposedly removing disguises, ceaselessly multiplies them; in his writings she exists only in her appearing, not behind it. If, when a final veil is lifted, the initiate was confronted with nothing, for Nerval it would be because the deepest secret of the endlessly self-manifesting mother is, like the secret of poetry Hegel discovered and forgot or repressed, that there is no secret. To read this proliferation of masks over an initial maternal lack as the fetishist's response to the castration complex, the constant, metonymically sutured displacement of his frightened gaze over a field of partial objects intended but never able to disguise an originary, phallic lack, would in some respects be appropriate. The generation of masks would be an attempt to restore an apotropaic maternal plenitude in face of a castrating threat to the *je* as child, a threat that hovers over the latter's attempt to regain the maternal body and integrate his pleasure into discourse.[62] A normative psychoanalytic narrative would identify this fetishization as an irresolution of the Œdipus complex, which should come to an end through a semiotization of castration rather than of its refusal. Without disputing the possibility or even the legitimacy of such an interpretation, it is possible to question its normative valence. This questioning, it will become apparent, is part of the undercurrent of *Aurélia*, whose alienated "reasoning," or *raisonnement*, articulates a critical noncompliance with a preexistent metaphysical tradition, as symbolized in the German sublimation of Isis, and also, as we shall argue later, with an as-yet-unformulated psychoanalytic discourse.

In a vision from the fifth chapter of the second section of *Aurélia*, the goddess appears to the author, but only as a voice. He has fallen asleep after purchasing a velvet screen covered with hieroglyphics, an event he considers a sign of pardon from above. "It seemed to me," he then writes, "that the goddess appeared to me, saying, 'I am the same [*la même*] as Mary, the same as your mother, the same one, too, that in all forms you have always loved. At each of your trials I have abandoned one of the masks with which I veil my features [*traits*], and soon you will see me as I am.'"[63] The illegible but material hieroglyph—and Nerval draws attention to its materiality by referring to the velvet substrate on which it is written—the unreadable text in its physicality, is seen as a sign of pardon, and this is in turn associated with a dream of the mother goddess. The latter reveals her identity to be discernible not behind but among the different masks she wears: she is the same—*la même*—as them, and her ipseity, her self-sameness, lies here not outside of nor as other than her various figurations as Marie, his mother, or any of his beloveds, but rather in her very identity to them and their consequent identity to one another. The actor of the verb who will disclose the nature of the maternal goddess is not the goddess herself, it is rather the author, who will see. Strictly, grammatically speaking, the appearance of the goddess comes not when she appears but when the visionary *sees*. As the sign of pardon seems to lie in the sheer physicality of an inscrutable text illegible on its semantic or referential levels, so the meaning of the mother goddess, that which the female figures figure, seems to lie in her very figuration itself. She is already there, in her masks, the same as them. Her *traits* are not manifested elsewhere than in the veil—and nowhere here does she say that she will disclose her true identity by lifting a final disguise. She says instead that soon the dreamer will see her as she is. Her *traits* are then *le trait* as such, the identifying characteristic that in modelling the individual as recognizable individual also situates her in a preexisting system of characterization that necessarily introduces a certain repetition within variance, and this repetition is the self-sameness that makes of the *trait* itself a *trait*. She is the sameness among women, revealing itself as a mode of manifestation: the possibility of recognizing resemblance among difference. For all its insistence on the visual, on masks and seeing, this revelation comes only in a voice: "je n'entendais que sa voix... " It happens in words. In short, the maternal represented, for Nerval, an origin immanent to the processes of representation themselves.[64]

Associated with the materiality of the illegible hieroglyph, the mother is the *trait* that draws together multiple manifestations in the masklike figures of female deities. She also, and probably most significantly, appears in what must be the most horrific of the author's visions as a kind of writing, and here, as in the hieroglyphs, the emphasis is placed on the physicality of the text, which has now become grotesque. Placed in a small summer house, through the trellis of whose door an oneiric landscape has already taken shape, Nerval turns his attention to the images beginning to form near him, in the interior of the room:

> Little by little a bluish light penetrated the pavilion and brought out bizarre images. I thought myself in the midst of a vast charnel house where universal history had been written in strokes of blood [en traits de sang]. The body of a gigantic woman was painted across from me, only her various parts had been sliced off as if by a saber; other women of various races, and whose bodies loomed ever higher over me, presented on the other walls a bloody jumble of heads and members, starting with empresses and queens down to the most humble peasants. It was the history of every crime [l'histoire de tous les crimes], and one had only to fix one's eyes on a given spot to see some tragic spectacle illustrated. "This," I told myself, "is the result of deferring power to men. Little by little they have destroyed and slashed into a thousand pieces the eternal type of beauty, so that the races lose still more power and perfection..."[65]

In the bluish light there appears to the visionary a writing whose *traits* bring together different races into a universal history whose synthetic text is written in the blood and bodies of women. This universal material order is itself the eternal type of beauty, which the three flamelike sisters had been said to resemble, and this indicates that the world is drawn together as they were, in the very process of self-manifestation. This narrative is written in and as the globalization of the maternal body, but it is a body under violence. And it is precisely men who have disarticulated the universal maternal text, who have penetrated and dismembered it with their sabers, who have made of universal history a history of every crime. These rigid sabers that penetrate the maternal body and slice it open, violating its original integrity, recall the ithyphallic bar that had prevented the dreamer from uttering the sign of his own legitimacy at the end of the text's first section. There it was the father's weapon that prevented the *je* from reintegrating himself and his pleasure in himself into a coherent discursive organization of the material world, while here it is the blade of the father that prevents the coherent intelligibility of the maternally material world from appearing to the visionary and which consequently excludes him from it. The insertion of the paternal principle into the maternal body is not therefore to be understood in Nerval's terms as the beginning of history or its furtherance but rather as its end or incoherence. Within this context, to explain or historicize the birth of the *je* through an intercourse between a mother and a potent, ithyphallic father would make of his advent a crime, would unleash apocalypse, and would convert natural and human history into a universal charnel house. It would be to initiate the son into language as corpse into death. For this reason, the son, if he is to account for and integrate his experience into discourse as its meaning instead of as an inexplicable lacuna in it always threatening to bring an end to narrative and always, therefore, negated by the language that speaks it, must find a parthenogenic model for procreation, and this is precisely what the creation myths attempt.

Creation Stories

In repeated visions Nerval is witness to that which can have no witness, the creation of the world. Since the originary forces of the universe are analogues to mothers and fathers, what the *je* observes in these scenes is also his own conception and birth—the missing sign. Certain characteristic features and stylistic traits unify the different versions, but within them there is visible also a certain tension, reminiscent of that between the manuscript and published resolutions of the question concerning God's existence. The predominant variant of the creation narrative in *Aurélia* recounts the parthenogenic origination of the world from a female principle, but this version is troubled by the possibility that such a birth would in itself be monstrous and teratogenic. This trouble, or resistant anxiety, generates its own subnarrative in which the father is restored to his procreative rights, but despite this objection to it, it is the subversive, fatherless account of creation that prevails at the end, as throughout the text.

In the seventh and eighth chapters of the first section one finds the initial and most fully developed creation narrative. Interned in a clinic, Nerval is nonetheless able to appreciate the charms of its garden and the first signs of the onset of spring, and in this pleasant setting he attempts to set down in images the impressions left by his first series of dreams and visions. "One figure always predominated," he writes, "it was that of Aurélia, portrayed with the features of a divinity [sous les traits d'une divinité]." First he draws her in symbolic, hieratic frescos along the garden wall, but then he turns to the ground itself and attempts to model her body in the dirt. Already the author establishes both an identification through the *trait* between the beloved and the divinity, and a consubstantiality beween her body and the earth. Already, like the universal history written in female corpses and the ragged, diminishing moon that figured Isis, it is a body that others will harm and scatter, but here this violence is said to stem from a jealousy toward the author's happiness: "I attempted to figure the body of the woman I loved in the dirt; every morning I had to start again, for the madmen, jealous of my happiness, took pleasure in destroying its image."[66] Hers is the image of his happiness, and she, then, its materialization. The earthly body of the mother is also the locus of pleasure, constantly threatened by a jealousy that explains without itself needing an explanation and which appears in this text as a given, as the a priori state of things, similar to the original, prohibitive anger that drives God, at the end of the text's first section, to interpose his interdiction between the narrator and his pleasure in himself, as represented by an unutterable sign.

Blocked in this attempt to materialize his relation to an absent female body, the author then tries another, more common medium to represent the memories of his visions, and the struggle between a maternal corporeal plenitude and a paternal interdictive anger reasserts itself in this new medium, only now explicitly identified as an originary scenario that can account for the existence of the world and, consequently, the *je*. "I was given paper," he writes, "and for a long time I applied myself to representing, through a thousand figures accompanied by stories in verse and inscriptions in all known languages, a sort of history of the world, mixed with recollections from my studies and bits of dreams." Already the relation between language and what it represents is put into question—for the former must be capable of expressing its subject, and to write his history of the world no single extant language or genre will suffice. The vastness of that which is to be figured calls for a reinvention of the means of expression. The chronicler attempts to bring together poetry, narrative, and inscription as well as all different languages into a vast synthesis. Language itself must change to bear the weight of representing the universe. And the representation of the universe must pass through the *je*—for it is from his dreams and his recollections that it will be formulated. The knowledge of the universe is thus a form of self-knowledge, and the universal history will emerge from a kind of introspection. The sign of the origin is already written inside the *je*, and he already knows the language; it is a matter of being able to recall, to read himself, to work through the palimpsest that is memory to the palimpsest of languages and genres that holds the key of the self, already written, in the structures of the *je* itself. He must go farther back, beyond what is written by others, and consult his own experience of the origin, for it is still with him, marked in him, somehow: "I did not stop at the modern traditions of creation. My thought went further back: I glimpsed, as in a memory, the first pact that the genies struck by means of talismans." This kind of research, similar to the Kantian critical method in its attempt to base ontology in epistemology, and to the Hegelian dialectic in its attempt to base ontogenesis in introspection, provokes in the author a kind of visionary recollection the night before he is to set to work. "This system of history," he writes, "which I borrowed from Oriental traditions, began with a happy agreement among the Forces of nature, who formulated and organized the universe. During the night which preceded my work, I had believed myself transported onto a dark planet where the first seeds of creation were struggling."[67] The system is at once preexistent—borrowed—

and original to the experiences of the *je*. It is the recovery of lost universal truth in the immediacy of self-experience.

This first account of the origins of the world begins with the struggling of seeds on a dark planet. Where either the seeds or the planet came from is passed over in silence. The earth, or clay, is already figured as feminine, with a life-giving breast, and recalls the dirt with which the author had attempted to fashion a simulacrum of Aurélia. The seeds and the maternal body already exist, and the recollections can go no further back, can penetrate no deeper into the mystery of origination: in the beginning there is matter and the principle of life. From the earth's breast living things begin to grow:

> From the bosom of the still-soft clay there rose gigantic palm trees, venomous euphorbias and acanthus twisted around cactuses—the arid figures of rocks stood out like skeletons [squelettes] of that sketchy creation and hideous reptiles slithered, swelling or coiling themselves in the midst of an inextricable web [réseau] of wild vegetation. Only the pale glow of the stars illuminated that strange horizon's bluish perspectives; meanwhile, as these creations took shape, a brighter star drew from them the seeds [germes] of light.[68]

At first, everything remains attached to the maternal body, for in the initial moments of this vision all that distinguishes itself is either plant or stone. There is figuration and structure, but only in the lifeless forms of rocks, which are like so many skeletons. This use of the word *squelettes* indicates that in the first phases of this scene, life organizes itself in something like a body or bodies, and these then take on a certain independence from the earth in the form of reptiles, which will, in the following paragraph, be characterized as "monsters." The general tonality of this initial phase is overwhelming negative, with its bluish darkness, its venom-bearing plants, its monstrous saurians, its arid, skeletal rocks. But this is not yet creation itself—it is merely a sketch of creation, or a precreation. The vegetal *réseau* of this proto-world is not the *réseau magique* that will appear as the intelligible system of the world in a vision at the end of the text. Rather, it is an *un*intelligible, *in-extricable* confusion. While this hideous body is taking shape, however, something else is occurring. A principle of light is developing as one star begins to distinguish itself as a potential source of luminosity, vision, and intelligibility. What is remarkable here, though, is that instead of the earth drawing light from the star, the opposite occurs. On the basis of the solar-paternal identification that marks Nerval's writings, one would expect that it would be this privileged star that would inseminate the precreational material world with clarity and intelligence, but instead it is the earth that gives to the star the *germes* of light. If in the monstrous and entirely bodily precreation there is absolute uncertainty as to where the originating seeds come from, here there is no doubt, for they come explicitly, if unexpectedly, from the maternal body of the earth, so that however insemination may function in precreation, in creation itself it passes through something like female sperm.[69]

As if to mark the difference between precreation and creation, the paragraph cited above closes the seventh chapter of the first part of *Aurélia*, and the story of the origin of the world resumes under the heading of the eighth chapter. What the following paragraph describes is the advent of order in the world.

> Then the monsters changed form and, sloughing off their first skins, stood up more powerfully on gigantic paws; the enormous mass of their bodies smashed branches and prairies and in the disorder of nature they started battles in which I myself took part, for I had a body as strange [un corps aussi étrange] as theirs. All of a sudden a singular harmony resounded in our solitudes, and it seemed that the confused cries, roars and whistlings of the primitive beings thereafter tuned themselves [se modulassent] to that divine song. Infinite variations followed one another, little by little the planet brightened, divine forms could be made out in the greenery and in the depths of the thickets, and all the monsters that I had seen, now tamed, sloughed off their bizarre forms and became men and women; others put on, in their transformations, the figures of wild beasts, of fish and birds.
>
> Who then had performed this miracle? A radiant goddess guided, among these new *avatars*, the rapid evolution of humans. A distinction was then made among the races who, starting with the class of birds, included also the fish and reptiles. These were the Dives, the Peris, the water sprites and the Salamanders; every time that one of these beings died, it was born again immediately in a more beautiful form and sang the glory of the gods.[70]

As the star grows the world gives itself over to conflict and disorder. It is at this point in the narrative that the *je* appears, and its advent is rather striking, for it is not in the guise of an observer but as a participant that it intervenes, and there thus occurs a sort of doubling of the first person in which it observes itself in its corporeal alienation, in the strangeness of its *corps étrange*. The *je* advenes in an appreciation of the strangeness of its own disordered precreational body; it occurs as an awareness of the monstrousness of its unintelligible self; but such a recognition—of the unintelligible in its unintelligibility—must be premised on a reference to the intelligible, that is, to the nonmonstrous. The awareness that the disordered body is strange indicates that the adventitious *je* is ordered. Quite significantly, the eruption of the first person into the course of the narrative immediately precedes the sudden diegetic and narrative appearance of a singular harmony throughout the world. The advent of the *je* thus coincides with a realization of its own alienation from the unintelligible materiality of the precreational body and with the capacity to discern a universal harmony. This harmony brings order, light, and, through its pervasiveness and singularity, unity into the world. Difference becomes variation, like the metamorphoses of the *trait*, and races can form. The monstrous becomes human.

The sudden, miraculous occurence of the unifying voice comes, in narrative relation to its explanation, with something like the slight, *nachträglich* rejection of the harmonically originating *je* into the monstrous world that it excludes. At first it seems inexplicable, and attention is drawn to the harmonic effects on the material world, but in the following paragraph its nature and origin are revealed. It is the voice of a guiding female divinity who, like the star, is a source of light. The advent of the human, the advent of the intelligible and the intelligent, the advent of the *je*, are now shown to result from the intervention of a female voice which itself originates, as do all luminous principles, in the body of the mother. The order of the world, its intelligibility, is initiated in a voice originating from the mother's breast. If, in the physical, precreative initiation of life, the unmentioned possibility of paternal participation is not openly and definitively excluded, the accession of the *je* into the discursive structure of experience, on the other hand, depends entirely and solely on a maternal corporeality. That accession is what allows the *je* simultaneously to see himself in his own alienation, to see himself in otherness, and to see the extent to which he participates in a universal structure of intelligibility. If the history of the world can be revealed, as it is in this passage, through a process of recollection, it is because the *je* is and was always structured in and as the historicity, or discursive apprehensibility, of the world.

Something like a counter-narrative of male-dominated procreation then ensues. The appearance of a fifth race, which "it occurred to one of the Elohim to create," unleashes a period of bitter internecine struggle after which three of the races migrate to the southern hemisphere, taking with them the cabalistic secrets of the unity of the world. These "necromancers," as Nerval calls them, had discovered, among other things, a method to assure the immortality of their sovereigns, who would, every thousand years, withdraw into a sort of chrysalis where "powerful cabalists" would feed them elixirs until they were ready to be reborn in the person of one of their children. It is men who have taken over the mysteries of generation, which springs now not from the inner intelligibility of matter but from knowledge. The fatal fifth race is born of an idea, the sovereigns renewed through science. But it is not a process of true creation, since the cabalists are only able to preserve what is already alive, and even that at the sacrifice of the immortalized ruler's offspring, since certain of these latter will have to cede their very being to their fathers' will. And it is a regeneration reserved only for the most limited elite, the rulers of the races. The effect of this process is a general exhaustion of the earth, the original and true giver of life and knowledge. "Meanwhile," Nerval writes, "the vivifying forces of the earth were being exhausted to feed these families, whose blood, ever the same, flooded into new offspring." In the narcissistic self-perpetuation of the father in the face of death, even if it be at the expense of his sons, the world itself begins to die. The preservation of the isolated subject against dissolution and death, its refusal, unlike the *je* of Nervalian literature, to pass through death, through "Le Christ aux Oliviers" and "El Desdichado," entails, conversely, the death of the world. In its laboriously preserved finite self-identity, this subject premises itself on death, even if the death that comes is not its own, but that of everything else. Nerval expands, at some length, on the deleterious effects of this patriarchy: a generalized slavery and a withering of the earth beneath the heat of a devouring sun. "It was in the center of Africa . . . that these strange mysteries took place; for a long time I had been groaning there under captivity, along with part of the human race. . . . An implacable sun devoured these lands and the feeble children of these eternal dynasties seemed weighed down by the burden of life."[71] The paternal sun is now in ascendency; the solitary, abstract principle of intelligibility whose death had been explored across the trajectory of Nerval's poetic career has returned to live at the expense of its children, whom it devours, and the science of the father has revealed itself as the sacrifice of the child.

Despite all its archaizing eccentricity, this scenario of an egotistical law of the father that sacrifices its offspring to its own preservation while devouring the world in an insatiable desire to maintain itself infinitely as finite particular or immortal mortal, can be seen as the mystification of a more concrete and historically specific series of events which formed the context of the author's own life. This is the then-recent memory of a national trauma that had preceded his birth. France had known its own mass sacrifices during the Revolution, and Nerval speaks of himself as their offspring, as if he were the child not of a mother and father, but of legalized slaughter and cataclysm themselves. These recollections not only displace, or replace, the more distant visions of the origin of the world and an ensuing paternal tyranny into the specific personal history of the author and his own birth, they also draw into that nativity emblems and issues that formed the philosophical context of subjective theorization during Nerval's life, for it is in the guillotine's blade that Hegel found the iconography for the annihilating sublimation of individuality into the law of absolute, impersonal freedom. In the beginning of the second section of *Aurélia* Nerval speaks of "us, born in days of revolutions and storms, in which all beliefs were shattered," and an earlier version had referred to "us, the children of two revolutions."[72] It is in the rationalization that characterized and justified the upheavals following 1789 that faith had been broken, to be replaced only with abstract principles, and the revolutions, and especially *the* Revolution, have offered their children merely a theorization of self-interest and the ensuing evacuation of the concrete contents of experience in the annihilation of sensual existence. The author says he has never been able to find solace in this philosophy; he writes that in the liminal state between dream and life—that experiential realm of subjectivity that *Aurélia* has, since its first lines, undertaken to express—such an approach is without value:

> When the soul hovers uncertain between life and dream, between the disorder of the mind and the return to cold reflection, it is in religious thought that one must seek aid—I have never been able to find any in that philosophy which offers us only maxims of egotism or, at most, reciprocity, empty experience and bitter doubt. It combats sufferings of the spirit by annihilating sensation; like surgery, it can do no more than cut off the painful organ [elle lutte contre les douleurs morales en anéantissant la sensibilité; pareille à la chirurgie, elle ne sait que retrancher l'organe qui fait souffrir].[73]

Two kinds of discourse—religion and philosophy—are placed in opposition. The first is of practical significance to the subjective project that guides the text as a whole, the second is useless in that domain. It is, nonetheless, this second, philosophical discourse that is most fully described here and which is said to be characterized by its egotism, and as a systemization of egotism it is presumably premised on the finitude of the individual, like the narcissistic immortality of the chrysalis-spinning father and the death-based subjectivity of the metaphysical tradition.[74] As in the case of the cabalists, the maintenance of this egotistical subject supposes the annihilation of the sensual world, an annihilation that is figured in the ablation of an organ, which a surgeon severs. In its voiding of the material in favor of an empty (*vaine*) law of maxims, this sublimating surgical blade that institutes and institutionalizes the subject of philosophy, birthing it in the midst of revolution, functions identically to the guillotine of Hegel's reading of the Terror in *The Phenomenology of Spirit*, which had annihilated the punctual, concrete individual in favor of an abstract philosophical principle of liberty.[75] It also functions like the divine, castrating ithyphallic weapon which severed the pleasure of the *je* in itself and in the maternal body at the end of the first section of *Aurélia*. The blade of the surgeon, which encapsulates the gendered dynamics of the mystical Nervalian creation myths, thus also sutures two other subjective discourses: the metaphysical and the psychoanalytic, the Hegelian law of absolute impersonal freedom and, as will be more fully discussed, the Lacanian law of the castrating father.[76]

Beneath the guillotine countless heads have fallen to the sublimation of the individual in a metaphysics of freedom, and in looking back on this education in the law of terror, the *je* comes to a new conclusion regarding its overall value—such a law is death, for this meta-pedagogical reflection reveals to him that "the tree of knowledge [science] is not the tree of life."[77] Even knowing this, he acknowledges, it will be hard to regain what he has lost: "it is very difficult, once we feel the need, to reconstruct the mystic edifice that innocents and simple folk let into their hearts fully drawn [la figure toute tracée]."[78] Like the palimpsest of memory that allows the *je* to recall the origins of the world, the simple person, marked neither by the apotheosis of Reason in the Revolution's cult of the Supreme Being nor the legislation of metaphysical subjectivity in the Terror, finds life itself already figured in his own innermost being.[79]

One's Self in Love

In the last pages of the work, a dense series of seemingly disjointed but highly synthetic visions brings the most important elements of the text together into what the author himself identifies as a resolution, a pardon, and a cure. How these passages, which in their ebullience and apparent disconnection seem like the most manifestly "mad" in all of *Aurélia*, relate to each other and, more importantly, to the problems they are supposed to resolve, is not, however, self-evident. Still, by situating them in their immediate context and by attempting to identify their connection to the dominant concerns in the work as a whole, it becomes clear that their remarkably difficult style is an integral part of their curative properties. Certain now-familiar concerns resurface in these final pages: repeated narrations, more or less fragmentary, of the creation of the world, the presence of the goddess, the question of redemption, the revelation of the *réseau magique*. These are bound together now, however, not only by a very different expository mode, but also through the appearance of several new characters and the emergent centrality of a previously marginal theme, that of fraternity. To try to understand these last passages fully would be madness, but they are legible enough, in relation to the rest of the text, to reveal how they answer its primary question. One can see how they, in curing and pardoning, restore what was missing from the world and in so doing restore a universal harmony. The missing element is, of course, the sign that explains how the *je* entered language.

In something like a prologue to the final series of visions, the author himself gives the context from his daily life at the time they appeared. Something remarkable has occurred to him in the asylum at Passy, something that, in the lively impression it has made upon his mind, has drawn him, as he says, out of the "the monotonous circle of my sensations or inner sufferings." Among the cataclysms and revelations that have marked all of *Aurélia*, this determining event, which somehow initiates a final resolution to both his inner uncertainties and his apparent madness, seems strikingly ordinary: the author is moved to feelings of compassion and care for another human being. The person in question is a young man, formerly a soldier in the African compaigns, who has been interned at the clinic and who has steadfastly refused to speak, eat, or even open his eyes. Nerval describes as follows their first encounters:

> I would meet an indefinable being, taciturn and patient, seated like a sphinx at the supreme gates of existence. I took to him because of his unhappiness and his abandonment, and I felt myself uplifted by that sympathy and pity. He seemed to me, set as he was between death and life, like a sublime interpreter, like a confessor destined to hear those secrets of the soul that words would not dare transmit or could not succeed in rendering [*à rendre*]. He was the ear of God unmixed with the thought of another. I would spend whole hours examining myself mentally, my head leaning against his, his hands in mine. It seemed to me that a certain magnetism united our two spirits, and I was overjoyed the first time a word crossed his lips.[80]

It is in discovering sympathy and concern for another, whom he will soon refer to as a brother, that the author also learns to communicate with God, as if there were some essential relationship between fraternity, communication, and the father. The brother is the sublime interpreter, but also, because located between the living and the dead, the interpreter of the sublime, that one who mediates between the divine principle of transcendental intelligibility and the material world of imagination which it exceeds and annihilates. Now, between God and the author, as between death and life or between the paternal principle and the *je*, at the point previously defined by the guillotine or the castrating blade, an interpretive brother intervenes. The two incompossible states bridged by the *je* in the first paragraph of *Aurélia* are here mediated through this fraternal figure, as if the profound continuity of the *moi* was premised in another, to whom I am linked by a magnetic sympathy and compassion. And this mediation between experience and divine transcendental death is a pure, paternal listening, the unobstructed ear of God. The relation of life and death, the annihilating aporia of the sublime, is resolved when God listens, and this listening comes in the form of the compassion of the *je* for another. In his love for another as a brother the persistent impasse of Nerval's literary career, between death and life, between writing and experience, finds the promise of a resolution.

This brother figure begins to play a very active and central role in the visions that close *Aurélia*. The night after the young soldier speaks his first word, the author has a dream, full of the promise of redemption and reconciliation.

> That night I had a delightful dream, the first for a long time. I was in a tower, so deep on the earthward side and so high on the skyward that it seemed my whole existence must be consumed in climbing and descending. Already my forces were exhausted, and my courage was about to fail, when a lateral door happened to open; a spirit presented itself and said to me: "Come, brother!..." I don't know why the idea came to me that he was called Saturnin. He had the features [les traits] of the unfortunate invalid, but transfigured and intelligent.[81]

As the dream begins, the *je* is exhausting himself in an attempt to mediate or pass back and forth between heaven and earth by means of an enormous tower; emblem, elsewhere in Nerval's writings, of the father, it is here also the figure of the sublime impasse, the impossibility of uniting the intelligible and the sensual, the paternal and the maternal, in a single synthetic image. Like Savary's observer of the pyramids, quoted by Kant as an illustration of the sublime in *The Critique of Judgement*, the *je* of the dream must endlessly run back and forth trying to mediate between that which is imaginatively figurable and that which is intellectually comprehensible. The pyramids become sublime at precisely that moment when imagination, exhausted by the attempt to figure what it cannot, recognizes its limitation and concedes the unity of the subject to the abstract impersonal order of understanding, a concession that entails the annihilation of the sensible in the unification of the first person, a sublimation analogous to the egoism that unifies the subject in the surgical ablation of the organ of sense experience. It is at precisely this point of exhaustion in the apparently impossible attempt to mediate between the sensible and the intelligible that the *je* of the dream is shown an escape. The impasse is a product of the simple, vertical linearity of the sublime relation, and it is resolved when the *je* finds himself able to move laterally.

It is, quite significantly, a lateral familial relation, a brother, who reveals this other dimension of movement, this way out of the sublime aporia. Within the dynamics of the family, the brother represents an important variant on the two possible and antagonistic relations to the maternal body already depicted in the text. Brothers are in a relation of structural equality in reference to the mother, which is not at all the case with the father. As the dream proceeds, this equality is figured in a recension of the original moments of the first version of the creation narrative. The brothers leave the tower.

> We were in a landscape [nous étions dans une campagne] lit by the flames of stars; we stopped to contemplate this spectacle, and the spirit held out his hand against my forehead as I had done the day before in an attempt to magnetize my companion; immediately one of the stars that I could see in the sky began to grow, and the divinity of my dreams appeared to me. She was smiling,

dressed in an almost Indian costume, such as I had seen her before, and she walked between the two of us. The meadows turned green, the flowers and foliage rose up from the ground in her footprints... She said to me: "The trial to which you were subjected has come to an end; those numberless stairways which you exhausted yourself in descending or in climbing were themselves the bonds of past illusions that hindered your thought, and now, remember the day when you implored the holy Virgin and when, believing her dead, your spirit was seized by madness. It was necessary that your wish [vœu] be taken to her by a simple soul freed from the bonds of earth. That soul has been found close to you, and that is why I am allowed to come myself to encourage you." The joy which this dream spread through my soul procured for me a delightful awakening. Day was beginning to break. I wanted to have a material sign [un signe matériel] of the apparition which had consoled me, and I wrote on the wall these words: "Thou hast visited me this night [Tu m'as visité cette nuit]."

I inscribe here, under the title of *Mémorables*, the impressions of several dreams which followed the one I have just reported.[82]

As in the initial version of the creation narrative, the world is illuminated only by the light of the stars, one of which begins to grow until a female divinity appears. The witnessing *je* of the earlier account has now, however, become a *nous*, which shares the spectacle of the original world and the dream-deity. The goddess, who here plays the role taken before by the unifying maternal voice, places herself between the brothers, as if mediating between them, as if connecting and separating them by her very person, and from this position she makes three disclosures. First, she reveals that the stairs in which the dreamer had been trapped were in fact the figure for a mode of thinking, a specifically erroneous mode of thinking, which had been confusing the *je*. Second, she announces the ending of his trials. The pardon, the end of his period of expiation, thus comes contemporaneously with an innovation in his model for conceiving the relation between the intelligible and the material, an innovation that occurs in and as the advent of the fraternal. Third, the pardon, or at least the promise of pardon, was possible because of the intercession of someone, presumably the brother-figure Saturnin, freed from earthly bonds.

The vertiginous series of visions that bring the text to a close are initiated in and follow from the one here described, which thus plays a liminal function between the work and its conclusion. It is in this respect that the conceptual paradigm shift that this dream represents assumes its full importance, for the reconfiguration of the relations among the various elements of the sublime aporia entails a recasting of the relation between subject and language. And as the relation between heaven and earth is revolutionized here, so is the relation to the earth as maternal body. The brother, whose advent marks the revolution of literary subjectivity out of an aesthetics of the sublime, is the one who has broken free from an attachment to the earth. He is not detached from the maternal, and in fact, even here, his relation to the *je* is mediated through the very person of the mother-figure; nor does the maternal diminish in importance over the course of the following visions—quite the contrary. What the brother seems to represent is the model for a subtilization, rather than a sublimation, of the relation to the materiality of the mother in a principle of pure communication.[83] As the brother is the ear of God, so is he the mouthpiece of the *je*, who is able through him finally to express his desire, his *vœu*, to the virgin mother. The role of the material, like those of all the other elements and characters in the search for the sign of the origin of the *je*, has been displaced. On waking, the visionary wants a substantial sign of what he has seen, and he writes. It is only a brief line, it is merely on the wall, but its sheer primitiveness serves to underscore its true significance—it is in writing itself, in the stuff of pure communication, that the material now lies. From the dreamed advent of the fraternal comes the waking recognition of the materiality of the text.

Verbal Pleasure: "Les Mémorables"

This materiality seems particularly marked in "Les Mémorables," for there is no other part of *Aurélia* that is as given over to lyricism, whether it be in the almost musical use of repetition, in the preponderance of vocatives, or in the Symbolist density and rapidity of images, reminiscent of the style of "El Desdichado." The attempt to narrativize the various visions, which characterized the rest of the text, has here given way to the play of passing verbal images, and the paragraphs themselves are now brief iconographic gestures. The opening passage is exemplary of the style:

> Sur un pic élancé de l'Auvergne a retenti la chanson des pâtres. *Pauvre Marie!* Reine des cieux! c'est à toi qu'ils s'adressent pieusement. Cette mélodie rustique a frappé l'oreille des Corybantes. Ils sortent en chantant à leur tour des grottes secrètes où l'Amour leur fit des abris.—Hosannah! paix à la Terre et gloire aux Cieux!
>
> Sur les montagnes de l'*hymalaya*, une petite fleur est née: Ne m'oubliez pas!—Le regard chatoyant d'une étoile s'est fixé un instant sur elle et une réponse s'est fait entendre dans un doux langage étranger—*Myosotis!*—
>
> Une perle d'argent brillait dans le sable; une perle d'or étincelait au Ciel... Le monde était créé. Chastes amours, divins soupirs! enflammez la sainte mon-

254 *'Aurélia'*

tagne... car vous avez des frères dans les vallées et des sœurs timides qui se dérobent au sein des bois!

Bosquets embaumés de Paphos, vous ne valez pas ces retraites où l'on respire à pleins poumons l'air vivifiant de la Patrie. —"Là haut, sur les montagnes—le monde y vit content; —le Rossignol sauvage—fait mon contentement!"

On a lofty peak in the Auvergne the shepherds' song has resounded. *Poor Mary!* Queen of the heavens! it is thou whom they piously address. That rustic melody struck the ears of the Corybants. Singing in their turn they come out from the secret grottos where Love has made them shelters. —Hosannah! Peace on Earth and glory to the Heavens!

In the mountains of the *Himalaya* a little flower was born: Forget me not! —The shimmering glance of a star settled on it for an instant and an answer was heard in a gentle foreign tongue—*Myosotis!*—

A silver pearl gleamed in the sand; a golden pearl sparkled in the Heaven... The world was created. Chaste loves, divine sighs! enflame the holy mountain... for you have brothers in the valleys and timid sisters who hide in the bosom of the woods!

Perfumed thickets of Paphos, you cannot equal these retreats where one breathes freely the Fatherland's vivifying air.—"Up there, in the mountains—the world lives in happiness there—the wild nightingale—makes my joy!"[84]

These four paragraphs seem to go together as a complete section, both by their content and by their page layout, which sets them off by spaces.[85] They celebrate and synthesize two different originations: on the one hand, the echoes from the nativity sequence in the gospel according to Luke (2:8–20) and the apostrophe to Mary allude to the birth of Christ, the son, while on the other hand, the passage also speaks of the beginning of the world. Like the initial creation narrative, given in chapters 7 and 8 of the first section, this double origin of son and world involves singing, a goddess, and a reciprocity between the earth and a star, but here the female deity is identified with the sky rather than the earth. The latter, particularly its amorous recesses, has been given over to a fraternity, the followers of Cybele, goddess of a chaste love.[86] This idea of a brotherhood dwelling in the folds of the earth is repeated in the reference to "des frères dans les vallées" as the idea of nonerotic love is in the invocation of *chastes amours*. Still, though chaste, this love, like that of the virgin mother of Christ, still seems creative, for it is apostrophized directly after the words "the world was created." And if the renunciation of genital sexuality leads to the amorous relation between brothers and the unsubtilized recesses of the material, this latter has also incorporated a paternal principle in becoming "la Patrie." As the father sinks into the earth and the mother rises to the sky in her role as queen of the heavens, the parental couple describe, by their reciprocal exchange of places, a circulation figured in the mirroring of pearls, stars, and flowers. The familial system has been set into motion, and even the father has fallen under its mobile dynamics.

The *je* itself, however, appears here only implicitly, as the grammatical position of apostrophization, and though the body of the mother, with its loving invaginations and protective *sein*, has been given over to the father, a desexualized fraternity and a timid sorority, the *je* is now identified through a different sort of relation to the maternal: it is created out of the vocalization, the invocation and apostrophization of the mother—as in the words "*Poor Mary!* Queen of the heavens... thou."[87] Out of the communalization of the libidinized maternal body among father, brothers, and sisters, there emerges the subtle *je* in a textual gesture of address to the mother. Or rather, following the chronology of the narrative, it is the other way round. A song begins in the mouths of shepherds, and in identifying Mary as the addressee of the song, in referring to her as *toi*, or "thou," the *je* appears, dependently, obliquely, in the text. This address that initiates the *je* is then repeated by the Corybants, who emerge from an unsubtilized maternal body, which appears in the text only through their act of emerging from it, for like the song of the goddess that made the strangeness of the *je*'s own body apparent to it, the loving and creative folds of the mother become visible only in the song that initiates the first person. In this song, sung by a fraternity of shepherds who exist prior to the *je*, the body is made visible, intelligible, as a locus of communal material pleasure. The materiality of this body that emerges in the *toi* is like that which emerges from the *tu* of "thou hast visited me this night," for in both cases it is initiated by and perpetuated in the substantiality of a *signe matériel*. In a passage that celebrates the birth of a son who never figures thematically, the *je*, here, is shown to be born out of the text itself, out of a language already spoken by others, in the address to another. And the materiality of the text is the generative body of the mother, shared in the mouths of all, as a community of pleasure. The mystery of the "lost letter," the sign that would bind together the physical and the intelligible, language and experience, by accounting for the origin of the *je* is thus finally revealed: I am born out of the address to another, an address made in a language *both* material and intelligible, a language spoken communally before and after my birth, and which initiates me into a gathering of others, which initiates me as already there, among them, substantially, in these shared words that structure me and them. This passage, then, represents, or rather *is*, the pardon that has been sought throughout the text, the lost sign that accounts for the entrance of the *je* into language, for the latter is born out of a fraternal calling to be that already resonates in its own calling to the mother; it is born into the fraternal communality of language; and this materially intelligible world into which it is born is structured as language itself, is a form of language. The child, created not out of desire (excluded in the devaluation of Paphos, the island associated with Aphrodite) but from a loving evocation, is thus called to from the very language it speaks, and it recognizes in that language a primordial address to it, a preexistent linguistic position that makes of the world an interconnected system of material signs and that reveals experience as language directed to and from the first-person position. What this passage reveals and instantiates is, accordingly, a propositional subject, but one that is originated and grounded not in the finite "I" of Kantian apperception, but in the "Thou" that recognizes language as an address to and from a speaking other or others. While generating an implicit first-person position of address by uttering "toi," the *je* also recognizes the possibility of being addressed itself, of being interpellated, and there echoes in its words a calling into being as speaker from a preexistent community that is structured as language. The missing sign was the "toi" that prescribes the *je* in language, not as finite individual blocked off by death from the voices around it, but as already limitlessly outside itself and communal even in the form and material of is own experience.

The "Mémorables" are, in comparison to the rest of the text, remarkable for their use of the second person and the vocative, as if having discovered their power the author became intoxicated with it. But if one can demonstrate, with the detachment of a grammarian, that in the midst of a celebration of the birth of a divine son, the first-person position is introduced into the text by an effect of the relational dynamics inherent in the structures of language, one can by no means prove that the insistent use of apostrophe and the second person in this section is in fact determined by the ability of such structures to generate a locutor while positioning him in relation to a discursively articulated community; one cannot prove, in short, that the author consciously or unconsciously continues to use these formulations because they create the *je* or in order to create the *je*. One can, however, observe what is happening thematically in the text, and how it thereby relates to the elements of the maternally linguistic creation scene. The fragmentary visions of this section of the "Mémorables," through recurrent grammatical structures, stress the interlocutory relation between the first and second persons. They reiterate and vary fragments of the initial creation vision, such as the formula "Peace on Earth and glory to the Heavens!" and the passage beginning "In the mountains… " And they repeat the ideas of fraternity, pardon, and an original, originating song, like that which first introduces the *toi*. The passage as a whole, held together by these structures and themes, comes across as a lyrical expansion of what was held densely and *in nuce* in its four brief opening paragraphs. Most significant among the results of this expansion are the final characterization of the song and the further determination of the fraternal connection. The former is said to begin as the harmonization of two distinct notes out of the breast of darkness, and to conjoin the world in a "magic web." The latter, the fraternal, is extended to draw in other sons of gods—Jesus and Thor. The former signs with his blood the pardon of the world, whose unity the latter is incapable of destroying—in neither case do they represent a potentially successful threat to the maternal cohesiveness of the world. As Christ forgives Thor, brother pardons brother, and the *je* blesses the son of Odin, they are drawn together in relations of apostrophe and linguistic performativity with one another.[88] And when the visionary blesses Thor, the latter appears as fragmentarily displaced and dispersed among his family, as if his unity lay not in himself, but already among others, and as if what the *tu* represented were not an egoistically finite individual, but one spread among a community: "Blessed be thou, o Thor, the giant—the most powerful of Odin's sons! Blessed be thou in Hela, thy mother, for often the trespass is sweet—and in thy brother Loki, and in thy dog Garm."[89] The blessing, that which draws together interlocutors in a linguistic acting upon one another, also discloses the multiplicity of the other in language, even of the second person singular. Thor is addressed as son of Odin; he is acted upon, in language, in the persons of himself, his brother, his dog, and his mother. The mention of the latter elicits a reference to the sweetness of a forbidden act. Thor's crime was to attempt to break the unity of the world, a violence against the maternal body, a violence of the ithyphallic weapon, the hammer of the blacksmith-god. But it was an unsuccessful violence, for the mother is still intact, and the blessing of fraternity still possible. The attempt is sweet against the web, the sacred table, the materiality of language, the mother's body, even if the pleasure it procures entails castration, death, the end of fraternity. Often it is sweet, but here it has failed, and brother can still forgive brother, because language still works, holding one to another in the act of utterance and writing. Language still holds, the son of Odin can be blessed fraternally in his dispersion into those close to him, and the author will be able, in the second-to-last sentence of the work, to characterize his own cure as a return to his family: "The care which I received had already returned me to the affection of my family and friends." Through the discovery of a fraternal compassion in the person of Saturnin, the *je* has discovered and disclosed the secret turn that binds him to language, that explains and legitimizes his own pleasure as the very binding of that bond rather than as a fault or a "trespass"; he has discovered and disclosed his own birth into and as part of a world structured as a discursive community; and in the force of his discovery, the *je* gives himself over to forgiveness, compassion, and sharing. Language itself has been libidinized, it structures the world, and it structures the subject that is not a subject in the metaphysical sense, but which is a *je*, always already determined as a relating-to-others and a being-related-to by others, as a thing that insofar as it is in itself is already in others. In the *je*, I experience a world already structured by language, a language that makes me like other *je*'s, and as a thing structured in language, I am always already alien to myself. To know myself is to pass through a knowing of language and others, it must be always a knowing of myself in alienation, in otherness, in language. Before all things, and above all before the finitude of an egoistical misapprehension of myself, I am engaged to others as a *res loquens, scribens, legens*, living always in and as part of a community that is language. Before all things, I have become I in language, and that language is a precognitive bond to others, an ethics, a compassion, a pleasure.

In summarizing *Aurélia*, its author writes:

> Such were the inspirations of my nights; my days passed by gently in the company of the poor invalids, among whom I had made friends. The awareness that henceforth I was purified of the faults from my past life gave me infinite spiritual joy [des jouissances morales infinies]; the certitude of immortality and of the coexistence of all the people I had loved had come to me materially, so to speak [pour ainsi dire], and I blessed the fraternal soul who, from the heart of despair, had brought me back into the luminous paths of religion.[90]

He has found the assurance of forgiveness, immortality, and the community of the loved. There is no mention of a supreme being, the question of whose existence had so tormented him earlier, when he had spoken of the certitudes gained from his visionary experiences. Or rather, what had tormented him earlier was not so much the lack of such proof of an apotheosized father as his own attitude toward that lack.[91] That problem has fallen away, as has any mention of God, and instead there remains the pardon, that which preserves the unity of the world, and which in preserving that unity gives not the merely sweet pleasure of transgression but endless *jouissances*. Moral or ethical pleasures, infinite and intense, flow from the shared body of the mother that is community. And it is a body, even if a subtilized body, which holds together in love, for the assurance of its existence has itself come to him materially—*matériellement*. Nerval indicates, with the expression "pour ainsi dire," that it is an unusual kind of materiality he is speaking of, a subtilized concreteness and physicality, like that of the *signe matériel* which attested to the nocturnal visitation at the threshold of the "Mémorables." Language itself is revealed as both pleasure and meaning, as matter and sense together, and as such it comes from others. Nerval's return to this community arises from a fraternal intervention, and he, in turn, blesses the brother, participating in the act that sustains fraternity as a mode of relatedness through discourse.[92]

The Subject of Castration in Lacan

If *Aurélia* in general, and "Les Mémorables" in particular, revolt against a certain model of subjectivity, it is above all at the articulation between self and language that this revolution takes place, and what they are revolting against is a violent exclusion, a severing between a discursive world and self-experience, against the sublime subject. That exclusion has come through the agency of the father, or his surrogates, and has taken the form of what was earlier called a castrating threat: namely, the menace, figured in a weapon (the "long bar," for example),[93] of ablation of the sensual world, itself later figured in an unnamed organ. The result of that exclusion has been the son's submission to the recasting of the discursive world, the "magic web," as a humiliating divine law or law of the paternal. To appreciate what this revolt signifies, in or in relation to other discursive traditions of subjectivity, entails considering what such castration—to abbreviate—itself means within them. Nowhere, of course, is this concept so fully elaborated as in psychoanalytic theory, and this to a point where one can, within the present confines, only sketch out the main lines of the model within a single configuration.

As treated in Lacan, the question of castration is central to the relation of the subject to language, and in the paper "The Signification of the Phallus" he asserts that the functioning of the latter within an intersubjective economy raises the veil that had hidden its true role in the ancient mysteries. Again, as with Isis and the sublime, when speaking of the meaning of the phallus, of the relation that constitutes what has been referred to here as the *je*, it is a question returning to the ancients and lifting a veil. The castration complex itself, Lacan contends, has an articulatory importance as the nexus, or *nœud*, that draws together, on the one hand, the dynamic structure of symptoms in the various neurotic and pathological states, and on the other the installation, within the subject, of an unconscious position on which will depend the further elaboration of sexual self-identification.[94] Of more immediate interest than the gendering that devolves from it is the idea that the castration complex positions the subject. To understand how it does so, however, one must first understand the significance of that which is castrated: the phallus.

Needs, *les besoins*, are treated as primary by Lacan in this particular paper, and it seems that they can be understood in terms of basic infantile necessities, whether physical or affective. These needs are estranged from the needy one in their passage through language, where they become demands for something needed, and the article thus refers to "a deviation of man's needs from the fact that he speaks, in the sense that in so far as his needs are subjected to demand, they return to him alienated."⁹⁵ This impossibility of adequately expressing the need, of expressing it in a nonalienated way, constitutes a de facto primordial repression, the estrangement of the need, which returns as desire insofar as it is unexpressible. Desire is consequently that which is literally unspeakable; it is the very primordiality of need: "That which is thus alienated in needs constitutes an *Urverdrängung* (primal repression), an inability, it is supposed, to be articulated in demand, but it re-appears in something it gives rise to that presents itself in man as desire (*das Begehren*)."⁹⁶ Need is not merely unsatisfactorily unsatisfied, or insufficiently articulated in its linguistic instantiation as demand, it is also alienated, and this because language itself is other to that which needs. Language here appears as that other of the self, the unconscious, the place, paradoxically, of desire that cannot be expressed, a place that has its own structure and topology:

> It is a question of rediscovering in the laws that govern that other scene (*ein andere Schauplatz*), which Freud, on the subject of dreams, designates as being that of the unconscious, the effects that are discovered at the level of the chain of materially unstable elements that constitutes language: effects determined by the double play of combination and substitution in the signifier, according to the two aspects that generate the signified, metonymy and metaphor; determining effects for the institution of the subject. From this test, a topology, in the mathematical sense of the term, appears, without which one soon realizes that it is impossible simply to note the structure of a symptom in the analytic sense of the term.
>
> *It* speaks in the Other, I say, designating by the Other the very locus evoked by the recourse to speech in any relation in which the Other intervenes. If *it* speaks in the Other, whether or not the subject hears it with his ear, it is because it is there that the subject, by means of a logic anterior to any awakening of the signified, finds its signifying place.⁹⁷

It is the alienation of this other scene, language, that gives birth to the *rejeton* that is desire, the need in the impossibility of its satisfaction. This other scene, the symbolic order, is ruled by the laws of language that govern the unconscious, and these in turn generate the signified of language and institute the subject. This latter, then, is produced out of the expression of need in the demand, and the subject, like desire, is thus an offshoot of an entry into language, of the fact that *it* speaks in the Other.

The phallus itself is the sign of the initiating demand, the conjunction of logos and the advent of desire, or, as Lacan puts it: "The phallus is the privileged signifier of that mark in which the role of the logos is joined with the advent of desire."⁹⁸ It thus indicates the origin of what Lacan elsewhere calls the symbolic order, in distinction to the imaginary and the real, since the symbolic is precisely this endless displacement of unfulfillable desire which need has become through its expression in language.[99] Consequently, the phallus is the transcendental signifier, the signifier that signifies the signified as such, or, in Lacan's words, "it is the signifier intended to designate as a whole the effects of the signified, in that the signifier conditions them by its presence as a signifier."[100] The phallus itself is chosen, or forces its choice, as privileged signifier because it is the most obvious, salient aspect of sexual copulation, and because its turgidity is "the image of the vital flow as it is transmitted in generation."[101] This reasoning seems a little unclear, and the choice appears determined, or predetermined, in large part by Freud's observation of the penis as symbol both of sexual difference and the potential for bodily pleasure with the mother;[102] by referring to the organ's tumescence and to its role in sexual intercourse, Lacan seems to be recalling its functions within the Freudian system of the castration complex and appears to suggest that in its very rigidity, the penis is a unique and nonarbitrary sign of bodily desire, that in becoming erect it issues a protolinguistic demand, and thereby becomes semiotic.[103]

In thus becoming semiotic, the penis annuls its function as organ, for, as Lacan explains, the entry into the symbolic is achieved only through the cancellation of what is signified:

> All these propositions merely conceal the fact that it [the phallus] can play its role only when veiled, that is to say, as itself a sign of the latency with which any signifiable is struck, when it is raised (*aufgehoben*) to the function of signifier.
>
> The Phallus is the signifier of this *Aufhebung* itself, which it inaugurates (initiates) by its disappearance. That is why the demon of Αἰδώς (*Scham*, shame) arises at the very moment when, in the ancient mysteries, the phallus is unveiled (cf. the famous painting in the Villa di Pompeii).
>
> It then becomes the bar [*barre*] which, at the hands of this demon, strikes the signified, marking it as the bastard offspring of this signifying concatenation.
>
> Thus a condition of complementarity is produced in the establishment of the subject by the signifier—which explains the *Spaltung* in the subject and the movement of intervention in which that "splitting" is completed.
>
> Namely:
>
> (1) that the subject designates his being only by barring everything he signifies.[104]

The phallus only functions dissimulated, as the sign of the latency with which it strikes all that is signifiable. That is, in distinction to Nerval's version of the veils of Isis, which only hide that there is nothing to hide, here there is in fact something behind the phallic covering: all the world as it is a signifiable in language, as it is not yet or refuses language, as what language means. And for Lacan, this conversion into signifier, this veiling, is an *Aufhebung*; that is, it functions by the move of determinate negation that is the conceptual articulation holding the whole of the Hegelian dialectical system together. That *Aufhebung* of thing into sign is initiated by the disappearance or sublimation of the thing, for as soon as the thing appears, it must be veiled, which veiling makes of it a signifier insofar, only, as it is veiled. This veiling is a negation (*Aufhebung*), an abolition of what it covers, and the relation between the imaginary and real registers, on the one hand, and the symbolic, on the other, is thus analogous to the relation between the imagination and the understanding in the sublime moment, for in both cases the material figure, in becoming figure, figures its own annihilation as concrete particular object in a general annihilation of the specificities of the sensuous world. The symbolic order is, in short, like the egotistical philosophy of the Revolution that Nerval denounces for being premised on the ablation of the organ that knows the sensuous world, and this ablation, this separating off and annihilating, is itself what the phallus figures, in the form of a *barre* which strikes the signified sensuous world. The *barre* of a demon, like that which threatened the visionary when he was on the point of revealing the *signe* of his entry into language, it is also the *barre*, or line, that separates the signifier from the signified in the Saussurian algorithm of the sign: *Signifier/signified* or S/s.[105] This is the splitting (*Spaltung*) of the subject, incorporated as its alienation from itself through its inauguration as signifier. As subject, it is a linguistic construct, born of the castrating violence that makes of the phallus a signifier, marking the loss of the entire material world as that which is signifiable.[106]

Consequently, the disclosing of the significance of the phallus, its initiation as sign, comes in a disclosure of castration. First of all, without knowing yet what the sign is for his desire, and in fact because he does not know what the sign is, the child's call for love suffers from a nameless longing toward the mother. "The demand for love," Lacan writes, "can only suffer from a desire whose signifier is alien to it." Though that desire still knows no sign, because of the very structure of desire, which is formulated as a difference between being and having, the problem of the phallus already inheres in the relation to the mother: "If the desire of the mother *is* the phallus, the child wishes to be the phallus in order to satisfy that desire." The problem is that nothing the child *has* can substitute for *being* the desire of the mother, and this insufficiency perpetuates an unsatisfiable need that seeks a sign or an articulation with the *logos* or language. That sign appears, paradoxically, in its loss:

> Clinical experience has shown us that this test of the desire of the Other is decisive not in the sense that the subject learns by it whether or not he has a real phallus, but in the sense that he learns that the mother does not have it. This is the moment of the experience without which no symptomatic consequence (phobia) or structural consequence (*Penisneid*) relating to the castration complex can take effect. Here is signed the conjunction of desire, in that the phallic signifier is its mark, with the threat or nostalgia of lacking it.
>
> Of course, its future depends on the law [*la loi*] introduced by the father into this sequence.[107]

What is of interest here at present is not so much the potentially pathological consequences of the progression of the castration complex as the idea that the phallus, even if it has already been functioning semiotically in language and desire, is identifiable as the sign of their conjunction only in the moment that it is conceived as a lack, or as castrated. And it is in this identification of the phallus as the transcendental signifier through the disclosure of its inherent potential for loss that the law of the father is introduced. Or as Nerval wrote in a footnote he crossed out, but finally published: "We are born under the biblical law..."[108] The convergence of the two texts is clear if one reads that birth in terms of the global problematic of pardon in *Aurélia*, that is, as the birth of the *je*, or the inauguration of the subject into language, for in both Lacan's and Nerval's models of paternity, the subject is initiated into language through the castration of the sensuous or "organic" world that language would signify, and this castration is upheld as the humiliating and unnatural law of the father, which maintains that the relation between individual experience and its expression, between the particularity of the *je* and the language it uses to communicate with others and to identify itself, is an aporetic gap which can at best be pseudo-resolved through an annihilating sublimation, or sublation, of the sensuous, imaginary, or figurable world into an abstract and impersonal symbolization. In Nerval's paternal order, the child's birth, his own birth, is an insoluble mystery marked by the absence of a sign, an absence that falsifies the relation between universal history and the hieroglyphic language that would express it. It is a void protected by a reproachful series of father-figures, who perpetuate the incomprehensibility of the world to the *je* by substituting castration for a material sign when the link between language and individual threatens to reveal itself, as at the end of the first division of *Aurélia* or in the first chapter of the second division, where divine anger turns the author from his plans to reestablish a lost primordial harmony. As the Lacanian law of the father officiates at the castrating entry of the individual into the symbolic subjectivity that will negate him or her as sensuous particular and then upholds that negation, or alienation, through an incomprehensible shame or guilt, so too does the Nervalian law of the father.

In Lacanian terms, then, the subject that identifies itself in the symbolic order as a phallic demand for the fulfillment of its desire is always an alienated, split subject. The coherence given to it through desire is the articulation of a demand, which demand is initially expressed as the phallus. Because, however, language—even the semiotic phallus—is inherently other, by this very expression of desire the subject is alienated from itself in the same moment that it acquires symbolic coherence. In the signifying phallus, then, the subject designates its being—comprehends itself, but only at the price of reducing itself to pure sign, for "the subject designates its being only by barring everything he signifies."[109] This alienation is castration, the sign also of the separation from the integrity of the body, the ablation of the body, like the surgical ablation of an organ. Metaphysical, death-based subjectivity thus returns in the Lacanian subject, a subject constituted as a linguistic entity, in another place, in *einem anderen Schauplatz*, that is language, but who is constituted in language as the abolition of the sensible world. It is the return of the sublime subject, who sacrifices the physical, imaginable world, in the form of the imaginary and the real, not at the blade of the guillotine, but in its new avatar, the castrating bar of the signifier, the sign that constitutes the subject in semiotizing the latter's alienation from pleasure, from the sensuous. The subject which is initiated in language through the castration of its attachments to the world maintains itself only through the signification of that loss, through the institution, in its heart, not of the sign of its participation in life, but of its split from itself and of its repudiation of itself as sensuous, material being.

The homology between the Kantian structure of the sublime as a negative relation between the faculties of the imagination and the understanding on the one hand and the Lacanian relation between an imaginary penis and a symbolic castration on the other is reinforced by a passage from "Subversion of the subject and dialectic of desire in the Freudian unconscious" where Lacan speaks of the limitation of *jouissance*, or intense pleasure, in its representation:

> It is the indication of that *jouissance* in its infinitude that, in itself [seule] brings with it the mark of its prohibition, and, in order to constitute that mark, involves a sacrifice: that which is made in one and the same act with the choice of its symbol, the phallus.
>
> This choice is allowed because the phallus, that is, the image of the penis, is negativity in its place in the specular image. It is what predestines the phallus to embody *jouissance* in the dialectic of desire.
>
> We must distinguish, therefore, between the principle of sacrifice, which

is symbolic, and the imaginary function that is devoted to that principle of sacrifice, but which, at the same time, veils the fact that it gives it its instrument.[110]

The sheer indication, or marking, of limitless pleasure brings with it a limitation to that pleasure and consequently entails the necessary sacrifice of that element which becomes the sign of pleasure. In giving body to such pleasure, in becoming an identifiable image of it, the phallus is excluded from *jouissance*. The image of the penis thus both signifies and conceals its own negation or sacrifice, much as the sublime moment, by figuring the transcendence of figuration in a finite indication of the infinite, both images the end of imagination and conceals that end in the image itself.[111] By becoming the transcendental signifier and representing the whole of the world, the penis loses its partiality, its fragmentary incompleteness as an element within the world, and with its fragmentary materiality goes its open-ended pleasure in the world. Again, the subject is construed as the loss of the moment, its sublimation into a transcendental subject that bears within itself as fear the impress of its own alienation. What was terror for Hegel and Kant and became *Angst* in Heidegger, reappears in Lacan as castration anxiety.

Aurélia represents, as it promises, a movement away from dominant metaphysical models of subjectivity, especially as they relate to the role of language in self-experience. The question of the finitude and structure of self-hood that had been articulated in terms of self and other or self and death in Nerval's earlier works is here overwhelmed by a question more global, more pressing, more basic, and in respect to which the question of the self shrinks. It is the question of the world. Of care for the world, of compassion. It is the engagement toward others, expressed as love and a primordial responsibility. Writing itself, and the writing of *Aurélia*, is identified by its author as such an act of compassion.[112] He writes to help others. And the world of others, the world of the relation to others, passes through, or rather *is*, writing and language. It is, moreover, a specifically poetic mode of writing, and poetry is thus the face, the life, the voice of the other, it is the place where we are already engaged in and composed by the other, by others, where we discover that we are infinitely open. There are risks to this, however, for if everything is a system, another can gain control, to evil ends, and if everything is a system, any wrong becomes global. What had been a game between genres, between novel and history, in the preface to *Les Filles du feu*, is here the game of the world, of all life and living creatures, of immortality and salvation. What was sport for a master like Dumas, has become a primordial ethical responsibility in which one has always already been involved, and in which, for this reason, one runs the possibility of already being guilty. At this point Nerval proposes not a paternally ordered semiotic law, but a fraternally/maternally ordered language, wherein the pardon comes as primordially as the *faute*. Since the latter was always about the entry into language, and into the body of the mother, it is also the original sin, the sin of origination, but in the Nervalian text that origination is cast in terms not of a violence and castration that would inaugurate self-identity as death-based subjectivity, but as a constant origination in the Edenic pleasure of language's nonsubjective and eternal community. The *je* is born through writing, in the back-and-forth mirroring—like star and flower, sky and earth—between the first-person author and the maternal body that is the text, manifest in its very repetitions, its *traits* (especially apparent in the "Mémorables"), and in its nonlinear visionary poetic structure. One is both alive and dead in this language that already mediates between the mediate and immediate, that is signifying pleasure, that is meaningful matter.

The mother appears here as the materiality of the discursive field, which produces its own intelligibility, like light emanating from the ground. She appears in the repetitive intelligibility of the *trait*, while God the father, the solitary lawgiver, has foundered in the vast system of the maternal text, in its echoes, masks, and repetitions. When, at the beginning of the second section, Nerval mentions God, he remarks: "The fatal system that had been created in my mind did not admit of that solitary royalty… or rather, he was absorbed into the sum of beings: he was the god of Lucretius, powerless and lost in his immensity."[113] This suppression of the father allows a movement toward fraternal dispersion, a critical displacement of the discourse of the self away from a castrating, paternally legislating Lacanian phallus as the structuring principle of (necessarily) linguistic subjectivity, away from the sublimating language of Hegel's guillotine, and into the fraternal order of community and chaste love, where pleasure becomes infinite *jouissance*. Instead of finding the origin of the subject in a Lacanian phallo-guillotine barring of life as the subjective semiotization of castration, an origin that the text recognizes as a possible but unsatisfactory explanation of the inauguration of the *je*, *Aurélia* consciously locates that inauguration elsewhere, in the preexisting, unviolated communality of language as universal, intelligible matter; in doing this, Nerval advances a model of subjectivity that establishes itself as intentionally and critically different from the formulations of death-based textual subjectivity elaborated already in Hegel and only later in psychoanalysis. As Hegel discovered but forgot, or repressed, the secret of the subject is language itself, not as a hiding or veiling of something else, but as the material character that exists only in its manifestation, and which in manifesting itself reveals that the "I" is structured already in and in relation to a discursive community of other similarly structured people.

In rejecting death-based subjectivity, *Aurélia* also calls into question Heidegger's characterization of Dasein as inauthentic if it should pseudo-ground itself in the unappropriated discoursing of an indeterminable "they." The "novel-vision," as its author refers to it, instead embraces precisely such indeterminacy and self-alienation as constitutive of its subject stance, and one can argue that in so doing, Nerval elaborates a subjectivity grounded in something similar to what the French philosopher Emmanuel Levinas, in a critique of the most fundamental bases of Heidegger's system, will describe as an ethical engagement. For Levinas the "I" originates in a calling question, much as the question of Being distinguishes Dasein in the opening pages of *Being and Time*. But Levinas's question functions differently from Heidegger's in significant ways and is, according to him, more primordial. He describes it as: "A calling into question in which the question springs forth older than the one about the meaning of the being of beings." The question itself is not "what is the meaning of being" but rather, "Is it just to be?" It is the question of the "legitimacy of being."[114] The answer will be "a meaning that cannot be defined simply by the formalism of the logical structure of reference, moving from any given signifier to its signified."[115] That meaning will come from what Levinas calls "fraternity," which he describes as a "concreteness" on which being's legitimacy is based. And this fraternity, the legitimacy of being whose call originates the individual "I" is in fact the very strangeness of the other that reveals itself in a human face: "Does that meaning not show itself as meaning precisely as secret of the face — open, that is, exposed, without defense? Strangeness of the other, in that it is precisely by that strangeness that he or she puts me in question by demanding of me with a demand that comes to me I know not whence, or from an unknown God who loves the stranger. Face or non-autochthony."[116] The call that determines the individual "I" in Levinas differs from the call of Being that distinguishes Heidegger's Dasein in that the former does not see the individual called to his individuality by abstractness and death, but rather by the specificity of its difference from concrete others. Levinas's individual "I" is constituted in its specificity by the recognition of the unknowableness of others, and he argues that from this recognition there ensues a responsibility toward those others and a primordial ethical engagement. While Heidegger's Dasein must eschew the signs of the unknowable in others as *Gerede*, or idle chatter, Levinas views them as a question and an appeal which constitute the subject.

Aurélia, however, constructs a subject constituted as the materiality of language, which is already a relation to the other. This is a move not only away from Hegel's self-experiencing subject but also away from Heidegger's finite individual Dasein, a move toward a subject whose specificity lies not in living always in face of its finitude and death but rather in a primordial gesture toward otherness. For Levinas that otherness comes as a face, for Nerval as voice and written words, in the gesture toward an other, that as gesture, as language, is already from an other, from the unavoidable self-alienation that is discourse. This gesture calls to and from the subject, to and from the other, in a calling or gesturing whose most primordial seme is one's own pleasure, the possibility of one's self announced from an indeterminable elsewhere in a voice that was already sounding, in a writing that was already underway. This is, then, the poetic subject, the place where language reveals itself as ethical matter, as *jouissance*.

8.   Death and Its Alternatives

Death, Hegel argued, is the most terrible of things but also the most human. By the simple thought of death, the human thought par excellence, we are awakened from the dusky somnolence of our animal existence and haled up into the luminous world of our own self-consciousness. Shaking off the stupefying burden of our own sensuousness, we open our eyes to an infinite world of absolutes and signs. Death comes bringing language, the uniquely human possibilities of representation and abstract thought, the capacity not only to think of a thing in its absence, but also to think its absence as such, and indeed, our thought by its very nature does away with the material object of its intention, leaving only the intention, the word, the gesture in its purest form as sign. Death is not merely one negative among others but the very possibility of signification itself, the transcendental mechanism, the final, culminating negative, not only chronologically but absolutely. It is the negative that negates the whole world, down even to the "I" and the Cartesian doubter. No word is spoken, no representation is possible but through death, and every word, every representation also signifies death in the very negativity of its operation. Mad people and animals, incapable of drawing themselves out of the inhuman sleep of the material world and into the adulthood of semiotic self-consciousness, live in a sensuous but meaningless and speechless dream. And like Descartes's ontological proof of the existence of God, with the idea of death comes its inevitability, the certain knowledge not only that it is possible but that it is necessary and that I must die. It is an inevitability that does not come from elsewhere—no one else can prove to me that I must die—but from the idea itself. I cannot speak of death, indeed I cannot speak, represent, or negate at all, without asserting that I too will die. And with the ineluctability of death comes, it would seem, the inevitability of understanding subjectivity *as* death, as the constant perishing of our own material existence into a realm of pure semiotic abstraction.

But Nerval's last work had argued that there were other ways of thinking of the *moi* and that the seemingly speechless world of sensuous existence did have its own language, a language that revealed a richer, more complete image of the self. In this sense, the pages of *Aurélia* represent an attempt to prepare for "Les Mémorables" and to establish their legibility as the instantation of a resistant, alternative subjectivity. One could say, in fact, that all of Nerval's work up to that point was more or less directed to the same end: writing the infinite openness of his mad self, opening his self into writing, and making that undertaking comprehensible in its originality and discursive specificity. Seen from the viewpoint of *Aurélia*, his earlier works had been an attempt not merely to write otherwise, and thereby to write himself in a resistant particularity of language use, but also to assert the legitimacy and validity of that other writing of the self. The origin of the "I" is revealed through the rediscovery of a hidden speech, a language always already there in the language that we use but cut off from us by the castrating sublimation of the sensuous into abstract signification. More than merely giving "a purer meaning to the words of the tribe," as Mallarmé had said of Edgar Allan Poe, Nerval had placed meaning itself in question.[1]

Certainly, others besides Nerval have imagined a self-identity not based on the negation of experience and the material plenitude of the evanescent moment. And others, too, have sought an "I" that would be grounded otherwise than in an identification with its own death. Marx, for instance, described his own project as a rectification of the fundamental flaw in Hegel's dialectical approach, which, he argued, understood the concrete and specific only as modalities of a more fundamental abstraction. He would, as he put it, set Hegel on his head by beginning with and retaining the material actuality of things.[2] More recently, and closer to Nerval's approach, are the works of Julia Kristeva, Piera Aulagnier, and Emmanuel Levinas, all of whom come close to articulating his insights and practice without being able to account for them; for while they all dispute, more or less, the seeming inevitability of death-based subjectivity, Nerval remains in crucial ways still other from them too.

Kristeva, Althusser, Aulagnier

Like Marx, Kristeva has sought to ground the subject in the concrete actuality of social practice, understood in a broad sense, but has focused on the primordiality of corporeal and linguistic or proto-linguistic rather than purely economic relations. And while Heidegger, as we have seen, also attempted to determine individual human identity, or Dasein, through its actual existence rather than its abstract essence, Kristeva's emphasis on the materiality of the subject differs from his approach too, for whereas Heidegger insisted on the isolation of authentic Dasein in a resolute being toward an unrelational death, she argues for the basic importance of interpersonal relations instantiated in social practice.[3] The subject "in process," as she puts it, is an open-ended textual function, embedded in its presymbolic (what she calls semiotic) aspect:

> This subject ... is consequently not a punctual location, a subject of enunciation [un sujet de l'énonciation], but it acts through the organization (the structure, the finitude) of the text, in which the *chora* of the process is figured. That *chora* is the *non-verbal semiotic articulation of the process*: a music or an architecture are metaphors which more aptly designate the grammatical, linguistic categories which it redistributes. It is the logic of the "concrete operations," of the "motility" ... that cross the practical body within social space (transformation of objects, relations to parents and to the whole of society).[4]

This is a subject that has not rejected the materiality of the discourse in which it exists but which instead functions within it as its most primordial, prethematic articulation, as its syntactic and grammatical distributions; because it operates through such primary, presemantic structures, and in this sense redistributes them, the subject in process cannot be known syntactically or metalinguistically any more than it can be identified thematically in language. This subject is a groping, a shaping of language before it has propositional sense, before the subject identifies itself through the meaning of its predicates, and in this, it functions in the concrete body of social practice, elaborating a prethematic world of interpersonal or transsubjective relations. Presymbolic, embedded in the materiality of the social body, it emphatically does not originate in the transcendental moment of castration. "Such a place, which we shall call a *chora*, is the representation which one can give to the subject in process," Kristeva writes, "but one must not think that it is constituted by A Cutting-off (castration)."[5] The subject in process, this subject born not from castration or sublimation but in the very movement of language itself, retains its transsubjective impersonality in a process of constant self-multiplication, since instead of coming to a finite, unified, and transcendental meaning, Kristeva's subject perpetuates itself as the condition of possibility of sense; and insofar as it is a range of presemantic acts articulating the materiality of language, there is no end to its production. The subject that creates itself in this activity of making language, rather than making sense, can only keep on making itself since, by its very nature, it will never arrive at a moment of synthetic self-recognition in which it would find itself designated or represented.[6]

If one accepts, with Kristeva, that the self creates itself in these preverbal acts of differentiation, then it seems that one must also accept the existence of a yet more primordial self, a self that acts and that traces itself through the *chora* in the motivation of its movement and tendencies. In this vaguest of all possible worlds, something seems to determine and choose, for in the articulating act there remains some form of agency, and this primordial, presymbolic mechanism which grounds all formulations of the social and the human in the material practice of language is itself reduced to the simple act of rejection. As Kristeva writes:

> In running over the lines of force in that mobile and heterogeneous, but semiotizable *chora*, where the process of signification deploys itself by rejecting stases, the transsubject exposes itself to becoming the very mechanism of this functioning, the "mode" of its repetition, without a signifying substance of its own, without interiority and without exteriority: without subject and without object, nothing but the movement of rejection [rejet].[7]

The subject is not yet a subject, is in process as a transsubject, but this very term indicates that what is in question here is social—it is part of a relation among language users, a between-subjects, that somehow precedes them. The sheer sociality of language, its transitivity, constitutes the materiality of the chora as the space-among from which subject and object will be determined; as such, it is a common matter. Across it, as gesture among subjects or subjects-to-be, the transsubject operates the most primordial of distinctions, from which will devolve subject and object, I and You, caller and called, inside and outside.[8] And although this transsubject does not have its own body, it exists substantially in the materiality of language; and by materiality Kristeva is referring not merely to syntactic articulations or grammatical functions, but also to the tactile, sensuous aspect of language, its buccal existence as breath, sound, murmuring, the meaningless "expectorations" even, in Artaud's poems or in infantile crowing. It is a language of the body. Blanchot had pointed to a similar sort of linguistic materiality in his canny continuation of Hegel's "Sense-certainty" analysis from the *Phenomenology*. The word "cat" may be the annihilation of the sensuous cat it represents, Blanchot argued, but it is not for all that the same as the annihilation of a dog; in these two abstractions something distinct remains, something grounded in the material specificity of the words themselves, a sensuous actuality that alone makes meaningful language possible, even if it cannot be reduced to a positivity.[9] Kristeva has taken farther, one could say, this material articulation that allows for abstract linguistic sense. The primordial distinction, the *rejet*, is grounded in the actuality of the social body, but this, in turn, is grounded in the materiality of another body, itself articulated and semiotized through the act of rejection. "By the new phonemic and rhythmic network that it produces," Kristeva writes, "the *rejet* becomes a source of 'aesthetic' pleasure. Without thereby abandoning the line of meaning, it cuts that line up and reorganizes it, imprinting on it the itinerary of the drive [la pulsion] across its own body: from the anus to the mouth."[10] The *rejet* is itself grounded in the practice of the body that defecates, which expels from itself and turns what is itself into another, or at least into *something* else. In this, the movement is proto-semiotic, for in the same act it establishes the separability of the self from the self, designates a point of reference by which the self becomes other, and creates the material object by which that difference can be indicated.[11] Grounded in the material alienation of feces rather than in the theoretical ablation of the phallus, the subject in process is grounded too in an act of pleasure and aesthesis, which is repeated in the determinations it enacts on language. From anus to mouth the trajectory is not self-evident, since it passes through the child's relation to the maternal breast. The proto-semiotic functioning of the anal sphincter serves, according to Kristeva, to make sense of the Kleinian relation between a desirable good breast and an aversive bad breast, between the infant's sucking and turning away.[12] It is a distinction that persists as an erotic charge of pleasure within language use and that undermines propositional production of meaning:

> The subject and its linear language, characterized by the concatenation of syntagmas into subject/predicate, are combated by a return to oral and glottal pleasure: suction or expulsion. Fusion with the maternal breast or the rejection [rejet] of it seem to be at the base of that erotization of the vocal apparatus and, through it, of the introduction into linguistic order of a pleasurable surcharge which is marked by the redistribution of the phonemic order, of morphological structure and even of syntax (cf. Joyce's portmanteau-words and Artaud's glossolalia).[13]

As in "Les Mémorables," the subject in process manifests itself as a resistance to the propositional sense of language use based in the superego, or in the internalization of castration anxiety and the law of the father. Through its nonsensical repetitions, parabases, and vocatives, Nerval's text had generated a material, maternally coded pleasure that undermined its linear, predicative production of meaning. For Kristeva, this semiotic articulation of preverbal matter would be grounded in the primordial judgement toward the breast, itself legible through the semiotic functioning of the anus. The mouth is filled erotically with words, but it also distributes and punctuates that vocal matter, enacting upon it in displaced form the turning to or from the breast, filling it too with the erotic pleasure of rejection or expulsion.

    The infant's first gestures in relation to the breast thus lay the groundwork for language and, at the same time, for the determination of a subject and its symbolic relation to the world. It is, however, the *rejet* rather than the sucking which is primordial to symbolic representation, for it is the pleasurable refusal that marks separation and judgement on matter, opening it not merely to the possibility of satisfaction but also to meaning. It is in the act of rejection that the child develops the key to abstraction. The infant's "initial movement of 'burrowing,' intended to assure contact, indeed its biologically indispensable fusion with the mother's body, obtains a *negative* value in the sixth month: at that age the rotation of the head indicates refusal before presenting an abstract, semantic 'no' in the fifteenth month."[14] The emergence of meaningful language use and the symbolic order is premised, according to Kristeva, on an original articulation of the body in pleasure, a body that does not yet distinguish between acting and meaning, between doing and representing, and which will erupt nonsensically in the poetic aspects of language, in avant-garde practice, in all aestheticization of discourse. This resistant, linguistic substance announces itself affectively as pleasure, and, as such, embeds the self in discourse not as the terrified negation of sensuous existence but as its voluptuous persistence in pleasure. One would hardly get a sense of this other aspect of language from reading Kant or Hegel, who seem to have driven all delight from the act of reading. This may derive from the fact that, on the basis of historical accounts at least, they did not appear to take any pleasure in writing, for although Kant worked on the *Critique of Pure Reason* for over twelve years, its actual composition took him about five months, which means it was formulated and put onto paper at about the rate that the hand moves. Hegel wrote the *Phenomenology* with similar haste. What this would indicate is that both works are the product of authors either ignorant of or defiant toward the possibility of the sort of meaningful linguistic aesthesis that Kristeva describes here. It is suggestive, on the other hand, that Nietzsche, who placed such emphasis on the plenitude of momentary experience and who derided the communicative aspects of language, should have been a much more stylistically conscientious author.[15]

    Significantly, however, Kristeva's theorization of the primordial judgement embodied in the *rejet* is itself grounded in a reading of Hegel. In the rotation of its head, the infant enacts a presymbolic negative (*négative*), which Kristeva distinguishes from the semantic or symbolic "no" that will emerge later. This earlier gesture is the semiotic, or "'genuine negation' (what we are calling negativity)" that she will oppose to the Lacanian, symbolic "no" of the castrating father which arises subsequently.[16] As Kristeva puts it:

> It is from Hegel that we derive the notion of negativity (*Negativität*) which seems to be the *pattern* [in English], the organizational principle of the *process*. Distinguished from nothingness (*Nichts*) as well as from negation (*Negation*), negativity is the concept which figures the indissoluble relation between an "ineffable" mobility and its "singular determination": it is mediation, the overcoming of "pure abstractions."[17]

We have seen, however, in Kojève and in Hegel's writings themselves, how unstable the line is between abstract and determinate negation, how easily the terror of the subjectifying face to face can veer into the meaningless Terror of sheer indeterminacy, and how difficult it is to read or track that difference.[18] And again, if one is to avoid relapsing into death-based subjectivity, one must look more closely at this subject in process that Kristeva describes as a *rejet*, a negation, even if it is a pleasurable one. It is founded in something more basic, something that is rejected—the materiality of language, the pleasure of the breast. Language, as materiality, grounds the subject in a mobile, circulating, fluid substance, for the breast is itself already not a mere impassive presence, but a giving of milk, an enactment. And if language is based on a turning away from the breast, a rejection of the breast by the mouth, that too is premised on a connection with the breast: it is the act of recognizing that the breast is other, that what fills the self comes from another; it is the moment of proto-recognition, of an unthematized, primordial awareness of the alterity that was already there, of the primacy of the ethical, the preexistence of the other in the self. And although an anally aggressive preverbal subject seems appropriate from Kristeva's reading of Artaud's texts, it seems inadequate to account for Nerval's work, where the materiality of language, the connection with another, appears as the basis in which is embedded the call from the other, the primordial articulation of that matter as sense. The semiotic, the most basic deployment of the sensuous, comes not from the aggressively material pleasure of rejection, from the voiding of the sphincter around the semiotic *néant*, or "nothingness," that separates the self from the sign that will represent it, but emerges instead from the mouth's closing around the song that comes from elsewhere, from other mouths, from the calling to the *je* to be, to take part. In Nerval's "Les Mémorables," the primordial articulation of matter, of the *chora*, is its nonthematic articulation as address.

But it is problematic to understand the subject as primordially related to the social body through a calling into being. Heidegger, we saw, conceived of Dasein as called upon by conscience to project itself authentically toward the isolation of its own death. For Althusser, to take an example closer to Kristeva, language is a material practice by which we are called into our subjectivity, but the entity that so interpellates us is, in his view, far more pernicious than Nerval's maternalized brotherhood. For Althusser it is an inherently repressive State apparatus that so addresses us, and subjectivity is, in turn, our self-recognition in imaginary structures of ideology, which form the set of relations between ourselves as individuals and other social agencies. "Ideology," as Althusser put it, "is a 'Representation' of the imaginary relationship of individuals to their real conditions of existence."[19] Since we are always already interpellated as subjects since before our birth, the individual, although spoken of as concrete, has no "substance" of its own, but functions in the actuality of social practices that preexist and, in a certain vague sense, await its advent; it does not impose its individuality, but has its individuality imposed on it by the social order.[20] The Lacanian scene of linguistic subjective alienation, the *andere Schauplatz*, is conceived here in terms of ideology, for the language in which the subject enacts itself is now oriented by a will to repress, on the one hand, and toward the reproduction, on the other, of the material or imaginary conditions necessary for the perpetuation of the State and its class relations. One can think of Althusser's description of the relation between individual and State ideology as something like a convergence of Foucault and Lacan, in which the Lacanian subject of language is taken as nontranscendent because the symbolic system in which it conceives itself is already the concrete actuality of social practice, and it is for this reason that Althusser speaks of these relations as imaginary rather than symbolic. Insofar as they are already ideological, the various manifestations of State will (*volonté*) exceed the individuals that enact them, and the subject emerges as the assumption of material practices by an individual in order to recognize itself in its individuality. The individual, however, preexists that recognition only as the abstract category that a set of behaviors are supposed to materialize, and it is for this reason that Althusser, in what would otherwise strike us as a paradox, contends that it is the individual who is abstract in relation to the subject.[21] The individual is that imaginary construct of actuality which is supposed to ground social relations, but which is only a result of them, whereas the seemingly abstract subject is the actuality of the intercourse by which that construct is pursued and enforced. Like Heidegger's "idle talk," ideological structures hide their facticity and conventionality in an apparent self-evidence. "It is indeed a peculiarity of ideology that it imposes (without appearing to do so, since these are 'obviousnesses') obviousnesses as obviousnesses, which we cannot *fail to recognize*."[22] It is for this reason that the abstractness of the individual seems counter-intuitive, for its ideological determination is hidden by the apparent self-evidence of individual self-experience. Unlike Heidegger's Dasein, however, there is nowhere else for Althusser's subject to turn, since there is no "outside" of ideology.[23] One is always already called into individual subjectivity, into self-identity, through the discursive practices that organize one's existence as an ineluctably social process. That ubiquitous and incessant call to be an individual represents, in turn, the impersonal interest of class structures and the reproduction of the State. One could say that Althusser has merely inverted the terms subject and individual, to produce an abstract self-identity grounded, like Kant's sublime subject, in abstract interest, or like Hegel's subject of the Terror, in the identification with the State.

Althusser offers several concrete examples of the sorts of social practice that call upon and instantiate the subject. There is the friend who knocks at the door and announces himself only, but adequately, with the words: "It's me."[24] There is the scene, developed at some length, of the policeman in the street who calls out: "You, there."[25] More interesting, for the present context, is his discussion of the birth of a child:

> That an individual is always-already a subject, even before he is born, is nevertheless the plain reality, accessible to everyone and not a paradox at all. Freud shows that individuals are always "abstract" with respect to the subject they always-already are, simply by noting the ideological ritual that surrounds the expectation of a "birth," that "happy event." Everyone knows how much and in what way an unborn child is expected. Which amounts to saying, very prosaically, if we agree to drop the "sentiments," i.e. the forms of family ideology (paternal/maternal/conjugal/fraternal) in which the unborn child is expected: it is certain in advance that it will bear its Father's Name, and will therefore have an identity and be irreplaceable.[26]

The advent of the child, the moment of its birth, is inscribed, according to Althusser, within an ideological system that predetermines its identity and responsibilities, which identifies it even before its birth as answerable, responsible, indebted. As in the moment of birth which submitted the child to a paternal law of grief in *Aurélia*, the uniqueness of Althusser's child weighs upon it like an account due to a discursive society. The subject is called to be, but to be as an atoning for itself, as a primordial debt to the State, which looks to the individual's originality not as an end in itself, but as a means to its own impersonal self-perpetuation. The call of love that appeared in "Les Mémorables" would be no more than an instance of the sentimental "forms of family ideology," and would simply represent, according to Althusser's argument, another manifestation of coercion.

The psychoanalyst Piera Aulagnier was concerned, too, with the call into subjectivity and focused on the social dynamics that articulate it around the event of childbirth, but unlike Althusser, she construed those dynamics, and the possibility of intelligible discourse, in terms of the primacy of desire and pleasure rather than ideology, which is to say that she would ground ideology in tactile experience. For Aulagnier, the child's inquiry into the origin of babies, its inevitable "how are children born [comment naissent les enfants]," is a question, above all, of how the child *itself* came to be.[27] The question of the origin of the *I* is always inherently the question, addressed not to experience itself but to others, of how the subject came into the discourse of those others, a question that, although it concerns the originality of the subject, cannot be answered by the subject itself, for its origin, its birth, is the crucially absent page of its own history. It is a question of the original insertion of the *I* into a discursive community formed by other, preexisting subjects. On the response, in word or behavior, to that question hang the child's relation to the world and the possibility that the child find him- or herself forced to adopt psychotic modes to represent it.[28] This is because, on a most basic level, the question is that of how meaning is possible, and its response will permit or impede the attachment of language to subjective experience, the possibility of making sense of pain or pleasure. As Aulagnier writes:

> As a first approximation we shall say that the question "how are children born" is equivalent to a "how is the 'I' born" and that the "I" expects the answer to provide the text for the first paragraph of the story in which he must be able to recognize himself, since that answer alone can give meaning to the succession of identificatory positions which he can in turn occupy. . . . Within the register of the subject's story, this first paragraph can no longer remain blank: what gives it its specific texture is the fact that, in this case, it can only be written by necessarily borrowing from the discourses of others, who can alone claim to know and to remember what the author is supposed to have lived in that distant time in which an "I was born... " was inscribed.[29]

The answer attests the child's inscription into sociolinguistic structures that Althusser would designate as ideological, but in order to operate this articulation between personal, experiential meaning and discourse, the I must, according to Aulagnier, be able to identify a sign that would represent that relation within discourse itself, that would establish, discursively, the pre-inscription of the self, the aptitude, as it were, of language for the subject. The problem of origins is not, then, so much the problem of finding a signifier for the *I* as for the relation between the *I* and a previously existing discursive community that it can thereby and therein recognize as having already potentially included it.[30] The sense of the *I*'s discourse, its capacity to express affect and sensation, thus finds its condition of possibility in the calling-into-being expressed to it by a preexisting discursive community. For Aulagnier, in the best of cases, this call will be articulated, *après-coup*, as the evidence of the parents' desire for one another and of their wish, before the child's origin, to express that desire in the child. In a more problematic scenario, which might lead to potentially schizophrenic states, the response to the question, delivered in discourse or behavior, would be that the child was conceived as a violence against the mother, through the imposition of an alien will, or in displeasure.

This relation between the *I* and the discursive community of others, originally represented by the parents, is grounded in physical experience and its primordial articulation as pleasure and displeasure. The child who finds its preexistent calling to be as an expression of desire for its existence grounded in the love of its parents for one another will, according to Aulagnier, be able to make sense of its own pleasure. Pleasure will in turn become the primary articulation between physical experience—the sensuous voluptuousness of the world—and the discursive community of others, or language:

> The cause of pleasure, of all pleasure, for and by the "I" will be connected to the pleasure which the fact that *he* exists procures for the couple [i.e. his parents], and, since the logic of the "I" will have to obey the principle of non-contradiction, the cause of displeasure will be able to separate itself off and contradict the postulate of the primary process, for which everything that exists is an effect of the omnipotence of the Other's desire. It is a separation which will allow the "I" to make displeasure compatible with his belief in the love that is borne him, by accepting that displeasure is no longer uniquely an experience decided by the desire of the Other, but something which can impose itself, despite and against that desire, and that it can have for cause the reality of the body, the existence of others, an error, a not-knowing [un non-savoir].[31]

The parents, before all others, represent the community of language, and when the child understands through their responses that its pre-inscription in that community stemmed from desire and pleasure, the child's own desire becomes the experiential mode through which it can identify and appropriate the story of its abstract, discursive preexistence into its actual existence, by which it can make personal sense of language. The answer to the question of the *I*'s sense always comes from others, always embeds the self in a more primordial, potentially ethical relation, always withdraws its primary capacity for meaning into the interests and voices of others. Through its own body, through its own experience of pleasure or pain, the child reapppropriates that alienated story of its capacity for lending meaning to language. For the desired child, pleasure makes sense of language, and allows language to articulate personal experience; pain, in this context, would be an incomprehensible and unsemiotic parasite in the system, an unwilled error that insinuates itself as an uncommunicable lapse in the social, the dreadful isolation of the victim of torture, punishment, or accident. Conversely, however, if the parents' discourse or behavior indicates to the child that it originated as or out of *dis*pleasure, then it is pleasure that appears as an error, a *non-savoir*, an unaccountable and meaningless gap in the system.[32] In this case, displeasure or rejection would appear as the primordial articulation of the semiotic chora that traverses the physical and social bodies. Language would take hold in the body through the aggressivity of the *rejet*, and in such cases

> the subject happens to be born in an ambient psychic milieu where his desire, which is constituted very precociously as the desire to be desired, can find no satisfactory response. . . . As early as his first encounters, a crack, a discordance, a too much or not enough all bear witness to the conflict which the arrival of the *infans* has reactivated and reactualized. That is why there will prevail, at the time of his encounter with what is outside the psyche, any representation that deals with rejection [rejet], nothingness [néant], or hatred: the pictogram of rejection [du rejet] is universal, it is the representation which the new child [l'originaire] will forge of everything that can be the source of an experience of displeasure. . . . The satisfaction of need and the experience of nursing will become something which silences need, but they cry out the privation of a libidinal pleasure which the mother cannot, or will not give.[33]

For Aulagnier's *I*, unlike Kristeva's "subject in process," the *rejet* is not invariably the primordial articulation between the sensuous body and its eventual symbolic representation, since it constitutes, in fact, the exception. Instead the parents' manifestation of desire for the child would normally resolve the unbearable impasse between immediate sensuous existence and mediate language in which Foucault had grounded Nerval's madness. Through their desire for one another and for the expected child, the world "makes sense" for the *I*, since the *I* can integrate its pleasure into the community of language, and Aulagnier thus grounds the call to be in the possibility of pleasure: the call and the world "make sense" in relation to the *I* if the call is affectively charged as pleasure. Rather than simply obeying, like Althusser's presubjected ideological individual, the *I* has the "option" of schizophrenic or potentially schizophrenic states, the "possibility" of refusing the sense of the world, of refusing an ideology of subjectivity by withdrawing into an ideolect that circulates like language but does not correspond to the experience of an *I*, in the way, for instance, that a person who had never had an orgasm could still reproduce and manipulate a received discourse that would disguise that experiential lack.[34] On the other hand,

Aulagnier's subject can in fact answer the call, can assume its subjectivity, if the call is genuinely appealing, if, in other words, it grounds the comprehensibility of the self in the experience of pleasure.

Levinas

Like Aulagnier and Kristeva, the French philosopher Emmanuel Levinas understood subjectivity to be grounded in a primordial, prethematic, and preconceptual relation to others. Steeped in Heidegger's phenomenological approach but deeply critical of its emphasis on negativity and isolation, Levinas rejected Heidegger's argument that we are marked by a fundamental, defining fear of absolute nothingness and contended instead that if we are, by our very nature, troubled, it is by the inescapable persistence and ubiquity of the vaguest sense of being. This he described as the *il y a*, or "there is," and likened it, in his early work, to the experience of insomnia.[35] In his later writings, Levinas would come to see this inescapable "medium" of existence more in terms of a relation to others, as an open-ended primordial communality from which such concepts as negativity, subject, and death would devolve. This sense of the community, the original and originating relation to others, is conceived, idiosyncratically, in terms of the infinite. "This book," Levinas wrote of *Totality and Infinity*, "presents itself as a defense of subjectivity, but it will apprehend subjectivity not on the level of its purely egotistical protestation against totality, nor in its anguish before death, but as founded in the idea of infinity."[36]

His approach to subjectivity is based on a reading of the ontological proof of God's existence from Descartes's *Meditations*. The idea of the infinite, since it exceeds me, the argument goes, must come from elsewhere than me. "Infinity," Levinas wrote, "is characteristic of a transcendent being as transcendent; the infinite is the absolutely other. The transcendent is the sole *ideatum* of which there can be only an idea in us; it is infinitely removed from its idea, that is, exterior, because it is infinite."[37] The infinite opens the subject up in a unique and precomprehensible way: the subject contains this idea, but because its *ideatum*, or meaning, is absolutely greater than the thinking subject, the latter finds itself paradoxically related, in the immediacy of thought, to something absolutely other to it, to something immediately other, in the sense that there is no median term between the finite and the infinite. This is the crux of what Levinas sees as the metaphysical and transcendental relationship to the Other, one that puts the Other into contact with me while allowing us to remain absolutely separate.[38] This relation is described as ethical, because it places the self, or *Même*, through its very self-experience as thinking subject, into a relation with the absolutely other, and just as the absolutely foreign can alone teach me, so too am I a genuinely concerned or good person only in respect to the absolutely other.[39] Levinas contrasts this engagement of the infinite with Totality, which he understands as a denial of the absolute particularity of the individual within a system that would engulf it. As part of a totality, in other words, one loses the absoluteness of one's difference from the social system through which one would identify that difference.[40]

Because they are determined by the limits of totalizing thought, Levinas views Kantian and Hegelian models of subjectivity as unsatisfactory accounts of self-experience that volatilize the specificity of the individual into the impersonality of abstract social relations. The fundamental problem of Hegel's approach lies, according to Levinas, in his misunderstanding of the infinite, a flaw that rendered his system incapable of accounting for, or even recognizing, genuine alterity. It is an "allergic" way of understanding human existence, as he put it, because it reduces the ethical relation to a modality of self-identity. Hegel's mistake was, in short, to understand the infinite as a totality, even if a positive one:

> Hegel returns to Descartes by maintaining the positivity of the infinite, but in so doing he posits the infinite as the exclusion of every "other" that might maintain a relation with the infinite and thereby limit it. The infinite can do no more than annex [englober] all relations. . . . The relation of a particular with the infinite would be equivalent to the entry of this particular into the sovereignty of State. It becomes infinite in negating its own finitude.[41]

By failing to recognize the full import of Descartes's insight, Hegel ended up construing the relation between the particular "I" and the infinite as a negation of the former. What would be, for Levinas, the ethical relation, in which the "I" absolves itself (*s'absout*) both from and in its very relatedness and in which, thereby, it preserves its independence, was for Hegel a sublimation in which the individual is absorbed and annihilated as individual. On this basis, one could say that all Idealist and most romantic subjectivities, indeed any model that conceives of the self, overtly or implicitly, in terms of sublimation or that understands the sublime moment as anything but a totalizing violence, would be open to Levinas's critique.[42]

This occurs in his analysis of the rationalized State, which one might understand in terms of Kant's moral order, Hegel's Terror, or Habermas's theory of communicative action.[43] When the social medium, that which relates a collectivity of individuals, is conceived of as reason, the individual soon vanishes as a meaningful term, according to Levinas. In such circumstances, he argues,

> each being is posited apart from all the others, but the will of each, or ipseity, from the start consists in willing the universal or the rational, that is, in negat-

ing its very particularity. In accomplishing its essence as discourse, in becoming a discourse universally coherent, language would at the same time realize the universal State, in which multiplicity is reabsorbed and discourse comes to an end, for lack of interlocutors.[44]

What Hegel had said of the Terror—"the individual consciousness . . . has put aside its limitation; its purpose is the general purpose, its language universal law"[45]—applies to Levinas's understanding of rationalized society in general. Absolute discursive transparency, in which the individual is perfectly comprehensible or coherent, would mean a community of absolutely impersonal, abstract individuals, since the only possible linguistic transparency is a purely universal, essentialized one.[46] For Levinas, this identification with the general constitutes a subtle, internalized form of ambient violence, which replaces more overt or spectacular ones, and although their understanding of subjectivity differed, Levinas, like Althusser, viewed its abstract imposition as an instrument by which the State perpetuated its power structures. Ontology, he wrote, "issues in the State and in the non-violence of the totality, without securing itself against the violence from which this non-violence lives, and which appears in the tyranny of the State. Truth, which should reconcile persons, here exists anonymously. Universality presents itself as impersonal; and this is another inhumanity."[47]

For Levinas, the subject is constituted neither through spontaneity nor through abstract law, but in the relation to an Other whose genuine alterity is revealed in the idea of the infinite. While preserving the centrality of transcendence for the concept of the subject, he argues against the sublimation of the individual in that transcendence, since, according to his terms, the self recognizes the absolutely other, the ethical relationship, but it does not *need* it, a fact manifested in the very possibility of atheism.[48] This is what he calls metaphysical desire; although it is a primordial and constitutional aspect of the subject it is nonetheless unnecessary for it, in the sense that, as a desire for the absolutely Other, it can never be satisfied. We are in this way preoriginally concerned with others through a disinterested interest, a recognition and approval of their alterity that does no violence to our own autonomy. For this reason, desire toward others, because it is an unneeded interest in them on the part of a satisfied "I," is understood by Levinas as a primordial goodness and justice. Whereas both Levinas and Lacan understand desire as inherently unsatisfiable, Lacan conceives of it as derivative of need, as that which cannot be fulfilled because its very neediness has been alienated into language. For Lacan, desire is a by-product of the origination of the subject in language, whereas for Levinas it is constitutive of the subject as a by-product of the ethical relation. In Lacan, desire is the sign of the unsatisfactory condition that is linguistic alienation, an alienation that constitutes the subject through its entry into the symbolic order; in Levinas, desire is a presymbolic surplus that, through its irreducible alienation, places the subject in relation to the infinite in the Other and confirms the ethical. Metaphysical desire, the ethical, is the desire which, one way or another, one assumes in its interminability *as* desire; it is, in this sense, a desire that Lacan's texts enunciate but do not recognize or account for. The Lacanian text, in other words, describes unsatisfiable desire, but does not explain the significance of that description itself, which is necessarily written from a different subjective standpoint than that of mere frustrated need.[49] The subject who is aware of the pointlessness of its own desire has a different relation to that desire than an unaware subject; this awareness is a position that Lacan himself occupies but does not theorize. Levinas, on the other hand, construes that awareness as an ethical appropriation of one's relation to the absolutely and interminably other, and in this respect, his subject of ethical goodness would seem to make more sense than Lacan's subject of castration and symbolic alienation.

Within Levinas's understanding of subjectivity as preoriginally related to an absolute but nonviolent Other, death loses its once defining importance. No longer deemed constitutive of a subject that would subsequently come upon others as if by accident, death is now understood to derive from the ethical relation. We never know the death that comes inexorably to us in itself but always only through the fear it arouses in us, and which announces its approach by falling, like the penumbra of an absolute void, across our sense of self. In view of this, Heidegger had tried to understand death by interpreting all that is experienced of it, that is, through an interpretation of the underlying anxiety that relates Dasein to its authentic projection into the world. Similarly, Levinas approached the significance of death not through the abstract category of negativity, but through an analysis of the fear it provokes and which alone tells us that we must die. And although death is, as Heidegger says, nonrelational, in the sense that we learn of its inevitability not from the death of others but from our own emotional anticipation of it, that anticipation is itself grounded, for Levinas, in our connection to others:

> Death threatens me from beyond. This unknown that frightens, the silence of the infinite spaces that terrify, comes from the other, and this alterity, precisely as absolute, strikes me in an evil design or in a judgment of justice. . . . Death approaches in the fear of someone, and hopes in someone. . . . A social conjuncture is maintained in this menace. It does not sink into the anxiety that would transform it into a "nihilation of nothingness." In the being for death of fear I am not faced with nothingness, but faced with what is *against me*, as though murder, rather than being one of the occasions of dying, were insepara-

ble from the essence of death, as though the approach of death remained one of the modalities of the relation with the Other.[50]

We should not be mislead by Levinas's use of the expression "as though" into thinking that this understanding of death as murder is somehow erroneous, or derivative of a more "accurate" and more authentic understanding of death. Although one can conceive, theoretically, of different kinds of death, death is always *experienced*, the passage argues, as violence against me from another. In this sense, death, as it can be most authentically known—that is, as genuinely in relation to me as an individual and not merely as my abstract, totalizing negation—comes from another. Insofar as it is absolute, death is so as a modality of a more fundamental relation to the absolute, that which comes to me in the experience of others, in the face, in language.[51]

The Other appears to me in his or her infinitude as a face, as a face that expresses and that I can recognize as expression even before I know what is expressed, before the thematization of things and concepts. Language, insofar as it embodies this primitive, prethematic expressivity, is itself the medium of the ethical relation, is itself transcendence.[52] This prethematic *parole* or utterance of the Other, which originates as an interpellation from a stranger, subsequently brings things and the world into existence by thematizing them, by proposing them, in propositions. "The world," Levinas writes, "is offered in the language of the Other; it is borne by propositions. The other is the principle of phenomena."[53] For this reason, when he speaks of language as ethical transcendence, he means not poetry but prose. Considered within the context of our readings of Nerval, Kristeva, and Aulagnier, however, the role that Levinas ascribes to language in the ethical grounding of the subject is problematic. First, his insistence on prose as opposed to the poetic aspects of language is somewhat surprising, given that his greatest interest lies in the prethematic expressivity of discourse, but he explicitly minimizes the importance of rhythmic effects, which he sees as a distraction of the relational value of language. In poetry, as in rational discourse, the interlocutors disappear, although now they are carried away by its sheer sensuous charm. "Discourse," he writes, "is rupture and commencement, breaking of rhythm which enraptures and transports the interlocutors—prose."[54]

Certainly, our readings would suggest, the limits of the self become vague in poetry, whether through the eruption of the Kristevan transsubject or in the endless indeterminacy of "El Desdichado." The poetic was, for us, the very insistence of our relatedness to others, the experience of our indefiniteness, grounded sensuously in our bodies. The voluptuousness of language that poetry instantiates reveals the persistence of meaningless matter even within rational discourse. In poetry, the subject founders, lost to itself, into the vague semiotic differentiations of pleasure that are the underlying community: *someone* is in pleasure, a pleasure that will later give sense to the language of the other, that will allow the other to express to me. The face, its corporeal language between meaning and presentation, must be recognized by me in order to express; its mute utterings come to me as such only because I too have a body, shaped in pleasure and displeasure, from whose original indeterminacy the other makes sense to me, appears as other, signifies and proposes. Just as the certitude of my own death can come to me from no one else, so the certitude of the other's pleasure, of his or her semiotic potential, his or her very faciality, comes to me only through the vagueness of a primordial pleasure that seemed to come to no one in particular and of which your sensation and mine are modalities. I can only engage in the ethical relation because I am not sure that your face was not originally mine and because mine is as strange as anyone else's.

Levinas also conceives of language in terms of presence, and the face that speaks, that expresses and finds words, is always one that is present before me, ready to explain the meaning of what I have not grasped, to answer my questions, simply to answer my call that it continue to express: "The interpellated one is called upon to speak; his speech consists in 'coming to the assistance' of his word—in being *present*."[55] His view of writing, on the other hand, conceives of it very much in terms of the linguistic sublime; it is a tyranny and universal depersonalization.[56] It is not clear, however, why this should be, why one cannot imagine language as itself already an indeterminate presence of the other. The very language I speak, that I read, whether or not I am alone, comes to me from elsewhere, is already a calling to me from others who do not need to be present otherwise than in these words for me to be aware that I am not alone, even in my own thoughts. Every word interpellates me as preexistent and as present in its materiality, in the voluptuousness of its poetic existence.

Conclusion: The Desired Self

Nerval's poetry, especially "El Desdichado" and "Les Mémorables," points to the possibility of a discontinuous existence, an unanswerable spontaneity, the senselessness of pain and pleasure and sensation. We are perhaps too quick to draw lessons from the meaningless, to understand it, as if pain and pleasure were not inherently incomprehensible. The plenitude of the moment resists the propositions that would determine it, surging up again in the language we speak, as its poetic incomprehensibility, its predicative indeterminacy, its syntax and grammar, its vocatives and rhetorical figures. But even in our meaningful existence we are not necessarily cut off from life; language is also pleasure, connectedness to others, the making of us as ones who, in speaking or in listening, in writing or reading, answer to the wanting of us to be, a wanting for us to be that stems from a longing not for control but for company. We are the ones who in speaking, even to ourselves, in our minds, bring others out of isolation, others who have wanted us to answer and to break the silence that would otherwise close about them like the tomb. By the use of language we answer the call of others' desire for us to be, of others' primordial loneliness, love, generosity.

Perhaps another invention of the nineteenth century allows us more tangible glimpses of this other discontinuous world that runs through language. The photograph, we could say, determines an instant and like a Nietzschean machine instantiates something approximating the eternal return. At first, however, photographic plates were not quick enough to grasp a moment, and the best human subjects were those who were dead or could, in their immobility, imitate the dead. Later, the action of the camera revealed another world under the continuity of meaningful existence, one that was submerged in the persistence of vision. A foreign moment emerged within the intimacy of the known, surging up in all of its ridiculousness and grotesquery. Gestures did not seem to find their goals or know what they were, faces grimaced, limbs and features distorted, the body twisted out of recognition. The links of Heideggerian potentiality and Dasein's temporality were cut—hands no longer reached for their own death, but simply appeared in the pleasure of vision.

Levinas's face, which expresses I know not what, is still a subject and comes as a refusal of the poetic. More troubling, but perhaps more significant, is the chaos of the world suggested by photography or the nonsense of Nerval's writing, a chaos to which we can lend ourselves, if only momentarily. This other self is a lawlessness, an unanswerableness that is not a breaking of laws but the failure to think oneself and a lingering instead in the experience of light or shadow, of song falling on our ears. From this madness, this play of sounds and light on dark, a voice comes together or a face takes shape, bearing with it the gift of myself, the I who will bring solace and joy to others. But it *is* a gift and not an obligation, because permanently or temporarily I can refuse the call to my own self, whether in madness, in drugs, in aesthetic distraction, or, perhaps, in a myriad other ways that slip unperceived in the apparent continuity of meaningful life. Nerval's poetry is such an offering and, at the same time, a reminder of the gratuitousness of the self, for out of a primeval confusion it calls up a language of the self, an expressiveness not of the face but of the materialized desire for us that language is and that we are in language.

Reference Matter

Notes

Preface

1. See Michel Foucault, "Technologies of the Self," pp. 19–22.
2. See Charles Taylor, *Sources of the Self*, pp. 495–513.

Chapter 1. History and Romantic Self-Identity

1. "Je suis tout ému d'avoir vu mon petit enfant pensif en face de la mer... En voyant, d'une part cette terrible image de l'infini, de l'autre ma fille, et cette attraction qui nous rappelle dans le gouffre de la nature, je sentais la fibre de l'individualité se déchirer. Le général, l'universel, l'éternel, voilà la patrie de l'homme. C'est à vous que je demanderai secours, mon noble pays; il faut que vous nous teniez lieu du Dieu qui nous échappe, que vous remplissiez en nous l'incommensurable abîme que le christianisme éteint y a laissé. Vous nous devez l'équivalent de l'infini. Nous sentons tous périr l'individualité en nous. Puisse recommencer le sentiment de la généralité sociale, de l'universalité humaine, de celle du monde! Alors peut-être nous remonterons vers Dieu." Entry for June 7, 1831, in Jules Michelet, *Journal*, vol. 1, p. 83. All translations mine unless otherwise noted.
2. Taine, for example, also attempted to explain individual artistic creation through the mediating influence of *race*, *milieu*, and historical moment, although unlike Michelet he did not express his motivation to do so as fear.
3. See Hegel's characterization of this abstract worship in the Revolution: "The *beyond* of this its actual existence hovers over the corpse of the vanished independence of real being, or the being of faith, merely as the exhalation of the stale gas, of the vacuous *Etre suprême*" (*Phenomenology*, p. 358).
4. In the *Conflict of the Faculties* Kant speaks of an event that would reveal history as progress: "There must be some experience in the human race which, as an event, points to the disposition and capacity of the human race to be the cause of its own advance toward the better, and (since this should be the act of a being endowed with

freedom), toward the human race as being the author of this advance.... Therefore, an event must be sought which would allow progress toward the better to be concluded as an inevitable consequence. This conclusion then could also be extended to the history of the past (that it has always been in progress) in such a way that that event would have to be considered not itself as the cause of history, but only as an intimation, a historical sign (*signum rememorativum, demonstrativum, prognostikon*) demonstrating the tendency of the human race" (p. 151); this event is in fact the disinterested interest of an observer toward certain episodes in human concourse and is exemplified for Kant by the French Revolution: "This event consists neither in momentous deeds nor crimes committed by men whereby what was great among men is made small or what was small is made great, nor in ancient splendid political structures which vanish as if by magic while others come forth in their place as if from the depths of the earth. No, nothing of the sort. It is simply the mode of thinking of the spectators which reveals itself publicly in this game of great revolutions, and manifests such a universal yet disinterested sympathy for the players on one side against those on the other, even at the risk that this partiality could become disadvantageous for them if discovered. Owing to its universality, this mode of thinking demonstrates a character of the human race at large and all at once; owing to its disinterestedness, a moral character of humanity, at least in its predisposition, a character which not only permits people to hope for progress toward the better, but is already itself progress in so far as its capacity is sufficient for the present. The revolution of a spirited people [Die Revolution eines gestreichen Volks] which we have seen unfolding in our day may succeed or miscarry ... this revolution, I say, nonetheless finds in the hearts of all spectators (who are not engaged in this fame themselves) a wishful participation that borders closely on enthusiasm, the very expression of which is fraught with danger; this sympathy, therefore, can have no other cause than a moral predisposition in the human race" (Kant, *Conflict*, p. 153, trans. modified). Although Kant asserts that as a past occurrence this event can have only symbolic or revelatory power, when speaking of the disinterested but sympathetic spectators of the French Revolution he contends that their affective relation to the object of their concern, because distinterested, already constitutes an act of historical progress: the observers, at potential risk to themselves as individuals, are concerned with humanity as such and thereby demonstrate and enact a historical consciousness, and this latter, since it is concerned for humanity as such, makes possible an amelioration or progress of the human condition. In this sense, moments such as the Revolution allow the inauguration of history; and it is in this sense that Kant asserts that the observer's disinterestedness "is already itself progress."

5. Similarly, in the domain of art history, Michael Baxendall has argued that the attention to optical peculiarities of the field of vision (for instance, plunging perspectives, the curvature at the edges of paintings) in the romantic painter Caspar David Friedrich can be understood as a conscious attempt to represent the universal laws of sight or the formal synthetic conditions of perception (lecture at Cornell University, April 10, 1986).

6. Kant, *Pure Reason*, p. 158: "But the pure form of intuition in time, merely as intuition in general, which contains a given manifold, is subject to the original unity of consciousness, simply through the necessary relation of the manifold of the intuition to the one '*I think*,' and so through the pure synthesis of understanding which is the *a priori* underlying ground of the empirical synthesis. Only the original unity is objectively valid." Later, in the "Paralogisms of Pure Reason," Kant will specifically refer to this apperceptive agency as the subject (*Pure Reason*, pp. 327–83, esp. p. 377).

7. This foundational centrality of the Subject in relation to history also appears in the Preface to Hegel's *Phenomenology*. For a discussion of this point, see Chapter 6.

8. *Pure Reason*, pp. 378, 380.

9. See *Pure Reason*, pp. 152–53, where, in the paragraph entitled "The Original Unity of Apperception," Kant writes: "It must be possible for the 'I think' to accompany all my representations; for otherwise something would be represented in me which could not be thought at all, and that is equivalent to saying that the representation would be impossible, or at least would be nothing to me. That representation which can be given prior to all thought is entitled intuition. All the manifold of intuition has, therefore, a necessary relation to the 'I think' in the same subject in which this manifold is found. But this representation is an act of *spontaneity*, that is, it cannot be regarded as belonging to sensibility. I call it *pure apperception*, to distinguish it from empirical apperception, or, again, *original apperception*, because it is that self-consciousness which, while generating the representation '*I think*' (a representation which must be capable of accompanying all other representations, and which in all consciousness is one and the same), cannot itself be accompanied by any further representation. The unity of this apperception I likewise entitle the *transcendental* unity of self consciousness."

10. This is taken from the second (1787) edition's version of this argument, in Kant, *Pure Reason*, p. 377.

11. In the earlier version of this chapter, from the 1781 edition, Kant seems to propose a less radical version of the subject's unknowability. There he appears to argue that, like any other *noumenon*, the subject, while unapprehensible in itself, can nonetheless be intuited as a representation, that is, as transformed according to the laws of perception into a perceived thing. See, for example, *Pure Reason*, pp. 346–47: "There can be no question that I am conscious of my representations; these representations and I myself, who have the representations, therefore exist. External objects (bodies), however, are mere appearances, and are therefore nothing but a species of my representations, the objects of which are something only through these representations. Apart from them they are nothing. Thus external things exist as well as I myself, and both, indeed, upon the immediate witness of my self-consciousness. The only difference is that the representation of myself, as the thinking subject, belongs to inner sense [that is, time] only, while the representations which mark extended beings also belong to outer sense [that is, space]." By treating the subject as a representation of something rather than as the formalism of pure

thought, Kant here risks slipping into a substantialist view of it, a threat that seems to have led to his rewriting of the whole chapter in the 1787 edition and his insistence in that later version on the sheer formalism of the subject.

12. Kant, *Pure Reason*, pp. 371–72.
13. Ibid., pp. 157–58.
14. See for example, the discussions of death-based subjectivity in Heidegger and phallic subjectivity in Lacan in Chapters 2 and 7.
15. Or "diese einzige schreckliche, *was er nur muß und nicht will.*" Friedrich von Schiller, *On the Sublime*, p. 194. German edition: "Ueber das Erhabene" in *Schillers Werke: Nationalausgabe*, p. 38.
16. Schiller, *On the Sublime*, p. 208.
17. Ibid., p. 210.
18. Ibid., pp. 205–6.
19. Kant, *Judgement*, p. 113. German version: *Kritik der Urtheilskraft*, vol. 5, p. 263.
20. *Judgement*, pp. 113–14; *Kritik*, p. 263.
21. *Judgement*, p. 114; *Kritik*, p. 264.   22. *Judgement*, p. 119; *Kritik*, p. 267.
23. *Judgement*, p. 118; *Kritik*, p. 268.   24. *Judgement*, p. 123; *Kritik*, p. 271.
25. *Judgement*, p. 120; *Kritik*, p. 269.
26. *Judgement*, p. 122, original emphasis; *Kritik*, p. 270.
27. *Judgement*, pp. 120–21 (trans. modified); *Kritik*, p. 269.
28. *Judgement*, p. 123.
29. The disinterested nature of this safety is articulated in the continuation of the passage. The security of the "he" has no relation to personal well-being: "Rather is it [the astonishment bordering on terror] an attempt to gain access to it [the sublime vista] through imagination, for the purpose of feeling the might of this faculty in combining the movement of the mind thereby aroused with its serenity, and of thus being superior to internal and, therefore, to external, nature, so far as the latter can have any bearing upon our feeling of well-being. For the imagination, in accordance with laws of association, makes our state of contentment dependent upon physical conditions" (*Judgement*, p. 121; *Kritik*, p. 269). Moreover, the interest here negated is of a specifically physical character.
30. This is not the only time he uses the term: in an earlier passage he had stated that "without the development of moral ideas, that which, thanks to preparatory culture, we call sublime, merely strikes the untutored man as terrifying [abschreckend]" (p. 115).
31. *Judgement*, p. 121.
32. *Phenomenology*, p. 357. German edition: *Phänomenologie des Geistes*, p. 433.
33. In comparing rational comprehension to imaginative apprehension in "The Analytic of the Sublime," Kant uses the cognate terms "zusammenfaßen" and "fassen" to designate the synthetic, totalizing conception which Reason gives (*Kritik*, p. 259). Earlier he had contrasted the "progressiv" quality of "Auffaßung [apprehension]" with the "comprehensiv" quality of "Zusammenfaßung" and the verb *fassen* (p. 254).

34. Hegel, *Phenomenology*, pp. 359–60; *Phänomenologie*, p. 436. For a further articulation of this opposition between atomic consciousness and universal thought, see p. 363 (p. 440): "the *universal will* is its [consciousness's] *pure knowing and willing* and *it* is the universal will *qua* this pure knowing and willing. It does not lose *itself* in that will, for pure knowing and willing is much more *it* than is that atomic point of consciousness. It is thus the interaction of pure knowing with itself; pure *knowing qua essential being* is the universal will."

35. This is particularly clear when one compares this metaphorics with Hegel's discussion of animals eating in the "Sense Certainty" chapter of the *Phenomenology*. There, close consideration of the functioning of language is shown to reveal that "what consciousness will learn from experience in all sense-certainty is, in truth, only what we have seen viz. the This as a *universal*, the very opposite of what that assertion affirmed to be universal experience" (p. 65; *Phänomenologie*, pp. 90–91). He goes on to contend that "even the animals are not shut out from this wisdom but, on the contrary, show themselves to be most profoundly initiated into it; for they do not just stand idly in front of sensuous things as if these possessed intrinsic being, but, despairing of their reality, and completely assured of their nothingness, they fall to without ceremony and eat them up" (p. 91).

36. *Phenomenology*, p. 357; *Phänomenologie*, p. 433.

37. That this identification with the language of the law should be an identification with the specifically *moral* in Hegel as well as in Kant is clear from the fact that the form of *Geist* to which this sublimation gives rise is morality itself. The chapter of the *Phenomenology* following "Absolute Freedom and Terror" is entitled "Spirit That Is Certain of Itself: Morality." The relation between the French Revolution and the aesthetics of the sublime has also been the object of recent work by Marie-Hélène Huet, who has emphasized the theatrical or representational aspects of the Terror (see "The Revolutionary Sublime").

38. *Phenomenology*, p. 363; *Phänomenologie*, p. 440.

39. The German term translated as "laid hold of" is in fact *erfaßt*, which means "grasped," in either a physical or an intellectual sense, and in the latter case is a synonym for "comprehended." This ambiguity of the verb *erfaßen* itself, this equivocality between the material and the immaterial, holds in itself the very ambiguity that marks the pseudo-specificity and pseudo-materiality of the atomic individual: what cannot be grasped in the hand is comprehended in the intellect .

40. *Phenomenology*, p. 362; *Phänomenologie*, p. 439. Cf. also this passage: "it [the negation that is the death without meaning] is the *universal will* which in this its ultimate abstraction has nothing positive and therefore can give nothing in return for the sacrifice. But for that very reason it is immediately one with self-consciousness, or it is the pure positive, because it is the pure negative; and the meaningless death, the unfulfilled negativity of the self, changes round in its inner Notion into absolute positivity" (p. 362; pp. 439–40). This positivity, since it is absolute, is nonetheless still absolute negativity from the point of view of the annihilated individual.

41. *Phenomenology*, p. 360; *Phänomenologie*, p. 436.

42. *Phenomenology*, p. 362; *Phänomenologie*, p. 439. Cf. Emmanuel Levinas's discussions of the tyranny of the abstract in *Totality and Infinity*, pp. 251–53 and 300–301; *Totalité et infini*, pp. 281–84 and 334–35. See also Chapter 8.

43. Deconstruction brought with it a resurgence of interest in the sublime, marked by such collections as Neil Hertz, *The End of the Line*, Silverman and Aylesworth, *The Textual Sublime*, and Courtine et al., *Of The Sublime*. The essays in these three volumes tend to focus on the relation of the sublime to literary, stylistic, or rhetorical structures rather than emphasizing issues of textuality and reference, as is the case with the present reading of Hegel.

44. *Phenomenology*, p. 60.

45. Ibid., p. 62.

46. "It is as a universal too that we *utter* what the sensuous [content] is. What we say is: 'This,' i.e. the *universal* This; or 'it is,' i.e. *Being in general*. Of course, we do not *envisage* the universal This or Being in general, but we *utter* the universal; in other words, we do not strictly say what in this sense-certainty we *mean* to say. But language, as we see, is the more truthful; in it, we ourselves directly refute what we *mean* to say, and since the universal is the true [content] of sense-certainty and language expresses this true [content] alone, it is just not possible for us ever to say, or express in words, a sensuous being that we *mean*" (*Phenomenology*, p. 60).

47. *Phenomenology*, p. 60. Cf. the discussion of language in *Hegel's Philosophy of Mind*: "the word gives to thoughts their highest and truest existence" (p. 221); and "The word as *sounded* vanishes in *time*; the latter thus demonstrates itself in the former to be an *abstract*, that is to say, merely *destructive*, negativity" (pp. 220–21).

48. As Hegel writes later in the *Phenomenology*: "Language is self-consciousness existing *for others*, . . . [where] the self separates itself from itself" (p. 395).

49. The description of nondialectical death is part of an account of the unfortunate outcome should two masters encounter one another; the loser reverts to the simple immediacy to itself of an inanimate thing, an immediacy that is not possible for consciousness (see the section on the *Akzidentelle* in Chapter 7) and from which no progress is possible: "They [that is, the two mutually slaughtering combatants, or masters] put an end to their consciousness in its alien setting of natural existence, that is to say, they put an end to themselves, and are done away with as *extremes* wanting to be *for themselves*, or to have an existence of their own. But with this there vanishes from their interplay the essential moment of splitting into extremes with opposite characteristics; and the middle term collapses into a lifeless unity which is split into lifeless, merely immediate, unopposed extremes; and the two do not reciprocally give and receive from each other consciously, but leave each other free only indifferently, like things. Their act is an abstract [that is, neither a determinate nor dialectical] negation, not the negation coming from consciousness, which supersedes in such a way as to preserve and maintain what is superseded, and consequently survives its own supersession" (*Phenomenology*, pp. 114–15).

50. On language in Hegel: "One of the profound defects in Hegel's thought is revealed perhaps in his philosophy of language and his conception of specificity,

which banished 'specific souls' because they are ineffable. For Hegel, specificity is a *negation* rather than an irreducible *originality*; it either manifests itself through a determination which is a negation or, qua genuine specificity, it is the *negation* of *negation*, an internal negation—which may indeed lead us to a *universal subject* but which tends to eliminate *specific existents*" (Hyppolite, *Genesis*, p. 86n; *Genèse*, p. 87n). On the problematic role of the Terror in Hegel's system: "What we have here is an internalization of absolute freedom, which cannot exist immediately, that is, as a nature. Hegel's thought is quite obscure here. Although it could well culminate in a justification of the revolution, in fact, it interprets the failure of that revolution. Nor, it seems, does Hegel's thought lead us to a City of God above, or parallel to, the terrestrial city. For the 'moral world view' fails in turn. Hegel's solution is not easily ascertainable" (*Genesis*, p. 455; *Genèse*, p. 441). On Hegel's theories of language and semiotics see Derrida's "The Pit and the Pyramid: Introduction to Hegel's Semiotics" in *Margins of Philosophy*; Lamb, *Language Perception*; McCumber, *The Company of Words*; Cook, *Language*; and Pippin, *Hegel's Idealism*, pp. 116–42.

51. "But we must return in a little more detail to what happened at the end of the eighteenth and the beginning of the nineteenth century: to that too sketchily outlined mutation of Order into History" (Foucault, *Order of Things*, p. 220; *Les Mots*, p. 232).

52. *Order of Things*, p. 225 (trans. modified); *Les Mots*, p.237. Foucault further states: "Wealth is always a functioning representative element: but, in the end, what it represents is no longer the object of desire; it is labour" (p. 223; p. 235); and that with the concept of work, Smith "formulates a principle of order that is irreducible to the analysis of representation" (p. 225; p. 237).

53. *Order of Things*, p. 225; *Les Mots*, p. 238.

54. *Order of Things*, p. 300; *Les Mots*, p. 313.

55. See the sections "Ideology and Criticism" and "Objective Syntheses" in *Order of Things*, pp. 236–49; *Les Mots*, pp. 249–61.

56. See discussion of Hegel's *Aesthetics*, Chapter 7.

57. Cf. Saussure, *Course*, p. 14; *Cours*, p. 30: "In separating language from speaking [la langue de la parole] we are at the same time separating: (1) what is social from what is individual; and (2) what is essential from what is accessory and more or less accidental." In Hegel's "Sense Certainty" chapter, the annihilating abstractive force of language is instantiated in its written form: "a truth cannot lose anything by being written down" (*Phenomenology*, p. 60).

58. On the purely grammatical positionality of the subject in the *Phenomenology*, see Chapter 6.

Chapter 2. Death-Based Subjectivity

1. See, for example, Mikkel Borch-Jacobsen's interpretation of the Freudian subject as the nothingness of death, which makes itself known through terror ("The Freudian Subject" in Cadava, *Who Comes After the Subject*, pp. 73–76).

2. "La pensée et le discours, révélateur du Réel, naissent de l'Action négatrice qui réalise le Néant en anéantissant l'Etre: l'être-donné de l'Homme. . . . C'est donc dire que l'être humain lui-même n'est pas autre chose que cette Action; il est la mort qui vit une vie humaine" (Alexandre Kojève, *Lecture*, p. 550).

3. "Le *Jeune-France* est gai, mais d'une gaîté putride. Dans la journée, il a vu les Catacombes, le Père-LaChaise et la Chambre des Pairs; il devise sur Montfaucon et le cabinet d'anatomie; aux jeunes dames il montre un os, et leur dit: 'Vous en avez autant sous vos gazes et vos mousselines. Ainsi vous marchez toujours en compagnie d'un squelette, vous avez la mort sous vos jupes: voyons la mort.'" (*Figaro*, Aug. 30, 1831, cited in Philothée O'Neddy, *Feu et flamme*, p. xiii).

4. I am deeply indebted to Alphonso Lingis's important *Deathbound Subjectivity*, which examines the relation between death and subjectivity in key philosophers (and Lacan) since Kant. Our approaches differ in several important respects. Lingis is, above all, interested in the subjective significance of the death of the other, and he writes, for instance, that the "relationship with the dying of the other is prior to language and to silence, insofar as silence among humans is a punctuation of, and invitation to, discourse" (p. 188); I, on the other hand, have concentrated on the death of the self, and for this reason, perhaps, I place much more emphasis on Hegel, who appears at best only peripherally in Lingis's work. Also, whereas I examine death as abstraction, Lingis seems to view it, at least in reference to Lacan, more as determinate of the sensuous and "real": "Do we not hear the laughter, weeping, blessing, and cursing with which the infancy that returns encounters the real other beneath the uniform of mother and that of father—the deathbound flesh of the other?" (p. 175).

5. The romantic period's attitude toward mortality can, however, be understood as part of a larger cultural movement. The historian Philippe Ariès writes of a change in the relation between individual and death during the period from the year one thousand to the thirteenth century: "We can here grasp that change in the mirror of death: *speculum mortis*, we could say, in the manner of the writers of the time. In the mirror of his own death each man rediscovered the secret of his individuality. . . . Since the height of the Middle Ages, rich Western man, powerful or literate, has recognized himself in his death: he has discovered the *death of the self*" (*Essais sur l'histoire de la mort*, p. 45, original emphasis); and "a connection was made among three categories of mental representations: those of death, those of the individual's knowledge of his own biography, and those of the passionate attachment to the things and beings possessed during life. Death became the place where man best became conscious of himself" (p. 41). In Hegel, Heidegger, and the other authors discussed in this chapter, one can see the full theorization of an attitude to death which arose during the late Middle Ages, with the important distinction that while for the medieval consciousness death allowed the individual to *rediscover* the secret of his therefore preexistent particularity, for the moderns death would have been the condition of possibility of that particularity and would thus be *prior* to the individual.

6. *Phenomenology*, pp. 6–7.

7. *Order of Things*, p. 225; *Les Mots*, p. 237.

8. *Order of Things*, p. 225; *Les Mots*, p. 238.

9. Michel Foucault, *Discipline*, p. 3; *Surveiller*, p. 9.

10. *Discipline*, pp. 44–45; *Surveiller*, p. 48.

11. *Discipline*, p. 45; *Surveiller*, p. 49.

12. See Gilles Deleuze and Félix Guattari, *Anti-Oedipus*, pp. 1–50; *L'Anti-œdipe*, pp. 7–59, and Louis Althusser, "Ideology and Ideological State Apparatuses" in *Lenin and Philosophy*, pp. 121–173; "Idéologie et appareils idéologiques d'état" in *Positions*, pp. 67–125.

13. Cited in Foucault, *Discipline*, p. 4; *Surveiller*, p. 10 (emphasis added).

14. *Discipline*, pp. 51–53; *Surveiller*, pp. 55–56.

15. Quoted in Daniel Arasse, p. 11.   16. Ibid., p. 16.

17. Ibid., p. 17.   18. Quoted in ibid.

19. Ibid., p. 35.

20. Quoted in ibid. Original in *Œuvres complètes de Cabanis*, vol. 2, p. 180. It is significant that Cabanis framed this whole discussion of the guillotine in terms of the subjectivity of the victim: "We are speaking here of the sensations relating to the *I* of the individual, which are the only ones which concern us" (p. 168n). The moment of the guillotine is seen to raise questions about the very essence of the self, questions that are now considered to be the province of medicine and philosophy rather than, say, theology.

21. "*Death*, this change of state so remarked on, so feared, is, in Nature, no more than the last nuance of a previous being; the necessary progress of our body's decline brings this step with it as it has all the others which preceded it. Life begins to end long before it has ended entirely; and in reality, there is perhaps a greater distance from old age to youth than there is between decrepitude and death, for one must not consider life here as an absolute thing but as a quantity susceptible to augmentation, diminution and, finally, necessary destruction" (*Encyclopédie*, vol. 10, p. 716).

22. Ibid.   23. Ibid.

24. Quoted in Arasse, pp. 22–23.   25. Quoted in ibid., p. 26.

26. Reproduced in ibid., pp. 184–85.

27. Jean-Paul Marat, *Textes choisis*, pp. 183, 184–85.

28. "Sur la police générale, sur la justice, le commerce, la législation et les crimes des factions" in *Discours et rapports*, ed. Albert Soboul (Paris: Editions Sociales, 1988), p. 183; see also 190: "Think only to strengthen that equality [of the people] by the vehemence of a pure government which, by means of a vast and judicious police, shall assure that all rights are respected; let the law be utterly rigid towards enemies of the homeland, let it be gently maternal towards the citizens." Of course, it is the crime itself that in most cases separates the enemy from the citizen.

29. Ibid., p. 195. On the beginning of the Republic, see p. 186: "What would have become of a Republic that had been indulgent towards its enraged enemies? We have set sword against sword and laid the foundations of liberty; sprung from

the heart of storms she shares her origins with the world, sprung from chaos, and with Man, who is born in tears."

30. From a speech to the Convention on Nov. 13, 1792, in ibid., p. 68.

31. See Robespierre's "Rapport sur les principes de morale politique qui doivent guider la Convention," Feb. 5, 1794: "as the essence of the republic or of democracy is equality, it follows that love of the homeland necessarily embraces the love of equality. It is also true that this sublime feeling supposes a preference for the public interest over all particular interests" (in *Discours et rapports*, p. 327); and Desmoulins's "Fragment de l'histoire secrète de la Révolution": "Those who destroyed royalty's prestige and sent a king of France to the scaffold because he was king will not be vilified in the opinion of peoples. We have tried a sublime experiment and one in which we would have gained eternal glory even by failing, that of making the human race happy and free" (in *Œuvres*, vol. 1, p. 349). Saint-Just declared: "One must be a sublime man to hold his country together" (*Discours et rapports*, p. 195). See also Marie-Hélène Huet's important analysis of the sublime theatrics of the Terror in "The Revolutionary Sublime," pp. 51–64.

32. Arasse, p. 91.

33. Kant makes a very similar argument in his moral writings, where he contends that the individual will does not represent the spontaneous interest of the particular person but instead the individual's conformity to the abstraction of law. "Only a rational being," he writes, "has the power to act according to his conception of laws, i.e., according to principles, and thereby has he a will" (*Grounding for the Metaphysics of Morals* in *Ethical Philosophy*, p. 23). In this sense, as a conformity to the laws of reason, the subject is in fact an impersonal objectification: "If reason infallibly determines the will, then in the case of such a being actions which are recognized to be objectively necessary are also subjectively necessary, i.e., the will is a faculty of choosing only that which reason, independently of inclination, recognizes as being practically necessary, i.e., as good" (p. 23). In order to be fully rational, and therefore free, a person must, in short, forego his or her interest in the sensuousness of the world to identify with an abstract and objective principle.

34. Hegel, *Phenomenology*, p. 299.

35. In speaking of those who might one day come across the manuscripts he leaves behind, the prisoner writes: "Perhaps reading these will slow their hand when it is again question of tossing a head that thinks, a man's head, into what they call the scales of justice? Perhaps the wretches have never considered the slow succession of tortures encapsulated in the curt pronouncement of a death sentence" (Victor Hugo, *Last Day*, pp. 42–43 (trans. modified); *Le Dernier Jour*, p. 286).

36. Hugo, *Last Day*, p. 34 (trans. modified); *Le Dernier Jour*, p. 274.

37. Death is in fact conceived of as a *néant* or void in the novel. For example, the prisoner exclaims, in weighing the guillotine against a lifetime of forced labor: "The galleys! No, death is infinitely to be preferred to this, the scaffold to the convict station, and nothingness [*le néant*] to such hell on earth!" (*Last Day*, p. 57, trans. modified; *Le Dernier Jour*, p. 306).

38. *Last Day*, p. 47 (trans. modified); *Le Dernier Jour*, p. 292.

39. "Literature and the Right to Death" in *Fire*, p. 323; *Feu*, p. 313.

40. *Last Day*, pp. 28–29 (trans. modified); *Le Dernier Jour*, pp. 397–98. Cf. Büchner's description of the National Assembly during the Terror in *Danton's Death*: "Equality swings its sickle over the heads of all, the lava of revolution flows, the guillotine makes republicans, eh Lacroix? The gallery claps, the Romans rub their hands; they don't hear that every word is the death-rattle of a victim. Follow your fine phrases through to the point where they become incarnate. Look around you: this is what you've been saying. It's all a mimic translation of your words. These wretches, their hangmen, and their guillotine are your speeches turned to life. You built your system, like the sultan Bajazet his pyramids, out of human heads" (*Danton's Death*, pp. 47–48). On the relation between subject and language in *Le Dernier Jour* see also the excellent article by Marie-Claire Vallois, "Ecrire ou décrire: L'Impossible histoire du 'sujet' dans *Le Dernier Jour d'un condamné* de Victor Hugo," in *Romantisme* 48: 2 (1985), pp. 91–104.

41. Hugo was concerned, and at a certain point virtually obsessed, with the language of the dead. In *Le Dernier Jour*, the prisoner is given a dream which apparently repeatedly troubled Hugo himself; it is an attempt to make someone speak, eventually by resorting to torture. Then there were the table-rapping sessions at Jersey, where, from 1853 to 1855, the family spent hours each day questioning the dead and tabulating their responses by counting the strokes of the table leg. Hugo himself would spend the nights transcribing these numeric responses into French. The dead continued, in short, to speak, their language was that of the living—it was the bridge, the sole bridge, between the living and the dead, and in it, disembodied, they could continue to think. See Jean De Mutigny, *Victor Hugo et le spiritisme*.

42. Hugo, *Last Day*, p. 39 (trans. modified); *Le Dernier Jour*, p. 280.

43. On the spectacular isolation of the protagonist as the one who is going to die, see, for example, a scene that takes place in the prison courtyard, as the condemned watches the other prisoners chained together for the journey to Toulon: "Then all eyes turned towards my window. 'Death Row! Death Row!' they shouted, all pointing at me; and their bursts of merriment grew louder. I stood petrified. . . . I was sunk even lower than they, and it filled them with respect. I shuddered. . . . A few days later it would have been my turn to put on a show for them. . . . Then it seemed that the horrible voices of the convicts had drawn closer. Convinced I could see their horrid heads rising above the sill of my window, I screamed out once more in dread and fell into a swoon" (*Last Day*, pp. 54–55 [trans. modified]; *Le Dernier Jour*, p. 303). While the prisoners hail him as their comrade, it is the condemned man's awareness of his separation from even these, society's excluded, that seems to terrify him. He is an object of interest not because he is like them, but because, through his relation to death, he is different. This is the sense of the honor here that so petrifies the character.

44. See *Totality and Infinity*, pp. 234–36; *Totalité et infini*, pp. 260–62; and Chapter 8 in this volume.

45. In his journal of Mar. 6, 1882, Edmond de Goncourt noted a remark made to him by Zola: "There are nights when I [Zola] leap up out of bed and stand there a moment in a state of unspeakable dread" (quoted in Emile Zola, *Les Rougon-Macquart*, vol. 3, p. 1786). Louis de Robert wrote of Zola's attitude toward death: "It was in his case a terror which turned at times to obsession, keeping him awake through the hours of the night. Mme Zola told me one day that her husband's fear of death led him at times to burst into tears" (quoted in *Les Rougon-Macquart*, pp. 1786–87). According to Goncourt, it was this fear of death which lay at the origin of the novel *La Joie de vivre*, for which Zola had initially considered the title *La Douleur* or "suffering": "he says that this obsession with death [ce hantement de la mort] and, perhaps, an evolution in his philosophical ideas brought about by the demise of one who had been dear to him, he is thinking of fitting it into a novel, which he would entitle something like *La Douleur*. This novel, he's groping about for it at this very moment" (*Journal*, entry for Feb. 20, 1883, quoted in *Les Rougon-Macquart*, p. 1751).

46. *Les Rougon-Macquart*, p. 843.

47. Ibid., p. 1055.

48. Ibid., p. 1057. Cf. also: "The truth of the matter was that his constant preoccupation with death each day stole more of his taste and will for living. He fell back into his old 'What's the use?'" (p. 1055); "His continual worry about the morrow spoiled the present moment" (p. 1056); and, "But, lording it over and wrecking everything was his boredom, grown to monstrous proportions, the boredom of an unbalanced mind which the ever-present thought of impending death had left disgusted with action and capable only of wallowing in its own futility, which he blamed on the emptiness of life" (p. 1057).

49. Ibid., p. 1795.

50. Ibid., p. 1055. Cf. also Zola's note to himself on Lazare's degenerating condition: "First take back up and emphasize the elements of the first phase. The idea of the eternal, of the nevermore, we part never to meet again" (p. 1795). Edmond de Goncourt noted in his journal on Feb. 20, 1883: "This idea of death comes to him [Zola] more frequently since the death of his mother; and, after a moment's silence, he adds that her death has punched a hole in the nihilism of his religious convictions, so dreadful is it for him to think of an eternal separation" (quoted in ibid., p. 1751).

51. One should perhaps say, rather, that these characteristics were represented *to Zola* as pathological, and that he was in fact simply describing something close to his own experiences. Before his domineering fear of death Lazare begins to exhibit behavior that strikes a modern reader as decidedly obsessive-compulsive (see ibid., pp. 998–1000) and which had manifested itself in the life of the author himself. In 1896 Dr. Toulouse gave a detailed description of Zola's condition, which he diagnosed as "arithmomanie" (see the report by Dr. Toulouse quoted in ibid., pp. 1796–97).

52. See Enid Starkie, *Pétrus Borel*, and Gautier, *History of Romanticism*, in *Works*, vol. 16, pp. 30–64 (*Histoire*, vol. 11 of *Œuvres complètes*, pp. 14–43).

53. As Valéry Larbaud pointed out, Dondey's poetic works were no slimmer than Alfred de Vigny's, but the great bulk of them only appeared posthumously. *Feu et flamme* was reedited once after its original and financially disastrous 1833 publication. This was in 1926, where it appeared under the name of Philothée O'Neddy as vol. 13 of the *Bibliothèque romantique*, ed. Henri Girard, and included letters between Dondey and Ernest Havet not previously published. Two years after his death appeared the volume of *Poésies posthumes de Philothée O'Neddy (Théophile Dondey)*, and a year later *Œuvres en prose: Romans et contes—critique théâtrale—lettres*. There is very little criticism devoted to Dondey. His lifelong friend Ernest Havet published a *Notice sur Philothée O'Neddy*. Théophile Gautier included a brief "medallion" on the poet in his *History of Romanticism* and Valéry Larbaud devoted a short monograph to him entitled *Théophile Dondey de Santeny (1811–1875)*.

54. God is "le moi de l'infini [the 'I' of the infinite]" (*Poésies posthumes*, p. 456).

55. See the 1837 fragment entitled "Fièvre de l'époque" (Fever of our times): "Or, chacun d'entre nous, dans sa prose ou ses vers, / A quotidiennement le malheureux travers / De mettre à nu son *moi*, de décrire les phases / De son cœur—d'en trahir les occultes emphases / …A l'excès, pour ma part, j'ai ce tempérament, / Je prends mon *moi* pour thème avec emportement. / Volontiers je traduis, en phrases cadencées, / Le rhythme intérieur du bal de mes pensées [Now, each of us, in his prose or his verse, / Has the daily misfortune / Of laying bear his *I*, of describing the movements / Of his heart—betraying its hidden obsessions / …For my part, I'm all too much this way / And enthusiastically take my *I* for theme. / I willingly set in measured lines / The rhythm that guides the danse of my thoughts]" (Théophile Dondey, *Poésies posthumes*, p. 145); and: "Voici l'un de ces chants: mon *moi*, ma fantaisie, / Ont un fidèle écho dans cette poésie. / Artistes incomplets, mes frères,—puissiez-vous / Y sentir palpiter le mal qui nous tient tous! [Here is one of those songs: my *I*, my fantasy / Find a faithful echo in this poetry. / Incomplete artists, brothers,—may you feel / The lines pulse with the sickness that grips us all]" (p. 146).

56. Ibid., p. 443 (original emphasis).

57. Ibid., p. 442.

58. "Descartes reste encore sublime [Descartes still remains sublime]" (ibid., p. 443).

59. This absolute distinction between thought and sensuous existence is also expressed in lines from "Les Rhapsodies du Vidame," composed from 1838–46: "Vois-tu, je suis de ceux qui ne peuvent pas croire / Que la pensée—un bien qui prime et passe en gloire / Les beautés, les splendeurs, les miracles divers / Que paraît contenir le visible univers— / Habite seulement dans la machine humaine, / Et n'ait pas l'infini, l'absolu pour domaine [Do you see, I am one of those who cannot believe / That thought—a good whose glory exceeds / All diverse beauties, splendours and miracles / That the visible universe seems to contain— / Only inhabits the human machine, / And has not the infinite, the absolute, for domain]" (*Poésies posthumes*,

p. 250). Thought, that absolute which grounds the subject in the *Viélléités philosophiques*, is here opposed to the variorum of sensuous existence.

60. Ibid., p. 476.
61. Ibid., p. 477.
62. On Dondey's funeral, see Valéry Larbaud, *Dondey de Santeny*, p. 37.
63. *Poésies posthumes*, pp. 262–63.
64. " . . . je n'ai créé mon œuvre que par *élimination*, et toute vérité acquise ne naissait que de la perte d'une impression qui, ayant étincelé, s'était consumée et me permettait, grâce à ses ténèbres dégagées, d'avancer profondément dans la sensation des Ténèbres absolues. La Destruction fut ma Béatrice" (Stéphane Mallarmé, *Correspondance 1862–1871*, pp. 245–46). Cf. also the letter to Villiers de L'Isle-Adam of the same year: "unlike you . . . I have not had a Spirit at my disposal—and you will be terrified to learn that I have arrived at the Idea of the Universe entirely through sensation (and that to preserve an indelible notion of the pure Void, for example, I have had to impose on my mind the feeling of absolute emptiness). The mirror in which I have found Being reflected has been, for the most part, Horror [je n'ai pu . . . comme vous disposer d'un Esprit—et vous serez terrifié d'apprendre que je suis arrivé à l'Idée de l'Univers par la seule sensation (et que, par exemple, pour garder une notion ineffaçable du Néant pur, j'ai dû imposer à mon cerveau la sensation du vide absolu). Le miroir qui m'a réfléchi l'Etre a été le plus souvent l'Horreur]" (p. 259).
65. Stéphane Mallarmé, *Œuvres*, p. 434.
66. "And of Midnight the presence remains in the vision of a room from when the mysterious furniture arrests a vague shuddering of thought . . . while freezes (within a moving limit) the former place where fell the hour in a calm narcotic of *I* long known in dreams" (ibid., p. 435).
67. "It is the pure dream of a Midnight, vanished in itself, and whose identifiable Light, which alone remains at the heart of its finishing, and that plunged in darkness, summarizes its barrenness on the pallor of an open book the table offers up" (ibid.).
68. "The character who, believing only in the existence of the Absolute, imagines himself to be everywhere in a dream (he acts from the point of view of the Absolute), thinks action futile, for there is and there is not chance—he reduces chance to *Infinity*" (ibid., p. 442).
69. "Infinity at last escapes the family, who have suffered from it—old space—no chance. They were right to deny it—his life—that there might be the absolute. This was supposed to take place through the permutations of Infinity in relation to the Absolute" (ibid., p. 434).
70. Ibid., p. 442.
71. Ibid., pp. 457–77.
72. *Hasard*, whether a particular event should seem to confirm or deny it, is always affirmed as Idea, as Infinite, beyond the vicissitudes of actual existence: "Bref dans un acte où le hasard est en jeu, c'est toujours le hasard qui accomplit sa propre

Idée en s'affirmant ou se niant. Devant son existence la négation et l'affirmation viennent échouer. Il contient l'Absurde—l'implique, mais à l'état latent et l'empêche d'exister: ce qui permet à l'Infini d'être. [In short, in an action which puts chance into play, it is always chance which accomplishes its own Idea by affirming or denying itself. Confronted with its existence, negation and affirmation both fail. Chance contains the Absurd—implies it, but at a latent stage, and prevents it from existing; this allows the Infinite to be]" (ibid., p. 441).

73. Cf. "Crise de vers": "L'œuvre implique la disparition élocutoire du poëte, qui cède l'initiative aux mots, par le heurt de leur inégalité mobilisés; ils s'allument de reflets réciproques comme une virtuelle traînée de feux sur des pierreries, remplaçant la respiration perceptible en l'ancien souffle lyrique ou la direction personnelle enthousiaste de la phrase. [The work implies the elocutory disappearance of the poet, who yields the initiative to words, set into motion by the jostling of their inequality; they light up with reciprocal reflections like a virtual string of fires across jewel stones, replacing the respiration perceptible in the breath of ancient lyric or the enthusiastic personal direction given to the line]" (ibid., p. 366).

74. In *Revolution*, Julia Kristeva sees Mallarmé's poetic practice, exemplified by the syntax of "Un coup de dés," as constituting an ethics: "*Igitur*—the wild panic of reason, the logical conclusion of madness—will not take place: what takes its place so as to bring about the expenditure of logic is the syntax of *A Throw of the Dice*" (p. 231; *La Révolution*, p. 202); this logical expenditure is, in Kristeva's terms, a practice, and as such, a negation of the narcissism of the semiotic, a gesture towards the other, and, consequently, an ethics: "'Ethics' should be understood here to mean the negativizing of narcissism within a *practice*. . . . Practice, such as we have defined it, positing and dissolving meaning and the unity of the subject, therefore encompasses the ethical. . . . Finally, our notion of the ethical as coextensive with textual practice separates us from the 'scientific morality' that would like to found a normative, albeit apparently libertarian, ethics based on knowledge" (pp. 233–34; 203–4). See also "Le sujet en progrès" in *Polylogue*, pp. 68–69. This understanding of linguistic practice and ethics will be taken up in the last chapter.

75. " ...until at last, my hands drawn a moment from my eyes, where I had laid them so as not to see my face disappear into a dreadful sensation of eternity, in which the room seemed to expire, it appeared to me to be the horror of that eternity. And when again I opened my eyes to the depths of the mirror I saw the character of horror, the ghost of horror absorbing little by little what remained of feeling and of pain into the glass, feeding its horror on the ultimate shudders of the illusions and on the instability of the hangings, and taking shape by rarifying the mirror to an unheard-of purity" (Mallarmé, *Œuvres*, pp. 440–41). Like Zola in relation to Lazare, Mallarmé seems to have depicted his own anxieties in his character. In a letter of May 14, 1867, he wrote to Henri Cazalis, "je tombai, victorieux, éperdument et infiniment—jusqu'à ce qu'enfin je me sois revu un jour devant ma glace de Venise, tel que je m'étais oublié plusieurs mois auparavant. J'avoue du reste, mais à toi seul, que j'ai encore besoin, tant ont été grandes les avanies de mon tri-

omphe, de me regarder dans cette glace pour penser et que si elle n'était pas devant la table où je t'écris cette lettre, je redeviendrais le Néant. C'est t'apprendre que je suis maintenant impersonnel et non plus Stéphane que tu as connu,—mais une aptitude qu'a l'Univers spirituel à se voir et à se développer, à travers ce qui fut moi [I fell, victorious and lost, endlessly—until at last one day I saw myself again in front of my Venetian glass, the same person that I had forgotten several months before. I will admit, moreover—although to you alone—that my victory has been so humiliating that I still need to look at myself in that mirror in order to think and that were it not in front of the table where I am writing you this letter, I would once again become Nothingness. This is to tell you that I am now impersonal and no longer Stéphane whom you have known—but an aptitude which the spiritual Universe has for seeing itself and for developing itself across what was I]" (*Correspondance*, pp. 241–42). Mallarmé has attributed feelings to his fictional character, however, which are significantly different from his own, as expressed here. In the letter the mirror is a reassurance; in *Igitur* it is an image of the devouring Néant itself. One could say that Mallarmé has displaced into fictional representation an expression of a fear about representation itself, the moment when even the mirror reveals itself as a form of alienated permanence and writing.

76. There is, however, in Mallarmé's writings, an understanding of literature as the means for restoring the material "truth" to language, as if to mitigate, in some way, its grim negativity. In *Crise de vers*, for example, he regrets "que le discours défaille à exprimer les objets par des touches y répondant en coloris ou en allure, lesquelles existent dans l'instrument de la voix, parmi les langages et quelquefois chez un. A côté d'*ombre*, opaque, *ténèbres* se fonce peu; quelle déception, devant la perversité conférant à *jour* comme à *nuit*, contradictoirement, des timbres obscur ici, là clair. Le souhait d'un terme de splendeur brillant, ou qu'il s'éteigne, inverse; quant à des alternatives lumineuses simples—*Seulement, sachons n'existerait pas le vers*: lui, philosophiquement rémunère le défaut des langues, complément supérieure [that discours falters when called on to express objects by strokes corresponding to them in coloring or aspect, which exist in the instrument of the voice, among languages and sometimes within a single one. Next to the opacity of *shadow*, the word *darkness* scarcely dims; what disappointment when faced with the perversity that confers on *day* and *night*, against their nature, tones here obscure, there clear. The longing for some term of brilliant splendour, or, conversely, its extinction; as for simple luminous alternatives—*Simply, we should be aware, verse would not exist*, for it, their superior complement, redeems philosophically the failings of tongues]" (*Œuvres*, p. 364). Still, it is a "philosophical" mitigation, which suggests a return to the negativity of abstract thought.

77. For example, Maurice Blanchot's chapter on "Literature and the Right to Death" contains a passage specifically connecting *Crise de vers* with the "Sense Certainty" section from the *Phenomenology* (see *Fire*, pp. 322–28; *Feu*, pp. 312–17). See also Blanchot's "L'Expérience de Mallarmé" and "L'Expérience d'Igitur" in *L'Espace littéraire*, pp. 32–48 and 133–49; Paul de Man, "Le Néant poétique: commentaire

d'un Sonnet hermétique de Mallarmé," pp. 63–75; Jean-Pierre Richard, *L'Univers imaginaire de Mallarmé*; Georges Poulet, "La 'Prose' de Mallarmé" in *Les Métamorphoses du cercle*, pp. 439–57; Andrzej Warminski, "Dreadful Reading." In *Théories du sujet* (Paris: Seuil, 1982), Alain Badiou speaks of Mallarmé as one of the great French dialecticians. The reading of Mallarmé as poet of the absolute has come under question in Vincent Kaufmann's *Le Livre et ses adresses*. It has been deconstructed in Derrida's reading of "Mimique" through, for example, the "cheville syntactique" that complicates the absolute difference between syntax and reference and through his reading of the fold ("The Double Session" in *Dissemination*, pp. 227–85; "La double séance" in *La Dissémination*, pp. 257–317). Whether or not this absolute sublimation works is not the question here; rather we are interested in the sheer perception that such an absolute difference exists in self-identity and the reaction to that perception.

78. Cf. for example, Roger Dragonetti, "Métaphysique et poétique dans l'œuvre de Mallarmé (*Hérodiade, Igitur, Le Coup de dés*)," p. 371: "Neither Hegelian nor Platonic nor Cartesian, the speculation of Mallarmé's mirror withdraws from the traditional dialectic of truth, becoming the empty site of a prismatic dissolution of all the subject's imaginary identities: of all images and, equally, of all thought open to its ontological mystery. Depersonalized, the author thus becomes a pure, vacuous center, an anonymous aptitude for receiving Language's most secret summations. This process of effacement, inseparable from the emergence of Language as an autonomous producer of sense-effects, corresponds to Mallarmé's idea of Literature as the *Science* of the text." While I would certainly agree that the impersonal void of the subject is not Hegelian according to the popular understanding of the term, which thinks of it as a conversion of conceptual negativity into historical positivity, I would also argue that Mallarmé, if unbeknownst to himself, is part of an ongoing reading of Hegel. I would also differ from Dragonetti's brilliant interpretation in his restriction of this subjective negativity to a particular literary practice—it is rather, as I am attempting to demonstrate, the general condition of thought for Mallarmé.

79. "Mallarmé, Yeats and the Post-Romantic Predicament," Ph.D. diss., Harvard University, 1961.

80. *Birth of Tragedy*, p. 52 (original emphasis). Cf. *The Gay Science*, p. 163: "As an aesthetic phenomenon existence is still *bearable* for us."

81. Cf. Emmanuel Levinas, "The Meaning of Meaning" in *Outside the Subject*, pp. 90–95; and Chapter 7 of this volume.

82. "Insofar as the subject is the artist, however, he has already been released from his individual will, and has become, as it were, the medium through which the one truly existent subject celebrates his release in appearance" (p. 52).

83. *Daybreak*, p. 76.

84. "Rhetoric of Tropes (*Nietzsche*)" in *Allegories of Reading*, pp. 103–18.

85. *The Gay Science*, p. 297. Nietzsche early asserts that consciousness, this mirroring of the self, is normally understood to constitute the unity or "kernel" of the individual (see p. 85).

86. " ...the subtlety and strength of consciousness always were proportionate to a man's (or animals's) *capacity for communication*, and as if this capacity in turn were proportionate to the *need for communication*" (*The Gay Science*, p. 298). "Supposing that this observation is correct, I may now proceed to the surmise that *consciousness has developed only under the pressure of the need for communication*" (p. 298). "Consciousness is really only a net of communication between human beings" (p. 298). "Man, like every living being, thinks continually without knowing it; the thinking that rises to *consciousness* is only the smallest part of all this—the most superficial and worst part—for only this conscious thinking *takes the form of words, which is to say signs of communication*, and this fact uncovers the origin of consciousness" (p. 299).

87. "That our actions, thoughts, feelings, and movements enter our own consciousness—at least a part of them—that is the result of a 'must' that for a terribly long time lorded it over man" (ibid., p. 298). Cf. also the section entitled "A firm reputation" (p. 230) and the following passage, in which Nietzsche even more explicitly identifies the persistence of subjective identity with the coercion of responsibility: "You must be recognizable, express your intimacy by *precise* and *constant* signs—otherwise you will be dangerous; and if you are evil, your capacity for disguising yourself will be the worst thing of all for the herd; we despise the secret, unknowable being. Consequently, the requirement of truth presupposes knowability and the persistence of the person" (quoted in Pierre Klossowski, p. 317).

88. *The Gay Science*, p. 299. Cf. also: "Owing to the nature of *animal consciousness*, the world of which we can become conscious is only a surface- and sign-world, a world that is made common and meaner; whatever becomes conscious *becomes* by the same token shallow, thin, relatively stupid, general, sign, herd signal; all becoming conscious involves a great and thorough corruption, falsification, reduction to superficialities, and generalization. Ultimately, the growth of consciousness becomes a danger; and anyone who lives among the most conscious Europeans even knows that it is a disease" (pp. 299–300).

89. "At Noon," in *Thus Spoke Zarathustra*, p. 278; see also from the same section: "What has happened to me? Listen! Did time perhaps fly away? Do I not fall? Did I not fall—listen!—into the well of eternity?" (p. 277). Cf. also Zarathustra's denunciation of contempt towards the earthly, towards the moment: "Alas, do you preach patience with the earthly? It is the earthly that has too much patience with you, blasphemers!... As yet he knew only tears and the melancholy of the Hebrew, and hatred of the good and just—the Hebrew Jesus: then the longing for death overcame him. Would that he had remained in the wilderness and far from the good and the just! Perhaps he would have learned to live and to love the earth—and laughter too" ("On Free Death," p. 73).

90. Quoted in Klossowski, *Nietzsche*, p. 318. On the Eternal Return see "On the Vision and the Riddle" in *Thus Spoke Zarathustra*: "'Behold,' I continued, 'this moment! From this gateway, Moment, a long eternal lane leads *backward*: behind us lies an eternity. Must not whatever *can* walk have walked on this lane before? Must not whatever *can* happen have happened, have been done, have passed by before?...

and I and you in the gateway, whispering together, whispering of eternal things—must not all of us have been there before? And return and walk in that other lane, out there, before us, in this long dreadful lane—must we not eternally return?' " (p. 158). That its revelation is at the heart of the jubilant experience of high noon and that this experience was, moreover, one which Nietzsche himself had known, seem to be confirmed by a letter written by him at Sils-Maria on Aug. 14, 1881 (quoted in Klossowski, pp. 91–92). Klossowski gives an analysis, at once profound and brilliant, of the disruptive implications of the Eternal Return on the Aristotelean principle of identity, summarized in his assertion, "What the Eternal Return implies as a doctrine is no more and no less than the insignificance of the *once and for all* of the principle of identity and non-contradiction, the basis of human understanding" (p. 314). This undermining of the identity principle would apply, according to Klossowski, to subjectivity itself, bringing the philosopher to understand himself as something frighteningly other than the vulgar mask by which others knew him: "Ce masque, que Nietzsche rejette comme une falsification de soi, couvre l'horrifiant hasard que Nietzsche est à lui-même. Jusqu'à ce que Nietzsche en vienne à adhérer à la discontinuité et le hasard cesse d'être horrifiant et devient une fortuité joyeuse [This disguise, which Nietzsche rejected as a self-falsification, covers over the horrifying happenstance that Nietszche is to himself. Until Nietzsche is able to adhere to discontinuity and chance ceases to be horrifying and becomes a joyous accident]" (p. 280).

91. On the importance of Kojève for postwar French thought see Louis Althusser, "The Return to Hegel" in *Specter of Hegel*, pp. 173–84; Vincent Descombes, *Le Même et l'Autre*; and *Parallax* 4 (Feb. 1997). On his role as statesman and *éminence grise* under de Gaulle, see Dominique Auffret, *Alexandre Kojève: La Philosophie, l'Etat, la fin de l'Histoire*, and Shadia B. Drury, *Alexandre Kojève: The Roots of Postmodern Politics*. In *Lacan—Le Maître absolu*, Mikkel Borch-Jacobsen offers a detailed description of Kojève's influence on Lacanian theory; see especially his discussion of subjectivity in Lacan's writings (pp. 221–33).

92. " . . . to accept the fact of death without dissembling [*sans détours*] and to describe, on the three philosophical registers, its significance and import. Now, this is precisely what the philosophers before Hegel neglected to do" (Kojève, p. 548).

93. "Man accedes to God only *after his death*, and it is only then that he fully manifests his 'spirituality.' Now, according to Hegel, 'spiritual' or 'dialectical' being is necessarily *temporal* and *finite*. The Christian notion of an infinite and eternal Spirit is a contradiction in itself: an infinite being is of necessity given-static-Being that is 'natural' and eternally identical to itself; and a created or created 'dynamic' being is necessarily limited in time, which is to say essentially mortal" (Kojève, p. 537).

94. On Kant, see *Conflict*, p. 151, and the discussion in Chapter 1.

95. Emmanuel Levinas will hold a similar view of the relation between death and history, but in his case that relation would lead not to a definition of the human, but instead to a devaluation of history. See *Totality and Infinity*, p. 182; *Totalité et infini*, p. 199: "The surplus that language involves with respect to all the works and labors that manifest a man measures the distance between the living man and

the dead—who, however, is alone recognized by history, which approaches him objectively in his work or his heritage"; and p. 52; 45: "When man truly approaches the Other he is uprooted from history."

96. "The sense-*essence* of a thing is, as they say, that thing itself less its *existence*. Now, the 'subtraction' which removes being from Being is none other than Time, which forces Being out of the present, in which it *is*, and into the past, in which it *is not* (is no longer), and in which it is nothing but pure *sense* (or essence without existence).... By the same token, since it is the same past Being which is in the present and will be in the future (where, *not yet being*, it is also essence without existence), one can say that Being has a goal (and this goal, which is the transformation of the future into the present or the bestowing of existence on essence, is nothing but the transformation of the present into past, which is to say of Being into Concept): which can also be expressed by saying that the very being of Being has a sense" (Kojève, p. 544).

97. Ibid., pp. 541–42.

98. "Action reverses the 'natural' flow of Time in which the given-Being which is temporal or which has a sense endures. Action introduces the primacy of the *future* into Time, in which Being *is* and is *given* only in the present. For the present of Action is the realization of a project for the future: in and by Action (or better: as Action), the future has a *real presence* as future. Certainly, the project *realizes* itself in the present and it is in the past insofar as it is already *realized*. But the present, and therefore the past, of the project are penetrated and determined by the future, which subsists in it under the form of discourse" (p. 547n). See also p. 548.

99. Ibid., p. 531.

100. Ibid., p. 546. Cf.: "If *Substance*, conceived of as natural given-static-Being (*Sein*), has Identity (with itself) for its ontological grounding, the *Subject* of Discourse which reveals that being and itself, or in other words Man, has Negativity for its ultimate basis" (p. 531).

101. Ibid., p. 546.

102. See the discussion in Chapter 6 of the split subject in Lacan.

103. Kojève, p. 565. Cf.: "And the entity which in its very being is Action 'appears' (on the phenomenological level) to itself and to others as irreducibly *mortal*. That is why, in the text just cited, Hegel can call *death* that "unreality" which is Negativity or the 'negative-or-negating-entity.' But if Man is Action, and if Action is Negativity 'appearing' as death, Man, in his human or verbal existence, is nothing but a *death* that is conscious of itself and more or less differed. Therefore: to account philosophically for Discourse, or for Man insofar as he is verbal, is to accept the fact of death without dissembling [sans détours] and to describe, on the three philosophical registers, its significance and import. Now, this is precisely what the philosophers before Hegel neglected to do" (p. 548).

104. Ibid., p. 564. Cf.: "Hegel repeatedly insists on the fact that it is death which is the ultimate manifestation and, one might say, 'realization' of the Universal in empirical existence" (p. 564).

105. Ibid., p. 550.

106. See ibid., p. 553: "Man . . . can spontaneously transcend himself and go, of his own, beyond his 'innate nature,' even while remaining what he is, which is to say a *human* being. But, for the animal which serves him as a support, such transcendance means death. Only, in the *human* animal, that death is no longer external: he is himself (insofar as he is a man) the cause of his death (insofar as he is an animal)."

107. Ibid., p. 548. See also: "Consequently Hegel's 'dialectical' or anthropological philosophy is, in the final analysis, *a philosophy of death* (or, which is the same thing, of atheism)" (p. 539).

108. On the first page of the "Remarques préliminaires" one reads: "The Absolute is real neither insofar as it is essence ('Logic') nor insofar as it is Nature (existence). Nature is abstract because it sets aside Spirit as an abstraction. Only the Synthesis is concrete, which is to say, Man, in whom the essence of the Absolute is fully realized and revealed as such" (ibid., p. 37). On the following page Kojève identifies this synthesis as absolute Philosophy: "Absolute Philosophy has, as it were, no object, or rather it is itself its own subject. The All [the synthesis of existence and essence] alone possesses a concrete reality. Philosophy, by studying that concrete reality, consequently studies Totality. That Totality implies consciousness as well as absolute Philosophy (since it is effectively realized by Hegel)" (p. 38).

109. Ibid., p. 539.

110. See this chapter, note 51.

111. Kojève, pp. 531–32.

112. "What we have here [in Hegel's interpretation of the Terror] is an internalization of absolute freedom, which cannot exist immediately, that is, as a nature. Hegel's thought is quite obscure here. Although it could well culminate in a justification of the revolution, in fact, it interprets the failure of that revolution. Nor, it seems, does Hegel's thought lead us to a City of God above, or parallel to, the terrestrial city. For the 'moral world view' fails in turn. Hegel's solution is not easily ascertainable" (*Genesis*, p. 455; *Genèse*, p. 441).

113. Kojève, p. 557.

114. *Fire*, p. 320; *Feu*, p. 310.

115. "Now, we have seen [in the analysis of the Master/Slave dialectic] that death, when braved voluntarily in a negating struggle, is precisely the most authentic realization and manifestation of absolute individual liberty. It is thus clearly in and by Terror that this liberty is propagated throughout society, and it cannot be attained within a 'tolerant' State, which does not take its citizens seriously enough to assure them their political right to death [qui ne prend pas ses citoyens au sérieux pour leur assurer leur droit politique à la mort]" (Kojève, p. 558).

116. *Phenomenology*, p. 360. See our discussion of this passage in Chapter 1.

117. *Genesis*, p. 455; *Genèse*, p. 441.

118. As Kojève quotes Hegel: "War and the condition-of-being-a-soldier are the objectively-real sacrifice of the personal-I, the danger of death for the particular which is the contemplation (Anschauen) of his abstract immediate Negativity; just

as war is equally the immediately positive personal-I of the particular... such [that in it] each individual, insofar as it is a present particular, creates (macht) itself as absolute power (Macht), contemplates itself as [being] absolutely free, as universal Negativity [existing] for itself and really against another (Anderes). It is in war that this is granted (gewärht) to the particular: war is [a] crime [committed] *for the Universal* [= the State]; the goal [of war is] the conservation [mediated by the negation] of everything [= the State] against the enemy, who is preparing to destroy that everything. This alienation (Entäusserung) [of the Particular from the Universal] must have precisely that abstract form, and be deprived-of-individuality; death must be received and given coldly; not by means of a commented (statarische) combat, in which the particular perceives the adversary and kills him out of immediate hatred; no, death is given and received in-the-void (leer),—*impersonally*, out of the smoke and powder [La condition-de-soldat et la guerre sont le sacrifice objectivement-réel du Moi-personnel, le danger de mort pour le particulier,—cette contemplation (Anschauen) de sa Négativité abstraite immédiate ; de même que la guerre est également le Moi-personnel immédiatement positif du particulier,... de sorte [qu'en elle] chacun, en tant que ce particulier-ci, se crée (macht) soi-même comme puissance (Macht) absolue, se contemple comme [étant] absolument libre, comme Négativité universelle [existant] pour soi et réellement contre un autre (Anderes). C'est dans la guerre que ceci est permis (gewärht) au particulier: elle est [un] crime [commis] pour l'Universel [= l'Etat]; le but [de la guerre est] la conservation [médiatisée par la négation] du tout [= Etat] contre l'ennemi, qui s'apprête à détruire ce tout. Cette aliénation (Entäusserung) [du Particulier à l'Universel] doit avoir précisément cette forme abstraite, être privée-d'individualité; la mort doit être reçue et donnée froidement; non pas par un combat commenté (statarische), où le particulier aperçoit l'adversaire et le tue dans une haine immédiate; non, la mort est donnée et reçue dans-le-vide (leer),—impersonnellement, à partir de la fumée de la poudre]" (p. 560).

119. Kojève, p. 560.
120. *Phenomenology*, p. 362.
121. *Being and Time*, p. 351.
122. In Kant, for example, "the ontological concept of the subject *characterizes not the Selfhood of the 'I' qua Self, but the selfsameness and steadiness of something that is always present-at-hand*. To define the 'I' ontologically as '*subject*' means to regard it as something always present-at-hand. The Being of the 'I' is understood as the Reality of the *res cogitans*" (*Being and Time*, p. 367). Cf. also: "How are we to conceive this unity? How can Dasein exist as a unity in the ways and possibilities of its Being which we have mentioned? Manifestly, it can so exist only in such a way that it *is itself* this Being in its essential possibilities—that in each case I am this entity. The 'I' seems to 'hold together' the totality of the structural whole. In the 'ontology' of this entity, the 'I' and the 'Self' have been conceived from the earliest times as the supporting ground (as substance or subject)" (p. 365).
123. See "The Being of the Entities Encountered in the Environment" and "How the Worldly Character of the Environment Announces Itself in Entities

Within-the-World," in *Being and Time*, pp. 95–107. On circumspection, see pp. 98, 159–60.

124. "Care is Being-towards-death. We have defined 'anticipatory resoluteness' as authentic Being towards the possibility which we have characterized as Dasein's utter impossibility" (*Being and Time*, p. 378).

125. Ibid., p. 362.

126. Ibid., p. 330.

127. Ibid. (trans. modified).

128. Ibid., p. 374. Cf. also: "Temporality makes possible the unity of existence, facticity, and falling, and in this way constitutes primordially the totality of the structure of care" (p. 376).

129. Ibid., p. 373.

130. Ibid. Cf. also: "Primordial and authentic temporality temporalizes itself in terms of the authentic future and in such a way that in having been futurally, it first of all awakens the present. *The primary phenomenon of primordial and authentic temporality is the future*" (p. 378).

131. "'As long as' Dasein factically exists, it is never past [vergangen], but it always is indeed as already having *been*, in the sense of the 'I *am*-as-having-been.' On the other hand, we call an entity 'past,' when it is no longer present-at-hand. Therefore Dasein, in existing, can never establish itself as a fact which is present-at-hand, arising and passing away 'in the course of time,' with a bit of it past already" (ibid., p. 376).

132. Kojève, p. 548.

133. *Being and Time*, p. 331.

134. "The appeal [of conscience] calls back by calling forth; it calls Dasein *forth* to the possibility of taking over, in existing, even that thrown entity which it is; it calls Dasein *back* to its thrownness so as to understand this thrownness as the null basis which it has to take up into existence. This calling-back in which conscience calls forth, gives Dasein to understand that Dasein itself—the null basis for its null projection, standing in the possibility of its Being—is to bring itself back to itself from its lostness in the 'they'; and this means that it *is guilty*" (ibid., p. 333).

135. Ibid., p. 334.

136. "This fleeing has been described as a fleeing in the face of the uncanniness which is basically determinative for individualized Being-in-the-world. Uncanniness reveals itself authentically in the basic state-of-mind of anxiety; and, as the most elemental way in which thrown Dasein is disclosed, it puts Dasein's Being-in-the-world face to face with the 'nothing' of the world; in the face of this 'nothing,' Dasein is anxious with anxiety about its ownmost potentiality-for-Being" (ibid., p. 321).

137. Ibid., p. 369.

138. "In the prevalent way of saying 'I,' it is constantly suggested that what we have in advance is a Self-Thing, persistently present-at-hand; the ontological question of the Being of the Self must turn away from any such suggestion. *Care does not need to be founded in a Self. But existentiality, as constitutive for care, provides the ontological*

constitution of Dasein's Self-constancy, to which there belongs, in accordance with the full structural content of care, its Being-fallen factically into non-Self-constancy. When fully conceived, the care-structure includes the phenomenon of Selfhood" (ibid., p. 370).

139. Ibid., p. 346. Cf. also: "As resolute, Dasein is already *taking action*. The term 'take action' is one which we are purposely avoiding. For in the first place this term must be taken so broadly that 'activity' [Aktivität] will also embrace the passivity of resistance... " (p. 347).

140. See Elaine Scarry's *The Body in Pain*, p. 35: "Intense pain is also language-destroying: as the content of one's world disintegrates, so the content of one's language disintegrates; as the self disintegrates, so that which would express and project the self is robbed of its source and its subject. World, self, and voice are lost, or nearly lost, through the intense pain of torture."

141. *Being and Time*, p. 378. Cf. also: "Resoluteness does not just 'have' a connection with anticipation, as with something other than itself. *It harbours in itself authentic Being-towards-death, as the possible existentiell modality of its own authenticity*" (p. 353).

142. Ibid., p. 356.

143. Ibid., p. 354.

144. "*But the state-of-mind which can hold open the utter and constant threat to itself arising from Dasein's ownmost individualized Being, is anxiety*. In this state-of-mind, Dasein finds itself *face to face* with the 'nothing' of the possible impossibility of its existence. Anxiety is anxious *about* the potentiality-for-Being of the entity so destined [des so bestimmten Seienden], and in this way it discloses the uttermost possibility. Anticipation utterly individualizes Dasein, and allows it, in this individualization of itself, to become certain of the totality of its potentiality-for-Being... Being towards death is essentially anxiety" (ibid., p. 310).

145. Ibid., p. 295.

146. A recent book demonstrates the pervasive and continuing reluctance to recognize the fundamental role of death in Heidegger's thinking on subjectivity. François Raffoul, in his otherwise excellent *Heidegger and the Subject*, does not list "death" in his index. One can also note that the relation between the individual and the *Gerede* of the "they" in Being and Time is very similar to the relation between language and the I in Sartre's *Being and Nothingness*, especially pp. 413–30; *L'Etre et le néant*, pp. 484–503. On the "face-to-face" with death in Hegel, see Chapter 6.

Chapter 3. Nerval in Context: The Authority of Madness

1. Théophile Gautier, "Gérard de Nerval," in *Portraits*, pp. 35–36.
2. Théophile Gautier, *History of Romanticism* in *Works*, vol. 16, pp. 17–18; *Histoire du romantisme* in *Œuvres*, vol. 9, p. 3. For a general description of the Bousingos, see Enid Starkie, *Pétrus Borel*.
3. *History*, pp. 100–101; *Histoire*, p. 74.
4. *History*, p. 101; *Histoire*, p. 74.

5. "La littérature excentrique" developed into a subgenre in the Paris of the mid-nineteenth century. See, for example, Charles Nodier, "Bibliographie des Fous"; Lorédan Larchey, *Les Excentricités du langage*; and Daniel Sangsue, *Le Récit excentrique*.

6. Nerval, "A Jules Janin" in *Lorely* in *Œuvres*, vol. 3, p. 4. In the article itself (*Journal des débats*, March 1, 1841), Janin speaks of himself as writing an "elegy which is more than a posthumous elegy—a hundred times more sad and far more solemn."

7. Nerval, "A Alexandre Dumas" in *Les Filles du feu* in *Œuvres*, vol. 3, p. 458.

8. Théophile Gautier, *Portraits*, pp. 65–66.

9. E.g. in *Portraits*: "Gérard's style was a lamp bringing light into the darkness of thought and words" (p. 12); "the pure and limpid style of these works" (p. 22); "Gérard's mental balance had undoubtedly been off long before any of us noticed it. This was all the more difficult to suspect, for never had a style been more clear, more limpid, more reasonable, in a word, than his; even when his sickness had incontestably reached his mind, all the qualities of his intelligence still remained intact. Not a mistake, not an error, not an impropriety betrayed the disorder of his intellectual faculties. Until the end he remained impeccable" (pp. 36–37).

10. "Si un écrivain . . . a cherché à se définir laborieusement à lui-même, à saisir, à éclairer des nuances troubles, des lois profondes, des impressions presque insaisissables de l'âme humaine, c'est Gérard de Nerval" (Proust, *Contre Saint-Beuve*, p. 237).

11. "Cette folie est tellement le développement de son originalité littéraire dans ce qu'elle a d'essentiel, qu'il la décrit au fur et à mesure qu'il l'éprouve" (ibid., p. 234).

12. Gautier, *Portraits*, p. 23.

13. On Nerval's interest in *contrefaçon*, or literary piracy, see Jules Janin, "Gérard de Nerval," in *Le Journal des débats*. See also the letter to his father written from Vienna at the end of November 1839: "Three pirated editions of my work [*Léo Burckart*] have appeared in Belgium, Holland and Stuttgart" (Nerval, *Œuvres*, vol. 1, p. 1327); the letter to his father from Liège on Nov. 17, 1840: "I have taken advantage of my stay in Brussels to do a work on literary piracy; I believe I have found a way to solve the problem and I shall present a paper on it when I return. It is simply a matter of obtaining from the House that literary products be assimilated to industrial products and that one be able to obtain, so to speak, an import license. I have seen Mr. Rogier, the minister of Public Works, about this and he raised no serious objections" (p. 1361); the letter to Godefroy, from Passy, Sept. 23, 1854: "would you be so good as to write to England and Spain to insure rights there [pour m'y assurer la propriété] for my new book, entitled *Aurélia*" (vol. 3, p. 891).

14. Cf. for example, the following passage in a letter from Hölderlin to his brother, cited by Heidegger: "Man comes together in it [poetry] and it gives him calm, not an empty but a living calm, in which all his powers are alert and, by their inner harmony alone, can be recognized outside their exercise. Poetry draws men close and brings them together, *not like play, in which they are simply united, with*

everyone forgetting himself and no one's living features coming to light [sammelt sich der Mensch bei ihr [der Poësie] und sie gibt ihm Ruhe, nicht die leere, sondern die lebendige Ruhe, wo alle Kräfte regsam sind, und nur wegen ihrer innigen Harmonie nicht als thätig erkannt werden. Sie nähert die Menschen und bringt sie zusammen, *nicht wie das Spiel, wo sie nur dadurch vereiniget sind, dass jeder sich vergisst und die lebendige Eigenthümlichkeit von keinem zum Vorschein kommt*]" (Martin Heidegger, "Hölderlins Hymnen 'Germanien,'" p. 8, emphasis added).

15. Cf. Gilles Deleuze, *The Fold*, p. 30; *Le pli*, p. 42.

16. Michel Foucault, *Histoire*, p. 371. The pages quoted here and following do not appear in the English translation (*Madness and Civilization*).

17. Foucault, *Histoire*, p. 371.

18. Ibid., p. 372.

19. Ibid., emphasis added.

20. It is in these same terms of questioning, penetrating, and disrupting that Foucault describes the relation between the silent discourse of madness and the coherence of an artwork when he speaks of Nietzsche, Van Gogh, and Artaud at the end of his study. The difficult, interrogatory language of madness can only be discerned, he contends, when the discontinuity and disunity of a work are allowed into consideration as elements in their own right and with their own semiotics rather than merely as deficiencies to be reworked into a general aesthetic coherence. "By the madness which interrupts it," he writes, "a work opens a void, a period of silence, a question without answer. It provokes an unreconcilable split in which the world is forced to question itself" (ibid., p. 556).

21. Quoted in Robert Castel, *The Regulation of Madness*, p. 1. For Pinel's own description of his work at *La Salpêtrière*, see his *Traité médico-philosophique sur l'aliénation mentale*. On Hegel's reference to the madness provoked by the Revolution, see *Philosophy of Mind*, p. 135: "In the French revolution... the almost complete collapse of civil society caused many people to become insane." On the history of madness in this period, see Foucault, *Madness and Civilization*, pp. 241–78 (*Histoire de la folie*, pp. 440–530); his *Birth of the Clinic* (*La Naissance de la clinique*); and Daniel Berthold-Bond, *Hegel's Theory of Madness*, pp. 9–35. Berthold-Bond has performed the remarkable feat of convincingly extracting such a "theory" from the handful of pages that Hegel devoted to the topic of insanity.

22. On madness and romantic or metaphysical medicine, see Berthold-Bond, pp. 13–14.

23. See *Lenin and Philosophy*, pp. 136–37; *Positions*, pp. 82–83.

24. See the section on Zola in Chapter 2.

25. *Philosophy of Mind*, pp. 124 and 130.

26. Ibid., pp. 126 and 128.

27. In *Hegel's Theory of Madness* (pp. 26–29), Berthold-Bond argues that insanity represents for Hegel a regression toward an indeterminate state of nature or, as Hegel puts it, in madness the "natural self... gains the mastery over the objective, rational, concrete consciousness" (*Philosophy of Mind*, p. 130). The mad self has thus

surrendered itself to "earthly elements" (p. 124). Again, insanity appears as a resistance to language and sublimation. On madness as an obstruction to totalization, see *Philosophy of Mind*, p. 123: the mad self becomes "engrossed with a single phase of feeling... [and] it fails to assign that phase its proper place"; consequently it "finds itself in contradiction between the totality systematized in its [healthy] consciousness, and the single phase or fixed idea which is not reduced to its proper place."

28. Gérard de Nerval, *Les Filles du feu* in *Œuvres*, vol. 3, p. 449.
29. Letter to Jules Janin, Aug. 24, 1841 (ibid., vol. 1, p. 1380).
30. Ibid., vol. 3, pp. 449–50.
31. Ibid., p. 450.
32. Ibid., pp. 449 and 458.
33. Ibid., p. 458. Although in letters to friends he spoke of the incident as his "maladie," or sickness, in print he continued to reject the contention that he had gone mad. Instead, in the preface, he stated, "I was *thought* mad [*on* m'a cru *fou*]" (emphasis added), and insisted that when the story of his recent experiences was told in full, it would be seen that "it has not entirely lacked reasoning though it has always been free of reason."
34. Cf. the letter to his father from Strasbourg, dated June 4, 1854: "Still, I feel ten times better, whatever people might tell or write you. Rest assured about it. The proof, besides, is that I live as I like and that I am able to write you, as you see, easily and logically enough. Take care of yourself, I shall write my cousin to go see you and to bring you a longer letter since, I must admit, I'm still a bit shaky, and you should take this as a testimony to my good sense, bearing in mind that the weather here has been very bad recently" (ibid., p. 861); to Dr. Blanche, from Cassel, July 1854: "Whether my health is as good as I believe, that must be proved by my work" (p. 882). Cf. also Kofman, p. 22: "with a few exceptions, writing would be for him an effort to block off his delirium, to wipe away every last trace of his madness. Writing would be an *attempt to demonstrate the health of his mind*" (original emphasis).
35. Paul de Man, "Ludwig Binswanger and the Sublimation of the Self" in *Blindness and Insight*, p. 39.
36. *Œuvres*, vol. 3, p. 450.
37. Ibid., pp. 450–51. Nerval also speaks about his tendency to identify with his characters in *Promenades et Souvenirs* (Walks and memories). Cf. ibid., pp. 685–86.
38. Nerval, *Les Filles du feu* in ibid., p. 451.
39. Ibid., p. 458.
40. In ibid., vol. 1, p. 1742. The letter had already been published in 1844 under the title *Le Roman tragique* (The tragic novel) and accompanied by the following note, indicating that there too, it was presented by its author as a fragment, the foretaste of what would turn out to be another *livre infaisable*: "This letter is the preamble to a story which will continue [Scarron's] *Roman comique* by depicting the mores of actors in the time of Louis XIV" (p. 701).
41. Nerval, *Œuvres*, vol. 3, p. 856.

42. "Mes idées sont singulières; ma passion s'entoure de beaucoup de poésie et d'originalité; j'arrange ma vie volontiers comme un roman, les moindres désaccords me choquent" (*Œuvres*, vol. 1, p. 1751). The *Lettres d'amour* are so called by the editors of the Pléiade edition, not by Nerval himself.

43. Ibid., vol. 3, p. 4.

44. Ibid., vol. 1, p. 1380 (original emphasis).

45. On the importance of *charme*, or charm, as a property between the rhetorical and the epistemological in Nerval's texts, see Kofman.

46. *DSM-IV*, for example, lists as the primary psychotic feature in schizophrenic disorders "bizarre delusions" (American Psychiatric Association, *Diagnostic and Statistical Manual*, p. 285) and qualifies these by stating: "Although bizarre delusions are considered to be especially characteristic of Schizophrenia, 'bizarreness' may be difficult to judge, especially across different cultures. Delusions are deemed bizarre if they are clearly implausible and not understandable and do not derive from ordinary life experiences" (p. 275). The primary psychotic characteristic here is thus a subjective, phantasmic experience.

Chapter 4. Playing with Death: 'Les Faux Saulniers'

1. "Ludwig Binswanger and the Sublimation of the Self" in de Man, *Blindness*, pp. 49–50.

2. "Function and Field of Speech and Language" in *Ecrits: A Selection*, pp. 41–42 (trans. modified); "Fonction et champ de la parole" in *Ecrits*, p. 249 (original emphasis).

3. The sublime, typically theorized during this period as a relation between two faculties of the human mind, came almost invariably to be associated with the figure of Isis. In the third critique, Kant asserts: "Perhaps there has never been a more sublime utterance, or a thought more sublimely expressed, than the well-known inscription upon the Temple of *Isis* (Mother *Nature*): 'I am all that is, and that was, and that shall be, and no mortal hath raised the veil from before my face'" (*Judgement*, p. 179). In Schiller's *The Veiled Image at Sais* (1795), the concealed statue of the goddess represents knowledge of the abstract universal ("[The truth,] 'tis changeless, indivisible (Ist sie [die Wahrheit] nicht eine einz'ge, ungeteilte?)" (in *The Poems of Schiller*, p. 191), and it kills the worshipper who confronts it face to face. Also, in Novalis's *The Novices of Sais* the confrontation/revelation of the deity to the initiate serves as a figure for the relation between the individual and the annihilating presence of the absolute. For a detailed description of this relation in terms of the sublime, see Chapter 1.

4. Ora Avni, p. 220.

5. Cf. the discussion of Foucault in Chapter 3.

6. *Les Faux Saulniers* in *Œuvres*, vol. 2, p. 30.

7. Jules Janin, "Gérard de Nerval" in *Le Journal des débats*, Mar. 1, 1841.

8. Interestingly, Jean Hyppolite has asserted that madness reaches its most ex-

treme limit when the individual "does not wish to speak anymore" and "withdraws [in]to itself and rejects all communication"; for Hyppolite, this retreat into silence is the realization of the death instinct ("Hegel's Phenomenology and Psychoanalysis," p. 70). Nerval's silence would appear to signify just the opposite, that is, a retreat from death.

9. Nerval, *Les Faux Saulniers* in *Œuvres*, vol. 2, p. 112.

10. Cf. Ross Chambers, "Literature Deterritorialized," in Denis Hollier, *A New History*, pp. 710–16.

11. See the "Note sur le texte" by Jacques Bony in Nerval, *Œuvres*, vol. 2, p. 1328.

12. Nerval, *Œuvres*, vol. 2, p. 10.

13. Raymond Jean, *La Poétique du désir*, p. 94.

14. Ibid., p. 97.

15. Ibid.

16. Ibid., p. 94.

17. Ibid., p. 95.

18. Sarah Kofman, *Nerval*, p. 22. Without giving a detailed analysis of *Angélique*, Kofman nonetheless draws attention to its most interesting and troubled aspects. "A single time . . . , with *Angélique*," she writes, "Nerval would allow himself the pleasure of writing an eccentric text. . . . He would not fear delirium or wandering, a vagabond like Ulysses. He would not hesitate to undo, like Penelope, at night, the cloth woven during the day. Indefinitely" (p. 21). This pointless, delirious wandering and weaving that characterize the text are specifically anti-Hegelian for Kofman, precisely because they do *not* offer the prospect of a return, or a recollection. In a footnote to the lines quoted above, she draws attention to a passage at the end of *Angélique*, that point which in the *Faux Saulniers* marks the shift from Nerval's account of his search for the biography to his retelling of it. Having finally found the book, after so many digressions and peregrinations, he compares himself to both Ulysses and Penelope at the moment of the hero's return to Ithaca, but this comparison, instead of reenforcing the closure of a text in which Nerval set his identity at play, interpretively reopens the ending of the Homeric epic. In this comparison between his own and the Homeric texts, according to Kofman, "the *Odyssey*—with its voyage of Ulysses made of endless turns and detours, with Penelope, who undoes each night what she had woven during the day—is given as the paradigm for the *unravelled* [décousu] and vagabond text, a rhapsodic text-ile made of bits and pieces. One could oppose that reading of the *Odyssey*, which accentuates its variety, detours, digressions and delirium, to the Hegelian reading, according to which the *Odyssey* is the very metaphor of spirit's journey away from itself, marked above all by the nostalgia for a return to the native land: a journey that is a false journey; the turns and detours are here fictions in that one always already knows he will return home; the return is guaranteed before the departure which, by this very fact, is a false departure" (p. 21).

19. Nerval, *Œuvres*, vol. 2, p. 139.

20. Ibid., vol. 1, p. 693.

21. Ibid., vol. 2, p. 839. The idea that the only thing holding the "real adventures" together in a unified whole is the binding of the two volumes ("réunis dans ces deux volumes," the events are *liés*, or "bound," by their *réliure*, or "binding") recalls the re-

mark attributed by Gautier to Nerval, that the latter wished to "travel through life along an endless band of paper that should roll itself up behind him, and upon which he would note the thoughts that occurred to him, so that at the end of his road they would form a single volume with a single line" (*History*, p. 97; *Histoire*, p. 73).

22. *Voyage en Orient*, in *Œuvres*, vol. 2, pp. 790–91.

23. Gautier, *History*, p. 97; *Histoire*, p. 71. See note 21 to this chapter.

24. My readings of *Les Faux Saulniers*, and of Nerval's writings in general, are deeply indebted to the seminal work of Ross Chambers, who has done more than perhaps anyone else to show Nerval's literary and cultural significance. Developing a theme first elaborated in *Gérard de Nerval et la poétique du voyage*, Chambers has pointed to Nerval's elusive "nomadism" in *Room for Maneuver*, pp. 102–43, and "Literature Deterritorialized" to show how the style of *Les Faux Saulniers* enacts a subjective resistance to discursive authority (for instance, legal impositions).

25. Cf. *Œuvres*, vol. 2, p. 1688. The failed suicide that serves as pretext for the hallucinations in the "Mort-Vivant" does bear a close resemblance to the program of Berlioz's "Symphonie Fantastique" (1830), but the content and import of those visions are altogether different in the two works. The editors of the Pléiade edition were unable to find any text that corresponds to the title and author given by Nerval, and those of the same title varied largely in detail from the synopsis given in the feuilleton.

26. "What then is Death / Death, name without object, whether feared or desired / Is pure abstraction" (*Œuvres*, vol. 1, p. 476).

27. Ibid., vol. 3, p. 620. As has been pointed out by Nicolas Popa, Nerval's own version of "Isis" is an adaptation and, in parts, translation of *Die Isis-Vesper* by the German Carl A. Böttinger (see "Les sources allemandes de deux *Filles du feu*"). The reference to the unveiling of the goddess of Sais recalls, also, a *topos* of German romanticism that undoubtedly influenced Nerval here. See the discussion of Isis in romantic aesthetic theory, note 3 in this chapter.

28. *Œuvres*, vol. 3, pp. 619–20.

29. Ibid., p. 619, emphasis added.

30. On the author's pseudonyms and the various names he momentarily adopted before settling on Gérard de Nerval, see Jean Richer, *Expérience*, pp. 31, 44–45; and Huguette Brunet and Jean Ziegler, vol. 4.

31. "La loi du 16 juillet 1850, art. 3, amendement Tingy." See also Jacques Bony, *Le récit nervalien*, p. 188n, and Ross Chambers, "Literature Deterritorialized." Susan Dunn has argued that the Riancey amendment functions as a metaphor for Nerval's feelings of guilt and transgression, his internalization of what one, if not she, might refer to in Lacanian terms as the symbolic order, a system of limitations and statutes involving his relations to the law, his father, and his feelings of responsibility over the death of his mother. In internalizing his opponent—the one who limits his free-play—as Nerval does in many passages from *Les Faux Saulniers*, the author shows himself elaborating a space in which he can redistribute, or recirculate, the symbolic order and his role in it. The game thus has the *noms du père* as internalized

opponent, and Nerval plays not only to establish his position within the symbolic order, but to redefine the symbolic order itself. In this light, the relation between the struggle in the *Faux Saulniers* to establish the right of literature rather than of the "administration du Timbre" to legislate genres, and Nerval's attempts to justify the value of literature in letters to his father, would be of the utmost significance. Cf. Susan Dunn, "Transgression and the *Amendement Riancey*," pp. 86–95.

32. Letter of May 4, 5, or 6, 1849, in *Œuvres*, vol. 1, p. 1429.

33. *Œuvres*, vol. 2, pp. 1199–200.

34. Ibid., p. 72.

35. This is not an isolated example of such a conflation of *l'homme* and *l'œuvre*. Cf. for example a passage toward the beginning of the text where Nerval, speaking of the abbot's biography rather than the person himself, writes: "This eccentric and eternally fugitive character cannot forever escape a rigorous investigation" (ibid., p. 10).

36. Ibid., p. 28. Emphasis and all punctuation in original.

37. One could see this narrative position as related to Nerval's fascination with actresses, notably Jenny Colon. In potentially embodying any and all women as so many masks, the actress could be considered a synthetic force operating like the syncretic figure of Isis, who embodies all female deities. Similarly, the role would function, though in a disembodied way, to the same end, subordinating all individual performers to a principle of identity.

38. Sarah Kofman offers an antiphrastic description of Nerval's discursive subjectivity in "Angélique," contending that it had been imposed on him by the fact that adopting a more normal, continuous, and coherent style would have meant "renouncing, then, a 'style' more appropriate for describing a 'being' subject to every sort of metamorphosis [un 'être' sujet à toutes les métamorphoses] . . . varied and unravelled stories. . . . Renouncing a type of writing which 'lacked' a central subject, where digression was the rule; renouncing digressions which, because they don't take a straight path oriented and finalized by a single central subject, are always delirious, just as people who suddenly go from one idea to another are suspected of madness" (p. 22).

39. Ibid., p. 29.

40. Ibid.

41. On Nerval's use of pseudonyms see Huguette Brunet and Jean Ziegler, and Richer, *Expérience*, pp. 33–38.

42. That this appearance of another Gérard was not merely coincidental is strongly suggested by available evidence, which tends to show that Nerval invented this other individual in order to hide the fact that it was indeed he who had done what he here attempts to disavow. See Jacques Bony's notes to the Pléiade edition, *Œuvres*, vol. 1, pp. 1339–40.

43. Ibid., vol. 2, pp. 42 and 86.   44. Ibid., p. 12.

45. Ibid., p. 66.   46. Ibid., p. 10.

47. "Just as it is good in a symphony, even a pastoral one, to bring back the main

motive from time to time . . . I think it is useful to speak with you again of the Abbé de Bucquoy" (ibid., p. 93).

48. Ibid., p. 94. Cf. p. 125: "he got into a quarrel and wounded a man who had insulted him. This unhappy accident led him to return to the religious life. He felt himself obliged to shed his outfit in aid of a poor man, and it was then that, moved by the doctrines of Saint Paul, he founded a community or seminary in Rouen, which he directed under the name of *the Dead Man*. This name symbolized for him the forgetting of life's sorrows and the desire for eternal rest."

49. For example Hegel, perhaps the preeminent philosopher of death, views the latter as a pure abstraction, since in it self-consciousness shows "that it is not attached to any specific existence, not to the individuality common to existence as such, that it is not attached to life" (*Phenomenology*, p. 113).

50. Cf. the anonymous *Evénement des plus rares*, where the author refers only in passing to the name, citing it as an example of the Abbé's imagination: "This name of the Dead Man (for example), which he adopted at a seminary in Rouen to remind him always that he must die" (p. 202). From the original text Nerval also developed—retained, doubled, and displaced in reference—the idea of exemplarity, which appears in the source as a mere parenthetical aside.

51. *Œuvres*, vol. 3, p. 458.

52. Cf. Jacques Derrida, "Plato's Pharmacy," in *Dissemination*, pp. 61–171; "La Pharmacie de Platon," in *Dissémination*, pp. 69–198.

53. *Œuvres*, vol. 2, p. 57. A similar description of memory as a process of invisible inscription marking the core of one's being and brought to light only in midlife occurs in Nerval's biography of Restif de la Bretonne: "Until the age of thirty, the pains of love slide over the heart, which they press without penetrating; after the age of forty, each momentary sorrow reawakens past sorrows, and the man who has reached the full development of his being suffers doubly from his injured feelings and his wounded dignity" (p. 1013).

54. It would be easy to see this as simply a model for the unconscious, to take the writing and the book as early and somewhat defective versions of Freud's mystic writing-pad (cf. "A Note Upon the 'Mystic Writing-Pad'" in *The Standard Edition*, vol. 19, pp. 225–32), or certain Lacanian models, e.g.: "the unconscious is that part of the concrete discourse, in so far as it is transindividual, that is not at the disposal of the subject in re-establishing the continuity of his conscious discourse"; and "the unconscious is that chapter of my history that is marked by a blank or occupied by a falsehood: it is the censored chapter. But the truth can be rediscovered" (from "Function," in *Ecrits: A Selection*, pp. 49 and 50; "Fonction," in *Ecrits*, pp. 258 and 259), but this would be a return to a *lectio facilior*, for, in their specificity as book and writing, these metaphors represent a concern that Nerval elaborates at length. They recall and condense an elementary image of the *Faux Saulniers*, one that has returned over and over in varying forms throughout the length of the feuilleton: the palimpsest, the book of different writings. It had already appeared in the police dossiers of the Bibliothèque Nationale, where Nerval, literally reading between the

lines, had tried to grasp the significance of the three different hands that seemed to write in dialogue. He comments on a passage in the reports: "The sentence had thus been finished in the writing of the secretary, who had copied the report. Another, less practiced hand had added to the words: 'lit every evening' these: 'quite so.' In the margin could be found these words, evidently by Minister Pontchartrain: 'By all means'" (*Œuvres*, vol. 2, p.13). The idea of the overwritten document reappears obliquely in the guise of a paleographer who offers assistance to the narrator at the library (ibid., p. 11), then later in the manuscript of the story of Angélique de Longueval's life, which is begun in Angélique's own hand but finished in that of her cousin. Cf. also Bruno Tristmans, pp. 260–73.

55. "A Alexandre Dumas" in *Les Filles du feu*, in *Œuvres*, vol. 3, p. 451.

56. Cf. Jacques Bony, *Le Récit nervalien*, p. 217 ("Could the anti-novel be primarily a *pot-pourri*? It could be, if the narrator did not insure the indispensable linkage among all of its pieces").

57. *Œuvres*, vol. 2, pp. 118–19.

58. There are, just to cite a few examples, the *Roman à faire* (Novel to be written) (*Œuvres*, vol. 1, pp. 692–700); the "livre infaisable," or "book that cannot be done," on Brisacier (vol. 3, pp. 451–58); and the "livre devenu impossible," or "now impossible novel," detailed in the "Observations" section of the *Faux Saulniers* (vol. 2, pp. 136–41).

59. Cf. de Man, "Ludwig Binswanger and the Sublimation of the Self," and the discussion of this in relation to Nerval.

60. Hegel, *Aesthetics*, pp. 1119–20. The expression "poetizing subjectivity [die dichtende Subjektivität]" appears in an earlier discussion of the lyric author, on pp. 49ff.

61. Ibid., p. 1129.

62. For an explanation of the relation between individual experience and concrete content in Hegel's *Phenomenology of Spirit*, see Heidegger's *Hegel's Concept of Experience*.

63. Hegel, *Aesthetics*, vol. 2, p. 1126.

64. Ibid., p. 1123.

65. See "The Sonnet as a Hegelian Misstep," in Chapter 6.

66. For the discussion of Foucault's formulation of Nerval's madness, see Chapter 3.

67. See Thomas Aquinas's *Quaestiones disputatae de veritate*, qu. 1, art. 1, and the discussion of this in Heidegger's *Being and Time*, pp. 257–61.

68. From "Odd or even? Beyond intersubjectivity," in *Seminar 2*, p. 178 (trans. modified); "Pair ou impair? Au-delà de l'intersubjectivité," in *Le Séminaire 2*, p. 210. A similar theory of discursive subjectivity appears in the earlier thinking of Foucault, as when he writes: "First of all, we can say that today's writing has freed itself from the dimension of expression. Referring only to itself, but without being restricted to the confines of its interiority, writing is identified with its own unfolded exteriority. This means that it is an interplay of signs arranged less according to its

signified content than according to the very nature of the signifier. Writing unfolds like a game [*jeu*] that invariably goes beyond its own rules and transgresses its limits. In writing, the point is not to manifest or exalt the act of writing, nor is it to pin a subject within language; it is rather a question of creating a space into which the writing subject constantly disappears" ("What Is an Author?," in Josué V. Harari, ed., *Textual Strategies*, p. 142).

69. *Seminar 2*, p. 163; *Séminaire 2*, p. 195.

70. *Seminar 2*, pp. 169–70; *Séminaire 2*, p. 202.

71. Bruce Fink, in his wonderfully lucid and insightful *The Lacanian Subject*, argues against the permanence of the subject in Lacan: "The unconscious as a continual playing out of a signifying chain excluded from consciousness . . . in which knowledge of a certain kind is embodied, is permanent in nature; in other words, it subsists throughout an individual's life. Yet its subject is in no sense permanent or constant. The unconscious as chain is not the same as the *subject* of the unconscious" (p. 41). The passage from *Séminaire 2* quoted here indicates, however, that although the subject is not the signifying chain as such, it does attain permanence *through* the functioning of the signifying chain.

72. This pure differentiality of the signifier, which Lacan refers to above as the "most material aspect" of the sign, is based on Saussure's conception of linguistic systems in his *Course in General Linguistics*. The following observations from the section "Linguistic Value from a Material Viewpoint [La valeur linguistique considérée dans son aspect matériel]" should clarify Lacan's terminology and his structural presuppositions about language, as would more fully an examination of the whole chapter (*Course*, pp. 117–22; *Cours*, pp. 163–69): "The conceptual side of value is made up solely of relations and differences with respect to the other terms of language, and the same can be said of its material side. The important thing in the word is not the sound alone but the phonic differences that make it possible to distinguish this word from all others, for differences carry signification. This may seem surprising, but how indeed could the reverse be possible? Since one vocal image is no better suited than the next for what it is commissioned to express, it is evident, even *a priori*, that a segment of language can never in the final analysis be based on anything except its noncoincidence with the rest" (pp. 117–18; p. 163); and: "Everything that has been said up to this point boils down to this: in language there are only differences. Even more important: a difference generally implies positive terms between which the difference is set up; but in language there are only differences *without positive terms*" (p. 120; p. 166).

73. *Seminar 2*, p. 170 (trans. modified); *Séminaire 2*, p. 202.

74. On the relation between ego and subject in Lacan, see, for example, his discussion of the mirror stage from *Seminar 2*: "This *image* of his body is the principle of every *unity* he [man] perceives in objects. Now, he only perceives the unity of this specific image from the outside, and in an anticipated manner. Because of this double relation which he has with himself, all the objects of his world are always structured around the wandering shadow of his own ego [*moi*]. This will all have a

fundamentally anthropomorphic character, even *egomorphic* we could say. Man's ideal unity, which is never attained as such and escapes him at every moment, is evoked at every moment in this perception. The object is never for him definitively the final object, except in exceptional experiences. But it thus appears in the guise of an object from which man is irremediably separated, and which shows him the very figure of his dehiscence within the world. . . . If the object perceived from without has its own identity, the latter places the man who sees it in a state of tension, because he perceives himself as desire, and as unsatisfied desire. Inversely, when he grasps his unity, on the contrary it is the world which for him becomes decomposed, loses its meaning, and takes on an alientated and discordant aspect. It is this imaginary oscillation which gives to all human perception the dramatic subjacency experienced by a subject, in so far as his interest is truly aroused" (p. 166; *Séminaire 2*, pp. 198–99, emphasis added).

75. Cf. the discussions of knot theory used to explain the relations among the three registers of the real, imaginary, and symbolic given in lectures at Yale (Nov. 25, 1975), Columbia (Dec. 1, 1975), and MIT (Dec. 2, 1975), and published in *Scilicet* 6–7, pp. 38–63.

Chapter 5. The Subject Writes After Its Own Death: "Le Christ aux Oliviers"

An earlier version of this chapter previously appeared in *Romanic Review* 88, no. 1 (1997).

1. A similar opinion was held by Gautier, who also spoke of romanticism as distinguishable from earlier periods in being essentially narrative. He remarked that sculpture, of all the arts, lent itself least to romanticism because it is "that austere art which will not yield to fancy, because, feeling itself looked at under every one of its aspects, it may not scamp or conceal anything" (*History*, p. 48; *Histoire*, p. 30).
2. Hegel, *Aesthetics*, vol. 1, p. 576. Original version from *Ästhetik*, vol. 2, p. 198.
3. See the discussion in Chapter 6.
4. Hegel, *Aesthetics*, vol. 1, p. 588 (trans. modified).
5. See, for example, *Œuvres*, vol. 1, p. 1751: "I intentionally arrange my life like a novel, for the slightest discordance shocks me."
6. Hegel, *Aesthetics*, vol. 1, p. 588.
7. Ibid.
8. Ibid., p. 586.
9. "Hope has fled, like a dream / And alone my love has stayed with me / It has stayed like an abyss / Between my life and happiness" (*Œuvres*, vol. 3, p. 412).
10. Ibid., p. 414.
11. Ibid., pp. 648–49.
12. Kojève, p. 539.
13. "There exists in the archives of France a love letter written by a great Lady of the eighteenth century to an officer in combat at Rosbach. That letter contained a lock of beautiful blond hair which never reached its address, since the officer had

perished in the battle, and the letter was sent back to the central post office, where it was opened and later given to the archives as a curiosity. Poor letter! poor blond hair of a beautiful body now destroyed, sad knot of love cut off and unveiled before the world! Whoever dared fix a bit of story to your poetic existence would be an ill-inspired poet indeed. And besides, does the world not have enough novels already? Here is one less to read and one more to dream of" (Œuvres, vol. 1, p. 700).

14. Robert Graves, vol. 1, p. 315.
15. Ibid., p. 156.
16. Giulia Sfameni Gasparro, p. 42.
17. Cf. Graves, vol. 1, pp. 116–17, 157, 316.
18. See James George Frazer, vol. 1, pp. 261–317.
19. The loss of the phallus and its relation to subjectivity will be discussed in Chapter 7.
20. Œuvres, vol. 1, p. 1380 (original emphasis).
21. Published in *L'Artiste* of May 13, 1855, included in Œuvres, vol. 3, pp. 779–83. The editors of the Pléiade edition are guarded about the attribution of this text to Nerval (see Œuvres, vol. 3, pp. 1393–95). The publication of these "pensées" seems to have been overseen by Arsène Houssaye; that they were *not* in fact by Nerval would, in a sense, be only the more revealing, as they would then most likely represent things his friends, like Houssaye, had heard him say or which would be identifiable by his circle as typical of him.
22. Cf. Chapter 7.
23. Cited by Arsène Houssaye in "Figures parisiennes" in *Les Confessions*, vol. 3, p. 309. Although it summarizes the contents of Blanche's attestation, the formula is, unfortunately, the invention of Houssaye himself. For a copy of the actual attestation see Claude Pichois and Michel Brix, p. 371.
24. Cf. Chapter 1, note 18; similarly, Kant spoke of Nature's inability to attain to ideas as the starting point of the sublime.

Chapter 6. The Lyric First Person: "El Desdichado"

Portions of this chapter previously appeared in *L'Esprit Créateur* 35, no. 4 (1995).

1. The unification of a self-image through the desire for a lost object is a *topos* that dates back to the earliest French lyric—the highly personal poetry of the twelfth-century *trouvères*. For an interpretation of this sonnet as proto-Symbolist, see Emilie Noulet, "L'Hermétisme dans la poésie moderne," p. 30: "This new man writes *Les Chimères*, which contain two sonnets whose vocabulary, workmanship and resonance the Symbolists and all of modern poetry will not cease to recall."
2. Le Breton, *Nerval*, p. 21.
3. Ibid., p. 51.
4. *Aurélia*, in Œuvres, vol. 3, p. 699.
5. In an essay on Nerval's prosody, Henri Meschonnic, for example, remarks

that even in his most youthful lyric attempts "the poet piles up chevilles linked by nothing" and that by the end of his life, "in his mature work, he ends up writing stanzas only for the eye. The stanza has become the place to juxtapose verses that follow one another—or that don't. Each verse is constructed as if it were meant to be an entire poem" ("Poétique de Gérard de Nerval," pp. 13 and 21). Since Meschonnic's purpose is to expose and analyze Nerval's poetics rather than to determine their meaning, he does not attempt to give a sense to this metrical disjunctiveness.

6. Jacques Dhaenens, *Destin d'Orphée*, p. 10.
7. Dhaenens, p. 11.
8. Jean-Pierre Richard, "Le nom et l'écriture," in *Microlectures*, p. 23.
9. Ibid.
10. *Black Sun*, p. 146 (trans. modified); *Soleil noir*, p. 157.
11. *Black Sun*, p. 162; *Soleil noir*, p. 173.
12. *Black Sun*, p. 171; *Soleil noir*, p. 182.
13. Jean Guillaume, *"Les Chimères" de Nerval*. Since significant variance among the different texts of the sonnet will be noted here only when it bears on the present interpretation, the reader is referred to Guillaume for an exhaustive exposition of the variants. The various original editions of the poem will be referred to in the text by the following abbreviations: the *Mousquetaire* version of 1853 as (M.); the Alfred Lombard manuscript as (ms. AL); the Paul Eluard manuscript as (ms. PE); and the 1854 version from the *Chimères* as (C.).
14. Guillaume, p. 42.
15. For a study of the various possible influences on the sense of this title, cf. Dhaenens, pp. 13–17. The textual antecedents given there argue overwhelmingly for a translation of the Spanish as "disinherited" rather than the other possibilities: "unhappy," "miserable," or "distressed."
16. Le Destin is also the name given by his mistress to the imprisoned comedian of Scarron's *Roman comique*; she herself goes by the name L'Etoile. A continuation of Scarron's work figures in the letter-preface to the *Filles du feu*, where it forms the bulk of Nerval's response to the article by Dumas that had accompanied the first publication of "El Desdichado." In the preface Nerval has his hero write: "Here I am once more in my prison, madam; still imprudent, still guilty it seems, and still trusting, alas! in that beautiful *star* [étoile] of the stage, who had for one moment deigned to call me her destiny [destin]. Star and Destiny: what an amiable couple in the poet Scarron's novel! but it is difficult to play those two roles appropriately today" (*Œuvres*, vol. 3, p. 451). The relation between *je* and the *étoile* in "El Desdichado" would seem to have been somehow analogous, in Nerval's mind, to the relation between the two lovers in the letter.
17. For the importance of lineage, race, and family to Nerval, see Richer's analysis of the genealogy the poet drew up for himself (*Expérience*, pp. 29–52), Richard's article on the same subject (pp. 13–24), and the discussion of Nerval's wanderings through the Valois region in *Les Faux Saulniers* (*Œuvres*, vol. 2, pp. 40–118).
18. Noulet, "L'Hermetisme," p. 33.

19. *Œuvres*, vol. 3, pp. 824–25.
20. For the genealogy, see Richer, *Expérience*, pp. 29–52.
21. See ibid., pp. 33–35.
22. Richard, *Microlectures*, p. 14.
23. *Œuvres*, vol. 3, p. 15.
24. In *Le Messager* of Sept. 18, 1838. Reproduced in *Œuvres*, vol. 1, p. 456. Cf. also the description of the "tour d'ivoire" in *Sylvie*: "There remained no other refuge for us but that ivory tower of poets, where we climbed ever higher to isolate ourselves from the crowd. From those lofty points where our masters led us, we breathed at last the pure air of solitudes, we drank oblivion [nous buvions l'oubli] from the golden cup of legend, we were drunk on poetry and love" (p. 538); here, of course, the tower does not serve to synthesize the past but to abolish it; it is a terminal point that detaches itself from all that has led to it, a "tour d'oubli" which, like the "tour abolie," negates what has gone before.
25. *Black Sun*, p. 149; *Soleil noir*, p. 161.
26. Noulet, p. 35.
27. In *Pandora*, for example, Nerval refers to the eponymous object of his desires as "ma froide *Etoile*" (*Œuvres*, vol. 3, p. 660).
28. Dhaenens, p. 45.
29. *Black Sun*, pp. 145–46; *Soleil noir*, p. 157.
30. *Œuvres*, vol. 3, p. 458.
31. This constructs the first person, in other words, as a subject of desire. The role of desire in structuring or organizing subjectivity is exemplified by *The Phenomenology of Spirit*, where it functions as the origin and movement of the Hegelian dialectic of self-identity. According to Hegel, "self-consciousness is Desire" (p. 109) while work is "desire held in check" (p. 118); and one can understand this desire as something close to a logical aporia that would be inherently and endemically troubling to consciousness: "But that an accident as such, detached from what circumscribes it, what is bound and is actual only in its context with others, should attain an existence of its own and a separate freedom—this is the tremendous power of the negative; it is the energy of thought, of the pure 'I'... Spirit is this power only by looking the negative in the face, and tarrying with it. This tarrying with the negative is the magical power that converts it into being. This power is identical with what we earlier called the Subject" (p. 19). That a nonessential or accidental element of Spirit should develop independence or a separate freedom as an individual and thereby give concrete content to absolute Spirit is possible only through its being self-identical (see *Phenomenology*, pp. 12–13), but consciousness is in the unique position that to be self-same to itself it must be different from itself as consciousness and consciousness of that consciousness (see pp. 54–55): it is doubled and different *by* its very identity, and for it to be self-same is to be self-different. This difference of the same is the desire that is self-consciousness and it is this desire that must be worked out in the course of the history of Spirit. For other interpretations of Hegelian desire in relation to subjectivity, see Lacan, "The Subversion of the Sub-

ject and the Dialectic of Desire" in *Ecrits: A Selection*, pp. 292–325 (*Écrits*, pp. 793–827); and Judith Butler, *Subjects of Desire*.

32. In *Analyse structurale des Chimères de Nerval*, Jacques Geninasca, with little other explanation than the remark "the sphere of fixed stars is found to be, in the poetic tradition which prolongs an earlier cosmology, that of eternity (of *non-time*)," also notes the suspended temporality of this first stanza: "The abolition of the tower and the death of the star correspond to a fall into a non-oriented time that is burst into a succession of unlinked instants, the time of melancholy" (p. 60).

33. See, for example, chapter 10 of Lucien de Samosate's *De l'astrologie*: "Indeed, to honor it [the lyre of Orpheus] the Greeks assigned it a place in the sky, and the grouping of several stars took the name Lyre of Orpheus" (quoted in Richer, *Expérience*, p. 528; on Nerval's knowledge of Lucien de Samosate's works, see pp. 569–70).

34. Cf. for example Dom Antoine-Joseph Pernety's *Les Fables égyptiennes et grecques*, a work to which Nerval refers in *Les Illuminés* and which includes the following remark: "the sound of the lyre of Orpheus was nothing else than the harmony of his poetry" (vol. 2, p. 142); according to Lucien de Samosate's *De l'astrologie*, the "the seven-stringed lyre produced a harmony that was like the symbol for that of the planets" (quoted in Richer, *Expérience*, p. 528).

35. Cited in Richer, *Expérience*, p. 532. On the symbolic use of the lyre in reference to Ficino, see p. 534.

36. Ibid., p. 533.

37. Karlheinz Stierle, p. 109. The two figures, the dynamic lute and the lapidary mosaic, seem reconciled in Mallarmé's description of "the elocutory disappearance of the poet, who yields the initiative to words, set into motion by the jostling of their inequality; they light up with reciprocal reflections like a virtual string of fires across jewel stones" (*Œuvres*, p. 366). The image further evokes the stars in Nerval's "luth constellé."

38. Although she does not refer to the article, Kristeva's ideas of the "symbolic cannibalism" (*Black Sun*, p. 162; *Soleil noir*, p. 173) and poetic "incarnation" (p. 171; p. 182) with which Nerval lyrically transforms the loss of a primary prelinguistic object into the musicality of a sonnet apparently derive from the concept of incorporation elaborated by Abraham and Torok in "Mourning *or* Melancholy: Introjection versus Incorporation" from *The Shell and the Kernel* ("Deuil *ou* mélancolie Introjecter—incorporer," in *L'Ecorce et le noyau*). The terminology of encryptment, used in the latter article, does in fact seem especially resonant with the Nerval of "El Desdichado." Incorporation, like Kristeva's "incarnation," is an unconscious attempt to compensate for a loss not by signifying it but by replacing it materially. However, Abraham and Torok argue that in incorporation, "the impossibility of introjection [that is, the impossibility of signifing or metaphorizing loss through language] is so profound that even our refusal to mourn is prohibited from being given a language" (p. 130; pp. 265–66). Obviously, this is not the case of the sonnet, which is a verbalization of nothing *but* loss and mourning.

39. On Nerval's acquaintance with Ficino's works, see Richer, *Expérience*, p. 534.

40. André Chastel, p. 44. Ficino himself explicitly describes the melancholic condition as a withdrawal from external attachments: "The third mode [of *vacatio mentis*] derives from the contraction of melancholic humor, which draws the soul away from outside concerns, with the result that the soul is just as absent when a man is in a waking state as it normally is when he is asleep" (Ficino, vol. 2, p. 219).

41. Richer, *Expérience*, p. 571.

42. On the aesthetic of fragmentation and its theorization during the romantic period, see Philippe Lacoue-Labarthe and Jean-Luc Nancy, pp. 57–178.

43. "Octavie" in *Œuvres*, vol. 3, p. 608.

44. Ibid.

45. The relation between the site and death also has literary antecedents, since the Posilipo is the site of Cumae and the entrance into the underworld described in Book 4 of the *Aeneid*.

46. According to Cellier: "For those who understand Nerval, 'dans la nuit' refers indisputably to 'rends-moi'. . . . But Mme [Jeanine] Moulin connects it to 'consolé'" (cited in Dhanaens, p. 39). For Dhanaens, "'Rends-moi' and 'toi qui m'as consolé' can both refer to 'la nuit du tombeau'" (p. 40).

47. Nerval does in fact use the verb in this sense at the end of *Aurélia*: "He seemed to me, placed as he was between life and death, like a sublime interpreter, like a confessor predestined to hear those secrets of the soul which words would not dare transmit or could not succeed in rendering [ou ne réussirait pas à rendre]" (*Œuvres*, vol. 3, p. 744).

48. The connection tomb-poetry-Posilipo is further determined by the fact that classical legend locates the tomb of Virgil on the promontory.

49. Dhanaens, p. 44.

50. Geninasca views the difference between the Object of the first stanza and that of the second stanza as the difference between an "object connected to Ego" and an "autonomous object (communicable by 'toi')" (p. 58), basing his argument on the observation that the "étoile" is a property of Ego, while the "fleur" is a property at the disposal of a "toi." His analysis seems to fall victim here to its own structural rigor by being unable to accommodate the "mad" possibility of an identity alienated from itself, an Ego who has objectified his subjectivity in a "fleur" or an "étoile." Yet this is precisely the essence of Nerval's idea of subjectivity here, and it is entirely consistent with his other writings, where figures of the double, the doubled personality, and the *doppelgänger* play a frequent and decisive role (see Heidi Uster, *Identité et dualité*).

51. For Richer this identity of "fleur" and "étoile" is determined by a passage from *Aurélia* where Nerval asserts that "the flower is an image of the star which contemplates it" (*Nerval et les doctrines ésotériques*, pp. 23–24). In support, Dhanaens adds the following citation: "apple trees whose flowers I've often see burst open in the night like stars of the earth" (p. 44n). For Geninasca, they both represent an unidentified woman (Geninasca, p. 53).

52. Cited in Dhanaens, p. 45.

53. Similarly, the figure of death evoked in *Octavie* is "crowned with *pale* roses" (*Œuvres*, vol. 3, p. 608, emphasis added). It is the pallor of the rose, not its rose-ness alone, which makes it here an attribute of death.

54. *Œuvres*, vol. 3, p. 568. This imagery of a disorderly room came to hold an increasing significance for Nerval toward the end of his life. In many ways the image of the resumptive tower-*telos* that reveals the order of an existence from its lofty culminating point is replaced by the image of a cluttered room that holds the various *disjecta* that chance has salvaged from the poet's personal past. Cf. a passage earlier in *Sylvie*, where the narrator describes his room: "In the midst of all these splendors of *bric-a-brac* which it was the custom at that period to collect [réunir], in order to restore an antiquated apartment [un appartement d'autrefois] to its local color, there shone with a rejuvenated gleam one of those tortoise-shell clocks from the Renaissance, whose gilt dome, surmounted by the figure of Time, is supported by caryatids in the Medici style, resting, in their turn, on half-rearing horses.... The works, probably excellent, had not been wound for centuries.—I had not bought that clock in Touraine in order to tell the time" (*Œuvres*, vol. 3, pp. 543–44, emphasis added; for an excellent analysis of this passage in the context of symbolic language and historicity, see Kevin Newmark, "The Forgotten Figures of Symbolism: Nerval's *Sylvie*"). Again it is a question of the joining or "réunion" of disparate elements in an attempt to restore the past. This restoration is here indissociable from a defiance of time, a rejection of its progress, both in the recreation of an "appartement d'autrefois" and in the refusal to rewind the clock that forms the center of the tableau. Cf. also the passage from the end of *Aurélia* in which Nerval describes the room he set up for himself at the sanitorium of Doctor Blanche: "I've found there all the debris of my diverse fortunes, the confused remains of several sets of furniture dispersed or sold twenty years ago. It is a clutter worthy of Dr. Faust.... With what pleasure I was able to arrange the piles of my notes in my drawers, my bits of correspondence that chance encounters or the distant countries I have travelled fated to remain private or public, obscure or famous. In rolls of paper better protected than others I find once more Arab letters, relics from Cairo and Istambul. Oh happiness! Oh mortal sadness! These yellowed characters, these rubbed-out drafts, these half-crumpled letters, they are the treasure of my only love... Let us read once again... So many letters are missing, so many others torn or crossed-out; here is what I find" (pp. 742–43). These rooms become metaphors of objectified memory and images of the self across its chance itinerary. It is in this passage from *Aurélia* that the importance of the disorder of the past, its haphazard and accidental nature, its incompleteness and fragmentation, become most evident. It is here, among all of Nerval's works, that the series of concerns hinted at in the alliance between *rose* and *pampre* is most exhaustively verbalized. It is also a description taken up again—in some places almost verbatim—and recast by Baudelaire when he used the image of himself as a "vieux meuble à tiroirs [old chest of drawers]" to elaborate a disjunctive subjectivity in "Spleen II" (for an interpretation of this poem as a coherent aes-

theticization of an incoherent self see the reading by Hans Robert Jauss in *Towards an Aesthetic*, especially p. 164).

55. André Lebois, for example, also notes this geographically unifying force, extending it to other poems in the *Chimères* as well: "Starting with the second quatrain, the bay of Naples rises up, present also in *Corilla*, *Octavie* and *Isis*. Another factor of unity in the *Chimères*, which are truly *situated* [situées] close to the Posilipo" (*Vers une élucidation*, p. 6).

56. Geninasca also notes the structural parallelism between the lute and the arbor ("treille") as the site and support of a union (p. 56). He remarks, too, on the nonnarrative aspect of the first two stanzas, which he contrasts with the discursive structure of the tercets to formulate the "correlation Q[uatrain] / T[ercet] :: *axiological network / narrative structure*" (p. 49). One would have to disagree, however, with Geninasca's and Kristeva's (*Black Sun*, pp. 159–60; *Soleil noir*, p. 171) characterizations of the tercets as narrative.

57. As the "third letter" of the *Roman à faire*, which appeared in *La Sylphide* of Dec. 24 or 25, 1842 (*Œuvres*, vol. 1, p. 695); in the "Lettres d'amour" (p. 723); and in the version from *Octavie* (*Œuvres*, vol. 3, p. 608).

58. Geninasca, pp. 57–58. Dhaenens, pp. 39–41.

59. *Black Sun*, p. 152 (trans. modified); *Soleil noir*, p. 164.

60. On the relations between first and second persons, cf. Emile Benveniste, "Relationships of Person in the Verb" in *Problems in General Linguistics*, p. 197 ("Structures des relations de personne dans le verbe" in *Problèmes de linguistique générale*, vol. 1, p. 228): "In the first two persons, there are both *an implied person* and a discourse concerning that person. 'I' designates the one who speaks and at the same time implies an utterance about 'I'; in saying 'I,' I cannot but be speaking of myself. In the second person, 'you' is necessarily designated by 'I' and cannot be thought of outside a situation set up by starting with 'I'; and at the same time, 'I' states something as the predicate of 'you'" (trans. modified and emphasis added). The second person thus implies a relation, inherent and present in the language itself, to the first person. A process of exceeding death by addressing someone from beyond the grave, similar to that evoked in the sonnet, is described in a passage from Nerval's biography of Restif de la Bretonne. The story, according to Nerval, is taken from Restif's last work, "entitled *Letters from the Tomb, or les Posthumes*" and tells of a young man who learns, shortly after his marriage, that he has only a year to live. In order to keep his wife from remarrying, he writes a series of letters which he arranges for friends to dispatch periodically after his death so as to create the illusion that his continued absence is solely attributable to the exigency of the government, which perpetually sends him from distant land to distant land in its diplomatic service. There is a certain irony in Nerval's description of the letters' contents: "These letters, entrusted to reliable friends, did in fact follow one another for several years, bringing consolation to that *unwitting* widow. The posthumous correspondent had but one thought, which was to prove to his wife, who was somewhat given over to the materialist ideas of the times, that the soul survives the body and finds

again, in other regions, all the persons it had loved" (*Œuvres*, vol. 2, pp. 1069–70). The very existence of the letters themselves proves, however, that something does in fact survive the body and does find its way to the beloved, and to this extent the afterlife granted to the young Fontlèthe is not illusory. Here, as in the sonnet, it is the delayed address to another, allowed by writing but impossible in conversation, that produces the posthumous, literary simulacrum of an existence speaking from beyond the tomb.

61. Lebois, *Vers une élucidation*, p. 4.

62. Ibid., pp. 3–4; and Richer, *Expérience*, pp. 539–44.

63. On the relation between Nerval's ancestors and the Lusignan family, see Fernand Verhesen, p. 11.

64. Léon Cellier has suggested a character of that name from *Love's Labours Lost* on the basis of two other, slender intertextual similarities—the existence of a play by Nerval (*La Polygamie est un cas pendable*) which appears to draw on the earlier text, and a supposed resemblance between the Shakespearian hero and contemporary descriptions of Nerval's personality (Cellier, pp. 146–53). Norma Rinsler, in an article devoted to the question, offers five other possibilities: the legendary Biron, who figures in the "Chanson de Biron" quoted by Nerval in his *Chansons et légendes du Valois*; the English poet; Armand de Gontaut, baron de Biron, a well-known soldier born in Périgord in 1524; his son, Armand de Gontaut, duc de Biron, who was beheaded for conspiring against Henri IV; finally, Louis de Gontaut, duc de Biron, known also under the name of duc de Lauzun, who was beheaded during the Revolution. Rinsler concludes that "Nerval is not only Biron, but all the Birons" and that as such "Biron is the archetype of the man who is brave and carefree, adventurous and gay, possessing that fire of virile power which permits him to conquer women and father children; an immoral Don Juan if you like, but passionate and tender" (Rinsler, pp. 405–10).

65. Robert Faurisson, for example, proposes "Catherine de Médicis, who died in 1589 and to whom Biron was devotedly attached" (Faurisson, p. 23), while Cellier suggests the "French princess" who figures in *Love's Labours Lost* (Cellier, p. 151).

66. "dans cet espace d'apparent égarement, une écriture, à la recherche d'une identité, se noue peut-être, s'attache toujours plus fortement, plus nécessairement, se tisse à elle-même. Arbre-tissu. Feuille-famille" (Richard, *Microlectures*, p. 24).

67. It is precisely these connections that have led mythographers to speculate on a historical parentage among the various stories evoked in this line. According to Pierre Martin-Civet: "It is impossible not to draw a connection between the episode of Raymondin [Lusignan's] betrayal and the Greek myth of Eros and Psyche. Borrowing the theme from the old romance *de Parthonopéus de Blois*, Jehan d'Arras reversed the roles as well, but he returned to the major outline of Apuleius's story. For him, it is Raymondin's brother who plays the role of the evil counselor which Psyche's sisters assume in Apuleius's tale, and it is Mélusine, rather than the son of Venus, who is victim of a broken vow. If Psyche loses the handsome Eros for wanting to see his delicate beauty by lamplight, Raymondin loses Mélusine for

wanting to see her one Saturday" (Martin-Civet, p. 7). Similarly, Jean Markale notes the resemblances between the French fable and the story of Orpheus and Eurydice (Markale, pp. 150–52).

68. Heine, *Poëmes et légendes* (1892), p. 121 (cited in Rinsler, p. 408).

69. The word "tombeau" of the fifth line bears the annotation "Mausole" (ms. P.E.). That reference, as well as the fact that another of the *Chimères* is entitled "Artémise," has led some critics to construe Nerval himself as the tomb of the beloved "toi" in the second quatrain. The idea, however, of incorporating the dead into a living substance seems more to indicate a desire to animate the repository of the deceased and to find a poetic memorialization or language that would not annihilate but revivify the individual, even if such a memorialization entailed the radical rethinking of the limits and structure of individuality proposed in the last stanza of the poem.

70. Working within a Hegelian model of self-consciousness, Georges Bataille speaks of precisely such an incorporation of the death of another as symbolic of the death of the self and as, consequently, an essential moment of self-consciousness: "In order for Man to reveal himself ultimately to himself, he would have to die, but he would have to do it while living—watching himself ceasing to be. . . . In a sense, this is what takes place . . . by means of a subterfuge. In the sacrifice, the sacrificer identifies himself with the animal that is struck down dead. And so he dies in seeing himself die, and even, in a certain way, by his own will, one in spirit with the sacrificial weapon. But it is a comedy! At least it would be a comedy if some other method existed which could reveal to the living the invasion of death: that finishing off of the finite being, which *his* Negativity—which kills him, *ends* him and definitively suppresses him—accomplishes alone and which it alone can accomplish" ("Hegel, Death and Sacrifice," p. 19; "Hegel, la mort, et le sacrifice" in *Œuvres complètes*, vol. 12, p. 336). In Batailleian terms, Cain bears the mark of his own theatricalized self-constituting negativity. What is significant, in the present context, is that it is a mark: that which replaces what it stands for and negates it, which always designates it as absent. In a convergence of specific meaning and general semiotic function, the mark of Cain is the self-designating sign (I am Cain...), the sign that designates the death of the self (...who have seen my own death...), and the sign that is, in fact, the self as death of the self (...but who in seeing my death have grounded myself in it, and have thus seen my essence as a sign, this sign, that negates me).

71. Cain, in the "Story of Solomon and the Queen of the Morning" is spoken of as the founder of a long race of artists: "It is to our race... ," he asserts, "that they [the children of Jehovah] owe all the arts" (Nerval, *Œuvres*, vol. 2, p. 724). The portrayal of his descendant Adoniram, the hero of the "Story," constitutes something like a narrative study of the creative psyche, and while he is said to be sublime (p. 699), this stature seems to have left him impersonal and heartless, insofar as he has given himself up entirely to the dictates of his art: "His heart was silent; the activity of the artist alone animated his hands, which were made to mold the world, and

bowed down his shoulders, which were made to raise it up [Son cœur était muet; l'activité de l'artiste animait seule des mains faites pour pétrir le monde, et courbait seule des épaules faites pour le soulever]" (p. 673).

72. "It has been many years since the tomb closed over the author of these letters which we are about to excerpt. And indeed, can one really say the tomb? The chevalier Dubourjet having died in 1808, during a crossing to Santo Domingo, we are afraid that he had none but the blue bosom of the Ocean, which offers to the dying not even the hope of having his name engraved on a stone and of feeling a few tears filter down through a blessed soil. Perhaps it is a work of piety to snatch from oblivion one of those names which it so quickly lays hold of" (*Œuvres*, vol. 1, p. 692). The relation between the sea and rootless anonymity is further developed in Nerval's descriptions of the French capital: "I'm very fond of Paris, where chance dictated that I should be born — but I could just as easily have been born on a ship, and Paris, which bears in its coat of arms the bari, or mystical boat of the Egyptians, has not within its walls a hundred thousand true Parisians. A man from the South who by chance joins himself there to a woman from the North cannot produce a child of a Lutecian nature. 'So what!' one might ask. But ask about a little among people from the provinces whether it matters to be from such or such a place" ("Promenades et souvenirs" in *Œuvres*, vol. 3, p. 687). Nerval's belief that the name of Paris derived from an Egyptian root seems to be based on a theory of Court de Gébelin, to whom Nerval referred at several points in his writings (e.g., "Cagliostro" from the *Illuminés*) and who further identified the "bar" or "bari" with worship of the goddess Isis. The earlier writer had contended that the "name of Paris comes from Par or Bar, which designates a Boat and anything that serves for crossings. . . . This people [i.e. the Parisii] then worshipped Isis, who was the Goddess of Navigation and whose symbol was a Vessel" (Court de Gébelin, p. 165). Thus, etymologically, the ocean represents not only instability and passage, but an instability and passage specifically associated with the goddess of sublime, annihilating abstraction.

73. Jehan d'Arras, p. 332. The passage is quoted from an edition published the year after "El Desdichado" appeared in the *Mousquetaire*, but it reproduced a version widely available in the Paris libraries. Contemporary culture seemed to have reinforced the siren-Mélusine identification: current iconography represented the fairy in the shape of a siren, with her lower extremity more like the tail of a fish than a snake. Cookies representing Mélusine, popular in the first half of the nineteenth century, depicted her with a fish's tail: cf. images from the 1840 *Bulletin de la Société des Antiquaires de l'Ouest* reproduced in Martin-Civat, p. 109. Given Nerval's familiarity with Heinrich Heine and his works, the comb used by Mélusine in the bathing scene (and represented on the cookies) could not have failed to recall for him the line from Heine's most famous poem, "Die Lorelei," which evokes a siren-figure of German mythology also combing her hair: "Sie kämmt ihr goldenes Haar" (Heine, vol. 15, p. 200). Nerval in fact entitled an essay on his travels in western Germany with the French transliteration of the name: "Lorely."

74. Rousseau plays an important role in *Les Faux Saulniers*, and their style seems, at least in part, to have been inspired by the descriptions of wanderings in the Valois from *Reveries* (*Les Rêveries d'un promeneur solitaire*). On Rousseau's influence in Nerval's work, see Monique Streiff Maretti, *Le Rousseau de Gérard de Nerval*.

75. *Œuvres*, vol. 1, p. 700.

76. Virgil, p. 231 (emphasis added, my translation).

77. *Œuvres*, vol. 3, p. 855. The quoted verses are from Moline's libretto to Gluck's *Orphée*, Act II, scene xxii (see Nerval, *Œuvres*, vol. 3, p. 855n).

78. On Nerval's knowledge of this particular work by Pernety, see Georges Le Breton, who argues that the work is the source and key of "El Desdichado" as well as several other of the *Chimères*.

79. Dom Antoine-Joseph Pernety, vol. 2, pp. 460–61.

80. Dante, *Inferno*, pp. 60–61.

81. *Œuvres*, vol. 3, p. 451.

82. For example: "hanc [*sc.* lyram]... plectro modulatus eburno" (cited in the *Oxford Latin Dictionary*); and, in the sense of "versify": "verba ... fidibus modulanda Latinis" (Horace, Ep. 2.2.143, cited in *Oxford Latin Dictionary*).

83. " ... le premier a montré aux hommes la manière de coucher par écrit leurs pensées, et de mettre leurs expressions en ordre, pour qu'il en resultât un discours suivi. ... Il donna des noms convenables à beaucoup de choses ... inventa la musique ... la lyre à trois cordes" (Pernety, vol. 1, p. 268).

84. D'Arras, p. 359.

85. Dhanaens, p. 78.

86. Cf., for example, the identification Aurélie-Adrienne in *Sylvie*, the "young woman who resembled you" of *Octavie* (*Œuvres*, vol. 3, p. 608), the play of resemblances in *Corilla*, etc. On this subject see also Shoshana Felman, "Gérard de Nerval: Writing Living, or Madness as Autobiography" in *Writing and Madness*, pp. 59–77 ("Gérard de Nerval: Folie et répétition" in *La Folie*, pp. 61–96).

87. The verb "moduler" does not appear in Furetière's dictionary of 1690, although there is an entry for "modulation," which is given only the musical meaning of a change of key. Littré, who began publication of his dictionary (1863–73) some eight years after Nerval's death, gives the following definitions: "1. In formal style, to sing, to compose verses . . . 2. To give to style a character compared to musical modulation. To modulate one's phrases . . . 3. Musical term. To move the melody or harmony into different keys or modes" ["1. Dans le style élevé, chanter, composer des vers . . . 2. Donner au style un caractère comparé à la modulation musicale. Moduler ses phrases . . . 3. Terme de musique. Faire passer le chant ou l'harmonie dans des tons ou des modes différents"]. None of the examples of the first meaning actually indicate that the word was in fact used in the sense of "chanter." The Latin verb does not have that meaning. In fact, that sense seems to have arisen after Nerval's use of the word in this poem, perhaps as a result of it. The Robert, for example, gives the figurative definition "chanter," but then attests it only with the lines in question from "El Desdichado." That Nerval himself did not intend the word in this

sense seems clear from the fact that he originally used *both* the verb "moduler" and the verb "chanter."

88. Cf. Ovid's version of Orpheus's dismemberment: "Membra iacent diversa locis . . . / Iamque mare invectae flumen populare relinquunt" (*Metamorphoses*, Book 11, ll. 50–54).

89. Preface to the *Filles du feu* in *Œuvres*, vol. 3, p. 458. Nerval sounds a similar note in an article from 1845, when he speaks of a Moldavian prince who "arrived from Germany, where he had more studied than understood Hegel" (*Œuvres*, vol. 1, p. 917). These somewhat ironic references to German obscurantism are not, however, the only times that Nerval mentions the German philosopher, and elsewhere he suggests, at least, a more sober and comprehensive understanding of the Hegelian system: in "Les confidences de Nicolas" he speaks of Restif de la Bretonne as "a writter who lacked only a genius for elucidating his inspirations, in which can be found all the elements of Hegel's doctrine" (*Œuvres*, vol. 2, p. 1035). In an article on a marionette theatre from 1846 one finds him referring explicitly to a thesis from Hegel's *Aesthetics*, translated into French six years before by Charles Bénard: "Hegel, whom we must always cite when it is a question of aesthetics, has proved at length that in art nothing is frivolous" (*Œuvres*, vol. 1, p. 1101).

90. Virgil, pp. 230–31 (emphasis added, my translation).

91. A similar story is related concerning Adonis, whose partial victory over death was already noted in relation to "Le Christ aux Oliviers" and who seemed to represent an important figure of resurrection for Nerval. According to Dom Pernety's *Fables égyptiennes et grecques*, the goddess Venus fell in love with the young mortal, who was killed through the machinations of a jealous Mars. On the boy's death, Proserpina fell in love with him too. Venus "asked Jupiter for his [Adonis's] return to earth; Proserpina did not want to relinquish him. Jupiter left the decision to the muse Calliope, who determined that these two goddesses would enjoy him alternately for six months each" (vol. 2, p. 297).

92. See Heidi Uster, *Identité et dualité*.
93. Cited in Richer, *Expérience*, p. 540.
94. Hegel, *Phenomenology*, p. 19.
95. On this passage from the Preface, as well as the "failure" of absolute philosophy's synthetic aspirations, see the discussion of Kojève in Chapter 2.
96. On the *object little a*, see Anika Lemaire, p. 129.
97. *Black Sun*, p. 152 (trans. modified); *Soleil noir*, p. 164.
98. *Phenomenology*, pp. 12–13.
99. Ibid., p. 12.
100. Ibid., p. 15.
101. See "Naming Death" in Chapter 4.
102. Ibid., p. 14.
103. Ibid.
104. Ibid.
105. Ibid., p. 15.
106. Ibid., p. 17.
107. Ibid.
108. Ibid., p. 16.
109. Ibid., p. 17.

338 *Notes to Chapter 7*

110. Ibid., p. 16.
111. Ibid., pp. 18–19 (trans. modified).
112. "This tarrying with the negative is the magical power that converts it into being. This power is identical with what we earlier called the Subject" (*Phenomenology*, p. 19).
113. *Being and Time*, p. 212.
114. Ibid., p. 311 (original emphasis).

Chapter 7. 'Aurélia': The Signs of Others

1. "Le Rêve est une seconde vie. Je n'ai pu percer sans frémir ces portes d'ivoire ou de corne qui nous séparent du monde invisible. Les premiers instants du sommeil sont l'image de la mort; un engourdissement nébuleux saisit notre pensée, et nous ne pouvons déterminer l'instant précis où le moi, sous une autre forme, continue l'œuvre de l'existence. C'est un souterrain vague qui s'éclaire peu à peu, et où se dégagent de l'ombre et de la nuit les pâles figures gravement immobiles qui habitent le séjour des limbes. Puis le tableau se forme, une clarté nouvelle illumine et fait jouer ces apparitions bizarres;—le monde des Esprits s'ouvre pour nous" (Nerval, *Œuvres*, vol. 3, p. 695).
2. One should note that Nerval was working on a project for his *Œuvres complètes* at the time of writing this (see vol. 3, p. 1396–97), and *œuvre* should certainly be read in that sense also.
3. The concepts of use and mention values in language are derived from the difference between phatic and rhetic acts in J. L. Austin's *How To Do Things with Words*, pp. 94–98.
4. The first three reasons that Descartes, in the initial meditation, finds for casting doubt on the apparent certainties of his experience are, in order: that the senses sometimes deceive, that *insensés*, or madmen, take for indubitable things that are manifestly false, and that human beings dream. This last point he expresses as follows: "I must remember that I am a man, and that consequently I am in the habit of sleeping, and in my dreams representing to myself the same things or sometimes even less probable things, than do those who are insane in their waking moments" (*Meditations*, p. 46; *Méditations*, p. 69). Dreaming in its epistemologically primary destructiveness to self-certainty is thus analogous to—and in the course of the argument given as understandable in reference to—madness.
5. Hegel described madness as "*dreaming while awake*" (*Philosophy of Mind*, p. 126) and asserted: "Between [sanity] and insanity the difference is like that between waking and dreaming: only that in insanity the dream falls within the waking limits" (p. 123). In his *Versuch über die Krankenheiten des Kopfes*, Kant writes that "the madman is a waking dreamer" (in *Gesammelte Schriften*, vol. 2, p. 265). On the relation between dreaming and madness during the late eighteenth and early nineteenth centuries, see Berthold-Bond, pp. 28–29.
6. *Œuvres*, vol. 3, p. 708. The modern tendency might well be to read the text

with *Aurélia* in one hand and the *DSM* in the other. On that basis, a possible diagnosis might be ICM: 295.40 (Schizophreniform Disorder) or 295.70 (Schizoaffective Disorder).

7. Cf. the letter to Antony Deschamps of Oct. 12, 1854 (*Œuvres*, vol. 3, p. 900): "I officially acknowledge that I have been ill. I cannot acknowledge that I have been *mad* [fou] or even that I have hallucinated."

8. The degree of communality between the two kinds of discourse at this time, especially in face of madness, is apparent through the title of Pinel's *Traité médico-philosophique sur l'aliénation mentale*.

9. *Œuvres*, vol. 3, p. 705.

10. Ibid., p. 458.

11. Ibid., p. 695.

12. *Aesthetics*, vol. 2, p. 997. On the following page, Hegel again contrasts poetry with the other arts, asserting: "But in the case of the other arts, the manner of conception remains, with its inner creative activity, in continual connection with the execution of its designs in a specific perceptible material" (p. 998).

13. Ibid., p. 997.

14. This idea of a perfect adequation between language, specifically *poetic* language, and subjectivity is yet more forcefully expressed in the following passage from the same text: "poetry is the art which *can exhaust all the depths* of the spirit's whole wealth, and therefore the poet is required to give the deepest and richest inner animation to the material that he brings into his work... The range of what the poet has to experience in himself stretches further [than for the other arts], because he has not only to polish an inner world of the heart and self-conscious ideas but to find for it a correspondent external appearance through which that ideal totality peeps in a fuller and more exhaustive way than is the case with the productions of the other arts. He must know both the inner and the external side of human existence and have absorbed the whole breadth of the world and its phenomena into his own mind, and there have felt it through and through, have penetrated it, deepened and transfigured it" (*Aesthetics*, p. 998, emphasis added). The poet therefore *lives his subject*, and his subject is ultimately himself, but a self which is in some way primordially poetic since its structures and secrets can be absolutely adequately exhausted in their poetic representation. Furthermore, what was cast in terms of consciousness in the preceding passage (discussed in the body of the text) is here expressed as "spiritual" content. The stakes in this passage are therefore not merely those of individual consciousness, but of the progress of Spirit as a whole.

15. Cf. Eluard's "Giorgio di Chirico" in Eluard, *Œuvres complètes*, vol. 1, p. 144. Hegel's construction is not as strange as it may seem to readers brought up with the idea of the Unconscious and the consequent belief that there are, in fact, depths of the psyche impenetrable to the light of consciousness and known to it only through representations. In Kant, for example, one encounters a formulation similar to Hegel's when he argues that the transcendental conditions of experience are not recognized as such (say, by the British empiricists) because they are only manifested in

experience, an appearing that seems to present them as manifestations rather than as manifestation itself (cf. *Pure Reason*, pp. 118, 164, 362, for example). The primary difference between the two is that in Kant, appearing—its transcendental characteristics—is hidden by appearances, while in Hegel's description of poetry the non-transcendental phenomenality of conciousness is hidden only by the idea that the apparent (poetry) must be different from what appears (consciousness), or in other words, appearance is hidden in appearances only by the belief that they differ. Consciousness is not, however, other than or to be abstracted out of poetry; rather, it *is* poetry. This is simply what Hegel wrote, not, or course, what he probably meant to write, since such a conception of consciousness would have rerouted the dialectic of self-consciousness into language theory and poetics; that is the path taken by Nerval, not by the philosopher. A certain caveat must be observed in close readings of Hegel's *Aesthetics*, since they were first published (in 1835) only after his death (in 1831) and on the basis of students' lecture notes edited by H. G. Hotho, not Hegel himself. Still, this is the text that has formed the received tradition.

16. For example: in respect to the other arts, lyric poetry has "on the contrary a higher vocation: its task, namely, is to liberate the spirit not *from* but *in* feeling" (*Aesthetics*, vol. 2, p. 1112).

17. Cf. Proust's remark about *Sylvie*: "one is obliged at every moment to turn the preceding pages to see where one is, whether it is the present or a recollection of the past" (*Contre Sainte-Beuve*, p. 238).

18. Cited in *Œuvres*, vol. 3, p. 1329. In fact, the Collection Spoelberch de Louvenjoul at the Bibliothèque de l'Institut de France contains a series of galleys for almost all of *Aurélia*, which bear a single correction by Nerval himself and, in several places, the notation "Lacune [gap]" in another hand.

19. The editors of the most recent Pléiade edition argue, however, for certain obvious mistakes in the *Revue de Paris* interpretation of Nerval's plans. The most significant would be Ulbach's use of a manuscript, found on the author at his death, to supplement rather than replace an existing section (see *Œuvres*, vol. 3, p. 1329).

20. Gautier's remarks on this subject appear in a note to Ulbach written in the margins of a scrap of the galleys (see *Œuvres*, vol. 3, pp. 1366–67).

21. On Dec. 2, Nerval wrote to Blanche: "My thoughts have always been pure, so grant me the liberty to express them. I am sending you two pages that should be added to those which I gave you yesterday. I shall continue this series of dreams if you like, or I shall set about writing a play—that would be more gay and would earn more"; to his father, on the same date: "I am undertaking to write and to take note of all the impressions which my illness has left behind in me. It will not be a study without value for observation and science"; and in a letter to Blanche the next day he spoke of his desire to "continue my work, which, I believe, can only be useful and honorable to your establishment. I am able in this way to free my head of all these visions which have peopled it" (*Œuvres*, vol. 3, pp. 831, 832, 833). The pages Nerval speaks of having given to Blanche on the first of December would probably have

been those that follow *Aurélia* in the Pléiade edition and which seem more closely related to *Pandora* in content than to the former work.

22. Letters to his father of May 31, 1854 (*Œuvres*, vol. 3, p. 859), to Blanche of June 11 and 25 (pp. 862 and 873), and to Liszt of June 23 (p. 871). The chronological and textual-critical information in this section is condensed from *Œuvres*, vol. 3, pp. 1170–73, 1182–89, 1267–76, 1325–36; and pp. 325–78 in Pichois and Brix.

23. *Œuvres*, vol. 3, p. 888.

24. *Œuvres*, vol. 3, p. 723.

25. "Toutefois, me disais-je, il est sûr que ces sciences sont mélangées d'erreurs humaines. L'alphabet, l'hiéroglyphe mystérieux ne nous arrivent qu'incomplets et faussés soit par le temps, soit par ceux-là mêmes qui ont intérêt à notre ignorance; retrouvons la lettre perdue ou le signe effacé, recomposons la gamme dissonante, et nous prendrons force dans le monde des esprits. C'est ainsi que je croyais percevoir les rapports du monde réel avec le monde des esprits. La terre, ses habitants et leur histoire étaient le théâtre où venaient s'accomplir les actions physiques qui préparaient l'existence et la situation des êtres immortels attachés à sa destinée" (ibid., p. 724).

26. "Comment, me disais-je, ai-je pu exister si longtemps hors de la nature et sans m'identifier à elle? Tout vit, tout agit, tout se correspond; les rayons magnétiques émanés de moi-même ou des autres traversent sans obstacle la chaîne infinie des choses créées; c'est un réseau transparent qui couvre le monde, et dont les fils déliés se communiquent de proche en proche aux planètes et aux étoiles. Captif en ce moment sur la terre, je m'entretiens avec le chœur des astres, qui prend part à mes joies et à mes douleurs!" (ibid., p. 740).

27. Ibid. Cf. Nerval's footnote at the bottom of page 705, which speaks of a similar *frémissement* (shudder) on perceiving the necessity of subordinating a system to laws.

28. This game of universal history bears a strong resemblance to Foucault's concept of discourse as a process of production regulated and contested by various, opposing wills. In "The Order of Discourse," for instance, he summarizes his global intellectual project with the following words: "Here is the hypothesis which I would like to put forward tonight in order to fix the terrain—or perhaps the very provisional theatre—of the work I am doing: that in every society the production of discourse is at once controlled, selected, organised and redistributed by a certain number of procedures whose role is to ward off its powers and dangers, to gain mastery over its chance events, to evade its ponderous, formidable materiality" (p. 52; *L'Ordre du discours*, pp. 10–11). He speaks of these articulatory procedures as being the expression and determination of power relations such as a will to truth, which functions much like Nietzsche's idea of a will to power: "if one asks the question what has been, what constantly is, through our discourses, that will to truth which has crossed so many centuries of our history, or what is, in its very general form, the type of division that rules our will to know, then it is perhaps something

like a system of exclusion (an historical, modifiable, institutionally constraining system) which can be seen taking shape" (p. 16).

29. "C'est ainsi que les dieux antiques ont été vaincus et asservis par des dieux nouveaux; c'est ainsi, me dis-je encore, en consultant mes souvenirs du monde ancien, que les nécromants dominaient des peuples entiers, dont les générations se succédaient captives sous leur sceptre éternel. O malheur! la Mort elle-même ne peut les affranchir! car nous revivons dans nos fils comme nous avons vécu dans nos pères,—et la science impitoyable de nos ennemis sait nous reconnaître partout. L'heure de notre naissance, le point de la terre où nous paraissons, le premier geste, le nom, la chambre,—et toutes ces consécrations, et tous ces rites qu'on nous impose, tout cela établit une série heureuse ou fatale d'où l'avenir dépend tout entier" (*Œuvres*, vol. 3, pp. 740–41).

30. "Mais si déjà cela est terrible selon les seuls calculs humains, comprenez ce que cela doit être en se rattachant aux formules mystérieuses qui établissent l'ordre des mondes. On l'a dit justement: rien n'est indifférent, rien n'est impuissant dans l'univers; un atome peut tout dissoudre, un atome peut tout sauver. O terreur! voilà l'éternelle distinction du bon et du mauvais. Mon âme est-elle la molécule indestructible, le globule qu'un peu d'air gonfle, mais qui retrouve sa place dans la nature, ou ce vide même, image du néant qui disparaît dans l'immensité? Serait-elle encore la parcelle fatale destinée à subir, sous toutes ses transformations, les vengeances des êtres puissants? Je me vis amené ainsi à me demander compte de ma vie, et même de mes existences antérieures. En me prouvant que j'étais bon, je me prouvai ainsi que j'avais toujours dû l'être. Et si j'ai été mauvais, me dis-je, ma vie actuelle ne sera-t-elle pas une suffisante expiation?" (ibid., p. 741). This idea of the interconnectedness of the universe and the relation of the *molécule* to it recalls Leibniz's formulation of the monad as representation of the totality of creation. Cf. the *Monadology* (in *Philosophical Essays*): "This interconnection or accommodation of all created things to each other, and each to all the others, brings it about that each simple substance [monad] has relations that express all the others, and consequently, that each simple substance is a perpetual, living mirror of the universe" (p. 220); and "composite substances are analogous to simple substances. For everything is a plenum, which makes all matter interconnected. In a plenum, every motion has some effect on distant bodies, in proportion to their distance. For each body is affected, not only by those in contact with it, and in some way feels the effects of everything that happens to them, but also, through them, it feels the effects of those in contact with the bodies with which it is itself immediately in contact. From this it follows that this communication extends to any distance whatsoever. As a result, every body is affected by everything that happens in the universe, to such an extent that he who sees all can read in each thing what happens everywhere, and even what has happened or what will happen, by observing in the present what is remote in time as well as in space" (p. 221). Were it not for his concern with issues of will and responsibility, one could understand the visionary Nerval in the garden of Dr. Blanche's clinic as Leibniz's "he who sees all."

31. See the section on Zola in Chapter 2.

32. *Œuvres*, vol. 3, p. 696.   33. Ibid., p. 739.

34. Ibid., p. 721.   35. Ibid., p. 720.

36. A footnote to the fourth chapter of the first section reveals an ambivalence on Nerval's part toward this same convergence of fear, the law, the father (here under the guise of God) and the questions of personal origination. The note ends with the words: "I shudder [je frémis] to go any farther, for in the Trinity resides a fearful mystery... We are born under the biblical law... " (ibid., p. 705n). The author's own conflicted attitude toward even identifying this nexus of issues seems to be indicated by the fact that in the manuscript version the text is crossed out but finally let stand, accompanied in the margins by the notation, "bon—en note [fine—in a note]" (p. 1343): it is written, withdrawn, then reasserted.

37. Ibid., p. 741.

38. Ibid.

39. On the importance of Blanche as a father figure, see Peter Dayan, pp. 65–108. In *Le Travail du négatif*, the psychoanalyst André Green also speaks of such an identification between Nerval's father and Blanche, "to whom he [Nerval] is bound by an authentic transference" (p. 327).

40. Quotations from *Aurélia*, (*Œuvres*, vol. 3, p. 730) and *Promenades et souvenirs* (*Œuvres*, vol. 3, p. 680).

41. *Œuvres*, vol. 3, pp. 680 and 681. For a novelized version of the crossing of the Berezina, see Balzac's *Adieu* in *La Comédie humaine*, vol. 10, pp. 961–1014.

42. See also *Œuvres*, vol. 3, p. 680.

43. Ibid., p. 1140. The text in question is the short story, *Le Monstre vert*, published for the first time in Nov. 1849.

44. Given the extremely striking resemblances between passages on souls in fusion from *Aurélia* and discussions of simple substances in works such as the *Monadology*, it seems likely that the Leibnizian resolution of the relation between the intelligible and the material through the mathematical structuring of the monadic universe affected Nerval's conceptions of the *molécule* (used to describe the soul also in *Œuvres*, vol. 3, p. 741) and the *âme* either directly or, more probably, through other writers who were influenced by it.

45. *Œuvres*, vol. 3, p. 703. Cf. Leibniz's *Monadology*: "But where there are no parts, neither extension, nor shape nor divisibility is possible. These monads are the true atoms of nature and, in brief, the elements of things" (p. 213); and "there is a world of creatures, of living beings, of animals, of entelechies, of souls in the least part of matter... Each portion of matter can be conceived as a garden full of plants, and as a pond full of fish. But each branch of a plant, each limb of an animal, each drop of its humors, is still another such garden or pond... And although the earth and air lying between the garden plants, or the water lying between the fish of the pond, are neither plant nor fish, they contain yet more of them, though of a subtleness imperceptible to us, most often... Thus there is nothing fallow, sterile, or dead in the universe, no chaos and no confusion except in appearance, almost like it looks

in a pond at a distance, where we might see the confused and, so to speak, teeming motion of the fish in the pond, without discerning the fish themselves... *But we must not imagine, as some who have misunderstood my thought do, that each soul has a mass or portion of matter of its own, always proper to or allotted by it, and that it consequently possesses other lower living beings, forever destined to serve it. For all bodies are in a perpetual flux, like rivers, and parts enter into them and depart from the continually*" (p. 222, emphasis added). There are many other versions, in *Aurélia*, of this image of a spiritual composite, or of a living community. Cf., for example, *Œuvres*, vol. 3, p. 739: "That thought led me to consider that there was a vast conspiracy of all animate beings to re-establish the world in its original harmony, and that communications took place by the magnetism of the stars, that an uninterrupted chain around the world linked intelligences devoted to that general communication, and that songs, dances, glances, drawn magnetically from one to the next, translated the same aspiration. The moon was for me the refuge of the fraternal souls who, freed from their mortal bodies, worked more freely towards the regeneration of the universe." In another passage he speaks of God as being swallowed up in the sum of all creatures: "The fatal system that had been created in my mind did not admit of that solitary royalty [God]... or rather, he was absorbed into the sum of beings: he was the god of Lucretius, powerless and lost in his immensity" (p. 722).

46. Passages from the "Seventh Walk" of the *Reveries* seem to prefigure in the negative Nerval's personal mythology of a metalworking, Cainite race dwelling in the bowels of the earth and, more immediately, the conjunction of metallurgy and a maternal earth seen in this paragraph from *Aurélia*: "In itself, the mineral realm has nothing lovely or attractive. Its riches, sealed up within the bosom of the earth, seem to have been removed from the sight of man so as not to tempt his cupidity. They are there, as though in reserve, to serve one day as a supplement to the true riches more within his reach and for which he loses taste to the extent that he becomes corrupted. Thus he must call on industry, labor, and toil to relieve his misery. He digs in the bowels of the earth. He goes to its center, at the risk of his life and the expense of his health, to seek imaginary goods in place of the real goods it freely offered him when he knew how to enjoy them. He flees the sun and the day which he is no longer worthy to see. He buries himself alive and does well, no longer deserving to live in the light of day. There, quarries, pits, forges, furnaces, an apparatus of anvils, hammers, smoke, and fire replace the gentle images of pastoral occupations. The wan faces of the wretches who languish in the foul fumes of the mines, of grimy ironsmiths, of hideous cyclopes are the spectacle the apparatus of the mines substitutes, in the bosom of the earth, for that of greenery and flowers, of azure sky, of amorous shepherds, and of robust plowmen on its surface" (*Reveries*, p. 96; *Œuvres*, vol. 1, pp. 1066–67). Here again the earth is seen as a living body, with breast and bowels; to enjoy the riches provided by the former is healthy while to penetrate the latter is a violence not merely against this maternally nourishing body but against nature itself.

47. *Œuvres*, vol. 3, p. 704.

48. Ibid., p. 702.

49. Ibid., p. 705.

50. Nerval speaks of two visits he makes to his father (ibid., pp. 733 and 736). A particularly strong reading of *Aurélia*, but for that reason also particularly susceptible to the limitations inherent in psychoanalytic approches—whose critique is proleptically formulated in Nerval's text itself—can be found in André Green, *Le Travail du négatif*, pp. 322–45, which includes an especially astute discussion of the relations—esp. the medical relations—between Nerval and his father.

51. Green does acknowledge that "the process of writing is integrated into his thought" (ibid., p. 330) but understands this condition as negative or pathological, insofar as it is part of a narcissistic problematic.

52. *Œuvres*, vol. 3, p. 723.

53. Ibid., p. 728.

54. Namely, in the paragraph at the end of the first chapter of the second section, where Nerval visits a sick friend, whom he feels to be in God's grace: "God is with him, I cried out... but he is no longer with me! O woe! I have driven him from me, I have threatened him, I have cursed him! It was certainly him, that mystical brother, who distanced himself farther and farther from my soul and who warned me in vain! That chosen husband, that king of glory, it is he who is judging me and condemning me, and who is carrying off forever into his heaven the woman whom he would have given me and of whom I am henceforth unworthy" (ibid., p. 725).

55. Ibid., p. 720.

56. So too, according to the Lacanian formulation of the semiotic phallus, must individuals alienate their bodies from their phallic representation, hiding the one from the other.

57. "J'aimais davantage [que mes médecins] ceux de mes amis qui, par une patiente complaisance ou par suite d'idées analogues aux miennes, me faisaient faire de longs récits des choses que j'avais vues en esprit. L'un d'eux me dit en pleaurant: 'N'est-ce pas que c'est vrai qu'il y a un Dieu?—Oui!' lui dis-je avec enthousiasme. Et nous nous embrassâmes comme deux frères de cette patrie mystique entrevue.—Quel bonheur je trouvai d'abord dans cette conviction! Ainsi ce doute éternel de l'immortalité de l'âme qui affecte les meilleurs esprits se trouvait résolu pour moi. Plus de mort, plus de tristesse, plus d'inquiétude" (*Œuvres*, vol. 3, p. 708).

58. "'. . . —Oui!' lui dis-je avec enthousiasme. [Mais cette idée souleva en moi plutôt ~~la conviction~~ des doutes étranges. La vie surnaturelle m'était prouvée, mais non l'existence d'un être unique tout puissant. Je ne mettais nulle impiété, nulle révolte à ce raisonnement funeste. C'était une crainte douloureuse et non l'espoir ténébreux du méchant qui redoute la main divine. Sans doute me disais-je] Quel bonheur . . . " (ibid., p. 1345). Brackets denote Nerval's deletions.

59. Ibid., p. 722.

60. Cf., in *Aurélia*, pp. 736 and 741. This tendency becomes a veritable outpouring in *Les Filles du feu* (ibid., p. 620). Even though Nerval uses this passage to

show the transformation of Isis into a Christian metaphysical principle, he himself refuses to subscribe unreservedly to such an interpretation of the goddess, and rather than propositionally identifying her with death, he poses such an identification as a question.

61. *Œuvres*, vol. 3, p. 608.

62. See Freud's "Fetishism" in *The Standard Edition*, vol. 21, pp. 152–57, and "Medusa's Head," vol. 28, pp. 273–74. In "Agency of the Letter in the Unconscious," Lacan applies the substitutive aspect of fetishization to the primary structures of language, and he describes the metonymic displacement of desire as a mechanism for continuously eliding signification, which is to say that by substituting one signifier for another according to the connection between them as signifiers, their possible relation to an object or significance is suspended: "the metonymic structure . . . is the connexion between signifier and signified that permits the elision in which the signifier installs the lack-of-being in the object relation, using the value of 'reference back' possessed by signification in order to invest it with the desire aimed at the very lack it supports. The sign—placed between () represents here the maintenance of the bar [*barre*]—which, in the original algorithm, marked the irreducibility in which, in the relations between signifier and signified, the resistance of signification is constituted" (*Ecrits: A Selection*, p. 164; *Ecrits*, p. 515). The illustration given by Lacan for this displacement which both hides and maintains the lack of an original or primary object of signification is fetishization, wherein what is hidden and preserved is an absence, namely, the missing maternal phallus, or rather absence as such, since it is the privileged absence that initiates the subject into the symbolic order and thereby inaugurates him or her as subject: "To fall back on a more limited incident, but one more likely to provide us with the final seal on our proposition, let me cite the article on fetishism of 1927, and the case Freud reports there of a patient who, to achieve sexual satisfaction, needed a certain shine on the nose (*Glanz auf der Nase*); analysis showed that his early, English-speaking years had seen the displacement of the burning curiosity that he felt for the phallus of his mother, that is to say, for that eminent *manque-à-être*, for that want-to-be, whose privileged signifier Freud revealed to us, into a *glance at the nose* [in English] in the forgotten language of his childhood, rather than a *shine on the nose* [in English]" (*Ecrits: A Selection*, p. 179; *Ecrits*, p. 522).

63. *Œuvres*, vol. 3, p. 736.

64. In another vision, from the sixth chapter of the first part, Nerval finds a different way to depict such a relation of identity among various female personages, and it too is articulated around the idea of the *trait*. In a dream he enters a room: "Three women were working in that room, and represented, without absolutely resembling them, relatives and friends from my childhood. It seemed that each one of the women had the features [*les traits*] of several of those people. The contours of their faces varied like the flame of a lamp, and at every moment something of one passed into the other; the smile, the voice, the color of her eyes, of her hair, her figure, familiar gestures were all exchanged as if they had lived from the same life, and

each one was in this way composed of all, similar to those types which painters imitate from several models in order to achieve a complete beauty" (ibid., p. 709). The oldest of the three will separate herself from her sisters to lead Nerval through a trellis and into a garden where she will then be transformed into a personification of the whole of the material world. She is, however, in a certain way inalienable from her sisters, since her appearance depends on a circulation of physical characteristics among them. They are separate yet the same, the endless metamorphosis of three individuals through the possible combinations of their features. They are bound together, in their mutual appearing, by a process of endless exchange which generates among them a certain resemblance. Like the combinatory logic of manifest resemblance that holds families together as race, these three sisters are identified with each other by a principle of sharing and repetition. In *Promenades et souvenirs*, written at about the same time as *Aurélia*, Nerval asserted that he never saw the original of his mother, only likenesses: "I've never seen my mother, her portraits were lost or stolen; I only know that she resembled an engraving of the time, after Prud'hon or Fragonard, which was called *Modesty*. The fever that killed her has seized hold of me three times, at moments that form unique and periodic divisions in my life. Always, at those moments, I felt my spirit struck by the images of mourning and desolation which surrounded my cradle" (ibid., p. 680). Again, the maternal original exists only through and as a result of reproduction. Cf. Shoshana Felman, "Gérard de Nerval: Writing Living, or Madness as Autobiography" in *Writing and Madness*, pp. 59–77 ("Gérard de Nerval: Folie et répétition" in *La Folie*, pp. 61–96).

65. *Œuvres*, vol. 3, pp. 743–44. A similar image of a dismembered universal mother can be found earlier in the text, at the end of Nerval's vision of creation: "Everywhere the suffering image of the eternal Mother was dying, weeping or languishing. Across the vague civilizations of Asia and Africa one could see constantly renewed a bloody scene of orgy and carnage which the same spirits reproduced in new forms. . . . For how many more years will the world have to suffer, for the vengeance of these eternal enemies must renew itself under other skies! These are the divided slices of the snake that surrounds the world... Separated by iron, they join up again in a hideous kiss cemented with the blood of men" (p. 715).

66. Ibid., p. 711.

67. Ibid., p. 712.

68. Ibid.

69. A belief in the existence of such a female sperm necessary for reproduction is attested, for example, in classical antiquity, where it was, however, considered a counterpart to male sperm; see Aline Rousselle, pp. 27–32.

70. *Œuvres*, vol. 3, pp. 712–13.   71. Ibid., p. 713.

72. Ibid., p. 722.   73. Ibid.

74. See the discussion of death-based subjectivity at the end of Chapter 6, above.

75. See above, Chapter 1, the discussion of the guillotine as subject.

76. The fact that it is *la chirurgie* which severs the organ of sensual existence is

itself significant, especially to a psychoanalytic reading of this text, since Nerval's father was himself a surgeon. For the importance of this latter fact to the medical-paternal subtext of *Aurélia*, see André Green, *Le Travail du négatif*, pp. 322–45.

77. See Chapter 1.

78. *Œuvres*, vol. 3, p. 723.

79. Nerval later offers another version of the creation which levels all that is remarkable in the earlier account: "Without troubling the impenetrable mystery of the worlds' eternity, my thoughts traveled back to the time when the sun, like the plant which represents it and which, with tilted head, follows the revolution of its celestial progress, sowed on the earth the fecond seeds of plants and animals. It was none other than fire itself, which, being a composite of souls, instinctively formulated the common dwelling. The spirit of the God-Being, which was reproduced and, so to speak, reflected on the earth, became the common type of human souls, each one of which, consequently, was at the same time man and God. Such were the Elohim" (ibid., p. 724). This flattened, amended version does not last long. Virtually everything else in the text militates against it, and it is swept away, at the end of *Aurélia*, in the explosive divulgence of the "magic web," and in the final lyricizations of the female parthenogenic version that mark the closing fragments called "Les Mémorables." The motivation for the brief, seemingly insignificant detour that the paternally amended version of the creation scenario constitutes would appear to be explained by its context. The author is here proposing a nonblasphemous version of origination, a version that would be acceptable to a Christian Father-God who expects servile humility from his sons.

80. Ibid., p. 744.

81. Ibid., p. 745.

82. Ibid.

83. Cf. Lacan, "Function" (*Ecrits: A Selection*, p. 87; *Ecrits*, p. 301): "Speech is in fact a gift of language, and language is not immaterial. It is a subtle body, but body it is." For Lacan, however, this very materiality makes of language a substance for ego-identifications, that is, exactly those "corporeal images" which are negated by the subject. By not accounting for the difference between subtilized and sublimated body, Lacan reintegrates the materiality of language into an annihilating relation between abstract subject and concrete—or material—individual, an annihilation that Nerval is attempting to find his way out of here.

84. *Œuvres*, vol. 3, pp. 745–46.

85. This is apparently true also of the manuscript version of this passage, referred to as Planche 13 (PA 13) by the editors of the Pléiade edition.

86. The Corybants were quite literally desexed. During the Roman festival of the Hilaria they would castrate themselves in imitation of Attis in order to draw nearer to the goddess Cybele. This is very different from the logic of paternal castration as it figures in the Freudian formulation of the Oedipus complex. In the latter, the putative or symbolic castration comes at the hands of the father and is intended to separate the child from the libidinized maternal body. In the former, the

real castration comes at the hands of the initiate himself, who thereby strengthens his bond to the mother. That this latter castration is not a desexualization but rather an intensification and enlargement of the libidinal field, has been argued by André Green and Bruno Bettelheim. See Green's *Le complexe de castration*, pp. 19–20: "Among the priests of Cybele, self-mutilation involves both sexes, although it is more frequent among men. It is remarkable that self-emasculation took place in an orgiastic atmosphere, as if the change of sex towards the feminine signified an accession to a higher *jouissance*. One thinks, here, of Tiresias and the issue of the disproportion between masculine *jouissance* and feminine *jouissance*, the latter being thought to be nine times more powerful... It is not easy to understand the meaning of emasculation intended to please the Mother-Goddess. Why would she demand the sacrifice of virility? Is it to affirm the feminine-maternal predominance of an entirely feminized universe, that is, one subjected to a maternal law? How is one to reconcile that emasculation—that is to say desexualization—with the feminine orgying supposed to follow the self-mutilation? Is it a matter of *a*sexualizing or of *over*sexualizing by means of devirilization? Should one see in these cults of Mother-Goddesses stages 'anterior' to the cults of masculine Gods or are they different contexts?" See also Bruno Bettelheim, pp. 154–64. For the sake of brevity, this generalized libidinization in the "Mémorables" (marked certainly by the free access now granted the Corybants to "the secret grottos where Love has made them shelters") will be referred to as a "chaste love."

87. On the implication of a first person in the second person, see Emile Benveniste, "Relationships of Person in the Verb" in *Problems*, pp. 195–204 ("Structures des relations de personne dans le verbe" in *Problèmes de linguistique générale*, vol. 1, pp. 225–36).

88. For the idea of pardon and blessing as speech acts, see the discussion of explicit performatives in Austin, esp. p. 45.

89. *Œuvres*, vol. 3, 749.

90. Ibid.

91. Cf. ibid., p. 708.

92. This idea of a community held together in love appears in germ throughout the text in its various expressions of what one might call compassion. There is the concern Nerval feels towards the police who arrest him: "A night watch surrounded me—I had, at that moment, the idea that I had become very big, and that, completely flooded with electric forces, I was going to knock over anyone who approached me. There was something comic in the care which I took to protect the forces and the lives of the soldiers who had picked me up" (*Œuvres*, vol. 3, p. 700); he speaks of the sympathy which one's own suffering engenders: "When one is unhappy, one thinks of others' unhappiness" (p. 724); he justifies his publication of *Aurélia* as an aid to others who might be in despair: "Despair and suicide are the result of certain situations fatal to anyone who, in his sorrows and his joys, does not have faith in immortality—I believe I will have done something good and useful by naively laying out the succession of ideas by which I regained a calm and a new force

350 Notes to Chapter 7

to set against the future misfortunes of life" (p. 731); he expresses his profound aversion for all philosophies of egotism: "it is in religious thought that one must seek aid—I have never been able to find any in that philosophy which offers us only maxims of egotism or, at most, reciprocity, empty experience and bitter doubt" (p. 722).

93. Œuvres, vol. 3, p. 720.

94. See "The Signification of the Phallus" in Ecrits: A Selection, p. 281 (Ecrits, p. 685).

95. Ecrits: A Selection, p. 286; Ecrits, p. 690.

96. Ecrits: A Selection, p. 286; Ecrits, p. 690.

97. Ecrits: A Selection, p. 285; Ecrits, p. 689.

98. Ecrits: A Selection, p. 287; Ecrits, p. 692.

99. On what Lacan will elsewhere call the "symbolic concatenation" ("Situation de la psychanalyse en 1956" in Ecrits, p. 464), see the opening page of his "Séminare sur 'La Lettre volée'," where he describes the relation between the imaginary and the "symbolic chain," which he characterizes as an activity of displacement or Entstellung (Ecrits, p. 11). The elision on this page between the terms "symbolic chain" and "signifying chain" indicates the importance of any subsequent discussion of the signifier for the question of subjectivity: since the latter emerges as a product—or the production—of the symbolic order, which is itself inaugurated in the oedipal fear of castration, discussions of the signifying chain, insofar as they can also be understood as discussions of the symbolic, serve to determine the structure and processes of the subject. The observation is basic but for that reason indispensable to an understanding of Lacan, and it is in its light that one should read such passages as the following: "I think where I am not, therefore I am where I do not think. Words that render sensible to an ear properly attuned with what elusive ambiguity the ring of meaning flees from our grasp along the verbal thread" ("Agency of the Letter" in Ecrits: A Selection, p. 166; Ecrits, p. 517). Conversely, discussions of symbolic effects must be understood in terms of the differential activity of signifiers, as in the following quotation: "This is precisely where the Oedipus complex—in so far as we continue to recognize it as covering the whole field of our experience with its *signification*—may be said, in this connexion, to mark the limits that our discipline assigns to subjectivity: namely, what the subject can know of his unconscious participation in the movement of the complex structures of marriage ties, by verifying the *symbolic* effects in his individual existence of the tangential movement towards incest that has manifested itself ever since the coming of a universal community" ("Function" in Ecrits: A Selection, p. 66; Ecrits, p. 277, emphasis added). Bruce Fink makes too little of the role of castration in Lacanian subjectivity, reducing it to something of a subcategory (see The Lacanian Subject, pp. 72–73). Although Lacan's approaches to subjectivity shifted over the years, which Fink details admirably, this last quotation nonetheless indicates the central and original role of castration in *entirely* covering and delimiting the field of subjectivity.

100. "Signification" in Ecrits: A Selection, p. 285; Ecrits, p. 690.

101. Ecrits: A Selection, p. 287; Ecrits, p. 692.

102. On the penis as the organ of sexual difference, see notably "Female Sexuality" (*Standard Edition*, vol. 21, pp. 225–43) and "The Infantile Genital Organization (An Interpolation into the Theory of Sexuality)" (vol. 19, p. 145): "At the stage of the pre-genital sadistic-anal organization, there is as yet no question of male and female; the antithesis between *active* and *passive* is the dominant one. At the following stage of infantile genital organization, which we now know about, *maleness* exists, but not femaleness. The antithesis here is between having *a male genital* and being *castrated*. It is not until development has reached its completion at puberty that the sexual polarity coincides with *male* and *female*. Maleness combines [the factors of] subject, activity and the possession of the penis; femaleness takes over [those of] object and passivity. The vagina is now valued as a place of shelter for the penis; it enters into the heritage of the womb." In "The Dissolution of the Œdipus Complex" (vol. 19, pp. 173–79), Freud speaks of the penis as the organ fantasmatically identified as the instrument for taking pleasure in the mother's body: "As can be clearly shown, [the child] stands in the Œdipus attitude to his parents; his masturbation is only a genital discharge of the sexual excitation belonging to the complex, and throughout his later years will owe its importance to that relationship. The Œdipus complex offered the child two possibilities of satisfaction, an active and a passive one. He could put himself in his father's place in a masculine fashion and have intercourse with his mother as his father did, in which case he would soon have felt the latter as a hindrance; or he might want to take the place of his mother and be loved by his father, in which case his mother would become superfluous. The child may have had only very vague notions as to what constitutes a satisfying erotic intercourse; but certainly the penis must play a part in it, for the sensations in his own organ were evidence of that" (p. 176). An organic, quasi-evolutionary argument for the privileging of the penis is offered in "Some Psychical Consequences of the Anatomical Distinction Between the Sexes" (in vol. 19, pp. 248–58): "Since the penis . . . owes its extraordinarily high narcissistic cathexis to its organic signification for the propagation of the species, the catastrophe of the Œdipus complex (the abandonment of incest and the institution of conscience and morality) may be regarded as a victory of the race over the individual" (p. 257). It may be remarked in passing that the impersonality of the subject constituted by castration anxiety, which will integrate Lacanian theory into the tradition of death-based subjectivity exemplified by Kant's sublime, Hegel's subject, and Heidegger's Being-unto-death, is already suggested in the sacrifice of individual to race described in this 1925 article.

103. This interpretation flies in the face, it must be said, of most readings of Lacan, which hold that whatever else it may be, the phallus is certainly not related to the penis. As Fink, for example, writes: "Castration, in this Lacanian context, clearly has nothing to do with biological organs or threats thereto" (Fink, p. 73). It is hard to imagine what sense could be made, in that light, of this passage from "The Signification of the Phallus," where even scrupulous and close readers of Lacan acknowledge some puzzlement. See, for example, Muller and Richardson, p. 336.

104. "Signification" in *Ecrits: A Selection*, p. 286; *Ecrits*, pp. 692–93.

105. That the bar has this other sense is not immediately clear from the paper in question, which seems to draw, elliptically, on other, more explicit treatments of the issue in Lacan's writings. The subject that is instantiated through this barring is thus often referred to as the barred-S subject, and represented with the sign: $. See "The Subversion of the Subject" in *Ecrits: A Selection*, pp. 292–325 (*Ecrits*, pp. 793–827). For the original formulation of the sign in Saussure, see *Course*, pp. 111–22 (*Cours*, pp. 155–69). It is true that Lacan speaks of a "franchissement," or crossing, of the bar S/s by the subject: "This crossing expresses the condition of passage of the signifier into the signified that I pointed out above, although provisionally confusing it with the place of the subject" (*Ecrits: A Selection*, p. 164; *Ecrits*, pp. 515–16). It should be understood, however, that this crossing is in fact the metaphoric substitution of another signifier for a signified and that the so-called crossing only throws the subject back onto the level of the signifier.

106. In a curiously unsubstantiated argument on symbolic castration, Julia Kristeva, in *New Maladies of the Soul*, contends that the separation between thought and affect, or between the *I* as "*Subject of the cogito*" and the affective *ego* (pp. 93–94; *Les Nouvelles maladies*, pp. 144–45), can result from a refusal of castration (p. 95; pp. 146–47). It would be interesting to see the theoretical justifications for this approach spelled out, since, as shown above, castration itself already is just such a separation.

107. *Ecrits: A Selection*, p. 289; *Ecrits*, pp. 693–94.

108. *Œuvres*, vol. 3, p. 705n. Elsewhere, Lacan states: "It is in the *name of the father* that we must recognize the support of the symbolic function which, from the dawn of history, has identified his person with the figure of the law" (*Ecrits: A Selection*, p. 67; *Ecrits*, p. 278). On the interrelation among the symbolic bar of castration, the law of the father, and pleasure, see "Subversion of the Subject" in *Ecrits: A Selection*, p. 319 (*Ecrits*, p. 821): "But it is not the Law itself that bars the subject's access to *jouissance*—rather it creates out of an almost natural barrier a barred subject."

109. *Ecrits: A Selection*, p. 288; *Ecrits*, p. 693.

110. *Ecrits: A Selection*, p. 319 (trans. modified); *Ecrits*, p. 822.

111. There has been much recent interest in the relation between the sublime and issues of representation or figurability, since the sublime is normally taken as the figure of the end of figures; this relation is here, in reference to Lacan, understood as the semiotic negation of the sensuous, imaginable world. See also, Marie-Hélène Huet's "The Revolutionary Sublime"; Jean-Luc Nancy's "The Sublime Offering" in *Of the Sublime* (pp. 25–53); and Jean-François Lyotard's "The Sublime and the Avant-Garde" in *The Lyotard Reader* (pp. 196–211). The historian Daniel Arasse's observation that to thinkers of the late eighteenth century the problem of the guillotine as public spectacle and aesthetico-epistemological conundrum is that in the discreet instantaneity of its execution *there is nothing to see*, would be in utter conformity with the unrepresentability of the sublime moment in its most purely terrible form: in the lack of spectacle characterizing this mechanized death lies the utter ablation of all figuration and its reduction into the purely intelligible, semiotic instant

that shows nothing but means everything (see *La Guillotine et l'imaginaire de la Terreur* and the discussion in Chapter 2, above).

112. See *Œuvres*, vol. 3, p. 731.
113. Ibid., p. 722.
114. "The Meaning of Meaning" in *Outside the Subject*, p. 92.
115. Ibid., p. 94.
116. Ibid.

Chapter 8. Death and Its Alternatives

1. "Le Tombeau d'Edgar Poe" in Mallarmé, *Œuvres complètes*, p. 70.
2. "But because Hegel has conceived the negation of the negation, from the point of view of the positive relation inherent in it, as the true and only positive, and from the point of view of the negative relation in it as the only true act and spontaneous activity of all being, he has only found the *abstract, logical, speculative* expression for the movement of history, which is not yet the *real* history of man as a given subject" (*Economic and Philosophic Manuscripts of 1844*, in Marx and Engels, vol. 3, p. 328). Marx's critique of Feuerbach centered, too, on the transcendental abstraction that grounded the latter's understanding of human intercourse. See the *Theses on Feuerbach* (in *The Marx-Engels Reader*, pp. 143–45).
3. On Heidegger, see Chapter 2 above.
4. Julia Kristeva, *Polylogue*, p. 69.
5. Ibid., p. 57. See also: "'genuine negation' (what we are calling negativity) presupposes 'impersonal thought,' a vanishing of the unitary subject, while symbolic negation, the 'no,' is nothing but the symbolic function itself positing the unitary subject. Lacan says that it is the Father who says: 'No'" (p. 65).
6. "It concerns the movement of an impersonal 'thinking' which is precisely the destruction of thought, the only possible destruction of *thought* . . . without the *process of signification* being lost, since the subject is not lost in it, but rather, multiplied" (ibid.).
7. Ibid., p. 101.
8. "The *rejet* has not yet, therefore, dissociated the subject from the object, but travels over the body and the surrounding milieu to a rhythm whose logic is a-representative: it binds, articulates, disposes, organizes, but does not represent in the presence of a subject coagulated in face of an object. Such a pre-verbal logic structures the space from which the subject/object separation will detach itself" (ibid., p. 96).
9. *La Part du feu*, pp. 314–17.
10. *Polylogue*, p. 75.
11. "The 'normal,' oedipal path consists in an identification between the child's own body and one of the parents during the oedipal phase. Simultaneously, the rejected object separates itself off definitively; it is not merely rejected, but suppressed as material object. It is the 'opposing other [l'autre en face],' with which a single re-

lation is possible: the sign, the symbolic relation *in absentia*. The *rejet* is thus on the way towards the object's becoming a sign, which will happen when the object is detached from the body and isolated as a real object; in other words and simultaneously, the *rejet* is on the way towards the imposition of the *superego*" (ibid., pp. 71–72).

12. There is some ambiguity in Kristeva's text concerning the chronology of corporeal semiotization; although she speaks of the "the itinerary of the drive [*la pulsion*] across its own body: from the anus to the mouth" (*Polylogue*, p. 75) and seems to view buccal erotization as a displacement of anal pleasure, Kristeva also describes the mouth as the "earliest developed organ of perception and the one which assures the nursing infant's first contact with the exterior" (p. 74n). What is clear, however, is that anal expulsion, whether pedagogically or developmentally, makes sense of oral pleasure.

13. Ibid., p. 74.

14. Ibid., p. 74n.

15. See Walter Kaufmann, *Goethe, Kant, and Hegel*, vol. 1 of *Discovering the Mind*, pp. 173–85 and 215–16.

16. *Polylogue*, p. 65.

17. Ibid., p. 61.

18. One thinks, for instance, of the difficulty that Kojève and Hyppolite both encountered with the passage on "Absolute Freedom and Terror" from the *Phenomenology* (see above, discussion of Kojève in Chapter 2).

19. "Ideology" in Louis Althusser, *Lenin and Philosophy*, p. 152 (trans. modified); "Idéologie" in Althusser, *Positions*, p. 101.

20. " . . . you and I are *always already* subjects, and as such constantly practice the rituals of ideological recognition, which guarantee for us that we are indeed concrete, individual, distinguishable and (naturally) irreplaceable subjects." (*Lenin and Philosophy*, pp. 161–62; *Positions*, p. 112).

21. "As ideology is eternal, I must now suppress the temporal form in which I have presented the functioning of ideology, and say: ideology has always-already interpellated individuals as subjects, which amounts to making it clear that individuals are always-already interpellated by ideology as subjects, which necessarily leads us to one last proposition: *individuals are always-already subjects*. Hence individuals are 'abstract' with respect to the subjects which they always-already are. This proposition might seem paradoxical" (*Lenin and Philosophy*, p. 164; *Positions*, p. 115).

22. *Lenin and Philosophy*, p. 161; *Positions*, p. 111. On the individual as an abstract category see pp. 164–65 and 166n; 115 and 117n. On the materiality of the system, see p. 158; 108: "I shall therefore say that, where only a single subject (such and such an individual) is concerned, the existence of the ideas of his belief is material in that *his ideas are his material actions inserted into material practices governed by material rituals which are themselves defined by the material ideological apparatus from which derive the ideas of that subject*."

23. "Those who are in ideology believe themselves by definition outside ideol-

ogy: one of the effects of ideology is the practical *denegation* of the ideological character of ideology by ideology: ideology never says, 'I am ideological'" (*Lenin and Philosophy*, pp. 163–64; *Positions*, p. 114). See also p. 161; 112: "you and I are *always already* subjects, and as such constantly practice the rituals of ideological recognition."

24. *Lenin and Philosophy*, p. 161; *Positions*, pp. 111–12.

25. "I shall then suggest that ideology 'acts' or 'functions' in such way that it 'recruits' subjects among the individuals (it recruits them all), or 'transforms' the individuals into subjects (it transforms them all) by that very precise operation which I have called *interpellation* or hailing, and which can be imagined along the lines of the most commonplace everyday police (or other) hailing: 'Hey, you there!' Assuming that the theoretical scene I have imagined takes place in the street, the hailed individual will turn round. By this mere one-hundred-and-eighty-degree physical conversion, he becomes a *subject*. Why? Because he has recognized that the hail was 'really' addressed to him and that 'it was *really him* who was hailed'" (*Lenin and Philosophy*, pp. 162–63; *Positions*, p. 113). On the somewhat confusing use of the terms "individual" and "subject here," see p. 166n; 117n: "Although we know that the individual is always already a subject, we go on using this term, convenient because of the contrasting effect it produces."

26. *Lenin and Philosophy*, p. 164; *Positions*, p. 115.

27. Aulagnier, *La Violence de l'interprétation*, p. 227.

28. "We are designating by the terms schizophrenia and paranoia those two modes of representation which, under certain conditions, the 'I' forges from his relation to the world, constructions which have in common the characteristic of being based on a discourse [énoncé] about origins which is substituted for the discourse shared by the collectivity of other subjects" (Aulagnier, p. 222).

29. Ibid., p. 227.

30. "The 'I' must have at his disposal a sign indicating to him the cause of his utterable and intelligible feelings, even if he is the only one to understand that intelligibility" (ibid., p. 231); and: "We have seen, in relation to the question of origins, that it is only if the 'I' can find an answer, which he can name and invest, for the cause of the 'I''s own existence, that he can fashion from it a fundamental discourse [énoncé] which will allow him to place into a context of meaning his conception of the world and of his relation to the world" (p. 242).

31. Ibid., pp. 228–29.

32. Ibid., pp. 232–33.

33. Ibid., pp. 234–35.

34. Aulagnier refers to certain fundamentally incomprehensible but firmly believed discourses which a potentially schizophrenic subject might produce: "as soon as one listens closely one realizes that this conviction [of the analysand in the meaning of his or her own discourse] places the origin of the body, the origin of the world and the temporal order which founds genealogical order all radically into question. This can be proven by a test which any analyst can try: if he attempts, be-

ginning with that apparently 'punctual' conviction, to consider the logical implications which follow from it, he will observe that they lead up to a representation of reality which is in every point heterogeneous to the model which discourse gives of the subject-world relation. 'Bizarreness,' in these cases, replaces causal order, to which the whole appeals in order to designate the origin of itself and of the world—that 'bizarreness' is an interpretation which connects the origin to a cause incompatible with the models according to which the whole functions. It is this characteristic that marks for us the presence of primary delirious thought [pensee délirante primaire]" (ibid., p. 258).

35. See, for example, Heidegger's "What Is Metaphysics": "If Dasein can relate itself to beings only by holding itself out into the nothing and can exist only thus; and if the nothing is originally disclosed only in anxiety; then must we not hover in this anxiety constantly in order to be able to exist at all?" (*Basic Writings*, p. 104). Cf. Levinas's *Existence and Existents*, p. 27 (*De l'existence à l'existant*, p. 36): "Concern is not, as Heidegger thinks, the very act of being on the brink of nothingness; it is rather imposed by the solidity of a being that begins and is already encumbered with the excess of itself." On the *il y a* and insomnia see pp. 57–64 and 65–67 (93–105 and 109–13).

36. Levinas, *Totality and Infinity*, p. 26 (trans. modified); *Totalité et infini*, p. 11.

37. *Totality and Infinity*, p. 49; *Totalité et infini*, p. 41. Cf. also: "Our analyses are guided by a formal structure: the idea of Infinity in us. To have the idea of Infinity it is necessary to exist as separated. . . . But the idea of Infinity is transcendence itself" (pp. 79–80; p. 78).

38. "Metaphysics, the relation with exteriority, that is, with superiority, indicates, on the contrary, that the relation between the finite and the infinite does not consist in the finite being absorbed in what faces him, but in remaining in his own being, maintaining himself there, acting here below. The austere happiness of goodness would invert its meaning and would be perverted if it confounded us with God" (*Totality and Infinity*, p. 292; *Totalité et infini*, pp. 324–25). "[Metaphysical D]esire is desire for the absolutely other" (p. 34; 23).

39. "The absolutely foreign alone can instruct us" (*Totality and Infinity*, p. 73; *Totalité et infini*, p. 71).

40. "But transcendence precisely refuses totality, does not lend itself to a view that would encompass it from the outside" (*Totality and Infinity*, p. 293; *Totalité et infini*, p. 326); and "the metaphysician and the other can not be *totalized*. The metaphysician is absolutely separated" (p. 35; 24). Levinas also sees this totality theorized in traditional metaphysics and actualized in the social practice of war: "The visage of being that shows itself in war is fixed in the concept of totality, which dominates Western philosophy" (p. 21; 6); and: "does not the experience of war and totality coincide, for the philosopher, with experience and evidence as such?" (p. 24; 9).

41. *Totality and Infinity*, p. 196 (trans. modified); *Totalité et infini*, p. 214.

42. Such models, based on the sublimation of the sensuous aesthetic itself, can be seen in modern and postmodern art theory. See, for example, Jean-François

Lyotard, "The Sublime and the Avant-Garde" and "Newman: The Instant," in *Reader*, pp. 196–211 and 240–49. His interpretations in these cases are based on the painter Barnett Newman's own writings about his work; see especially "The Plasmic Image," "The New Sense of Fate," and "The Sublime is Now" in Newman's *Writings*, pp. 138–55, 165–69, 171–73. It should be noted that Yve-Alain Bois has vigorously and persistently opposed such interpretations of Newman's work, which would reduce it to representations of abstract ideas (see, for example, "Perceiving Newman" in *Barnett Newman*, esp. pp. i–iii and "Barnett Newman's Sublime = Tragedy" in *Negotiating Rapture*, pp. 138–39).

43. See Jürgen Habermas, *The Theory of Communicative Action*.

44. *Totality and Infinity*, p. 217; *Totalité et infini*, p. 239. Cf. also: "When the I is identified with reason, taken as the power of thematization and objectification, it loses its very ipseity. . . . Reason makes human society possible; but a society whose members would be only reasons would vanish as a society" (p. 119; 124).

45. Hegel, *Phenomenology*, p. 433.

46. Such an absolute transparency was, in fact, a Jacobin goal, enunciated by Robespierre, among others. See Susan Maslan, "Robespierre's Eye: Surveillance and the Modern Republican Subject," in *Representation and Theatricality in French Revolutionary Theater and Politics*, Ph.D. diss., Johns Hopkins University, 1997.

47. *Totality and Infinity*, p. 46; *Totalité et infini*, p. 37. Its self-identity based on abstract persistence, the Kantian apperceptive subject represents one example of that violent internalization. By condensing identity into the formula "I think," Kant defines the subject in terms of propositional reason. "We call it 'the same' because in representation the I precisely loses its opposition to its object; the opposition fades, bringing out the identity of the I despite the multiplicity of its objects, that is, precisely the unalterable character of the I. To remain the same is to represent to oneself. The [Kantian] 'I think' is the pulsation of rational thought" (p. 126; 132). See also pp. 125–26; 131: "The fact that in representation the same defines the other without being determined by the other justifies the Kantian conception according to which the unity of transcendental apperception remains an empty form in the midst of its synthetic work." The apperceptive subject of representation gains its persistence in face of the variorum of its experiential objects by identifying with a universal law, or in other words with the abstract indifference to experience that is reason. But in so doing, the subject vanishes as individual: "The I of representation is the natural passage from the particular to the universal. Universal thought is a thought in the first person. This is why the constitution that for idealism remakes the universe starting from the subject is not the freedom of an I that would survive this constitution free and above the laws it will have constituted" (p. 132).

48. "We then understand that the idea of infinity, which requires separation, requires it unto atheism, so profoundly that the idea of infinity could be forgotten. The forgetting of transcendence is not produced as an accident in a separated being; the possibility of this forgetting is necessary for separation" (*Totality and Infinity*, p. 181; *Totalité et infini*, p. 197).

49. On the Lacanian alienation of desire in language, see, above, the section on Lacan from the end of Chapter 7.

50. *Totality and Infinity*, p. 234; *Totalité et infini*, p. 260. The fear of death also attests, for Levinas, the limits of previous conceptions of subjectivity: "In the horror of the radical unknown to which death leads is evinced the limit of negativity. This mode of negating, while taking refuge in what one negates, delineates the same or the I. The alterity of a world refused is not the alterity of the Stranger but that of the fatherland which welcomes and protects. Metaphysics does not coincide with negativity. . . . Negativity is incapable of transcendence" (p. 41, trans. modified; 31).

51. Levinas's understanding of death is sometimes ambiguous. He asserts, for example: "To die for the invisible—this is metaphysics" (*Totality and Infinity*, p. 35; *Totalité et infini*, p. 23). As our reading of *Totality and Infinity* should make clear, however, Levinas refused to ground subjectivity, the Other, and the ethical relation in the alterity of death. For this reason I would disagree with Alphonso Lingis's suggestion to the contrary: "Levinas names this axis which is not a fifth dimension in a world spread out in geometrical space-time or infinitely open horizons, God, and takes this name to cover the irreversibility of the relationship with the other, the unending demand the other's existence puts on me. Yet this illeity, this God, this infinity, is perhaps that of dying, or at least its transcendence to the world is manifest in me as the unending departure of the other" (*Deathbound Subjectivity*, p. 189). To understand the Other, *ille*, as death or dying is, in fact, to undo much of what is most important in Levinas's work by construing it as a mere continuation of the tradition which it rejects.

52. "For language accomplishes a relation such that the terms are not limitrophe within this relation, such that the other, despite the relationship with the same, remains transcendent to the same. The relation between the same and the other, metaphysics, is primordially enacted as conversation, where the same, gathered up in its ipseity as an 'I,' as a particular existent unique and autochthonous, leaves itself" (*Totality and Infinity*, p. 39; *Totalité et infini*, pp. 28–29). See also: "A relation between terms that resist totalization, that absolve themselves from the relation or that specify it, is possible only as language" (p. 97; 99); and "Absolute difference, inconceivable in terms of formal logic, is established only by language. . . . Better than comprehension, *discourse* relates with what remains essentially transcendent" (p. 195; 212).

53. *Totality and Infinity*, p. 92; *Totalité et infini*, p. 92.

54. *Totality and Infinity*, p. 203; *Totalité et infini*, p. 222.

55. *Totality and Infinity*, p. 69; *Totalité et infini*, p. 65.

56. The impersonal and abstract concept of liberty, for example, can only exist in writing: "Hence freedom would cut into the real only by virtue of institutions. Freedom is engraved on the stone of the tables on which laws are inscribed—it exists by virtue of this inscrustation of an institutional existence. Freedom depends on a written text, destructible to be sure, but durable, on which freedom is conserved for man outside of man" (*Totality and Infinity*, p. 241; *Totalité et infini*, p. 270). Sim-

ilarly, written works are by their very nature alienated: "the will now knows another tyranny, that of works alienated, already foreign to man" (p. 242; pp. 270–71). The status of writing in relation to the Other is somewhat ambiguous, however, and at the end of *Totalité et infini*, Lévinas allows for the possibility of addressing a reader as that Other: "The relation between the 'fragments' of separated being is a face to face, the irreducible and ultimate relation. An interlocutor arises again behind him whom thought has just apprehended—as the certitude of the *cogito* arises behind every negation of certitude. The description of the face to face which we have attempted here is told to the other [l'Autre], to the reader who appears anew behind my discourse and my wisdom" (p. 295; 329).

Works Cited

Abraham, Nicolas, and Maria Torok. "Deuil ou mélancolie introjecter—incorporer: Réalité métapsychologique et fantasme." In *L'Ecorce et le noyau*. Paris: Aubier-Flammarion, 1978.
——. *The Shell and the Kernel: Renewals of Psychoanalysis*. Trans. Nicholas T. Rand. Chicago: University of Chicago Press, 1994.
Althusser, Louis. *Lenin and Philosophy and Other Essays*. Trans. Ben Brewster. London: NLB, 1971.
——. *Positions (1964–1975)*. Paris: Editions Sociales, 1976.
——. "The Return to Hegel." In *Specter of Hegel: Early Writings*. Trans. G. M. Goshgarian. New York: Verso, 1997, pp. 173–84.
American Psychiatric Association. *Diagnostic and Statistical Manual of Mental Disorders*, 4th ed. Washington, D.C.: APA, 1994.
Arasse, Daniel. *The Guillotine and the Terror*. Trans. Christopher Miller. London: Allen Lane, 1989.
Ariès, Philippe. *Essais sur l'histoire de la mort en Occident: Du moyen âge à nos jours*. Paris: Seuil, 1975.
Auffret, Dominique. *Alexandre Kojève: La Philosophie, l'Etat, la fin de l'Histoire*. Paris: Bernard Grasset, 1990.
Aulagnier, Piera. *La Violence de l'interprétation: Du pictogramme à l'énoncé*. Paris: Presses Universitaires de France, 1975.
Austin, J. L. *How To Do Things with Words*. Ed. J. O. Urmson and Marina Sbisà. Oxford: Oxford University Press, 1975.
Avni, Ora. *The Resistance of Reference: Linguistics, Philosophy, and the Literary Text*. Baltimore: Johns Hopkins University Press, 1990.
Badiou, Alain. *Théories du sujet*. Paris: Seuil, 1982.
Balzac, Honoré de. *La Comédie humaine*. Vol. 10. Ed. Pierre-Georges Castex, Thierry Bodin, Pierre Citron, Madeleine Ambrière, Henri Gauthier, René Guise, and Moïse Le Yaouanc. Paris: Gallimard [Pléiade], 1979.

Bataille, Georges. "Hegel, la mort, et le sacrifice." In *Œuvres complètes*, vol. 12. Ed. Sibylle Monod. Paris: Gallimard, 1988. Trans. Jonathan Strauss as "Hegel, Death and Sacrifice." *Yale French Studies* 78 (1990): 9–28.

Benveniste, Emile. *Problèmes de linguistique générale*. 2 vols. Paris: Gallimard, 1966.

———. *Problems in General Linguistics*. Trans. Mary Elizabeth Meek. Coral Gables, Fla.: University of Miami Press, 1971.

Berthold-Bond, Daniel. *Hegel's Theory of Madness*. Albany: State University of New York Press, 1995.

Bettelheim, Bruno. *Symbolic Wounds: Puberty Rites and the Envious Male*. Glencoe, Ill.: The Free Press, 1954.

Blanchot, Maurice. *De Kafka à Kafka*. Paris: Gallimard, 1981.

———. *La Part du feu*. Paris: Gallimard, 1949. Trans. Charlotte Mandel as *The Work of Fire*. Stanford, Calif.: Stanford University Press, 1995.

Bois, Yve-Alain. *Barnett Newman: Paintings: April 8–May 7 1988*. New York: Pace Gallery, 1988.

———. "Barnett Newman's Sublime = Tragedy." In *Negotiating Rapture: The Power of Art to Transform Lives*. Ed. Richard Francis. Chicago: Museum of Contemporary Art, 1996, pp. 138–39.

Bony, Jacques. *Le Récit nervalien: Une Recherche des formes*. Paris: José Corti, 1990.

Borch-Jacobsen, Mikkel. *Lacan: Le Maître absolu*. Paris: Flammarion, 1990.

———. "The Freudian Subject." In *Who Comes After the Subject*. Ed. Eduardo Cadava, Peter Connor, and Jean-Luc Nancy. New York: Routledge, 1991, pp. 73–76.

Brunet, Huguette, and Jean Ziegler. *Nerval et la Bibliothèque Nationale*. In *Etudes nervaliennes et romantiques*, vol. 4. Namur: Presses Universitaires de Namur, 1982.

Büchner. *Danton's Death, Leonce and Lena, Woyzeck*. Trans. and intro. Victor Price. Oxford: Oxford University Press, 1971.

Butler, Judith. *Subjects of Desire: Hegelian Reflections in Twentieth-Century France*. New York: Columbia University Press, 1987.

Cabanis, Pierre Jean Georges. *Œuvres complètes de Cabanis*, vol. 2. Paris: Bossagne Frères and Firmin Didot, 1823.

Castel, Robert. *The Regulation of Madness: The Origins of Incarceration in France*. Trans. W. D. Halls. Berkeley: University of California Press, 1988.

Cellier, Léon. "Sur un vers des Chimères, Nerval et Shakespeare." *Cahiers du Sud* 311 (1952): 146–53.

Chambers, Ross. *Gérard de Nerval et la poétique du voyage*. Paris: José Corti, 1969.

———. "Literature Deterritorialized." In *A New History of French Literature*. Ed. Denis Hollier. Cambridge, Mass.: Harvard University Press, 1989, pp. 710–16.

———. *Room for Maneuver: Reading (the) Oppositional (in) Narrative*. Chicago: University of Chicago Press, 1991.

Chastel, André. *Marsile Ficin et l'art*. Geneva: Droz, 1975.

Cook, David C. *Language in the Philosophy of Hegel*. The Hague: Mouton, 1973.
Courtine, Jean-François, Michel Deguy, Eliane Escoubas, Philippe Lacoue-Labarthe, Jean-François Lyotard, Louis Marin, Jean-Luc Nancy, and Jacob Rogozinski. *Of the Sublime: Presence in Question*. Trans. Jeffrey S. Librett. Albany: State University of New York Press, 1993.
Dante. *Inferno*. Trans. John D. Sinclair. New York: Oxford University Press, 1979.
d'Arras, Jehan. *Mélusine*. Preface by M. Ch. Brunet. Paris: P. Jannet, 1854.
Dayan, Peter. *Nerval et ses pères: Portrait en trois volets avec deux gonds et un cadenas*. Geneva: Droz, 1992.
de Gébelin, Court. *Le Monde primitif, analysé et comparé avec le monde moderne*, vol. 1. Paris: Chez l'auteur, 1781.
de Man, Paul. *Allegories of Reading: Figural Language in Rousseau, Nietzsche, Rilke, and Proust*. New Haven: Yale University Press, 1979.
——. *Blindness and Insight: Essays in the Rhetoric of Contemporary Criticism*. Minneapolis: University of Minnesota Press, 1983.
——. "Mallarmé, Yeats and the Post-Romantic Predicament." Ph.D. diss., Harvard University, 1961.
——. "Le Néant poétique: Commentaire d'un sonnet hermétique de Mallarmé." *Monde nouveau* 88 (Apr. 1955): 63–75.
Deleuze, Gilles. *Le Pli: Leibniz et le Baroque*. Paris: Editions de Minuit, 1988. Trans. Tom Conley as *The Fold: Leibniz and the Baroque*. Minneapolis: University of Minnesota Press, 1993.
Deleuze, Gilles, and Félix Guattari. *Capitalisme et schizophrénie: L'anti-Œdipe*. Paris: Minuit, 1972. Trans. Robert Hurley, Mark Seem, and Helen R. Lane as *Anti-Oedipus: Capitalism and Schizophrenia*. Minneapolis: University of Minnesota Press, 1983.
Derrida, Jacques. *La Dissémination*. Paris: Seuil, 1972. Trans. Barbara Johnson as *Dissemination*. Chicago: University of Chicago Press, 1981.
——. *Marges de la philosophie*. Paris: Minuit, 1972.
Descartes, René. *Méditations métaphysiques*. Ed. Jean-Marie Beyssade and Michelle Beyssade. Paris: Garnier-Flammarion, 1979.
——. *Meditations on First Philosophy: In Focus*. Trans. Elizabeth S. Haldane and G. R. T. Ross. Ed. Stanley Tweyman. London: Routledge, 1993.
Descombes, Vincent. *Le Même et l'autre*. Paris: Minuit, 1979.
Desmoulins, Camille. *Œuvres de Camille Desmoulins*, vol. 1. Ed. M. Jules Claretie. Paris: Charpentier, 1874.
Dhaenens, Jacques. *Le Destin d'Orphée, étude sur "El Desdichado" de Nerval*. Paris: Minard (Lettres Modernes), 1972.
Dondey, Théophile (pseudonym: Philothée O'Neddy). *Feu et flamme*. Vol. 13 of *Bibliothèque romantique*, ed. Henri Girard. Paris: Edition des Presses Françaises and "Les Belles Lettres," 1926.
——. *Œuvres en prose: Romans et contes—critique théâtrale—lettres*. Paris: G. Charpentier, 1878.

———. *Poésies posthumes de Philothée O'Neddy (Théophile Dondey)*. Preface by Ernest Havet. Paris: G. Charpentier, 1877.
Dragonetti, Roger. "Métaphysique et poétique dans l'œuvre de Mallarmé (Hérodiade, Igitur, Le Coup de dés)." *Revue de métaphysique et de morale* 84 (1979): 366–96.
Drury, Shadia B. *Alexandre Kojève: The Roots of Postmodern Politics*. New York: St. Martin's Press, 1994.
Dunn, Susan. "Transgression and the Amendement Riancey." *Nineteenth Century French Studies* 12:1–2 (1983–84): 86–95.
Eluard, Paul. *Œuvres complètes*, vol. 1. Ed. Marcelle Dumas and Lucien Scheler. Paris: Gallimard [Pléiade], 1968.
Encyclopédie ou dictionnaire raisonné des sciences et des métiers, vol. 10. Neufchastel: Samuel Faulche, 1765.
Evénement des plus rares ou l'histoire du Sr. abbé comte de Buquoy singuliérement son évasion du Fort-L'Evêque et de la Bastille. Bonnefoy: Jean de la Franchise, 1719.
Faurisson, Robert. *La Clé des chimères et autres chimères de Nerval*. Paris: J. J. Pauvert, 1977.
Felman, Shoshana. *La Folie et la chose littéraire*. Paris: Seuil, 1978. Trans. Martha Noel Evans, Shoshana Felman, and Brian Massumi as *Writing and Madness (Literature/Philosophy/Psychoanalysis)*. Ithaca, New York: Cornell University Press, 1985.
Ficino, Marsilio. *Théologie platonicienne de l'immortalité des âmes*, vol. 2. Ed. and trans. Raymond Marcel. Paris: Les Belles Lettres, 1964.
Fink, Bruce. *The Lacanian Subject: Between Language and Jouissance*. Princeton, N.J.: Princeton University Press, 1995.
Foucault, Michel. *Histoire de la folie à l'âge classique*. Paris: Gallimard, 1972. Trans. Richard Howard as *Madness and Civilization: A History of Insanity in the Age of Reason*. New York: Vintage, 1973.
———. *Les Mots et les choses: Une Archéologie des sciences humaines*. Paris: Gallimard, 1966. Trans. as *The Order of Things: An Archaeology of the Human Sciences*. New York: Vintage, 1973.
———. *Naissance de la clinique: Une archéologie du regard médical*. Paris: Presses Universitaires de France, 1972. Trans. A. M. Sheridan Smith as *The Birth of the Clinic: An Archeology of Medical Perception*. New York: Pantheon, 1973.
———. *L'Ordre du discours*. Paris: Gallimard, 1971. Trans. as "The Order of Discourse." In *Untying the Text*. Ed. Robert Young. London: Routledge and Kegan Paul, 1981, pp. 51–77.
———. *Surveiller et punir: Naissance de la prison*. Paris: Gallimard, 1975. Trans. Alan Sheridan as *Discipline and Punish: The Birth of the Prison*. New York: Pantheon, 1977.
———. "Technologies of the Self." In *Technologies of the Self: A Seminar with Michel*

Foucault. Ed. Luther H. Martin, Huck Gutman, and Patrick H. Hutton. Amherst: University of Massachusetts Press, 1988, pp. 19–22.

———. "What Is an Author?" In *Textual Strategies: Perspectives in Post-Structuralist Criticism*. Ed. Josué V. Harari. Ithaca: Cornell University Press, 1979, pp. 141–60.

Frazer, James George. *Adonis, Attis, Osiris: Studies in the History of Oriental Religion*, vol. 1. London: Macmillan, 1927.

Freud, Sigmund. *The Standard Edition of the Complete Psychological Works of Sigmund Freud*. 24 vols. Ed. and trans. James Strachey et al. London: The Hogarth Press, 1961.

Gasparro, Giulia Sfameni. *Soteriology and the Mystic Aspects in the Cult of Cybele and Attis*. Leiden: E. J. Brill, 1985.

Gautier, Théophile. *Portraits et souvenirs littéraires*. Paris: Michel Lévy Frères, 1875.

———. *Œuvres complètes*. Geneva: Slatkine Reprints, 1978.

———. *The Works of Théophile Gautier*. 24 vols. Trans. and ed. F. C. de Sumichrast. Cambridge, Mass.: Jenson Society, 1907.

Geninasca, Jacques. *Analyse structurale des Chimères de Nerval*. Neuchatel: La Baconnière, 1971.

Graves, Robert. *The Greek Myths*, vol. 1. New York: Viking Penguin, 1960.

Green, André. *Le Complexe de castration*. Paris: Presses Universitaires de France, 1990.

———. *Le Travail du négatif*. Paris: Minuit, 1993.

Guillaume, Jean. *"Les Chimères" de Nerval: Édition critique*. Brussels: Académie Royale de Langue et de Littérature Françaises, 1966.

Habermas, Jürgen. *The Theory of Communicative Action*. 2 vols. Trans. Thomas McCarthy. Boston: Beacon Press, 1984–87.

Havet, Ernest. *Notice sur Philothée O'Neddy*. Paris: G. Charpentier, 1877.

Hegel, G. W. F. *Vorlesung über die Ästhetik*. 3 vols. Frankfurt am Main: Suhrkamp, 1970. French trans. S. Jankélévitch as *Esthétique*. 4 vols. Paris: Flammarion, 1979. English trans. T. M. Knox as *Aesthetics: Lectures in Fine Arts*. 2 vols. Oxford: Oxford University Press, 1975.

———. *Phänomenologie des Geistes*. Ed. Eva Moldenhauer and Kark Markus Michel. Frankfurt am Main: Suhrkamp, 1970. Trans. A. V. Miller as *Phenomenology of Spirit*. Oxford: Oxford University Press, 1981.

Heidegger, Martin. *Basic Writings: From Being and Time (1927) to The Task of Thinking (1964)*. Ed. David Farrell Krell. New York: HarperCollins, 1977.

———. *Being and Time*. Trans. John Macquarrie and Edward Robinson. New York: Harper & Row, 1962.

———. *Hegel's Concept of Experience*. New York: Harper & Row, 1970.

———. *Hölderlins Hymnen "Germanien" und "Der Rhein."* Frankfurt am Main: Vittorio Klostermann, 1980.

Heine, Heinrich. *Dichtungen*. In *Sämmtliche Werke*, vol. 15. Hamburg: Hoffman und Campe, 1862.

Hertz, Neil. *The End of the Line: Essays on Psychoanalysis and the Sublime*. New York: Columbia University Press, 1985.
Houssaye, Arsène. *Les Confessions: Souvenirs d'un demi-siècle 1830–1880*. 3 vols. Geneva: Slatkine Reprints, 1971.
Huet, Marie-Hélène. "The Revolutionary Sublime." In *Eighteenth-Century Studies: Eighteenth-Century Culture and the Disciplines* 28:1 (Fall 1994): 51–64.
Hugo, Victor. *Le Dernier Jour d'un condamné précédé de Bug-Jargal*. Ed. Roger Borderie. Paris: Gallimard [Folio], 1970. Trans. Geoff Woollen as *The Last Day of a Condemned Man and Other Prison Writings*. Oxford: Oxford University Press, 1992.
Hyppolite, Jean. *Genèse et structure de la phénoménologie de l'esprit de Hegel*. Paris: Aubier Montaigne, 1946.
——. "Hegel's Phenomenology and Psychoanalysis." Trans. Albert Richer. In *New Studies in Hegel's Philosophy*. Ed. Warren E. Steinkraus. New York: Holt, Rinehart, Winston, 1971, pp. 57–70.
Janin, Jules. "Gérard de Nerval." *Le Journal des débats*, Mar. 1, 1841.
Jauss, Hans Robert. *Towards an Aesthetic of Reception*. Trans. Timothy Bahti. Minneapolis: University of Minnesota Press, 1982.
Jean, Raymond. *La Poétique du désir: Nerval Lautréamont Apollinaire Éluard*. Paris: Seuil, 1974.
Kant, Immanuel. *Conflict of the Faculties*. Trans. Mary J. Gregor. New York: Abaris Books, 1979.
——. *Critique of Pure Reason*. Trans. Norman Kemp Smith. New York: St. Martin's Press, 1965.
——. *Grounding for the Metaphysics of Morals in Ethical Philosophy*. Trans. James W. Ellington. Indianapolis: Hackett, 1983.
——. *Kritik der Urtheilskraft*. In *Kants Werke*. Akademie-Textausgabe, vol. 5. Berlin: Walter de Gruyter, 1968. Trans. James Creed Meredith as *The Critique of Judgement*. Oxford: Oxford University Press, 1957.
——. *Versuch über die Krankenheiten des Kopfes*. In *Gesammelte Schriften*, vol. 2, ed. Preussische Akademie der Wissenschaft. Berlin: Georg Reimer, 1955 (1902).
Kaufmann, Vincent. *Le Livre et ses adresses: Mallarmé, Ponge, Valéry, Blanchot*. Paris: Klincksieck, 1986.
Kaufmann, Walter. *Goethe, Kant, and Hegel*. Vol. 1 of *Discovering the Mind*. New Brunswick: Transaction, 1990–92.
Klossowski, Pierre. *Nietzsche et le cercle vicieux*. Paris: Mercure de France, 1969.
Kofman, Sarah. *Nerval: Le charme de la répétition: Lecture de Sylvie*. Lausanne: L'Age d'homme, 1979.
Kojève, Alexandre. *Introduction à la lecture de Hegel: Leçons sur la "Phénoménologie de l'Esprit" professées de 1933 à 1939 à l'Ecole des Hautes Etudes*. Ed. Raymond Queneau. Paris: Gallimard, 1947.
Kristeva, Julia. *La Révolution du langage poétique*. Paris: Seuil, 1974. Trans. Margaret

Waller as *Revolution in Poetic Language*. New York: Columbia University Press, 1984.
——. *Les Nouvelles Maladies de l'âme*. Paris: Fayard, 1993. Trans. Ross Guberman as *New Maladies of the Soul*. New York: Columbia University Press, 1995.
——. *Polylogue*. Paris: Seuil, 1977.
——. *Soleil noir: Dépression et mélancolie*. Paris: Gallimard, 1987. Trans. Leon S. Roudiez as *Black Sun: Depression and Melancholy*. New York: Columbia University Press, 1989.
Lacan, Jacques. *Ecrits*. Paris: Seuil, 1966. Trans. Alan Sheridan as *Ecrits: A Selection*. New York: W. W. Norton, 1977.
——. *Le Séminaire, livre II: Le Moi dans la théorie de Freud et dans la technique de la psychanalyse*. Ed. Jacques-Alain Miller. Paris: Seuil [Champ freudien], 1978. Trans. Sylvana Tomaselli as *The Ego in Freud's Theory and in the Technique of Psychoanalysis 1954–1955*. Book 2 of *The Seminar of Jacques Lacan*. Ed. Jacques-Alain Miller. New York: W. W. Norton, 1988.
Lacoue-Labarthe, Philippe, and Jean-Luc Nancy. *L'Absolu littéraire: Théorie de la littérature du romantisme allemand*. Paris: Seuil, 1979.
Lamb, David. *Language Perception in Hegel and Wittgenstein*. England: Avebury, 1979.
Larbaud, Valéry. *Théophile Dondey de Santeny (1811–1875)*. Tunis: Editions de Mirages, 1935.
Larchey, Lorédan. *Les Excentricités du langage*. Paris: E. Denta, 1863.
Le Breton, Georges. *Nerval, poète alchimique, la clef des chimères et des mémorables d'Aurélia: Le Dictionnaire mytho-hermétique de Dom Pernety*. Paris: Curandera, 1982.
Lebois, André. *Vers une élucidation des Chimères de Nerval*. Paris: Lettres modernes, 1957.
Leibniz, Gottfried Wilhelm. *Monadology*. In *Philosophical Essays*. Ed. and trans. Roger Ariew and Daniel Garber. Indianapolis: Hackett, 1989.
Lemaire, Anika. *Jacques Lacan*. Trans. David Macey. London: Routledge and Kegan Paul, 1977.
Levinas, Emmanuel. *De l'existence à l'existant*. Paris: J. Vrin, 1978. Trans. Alphonso Lingis as *Existence and Existents*. The Hague: Martinus Nijhoff, 1978.
——. *Outside the Subject*. Trans. Michael B. Smith. Stanford, Calif.: Stanford University Press, 1994.
——. *Totalité et infini. Essai sur l'extériorité*. La Haye: Martinus Nijhoff, 1971. Trans. Alphonso Lingis as *Totality and Infinity: An Essay on Exteriority*. Pittsburgh: Duquesne University Press, 1969.
Lingis, Alphonso. *Deathbound Subjectivity*. Bloomington: Indiana University Press, 1989.
Lyotard, François. *The Lyotard Reader*. Ed. Andrew Benjamin. Oxford: Basil Blackwell, 1989.
Mallarmé, Stéphane. *Correspondance 1862–1871*. Ed. Henri Mondor and Jean-Pierre Richard. Paris: Gallimard, 1959.

———. *Œuvres complètes*. Ed. Henri Mondor and G. Jean-Aubry. Paris: Gallimard, 1945.
Marat, Jean-Paul. *Textes choisis*. Intro. Michel Vovelle. Paris: Editions Sociales, 1975.
Maretti, Monique Streiff. *Le Rousseau de Gérard de Nerval: Mythe, légende, idéologie*. Paris: A. G. Nizet, 1976.
Markale, Jean. *Mélusine ou l'androgyne*. Paris: Retz, 1983.
Martin-Civet, Pierre. *La Mélusine, ses origines et son nom, comment elle est devenue la mythique aïeule des Lusignan*. Poitiers: Oudin, 1969.
Marx, Karl, and Frederick Engels. *Economic and Philosophic Manuscripts of 1844*. In *Complete Works*, vol. 3. Ed. Jack Cohen et al., trans. Martin Milligin and Dirk J. Struik. New York: International Publishers, 1975.
———. *The Marx-Engels Reader*. Ed. Robert C. Tucker. New York: W. W. Norton & Co., 1872.
Maslan, Susan. "Representation and Theatricality in French Revolutionary Theater and Politics." Ph.D. diss., Johns Hopkins University, 1997.
McCumber, John. *The Company of Words: Hegel, Language, and Systematic Philosophy*. Evanston, Ill.: Northwestern University Press, 1993.
Meschonnic, Henri. "Poétique de Gérard de Nerval." *Europe* (Sept. 1958): 10–33.
Michelet, Jules. *Journal*, vol. 1. Ed. Paul Viallaneix. Paris: Gallimard, 1959.
Muller, John P., and William J. Richardson. *Lacan and Language: A Reader's Guide to "Ecrits."* New York: International Universities Press, 1982.
Mutigny, Jean de. *Victor Hugo et le spiritisme*. Paris: Fernand Nathan, 1981.
Nancy, Jean-Luc. "The Sublime Offering." In *Of the Sublime: Presence in Question*. Ed. Jean-François Courtine et al.; trans. Jeffrey S. Librett. Albany: State University of New York Press, 1993, pp. 25–53.
Nerval, Gerard de. *"Les Chimères" de Nerval: Édition critique*. Ed. Jean Guillaume. Brussels: Académie Royale de Langue et de Littérature Françaises, 1966.
———. *Œuvres complètes*, 3 vols. Ed. Jean Guillaume et al. Paris: Gallimard [Pléiade], 1984 (1989, 1993).
Newman, Barnett. *Newman's Selected Writings and Interviews*. Ed. John P. O'Neill. Berkeley: University of California Press, 1990.
Newmark, Kevin. "The Forgotten Figures of Symbolism: Nerval's Sylvie." *Phantom Proxies, Yale French Studies* 74 (1988): 207–30.
Nietzsche, Friedrich. *Birth of Tragedy*. Trans. Walter Kaufmann. New York: Vintage, 1967.
———. *Daybreak*. Trans. R. J. Hollingdale. Cambridge: Cambridge University Press, 1982.
———. *The Gay Science*. Trans. Walter Kaufmann. New York: Random House, 1974.
———. *Thus Spoke Zarathustra: A Book for All and None*. Trans. Walter Kaufmann. New York: The Modern Library, 1995.
Nodier, Charles. "Bibliographie des fous: De quelques livres excentriques." *Bulletin du bibliophile* (Nov. 1835).

Noulet, Emilie. "L'Hermétisme dans la poésie moderne." *Etudes littéraires*. Mexico: 1944.
O'Neddy, Philothée (pseudonym for Théophile Dondey). *Feu et flamme*. Ed. Marcel Hervier. Paris: Editions des Presses Française, 1926.
Ovid. *Les Métamorphoses.* 3 vols. Ed. and trans. Georges Lafaye. Paris: Les Belles Lettres, 1930.
Parallax: A Journal of Metadiscursive Theory and Cultural Practices 4 (Feb. 1997).
Pernety, Dom Antoine-Joseph. *Les Fables égyptiennes et grecques dévoilées et réduites au même principe avec une explication des hiéroglyphes et de la guerre de Troye.* 2 vols. Paris: Delalain l'aîné, 1786.
Pichois, Claude, and Michel Brix. *Gérard de Nerval*. Paris: Fayard, 1995.
Pinel, Philippe. *Traité médico-philosophique sur l'aliénation mentale ou la manie.* Paris: Richard, Caille & Ravier, 1801.
Pippin, Robert B. *Hegel's Idealism: The Satisfactions of Self-Consciousness*. Cambridge: Cambridge University Press, 1989.
Popa, Nicolas. "Les Sources allemandes de deux *Filles du feu.*" *Revue de littérature comparée* (July–Sept. 1930).
Poulet, Georges. *Les Métamorphoses du cercle*. Preface by Jean Starobinski. Paris: Flammarion, 1961.
Proust, Marcel. *Contre Sainte-Beuve*. Ed. Pierre Clarac and Yves Sandre. Paris: Gallimard, 1971.
Raffoul, François. *Heidegger and the Subject*. Trans. David Pettigrew and Gregory Recco. Atlantic Highlands, N.J.: Humanities Press International, 1998.
Richard, Jean-Pierre. *L'Univers imaginaire de Mallarmé*. Paris: Seuil, 1961.
——. *Microlectures*. Paris: Seuil, 1979.
Richer, Jean. *Nerval et les doctrines ésotériques*. Paris: Griffon, 1947.
——. *Nerval, expérience et création*. Paris: Hachette, 1963.
Rinsler, Norma. "Nerval et Biron." *Revue d'histoire littéraire de la France* (July–Sept. 1961): 405–10.
Robespierre, Maximilien de. *Discours et rapports de Robespierre*. Intro. Charles Vellay. Paris: Charpentier and Fasquelle, 1908.
Rousseau, Jean-Jacques. *Œuvres complètes*. 5 vols. Ed. Bernard Gagnebin and Marcel Raymond. Paris: Gallimard [Pléiade], 1959.
——. *The Reveries of the Solitary Walker*. Trans. Charles E. Butterworth. Indianapolis: Hackett, 1992.
Rousselle, Aline. *Porneia: On Desire and the Body in Antiquity*. Trans. Felicia Pheasant. Oxford: Basil Blackwell, 1988.
Saint-Just, Louis-Antoine-Léon de. *Discours et rapports*. Ed. Albert Soboul. Paris: Editions Sociales, 1988.
Sangsue, Daniel. *Le Récit excentrique: Gautier—De Maistre—Nerval—Nodier*. Paris: J. Corti, 1987.
Sartre, Jean Paul. *L'Etre et le néant*. Paris: Gallimard, 1943. Trans. Hazel E. Barnes as

Being and Nothingness: An Essay on Phenomenological Ontology. New York: Philosophical Library, 1956.
Saussure, Ferdinand de. *Cours de linguistique générale*. Ed. Tullio de Mauro. Paris: Payot, 1982. Trans. Wade Basking as *Course in General Linguistics*. Ed. Charles Bally and Albert Sechehaye. New York: Philosophical Library, 1959.
Scarry, Elaine. *The Body in Pain: The Making and Unmaking of the World*. New York: Oxford University Press, 1985.
Schiller, Friedrich. *On the Sublime*. Trans. Julius A. Elias. New York: Frederick Ungar, 1966.
———. *The Poems of Schiller*. Trans. Edgar A. Bowring. London: George Bell & Sons, 1900.
———. *Schillers Werke: Nationalausgabe*, vol. 21. Ed. Lieselotte Blumenthal and Benno von Wiese. Weimar: Hermann Böhlaus Nachfolger, 1963.
Silverman, Hugh J., and Gary E. Aylesworth, eds. *The Textual Sublime: Deconstruction and Its Differences*. Albany: State University of New York Press, 1990.
Soboul, Albert, ed. *Discours et rapports*. Paris: Editions Sociales, 1988.
Starkie, Enid. *Pétrus Borel the Lycanthrope: His Life and Times*. London: Faber and Faber, 1954.
Stierle, Karlheinz. *Dunkelheit und Form in Gérard de Nervals "Chimères."* Munich: Wilhelm Fink, 1967.
Taylor, Charles. *Sources of the Self: The Making of the Modern Identity*. Cambridge, Mass.: Harvard University Press, 1989.
Tristmans, Bruno. "Les Métamorphoses du palimpseste: Souvenir et regénération chez Gérard de Nerval." *Revue romane* 21:2 (1986): 260–73.
Uster, Heidi. *Identité et dualité*. Zurich: Juris Druck, 1970.
Vallois, Marie-Claire. "Ecrire ou décrire: L'Impossible histoire du 'sujet' dans *Le Dernier Jour d'un condamné* de Victor Hugo." *Romantisme* 48:2 (1985): 91–104.
Verhesen, Fernand. *Gérard de Nerval, "El Desdichado."* Rodez: Feuillets de l'Ilot, 1938.
Virgil. *Opera*. Ed. R. A. B. Mynors. Oxford: Oxford University Press, 1969.
Warminski, Andrzej. "Dreadful Reading." *Yale French Studies* 69 (1985): 267–75.
Zola, Emile. *Les Rougon-Macquart: Histoire naturelle et sociale d'une famille sous le second empire*, vol. 3. Ed. Henri Mitterand. Paris: Gallimard [Pléiade], 1964.

Index

In this index an "f" after a number indicates a separate reference on the next page, and an "ff" indicates separate references on the next two pages. A continuous discussion over two or more pages is indicated by a span of page numbers, e.g., "57–59." *Passim* is used for a cluster of references in close but not consecutive sequence.

absence, 142, 144
abstraction, 35–41, 56–57, 60, 65, 112, 119, 121, 189, 200, 270, 274
Aeneid, 184–85, 191–92, 219
affect, 3, 109–10, 222
alienation, 41, 46, 53, 99, 204, 208f, 245–46, 258, 260, 264, 268, 273, 276, 283f
alterity, 89, 96, 125, 275
Althusser, Louis, 53, 83, 276–83 *passim*, 309, 354f
annihilation, 18, 112, 130, 132, 137–53, 168, 192, 237, 239, 250f, 262, 272; of self, 7, 21, 183, 282
anonymity, 69, 114, 119, 121, 146
anticipation, 67
anxiety, 64, 72, 265, 273, 284
Arasse, Daniel, 30–31, 34–35
Artaud, Antonin, 80, 272f, 275
astonishment, 12
Aufhebung, 15, 18, 262
Aulagnier, Piera, 26, 270, 278–81, 285, 355–56
authenticity, 68–71
authorship, 22, 79, 88, 90–94 *passim*, 99, 101–8 *passim*, 112, 114, 122–23, 125, 265, 274
autobiography, 78–79, 87, 90, 97, 104, 140, 151–52
Avni, Ora, 101–2, 126

Bataille, Georges, 334
beauty, 193, 202, 241
being, 64–73, 98, 267, 281, 310
Bell, Georges, 94, 184
Blanche, Esprit, 80, 85, 153, 198f, 216, 218, 229, 317, 326, 331, 340–43
Blanchot, Maurice, 23, 38, 60f, 272f, 306
body, 28–29, 167, 180, 244, 246, 278, 280, 286; female (maternal), 237–39, 241–46, 253–58 *passim*, 266, 274
Bony, Jacques, 105f, 123, 125, 230
Borel, Petrus, 74, 302
breast, maternal, 273–75
Bucquoy, Abbé de, 89–90, 104–8, 115–21, 124–25, 133, 159, 194, 197, 322
Byron, Lord, 177–79, 181, 196, 198

Cabanis, Pierre Jean Georges, 31f
capital punishment, *see* execution

care, 64f, 67, 70–72, 265
castration, 239, 248, 250, 259, 261–66, 270–71, 273, 284
chance (*hasard*), 49–50, 59, 145
Chastel, André, 168, 330
Chateaubriand, François-René, Vicomte de, 119
chora, 271–72, 275, 280
Christ, 112–13, 136–53 *passim*, 185–86, 219, 254, 257
city, 220f
coherence, 157
Colon, Jenny, 175, 180, 321
community, 278, 281, 286, 349
conscience, 69
consciousness, 46, 53–54, 121, 202, 283, 307
creation, 242–46, 249, 348
Crusades, 134–36

Damiens, R.-F., 28–29, 33
Dante, 48, 185–86, 219
d'Arras, Jehan, *see Mélusine*
Dasein, 63–72, 203–4, 267, 271, 276–77, 284, 287, 313–14, 336
death, 7, 14–16, 26f, 31, 35, 37–39, 42–43, 47, 50, 55, 100f, 104, 111, 113, 148, 152f, 169–71, 190, 208, 238, 241, 247, 250, 267, 271, 276, 281, 284–85; and Hegel, 19, 55, 190, 193, 200–202, 207, 269; nature of, 20, 45, 60–63, 71, 121, 137, 183, 286; fear of, 23, 32, 40–41; and Kojève, 59, 63, 72; and Heidegger, 70–73, 203, 207; linguistic, 100–101; and writing, 104, 111; and the underworld, 162, 183–86, 191, 219; triumph over, 174, 186, 190, 194f, 237
de Man, Paul, 51f, 88, 98–100, 120, 125, 190, 306
Descartes, René, 40, 43–44, 209, 270, 281–82
desire, 120, 165–66, 172, 189, 256, 260–64, 278–80, 283, 287, 328, 338
Desmoulins, Camille, 34
Dhaenens, Jacques, 156–65 *passim*, 175, 191, 327, 330

Diderot, Denis, 80, 124
discourse, 56–57, 98, 207, 237, 268, 278–79, 283; and madness, 75–78, 84–86, 98; mediation of, 190, 258; medical, 83, 210–12, 237
dispossession, 162, 168
domination, 223–24
Dondey, Théophile, 24–25, 42–48, 303–4
doubt, 43–45, 145–51 *passim*, 162, 167, 172, 186, 237–38, 269
dreams and dreaming, 157, 207, 209–10, 215–18, 226, 230–32, 237, 248, 250–52, 270, 338
Dubourjet, chevalier, 183, 335
Du Camp, Maxime, 218
Dumas, Alexandre, 85–86, 89f, 94–96, 125, 165, 218f, 223, 265

Eluard, Paul, 213, 339; "El Desdichado" (manuscript), 160–62, 172, 182, 187ff, 327
ethics, 41, 53, 225, 258, 265, 267f, 275, 281–85, 305
exchange, 20
execution, 34, 37–39, 61, 300–301; torture-execution, 24, 27–29
executioner, 29–30, 33
expiation, 225–29, 252

family, 162, 164, 229–34, 247, 251, 255, 277
father, 233–38, 241–42, 246–48, 254–55, 263, 277
fear, 9, 52, 64, 73, 284
Ficino, Marsilio, 167f, 330
first-person singular, 206–8, 220, 223, 225–27, 251, 256
folie, see madness
Foucault, Michel, 19–21, 27–28, 75, 79–82, 86–87, 92, 98–101, 120, 128, 214, 276, 341
fragmentation, 135, 153
fraternity, 237–38, 250–52, 256–58, 267
freedom, 7, 11ff, 15, 34f, 247, 358
French Revolution, 1ff, 23, 26, 30–31, 36, 66, 83, 247–49, 262, 292, 295, 316

Freud, Sigmund, 131, 159, 260–61, 264, 277, 346, 351
future, 68, 220

Gasparro, Giulia, 149
Gautier, Théophile, 25, 74–77, 84, 88f, 110, 121, 158, 217, 325, 340
Geninasca, Jacques, 175, 329f, 332
God, 1, 9, 11, 43, 91, 122, 142–47 *passim*, 153, 172, 198, 216, 235–38, 242f, 250, 253, 258, 266, 270, 348; death of, 24, 26, 140–45 *passim*, 158, 168, 186
goddess, 228f, 240, 245f, 252, 254
Goethe, Johann Wolfgang von, 74
Goncourt, Edmond de, 41, 302
Guillaume, Jean, 160, 218
Guillotin, Joseph Ignace, 30–31
guillotine, 13–16, 24, 27, 30–37, 58–61, 63, 83, 248, 250, 264, 266, 299. See also Terror, the
guilt, 69, 70, 224–26, 238

Habermas, Jürgen, 282
hasard (chance), 49–50, 59, 145
Hegel, G. W. F., 18–19, 55–57, 69, 190, 193f, 206–11 *passim*, 234, 247, 265–66, 270, 274f, 294; and the Terror, 11–16, 19, 35, 37, 55, 60ff, 248, 277, 282–83, 311; *Phenomenology of Spirit*, 12, 16–18, 21, 25, 34–35, 38, 59, 60, 63, 133, 135, 141, 192ff, 198–204, 272, 274, 295–96, 328; *Aesthetics*, 12, 21, 126–29, 134f, 212–14, 239, 337, 340. See also Kojève, Alexandre
Hegelianism, 108, 128, 162, 191–95 *passim*, 243, 262
Heidegger, Martin, 79–81, 120, 194, 203, 265, 267, 271, 276–77, 284, 287
Heine, Heinrich, 179
Hercules, 184, 185–86
hero, 116, 184
hieroglyphics, *see* semiotics
history, 3, 19, 36, 55, 58ff, 63, 106, 122, 124, 141, 201, 235, 241, 243, 291, 309
Hölderlin, Friedrich, 79–82, 128, 135, 315
Houssaye, Arsène, 153, 326

Hugo, Victor, 37–39, 42, 74, 112
Hyppolite, Jean, 19, 60ff, 318f

"I", the, 6, 16–18, 24f, 36, 41–50 *passim*, 57, 70, 87–88, 96, 105, 132, 137–38, 151, 193, 207, 256, 266f, 269f, 278–83; narrative, 94, 110, 115f, 159
Icarus, 148–49
identity, 29, 100, 131, 151, 195, 282
ideology, 276f, 280, 354
imaginary, 99
imagination, 11
immediacy, 281
incoherence, 157–58
individual, 11, 24, 54, 111, 119, 121f, 128, 190, 201, 249, 267, 277, 282
individuality, 26f, 35, 63, 117, 202
insanity, *see* madness
intuition, 4–6
invention, literary, 90–94, 104, 106, 110, 122–23, 223
Isis, 112–13, 153, 189, 228, 230, 239, 242, 259, 262, 318, 320f, 346

Janin, Jules, 75, 85, 95, 102, 104, 126, 133, 152f, 215, 315
je, the, 243–51, 253–59 *passim*, 263, 266
Jean, Raymond, 108, 110, 123, 125
Jeunes-France, 24–25, 36, 75, 298
jouissance, 258, 264–66, 268, 349

Kant, Immanuel, 3–15 *passim*, 35, 209, 239, 243, 265, 274, 282; *Conflict of the Faculties*, 3, 36, 291; *Critique of Pure Reason*, 3f, 21, 274, 293; and the subject, 3, 5, 13, 21, 197f, 256, 282; and the sublime, 7–18 *passim*, 36, 40, 100, 264; *Critique of Judgement*, 9–12, 34–35, 40, 202, 251, 294
Karr, Alphonse, 102
Kofman, Sarah, 108, 319, 321
Kojève, Alexandre, 24–25, 54–62, 68, 142, 275, 309–12
Kristeva, Julia, 26, 159–68 *passim*, 175, 194, 197–98, 270–76, 280–81, 285, 305, 329, 332

La Boderie, Guy Le Fèvre de, 167
labor, 27
Lacan, Jacques, 26, 54, 99, 129–33, 197, 248, 259–66, 275–76, 283–84, 323–25, 346, 350f
Lamartine, 74
language, 36, 38–39, 46, 52–56 *passim*, 81, 96, 99, 101, 103–5, 111, 113, 121, 125–26, 135, 153, 165, 190, 198, 204, 206f, 211, 221–22, 226, 234, 243, 252, 256–80, 283–87, 297, 346; failure of, 188, 195, 214; entry into, 207, 224, 229, 249, 255–56, 260, 278; poetic, 212–13, 274, 285, 339
Larbaud, Valéry, 42, 303
law, 10ff, 260, 266, 283; of the father, 224, 227, 238, 247, 259, 263f, 266, 273, 277, 352; of nature, 227–28, 237
lawlessness, 7, 287
Lebois, André, 177
Le Breton, Georges, 156–57
lectio difficilior, 77–78, 82, 86
Lefébure, Eugène, 48
Leibniz, Gottfried Wilhelm, 342f
Levinas, Emmanuel, 26, 39–41, 55, 60, 267–68, 270, 281–87, 309, 358–59
liberty, *see* freedom
Liszt, Franz, 218
literary theory, 98, 100
literature, 20–21, 61, 106, 183
Lombard, Alfred, "El Desdichado" (manuscript), 160–61, 327
lyre of Orpheus, 166–67, 181, 187–92, 196, 198, 204. *See also* subject, lyric

madness, 52, 73–98, 100–105 *passim*, 120, 122, 126, 151–53, 165, 173, 184, 197, 270, 287, 316ff, 338
Mallarmé, Stéphane, 43, 48–52, 270, 304–7
Marx, Karl, 270f, 353
materiality, 57, 132, 136, 141, 196–98, 232, 240, 245, 253–58 *passim*, 264–67, 271–73, 275, 286, 348
material world, 222, 224, 231–32, 241, 269

maternal, the, 240, 252, 347f. *See also* body, female; goddess; mother
melancholy, 168
Mélusine, 179–83, 187–88, 333, 335
memory, 121–22, 125, 249
metaphor, 38–39, 48, 50, 77, 92, 116, 121, 231, 260
Michelet, Jules, 1–4, 7, 16, 23
Montaigne, Michel de, 114
mother, 233, 238–42, 253–55, 257, 262, 280. *See also* maternal, the
muteness, 82, 84, 105, 121, 148, 150f, 183

narrator, 87, 106, 115, 125
nature, 9f, 40, 59, 100, 215, 221f, 228, 233
néant, *see* nothingness
negation, 42, 220, 262, 265, 282–83, 285
negativity, 15f, 24, 47, 51, 58, 60, 63, 68, 80, 162, 169, 192, 206, 269, 275, 281, 284, 310, 334
Nerval, Gérard de, 25–26, 99, 102–3; *Aurélia*, 76, 95, 133, 150, 152, 168, 181, 198, 205–68 *passim*, 277, 331; *Les Filles du feu*, 85–96, 105–12 *passim*, 122, 152, 160–61, 165, 169, 186, 189, 218ff, 223, 265; *Les Faux Saulniers*, 85, 98–133 *passim*, 135, 214; Brisacier (character), 89–91, 93–94, 104–5, 111, 115–16, 122; *Lettres d'amour*, 94, 109, 216; *Chimères*, 95, 159f, 178–82 *passim*, 188, 191; *Lorely*, 95, 164; *Les Illuminés*, 106; *Voyage en Orient*, 110f, 180f; *Un Roman à faire*, 122, 148; "Le Christ aux Oliviers," 137, 140–54, 235, 247; "Le Point noir," 138–44 *passim*, 231; juvenilia, 138–39; "El Desdichado," 138, 155–212 *passim*, 218ff, 247, 253, 283, 286, 336–37; family, 163, 178, 229, 232, 234–35, 327; *Octavie*, 169–74 *passim*; in Naples, 169–72, 174, 180; *Sylvie*, 173; institutionalization of, 209–10, 215–18, 221, 226, 229, 234, 242, 249. *See also* Blanche, Esprit
Nietzsche, Friedrich, 52–54, 73, 274, 287, 307–8

Nodier, Charles, 89
nothingness, 26, 37, 40, 45, 57f, 67f, 71, 224, 239, 275, 281, 284, 306
Noulet, Emilie, 163, 165, 326
noumena, 4, 293
Novalis, 100, 239, 318
nullity, *see* nothingness

objectivity, 92, 141, 144
obsession, 91
O'Neddy, Philothée, *see* Dondey, Théophile
originality, 78, 82, 89, 236, 278
Orpheus, *see* lyre of Orpheus

palimpsest, 121–23, 125, 243, 249
particularity, 17
Pascal, Blaise, 114
Passy, *see* Nerval, Gérard de, institutionalization of
paternity, 235, 254, 263. *See also* father
Paul, Jean, 24, 134, 140, 218
Pernety, Dom, 185, 187, 329, 337
phallus, 236–37, 259–66, 273, 345
Pinel, Philippe, 83, 316
piracy, 101–4, 315
Poe, Edgar Allan, 270, 353
poetics, *see under* language
poetry, 21, 127f, 155, 160, 171, 179, 188, 212–14, 234, 239, 285, 315
poet-savior, 147–48, 151, 158, 186
potentiality, 66–70 *passim*
projection, 66, 68
Promenades et souvenirs, 229
property, literary, 101–3, 113–14, 126
Proust, Marcel, 74, 78f, 85, 88f, 214
pseudonyms, 117–20, 320f
psychoanalysis, 76, 99, 129–30, 234, 239, 266
puns, 129–33

raisonnement, 75, 87, 96, 239
Rancé, Abbé de, 119
readers and reading, 47–48, 229, 234, 274, 287
reason, 75–77, 84, 86–88, 113, 153, 249

rebirth, 228
referentiality, 132
rejet, 273–75, 280, 353–54
representation, 128, 137, 196, 234, 243, 293
resoluteness, 70f
Restif de la Bretonne, Nicolas Edmé, 322, 332, 337
Riancey amendment, 105f, 109, 113f, 320
Richard, Jean-Pierre, 158–60, 164, 178
Richer, Jean, 156, 327–30
Robespierre, Maximilien de, 33–34, 300, 357
Rousseau, Jean-Jacques, 183, 231, 336

sacrifice, 10–12
Saint-Just, Louis-Antoine-Léon de, 34, 300
Sand, George, 163, 177, 192
Sanson, Charles Henri, 33, 38
Sartre, Jean-Paul, 207
Saussure, Ferdinand de, 21, 262, 324, 352
Schiller, Friedrich, 7ff, 50, 100, 153, 239, 318
science, 21
Scott, Walter, 162, 164
secularization, 24
self-consciousness, 5, 53, 122, 200f, 204, 269, 328
self-construction, 120
self-identification, 108, 155, 162, 196–97, 206, 259
self-knowledge, 87, 125, 141, 209, 211f, 219, 229, 243
self-representation, 99, 120
self-sameness, 17, 36, 148, 240
semiotics, 220–22, 226–27, 237, 240, 261–64, 266, 269–71, 274–75
sensuousness, 275, 285
signifier, 260–64, 267
signs, 225–28, 235–38, 242–43, 256, 261, 263, 269
silence, 82, 84, 142, 151, 196
Smith, Adam, 20, 27
solitude, 41–42, 91–92

spirit (and Spirit), 135–37, 193–94, 200–203, 328
state, the, 30, 33, 35f, 61ff, 276f, 282f
Stierle, Karlheinz, 167
subject, 4–6, 49, 51, 57, 60, 94, 99, 106, 144, 147f, 192f, 197, 224–26, 252, 267, 274, 276–86; propositional, 6f, 94, 137; sublime, 14–16, 126–27, 264, 277; and language, 109–16 *passim*, 123f, 129–32, 137, 140, 153–55, 165, 169, 198, 208, 222, 234; Lacanian, 130–32; lyric (and lyre-ic), 162, 168–69, 188, 192–98 *passim*, 208; interpellated, 276–77, 286; and the Other, 281–84
subjectivity, 21–26 *passim*, 35–37, 42–55 *passim*, 61, 88, 92, 97–98, 105, 117, 122, 126, 132, 137, 141, 144, 152–53, 158, 165–69, 180, 190, 196, 203, 205, 219, 229, 234, 236, 252, 265, 270, 277–81 *passim*; death-based, 23–73 *passim*, 99–100, 194, 206, 264, 266f, 270; and objectivity, 106, 108; literary, 111, 116, 120, 127, 133, 138, 157, 171, 204, 219; poetic, 206–7, 209, 213–14, 268
subjugation, 223–24, 235
sublimation, 13, 15, 35–36, 41, 44, 49, 51, 55, 61, 83f, 88, 98–100, 225, 247–49, 251, 262, 270–71, 282f
sublime, 4, 7–13, 34, 44, 56, 100, 126, 153, 286, 318, 352. *See also under* Kant, Immanuel
substitution, 118, 129, 136
suicide, 8, 169–71, 180, 349
Swedenborg, Emanuel, 191
symbolic, 262, 274f, 280, 350

Taine, Hippolyte, 291
temporality, 167
terror, 15, 33, 35, 42, 45, 51, 55, 60, 224–25, 249, 265, 275
Terror, the, 33–36, 55, 60–62, 249. *See also under* Hegel, G. W. F.
time, 19, 48, 56, 67, 145–48 *passim*
Tingy amendment, 113, 320
torture, *see under* execution
towers, 163–65, 217, 251, 328, 331
transcription, 212

Ulbach, Louis, 217ff, 340
unconscious, the, 130, 192, 260, 264, 322
unity, 5, 7, 189, 220, 251
universal, the, 57, 59, 122
universality, 2, 13–17 *passim*, 100, 102, 222, 283

vertigo, 92
victim, *see* execution
vision, 139f, 287
void, *see* nothingness

Wahl, Jean, 54
Walpurgisnacht, 88
war, 58, 62f
Warminski, Andrzej, 134
will, 13, 223, 246, 276
writing, 16f, 21f, 36, 43, 47–48, 99, 101, 114–15, 153–54, 183, 234, 240f, 250, 265, 274, 286f; and death, 47–48, 104, 111, 135, 137; and madness, 78, 85, 88, 96–97; and the self, 99, 122, 124f, 196, 270

Zola, Emile, 23, 39–43, 49, 83, 225, 302

Library of Congress Cataloging-in-Publication Data

Strauss, Jonathan.
    Subjects of terror : Nerval, Hegel, and the modern self / Jonathan Strauss
        p.   cm.
    Includes bibliographical references and index.
    ISBN 0-8047-3122-5
    1. Nerval, Gérard de, 1808–1855—Criticism and interpretation.
2. Hegel, Georg Wilhelm Friedrich, 1770–1831.   3. Self in literature.   4. Self (Philosophy)   5. Psychoanalysis and literature.   6. Psychoanalysis and philosphy.   I. Title.
PQ2260.G36Z8575   1998
848'.709—dc21   98-8339
                                                                                        CIP

∞ This book is printed on acid-free, recycled paper.

Original printing 1998
Last figure below indicates year of this printing:
07   06   05   04   03   02   01   00   99   98